Managing Human Resources

18th Edition

SCOTT A. SNELL
Professor of Business Administration,
University of Virginia

SHAD S. MORRIS
Associate Professor of Management,
Brigham Young University

CENGAGE

Australia • Brazil • Mexico • Singapore • United Kingdom • United States

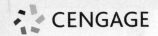

**Managing Human Resources,
Eighteenth Edition
Scott Snell and Shad Morris**

Senior Vice President: Erin Joyner

Product Director: Bryan Gambrel

Content Developer: Jamie Mack

Product Assistant: Rhett Ransom

Marketing Manager: Emily McLellan

Digital Content Specialists: Jennifer Chinn/
David O'Connor

Digital Production Services Manager:
Derek Drifmeyer

Project Management and Compostion:
SPi Global

Sr. Art Director: Michelle Kunkler

Text Designer: Red Hangar Design, LLC

Cover Designer: Red Hangar
Design, LLC

Cover Image: i3alda/Shutterstock.com

Intellectual Property
Analyst: Diane Garrity

Intellectual Property Project Manager:
Nick Barrows

For product information and technology assistance, contact us at
Cengage Customer & Sales Support, 1-800-354-9706

For permission to use material from this text or product, submit all
requests online at **www.cengage.com/permissions**

Further permissions questions can be emailed to
permissionrequest@cengage.com

Library of Congress Control Number: 2017945321

ISBN: 978-1-337-38962-4

Cengage
20 Channel Center Street
Boston, MA 02210
USA

Cengage is a leading provider of customized learning solutions with
employees residing in nearly 40 different countries and sales in more
than 125 countries around the world. Find your local representative at
www.cengage.com.

Cengage products are represented in Canada by
Nelson Education, Ltd.

To learn more about Cengage platforms and services, visit
www.cengage.com

To register or access your online learning solution or purchase materials for your course, visit **www.cengagebrain.com**

Printed in the United States of America
Print Number: 01   Print Year: 2017

Brief Contents

Contents

Chapter 7 Training and Development 241

Part 6   Expanding Human Resources Management Horizons

Chapter 15   International Human Resources Management   515

The 18th edition of *Managing Human Resources* will place your students at the forefront of understanding how organizations can gain a sustainable competitive advantage through people. Today's HR managers play an active role in the strategic planning and decision making within their organizations. Those managers who are good at it have a major impact on the success of their firms and elevate human resources in terms of its importance in the C-suites of their organizations. But human resources management is not limited to the HR staff. The best organizations recognize that managing people is the job of every manager, working in partnership with HR.

Each edition of the book highlights the changes human resources management is undergoing but reveals that the goal of utilizing an organization's talent in the best way possible never changes. Consequently, the purpose of this book is always twofold: (1) to equip students with the tools and practices of HR management and give them an appreciation for the changes they can make by understanding how best to manage people, and (2) to present the most current challenges and opportunities graduating students will face when it comes to today's human resources management environment. These challenges exist both for those who will become HR managers and those who will go on to become other types of managers.

Toward that end, the first chapter of the book lays out in broad terms the key challenges in HRM today. It includes a discussion of the HR strategies pursued by firms and the importance of retaining and motivating employees in the process. Other aspects broached include the strategies companies are using to continue to try to control health care costs; how social media is affecting hiring, human resources management, and employees' privacy rights; and how good human resources practices can help a firm achieve its corporate social responsibility and sustainability goals and make it an employer of choice. The chapter also discusses the important partnership with line managers and the competencies required of HR management. The textbook continues with the introduction, explanation, and discussion of the individual practices and policies that make up HRM. We recognize the manager's changing role and emphasize current issues and real-world problems and the policies and practices of HRM used to meet them.

Strategy and talent have become such central concerns of HR today that we continue to emphasize the topic in this edition of the book in Chapter 2. Chapter 5 focuses on expanding and managing the talent pool in organizations. Employee diversity and inclusion, and how firms can leverage all types of differences among their workers to their strategic advantage, are examined.

Organizations in today's competitive world are discovering that it is *how* the individual HR topics are combined that makes all the difference. Managers typically don't focus on HR issues such as staffing, training, and compensation in isolation from one another. Each of these HR practices should be combined into an overall system—one that furthers a firm's strategy by enhancing employee involvement and productivity. *Managing Human Resources* ends with a final chapter that focuses on how high-performance work systems (HPWSs) are used to implement these strategies. We outline the strategic processes used to implement HPWSs, including workflow design, HR practices, management processes, and supporting technologies as well as the outcomes of an HPWS that benefit both the employee and the organization as a whole.

Streamlined Coverage

Today's students are extremely busy. They want to know what they need to learn and be able to learn it as quickly as possible. Instructors also want to be able to cover all of the material they want to teach during a semester. To help both groups, we made a special effort to streamline our coverage in this edition. We did so without sacrificing key material but by shortening the copy to make it readable and deleting extraneous information reviewers have indicated may be "TMI" (too much information) for their students. Students and instructors will find that the copy is briefer, clearer, and more engaging.

New Cutting-Edge Content

As with other editions, a great deal of new information is provided in this revision to accurately reflect HRM in today's business world and help the reader understand today's HRM issues more effectively. Examples include the concerns of Millennial and Generation Z employees, and how Big Data, HR analytics, mobile technology, and social media are profoundly affecting the field, and the effects artificial intelligence and automation are having. Ever-changing international HR concerns are covered, including the work-visa challenges facing U.S. firms, immigration, human rights issues, global rights issues such as data protection, and intellectual property rights. The International Labor Organization's "Agenda 2030 for Sustainable Development," which places decent work for all at the heart of the ILO's current initiatives, resulted in numerous updates. Of course, the 18th edition also includes a complete update of all laws, administrative rulings and guidelines, and court decisions governing HRM. We also show a recent shift in the interest of Millennials who are seeing collective action through unions as much more aligned with their interests than previous generations.

Lastly, in addition to the changes we have already mentioned, to help instructors incorporate the new material discussed into their courses, the following is a list of chapter-by-chapter additions:

Chapter 1

- Updated discussion on international trade, Brexit, and the H-1B visa debate.
- The loss of middle-class jobs in the United States and new technology affecting HR, such as robotics and automation.
- New coverage on the employee experience.
- New coverage on Generation Z.
- Updated information on workforce demographic trends and the progress of women and minorities in the workplace.

Chapter 2

- Updated information on U.S. labor supply statistics.
- New section on a firm's primary and secondary stakeholders.
- New section and figure on the 4As model (**Alignment, Agility, Architecture, and Ability**).
- New case study on how a strategy change led to the formation of Nike.

Chapter 3

- New legal interpretations on what reasonable accommodation means for employees with disabilities.
- Updated information on how Title VII is being interpreted to prohibit discrimination based on gender identity or sexual orientation.
- A list of specific examples of unlawful discrimination against LGBTQ communities.
- New research showing how states that enact the federal Employment Non-Discrimination Act (ENDA) achieve higher levels of innovation than states that do not enact the act.
- We expand upon the term "disparate treatment."
- New material on how students in universities react to affirmative action.

Chapter 4

- New coverage of workflow analysis prior to job analysis.
- New discussion on how a firm's strategy affects its workflows and job design.
- New discussion of how companies are using fitness trackers, standing desks, and other devices to improve the ergonomics in their workplaces.
- New discussion on workplace democracy, and the work-life balance Millennials and the members of Generation Z are demanding.
- New case study on how Zappos eliminated all managerial positions and moved to a self-management model.

Chapter 5

- New section on retaining talent.
- New coverage on the use of games to attract applicants.
- New information on writing job postings to attract more candidates and the use of technology to detect biased job postings.
- New information on the virtual-assistant type technology some companies are beginning to use to automate the process of posting jobs, searching for candidates online, scheduling interviews with them, and notifying them of where they stand in the job hiring process.
- New case study on Scripps Health's lifecycle approach to training and retaining talent.

Chapter 6

- Updated information on the practice of using the Internet to prescreen candidates and the legal hazards of doing so.
- Updated information on the "ban the box" movement.

- New coverage on the use of technology and other best practices to eliminate bias when screening résumés and ranking candidates based on their interviews.
- New information on the use of Big Data and gamification in preemployment testing.

Chapter 7

- Updated coverage on how MOOCs are affecting corporate training.
- New coverage on experiential learning and the gamification of employee training.
- Updated information on social media's role in training.

Chapter 8

- New coverage reflecting the growing role of coaching rather than formal performance appraisals in organizations.
- New coverage of SMART goals.
- New coverage on how some firms are using technology to detect biased performance appraisals and get a better picture of how well employees are performing.
- New case study on why Adobe ended formal appraisals and what the company replaced them with.

Chapter 9

- How some companies like Zappos are moving from a traditional management structure to a system where work is organized around roles rather than titles and teams report to teams rather than supervisors.
- The movement by tech companies to using objectives and key results (OKR) systems to tie compensation to objectives.
- The push for health care professionals to be evaluated based on quality of care instead of a production model where it is more about quantity of care.
- New research that shows how competition and recessions can reduce employee wages.
- New coverage of locations, such as Glassdoor, to collect salary and other related data.
- A list of the highest paying jobs for 2017 in the United States.
- An updated discussion of minimum age required for employment.
- Salary rates for the fastest growing jobs in the United States.

Chapter 10

- Discussion of the new presidential administration's support for policies that reward government employees for merit, not just tenure.
- New discussion of how companies are gamifying incentives and rewards to improve performance.
- Updated research on how to design rewards to provide (1) autonomy, (2) opportunity, and (3) purpose.
- New research on public sentiment toward CEO pay.

Chapter 11

- Updated information on the current status of the Patient Protection and Affordable Care Act (PPACA).

- New discussion of workers' lack of awareness of the employer costs of their benefits.
- Updated information on employee leave programs as they relate to the Family Medical Leave Act.
- Expanded discussion on how companies can better meet the needs of Millennials by providing work-life benefits.

Chapter 12

- Updated research on the financial benefits of health and safety programs.
- Updated information on U.S. employee injury and safety statistics today.
- Updated information on how to enforce safety rules.
- Updated information on workplace violence and antibullying legislation.

Chapter 13

- Updated information on employee privacy rights at their place of employment.
- New figures on employer versus employee rights.
- New information on how employees are protected for blowing the whistle.
- New discussions and statistics of social media and how it is used and abused by employees.

Chapter 14

- A clearer introduction to the chapter that includes current sentiments in the United States toward unions.
- Discussion of how the last presidential election impacted unions and their traditional allegiance to the Democratic Party and U.S. sentiment toward international trade.
- New research showing how Millennials relate to collective action—where they agree and disagree with unions.
- Some evidence that more professionals are seeing unionization as a viable way to stabilize employment. A look at recent union movements that aren't just limited to companies but more related to social movements (e.g., Fight for 15 and Occupy Wall Street).
- Reorganized material to help with chapter flow.

Chapter 15

- Updated discussions on sentiments about globalization and free trade.
- Discussion surrounding the new gig economy where many workers are finding work globally online as independent contractors.
- Updated discussions of how companies like Microsoft are creating globally dispersed teams that must work virtually.
- Updated immigration and foreign worker discussions as they relate to H-1B visas.

Chapter 16

- New discussion on why higher compensation is generally required when implementing an HPWS.
- Updated case study on Whole Foods' HPWS and the challenges the company faces sustaining it and regaining a competitive advantage.

Features of the Book

Designed to facilitate understanding and retention of the material presented, each chapter contains the following pedagogical features:

- **Learning Outcomes** listed at the beginning of each chapter provide the basis for the Integrated Learning System. Each outcome is also listed in the margin of the chapter in which it appears, along with a thought-provoking question designed to get students thinking about how the related content applies to them personally. The outcomes are revisited in the chapter summary and discussion questions and in all of the book's ancillaries.
- **Small Business Application Boxes.** The boxes are designed to help entrepreneurs, small business owners, and managers think about how to organize, implement, and leverage talent and to draw attention to resources designed especially for them to do so. We feel the coverage is very important because many students today are very interested in entrepreneurship and will go on to found their own businesses. Moreover, small businesses provide most of America's jobs to workers.
- **Highlights in HRM.** This popular boxed feature provides real-world examples of how organizations perform HR functions. The highlights are introduced in the text discussion and include topics such as small businesses and international issues.
- **Key Terms** appear in boldface and are defined in margin notes next to the text discussion. The Key Terms are also listed at the end of the chapter and appear in the glossary at the end of the book.
- **Figures.** An abundance of graphic materials and flowcharts provides a visual, dynamic presentation of concepts and HR activities. All figures are systematically referenced in the text discussion.
- **Summary.** A paragraph or two for each Learning Outcome provides a brief and focused review of the chapter.
- **Discussion Questions** following the chapter summary offer an opportunity to focus on each of the Learning Outcomes in the chapter and stimulate critical thinking. Many of these questions allow for group analysis and class discussion.
- **HRM Experience.** An experiential activity designed to simulate HR activities is included in each chapter.
- **End-of-Chapter Cases.** Two case studies per chapter present current HRM issues in real-life settings that allow for student consideration and critical analysis.
- **Extended Cases.** Eleven extended cases are provided at the end of the main text. These cases use material covered in more than one chapter and provide capstone opportunities.

MindTap

Managing Human Resources, 18th edition, includes a brand new MindTap learning experience, powered by a rich array of online resources designed to deliver an all-in-one solution for learning and retaining the course topics. The following items are included in the MindTap learning path:

- An **engagement activity** designed to stimulate student interest and launch your classroom discussion.

- A **media-rich e-version** of the text enhanced with interactive versions of several figures in the text as additional video content for extra concept coverage and engagement.
- A comprehensive **auto-graded homework assignment** designed to guide students from basic comprehension to real-world application of concepts. Robust feedback is provided within each question to help reinforce understanding as students navigate through the new concepts of each chapter.
- Assignable version of Integrated Case assignments found at the end of the book. The assignments utilize the power of digital to engage students and grade open-ended question submissions easier with MindTap.
- **Brand new video "You Make the Decision"** exercises designed to enable students to think like HR managers and teach students to apply concepts taught within the classroom to real-world scenarios.
- Quiz assignment that delivers a myriad of question types to measure overall comprehension of chapter learning objectives.
- New Study App that helps students quiz themselves and prepare for upcoming exams. Practice questions are based on learning objectives within the course, and correlated to the test bank to provide students with a robust bank to utilize in their test preparation. Student have the flexibility to decide what chapters to study, and how many questions they will answer making on-the-go studying easier, quicker, and exactly what they need.

Instructor Materials

The following instructor support materials are available to adopters online at www.cengagebrain.com.

- *Instructor's Resource Guide.* The *Instructor's Resource Guide* contains a chapter synopsis and learning objectives; a very detailed lecture outline; answers to the end-of-chapter discussion questions, notes for decision activities, and end-of-chapter case studies; solutions to the extended cases in the textbook; and "Flip Tips" activities to provide ideas for the flipped classroom.
- *Test Bank.* Cengage Learning Testing powered by Cognero is a flexible, online system that allows you to:
  - Author, edit, and manage test bank content from multiple Cengage Learning solutions.
  - Create multiple test versions in an instant.
  - Deliver tests from your LMS, your classroom, or wherever you want.

  Each test bank chapter provides more than 100 questions, all tagged by learning objective, AACSB standards, and Bloom's taxonomy. There are true/false, multiple-choice, and essay items for each chapter.
- *PowerPoint™ Presentation Slides.* These presentation slides will add color and interest to lectures. Lecture slides also include engagement items such as video links and discussion questions to enhance the classroom learning experience.

Acknowledgments

Because preparation of manuscript for a project as large as *Managing Human Resources* is a continuing process, we would like to acknowledge the work of those colleagues who provided thoughtful feedback, and invaluable content expertise for this and the previous editions of the text. Our appreciation and thanks go to:

Ryan Hall, Chatfield College
Loren Kuzuhara, University of Wisconsin
Kim Fox-Marchetti, Lone Star College
Dale King, Lenoir-Rhyne University
Carol Decker, Tennessee Wesleyan University
Christie Hovey, Lincoln Land Community College
Tony Hunnicutt, College of the Ouachitas
Debra Moody, Virginia Commonwealth University
Dave Quirk, Northwest Christian University
Greg Berezewski, Robert Morris University of Illinois
Avan Jassawalla, SUNY Geneseo School of Business
Jeffrey Moser, Valley City State University
Jonathan Biggane, Fresno State University
Niesha Geoffroy, Golden Gate University
Julia Levashina, Kent State University
Jaime Simmons, Marlboro College Graduate School
Zhaoquong Qin, Langston University
Justin Wareham, Oklahoma City University
Kiristen Jefferson, Southern New Hampshire University
LaSondra Banks, Triton Community College
Misty Resendez, Ivy Tech
Neeley Shaw, Waynesburg University
Rimjhim Banerjee-Batist, Schenectady County Community College
Rhoda Sautner, University of Mary
Robin Sawyer, University of Maryland
Sandra Obilade, Bresica University
Shirley Rijkse, Central Carolina Community College
Weichu Xu, East Stroudsburg University
Steve Ash, University of Akron
Michael Bedell, California State University, Bakersfield
Brad Bell, Cornell University
Katherine Clyde, Pitt Community College
Mary Connerley, Virginia Tech University
Susie Cox, McNeese State University
Paula S. Daly, James Madison University
Sharon Davis, Central Texas College
Douglas Dierking, University of Texas, Austin
Suzanne Dyer-Gear, Carroll Community College
Joe J. Eassa, Jr., Palm Beach Atlantic University
Summer Zwanziger Elsinger, Upper Iowa University
Robert E. Ettl, SUNY Stony Brook
Diane Fagan, Webster University
Angela L. Farrar, University of Nevada, Las Vegas

Lou Firenze, Northwood University
Olene L. Fuller, San Jacinto College
Judith Gordon, Boston College
Rita G. Greer, Spalding University
Mike Griffith, Cascade College
Daniel Grundmann, Indiana University
Adrian Guardia, Texas A&M University, San Antonio
Xuguang Guo, University of Wisconsin, Whitewater
Sally Hackman, Central Methodist College
Kevin Hale, Lonestar College
Mike Hashek, Gateway Technical College
Rich Havranek, SUNY Institute of Technology
Kim Hester, Arkansas State University
Stephen Hiatt, Catawba College
Alyce Hochhalter, St. Mary Woods College
Madison Holloway, Metropolitan State College of Denver
David J. Hudson, Spalding University
Karen Jacobs, LeTourneau University
Avan Jassawalla, SUNY at Geneseo
Michelle Jetzer, Madison College
Nancy M. Johnson, Madison Area Technical College
Jeffrey Johnston, Alpena Community College
Pravin Kamdar, Cardinal Stritch University
Cheryl L. Kane, University of North Carolina, Charlotte
Jordan J. Kaplan, Long Island University
Steve Karau, Southern Illinois University at Carbondale
Joseph Kavanaugh, Sam Houston State University
John Kelley, Villanova University
Dennis Lee Kovach, Community College of Allegheny County
Kenneth Kovach, University of Maryland
Trudy Kroeger, Wisconsin Indianhead Technical College
Chalmer E. Labig, Jr., Oklahoma State University
Alecia N. Lawrence, Williamsburg Technical College
Scott W. Lester, University of Wisconsin, Eau Claire
J. Jonathan Lewis, Texas Southern University
Corinne Livesay, Bryan College
Beverly Loach, Central Piedmont Community College
L. M. Lockhart, Penn State Greater Allegheny
Gloria Lopez, New Mexico Highlands University
Barbara Luck, Jackson Community College
Larry Maes, Davenport University
Jennifer Malfitano, Delaware County Community College
Michael Matukonis, SUNY Oneonta
Doug McCabe, Georgetown University
Lee McCain, Seminole Community College
Marjorie L. McInerney, Marshall University
Veronica Meyers, San Diego State University
Robert T. Mooney, Texas State University
Julia Morrison, Bloomfield College

Jim Nichols, Crown College
Harold Nolan, Georgian Court University
Sue Norton, University of Wisconsin Parkside
David Nye, Kennedy-Western University
Paul Olsen, Saint Michael's College
Donald Otto, Lindenwood University
Charles Parsons, Georgia Institute of Technology
Dane Partridge, University of Southern Indiana
Bryan J. Pesta, Cleveland State University
Theodore Peters, Hartwick College
David Pitts, Delaware Technical and Community College
Amy Pogue, Valencia College
Alex Pomnichowski, Ferris State University
Victor Prosper, University of the Incarnate Word
Michael Raphael, Central Connecticut State University
Charles Rarick, Barry University
Eladio D. Reid, University of Houston Downtown
June Roux, Salem Community College
Robert Rustic, University of Findlay
Laura L. Sankovich, Capella University
Machelle Schroeder, University of Wisconsin–Platteville
Kelli Schutte, Calvin College
Mike Sciarini, Michigan State University
Tom Sedwick, Indiana University of Pennsylvania
Jim Sethi, University of Montana Western
Patricia Setlik, William Rainey Harper College
William L. Smith, Emporia State University
Norman Solomon, Fairfield University
Emeric Solymossy, Western Illinois University
Carol Spector, University of North Florida
Howard Stanger, Canisius College
Scott L. Stevens, Detroit College of Business
Michael Sturman, Cornell University
Nanette Swarthout, Fontbonne College
Michael T. Korns, Indiana University of Pennsylvania
Karen Ann Tarnoff, East Tennessee State University
Thomas Taveggia, University of Arizona
Donna Testa, Herkimer County Community College
Alan Tillquist, West Virginia State College
Sue Toombs, Weatherford College
Richard Trotter, University of Baltimore
William Turnley, Kansas State University
Catherine L. Tyler, Oakland University
Melissa Waite, The College at Brockport, SUNY
Harvell Walker, Texas Tech University
Barbara Warschawski, Schenectady County Community College
Steve Werner, University of Houston
Liesl Wesson, Texas A&M University
JoAnn Wiggins, Walla Walla University

Jim Wilkinson, Stark State College
L. A. Witt, University of New Orleans
Evelyn Zent, University of Washington, Tacoma
Ryan Zimmerman, Texas A&M University

In the manuscript for this edition, we have drawn not only on the current literature but also on the current practices of organizations that furnished information and illustrations relating to their HR programs. We are indebted to the leaders in the field who have developed the available heritage of information and practices of HRM and who have influenced us through their writings and personal associations. We have also been aided by students in our classes; by research assistants like Natalie Stoker, Kennerley Roper, and Ashley Fife; by former students; by the participants in the management development programs with whom we have been associated; by HR managers; and by our colleagues. In particular, we would like to express our appreciation to Amy Ray for her helpful insights, research, and editorial support for this edition of the text. She is a wonderful partner. We appreciate the efforts of everyone at Cengage who helped develop and produce this text and its supplements. They include: Bryan Gambrel, Product Director; Jamie Mack, Content Developer; Stephanie Hall, Learning Design Author; Carol Moore, Digital Content Designer; Michelle Kunkler, Sr. Art Director; and Rhett Ransom, Product Assistant.

We are also so grateful to our wives—Marybeth Snell and Mindi Morris—who have contributed in so many ways to this book. They are always sources of invaluable guidance and assistance. Furthermore, by their continued enthusiasm and support, they have made the process a more pleasant and rewarding experience. We are most grateful to them for their many contributions to this publication, to our lives, and to our families.

Lastly, we would like to say farewell and thank you to long-time coauthor, George Bohlander, who has been a valued partner for decades and the intellectual backbone of the franchise. With his departure from the author team, George leaves an enduring legacy. His experience and insight have given this book its voice for many editions, and his guidance, counsel, and leadership have proved invaluable. His passion for the field, his students, and the profession have been inspirational. He is a great mentor, and friend. And a wonderfully decent man. Thank you, George.

Scott A. Snell
University of Virginia

Shad S. Morris
Brigham Young University

Scott A. Snell

Scott Snell is the E. Thayer Bigelow Research Chair of business administration and former senior associate dean for executive education at the University of Virginia's Darden Graduate School of Business. Scott teaches courses in leadership and strategic management and works with management teams on aligning their human resource investments to better execute their strategies. Scott is the author of four books and was recently listed among the top one hundred most-cited authors in scholarly journals of management. He currently serves on the board of HR People + Strategy (SHRM), and previously has served on the boards of the Strategic Management Society's Human Capital Group, the Society for Human Resource Management Foundation, the Academy of Management's Human Resource Division, the *Academy of Management Journal*, and the *Academy of Management Review*.

Prior to joining the Darden faculty in 2007, Scott was professor and director of executive education at Cornell University's Center for Advanced Human Resource Studies and a professor of management in the Smeal College of Business at Pennsylvania State University. He received a BA from Miami University, as well as an MBA and PhD in business from Michigan State University. Originally from Ohio, Scott now lives in Charlottesville, Virginia.

Shad S. Morris

Shad Morris is the Georgia White Fellow and associate professor of management at the Marriott School of Business at Brigham Young University. He teaches courses in the areas of human resources management and international business. Prior to joining the Marriott School in 2013, Shad was an assistant professor of management and human resources at The Ohio State University and has held appointments at the Sloan School of Management at MIT, Copenhagen Business School in Denmark, China Europe International Business School (CEIBS) in China, and SKK Graduate School of Business in South Korea.

Shad's research focuses on strategic human resource management in a global environment. His research has been published in a number of journals, such as the *Harvard Business Review, MIT Sloan Management Review, Academy of Management Review, Journal of International Business Studies, Strategic Management Journal, Journal of Management,* and *Human Resource Management*. He has worked for the World Bank, Management Systems International, and Alcoa. He has consulted with numerous companies on their HR and knowledge practices. He is the recipient of the

International HRM Scholarly Research Award from the Academy of Management and is currently a faculty fellow at Cambridge University's Centre for International Human Resource Management. In addition, Shad currently serves on the board of the *International Journal of Human Resources Management* and is a founding editor of the *Journal of Microfinance*. He received a BS in psychology and a masters in organizational behavior from Brigham Young University, as well as a PhD in human resources management from Cornell University.

Rawpixel/Getty Images

CHAPTER **1**

The Rewards and Challenges of Human Resources Management

Learning Outcomes

After studying this chapter, you should be able to

LO ① Explain how human resource managers and other managers can have rewarding careers by helping their firms gain a sustainable competitive advantage through the strategic utilization of people.

LO ② Explain how good human resource practices can help a firm's globalization, corporate social responsibility, and sustainability efforts.

LO ③ Describe how technology can improve how people perform and how they are managed.

LO ④ Explain the dual goals HR managers have in terms of increasing productivity and controlling costs.

LO ⑤ Discuss how firms can leverage employee differences to their strategic advantage and how educational and cultural changes in the workforce are affecting how human resource managers engage employees.

LO ⑥ Provide examples of the roles and competencies of today's HR managers and their relationship with other managers.

1

We use a lot of words to describe how important people are to organizations. The terms *human resources, human capital, intellectual assets*, and *talent management* imply that it's people who drive the performance of their organizations (along with other resources such as money, materials, and information). Successful organizations are particularly adept at bringing together different kinds of people to achieve a common purpose. This is the essence of **human resources management (HRM)**. Human resources management involves a wide variety of activities, including analyzing a company's competitive environment and designing jobs and teams so a firm's strategy can be successfully implemented to beat the competition. This, in turn, requires identifying, recruiting, and selecting the right people for those jobs and teams; training, motivating, and appraising these people; developing competitive compensation policies to retain them; grooming them to lead the organization in the future—and the list goes on.

human resources management (HRM)
The process of managing human talent to achieve an organization's objectives.

LO ①
Think of a firm you do business with that is facing dramatic changes in order to survive. (Retailers such as Target and Macy's, which are facing stiff competition from online retailers are an example.) How do you think the firm's personnel can help it adapt? What role will the company's HR staff play in helping with that goal?

1.1 Why Should You Study Human Resources Management? Will It Pay Off?

Which of these activities would you like to engage in your career:

- Establishing the strategic direction your firm should take
- Attracting top-notch people to come to work for you and your firm
- Determining the right people to hire so your team and company are a success
- Helping and coaching people so they become top-notch performers

If you answered yes to these questions, a job managing people might be a rewarding career for you and an excellent reason why you should study human resources management. Having a good understanding of human resources management is important for managers and entrepreneurs of all types—not just human resources (HR) personnel. All managers are responsible for at least some of the activities that fall into the category of management. Managers play a key role in selecting employees, training and motivating them, appraising them, promoting them, and so forth. It's a job that can be incredibly rewarding—like a gardener helping his or her crops to grow. But what if you do a poor job of these activities? Believe it or not, many businesspeople with great business strategies, business plans, and products and services fail because they do not fully grasp the importance of human resources management. Laments one entrepreneur:

> My first year after investing in a small business that was failing, I tripled the amount of business the company did and made a lot of money. But I didn't pay my personnel enough or motivate them. They eventually abandoned me, and a larger competitor muscled me out of the marketplace. I now understand the important role personnel play in a business. They can make or break it.

In addition, great business plans and products and services can easily be copied by your competitors. Great personnel cannot. Their knowledge and abilities are among the

If an employer requested your Facebook login credentials, what would you do?

Rawpixel.com/Shutterstock

most distinctive and renewable resources upon which a company can draw. As Thomas J. Watson, founder of IBM, said, "You can get capital and erect buildings, but it takes people to build a business."[1]

Lastly, even if you never become a manager, understanding human resources management can help you understand your responsibilities and rights as an employee. For example, what if your employer asks for your passwords to Facebook or other social media sites? Do you need to provide the manager with that information? This textbook can help you answer questions such as these.

1.1a Human Capital and Organizational Culture

The idea that organizations "compete through people" highlights the fact that achieving success increasingly depends on an organization's ability to manage its *human capital*. The term **human capital** describes the employees' knowledge, skills, abilities, and other attributes (KSAOs) that have economic value to the firm. Although the value of these assets might not show up directly on a company's balance sheet, it nevertheless has tremendous impact on an organization's performance. The following quotations from notable CEOs and former CEOs illustrate this point[2]:

human capital
The knowledge, skills, and capabilities of individuals that have economic value to an organization.

- "The key for us, number one, has always been hiring very smart people." (Bill Gates, Microsoft)
- "Human resources isn't a thing we do. It's the thing that runs our business." (Steve Wynn, Wynn Las Vegas)
- "You gotta build a team that is so talented, they almost make you uncomfortable." (Brian Chesky, AirBnB)

Companies that *do* "win" because of the talent they find, hire, and manage include:

- Publix, which empowers its employees to make decisions—decisions that are good for an individual store, its customers, area growers, community, and the firm as a whole.

- Nordstrom's, which empowers its employees to go through near-heroics to satisfy customers.

- The Martin Agency, a Virginia-based advertising agency whose talented and creative personnel generate award-winning advertising campaigns like those for insurer Geico and cable-TV network Nickelodeon.

However, unlike physical capital and resources, human capital is intangible and cannot be managed the way organizations manage jobs, products, and technologies. One reason why this is so is because employees, *not* the organization, own their own human capital. If valued employees leave a company, they take their human capital with them, and any investment the company has made in training and developing these people is lost.

To build human capital in organizations, managers must continue to develop superior knowledge, skills, and experience within their workforces and retain and promote top performers.[3] Beyond the need to invest in employee development, organizations have to find ways to better utilize the knowledge of their workers. Too often employees have knowledge that goes unused. Human resource managers and programs are often the conduit through which knowledge is developed and transferred among employees. As Dave Ulrich, a noted expert in human resources, notes: "Learning capability is *g* times *g*—a business's ability to *generate* new ideas multiplied by its adeptness at *generalizing* them throughout the company."[4]

Why does knowledge go unshared and unused in organizations? Oftentimes it's because of a firm's organizational culture. **Organizational culture** refers to the shared values, beliefs, and assumptions people in an organization have. Organizational culture affects how people in an organization work and treat each other and customers. A negative organizational culture stifles employees and leads to lower productivity and morale. In contrast, a positive organizational culture helps employees not only acquire knowledge and skills, but also helps foster curiosity among employees, allows them to grow and thrive, and creates mission-driven teams that actually achieve success.

You probably understand organizational culture more than you realize. Are there businesses you like to shop with because they perform better and you enjoy the atmosphere and people? Are there other businesses that are similar but that you don't like to shop with? The difference is likely due to organizational culture. Marriott's culture is critical to its success. The hotel chain takes care of its employees. They, in turn, take care of the customers, who come back time and again.

Although "competing through people" and "organizational culture" are major themes of human resources management, on a day-to-day basis, managers of all types have to carry out the specific activities for a company to effectively do so. Figure 1.1 provides an overall framework of these activities.

What do you think are the biggest human resource–related challenges you would have to face as a manager or team leader? Professional organizations such as the Society for Human Resource Management (SHRM) conduct ongoing studies of the most pressing competitive issues facing firms. The top trends, or challenges, firms name today include those outlined in the sections that follow.

organizational culture
The shared values, beliefs, and assumptions people in an organization have.

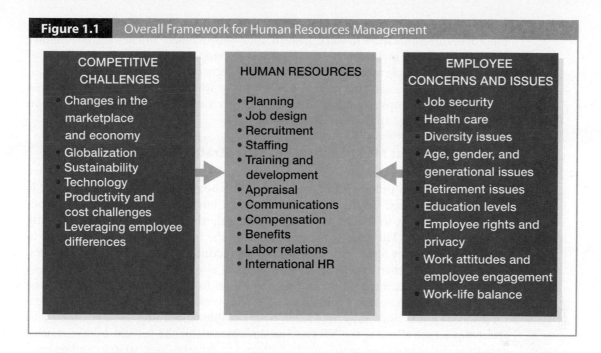

Figure 1.1   Overall Framework for Human Resources Management

COMPETITIVE CHALLENGES
- Changes in the marketplace and economy
- Globalization
- Sustainability
- Technology
- Productivity and cost challenges
- Leveraging employee differences

HUMAN RESOURCES
- Planning
- Job design
- Recruitment
- Staffing
- Training and development
- Appraisal
- Communications
- Compensation
- Benefits
- Labor relations
- International HR

EMPLOYEE CONCERNS AND ISSUES
- Job security
- Health care
- Diversity issues
- Age, gender, and generational issues
- Retirement issues
- Education levels
- Employee rights and privacy
- Work attitudes and employee engagement
- Work-life balance

1.2 Strategic and Global Challenges

LO ②
Does a company's HRM function need to be an integral part of its sustainability and corporate social responsibility efforts? Why or why not?

Organizations can rarely stand still for long. Being able to adapt has become the key to capturing opportunities and overcoming obstacles both domestically and abroad. In fact, it is often the key to the very survival of organizations. Many of the biggest 500 companies in the world 50 years ago (GE and GM included) are still in business. However, many others, such as Esmark Steel, are not. In fact, you may never have even heard of Esmark Steel. As a corollary, think about the species that populate our planet today. It's not necessarily the biggest and the strongest species, such as the dinosaurs, that have survived but those best able to adapt. This is true for not only species but individual employees and companies as well.

1.2a Responding Strategically to Changes and Disruptions in the Marketplace

Products and markets are evolving at a breakneck pace, disrupting what businesses produce, how they produce, and for whom. Changes in the stock market, world economic conditions, labor markets, and technology are making "business as usual" a thing of the past. So how do HR managers help their firms cope with ever-changing business conditions? One way is by helping redesign their firms to achieve agility.

Agility is a firm's ability make quick changes to gain a competitive advantage. Achieving agility often involves eliminating managerial layers that can slow down decision making and make an organization less nimble. Instead, project teams that can gear up fast, make their own decisions, and disband quickly are utilized to develop and get new products out the door while they're "hot." Many tech companies operate this way, and other firms are finding that the model can work for them.

agility
A firm's ability make quick changes to gain a competitive advantage.

The online shoe company Zappos has gone so far as to eliminate all of its managers. Employees aren't told how to work. Instead, they "self-manage" and belong to voluntary employee teams. Employees are motivated to develop new skills and capabilities so they can join multiple teams and work on new projects at a moment's notice. Successful companies, says Harvard Business School professor Rosabeth Moss Kanter, develop a culture that just keeps moving all the time.[5] It's been said that "No change means no chance." The change applies to HR managers, too.

Human Resources Managers and Business Strategies

In decades past, HR departments were often focused on performing administrative tasks, dealing with unions, and complying with labor laws. But HR management is vastly different today. Astute executives know that human resource professionals can help them improve, to comply with the law and help the bottom line by streamlining employment costs. HR professionals can improve the top line by redesigning work to foster innovation, by forecasting labor trends, by recruiting and motivating employees, and by measuring their effectiveness. HR managers also help their firms with business strategies, as well as mergers, acquisitions, and ways to enter new and global markets. "If you look at the evolution going back to when we called HR 'personnel,' it's come a long way as a function," says Art Mazor, with Deloitte Consulting. New HR tools and technologies are allowing the HR function to look outside the tactical, administrative reporting and data gathering to bring insights and to drive business strategy and results.[6] Mazor says.[6]

Sometimes changing a firm's strategy requires adjusting the labor force via downsizing, outsourcing, and offshoring. **Downsizing** is the planned elimination of jobs, and **outsourcing** simply means hiring someone outside the company to perform business processes that were previously done within the firm. **Offshoring**, also referred to as "global sourcing," involves shifting work to locations abroad.

A common denominator of all these strategies is that they require companies to engage in bringing about and managing both organizational changes and changes on the individual level. Although most employees understand that change is continuous—responsibilities, job assignments, and work processes change—people often resist it because it requires them to modify or abandon ways of working that have been successful or at least familiar to them. Successful change rarely occurs naturally or easily.

Some of the strategic changes companies pursue are reactive changes that result when external forces, such as the competition, a recession, a law change, or an ethical crisis (such as the backlash Volkswagen experienced in 2016 for cheating on its vehicles' emissions tests) have already affected an organization's performance. Other strategic changes are proactive changes, initiated by managers to take advantage of targeted opportunities, particularly in fast-changing industries in which followers are not successful.

Good HR managers know that they can be key players when it comes to driving the business strategies of their organizations to make changes. That is why forward-looking CEOs, including those of Southwest Airlines, Starbucks, and GE, make certain their top HR executives report directly to them and help them address key issues.

A rapidly growing number of companies, including Ford, Intel, United Technologies, and the gamemaker Electronic Arts, are assigning HR representatives to their core business teams to make certain they are knowledgeable about core business issues. In

downsizing
The planned elimination of jobs.

outsourcing
Contracting outside the organization to have work done that formerly was done by internal employees.

offshoring
The business practice of sending jobs to other countries.

shaunl/Getty Images

Some changes are reactive, such as those experienced by Volkswagen when it was revealed the company had cheated on its vehicles' emission tests.

addition, companies are increasingly rotating non-HR managers *into* HR positions and vice versa to give them exposure to different areas of the organization. Rather than emphasizing the administrative aspects of HR, these companies develop and promote their HR personnel and provide them with key business statistics and numbers they can use to measure the effectiveness of the workforce.

We will discuss more about competitive HR strategies and HR in Chapter 2. Meanwhile, keep in mind that HR's role is not all about providing advice to CEOs and supervisors. In addition to serving as a strategic partner to management, HR managers are also responsible for listening to and advocating on behalf of employees to make sure their interests are aligned with those of the firm and vice versa. A good deal of evidence suggests that this is one of the toughest parts of an HR manager's job. We will discuss more about this aspect of the job later in the chapter.

1.2b Competing, Recruiting, and Staffing Globally

Have you ever thought about working abroad or learning a second (or third) language? Doing so could give you a big advantage in today's workplace. Why? Because the strategies companies are pursing today increasingly involve one or more elements of globalization. The integration of world economies and markets has sent businesses abroad to look for opportunities, fend off foreign competitors domestically, and find the right kind of employees to help them do so. Consumers around the world today want to be able to buy "anything, anytime, anywhere," and companies are making it possible for them to do so. Want to buy a Coke in Pakistan? No problem. Coca-Cola has an elaborate delivery system designed to transport its products to some of the remotest places on the planet. In fact, the company has long generated more of its revenues abroad than it does in the United States

Importing and exporting goods and services is the easiest way to "go global." India has the world's second-largest population (1.2 billion people) and a growing middle class, so firms are increasingly trying to expand their exports to that country.[7] Apple is one of those companies. Although the iPhone dominates the U.S. market, only 5 percent of smartphones in India are iPhones. Partnerships, mergers, and takeovers are other ways companies are preparing for globalization.

Many American and foreign firms have partnered with Chinese firms to expand in China, which is the world's most populous country, with 1.3 billion people. In turn, Chinese and other foreign companies are merging with American firms, sometimes in industries you wouldn't expect. For example, in 2016, the Chinese firm Dalian Wanda Group bought U.S. film company Legendary, which produced *The Dark Knight, Jurassic World*, and *Straight Outta Compton*.[8]

As a result of globalization, the national identities of products are blurring, too. BMW is a German brand, but the automaker builds cars in the United States, China, and elsewhere. Likewise, you probably think of Budweiser as an American beer, but its maker (Anheuser-Busch) is owned by a Belgian company called InBev. Like many other companies, Anheuser-Busch InBev has been purchasing or partnering with factories and brands in other countries such China and Mexico to expand its sales.[9] After buying Legendary, Dalian Wanda Group produced *The Great Wall* starring Matt Damon, which was released in both China and the United States.

Numerous free-trade agreements forged between nations in the last half century have helped quicken the pace of globalization. The first major trade agreement of the twentieth century was made in 1948, following World War II. Called the General Agreement on Tariffs and Trade (GATT), it established rules and guidelines for global commerce between nations and groups of nations. Since GATT began, the growth in world trade has far outpaced the growth in the world's overall output. GATT paved the way for the formation of many major trade agreements and institutions, including the European Union in 1986 and the North American Free Trade Agreement (NAFTA) in 1994, encompassing the United States, Canada, and Mexico.

Although they have come under fire from people and politicians around the world, new free-trade agreements continue to be forged. The United Kingdom left ("Brexited") the European Union in 2016. Nonetheless, even the country's most vocal opponents of global trade are anxious to complete a new free-trade deal with India to do more business with that nation.[10]

How Globalization Affects HRM

Due to globalization, firms have to balance a complicated set of issues related to different geographies, including different cultures, employment laws, and business practices, and the safety of employees and facilities abroad. Human resource issues underlie each of these concerns. They include such things as dealing with employees today who, via the Internet and social media, are better informed about global job opportunities and are willing to pursue them, even if it means working for competing companies or foreign companies. Gauging the knowledge and skill base of workers worldwide and figuring out how best to hire and train them (sometimes with materials that must be translated into a number of different languages) is also an issue for firms. Relocating managers and training foreign managers abroad to direct the efforts of an international workforce is a challenge as well. In Chapter 15, we will explain how these challenges are tackled.

1.2c Setting and Achieving Corporate Social Responsibility and Sustainability Goals

Globalization has led to an improvement in people's living standards in the last half century. As a result of free trade, Americans are able to buy products made abroad more cheaply. Conversely people in low-wage countries that make those goods and services are becoming wealthier and are beginning to buy American-made products. Nonetheless, globalization stirs fierce debate—especially when it comes to jobs. Since the turn of the century, millions of U.S. jobs—both white collar and blue collar—have been exported to low-wage nations all around the world. Other people worry that free trade is creating a "have/have not" world economy, in which the people in developing economies and the world's environment are being exploited by companies in richer, more developed countries. This has sparked anti-free-trade protests in many nations.

Concerns such as these, coupled with corporate scandals over the years, including the use of sweatshop labor in third-world countries, have led to a new focus on **corporate social responsibility**, or good corporate citizenship. Many firms and professional associations also have ethics codes, or codes of conduct. The codes are written guidelines that clarify right and wrong behaviors an organization endorses or prohibits. Highlights in HRM 2 shows the codes of ethics adopted by the Society for Human Resources Management. Other firms have gone so far as to appoint "chief ethics officers" to try to ensure that ethical breaches by employees don't adversely affect their companies. Chief ethics officers and ethics are discussed in more detail in Chapters 7 and 13.

Companies are learning (sometimes the hard way) that being ethical and socially responsible both domestically and abroad can not only help them avoid lawsuits but also improve their earnings. For example, researchers at Boston College's Center for Corporate Citizenship found that as a company's reputation improved, so did the percentage increase in the number of people who would recommend that firm. Nearly two-thirds of

corporate social responsibility
The responsibility of the firm to act in the best interests of the people and communities affected by its activities.

After an unsafe factory collapsed, killing hundreds of textiles workers in Bangladesh in 2013, approximately 70 retailers, mostly European, signed an agreement to inspect factories they offshore work to and finance safety upgrades for them.

MUNIR UZ ZAMAN/AFP/Getty Images

the members of the 80-million-strong millennial generation (people born in the 1980s and 1990s) consider a company's social reputation when deciding where to shop, and 9 of 10 say they would switch brands based on their perceptions of a company's commitment to social responsibility.[11] Moreover, prospective workers are saying corporate responsibility is now more important to their job selection. They want to work for companies that are concerned not only with profits but also making the world a better place for everyone, both rich and poor.

sustainability
Doing business in a way that does as little harm to the environment and depletes as few natural resources as possible.

Sustainability is closely related to corporate social responsibility. Sustainability refers to a company's ability to produce goods or services without depleting the world's resources and doing the least amount of harm to the environment as possible. Achieving complete sustainability is nearly impossible, but companies are making strides to reduce their "carbon footprints." Those that are not are finding themselves under pressure from consumers and groups determined that they do.

Consider what happened to Hewlett-Packard (HP). After HP broke a promise to eliminate toxic materials in its computers, Greenpeace activists painted the words "Hazardous Products" on the roof of the company's headquarters in Palo Alto, California. Meanwhile, a voicemail message from *Star Trek* actor William Shatner was delivered to all of the phones in the building. "Please ask your leader [HP's CEO] to make computers that are toxin free like Apple has done," Shatner said in the recording. The stunt and publicity it generated worked. HP got the message and later delivered on its promise.[12]

One of HR's leadership roles is to spearhead the development and implementation of corporate citizenship throughout their organizations, especially the fair treatment of workers.[13]

LO ③

In what ways can the HR managers and employees of small firms facilitate their competitiveness relative to firms with superior technology? Why are employees still key?

1.3 Technology Challenges

Advancements in information technology have enabled organizations to take advantage of the information explosion. Computer networks and "cloud computing" (Internet computer services and data storage) have made it possible for nearly unlimited amounts of data to be stored, retrieved, and used in a wide variety of ways anywhere and at any time. Software that allows workers to work with and share information with one another electronically anywhere, any time—social media, wikis, document-sharing platforms such as Google Docs, online chat and instant messaging, and web- and videoconferencing—have changed how and where people and companies do business. For example, BNSF Railway uses the social media site Yammer to help employees collaborate on ideas and provide each other with praise and feedback.

Social media networking has also become the way workers find jobs and employers recruit candidates and screen them today. Companies are hiring firms such as Social Intelligence, which combs through Facebook, LinkedIn, Twitter, Instagram, YouTube, and "thousands of other sources" to create reports about the "real you"—not the "you" you have presented in your resume.[14] (Care to change your Facebook page, anyone?)

HR managers are often responsible for developing Internet and social media policies for employees, including how much time employees should be allowed to spend online, the sites they should be allowed to visit, and whether or not an employee can use his or her own electronic devices (mobile phones, tablets, etc.) for work purposes. Other issues include what apps employees can use. Deutsche Bank doesn't allow its employees to use unapproved apps such as Google Talk and What's App for business purposes on either their work or personal phones.[15]

From Touch Labor to Knowledge Workers

Technology—and automation in particular—have reduced the number of jobs that require routine tasks and little skill and have increased the number of jobs that require considerable skill. In 1979, approximately 40 percent of Americans held routine-task-type jobs. Today, only about 30 percent do as a result of automation and robotics.[16] This change has been referred to as a shift from "touch labor" to **knowledge workers**, in which employee responsibilities expand to include a richer array of nonroutine activities that involve analyzing information and problem-solving.[17] Fewer good "middle class" type jobs are available to U.S. workers today as a result, disrupting the labor market. "One of our retail utility customers in the U.K. has about 300 robots doing 600 people's worth of work," says Alistair, the CEO of Blue Prism, a company that helps automate business functions. "Before you needed a building to house 600 people, but all that gets crushed down to one cabinet in the corner of a data center."[18]

But it's not just routine jobs and blue-collar jobs that are affected by automation. News organizations are using web robots ("bots") to gather information and write basic stories about corporate earnings and sports recaps. Many of the entries on Wikipedia aren't written by people but by bots that comb the Web for information and compile the information you see on the site. Or consider the IBM robot Jill Watson. In 2016, Georgia Institute of Technology used Jill as an online teaching assistant in an experiment with an artificial intelligence class. Most students never figured out Jill wasn't human—although some of them said they were suspicious she was because she seemed to answer their questions way too fast.[19]

knowledge workers
Workers whose responsibilities extend beyond the physical execution of work to include planning, decision-making, and problem-solving.

Ordering kiosks like this one in a New York City store are likely to replace some workers.

Sorbis/Shutterstock

Clearly, no one is immune to the changes automation and technology bring. But that doesn't mean that all jobs are going away because of it. A recent study found that about 50 percent of workers' tasks today could be eliminated with current technology and technology being developed. However, only 5 percent of jobs could be.[20] More likely, humans will work with the help of virtual assistants similar to Siri, Cortana, and Amazon's Echo device.

Knowledge-based training is critical to the business model of Manpower, the largest employment agency in the United States. Manpower offers free information technology training to its employees through its online university. The site features thousands of hours of instruction in technology applications, along with professional development, business skills, and telecommunications courses, seminars, and chat rooms with mentors. "Just-in time" learning is delivered via the Internet to Manpower's employees' mobile phones, tablets, and computers.

Firms and their employees are also utilizing massive open online courses (MOOCs) created by colleges and educational firms. A MOOC is a noncredit, often free course anyone can take online, and enrollment is unlimited. MOOCs can help employees get training quickly as well as stretch a company's training budget.

Virtual learning is taking place as well. IBM, Cisco, Kelly Services, and Manpower are among the many companies that have built training facilities, offices, and meeting rooms inside the online reality game Second Life. The spaces these companies build online enable them to do certain things more easily and cheaply than they can in the real world—for example, bringing people from several continents into one room for training or new hires for orientation.[21] Augmented reality devices such as Google Glass and "wearables" such as the Apple Watch are helping employees get information when and where they need it, too. At AGCO, a manufacturer of agricultural equipment, factory workers wear augmented reality glasses, which display diagrams and instructions to help them conduct quality checks.[22]

Technology's Effect on HRM

human resources information system (HRIS)

A computerized system that provides current and accurate HR-related data for the purposes of control and decision-making.

Perhaps the most central use of technology in HRM is an organization's **human resources information system (HRIS)**. HR affects the entire workforce—everyone who works for the company must be hired, trained, paid, and promoted, usually through HR. Human resources information systems are used for everything from automating payroll processing to administering benefits programs. The systems allow managers to access employee records for administrative purposes and employees to access and change their own benefits and other personal information on either an intranet or a secure website.

Firms use human resources information systems to recruit, screen, and pretest applicants online before hiring them as well as to train, track, and promote employees once they have been hired. The drugmaker Merck's HRIS captures information from job recruiting sites and social network sites like LinkedIn, scans applicants' resumes, and makes the information immediately accessible to managers so they can search systematically for the people whose skills they want. Managers can search online for internal and external talent by running searches of candidates who have been categorized by skill set.[23] The HRIS system of the consumer-products maker Procter and Gamble (P&G) makes good internal candidates visible to managers instead of the managers having to scour the company to find them. The system contains information about its 100,000-plus employees worldwide for promotion purposes at the country, business category, and regional levels.

Corning Inc. uses HR software, among other things, to set the developmental goals of its employees once they have been hired and to gauge how well they are meeting them. Employees can look online to see their own goals and mark their progress as well as see everyone else's goals in the command chain, from the CEO down to their immediate supervisors. This "cascading" of goals has helped Corning's employees align their personal goals with the organization's overall objectives, to reach higher levels. "Like any large company, we tended to get 'silo-ed' and fragmented the more we grew," said one vice president at a company using a system similar to Corning's. "We needed a better way to pull our global team together and get people focused on what the priorities are for our business."[24]

One of the newer HRIS applications is the use of big data. *Big data* is a buzzword that describes the massive amounts data available online and offline today that can be "crunched" to make decisions. Marketing departments have very successfully used big data to detect people's buying patterns. By analyzing its customers' buying habits, Target was able to predict which of them were pregnant, sometimes before they had even told their families. The company then sent the customers ads and coupons for baby products.

Now companies are doing the same thing to analyze HR information, a process that's referred to as **workforce (HR) analytics**. Using HR data, such as employee demographic information, performance ratings, pay, employee surveys, academic history, years of service, and so on, a firm can definitely answer questions like the following:

workforce (HR) analytics
The process of gathering and analyzing data to improve a firm's human resources management.

- Do employees with degrees from Ivy League schools perform better—or not?
- Exactly how much more do top performers need to be paid to stay with our firm?
- Which job applicants are likely to perform better?
- Which employees are most likely to quit?

Traditionally, questions such as these have been answered based on anecdotal evidence or the "gut" feelings of HR professionals. But workforce analytics can provide more definitive answers. For example, a major customer service provider analyzed more than 7,000 of its employees and found that "relevant job experience" in the customer service area had no impact on how well they performed and stayed with the company. As a result, the company altered its hiring criteria.[25] Gathering and analyzing HR data may sound like a daunting task, but HR software providers are including data analysis tools in their programs that make it easier to gather and visualize HR data in a meaningful way.

So what sort of HRIS should HR professionals choose among the many options available to them? One of the first steps in choosing a HRIS is for HR personnel to evaluate the biggest "headaches" they experience, or the most time-consuming tasks, and then choose the applications that can have the strongest impact on the firm's financial measures—that is, the ones that get the "biggest bang for the buck." Off-the-shelf HR Web-based solutions are as commonly used as custom-designed systems. Free open-source HRIS software is also available on the Web. OrangeHRM is an example. Open-source software can be a good solution for startup and small businesses looking for a low-cost HRIS solution. Highlights in HRM 1 shows the other factors that need to be evaluated.

Factors to Consider When Evaluating a Human Resources Information System

- *Fit of the application to the firm's employee base.* If many of the firm's employees work on a factory floor, is the system appropriate, or does HR need to install kiosks in employee areas? Will employees be able to access the HRIS offsite on the Internet or on their mobile phones? How will the information be secured? Will employees need to be assigned passwords?

- *Ability to upgrade or customize the application.* What sorts of costs will be involved to upgrade the application in the coming years?

- *Compatibility with current systems.* Does the HRIS link into existing, or planned, information systems easily and inexpensively?

- *User friendliness.* Does the application provide additional features such as links to learning resources or help for managers or employees who might need it?

- *Collaboration.* Does the system connect employees and allow them to collaborate on solutions to problems and projects?

- *Workforce analytics.* Does the system make it easy to gather HR data and visualize its implications?

- *Survey capabilities.* Does the system have an app that allows employees to be surveyed electronically?

- *Recruiting and applicant tracking.* Does the system make it easy to find, recruit, and track applicants and a company's current employees for hiring purposes?

- *Scheduling.* Does the system have scheduling ability to ensure employees are in the right places, working the right times, and on the right projects?

- *Availability of technical support.* Should the HRIS system be supported internally, or should the vendor host it? Will it be cloud based?

- *Time required to implement and train staff members to use the HRIS, including HR and payroll personnel, managers, and employees.* Who is responsible for training employees, and how will it be done?

- *Initial costs and annual maintenance costs.* Is a "suite" of apps needed or just a few key apps? Experts advise HR managers to price each application separately and then ask vendors for a "bundled" price.[26]

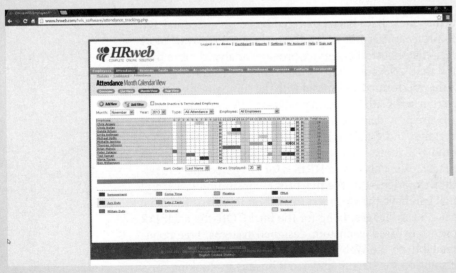

HRweb (shown here) is an example of one of the many HRIS systems available for firms to manage HR-related tasks.

HRWeb.com

Ultimately, however, an HRIS should provide HR personnel with analytical information—statistics, metrics, and so forth—that helps them analyze, refine, and better implement a firm's strategic direction. This can include forecasting personnel needs (especially for firms planning to expand, contract, or merge), planning for career and employee promotions, and evaluating the impact of the firm's policies—both those related to HR functions and other functions.

1.4 Productivity and Cost Challenges

Labor costs are often the largest expenditures companies make, particularly in service- and knowledge-intensive firms. How can companies actually spend more money on employees and still drive overall costs lower? The answer: via higher employee productivity. Employee productivity is the result of a combination of employees' abilities, motivation, and work environment, and the technology they use to work.

LO 4
As a manager, do you think it would be possible to maintain the morale of your firm's employees in the face of shrinking budgets and benefits? How might you do so?

1.4a Maximizing Productivity

Productivity can be defined as "the output gained from a fixed amount of inputs." Organizations can increase their productivity either by reducing their inputs (the cost approach) or by increasing the amount that employees produce by adding more human and/or physical capital to the process. Companies such as Southwest Airlines, Nucor, and the manufacturing and technology firm Danaher achieve low costs in their industries not because they scrimp on employees but because they are the most productive.

United States is still by far the world's most productive nation in terms of the total value of all goods and services it produces, even when it comes to manufacturing. China ranks second. Apparel and textile manufacturing are far smaller industries in the United States than what they once were, but they have been replaced by industries that rely more on technological precision and brainpower than on low-skilled labor—industries for aircraft, sophisticated machinery, medical devices, and so on.[27] However, the growth in output per worker is now climbing fast in countries such as China that in the past have lacked the amount of technology available to U.S. workers. When the investment in faster computers and more efficient machine tools levels off, this limits how much assistance technology can offer employees in terms of their productivity. Any additional productivity will have to come from the enhanced ability of employees, their motivation, and their work environment, which makes the job of the HR manager in the coming years all the more crucial.[28]

1.4b Managing the Size of the Workforce

Part of managing productivity is matching the size of the workforce to the demand requirements of a firm given technology, the firm's strategic direction, and global competition. Sometimes this task entails hiring additional personnel to expand a firm's capacity. At other times, offshoring is used to increase capacity. Offshoring can help a firm deliver products more quickly if people across the globe are working around the clock on them. For example, to keep up with demand as well as lower costs, some U.S. clinics and hospitals have offshored the task of reading X-rays to radiologists in other countries such as India. X-rays taken in the day are read at night abroad and delivered the next day to the hospitals and clinics.[29] Offshoring is also used when companies want to expand to other countries and capture market share there. Apple is trying to do this by opening an iPhone manufacturing facility in India.

Outsourcing can help a firm manage the size of its workforce, reduce costs, and focus on the activities it does best. For example, companies hire advertising firms to handle their promotions, software firms to develop data-processing systems for them, and law firms to handle their legal issues rather than do them in-house. Maintenance, security, catering, and payroll (and in small companies, sometimes entire HR departments) are outsourced to increase the organization's flexibility and manage the size of the workforce.

Despite the advantages offshoring and outsourcing offer, a growing number of firms are moving jobs back to their domestic markets or in-house. Delta Air Lines is among the firms that returned its call-center operations to the United States after customers complained about the service they received from personnel in foreign countries. Other companies are **nearshoring**, which is the practice of bringing jobs closer to domestic countries, and **homeshoring**, which is the practice of outsourcing work to domestic workers who work out of their homes.

Downsizing is, of course, another way to manage the size of the workforce as is furloughing. **Furloughing** is the practice of requiring employees to take time off for either no pay or reduced pay. More diligent workforce planning may be a better solution than either downsizing or furloughing, says John Sullivan, an HR expert and consultant. Business revenues seldom fall off overnight. Sullivan says the best managers develop a process that pinpoints skills the company no longer needs, low-impact jobs, and poor performers in advance of a crisis. Instead, part-time or contract employees can be hired and their hours of service adjusted as needed.[30]

1.4c Managing Pay and Benefits

Most firms closely monitor employee pay and benefit programs. Skyrocketing health care costs are perhaps the biggest concerns companies are facing when it comes to compensation and benefits. Companies are taking many different approaches to try to keep health care costs in check, including charging employees higher premiums for covering their spouses if they are able to obtain insurance through their own employers. Yet another approach is giving employees a set amount of money they can use to purchase health insurance on their own. Walgreen's and Darden Restaurants, which operates the Olive Garden and Red Lobster chains, have taken this approach. A more proactive approach is to offer employees incentives to get healthy—for example, by quitting smoking, losing weight, or exercising.[31]

Another way firms are managing benefits is by using employee leasing. When **employee leasing** is used, a firm signs an agreement with a professional employer organization (PEO). The PEO—typically a larger company—takes over the management of the smaller company's HR tasks and becomes a coemployer to its employees. The PEO performs all the HR duties of an employer—hiring, payroll, and performance appraisal. Because PEOs can coemploy a large number of people working at many different companies, they can provide employees with benefits that small companies cannot afford, such as 401(k) and health care plans, workers' compensation, and even adoption assistance.

Another strategy to manage pay and benefits is to hire freelancers, part-time employees, independent contractors, and consultants, who work in what's being called the "gig economy." In the gig economy, people earn income from various nonpermanent "gigs," or jobs, and work independently, rather than full time for a single employer. An Uber driver is an example of a person participating in the gig economy. The gig economy isn't new, but it's definitely a growing trend.

nearshoring
Occurs when a firm relocates jobs abroad to nations closer to its domestic market.

homeshoring
The practice of outsourcing work to domestic workers who work out of their homes.

furloughing
A situation in which an organization asks or requires employees to take time off for either no pay or reduced pay.

employee leasing
The process of eliminating the jobs of employees who are then hired by a leasing company (which handles all HR-related activities) and contracting with that company to lease back the employees.

Some companies, such as Google, are able to hire talented employees by offering them great pay and fantastic benefits. However, most companies, especially small ones or ones that are struggling, find it hard to compete with bigger firms like Google with deluxe benefit packages. What can small companies do to attract employees yet contain costs? Many companies are finding that providing work flexibility is a good way to improve the productivity and motivation of valuable employees, especially when giving them larger benefit packages is not an option. For example, when gasoline prices shot up to over $4/gallon during the last recession, most small companies weren't able to increase their employees' pay because they were facing higher transportation costs themselves for the goods and services they had to buy. But some companies began letting employees telecommute (work from home) or, like the state of Utah did, work 10 hours per day, 4 days a week.

Small Business Application

A Small Business Built on Helping Small Businesses

As experienced and highly respected HR professionals, Delise West and Tonya Rochette could have easily furthered their careers by pursuing positions in large corporations or academia. Instead, they chose to forge a new path for themselves by founding Human Resource Partners, a small human-resources consulting firm located in Dover, New Hampshire. Friends and family thought they were both a little crazy to enter the "risky" world of owning a small business, but since joining forces 12 years ago, they have been very successful at serving other small, entrepreneurial businesses just like theirs.

West and Rochette both recognized early on that small businesses need to address HR issues just as much as larger businesses, yet small-business owners usually do not have the time or expertise to devote to these issues themselves and often do not have the financial resources to hire a full-time, knowledgeable HR manager. This pair of entrepreneurs saw that reality as an opportunity to provide a full spectrum of HR services to companies in need.

"There are so many companies who don't have the right HR infrastructure in place," said West, whose firm works mostly with companies under 70 employees. "Oftentimes, an owner of a growing business will come to me and simply say, 'I can't do it anymore because it has become too time consuming.' Some of the companies that have turned to West and Rochette for help with HR functions and strategy include a major car dealership, a regional construction company, and a local nursery.

Work with a new client typically begins with an evaluation of the firm's level of HR compliance and best practices, such as job description documentation, payroll systems, and legal interviewing practices. From there, Human Resource Partners develops strategies for the client to implement in the areas of recruiting, screening, interviewing, and hiring new staff; evaluating and recognizing current employee performance; and improving employee relations and developing supervisory skills.

By giving small firms the tools, services, and training they need, West and Rochette allow their clients to focus on their core business. Said West, Human Resource Partners lets small firms "realize the return on their investments in their greatest assets: their people."

Outsourcing a firm's HR isn't a new strategy for firms, big or small. Many companies have outsourced their pay and benefits functions for years. What is new is the growth in HR outsourcing. Currently, it's a $42.6 billion industry. By 2020, that number is expected to grow to $53.9 billion, a 25 percent increase.

The growth of HR outsourcing has been good news for West and Rochette. Human Resource Partners expanded quickly and now serves larger, midsize businesses as well. To help meet demand in Dover and other New Hampshire cities the two entrepreneurs also brought on additional HR professionals as partners. Because the outsourcing model gives small and midsize businesses senior-level HR expertise, West says she believes HRP will continue to grow.

Sources: Mark Feffer, "Meet the People Behind Your Outsourcing," *HR News* (July 1, 2016), https://www.shrm.org; Kim Murdoch, "Celebrating 10 Years: Concord- and Dover-based HRP Marks Milestone," *ConcordPatch* (May 24, 2013), http://concord-nh.patch.com; Michael McCord, "Outsourcing Frees Owners from Time Consuming Tasks," SeaCoastonline.com (January 10, 2011), http://www.seacoastonline.com; company website: h-rpartners.com.

LO ⑤

Think about some of the teams you have been a member of. Which of them performed better—those that were diverse or those that were not? What challenges and opportunities did the more diverse teams present? How do you think they translate to human resources management?

1.5 Employee Challenges

Do you think a company has a moral obligation to take care of its workforce? What kind of company would you like to work for? These are questions you are probably asking yourself as you prepare for your career. Clearly, in addition to the strategic challenges that companies face, they also must attend to some very important employee concerns. Those challenges span a wide range of important concerns such as job security, health care, diversity, and employee rights.

1.5a Responding to the Demographic and Diversity Challenges of the Workforce

To forecast trends to support the strategies of their organizations, HR managers frequently analyze the capabilities of different demographic groups and how well each is represented in both fast-growing and slow-growing occupations. Women, for example, are fairly well represented in fast-growing occupations such as health services but are also represented in some slow-growth occupations such as administrative jobs and computer and financial records processing jobs. Blacks and Hispanics have been heavily concentrated in several of the slow-growth and declining occupations. The U.S. labor force also grew more slowly in the last decade than it did in the previous one, a trend that is projected to continue. The labor force participation rate—that is, the number people employed or actively looking for work—is also declining in the United States. Figure 1.2 shows the U.S. labor force participation rate. The rate peaked in 2000 at about 67 percent; however, during the last recession, many people dropped out of the job market. The rate then fell before leveling off at about 62.7 percent.

But even with the economic recovery, the labor participation rate is predicted to fall because of declining birth rates and the aging U.S. population. By 2050, the U.S. Bureau of Labor Statistics (BLS) predicts the labor force participation rate will be about 60.2 percent. To accommodate shifts such as these, find qualified talent, and broaden their customer bases, businesses know it is absolutely vital to increase their

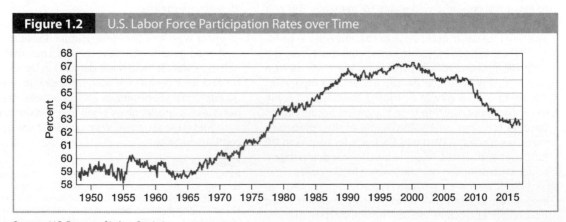

Figure 1.2   U.S. Labor Force Participation Rates over Time

Source: U.S. Bureau of Labor Statistics

efforts to recruit and train a more diverse workforce. And with a more diverse workforce comes more diverse expectations on the part of employees for their employers to meet.

Ethnic and Racial Diversity in the Workforce

Minorities in the United States are increasing relative to the total population. U.S. workers are becoming more diverse as well. Much of the growth of the minority workforce has been due to not only the arrival of immigrants but also high birth rates among some minority groups, such as Hispanics. By 2024, Hispanics are projected to make up nearly one-fifth of the labor force. By 2050, they are projected to make up about one-third of the labor force, as Figure 1.3 shows.[32]

Firms have been criticized for hiring immigrant workers—both legal and illegal—because people believe they prevent U.S. citizens from getting jobs. In addition, following the attack on the World Trade Center in 2001, the number of work visas issued to foreigners by the U.S. government was cut. Many American employers say this a problem because they lack the highly qualified workers they need for key positions. To bring in the talent it needs from abroad, Microsoft opened a facility in Canada, across from its Redmond, Washington, headquarters. However, critics of work visas, of which there are many, claim there isn't a shortage of qualified workers and that employers use the program to hire foreign workers they can pay less. The United States has been able to attract the best and brightest of the world's talent, which fueled the country's success. For example, in 2016, all American Nobel Laureates were immigrants. But as you will learn in Chapter 15, that is changing.[33]

It is not just the most highly educated who are in demand either. Some businesses, including those in the agricultural business, face labor shortages that would be even more severe without less-skilled immigrants willing to work for low pay and few or no benefits. The jobs these people do are often labor intensive and must be

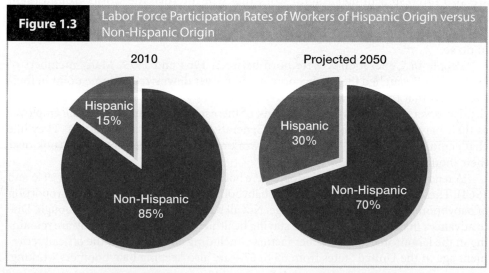

Figure 1.3   Labor Force Participation Rates of Workers of Hispanic Origin versus Non-Hispanic Origin

Source: U.S. Bureau of Labor Statistics

done in bad weather or in agricultural facilities in less-than-pleasant conditions, and involve work that many Americans don't want to do. Nonetheless, there is a concern that immigrants (both legal and illegal) are taking away jobs from Americans. Illegal immigrants make up about 5 percent of the labor force. They are concentrated in certain jobs, such as farming (26%), cleaning and maintenance (17%), and construction (14%).[34]

In recent years, the federal government and state and local governments have tried to make it harder for firms to hire illegal immigrants and passed laws making it more difficult for them to live, work, and drive in the United States. After Georgia and Alabama did so, crops rotted in the fields in those states because of a lack of workers to harvest them. Those states subsequently relaxed their rules. Later in the book we will discuss in more detail what companies are doing in response to minority and immigration challenges and opportunities.[35]

Age Distribution of the Workforce

The newest generation entering the workplace is Generation Z. The members of Generation Z were born in the mid-1990s and early 2000s. It's been estimated that by 2020, they will make up 20 percent of the workforce. These workers have never known life without smartphones and social media and they expect to be trained and managed with digital tools. They are also more comfortable with racial, cultural, and sexual diversity than other generations and want to change the world for the better. A large number of members of this generation say they want to start their own businesses. Others, having grown up during the last recession, want to go straight to work rather than incurring the cost of college.

The millennial generation (Generation Y) is having a big impact on the labor market right now. The group is also 75 to 80 million people strong, making it the largest generation ever. Millennials are generally regarded as having good technological knowhow and initiative, especially when it comes to starting their own businesses. (Facebook founder Mark Zuckerberg is a notable example.) Like Generation Z, they are also interested in meaningful work that will improve the world around them and want a good work-life balance. Neither generation wants to be pigeonholed into jobs. They want to try new jobs and new tasks, and they are quite willing to job hop to do so.

People in Generation X were born between 1964 and 1979. Many members of Generation X watched their babyboomer parents get downsized at some point in their lives. Now that they are raising children themselves, Generation Xers value job security. However, they are less likely to think of themselves as being wed to one employer as their parents were. The members of Generation X are also independent. They like challenging work rather than repetitive work and dislike supervisors who look over their shoulders.

A relatively large number of people were born after World War II (between 1946 and 1964). These people are members of the babyboom generation. A significant proportion of babyboomers have hit retirement age. Not all babyboomers are retiring, though. Due to advances in medicine, people are staying healthier as they age, and many are remaining in the labor force longer. Other factors—including an increase in the official retirement age in the United States from 65 to 67—are also keeping babyboomers working.

So are economic factors: Many babyboomers have not saved enough to retire, or their 401(k) retirement accounts have not grown as well as expected. Older workers tend to be dependable and remain on the job longer than younger workers, who operate more like free agents. Because their kids are grown up, older workers are also often willing to work flexible hours.

So, what will the workforce look like in years to come in terms of ages? Figure 1.4 shows older Americans—those hitting the 55-and-over age bracket—are the fastest growing segment of the workforce and will be for decades as the U.S. workforce continues to age. By contrast, the average annual growth rate of 16- to 24-year-olds in the labor force is projected to decline. Managers can find themselves challenged in terms of getting the four generations to work well together. Babyboomers sometimes categorize younger workers as having a poorer work ethic. Some younger workers have the perception that older workers are set in their ways and are technologically challenged. The situation can also create supervisory issues. How will a 55-year-old react to being managed by someone in their 20s or 30s? To help companies overcome these obstacles, HR departments and experts are developing programs to help the generations understand one another better so they can capitalize on one another's strengths rather than preying on one another's weaknesses.

Keep in mind that the three generations of workers we have described here are generalizations. Individual employees are vastly different from one another and motivated by different factors, even if they belong to the same generation. It is up to managers to figure out what drives each person so as to best utilize his or her talents and to meet the person's employment demands and career aspirations.

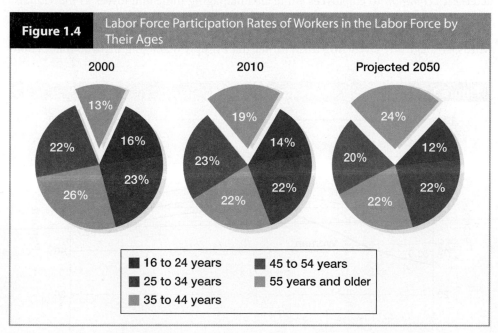

| Figure 1.4 | Labor Force Participation Rates of Workers in the Labor Force by Their Ages |

2000   **2010**   **Projected 2050**

- ■ 16 to 24 years
- ■ 25 to 34 years
- ■ 35 to 44 years
- ■ 45 to 54 years
- ■ 55 years and older

Source: U.S. Bureau of Labor Statistics

Gender Distribution of the Workforce

Following World War II, less than one-third of women were in the workforce. Currently, women constitute a little under half of the U.S. workforce. About 60 percent of women age 16 and older are in the labor force, and approximately 70 percent of mothers with school-age children are employed in some capacity. As Figure 1.5 shows, the number of women joining the U.S. labor force has tapered off some in recent years as it has for men and is expected to continue to do so.[36]

The educational attainment of women is also increasing relative to men. Today, three of every five college graduates are women. Women's wages have increased, too. In 1979, on average, women made 62 percent of what men made. Although the gap has not closed, it has narrowed. Women who are employed full time today make about 83 percent of what men employed full time make.[37]

However, some studies have found that younger women in urban areas make more than their male counterparts. One market research firm analyzing census data found that in 47 of the 50 biggest U.S. metropolitan areas, the median full-time salaries of young women were 8 percent higher than for men in their peer group.[38] Top executive positions are still dominated by men, though.

Employers wanting to attract the talent that women have to offer are taking measures to ensure they are treated equally in the workplace in terms of their advancement opportunities and compensation. In addition, more companies are accommodating working parents by offering them parental leave, part-time employment, flexible work schedules, job sharing, telecommuting, child and elder care assistance, and adoption assistance.

As we have suggested, harnessing a company's talent means being aware of characteristics *common* to employees while also managing these employees as *individuals*. It means not just tolerating or accommodating all sorts of differences but supporting, nurturing, and utilizing these differences to the organization's advantage—in other words, strategically leveraging them rather than simply managing them so that people

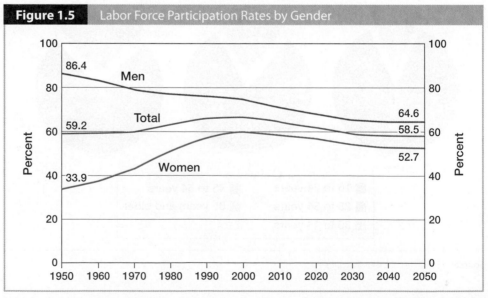

Figure 1.5   Labor Force Participation Rates by Gender

Source: U.S. Bureau of Labor Statistics

are treated equitably and "everyone gets along."[39] HR managers have to ask themselves the following questions: What is it about the experiences, mindsets, and talents of different groups of people that can be utilized in a strategic way? After all, despite our similarities, *all* of us are different in one way or another, aside from the obvious differences we have outlined in this section. These differences, too, can be the source of organizational strength. Later in the book, we will discuss more about the steps firms can take to leverage employee differences.

1.5b Educational Shifts Affecting the Workforce

Over the years, the educational attainment of the U.S. labor force has risen dramatically.[40] Figure 1.6 shows that a college education results in higher wages and lower unemployment rates. Despite the fact the educational attainment of the labor force has risen in general, American students' math and science test scores lag behind those of students in China, Japan, Singapore, Finland, and several other nations. The U.S. Department of Education has found that less than half of all high school seniors can handle mathematics problems involving fractions, decimals, percentages, elementary geometry, and simple algebra. American adults are struggling, too. In survey of adults in 24 developed countries, Americans scored below the average on literacy, math, and computer skills tests.[41] What does this mean for the United States? What will HR managers do? The best ones will find strategies to help their firms compete, despite these challenges.

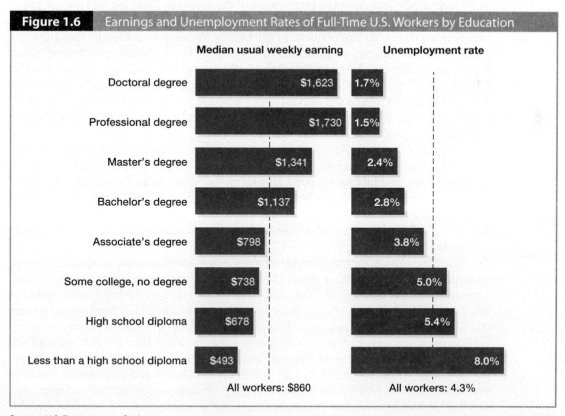

Figure 1.6   Earnings and Unemployment Rates of Full-Time U.S. Workers by Education

	Median usual weekly earning	Unemployment rate
Doctoral degree	$1,623	1.7%
Professional degree	$1,730	1.5%
Master's degree	$1,341	2.4%
Bachelor's degree	$1,137	2.8%
Associate's degree	$798	3.8%
Some college, no degree	$738	5.0%
High school diploma	$678	5.4%
Less than a high school diploma	$493	8.0%
	All workers: $860	All workers: 4.3%

Source: U.S. Department of Labor.

1.5c Adapting to Cultural and Societal Changes Affecting the Workforce

The attitudes, beliefs, values, and customs of people in a society are an integral part of their culture. Naturally, their culture and society affect their behavior on the job and the environment within the organization, influencing their reactions to work assignments, leadership styles, and reward systems. Cultural and societal changes are ongoing. HR policies and procedures therefore must be adjusted to cope with these changes.

Changing Employee Rights

Laws affecting employee rights are continually changing. In this book we will discuss the major laws affecting companies today. Among them are laws granting employees the right to equal employment opportunities (Chapter 3); union representation if they desire it (Chapter 14); a safe and healthful work environment (Chapter 12); unemployment and health care benefits as required by law and the regulation of pension plans by the government (Chapter 11); equal pay for equal work (Chapter 9); and so on. An expanded discussion of the specific areas in which rights and responsibilities are of concern to employers and employees will be presented in Chapter 13.

Privacy Concerns of Employees

HR managers and their staff members, as well as line managers in positions of responsibility, generally recognize the importance of discretion in handling all types of information about employees. Since the passage of the federal Privacy Act of 1974, increased attention to privacy has been evident, heightened by the increase in identity theft in recent years. While the act applies almost exclusively to records maintained by federal agencies, it has drawn attention to the importance of privacy and has led to the passage of additional privacy legislation, including the Health Insurance Portability and Accountability Act of 1996 (HIPAA) and the associated privacy rule issued by the U.S. Department of Health and Human Services, which protects the use and disclosure of personal medical information.

In addition to implementing privacy policies, most companies try to limit the use of social security numbers on employment forms. Companies also restrict access to employee files, conduct background checks on employees who have access to others' files, and contract with outside firms specializing in identity theft to prevent the abuse of employee information. Globalization has added another twist to privacy compliance. For example, EU countries prohibit the transfer of personal data to countries with inadequate data protection laws.[42]

The Electronic Communications Privacy Act of 1986 protects people's electronic communications such as their email. However, employers have a right to monitor their employees' emails, phone calls, texts, and Internet use while on the job. Camera surveillance in the workplace is also an issue, as is the use of the global positioning system (GPS). The nonprofit organization Workplace Fairness reports that employers are using GPS in company cars to track where workers are, how fast they are driving, and the length of their breaks by monitoring how long their vehicles have not moved. Employers are also using applications installed on workers' smartphones and employee ID cards to see where they are, if they have arrived at jobsites on time, and dispatch the closest ones to jobs.[43] In addition, employers are scrutinizing information employees post on the Web and social media. Some employers have gone so far as to demand job applicants give them their passwords to social media sites.

Tracking software and mobile apps are becoming more popular for employers to remotely track employees actions on their cell phones or computer to monitor their whereabouts and activities while on the job.

Is it legal to do these things? In many cases, yes. In most U.S. states it's legal for employers to require their employees to give passwords to social networking sites, and ask job applicants what they earned at their previous jobs, despite efforts by some legislators to prohibit the practice. And in most states, it's legal to monitor your employees without telling them.

But although legislators have not addressed all privacy situations, some of them are being decided in court. Firms that have disciplined or fired employees for making disparaging remarks about their organizations on the Internet have found themselves sued by the employees and labor organizations claiming the workers' rights to communicate and congregate freely were violated. Intrusive practices can also seriously erode employee morale and a firm's ability to attract top talent. In Chapter 13, we will discuss employer-implemented privacy programs and guidelines along with the privacy employees can expect while on the job.

Changing Attitudes Toward Work and How They Relate to Employee Engagement

Employees today are less likely to define their personal success only in terms of financial gains. Many employees, especially younger ones, believe satisfaction in life is more likely to result from balancing their work challenges and rewards with those in their personal lives. Though most people still enjoy work and want to excel at it, they tend to be focused on finding interesting work and are more inclined to pursue multiple careers. In fact, in a survey of more than 3,000 workers, 86 percent said work fulfillment and work-life balance were their top priorities. Only 35 percent of workers said being successful at work and moving up the ladder were their top priorities. Remaining with a single employer is no longer a top priority either. People also appear to be seeking ways of living that are less complicated but more meaningful.

employee engagement
The extent to which employees are enthused about their work and committed to it.

These new lifestyles cannot help having an impact on the way employees must be motivated, managed, and engaged. **Employee engagement** can be defined as the extent to which employees are enthused about their work and committed to it. Employee engagement is not easy to achieve. Many studies show that far fewer employees are engaged with their jobs than their firms would like.

Consequently, firms are rethinking what employee engagement means and how it can be achieved. A growing number of them are thinking about the "employee experience" like they do the "customer experience." For example, how can a firm excite its employees about their jobs and gain their loyalty like Apple does its iPhone customers? In other words, firms are using some of the insights of consumer marketing and applying them to HR.

To improve the employee experience, firms such as Whole Foods are allowing their workers to vote on firmwide initiatives and rate their company's HR practices—just like people rate restaurants, hotels, and movies on Yelp.[44] Improving the employee experience also includes allowing employees to test-drive new roles and jobs, just like customers test-drive different products. One HR manager predicts there will come a time when, after completing projects, workers will get computer messages that say something like: *If you enjoyed this type of work, you might also enjoy X type of work*—just like you get alternate product selections when you're shopping on the Web.

Balancing Work and Family

Even though new Census Bureau figures show couples postponing marriage and parenthood, balancing work and family continues to be a major concern for firms and their employees. Employees are already working more hours than they have at any time since 1973, and increasingly employees are tethered to their companies around the clock via communication technologies. Complicating the task is the fact that today's families are also more diverse. They can consist of two-wage-earner families, single-parent families, families headed by same-sex couples, and families in which multiple generations of adults are living under one roof.

Competitive organizations are finding it advantageous to provide employees with more family-friendly options. Those options include telecommuting, flexible work hours, day care, elder care, part-time work, job sharing, parental leave, adoption assistance, spousal involvement in career planning, and assistance with family problems. Most Fortune 500 companies, including Walmart and Exxon-Mobile, now provide same-sex-partner health-insurance benefits.[45]

Companies with programs such as these calculate that accommodating their employees' individual needs and circumstances is a powerful way to attract and retain top-caliber people. Aetna Life and Casualty, for example, cut its turnover by 50 percent after it began offering 6-month parental leaves, coupled with an option for part-time work when employees return to the job. Bank of America encourages all its employees to visit their children's schools or volunteer at any school—on company time.[46]

Family-friendly companies have to balance the benefits they provide to families versus their single employees, though. The majority of employees have no children under 18. A Conference Board survey of companies with family-friendly programs found that companies acknowledge that childless employees sometimes harbor resentment against employees with children who are able to take advantage of these programs when they cannot.[47]

1.6 The Role HR Managers Play and Their Partnership with Other Managers

So far in this chapter, we have outlined a number of challenges firms face. HR managers can play a key role in terms of helping their firms meet these challenges. For example, utilizing business statistics and surveys, HR managers can measure the engagement and effectiveness of their firms' workforces. How do employees think, learn, work, solve problems, manage their time, and deal with other people? By first seeing differences such as these, exploring them, and then discovering how they can provide value to the organization, HR managers can leverage those differences.

Similarly, by staying abreast of workforce trends and developments and gathering and analyzing data, HR managers can help theirs firms choose the best strategies when it comes to competing globally, selecting human resource systems that are ideal for a firm and its workers, maximizing productivity, managing benefits, and so on. For example, rather than cutting its health care benefits, HR personnel at Cerner Corp., a midsize Kansas City–based technology company, looked at statistics and other data to find out which diseases its workers were most likely to suffer from and adjusted its employee health-and-wellness programs accordingly. The company has been able to lower its health care costs as a result.

HR managers also serve as valuable partners to other managers, including **line managers**. Line managers are non-HR managers who are responsible for overseeing the work of other employees. Successful organizations combine the experience of line managers with the expertise of HR managers to develop and utilize the talents of employees to their greatest potential. HR programs in particular tend to more successful if they are "owned" by line managers *and* HR. When employees see HR as the sole owner of a program, they sometimes interpret it as an administrative or back-office rather than a strategic initiative.

Just as there are different types of line managers who specialize in different functions—operations, accounting, marketing, and so forth—there are different types of HR managers who specialize in different functions. Some of these workers specialize in employee training and development, recruitment, or compensation. Other HR employees specialize in studying the effects of industry and occupational trends, or concentrate on labor relations and prepare information for managers to use during negotiations with labor unions. By contrast, an HR generalist might handle all aspects of human resources work depending on his or her employer's needs. Figure 1.7 shows salary information for some of the HR positions we have discussed. The median pay for HR managers in 2015 was $104,440.

The Bureau of Labor Statistics has forecasted that the number of HR managers needed is expected to grow by 9 percent between 2014 and 2024, which is faster than the

LO 6

Explain the dual role HR managers play in terms of serving both management and staff. Have you ever found yourself in a similar situation at work or school? Were you able to keep both groups happy? How were the challenges you faced similar to those faced by HR managers?

line managers
Non-HR managers who are responsible for overseeing the work of other employees.

Figure 1.7	Positions in HR and Their Median Annual Wages

Position	Annual Wage
Training and development specialists	$ 58,210
Labor relations specialists	$ 58,820
Compensation, benefits, and job analysis specialists	$ 60,850
Training and development managers	$ 102,640
Compensation and benefits managers	$ 111,430

Source: U.S. Bureau of Labor Statistics.

average for all occupations. Nonetheless, we understand that most readers of this book will be line managers and supervisors rather than HR specialists. The text is, therefore, oriented to *helping people lead and manage people more effectively*, whether they become team leaders, first-line supervisors, HR managers, or chief executive officers.

1.6a Responsibilities of Human Resource Managers

The major activities for which HR managers are typically responsible include:

1. *Strategic advice and counsel.* HR managers often serve as in-house consultants to supervisors, managers, and executives. Given their knowledge of internal employment information and productivity metrics as well as their awareness of external trends such as economic and unemployment data and new legal and regulatory issues, HR managers are an invaluable resource for making decisions. In some companies, generally larger ones, chief compliance or ethics officers help employees wade through gray areas when it comes to right and wrong and ensure personnel comply with the laws and regulations that affect their industries. The firm's top HR manager is in a good position for this job. HR managers are also being relied on more heavily to advise compensation committees, which are more closely scrutinizing executives' pay than they have in years past.

2. *Service.* HR managers perform a host of service activities such as recruiting, selecting, testing, and planning/conducting training programs. Technical expertise in these areas is essential for HR managers as they design and implement talent-management programs.

3. *Policy formulation and implementation.* HR managers generally propose and draft new policies or policy revisions to cover recurring problems or to prevent anticipated problems. Ordinarily, the policies are proposed to the senior executives of the organization, who actually issue them. HR managers also monitor the firm's managers and employees to ensure they follow established HR policies, procedures, and practices. Perhaps more important, they are a resource to whom managers can turn for policy interpretation.

4. *Employee advocacy.* One of the enduring roles of HR managers is to serve as an employee advocate—listening to employees' concerns and representing their needs to managers—to make certain that the interests of employees and the interests of the organization are aligned with one another.

1.6b Competencies Human Resource Managers Require

As top executives expect HR managers to assume a broader role in overall organizational strategy, many of these managers will need to acquire a complementary set of competencies. These competencies are summarized here and shown graphically in Figure 1.8.

- *Business mastery.* As we have explained, HR professionals need to know the businesses of their organizations and their strategies thoroughly. This requires an understanding of an organization's customers and economic and financial capabilities to help a firm shape and achieve its strategic direction and adjust it as needed. Human resource managers who have good problem-solving skills and are also innovative and creative are a strategic asset to their firms.

- *HR mastery.* HR professionals are the organization's behavioral science experts. They should develop expert knowledge in the areas of staffing, development, appraisals, rewards, team building, performance measurement, and communication. Good interpersonal skills are essential.

- *Personal credibility.* Like other management professionals, HR professionals must establish personal credibility in the eyes of people internal and external to the firm. Credibility and trust are earned by developing good relationships with people both internal and external to the firm, demonstrating the values of the firm, standing up for one's own beliefs, and dealing with all parties equitably. Highlights in HRM 2 outlines the code of ethical and professional standards HR personnel should follow, according to the Society for Human Resource Management.

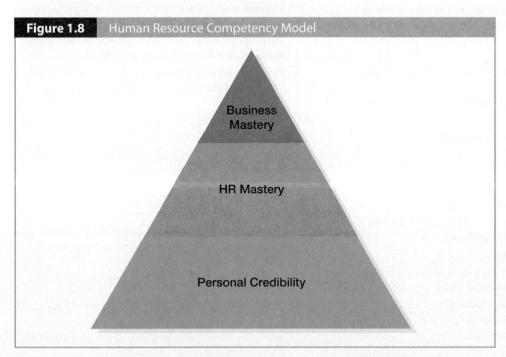

Figure 1.8 Human Resource Competency Model

Business Mastery

HR Mastery

Personal Credibility

Source: Adapted from Arthur Yeung, Wayne Brockbank, and Dave Ulrich, "Lower Cost, Higher Value: Human Resource Function in Transformation," reprinted with permission from Human Resource Planning, vol. 17, no. 3 (1994). Copyright 1994 by The Human Resource Planning Society, 317 Madison Avenue, Suite 1509, New York, NY 10017, (212) 490 6387.

SHRM Code of Ethical and Professional Standards in Human Resource Management

CODE PROVISIONS

Professional Responsibility

Core Principle

As HR professionals, we are responsible for adding value to the organizations we serve and contributing to the ethical success of those organizations. We accept professional responsibility for our individual decisions and actions. We are also advocates for the profession by engaging in activities that enhance its credibility and value.

Intent

- To build respect, credibility and strategic importance for the HR profession within our organizations, the business community, and the communities in which we work.
- To assist the organizations we serve in achieving their objectives and goals.
- To inform and educate current and future practitioners, the organizations we serve, and the general public about principles and practices that help the profession.
- To positively influence workplace and recruitment practices.
- To encourage professional decision-making and responsibility.
- To encourage social responsibility.

Guidelines

1. Adhere to the highest standards of ethical and professional behavior.
2. Measure the effectiveness of HR in contributing to or achieving organizational goals.
3. Comply with the law.
4. Work consistent with the values of the profession.
5. Strive to achieve the highest levels of service, performance and social responsibility.
6. Advocate for the appropriate use and appreciation of human beings as employees.
7. Advocate openly and within the established forums for debate in order to influence decision-making and results.

Professional Development

Core Principle

As professionals we must strive to meet the highest standards of competence and commit to strengthen our competencies on a continuous basis.

Intent

- To expand our knowledge of human resource management to further our understanding of how our organizations function.
- To advance our understanding of how organizations work ("the business of the business").

Guidelines

1. Pursue formal academic opportunities.
2. Commit to continuous learning, skills development and application of new knowledge related to both human resource management and the organizations we serve.
3. Contribute to the body of knowledge, the evolution of the profession and the growth of individuals through teaching, research and dissemination of knowledge.
4. Pursue certification where available, or comparable measures of competencies and knowledge.

Ethical Leadership

Core Principle

HR professionals are expected to exhibit individual leadership as a role model for maintaining the highest standards of ethical conduct.

Intent

- To set the standard and be an example for others.
- To earn individual respect and increase our credibility with those we serve.

Guidelines

1. Be ethical; act ethically in every professional interaction.
2. Question pending individual and group actions when necessary to ensure that decisions are ethical and are implemented in an ethical manner.
3. Seek expert guidance if ever in doubt about the ethical propriety of a situation.

4. Through teaching and mentoring, champion the development of others as ethical leaders in the profession and in organizations.

Fairness and Justice

Core Principle

As human resource professionals, we are ethically responsible for promoting and fostering fairness and justice for all employees and their organizations.

Intent

- To create and sustain an environment that encourages all individuals and the organization to reach their fullest potential in a positive and productive manner.

Guidelines

1. Respect the uniqueness and intrinsic worth of every individual.
2. Treat people with dignity, respect and compassion to foster a trusting work environment free of harassment, intimidation, and unlawful discrimination.
3. Ensure that everyone has the opportunity to develop their skills and new competencies.
4. Assure an environment of inclusiveness and a commitment to diversity in the organizations we serve.
5. Develop, administer and advocate policies and procedures that foster fair, consistent and equitable treatment for all.
6. Regardless of personal interests, support decisions made by our organizations that are both ethical and legal.
7. Act in a responsible manner and practice sound management in the country(ies) in which the organizations we serve operate.

Conflicts of Interest

Core Principle

As HR professionals, we must maintain a high level of trust with our stakeholders. We must protect the interests of our stakeholders as well as our professional integrity and should not engage in activities that create actual, apparent, or potential conflicts of interest.

Intent

To avoid activities that are in conflict or may appear to be in conflict with any of the provisions of this Code of Ethical and Professional Standards in Human Resource Management or with one's responsibilities and duties as a member of the human resource profession and/or as an employee of any organization.

Guidelines

1. Adhere to and advocate the use of published policies on conflicts of interest within your organization.
2. Refrain from using your position for personal, material or financial gain or the appearance of such.
3. Refrain from giving or seeking preferential treatment in the human resources processes.
4. Prioritize your obligations to identify conflicts of interest or the appearance thereof; when conflicts arise, disclose them to relevant stakeholders.

Use of Information

Core Principle

HR professionals consider and protect the rights of individuals, especially in the acquisition and dissemination of information while ensuring truthful communications and facilitating informed decision-making.

Intent

To build trust among all organization constituents by maximizing the open exchange of information, while eliminating anxieties about inappropriate and/or inaccurate acquisition and sharing of information

Guidelines

1. Acquire and disseminate information through ethical and responsible means.
2. Ensure only appropriate information is used in decisions affecting the employment relationship.
3. Investigate the accuracy and source of information before allowing it to be used in employment related decisions.
4. Maintain current and accurate HR information.
5. Safeguard restricted or confidential information.
6. Take appropriate steps to ensure the accuracy and completeness of all communicated information about HR policies and practices.
7. Take appropriate steps to ensure the accuracy and completeness of all communicated information used in HR-related training.

Summary

LO ① Understanding human resource management practices and issues can help you better compete in the marketplace—as an employee, manager, or HR manager. Employees and managers who have a good understanding of their firm's business can help it achieve its strategies—whatever they may be—through the effective utilization of people and their talents.

An organization's success increasingly depends on the knowledge, skills, and abilities of its employees. To "compete through people," organizations have to do a good job of fostering and managing human capital: the knowledge, skills, and capabilities that have value to organizations. Managers must develop strategies for identifying, recruiting, and hiring the best talent available; developing these employees in ways that are firm specific; helping them to generate new ideas and generalize them throughout the company; encouraging information sharing; and rewarding collaboration and teamwork among employees.

LO ② Globalization has become pervasive in the marketplace. It influences the number and kinds of jobs that are available and requires that organizations balance a complicated set of issues related to managing people working under different business conditions in different geographies, cultures, and legal environments. HR strategies and functions have to be adjusted to take into account these differences.

The fast pace of globalization along with corporate scandals over the years have led to a new focus on corporate social responsibility (good citizenship) and sustainability (a company's ability to produce a good or service without damaging the environment or depleting a resource). Companies are finding out that having a good reputation for pursuing these efforts can enhance their revenues and improve the caliber of talent they are able to attract. One of HR's leadership roles is to spearhead the development and implementation of corporate citizenship throughout their organizations, especially the fair treatment of workers.

LO ③ Technology has tended to reduce the number of jobs that require little skill and to increase the number of jobs that require considerable skill, a shift we refer to as moving from touch labor to knowledge work. This displaces some employees and requires that others be retrained. In addition, information technology has influenced HRM through human resources information systems (HRIS) that streamline HR processes, make information more readily available to managers and employees, and enable HR departments to focus on the firm's strategies. The Internet and social media are also affecting how employees are hired, work, and are managed.

LO ④ Productivity can be defined as "the output gained from a fixed amount of inputs." Organizations can increase their productivity either by reducing their inputs (the cost approach) or by increasing the amount that employees produce by adding more human and/or physical capital to the process. Companies such as Southwest Airlines, Nucor, and the manufacturing and technology firm Danaher achieve low costs in their industries not because they scrimp on employees but because they are the most productive.

To maximize productivity and contain costs, organizations have to manage the size of their workforce. Some of the techniques used to do so are offshoring, outsourcing, downsizing, furloughing, using part-time employees, and leasing them from professional employment agencies. HR's role is to not only implement these programs but consider the pros and cons of programs such as these and how they might affect a company's ability to compete, especially if they lead to the loss of talented staff members.

LO ⑤ The workforce is becoming increasingly diverse, and organizations are having to do more to address employee concerns and to maximize the benefit of different kinds of employees. HR managers have to keep abreast of the educational abilities of the talent available to their organization. Employee rights, privacy concerns, attitudes toward work, and efforts to balance work and family are becoming more important to workers as the cultural dynamics in the labor force shift. Companies are finding that accommodating employees' individual needs as a result of these shifts is a powerful way to attract and retain top-caliber people and improve employee engagement.

LO 6 HR managers play a number of important roles when it comes to meeting the challenges their firms face; they are called for strategic planning, advice and ethics counsel, various service activities, policy formulation and implementation, and employee advocacy. To perform these roles effectively, HR managers must have a deep understanding of their firm's operational, financial, and personnel capabilities and work with line managers and executive managers above and below them. HR managers who do and are creative and innovative can help shape a firm's strategies so as to respond successfully to changes in the marketplace. Ultimately, managing people is rarely the exclusive responsibility of the HR function. Every manager's job involves managing people. Consequently, successful companies combine the expertise of HR specialists with the experience of line managers and executives to develop and use the talents of employees to their greatest potential.

Key Terms

agility

corporate social responsibility

downsizing

employee engagement

employee leasing

furloughing

homeshoring

human capital

human resources information system (HRIS)

human resources management (HRM)

knowledge workers

line managers

nearshoring

offshoring

organizational culture

outsourcing

sustainability

workforce (HR) analytics

Discussion Questions

LO 1 Are people always an organization's most valuable asset? Why or why not? Suppose your boss asked you to summarize the major people-related concerns related to opening an office in India. What issues would be on your list?

LO 2 Name a company you hope to work for someday. What is its track record in terms of corporate social responsibility and sustainability? Are these factors important to you? Why or why not?

LO 3 Will technology eliminate the need for human resource managers?

LO 4 Do cost-containment pressures work against the effective management of people? Why or why not?

LO 5 What are the pros and cons of having a more diverse workforce? Is the United States in a better position to compete globally because of its diverse population?

LO 6 In your opinion, what is the most important role HR managers play?

CASE STUDY ❶   New HR Strategy Makes Lloyd's a "Best Company"

After more than 300 years in business, a few years ago, the global insurer Lloyd's of London finally set out to establish its first true HR strategy, starting with the hiring of HR Director Suzy Black. "I was brought in to transform the HR function from one modeled on an old-style personnel office to a function that is more cutting edge, business focused, and value adding," says Black.

Black's first order of business was to evaluate the current state of affairs, particularly how the corporation's senior managers perceived the HR role. With this information in hand, Black and her team began to develop an overarching strategic agenda as well as specific tactics, addressing everything from recruitment to performance management to basic policies to rewards and compensation.

Changing longtime employees' perception of HR took a bit of convincing, but employees quickly began to recognize the value of Black's actions. Gradually, they could see how the HR strategies were effectively creating conditions in which they could develop in their careers, be successful, and find meaning and value in their work. Today, Lloyd's employees list the company's challenging work environment, healthy incentive programs, and meaningful community outreach programs among the key reasons they enjoy working for the insurance giant.

Black's efforts also enhanced Lloyd's position as a desirable place to work. The average tenure of employees at the company is, incredibly, 21 years. The insurer has been named one of the "Top 100 Best Companies to Work For" (in the United Kingdom) by the *Sunday Times* and hailed as one of the United Kingdom's Top 40 Business Brands by an independent researcher.

Each year, new graduates scramble to get hired by Lloyd's. These new hires rotate through three to four different assignments within Lloyd's so they get a perspective of the company and the insurance market as well as a better idea of the departments in which they would like to ultimately work. Lloyd's also offers a graduate program in insurance, apprenticeships, and internships.

Work-life balance at the company is good. Although sometimes extra hours have to be worked, that's not the norm. Working mothers can choose to work part or full time. In addition, the company offers employees time to do charity and nonwork-related activities to further their personal growth, says Black. "Employees are very sophisticated people, and they have more drivers than just wanting to earn money," she notes.

Ironically, Black's position was the first HR position she had ever held, having risen through the ranks in other arenas in business. But her experience has given her a clear definition of the ideal characteristics of the HR professionals. "They must understand change and transformation, excel at operations, and balance tactical and strategic thinking and acting," she says. "They will have to be able to manage and navigate organizational complexity and ambiguities and not be afraid to say no occasionally in order to establish appropriate boundaries with the business."

Questions

1. What skills does Black think employees need, to work successfully in the area of HR?
2. What are some of the outcomes of the company's new HR strategy?
3. What do you think might be some of the challenges of establishing HR policies for a global company?
4. What types of situations do you think might require an HR manager to say "no"?

Sources: "Lloyd's of London Says India Reinsurance Branch to Open by April," *Reuters* (January 18, 2017), http://uk.reuters.com; "Careers," Lloyds.com (January 17, 2017), http://www.lloyds.com; "Lloyd's: A Top Place to Work," Lloyds.com (March 16, 2011), http://www.lloyds.com; Helen William, "City Slicker," *Personnel Today* (August 11, 2009): 10–11; *Digby Morgan Human Resourcefulness Newsletter* (February 2010), http://www.digbymorgannewsletter.com/story04_HR_02_10.htm; company website: www.lloyds.com.

CASE STUDY ❷   Shell's Top Recruiter Takes His Cues from Marketing

When Navjot Singh joined the global oil-and-gas company Shell, the company was facing an extraordinary challenge: The rate at which Shell's engineers were retiring meant the global firm needed to more than triple the number of new recruits it hired, which was about 2,500, to nearly 8,000. Yet at the time, Shell was not considered an employer of choice. The company needed to project a new image—fast. Says Singh, "In the same way marketers know they need to advertise to be a market leader, HR had to know how to create an employer brand. Marketing is the only way to ensure customers buy products. It was also the only way to ensure Shell got the best people coming to us first."

"Wait! Why would Shell's HR guy be talking about marketing?" you might be wondering. As both an HR and marketing expert, Singh saw a powerful synergy between the two. "I'm 50 percent a marketer—the rest is HR, communications, and recruitment," says Singh. Singh initially started out as VP of customer relationship management, but quickly joined the HR team when he recognized Shell's emerging need for new talent and the immense potential for him to use classic marketing techniques to help the company achieve its objectives. His vision, skill sets, and experience were a perfect match for the company's situation.

So in Singh's mind, addressing the company's need for new talent meant building a brand as an employer, which in turn meant creating a cohesive message. But Shell's global recruiting approach was anything but cohesive. "At the time we had 1,200 recruitment systems, 35 recruitment companies, and 400 executive search companies working for us," he recalls. "I attended a careers event at Cambridge University where there were three Shell stands beside each other—one from the UK, one from Malaysia, and another from Nigeria. This was a fragmented approach and tough for candidates to understand." Shell needed to create a unified outreach program if it was going to meet its need for numbers while fulfilling its desire for a global talent pool. The company recruits from among 90 different nationalities each year because it recognizes the benefits of cultural diversity.

"It's not enough to tell candidates why they should join Shell. We needed to demonstrate such reasons through the interviewing process and the whole candidate experience," explains Singh. "A motivating candidate experience—from the moment someone hears about Shell to the moment they have joined us—requires a coordinated approach across all the recruitment disciplines: marketing, operations, recruiters and line managers all need to work together." It also necessitated personnel take less of a more Shell-concentric perspective to one that focused on candidates.

Singh and his team set about applying various marketing techniques to the recruitment process, which have since resulted in an 80 percent cut in recruitment costs and a 20 percent reduction in the time to hire new staff. To attract talented graduates, Shell annually sponsors a popular competition that challenges student teams around the world to solve various food, water, and alternative energy problems. About a thousand teams compete annually.

The efforts have paid off. Shell has won more than 75 awards for its unique HR strategy. Better yet, in a recent global survey of 8,400 people in the oil-and-gas sector, Shell received the most mentions from respondents who were asked to name the employers they would most like to work for.

Despite Shell's recruiting success, Singh believes the war for talent will be ongoing: "In the future, companies will have to apply for skilled people to work for them rather than candidates applying to work at an organization. HR must still realize the strategic value it can bring."

Questions

1. What functions of HRM are similar to marketing functions? How can thinking about "marketing" a company's jobs improve the strategic focus of human resources personnel?

2. If you were planning to use marketing strategies to "brand" a company as an employer of choice, what are some of the factors you would consider?

3. Do you agree with Singh's statement that in the future, companies will have to apply for skilled people to work for them rather than candidates applying to work at an organization? Why or why not?

Sources: Jon Mainwaring, "Shell Q&A: What Makes an Ideal Employer in Oil, Gas?" *Rigzone* (November 16, 2016), http://www.rigzone.com; Jon Mainwaring, "Shell Takes First Place in Rigzone's Inaugural Ideal Employer Survey," *Rigzone* (November 16, 2016), http://www.rigzone.com; Don Wood, "Lateral Thinking," *Human Resources* (January 2010): 12–13; Christopher Van Mossevelde, "Views from the Top," *Employer Branding Today* (April 16, 2009), http://www.employerbrandingtoday.com; Peter Crush, "Shell UK Combines HR and Marketing to Sell the Brand," *HR Magazine* (August 25, 2009), http://www.hrmagazine.co.uk; Navjot Singh and Ana Maria Santos, "How Shell Recruited More for Less," *Marketing Society* (July 9, 2012), https://www.marketingsociety.co.uk.

Notes and References

1. T. J. Watson, Jr. *A Business and Its Beliefs: The Ideas That Helped Build IBM* (New York: McGraw-Hill, 1963).

2. Donald C. Busi, "Assignment Reviews (ARs): Moving toward Measuring Your Most Valuable Asset," *Supervision* 66, no. 1 (January 2005): 3–7.

3. David Lepak and Scott Snell, "Managing the Human Resource Architecture for Knowledge-Based Competition," in S. Jackson, M. Hitt, and A. DeNisi (eds.), *Managing Knowledge for Sustained Competitive Advantage: Designing Strategies for Effective Human Resource Management*, SIOP Scientific Frontiers Series (San Francisco: John Wiley & Sons, 2003), 127–54; David Lepak and Scott Snell, "Examining the Human Resource Architecture: The Relationship among Human Capital, Employment, and Human Resource Configurations," *Journal of Management* 28, no. 4 (2002): 517–43; Steve Bates, "Study Links HR Practices with the Bottom Line," *HRMagazine* 46, no. 12 (December 2001): 14; Ann Pomeroy, "Cooking Up Innovation: When It Comes to Helping Employees Create New Products and Services, HR's Efforts Are a Key Ingredient," *HRMagazine* 49, no. 11 (November 2004): 46–54.

4. Dave Ulrich, Steve Kerr, and Ron Ashkenas, *The GE Work-Out: How to Implement GE's Revolutionary Method for Busting Bureaucracy & Attacking Organizational Problems* (New York: McGraw-Hill Professional Publishing, 2002).

5. John P. Kotter, "Ten Observations," *Executive Excellence* 16, no. 8 (1999): 15–16.

6. Jared Lindzon, "Welcome to a New Era of Human Resources," *Fast Company* (May 20, 2015), https://www.fastcompany.com.

7. "Best Countries," *U.S. News & World Report* (2016), http://worldnews.com.

8. Ellen Sheng, "The Five Biggest Chinese Investments in the U.S. in 2016," *Forbes* (December 21, 2016), http://www.forbes.com.

9. Candice Choi and Bruce Schreiner, "Beam Being Acquired by Japan's Suntory," *Associated Press* (January 13, 2014), http://ap.org; "Beermaker Eyes Chinese Factories," *Fort Worth Star-Telegram* (December 28, 2010): 3C; Susan Meisinger, "Going Global: A Smart Move for HR Professionals," *HRMagazine* 49, no. 3 (March 2004): 6; "AB InBev Completes ModeloGrupo Deal," *St. Louis Post-Dispatch* (June 4, 2013), http://www.stltoday.com.

10. "U.K. Expresses Keenness to Have Free Trade Agreement with India," *The Tribune* (January 18, 2017), http://www.tribuneindia.com.

11. Laura McKnight, "For Companies, Doing Good Is Good Business," *Kansas City Star* (December 26, 2010), http://www.kansascity.com.

12. Jeff Tanner and Mary Anne Raymond, *Principles of Marketing* (Nyack, NY: FlatWorld Knowledge, 2010), Chapter 10.

13. Nancy R. Lockwood, "Corporate Social Responsibility: HR's Leadership Role," *HRMagazine* 49, no. 2 (December 2004): S1–11.

14. Carol Carter, *Keys to Business Communication* (Upper Saddle River, NJ: Pearson, 2012), 414.

15. "Text Messaging Curtailed at Bank," *Wall Street Journal* (January 14–15, 2017): B3.

16. Lauren Webber, "'Routine Jobs' Are Disappearing," *Wall Street Journal* (January 3, 2017), http://www.wsj.com.

17. "China Engineers Next Great Leap with Wave of 'Knowledge Workers,'" *Milwaukee Journal Sentinel* (December 31, 2003), http://www.jsonline.com; "Edward Yourdon's New Book Helps 'Knowledge Workers' Put Emotion Aside to Look at the Facts of the New Economic Reality," *PR Newswire* (October 4, 2004); Marshall Goldsmith, "Supervisors of the Smart," *BRW* 30, no. 20 (May 22, 2008): 57–57.

18. Christopher Mims, "Technology's Long-Term Toll on the Middle Class," *Wall Street Journal* (January 23, 2017): B1–B4.

19. Melissa Korn, "Imagine Discovering Your Teaching Assistant Is a Robot," *Wall Street Journal* (May 6, 2016), http://wsj.com.

20. Steve Lohr, "Robots Will Take Jobs, but Not as Fast as Some Fear, New Report Say," *New York Times* (January 12, 2017), https://www.nytimes.com.

21. Ben Worthen, "Measuring the ROI of Training," *CIO* 14, no. 9 (February 15, 2001): 128–36; Hashi Syedain, "Out of this World," *People Management* 14, no. 8 (April 17, 2008): 20–24.

22. Sarah Castellanos, "Augmented Reality in the Workplace," *Wall Street Journal* (December 13, 2016): B4.

23. Scott A. Snell, Donna Stueber, and David P. Lepak, "Virtual HR Departments: Getting Out of the Middle," in R. L. Heneman and D. B. Greenberger (eds.), *Human Resource Management in Virtual Organizations* (Columbus, OH: Information Age Publishing, 2002): 81–99; Samuel Greengard, "How to Fulfill Technology's Promise," *Workforce, HR Software Insights* (February 1999): S10–18.

24. Drew Robb, "Building a Better Workforce: Performance Management Software Can Help You Identify and Develop High-Performing Workers," *HRMagazine* 49, no. 10 (October 2004): 86–92.

25. Josh Bersin, "The Datification of Human Resources," *Forbes* (July 19, 2013), http://www.forbes.com.

26. Robb, "Building a Better Workforce," 86–92; "How to Implement an Effective Process for a New HR Management System," *HRFocus* (January 2005): 3–4; "New Study Finds HRIS Key to Reducing Costs," *Payroll Managers Report* 7, no. 5 (May 2007): 13.

27. Bruce Stokes, "Is There a Future for 'Made in America,'" *The Atlantic* (December 9, 2010), http://www.theatlantic.com.

28. Patrick Barta and Andrew Caffrey, "Productivity Leap Shows Potential of U.S. Economy—Rise at 8.6 Percent Pace, Positive for Profits, Doesn't Bode Very Well for Employment," *The Wall Street Journal* (May 8, 2002): A1; Jon E. Hilsenrath, "The Economy: Big U.S. Service Sectors Boosted Late 1990s Surge in Productivity," *The Wall Street Journal* (April 22, 2002): A2; Karen Lowry Miller, "Economy: Out of Steam—A Dip in U.S. Productivity Provokes Anxious Questions," *Newsweek International* (February 21, 2005): 34; Milan Yager, "Outsource to Gain Human Resources Expertise," *Hotel & Motel Management* 223, no. 7 (April 21, 2008): 14.

29. Pete Engardio, Michael Arndt, and Dean Foust, "The Future of Outsourcing," *BusinessWeek* (January 30, 2006): 50–58.

30. John Sullivan, "Employee Furloughs Can Be a Bad Alternative to Layoffs," ere.net (February 9, 2009), http://www.ere.net/.

31. Mike Stobbe, "Dieting Like It's Your Job: Does Paying for Healthy Habits Work?" *USA Today* (June 1, 2010), http://www.usatoday.com; Tom Murphy, "To Cut Health Costs, Firms Target Spousal Benefits," *Fort Worth Star-Telegram* (September 16, 2013): 1D.

32. Mitra Toossi, "Labor Force Projections to 2024: The Labor Force Is Growing, But Slowly," *Monthly Labor Review* (December 2015): 3–16.

33. Ibid.

34. Jeffrey S. Passel and D'Vera Cohn, "Share of Unauthorized Immigrant Workers in Production Construction Jobs Falls, since 2007," *Pew Research Center* (March 26, 2015), www.pewhispanic.org.

35. Irwin Speizer, "Diversity on the Menu: Rachelle Hood, Denny's Chief Diversity Officer, Has Boosted the Company's Image. But That Hasn't Sold More Breakfasts," *Workforce Management* 83, no. 12 (November 1, 2004): 41; Patrick Purcell, "Older Workers: Employment and Retirement Trends," *Journal of Pension Planning & Compliance* 34, no. 1 (Spring 2008): 32–48.

36. U.S. Bureau of Labor Statistics, "Occupational Employment," *Occupational Outlook Quarterly Online* (Winter 2013–2014), http://www.bls.gov.

37. Ibid.

38. U.S. Bureau of Labor Statistics, "Women in the Labor Force: A Databook," *BLS Reports* (December 2015), http://www.bls.gov.

39. Kathleen Iverson, "Managing for Effective Workforce Diversity," *Cornell Hotel and Restaurant Administration Quarterly* 41, no. 2 (April 2000): 31–38; Gail Johnson, "Time to Broaden Diversity Training," *Training* 41, no. 9 (September 2004): 16.

40. The U.S. Department of Labor's Bureau of Labor Statistics keeps up-to-date projections and percentages on educational requirements for different kinds of jobs. Interested readers can access this information at http://www.bls.gov; Louis Uchitelle, "College Degree Still Pays, but It's Leveling Off," *The New York Times* (January 13, 2005): C1.

41. Lyndsey Layton, "U. S. Adults Lag Most Countries in Literacy and Computer Skills," *Washington Post* (October 8, 2013), http://washingtonpost.com.

42. "Avoiding Identity Theft," *Aftermarket Business* 114, no. 12 (December 2004): 10.

43. "Your Rights: Surveillance at Work," *Workplace Fairness* (December 2010), http://www.workplacefairness.org.

44. Jeanne Meister, "The Employee Experience Is the Future of Work," *Forbes* (January 5, 2017), http://www.forbes.com; Rachel Emma Silverman, "Workplace Democracy Catches On, *Wall Street Journal* (March 28, 2016): B5.

45. Ashley Surdin, "Benefits for Same-Sex Couples Expanding," *Washington Post* (November 27, 2009), http://www.washingtonpost.com.

46. Todd Raphael, "The Drive to Down-shifting," *Workforce* 80, no. 10 (October 2001): 23; Jim Olsztynski, "Flexible Work Schedules May Make More Sense: One in Six Americans Qualifies as a Caregiver Who May Benefit from Flextime," *National Driller* 26, no. 2 (February 2005): 16–19; Karen Springen, "Cutting Back Your Hours," *Newsweek*, 151, no. 19 (May 12, 2008): 60.

47. Leah Carlson, "Flextime Elevated to National Issue," *Employee Benefit News* (September 15, 2004): 1–16.

CHAPTER **2**

Strategy and Human Resources Planning

Learning Outcomes

After studying this chapter, you should be able to

LO ❶ Explain how human resources planning and a firm's mission, vision, and values are integrally linked to its strategy.

LO ❷ Understand how an organization's external environment influences its strategic planning.

LO ❸ Understand why it is important for an organization to do an internal resource analysis.

LO ❹ Explain the linkages between competitive strategies and HR.

LO ❺ Understand what is required for a firm to successfully execute a strategy and assess its effectiveness.

LO ❻ Describe how firms evaluate their strategies and HR execution.

One of the clichés about the annual reports of companies is that they often claim that "people are our most important asset." Do you believe this is true? Historically managers often have not acted as though they themselves really believed it. Too often the focus has been on minimizing the number of a firm's employees rather than strategically utilizing their talents.

But for many firms, this is changing. Surveys show that 92 percent of chief financial officers now believe human capital affects an organization's customer service, 82 percent believe it affects profitability, and 72 percent believe it affects innovation.[1] And in a survey by the consulting firm Deloitte, nearly 80 percent of corporate executives said the importance of HRM in their firms has grown substantially over the years, and two-thirds said that HR expenditures are now viewed as a strategic investment rather than simply a cost to be minimized.

Forward-thinking companies are also demanding their human resource groups push past short-term projections and provide detailed forecasts for needs and the associated costs over a 2- to 3-year horizon. Even small companies are realizing that their employees are the key to ensuring their ability to compete and survive. As Apple's legendary founder Steve Jobs put it: "Hiring the best is your most important task."

2.1 Strategic Planning and Human Resources Planning

As we explained in Chapter 1, "competing through people" is the theme for this book. But the idea remains only a premise for action until put it into practice. To deliver on this promise, we need to understand some of the systems and processes in organizations that link human resources management with strategic management. A few definitions may be helpful upfront.

First of all, **strategic planning** involves a set of procedures for making decisions about the organization's long-term goals and strategies. In this chapter, we discuss strategic plans as having a strong external orientation that covers major portions of the organization. The plans especially focus on how the organization will position itself relative to its competitors, to ensure its long-term survival, create value, and grow. **Human resources planning (HRP)**, by comparison, is the process of anticipating and providing for the movement of people into, within, and out of an organization. Overall, its purpose is to help managers deploy their human resources as effectively as possible, where and when they are needed, to accomplish the organization's goals. **Strategic human resources management** combines strategic planning and HR planning. It can be thought of as the pattern of human resource deployments and activities that enable an organization to achieve its strategic goals.

HR planning is an essential activity of organizations. Consider CNA Financial Corp., a Chicago-based insurance company. CNA Financial discovered via HR planning that it would run short of underwriters—a key skill pool in the company—in just 2 years' time if their turnover rates continued at their current pace. The global strategies firms

Sidebar

LO 1

Why is HR planning integral to a firm's strategic planning? As an HR professional, what do you think you could do to tie the two functions together? What role might the firm's mission, vision, and values play?

strategic planning
Procedures for making decisions about the organization's long-term goals and strategies.

human resources planning (HRP)
The process of anticipating and providing for the movement of people into, within, and out of an organization.

strategic human resources management
The pattern of human resources deployments and activities that enable an organization to achieve its strategic goals.

increasingly pursue include mergers, joint ventures, offshoring, automating, relocating plants, and planning product innovations, thus making HR planning more critical and more complex for managers.

According to Walt Cleaver, an HR strategist and president of the Cleaver Consulting Group, increased global competitiveness in many industries has led to the commoditization of products based on price, which is making talent the "great differentiator" among firms. As we explained in Chapter 1, it is relatively easy for a competitor to copy your product and make it more cheaply. But duplicating the talents of your employees is much more difficult.[2] Globalization and shifts in the composition of the labor force that are occurring also require that HR managers become more involved in planning because these changes affect the full range of a company's HR practices (such as employee recruitment, selection, training, compensation, and motivation).

2-1a Strategic Planning and HR Planning: Linking the Processes

Good HR managers "marry" human resources planning to the strategic planning for their organizations as a whole. Human resources planning relates to strategic planning in several ways, but at a fundamental level, we can focus on two issues: strategy formulation and strategy execution. Human resources planning provides inputs into the strategic *formulation* process in terms of what is possible, that is, whether a firm has the types and numbers of people available to pursue a given strategy. For example, when Barnes & Noble executives contemplated the move into web-based commerce to compete with Amazon.com, one of the issues they had to address was whether they had the talent needed to succeed in that arena. Barnes & Nobles had to go through the same exercise again prior to launching its Nook reader.

In addition to strategy formulation, HRP is important in terms of strategy execution. In other words, once the firm has devised its strategy, the company's executives must make resource allocation decisions to implement that strategy, including decisions related to the firm's structure, processes, and human capital.[3] 3M's managers have the two aspects down to a science. Not only does the company engage in elaborate workforce planning, it has figured out how to utilize its employees to expand into markets worldwide. Once primarily a domestic company, today most of its products are sold abroad. The company is able to project the demand for any workforce category, in any business, in any part of the world.[4]

Figure 2.1, which will serve as a map for this chapter's discussion, shows how companies align their HRP and strategic planning in this way: A firm's business strategy, along with its overall purpose, goals, and values, establishes the context for its HR strategy and the number and types of people, the skills they must have, and the like. In other words, the firm's HR strategy follows the business strategy and helps to execute it: If the firm's strategy is based on efficiency, its HR strategy will focus on practices that encourage employees to look for better, faster, and more efficient ways for the company to do business. If the firm's strategy is based on innovation, its HR strategy will involve encouraging and incentivizing employees to be creative and innovative. For example, at GE, employees receive monetary incentives for developing and patenting products for the company.

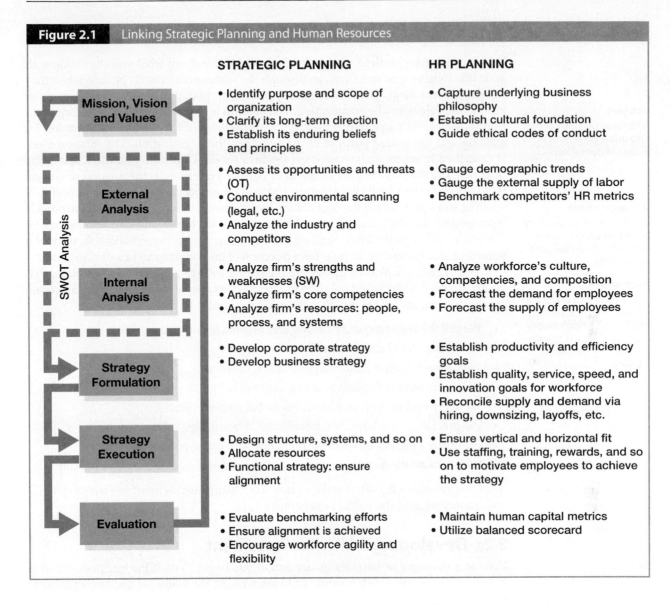

Figure 2.1 Linking Strategic Planning and Human Resources

	STRATEGIC PLANNING	HR PLANNING
Mission, Vision and Values	• Identify purpose and scope of organization • Clarify its long-term direction • Establish its enduring beliefs and principles	• Capture underlying business philosophy • Establish cultural foundation • Guide ethical codes of conduct
External Analysis	• Assess its opportunities and threats (OT) • Conduct environmental scanning (legal, etc.) • Analyze the industry and competitors	• Gauge demographic trends • Gauge the external supply of labor • Benchmark competitors' HR metrics
Internal Analysis	• Analyze firm's strengths and weaknesses (SW) • Analyze firm's core competencies • Analyze firm's resources: people, process, and systems	• Analyze workforce's culture, competencies, and composition • Forecast the demand for employees • Forecast the supply of employees
Strategy Formulation	• Develop corporate strategy • Develop business strategy	• Establish productivity and efficiency goals • Establish quality, service, speed, and innovation goals for workforce • Reconcile supply and demand via hiring, downsizing, layoffs, etc.
Strategy Execution	• Design structure, systems, and so on • Allocate resources • Functional strategy: ensure alignment	• Ensure vertical and horizontal fit • Use staffing, training, rewards, and so on to motivate employees to achieve the strategy
Evaluation	• Evaluate benchmarking efforts • Ensure alignment is achieved • Encourage workforce agility and flexibility	• Maintain human capital metrics • Utilize balanced scorecard

(SWOT Analysis encompasses External Analysis and Internal Analysis)

Although the firm's business strategy affects its HR strategy, it is not a one-way street. The type of people an organization has, and the culture and climate of the company, in turn will *constrain* what the firm is able to achieve strategically. So, HR planning and strategic planning are integral to one another: Strategic planning decisions affect—and are affected by—HR concerns. As James Walker, a noted HRP expert, puts it, "Today, virtually *all* business issues have people implications; *all* human resource issues have business implications."

Researchers Douglas Conger and Jeff Ready have studied businesses that lacked the talent to get their strategies off the ground. To underscore how important talent is to firms, they point to an instance in which a London real estate developer had to pass on a project worth more than $0.5 billion of reconstruction work because it hadn't groomed anyone capable of leading the project. Talent problems are all too common in firms.

2.2 Step One: Mission, Vision, and Values

mission

The basic purpose of the organization as well as its scope of operations.

When you entered college, you probably thought a lot about what you should do with your life. Believe it or not, firms go through the same sort of search process when they develop their strategic plans. The first step in strategic planning is establishing a mission, vision, and values for the organization. The **mission** is the basic purpose of the organization, as well as its scope of operations. It is a statement of the organization's reason for existing and the shared purpose of the people in the organization. The mission often is described in terms of the customers the firm serves. Depending on the scope of the organization, the mission may be broad or narrow. For example, the mission of Google is "to organize the world's information and make it universally accessible and useful."[5]

strategic vision

A statement about where athe company is going and what it can become in the future.

The **strategic vision** of the organization moves beyond the mission statement to provide a perspective on where the company is headed and what the organization can become in the future. Although the terms *mission* and *vision* often are used interchangeably, the vision statement ideally clarifies the long-term direction of the company and its strategic intent.

core values

The strong and enduring beliefs and principles that guide a firm's decisions and are the foundation of its corporate culture.

The organization's **core values** are the strong enduring beliefs and principles that guide a firm's decisions and are the foundation of its corporate culture.[6] The following are the core values for the organic grocer Whole Foods:

- We sell the highest quality natural and organic products available.
- We satisfy, delight, and nourish our customers.
- We support team member happiness and excellence.
- We create wealth through profits and growth.
- We serve and support our local and global communities.
- We practice and advance environmental stewardship.
- We create ongoing win-win partnerships with our suppliers.
- We promote the health of our stakeholders through healthy eating education.

Core values such as these indicate how a company intends to act toward its customers, employees, and the public in general.

2-2a Developing a Mission Statement

How as a manager or business owner would you begin to craft the business's mission statement? One way to begin would be to ask yourself the following questions and write down your answers to them:

- What is my organization's reason for being? What need do we fulfill that isn't already being met by another firm or could be better met?
- For whom will the firm fulfill the need? Who are our customers?
- Where is our market and our customers? Where will operate? Locally, geographically, or globally?
- What core values do the people in my organization share as part of our mission?
- How do these values differentiate us from other companies?

Once an organization or entrepreneur has the answer to these questions, they can begin to draft a mission statement that synthesizes the information. For example, Uber's mission, or vision statement, is to "make transportation as reliable as running water, everywhere, for everyone."

2-2b HR's Role in Establishing and Reinforcing a Firm's Mission, Vision, and Values

HR managers play a key role when it comes to formulating, vetting, and fine-tuning a firm's mission, vision, and values. Does the mission statement accurately reflect employees' beliefs or only upper management's? Does it accurately reflect the public's perception of the organization? If not, how should it be changed? A firm's mission statement keeps everyone on the "same page" and heading in the same direction. Hence, it needs to be accurate.

HR managers help embody the firm's mission, vision, and values within the organization by doing the following:

- Communicating them frequently, both informally and formally, via verbal and written communications such as employee meetings, emails, newsletters, bulletins boards, the firm's website, annual report, and employee orientations. Nordstrom's asks its employees to describe to new hires work incidents that demonstrate how they put the retailer's mission, vision, values into action. Doing so is more powerful and motivating than merely stating them or putting them into print.

- Recruiting and hiring employees whose values are consistent with the organization. This can also help organizations attract Generation Z and millennial workers, who place a high priority on finding employment meaningful to them and aligned with their goals and values in life.

- Translating the mission, vision, and values into job descriptions and specific behaviors and recognizing and rewarding employees based on them.

Like organizations themselves, firms have to be prepared to change their mission statements as conditions change over time. Monitoring those changes requires a firm to continually scan the environment for threats and opportunities, which we discuss next.

2-3 Step Two: External Analysis

Before you decided on your major, you probably looked at information about possible careers—whether there were many opportunities in those careers—or not. Were certain fields becoming more demanding than others or more profitable than others? Firms do something similar. On an ongoing basis, they analyze external opportunities and threats. A comparison of one's *strengths, weaknesses, opportunities*, and *threats* is referred to as a **SWOT analysis**. A SWOT analysis summarizes the major facts and forecasts derived from external and internal analyses. We'll discuss how to do a SWOT analysis later in the chapter. **Environmental scanning** is the systematic monitoring of major external forces influencing the organization, including forces in the business environment—which is sometimes called the remote environment—and the competitive environment, which we will discuss.[7]

Changes in the external environment directly impact the way organizations are run and people are managed. Some of these changes represent opportunities, and some of them represent real threats to the organization. By continuously scanning the environment for changes, managers can anticipate their impact and make adjustments early.

 LO 2

What external factors in the environment do you think firms are most likely to overlook when formulating their business strategies? How can an HR manager help its executive team get a fuller picture of the competitive environment in which a company operates?

SWOT analysis
A comparison of one's strengths, weaknesses, opportunities, and threats for strategy formulation purposes.

environmental scanning
Systematic monitoring of the major external forces influencing the organization.

2-3a The Business Environment

A firm's **business environment** consists of all of the external factors in the general environment—factors a firm cannot directly control but that can affect its strategy. The business environment includes forces that generally affect most, if not all, firms—forces over which they have virtually no control. Economic changes, technological changes, demographic changes, and legal and regulatory changes are examples. By and large, a firm can only adapt to these changes rather than influence them. In the next sections, we will look at these factors and how HR personnel can help their companies understand the business environment.

Economic Changes

All firms must react to local, regional, and global economic conditions. During economic booms, firms are more likely to expand. During recessions they generally contract. But this isn't true for all businesses. It depends upon their strategies. Dollar stores, such as Family Dollar and Dollar Tree, usually see their sales and stock prices rise during recessions as consumers cut back on their spending at regular retail stores. During the last recession, Family Dollar and Dollar Tree opened thousands of new stores and hired thousands of employees. Meanwhile, many other retailers scaled back their operations.[8]

Ecological Changes

Closely related to the economy are ecological conditions. To deal with climate change, farmers around the globe have had to adopt environmentally conscious techniques to combat erosion and depleted aquifers. No-till farming is one such technique: With this method, farmers don't ever till up the soil. Doing so depletes it of moisture and nutrients. Instead, growers just plant over any old plants from the year before.[9]

The catastrophic tsunami that struck Japan in 2011 is another example of an ecological change that affected thousands of different types of businesses and supply chains worldwide. One Japanese semiconductor manufacturer recovered more quickly than its peers from the tsunami, thanks to a strategy it had developed in the aftermath of an earlier earthquake: The company had created flexible manufacturing capabilities that allowed it to shift production to unaffected facilities in other parts of Japan and Asia.[10]

Technological Changes

Like economic and ecological changes, technological changes such as automation have a broad effect on businesses—changes that they have had to adapt to strategically. Many technology experts expect that in the future, 3D printers and other technological advances will dramatically change what products get made, how they get made, and by whom. The Internet, of course, has affected businesses in nearly every industry and in nearly every country. Think about travel agents. For decades they used to be the key resource people used to search for flights, hotels, rental cars, and the like. However, with the advent of online reservation systems, travel agents have had to adapt their approach. Today, they are more likely to compete based on the service they provide and the expertise they have about particular locations. Likewise, newspapers have had to adjust from print to digital subscribers and adjust their sales and revenues strategies to match the new medium or go out of business.

Demographic and Social Changes

Chapter 1 discussed demographic and labor market trends, including the age, composition, and literacy of the labor market, and immigration. From a strategic standpoint, changes in the labor supply can limit the strategies available to firms.

High-growth companies in particular may find it difficult to find the talent they need to expand their businesses. Unemployment rates vary by sector, but the shortage of talent in high-skill jobs continues to create strategic challenges for firms. The U.S. Department of Labor indicates that 11 of the 15 fastest growing occupations between now and 2024 will require some level of postsecondary education. These labor force trends illustrate the importance of monitoring demographic changes as a part of environmental scanning. It is a core responsibility of human resource managers.

Likewise, societal attitudes are constantly changing the business landscape for firms in all industries. We talked about social changes in Chapter 1 such as people's changing priorities toward work, the need for child care, elder care, adequate wages and job security, educational priorities, and environmental and sustainability concerns. How do these changes affect a firm's strategies, and HR strategies in particular?

Consider Walmart. For decades, selling products at low prices has been Walmart's main focus. But now the retailer and others are facing increasing social pressure to provide better pay for employees as are many fast-food companies. Offering low prices yet higher employee pay will be a strategic challenge for them.

Legal and Regulatory Changes

Finally, government and legislative issues, including laws and administrative rulings, have a broad effect on the business environment. Any one change can require firms and entire industries to dramatically adjust their strategic directions. For example, the U.S. government put a ban on slaughtering of horses in 2006. U.S. horse slaughterhouses were forced to exit this line of business or move their plants abroad, such as to Mexico—not an inexpensive proposition. And it's not just U.S. laws and regulations that are a part of the business environment, but the laws of other countries as well that affect businesses. Until recent years, Apple and other 4G smartphone makers were unable to sell devices in the lucrative Chinese market, because the Chinese government hadn't granted the country's major telecommunications companies licenses to build 4G networks there.[11]

2-3b The Competitive Environment

The competitive environment is narrower than the business environment, and firms have a greater ability to affect it. As Figure 2.2 shows, the **competitive environment** consists of a firm's specific industry, including the industry's customers, rival firms, new entrants, substitutes, and suppliers. Firms analyze their competitive environment to adapt to or influence the nature of competition. A general rule of thumb about this analysis is: The more power each of these forces has, the less profitable (and therefore attractive) the industry will be. Let us look at each of the five forces.

competitive environment
Consists of a firm's specific industry, including the industry's customers, rival firms, new entrants, substitutes, and suppliers.

Customers

A firm's strategy should focus on creating value for customers, who often want different things. For example, in the hotel industry, business travelers may want convenient locations with meeting facilities. Vacationers may want resort locations with swimming pools, golf courses, and luxury spas. Other travelers may just want an inexpensive room next to the highway. The point is that increasingly "one size does not fit all," so organizations need to know how they are going to provide value to customers. That is the foundation for strategy, and it influences the kinds of skills and behaviors needed from employees.

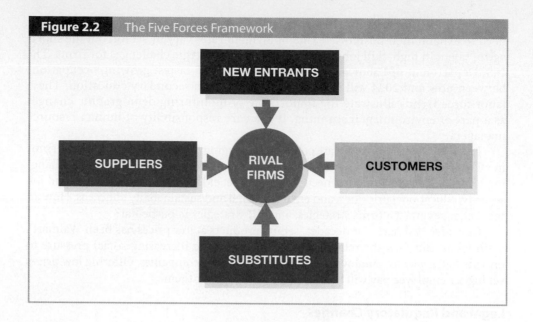

Figure 2.2   The Five Forces Framework

Rival Firms

Perhaps the most obvious element of industry analysis is examining the nature of competition. Who *is* the competition? Often the answer is clear to everyone, but sometimes it is not. For many years, Toys "R" Us viewed its main competitors to be other toy stores such as FAO Schwarz. However, other retailers such as Target and Walmart soon moved into this space very successfully. This had a direct effect on human resources planning for Toys "R" Us. While in the past, Toys "R" Us had been successful with a volume-based approach, bigger retailers like Walmart were even better at that game. As a consequence, Toys "R" Us had to modify its strategy to compete more on customer service and the expertise of its employees.

New Entrants

New companies can sometimes enter an industry and compete well against established firms, and sometimes they cannot. To protect their positions, companies often try to establish entry barriers to keep new firms out of their industries. However, when new firms do enter an industry it is often because they have a different—and perhaps better—way to provide value to customers. When Virgin America entered the airlines market, the company's goal was not just to sell cheap tickets. It promised to make "flying good again" by offering, among other perks, in-flight live concerts, free Wi-Fi, USB plugs at every seat, mood lighting, and top-notch customer service.[12] New entrants such as this can change the "rules of the game" in an industry.

Substitutes

At times, the biggest opportunity or threat in an industry does not come from direct competition but from buyers substituting other products. For example, people are increasingly disconnecting their cable-TV service and instead using streaming services such as Netflix and Hulu. That implies that firms may need to adjust their employee skill bases to support different technologies, or they may need to think about how they will compete in different ways.

Suppliers

Organizations rarely create everything on their own but instead have suppliers that provide them with key inputs. These inputs can include raw materials for production, money (from banks and stockholders), information, and people. This last factor—people, or labor as it is historically called—has direct implications for strategic planning and human resources planning.

Stakeholders

Stakeholders are key people and groups that have an interest in a firm's activities and can either affect them or be affected by them. A firm's primary stakeholders include its investors, employees, customers, suppliers, and creditors. Primary stakeholders have a direct stake in the firm and its success. A firm's *secondary stakeholders* have less of a stake but can nonetheless affect or be affected by the company. Secondary stakeholders include the community in which the firm operates, the government, business groups, and the media.

stakeholders
Key people and groups that have an interest in a firm's activities and that can either affect them or be affected by them.

Firms have to analyze and balance the interests of their various stakeholders. For example, laying off employees will often result in lower costs for a firm, at least in the short term. But if the cuts are too severe and affect a firm's service, for instance, customers are likely to suffer as will investors and creditors. The community could suffer as well.

One way a firm attempts to balance the interests of their shareholders is by determining how a strategic action is likely to impact each group. For which group is the action critical? For which group is the action less critical? As Figure 2.3 shows, the firm may want to involve or at least consult primary shareholders in major strategic actions. In contrast, secondary stakeholders can be monitored and informed. So, for example, if a firm is considering developing a new product, its suppliers, creditors, and employees should definitely be involved and consulted about the move. Secondary stakeholders, such as the community and the media, can merely be informed about the new strategy when appropriate and their responses monitored.

Figure 2.3   Primary Stakeholders versus Secondary Stakeholders

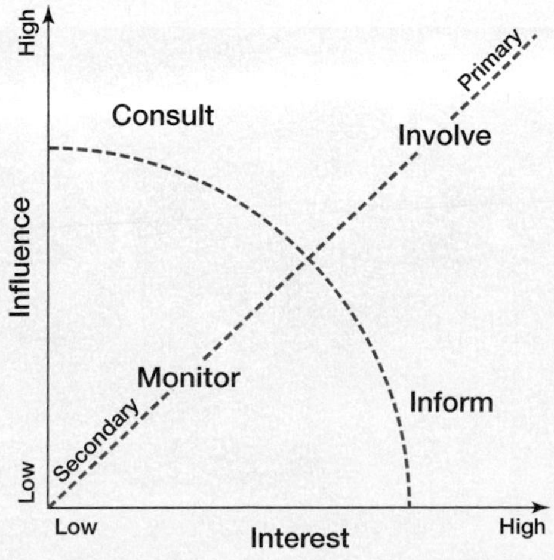

2-3c HR's External Analysis

benchmarking
The process of looking at your practices and performance in a given area and then comparing them with those of other companies.

Because strategic management is ultimately aimed at creating a competitive advantage, many firms also evaluate their performance against other firms. **Benchmarking** is the process of looking at your practices and performance in a given area and then comparing them with those of other companies. To accomplish this, a benchmarking team collects metrics on its own company's performance and those of other firms to uncover any gaps. The gaps help determine the causes of performance differences the team can use to map out a set of best practices.

The target company for benchmarking does not need to be a competitor. For example, when Xerox wanted to learn about excellent customer service, it benchmarked L.L. Bean. By working with noncompeting companies, Xerox was able to get access to information a competitor would not divulge.

Sources of information about the changes in a firm's external environment, particularly the external supply of labor, are invaluable for both operational and strategic reasons. HRP has to focus on both. At an operational level, labor-supply changes directly affect hiring plans in the area where the organization is located or plans to locate. To be closer to younger, educated workers, who will lead them into the digital future, as well as high-earning consumers, companies that moved to the suburbs decades ago are relocating to the cities or opening satellite offices there. In Detroit, Microsoft, Quicken Loans, and dozens of tech companies have relocated suburban facilities to the downtown area.[13]

Similarly, with a "maturing" workforce, HRP must consider the implications for recruitment and replacement policies. Other "barometers" of the labor market include migration in and out of the area and the mobility of the population, the firm's demand for specific skills, unemployment rates, educational level of the workforce, government labor regulations, and so on.

The analysis of the external labor market is aided by published documents. In the United States, unemployment rates, labor force projection figures, and population characteristics are reported by the U.S. Department of Labor.[14] The *Monthly Labor Review* and *Occupational Outlook Handbook*, both published by the Bureau of Labor Statistics (BLS), contain information on jobholder characteristics and predicted changes in the workforce. In addition, local chambers of commerce and individual state development and planning agencies can assist both large organizations and new business ventures by providing them with a labor market analysis of their areas. Offshore consulting firms such as IBM Global

Amazon.com has tested technology to deliver small packages to people's houses via drones. How might drone delivery change Amazon's competitive environment? What changes in customers, new entrants, substitutes, and suppliers might result? How would it affect the firm's HR practices?

Amazon/UPI/Newscom

Services and Accenture can be a good source for information about labor trends in other countries. 3M's HR team regularly consults with outside recruiters to learn about the talent supplies in various countries in which it does or wants to do business.

Part of conducting an external labor analysis includes gauging the talent in your own industry—in other words, looking at the competitive environment for labor. What schools are the top candidates being recruited from? What firms are attracting the most candidates and why? What firms end up hiring the best candidates and why? Astute HR managers who track their firms' hiring and recruiting metrics relative to the competition are an invaluable source of external labor "intelligence" such as this. Attending industry conventions and talking to your company's suppliers about business and employment trends are other good ways of gathering competitive intelligence. So are interviews with job candidates. Simply asking candidates who turned down job offers why they did so can yield a great deal of information. We will talk more about this aspect of HR in Chapter 5.

The HR benchmarks, or metrics, a firm collects fall into two basic categories: human capital metrics and HR metrics. Human capital metrics assess aspects of the workforce, whereas HR metrics assess the performance of the HR function itself. For its clients, the management consulting company PwC publishes monthly and annual human capital benchmarking information, which includes metrics from almost 900 companies.

Highlights in HRM 1 shows some of the basic HR metrics companies use. Most larger companies use software to track their HR metrics over time. Figure 2.4 shows an example of an HR "dashboard," which is software that tracks and graphically displays HR statistics so they can be viewed by managers at a glance (like you can your dashboard readings when driving a car).

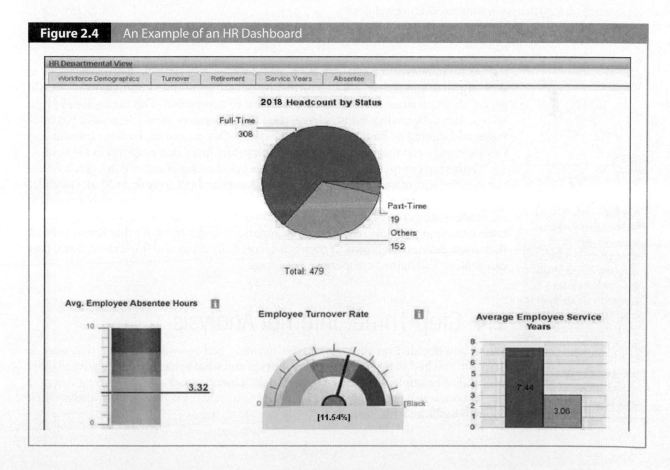

Figure 2.4 An Example of an HR Dashboard

HRM Metrics

Different companies rely on different HRM metrics, depending upon their strategic objectives. The following are some of the metrics mostly commonly used:

General

- Total payroll and benefits costs
- Payroll and benefits costs per employee
- Revenue earned per employee
- Average salary per employee
- Total employee hours worked
- Hours worked per employee
- Employees per department
- Average employee tenure
- Average employee age
- Employee absenteeism rate

Training and Development

- Total training costs
- Training costs per employee
- Average training hours provided to existing employees
- Average training hours provided to new hires

Hiring and Turnover

- Total separation costs (severance, etc.)
- Separation costs per employee
- Average time to fill (a position)
- Quality of fill
- Cost per fill
- Percentage of positions filled internally
- Percentage of new hires retained for 90 days
- Employee turnover rate
- Voluntary turnover rate
- Involuntary turnover rate

HR Department Metrics

- Number of employees per HR professional
- Total HR expenses
- HR expenses per employee
- Percentage of HR expenses spent on outsourced functions

As we have explained, today's HR managers can significantly enhance their worth to their organizations if they go a step further by gathering informal information, or "intelligence," about the strategic and HRM practices of their competitors. This can be done by legal means, such as by reading industry blogs, checking competitors' press releases and Facebook pages, and signing up for their newsfeeds, messages they put out on Twitter, LinkedIn, and Google email alerts that are triggered when competing firms' names appear in the news.

Gathering competitive intelligence and benchmarking alone will not give a firm a competitive advantage, though. According to author and HR consultant Mark Huselid, a competitive advantage is based on the unique combination of a company's human capital, strategy, and core capabilities—which differ from firm to firm. This means that HR managers cannot simply rely on the benchmarks and strategies of other firms. Instead, they must develop their own. If they can successfully do so and implement them, they can achieve a sustained competitive advantage.[15]

LO 3

Recall from Chapter 1 the discussion about autoparts makers having to look for new markets when car sales plummeted in the last recession. How do you think the autoparts makers assessed their ability to enter new markets? Do you think they looked first at new markets and then the capabilities of their employees and suppliers—or vice versa?

2.4 Step Three: Internal Analysis

When you decided on your major, you not only had to look at careers that were in demand, you had to take a hard look at yourself and what you're good at relative to other people. For example, software engineers make a lot of money and are in great demand. But do you have what it takes to become one? Similarly, organizations also analyze their own strengths and weaknesses.

2.4a Core Capabilities

A growing number of experts now argue that the key to a firm's success is based on establishing a set of **core capabilities**—abilities that distinguish an organization from its competitors and create value to customers. You can think of **value creation** as a cost–benefit scenario: value = benefits − costs. For example, what is driving, or would drive, a customer's willingness to buy from your firm versus another? What benefits do, or would, customers get from your firm relative to the costs they incur? In what areas does your organization excel as far as potential customers are concerned? Most firms recognize that there is a small set of three to six core capabilities that are most critical to differentiating them from competitors. Core capabilities can consist of a combination of three resources: (1) processes, (2) systems (technologies), and (3) people.

Processes are "recipes" or standard routines for how work will be done and results will be accomplished. For example, when Intermountain Healthcare (IHC), a hospital and clinic chain in Utah, analyzed the firm's capabilities, it found that less than 10 percent of its processes accounted for over 90 percent of the cost, time, and quality of a health care. Consequently, ICH chose to focus on these processes to enhance its core capabilities.

Top-notch systems are also part of the core capabilities equation. They include information systems, databases, proprietary technologies, and the like. Great systems and technologies are a core capability of Amazon.com—one that has resulted in a significant competitive advantage for the firm. UPS's Orion system is another example of a great system. The Orion system takes into account all of the packages a UPS driver has to deliver and determines out the fastest route for doing so.

Last, but certainly not least, people are a key resource that underlies a firm's core capabilities. Particularly in knowledge-based industries such as the software and information services industries, success depends on "people-embodied knowhow." Knowhow includes the knowledge, skills, and abilities of employees most critical for executing the firm's plan to create the most value for customers and whose skills are difficult to replicate or replace.

core capabilities
Integrated knowledge sets within an organization that distinguish it from its competitors and deliver value to customers.

value creation
What a firm adds to a product or service by virtue of making it; the amount of benefits provided by the product or service once the costs of making it are subtracted.

FedEx's workers support their employer's core capabilities. That helps FedEx stand out from its competitors and deliver added value to its customers.

Bloomberg/Getty Images

As a result, a number of companies that previously relied on standard plans for recruiting and managing their employees are designing more tailored plans to address the individual needs of employees so they will be in a better position to help execute their firms' strategies. Microsoft enables certain types of employees to design their own career paths. For example, the company offers software engineers both a management-focused and technical specialist career track and allows them to move back and forth between the two.

2.4b Sustaining a Competitive Advantage Through People

Organizations can achieve a sustained competitive advantage if they have resources—particularly people—that meet the following criteria[16]:

1. *The resources must be valuable.* People are a source of competitive advantage when they improve the efficiency or effectiveness of the company. Value is increased when employees find ways to decrease costs, provide something unique to customers, or some combination of the two. To improve the bottom line, REI and Southwest Airlines are among the companies that empower and motivate their workers to spark their creativity.

2. *The resources must be rare.* People are a source of competitive advantage when their knowledge, skills, and abilities are not equally available to competitors. Companies such as Facebook, Four Seasons Hotels, and Virgin America therefore invest a great deal to hire and train the best and the brightest employees to gain an advantage over their competitors.

3. *The resources must be difficult to imitate.* People are a source of competitive advantage when the capabilities and contributions of a firm's employees cannot be copied by others. Disney and Starbucks are each known for creating unique cultures that get the most from employees (through teamwork) and are difficult to imitate.

4. *The resources must be organized.* People are a source of competitive advantage when their talents can be combined and deployed to work on new assignments at a moment's notice. As you learned in Chapter 1, companies such as IBM, GE, and Procter & Gamble closely "track" employees and their talents. As a result, these firms are able to quickly reassign talent to different areas of their companies and the world as needed.

These four criteria highlight the importance of people and show the closeness of HRM to strategic management.

2.4c Types of Talent and Their Composition in the Workforce

A related element of internal analysis for organizations that compete on capabilities is determining the types of talent needed and their composition of a firm's current workforce. As we have indicated, managers need to determine whether people are available internally to execute an organization's strategy. Managers have to make tough decisions about whom to employ internally, whom to contract externally, and how to manage different types of employees with different skills who contribute in different ways to the organization.

Figure 2.5 shows that different skill groups in any given organization can be classified according to the degree to which they create strategic value and are unique to the

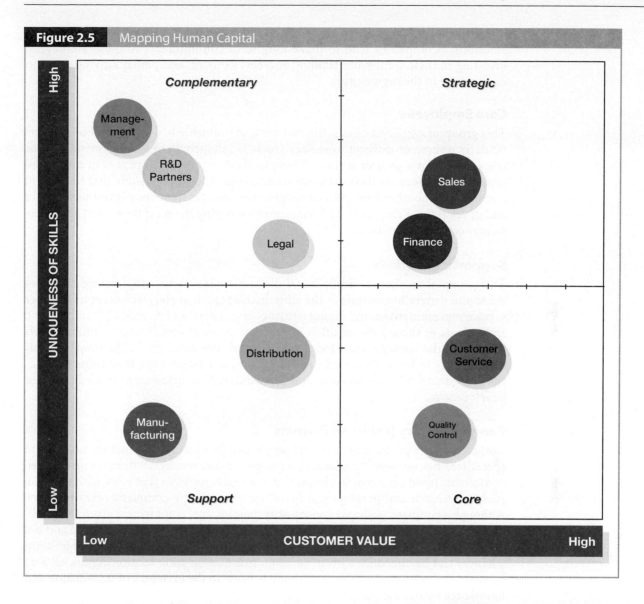

Figure 2.5 Mapping Human Capital

organization. This figure shows the departments for an Australian biotechnology firm and the quadrants those groups fall into. As a general rule, managers often consider contracting externally (or outsourcing) skill areas that are not central to the firm's core competence. HRP plays an important role in helping managers weigh the costs and benefits of using one approach to employment versus another. Evidence from research suggests that employment relationships and HR practices for different employees vary according to which segment they occupy in this matrix.

Strategic Knowledge Workers

This group of employees tends to have unique skills directly linked to the company's strategy and are difficult to replace (such as research and development scientists in a pharmaceuticals company or computer scientists in a software development company).

These employees typically are engaged in knowledge work that involves considerable autonomy. Companies tend to make long-term commitments to these employees, investing in their continuous training and development, and perhaps giving them an equity stake in the organization.

Core Employees

This group of employees has skills that are quite valuable to a company but not particularly unique or difficult to replace (such as salespeople in a department store or truckdrivers for a courier service). These workers tend to be employed in traditional types of jobs. Because their skills are transferable, it is quite possible that they could leave to go to another firm. As a consequence, managers frequently invest less to train and develop these employees and focus more on paying them for their short-term performance achievements.

Supporting Workers

This group of workers typically has skills that are less central to creating customer value and generally available in the labor market (such as clerical workers, customer service representatives, and manufacturing, operations, and distribution employees). Individuals in these jobs are often hired from external agencies on a contract basis to support the strategic knowledge workers and core employees. The scope of their duties tends to be limited, and their employment relationships tend to be transaction based and focused on rules and procedures. Less investment is made in their development.

Complementary (External) Partners

Complementary partners are external people and firms with skills that are unique and specialized but not directly related to a company's core strategy. Attorneys on retainer, consultants hired on a contract basis, and external companies that work with the firm, such as research and development firms, for example, are complementary partners. Although a company perhaps cannot justify their internal employment given their indirect link to the firm's strategy, these individuals have skills that are specialized and not readily available to all firms. As a consequence, companies tend to establish longer-term alliances and partnerships with them and nurture an ongoing relationship focused on mutual learning. Considerable investment is made in the exchange of information and knowledge with these people.[17]

2.4d Corporate Culture

cultural audits
Audits of the culture and quality of work life in an organization.

Think about our initial discussion of mission, vision, and values back at Step One. Because managers increasingly understand that their employees are critical to their success, they often conduct **cultural audits** to examine their values, attitudes, beliefs, and expectations. Can they make a difference in a firm's strategy? Yes. Cultural audits can help firms decide upon the strategic investments and maneuvers that their cultures lend themselves to. The audits can also be used to determine if the cultures of two companies will complement one another should the firms merge. As we will discuss later, many a merger has failed due to corporate "culture clashes" between companies that tried to join forces.

Conducting a Cultural Audit

To conduct a cultural audit, employees can be surveyed about how they feel about issues such as the following: How is business conducted within your organization? How do people communicate with one another? How are conflicts and crises resolved?

The cultural audit conducted by SAS, a business-analytics corporation that often ranks No. 1 on *Fortune* magazine's "Best Companies to Work For" list, includes detailed questions about the company's pay and benefit programs and a series of open-ended questions about the company's hiring practices, internal communications, training and recognition programs, health care and other benefits, and diversity efforts.[18] Cultural audits can also be used to determine whether there are different groups, or subcultures, within the organization that have distinctly different views about the nature of the work and how it should be done. To prevent legal and ethical breaches, some firms conduct cultural audits that ask employees questions about the degree of fear associated with meeting their firms' revenue goals and incentive plans that could encourage unethical or illegal behavior.[19]

Perhaps the most widely used cultural audit questionnaire is the Organizational Culture Assessment Instrument (OCAI), developed by Kim Cameron and Robert Quinn. The questionnaire helps identify four distinct types of corporate cultures, which are shown in Figure 2.6.

- The "clan" culture in which employees are closely knit and exhibit great concern for one another and their customers, and loyalty and cohesion are highly valued. Starbucks's culture can be categorized as a clan culture. Many small and midsize businesses fall into this category, too. Their HR strategies are more informal and focused on creating a family-type feel that binds employees emotionally to the organization.[20]

- The "adhocracy" culture, which is a culture characterized by risk-taking, innovation, and a spirit of entrepreneurship. Google clearly fits into this category.

- The "market" culture, which encourages competitive, result-oriented behaviors. Investment banks that closely focus on achieving their financial numbers are an example of firms with market cultures. The investment bank Goldman Sachs falls into this category.

- The "hierarchical" culture, which is characterized by formal structures and procedures and in which efficiency and stability are greatly valued. Utility-type companies and well-established companies such as railroads fall into this category.

Some cultures lend themselves more readily to certain strategies than others; however, almost all firms have elements of each of the four cultures. For example, W.L. Gore & Associates, which makes Gore-Tex fabric and other cutting-edge products such as space suits and surgical products, is highly entrepreneurial like an adhocracy is. However, the company, which was launched by entrepreneur Bill Gore and his wife, Vivien Gore, in their basement in the 1950s, remains privately owned and exhibits elements of the "clan" culture as well.

According to author James Clawson, leaders who target employees' values, attitudes, beliefs, and expectations are more effective than those who simply focus on workers' behaviors or thought processes. This makes sense. Recall from Chapter 1 the story about the entrepreneur who tripled his sales but, because he took his staff for granted, was then muscled out of the market by a competitor. If a firm lacks a clear idea of how employees view the organization, no matter how great the organization's plans are, those plans might never be successfully executed and sustained.

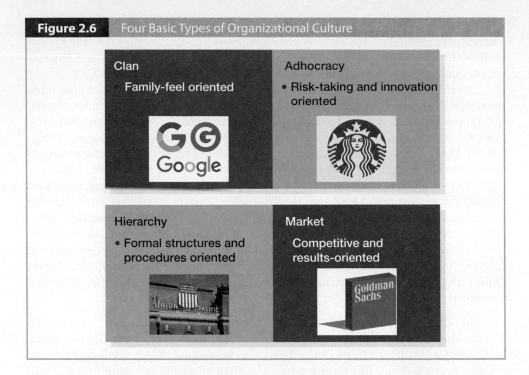

Figure 2.6 Four Basic Types of Organizational Culture

2.4e Forecasting

An internal analysis of an organization can reveal a great deal about where it stands today. However, things change. In an important sense, strategic planning is about managing that change. Managers must continually forecast both the needs and the capabilities of the firm for the future to do an effective job at strategic planning. As Figure 2.7 shows, managers focus on (at least) three key elements: (1) forecasting the demand for labor, (2) forecasting the supply of labor, and (3) balancing supply and demand considerations.

Consider for a moment the high costs of not forecasting—or forecasting poorly. If job vacancies are left unfilled, the resulting loss in efficiency can be very costly, particularly when you consider the amount of time it takes to hire and train replacement employees. As pointless as it may sound, it's not uncommon for employees to be laid off in one department while applicants are hired for similar jobs in another department. Poor forecasting that leads to unnecessary layoffs also makes it difficult for employees to accurately assess their own career prospects and development. When this happens, a firm's more competent and ambitious workers will be inclined to seek other employment where they feel they will have better career opportunities.[21]

On the plus side, accurate forecasting provides the kind of information managers need to make sound decisions. It can help them ensure that they have the right number and right kinds of people in the right places at the right times, doing things that provide value to both the organization and the employees.

Forecasting a Firm's Demand for Employees

As we have indicated, a variety of factors, including a firm's competitive strategy, technology, structure, and productivity, will affect its demand for labor. External factors such as business cycles—economic and seasonal trends—can also play a role. For example,

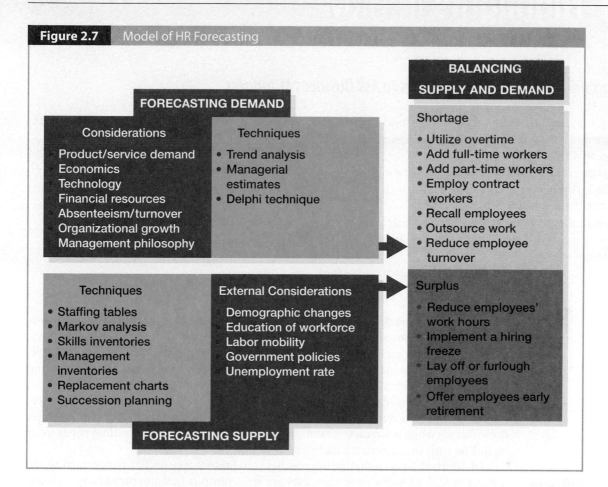

Figure 2.7 Model of HR Forecasting

BALANCING SUPPLY AND DEMAND

FORECASTING DEMAND

Considerations
- Product/service demand
- Economics
- Technology
- Financial resources
- Absenteeism/turnover
- Organizational growth
- Management philosophy

Techniques
- Trend analysis
- Managerial estimates
- Delphi technique

Shortage
- Utilize overtime
- Add full-time workers
- Add part-time workers
- Employ contract workers
- Recall employees
- Outsource work
- Reduce employee turnover

Techniques
- Staffing tables
- Markov analysis
- Skills inventories
- Management inventories
- Replacement charts
- Succession planning

External Considerations
- Demographic changes
- Education of workforce
- Labor mobility
- Government policies
- Unemployment rate

Surplus
- Reduce employees' work hours
- Implement a hiring freeze
- Lay off or furlough employees
- Offer employees early retirement

FORECASTING SUPPLY

retailers such as BestBuy, Bath & Body Works, and Target rely heavily on temporary employees between November and January, during the holiday season. There are two approaches to HR forecasting—quantitative and qualitative—which we discuss next.

Quantitative Approaches. Quantitative forecasting approaches involve the use of statistical or mathematical techniques. One commonly used method is a **trend analysis**, which plots a historical trend of a business factor, such as sales, in relation to the number of employees. The trend and its strength up or down will affect how many employees should be hired. Other, more sophisticated statistical planning methods include modeling or multiple predictive techniques.

Whereas a trend analysis relies on a single factor (such as sales) to predict employment needs, more advanced methods combine several factors, such as interest rates, gross domestic product, the disposable income of consumers, and sales, to predict employment levels. Factors such as a firm's strategy and "what if" scenarios can also be incorporated in the analysis. For example, if the firm wants to increase its sales by 10 percent, how many additional salespeople should it hire? Forecasting methods such as these are often used by larger companies with the help of analysts and statisticians. However, advances in data collection technology and software have made it easier and affordable for smaller businesses to use more sophisticated forecasting techniques.

trend analysis
A quantitative approach to forecasting labor demand based on a factor such as sales.

HR Planning and Strategy Questions to Ask Business Managers

- What are your current pressing business issues?
- What are our competitors' organizational strengths? How do we compare?
- What core capabilities do we need to win in our markets?
- What are the required knowledge, skills, and abilities we need to execute the winning strategy?
- What are the barriers to achieving the strategy?
- What types of skills and positions will be required or no longer required?

- Which skills should we have internally versus contract with outside providers?
- What actions need to be taken to align our resources with our strategy priorities?
- What recognition and rewards are needed to attract, motivate, and retain the employees we need?

Sources: Adapted from Agilent Technologies for The Conference Board and the Society for Human Resource Management.

Qualitative Approaches. Forecasting is frequently more of an art than a science, providing inexact approximations rather than absolute results. The ever-changing environment in which an organization operates contributes to this situation. For example, estimating changes in the demand for a firm's products or services is a basic forecasting concern, as is anticipating economic changes.

A firm's internal changes are critical, too. A community hospital anticipating internal changes in its technology or how the facility is organized or managed must consider these factors when it forecasts its staffing needs. Also, the forecasted staffing needs must be in line with the organization's financial resources.

In contrast to quantitative approaches, qualitative approaches to forecasting are less statistical. **Management forecasts** are the opinions (judgments) of supervisors, department managers, experts, or others knowledgeable about the organization's future employment needs. For example, at Souplantation and Sweet Tomatoes, a national soup, salad, and bakery chain, each restaurant manager is responsible for his or her store's employment forecasts. Another qualitative forecasting method, the Delphi technique, attempts to decrease the subjectivity of forecasts by soliciting and summarizing the judgments of a preselected group of individuals. HR personnel can do this by developing a list of questions to ask the managers in their companies. Highlights in HRM 2 contains some good questions to ask.

Ideally, forecasting should include the use of both quantitative and qualitative approaches. Numbers without context—including the context supplied by skilled HR professionals who understand the business and can analyze and interpret the data—are less useful. "The most important software is the one running between your ears," explains one HR director about the qualitative forecasting.[22]

management forecasts

The opinions (judgments) of supervisors, department managers, experts, or others knowledgeable about the organization's future employment needs.

Forecasting the Supply of Employees

Just as an organization must forecast its future requirements for employees, it must also determine whether sufficient numbers and types of employees are available to staff the openings it anticipates having. As with demand forecasts, the process involves both tracking current employee levels and making future projections about those levels.

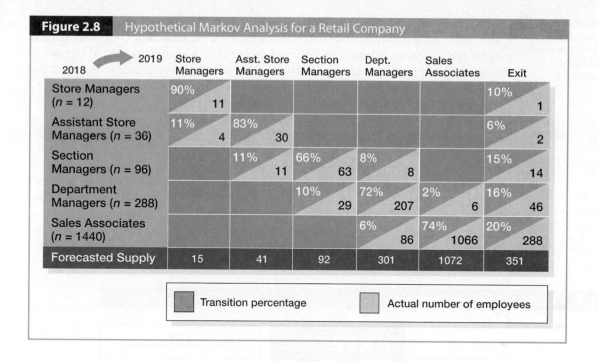

Figure 2.8   Hypothetical Markov Analysis for a Retail Company

2018 → 2019	Store Managers	Asst. Store Managers	Section Managers	Dept. Managers	Sales Associates	Exit
Store Managers ($n = 12$)	90% 11					10% 1
Assistant Store Managers ($n = 36$)	11% 4	83% 30				6% 2
Section Managers ($n = 96$)		11% 11	66% 63	8% 8		15% 14
Department Managers ($n = 288$)			10% 29	72% 207	2% 6	16% 46
Sales Associates ($n = 1440$)				6% 86	74% 1066	20% 288
Forecasted Supply	15	41	92	301	1072	351

■ Transition percentage   ■ Actual number of employees

Staffing Tables and Markov Analyses. An internal supply analysis can begin with staffing tables. A **staffing table** shows a firm's jobs, along with the numbers of employees currently occupying those jobs (and perhaps future employment requirements derived from demand forecasts). Another technique, called a **Markov analysis**, shows the percentage and actual number of employees who remain in each of a firm's jobs from year to year and the proportions of those promoted, demoted, transferred, or who have quit. As Figure 2.8 shows, a Markov analysis can be used to track the pattern of employee movements through various jobs and to develop a transition matrix for forecasting labor supply.

Forecasting the supply of human resources available to a firm requires managers to have a good understanding of employee turnover and absenteeism. We have included formulas for computing turnover and absenteeism rates in an appendix to this chapter. Also included in the appendix is a formula for calculating a metric called **quality of fill**. It was developed because managers understand that simply having "bodies" in place is not enough. The quality-of-fill metric attempts to measure how well new hires are performing so the company will have enough top performers to propel it toward its strategic objectives. We will show you how it is calculated in Chapter 5 when we discuss recruiting metrics.

Skill Inventories and Management Inventories. Staffing tables, a Markov analysis, turnover rates, and the like tend to focus on the *number* of employees in particular jobs. Other techniques are more oriented toward the *types* of employees and their skills, knowledge, and experiences. **Skill inventories** can also be prepared either manually or using a human resources information system that lists each employee's education, past work experience, vocational interests, specific abilities and skills, compensation history, and job tenure. The inventories allow an organization to quickly match forthcoming job openings with employee backgrounds. When data are gathered on managers, these inventories are called *management inventories*.

staffing table
A table that shows a firm's jobs, along with the numbers of employees currently occupying those jobs and future (monthly or yearly) employment requirements.

Markov analysis
A method for tracking the pattern of employee movements through various jobs in a firm.

quality of fill
A metric designed to measure how well new hires that fill positions are performing on the job.

skill inventories
Files of personnel education, experience, interests, skills, and so on that allow managers to quickly match job openings with employee backgrounds.

replacement charts
Listings of current job-holders and people who are potential replacements if an opening occurs.

succession planning
The process of identifying, developing, and tracking key individuals for executive positions.

talent reviews
strategic meetings to determine if a company has the human resources it needs to compete in the future.

Replacement Charts and Succession Planning. Skill and management inventories (talent inventories) can be used to develop employee **replacement charts**, which list current jobholders and identify possible replacements should openings occur. Figure 2.9 shows an example of how an organization might develop a replacement chart for the managers in one of its divisions. The chart provides information on the current performance and promotability of possible replacements.

A replacement chart can be used side by side with other pieces of information for **succession planning**—the process of identifying, developing, and tracking talented individuals so that they can eventually assume top-level positions. The strategy and consulting firm Accenture has developed an application listing its employees, where they are based, and their individual areas of expertise. The application helps managers with deployment decisions. It also makes it easier for Accenture's employees who do not necessarily know each other or work together to collaborate with one another. Succession planning and replacement charts are often developed in conjunction with **talent reviews**: strategic meetings to determine if a company has the human resources it needs to compete in the future.

Figure 2.9	An Executive Replacement Chart

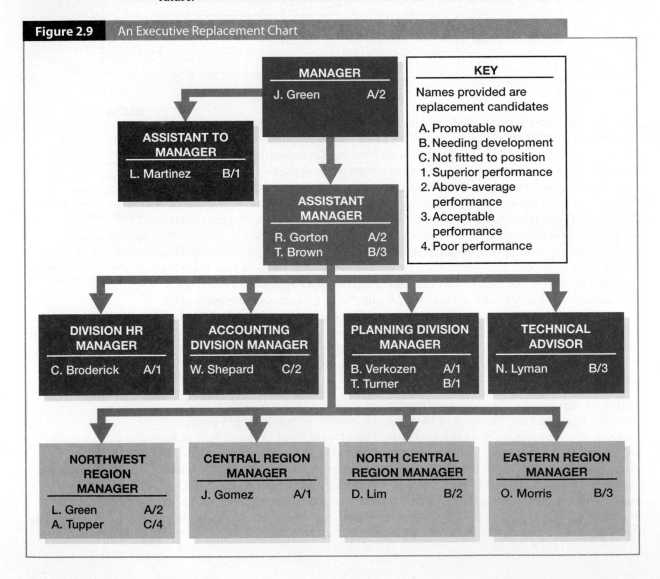

Small Business Application

Lack of Succession Planning Threatens Family Businesses

A certain mystique exists about family businesses being carried on for generations, But although 80 to 90 percent of U.S. businesses are family owned, less than a third of these companies continue to exist into the second generation, and just 10 percent survive into the third, according to one study. One reason this occurs is because only about one-quarter of family businesses have succession plans. It may take the death of a colleague or a sudden illness for business owners to realize that, like a will, they need a succession plan to keep a business going, continue to provide for their families, and keep their workers out of the unemployment line.

Business owners are sometimes reluctant to put succession plans in place for fear of relinquishing control, or they don't feel their successor is ready to take over the business. In some cases there is no clear successor. Sometimes the next generation just is not enthusiastic about joining the family business.

Even with a business owner willing to relinquish the reins and a well-chosen successor waiting in the wings, an actual transition plan is still needed. "[Any transition] needs to be carried out without causing any alarm to the other stakeholders—that is, financiers who may be worried that such a change may increase firm-specific risk," says Dr. Ashraf Mahate, an economist and expert on international trade and finance. "Suppliers may be concerned about providing future credit facilities or even doing business with the company. Customers may be fearful of long-term relationships with the company. Therefore, it is in everyone's interest to have an orderly change to the new structure."

Sources: Michael Cohn, "Most Family Businesses Lack Succession Plans," *Accounting Today* (January 14, 2017), http://www.accounting-today.com; "Next in Line: The Advantages of Succession Planning," *Forbes* (July 30, 2013), http://www.forbes.com; "Canada's Banks Eye Succession Plans for Boomers," Reuters (December 20, 2012), http://www.reuters.com; Manoj Nair, "Succession Planning Is the Key," gulf-news.com (January 19, 2011), http://gulfnews.com; Ernesto J. Poza, *Family Business* (Boston: South-Western/Cengage Learning, 2010), 85–89; Don Schwerzler, "Family Succession Plan First," http://www.family-business-experts.com/family-succession-plan.html.

Human resource managers frequently lament that they have trouble keeping managers, including CEOs, focused on succession planning. It's possible that because CEOs are increasingly being recruited from the outside, they are less concerned with internal succession planning than they are in "bringing in their own people." And, of course, because the workforce is becoming increasingly mobile, some managers wonder why they should develop employees internally who may eventually leave the organization when they can recruit qualified talent from the outside. Managers also get distracted by putting out immediate fires, especially in tough times, explains Ranjay Gulati, a Harvard Business School professor. Instead of planning for succession, they look externally for "savior" types of employees to rescue their organization because they have been unable to adapt to the competition.[23]

Not having a succession plan can imperil a small firm, as the small-business box in this chapter illustrates. Highlights in HRM 3 shows a checklist for evaluating how successful a firm's succession planning is.

2.4f Assessing a Firm's Human Capital Readiness: Gap Analysis

Once a company has assessed both the supply and demand for employee skills, talent, and knowhow, it can begin to understand its **human capital readiness**. Any difference between the quantity and quality of employees required versus the quantity and quality of employees available represents a gap that needs to be fixed.

Figure 2.10 shows how a pharmaceutical company approached its assessment of human capital readiness. Similar to our discussion in the preceding sections, managers

human capital readiness

The process of evaluating the availability of critical talent in a company and comparing it to the firm's supply.

Succession-Planning Checklist

RATE THE SUCCESS OF YOUR SUCCESSION PLANNING

For each characteristic of a best-practice succession-planning and management program appearing in the left column below, enter a number to the right to indicate how well you believe your organization manages that characteristic. Ask other decision makers in your organization to complete this form individually. Then compile the scores and compare notes.

Characteristics of a Best-Practice Succession-Planning and Management Program Your organization has successfully…	How Would You Rate Your Organization's Succession-Planning and Management Program on the Characteristic?				
	Very Poor (1)	Poor (2)	Neither Poor Nor Good (3)	Good (4)	Very Good (5)
1 Clarified the purpose and desired results of the succession-planning and management program.					
2 Determined what performance is required now for all job categories in the organization by establishing competency models.					
3 Established a means to measure individual performance that is aligned with the competencies currently demonstrated by successful performers.					
4 Determined what performance is needed in the future by establishing future competency models for all job categories.					
5 Created an ongoing means by which to assess individual potential against future competency models.					
6 Established a means by which to narrow gaps through the use of individual development plans (IDPs).					
7 Created a means to follow up and hold people accountable.					
8 Created a means by which to document competence and find organizational talent quickly when needed.					
9 Created and sustained rewards for developing people.					
10 Established a means by which to evaluate the results of the succession planning and management program.					

Total (add up the scores for items 1–10 and place in the box on the right)

SCORES

50–40	Congratulations. The succession-planning and management program in your organization conforms with best practices.
39–30	Pretty good. Your organization is on the way toward establishing a first-rate succession-planning and management program.

29–20	Okay. While your organization could make improvements, you appear to have some of the major pieces in place for a succession-planning and management program.
19–10	Not good at all. Your organization is probably filling positions on an as-needed basis.
9–0	Give yourself a failing grade. You need to take steps immediately to improve the succession-planning and management practices of your organization.

Source: From William J. Rothwell, "Putting Success into Your Succession Planning," *The Journal of Business Strategy* 23, no. 3 (May/June 2002): 32–37. Republished with permission—Thomson Media, One State Street, 26th Floor, New York, NY 10004.

begin by identifying a company's core capabilities and the key people and processes critical to those capabilities. The company identified nine key job "families." For each of these critical job families, managers identified the critical knowledge, skills, and behaviors necessary to build the core capabilities. They then determined the number of people required for these positions, as well as the number who are currently qualified. As the lower portion of the figure shows, the company's human capital (HC) readiness ranged between 63 percent for bioscientists and 100 percent for chemical and mechanical engineers. Once the assessment of a firm's human capital readiness is complete, managers have a much better foundation for establishing their strategy going forward and the specific requirements for developing the talent needed to execute the strategy.[24]

Figure 2.10	Assessing a Firm's Human Capital

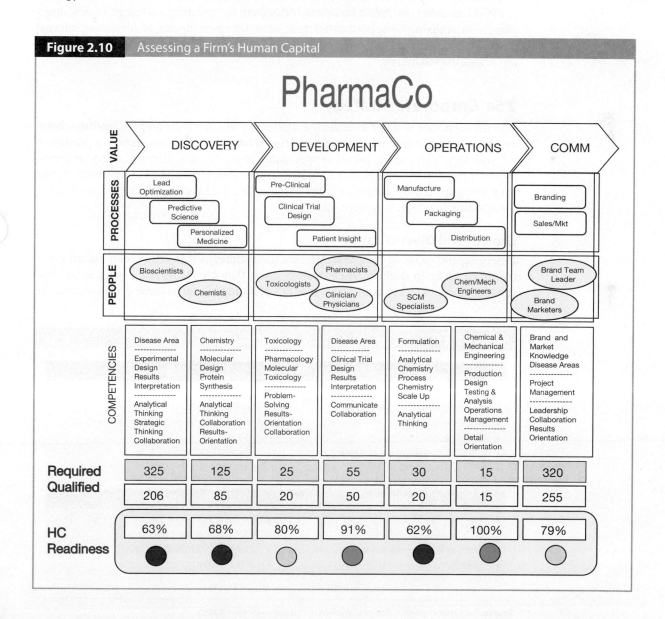

LO

Think about a firm you enjoy doing business with or one you don't. What competitive strategy does it pursue? Do you think its employees have the right skills given the strategy? Do you detect any mismatches?

2.5 Step Four: Formulating a Strategy

Think once again about your education, your major, and career choices. After you looked at possible careers, the opportunities they presented, and your ability and desire to do them, you probably had to formulate a strategy for pursuing one of them by choosing a college. When you graduate, you will have to formulate a strategy for successfully landing a job in your field. Similarly, after managers have analyzed the internal strengths and weaknesses of a firm, as well as external opportunities and threats, they have the information they need to formulate corporate, business, and HR strategies for the organization.

Strategy formulation builds on a SWOT analysis, discussed earlier in the chapter. A SWOT analysis can help a company move from formulating a strategy, to devising a plan, to capitalizing on opportunities, to counteracting on threats, to alleviating internal weaknesses. Figure 2.11 is an example of a SWOT analysis done for the women's clothing brand Liz Claiborne.

2.5a Corporate Strategy

A firm's corporate strategy includes the markets in which it will compete, against whom, and how. Some firms choose a concentration strategy that focuses on only a portion of the industry. Visteon Corporation specializes in electronics, climate, and powertrain technologies for the automotive industry. In contrast, Henry Ford at one time owned everything from the ore mines needed to make steel for his cars, all the way down to the showrooms in which they were sold.

Growth and Diversification

Emerging and growing companies execute their strategies differently than mature companies or those in decline. As companies grow, they often formulate geographic, volume, and product-expansion strategies. HR planning is vital to these decisions because

Figure 2.11	An Example of a SWOT Analysis for Liz Claiborne

Strengths	Weaknesses
• Brand Recognition • Understanding Customer Needs • New Product Lines • Advertising Scheme • Product Diversification Strategy • Tailor to Changing Needs • Preferences and Lifestyles	• Changing Consumer Needs • Highly Competitive Market • Long Lead Time Bringing New Styles to Market • Clothing Line Is Complete Success or Costly Mistake

Opportunities	Threats
• Overseas Markets • Worldwide Advertising • Entering the Large Size Consumer Market • Designing Mix-and-Match Outfits • Men's Sportswear	• Key Competitors • Strict Government Regulations • Changing Shopping Patterns • Quota Restrictions

Source: "Liz Claiborne SWOT Analysis," WikiSWOT, http://www.wikiswot.com.

achieving growth requires three related elements: (1) increased employee productivity, (2) a greater number of employees, and (3) employees developing or acquiring new skills. Thus, a firm's staffing, training, employee motivation efforts, and the like can either enable the company to grow or limit its potential.

As companies diversify into new businesses, managers are faced with a "make or buy" decision, just like Ford was. That is, should they develop the capabilities in-house to produce their products or contract externally for them or at least parts of them? When IBM entered the personal computer market in the early 1980s, it contracted with (then startup companies) Intel and Microsoft to make the hardware and operating systems for its PCs. The decision did not rest solely on human resource issues, but they were an important part of the equation.

Eventually IBM got out of the PC business altogether by selling its PC product lineup to the Chinese computer manufacturer Lenovo. Today IBM develops custom technology services for businesses, which it believes will be more profitable in the long run and a harder product for competitors to imitate. To help accomplish the strategy, IBM bought up dozens of business-service-related companies and hired their talent.

Some companies diversify far beyond their core businesses. At one time GE mostly produced electrical and home-appliance products. Today its products include those in the health, finance, truck and air transportation, oil and gas, and power and water industries. To manage such a diverse portfolio, GE has invested heavily in developing its talent and leadership abilities in contrast to its traditional focus on manufacturing, much of which it has outsourced.

Mergers and Acquisitions

As we have explained, the world has seen a host of mergers and acquisitions in recent years. They include such firms as AT&T and TimeWarner, Fiat and Chrysler, American Airlines and U.S. Airways, and others. When companies merge, they can often streamline their costs by eliminating duplicate functions, such as duplicate accounting, finance, and HR departments, for example.

However, many mergers end up being risky because they do not go well (measured by return on investment, shareholder value, and the like). Often the failure is due to cultural inconsistencies, as well as conflicts among the managers of each firm. The failure of the merger between the German firm Daimler-Benz (the manufacturer of Mercedes Benz vehicles) and Chrysler in 1998 is an example. Although the German portion of the firm had superior technology, reportedly it was less than eager to share its knowhow with its American counterparts. Problems like this one point directly to the importance of effective HR planning prior to—and during—the merger process.

Strategic Alliances and Joint Ventures

Sometimes firms do not acquire or merge with another firm but instead pursue cooperative strategies such as a strategic alliance or joint venture. Especially when firms enter into international joint ventures, the issues of culture (both company culture and national culture) become paramount. On the front end, HR plays a vital role in assessing the compatibility of cultures and potential problems. As the alliance is formed, HR helps select key executives and develops teamwork across the respective workforces. In addition, HR is typically involved in the design of performance assessment and mutual incentives for the alliance.

2.5b Business Strategy

While we think about corporate strategy as domain selection, business strategy is viewed in terms of domain navigation. It is more focused on how the company will compete against rival firms to create value for customers. Companies can increase the value they offer customers by decreasing the costs of their goods and services or by increasing the benefits their products provide (or some combination of the two). Their business strategies reflect these choices.

Low-Cost Strategy: Compete on Productivity and Efficiency

A low-cost strategy means keeping your costs low enough so that you can offer an attractive price to customers relative to your competitors. Organizations such as Dell, Walmart, and Spirit Airlines have been very successful competing based on a low-cost strategy by focusing on efficiency, productivity, and minimizing waste. These types of companies often are large and try to take advantage of economies of scale in the production and distribution of goods and services so they can sell them at lower prices, which leads to higher market shares, volumes, and (hopefully) profits. However, even a low-cost leader must offer a product or service that customers find valuable. As one CEO put it, "You can make a pizza so cheap that no one will buy it."[23] Ultimately organizations need to use a cost strategy to increase value to customers rather than take it away.

A low-cost strategy is linked to HR planning in several ways. The first has to do with productivity. A common misconception about low-cost strategies is that they inevitably require cutting labor costs. On the contrary, there are several good examples of companies that pay their employees "top dollar" but gain back cost advantages because of excellent productivity. That is, they get a terrific "bang for the buck." Either they produce more from the workforce they have, or they can produce the same amount with a smaller workforce.

According to Peter Cappelli, who heads the Center for Human Resources at the Wharton School at the University of Pennsylvania, the productivity of the best-performing staffs can be 5 to 20 *times* higher than the productivity of the worst-performing staffs, depending upon the industry. Both Costco and Sam's Club have low-cost, high-volume strategies. However, one study found that the pay and benefits to Costco's employees far outstripped those earned by Sam's Club employees, but so do Costco's profits per employee. In addition, employee turnover and the costs associated with it are much lower for Costco.[26] Similarly, Billy Beane, the general manager of the Oakland A's, became famous for making the most of the A's small payroll. Beane did so by carefully choosing and developing players and using them more strategically than other major league teams with bigger payroll budgets.

The second way that low-cost strategies are linked to HR pertains to outsourcing. Companies consider contracting with complementary (external) partners that can perform particular activities or services equally well (or better) at a lower cost. However, organizations need to have a clear understanding of their core processes and skills. Too often, a firm bases outsourcing decisions on costs alone. But this can lead to detrimental effects if the skills base of the firm's employees suffers and its core capabilities erode.

Differentiation Strategy: Compete on Unique Value Added

Another way to compete is by providing something unique and distinctive to customers, such as a high-quality product, innovative features, speed to market, or superior service. The Ritz-Carlton's commitment to quality and luxury, FedEx's focus on speed and flexible delivery, Neiman Marcus's commitment to high fashion and customer service, and Apple's emphasis on innovation and product development are all easily identifiable examples of differentiation strategies.

Each of these strategies is rooted in human resources management. Companies that focus on service, for example, need to identify and support ways to empower employees to serve customers better. Relative to companies that emphasize low cost and efficiencies, differentiating companies will bend the rules a bit more and customize products and services to let the customer "have it their way." In place of rigid rules, Starbucks looks for prospective employees with the ability to make good decisions on their own. Similarly, Nordstrom's employee handbook consists of just a single 5×8 index card that reads: "Welcome to Nordstrom. Rule #1. Use your good judgment in all situations. There will be no additional rules."

Billy Beane won more games by using statistics and other analytics to manage the Oakland A's.

2.5c HR Strategy

A firm's HR strategy must work in tandem with its corporate and business strategies. For example, decisions have to be made about the composition of the workforce. Getting the right number and kinds of people in right places at the right times doing things that benefit them and the firm is no small task. Too often firms focus on their core employees, such as knowledge workers, because they are in the best position to implement a firm's strategies. But core workers alone can't make or break a company. Engineering may develop a great product, but if the firm's customer service representatives do a poor job of helping customers with the good or service, its sales will suffer—as will the company.

Instead, the firm must focus on all of its talent, including support employees, contractors, temporary employees, and complementary partners and how they mesh with one another. Each group of workers differs in terms of the human capital they bring, the expectations placed on them, the extent to which they are trained and developed, and so on. Subcultures will also emerge from the various groups. The firm's engineers may have a whole different way of working and viewing the firm than, say, the company's customer representatives. HR managers have to examine and analyze these differences. They and line managers then have to formulate a plan that blends the firm's structure, culture, operations, technology, and "people management" practices in ways that facilitate a firm's competencies and drive its strategies forward.[27]

2.6 Step Five: Executing a Firm's Strategy

As the old saying goes, "Well begun is half done"—but only half. Like any plan, formulating the appropriate strategy is not enough. You can't be successful by just planning to go to college and formulating a strategy to get a career. You have to actually do it. As you know, this is easier said than done.

Similarly, strategy alone does not differentiate high- from low-performing firms. The true differentiator between winners and losers turns out to be, not what their

LO 5

Why is it difficult to translate a firm's strategy into HR deliverables that actually get the job done? What part of this endeavor do you think HR managers struggle with the most?

strategies were, but how well the strategy was executed. Yet half of managers in one survey said there is a gap between their organization's ability to develop a vision and strategy, and then actually execute it. Former Honeywell CEO Larry Bossidy noted in his book *Execution* that people believe they understand the concept—"it's about getting things done"—but when asked *how* they get things done, "the dialogue goes rapidly downhill."

Figure 2.12 shows the "4As" required to successfully execute a strategy. They are as follows:

- *Alignment.* Alignment occurs in an organization when it has a clear strategic intent, its staff has shared performance expectations, and are accountable for the results. We will talk about alignment more later in the chapter.

- *Agility.* Execution is not a "one and done event." It's also about competing tomorrow. The key to execution increasingly depends on being agile, nimble, and proactive in the face of change. As the great former hockey player Wayne Gretsky used to say, "I don't skate to where the puck is. I skate to where the puck is going to be."

- *Architecture.* A firm's architecture consists of its structures, processes, and systems. Ideally, they should be simple and streamlined so as to propel the firm to success. But too often a firm's architecture can end up being complicated and entangle a firm like a straightjacket.

- *Ability.* As we have explained, products and processes are easy to duplicate. Talent is not. Strategy execution (and ultimately growth, and profitability) depend on a firm's talent capacity—a talented group of leaders, managers, and employees working together in an engaged and collaborative way.

As the figure shows, execution is the process of combining these four elements of human capital and organizational capital.

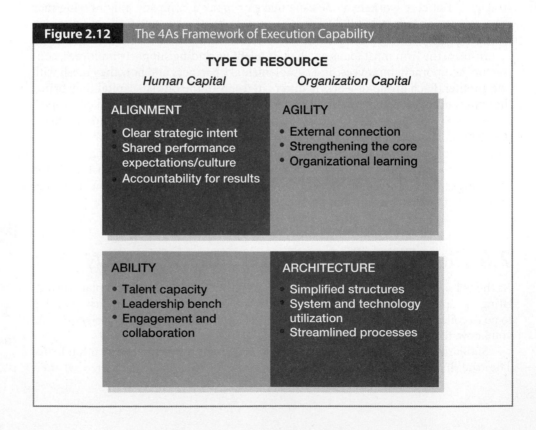

Figure 2.12   The 4As Framework of Execution Capability

TYPE OF RESOURCE

Human Capital   *Organization Capital*

ALIGNMENT
- Clear strategic intent
- Shared performance expectations/culture
- Accountability for results

AGILITY
- External connection
- Strengthening the core
- Organizational learning

ABILITY
- Talent capacity
- Leadership bench
- Engagement and collaboration

ARCHITECTURE
- Simplified structures
- System and technology utilization
- Streamlined processes

2.6a HR's Role in Strategy Execution

In addition to formulating corporate- and business-level strategies, managers need to "translate" strategic priorities into functional areas of the organization (such as marketing, manufacturing, human resources, and the like). Human resources management is instrumental to almost every aspect of strategy execution, whether it pertains to the organization's structure, systems, style, skills, staff, or shared values.

Remaining Agile

Like the firm as a whole, HR has to focus on ensuring agility when the environment changes. HR agility can be achieved in two primary ways: coordination agility and resource agility.

Coordination agility is the ability to rapidly reallocate resources to new or changing needs. Through HRP, managers can anticipate upcoming events, keep abreast of changes in legal regulations, forecast economic trends, spot competitors' moves, and the like. With advance notice, managers can move people into and out of jobs, retrain them for new skill requirements, and modify the kinds of incentives they use. The use of a contingency workforce composed of part-timers, temporary employees, and complementary partners also helps achieve coordination flexibility.[28]

Resource agility, on the other hand, results from having resources that can be used in different ways and people who can perform different functions in different ways. Cross-training employees, rotating them into different jobs, and using teams are all efforts that focus on building a flexible workforce.

Reconciling Supply and Demand

Part of remaining agile includes reconciling the firm's demand for its products with its supply of employees. Demand considerations are based on forecasted trends in business activity. Supply considerations involve determining where and how candidates with the required qualifications can be found to fill a firm's vacancies.

In an effort to meet their human resource demands, organizations have many staffing options, including recruiting and hiring full-time employees as well as reducing their turnover, having employees work overtime, recalling laid-off workers, using temporary or contract employees, and outsourcing or offshoring some of their business processes. Some of the ways firms say they are, or will, attract and retain babyboomers to avoid future labor shortages include offering employees flexible scheduling, health care, and long-term care benefits as they eventually retire.[29]

If its labor shortages are acute, a company may have to develop talent from the ground up. For example, knowing that about 40 percent of its aging workforce would be eligible for retirement in 5 years, Saudi Aramco, a Saudi-owned oil company, developed a system of hiring top high-school graduates in the country, sponsoring their college educations, and providing them with job training. The company employs 400 planners to analyze its workforce needs for the next decade and beyond.[30]

When forecasts show a surplus of employees, organizations often restrict their hiring, reduce their employees' work hours or furlough them, and consider layoffs. Across-the-board pay cuts are sometimes utilized in lieu of or in addition to layoffs. Some organizations try to reduce their workforces by relying on attrition, which is a gradual reduction of employees that occurs due to employee resignations, retirements, and deaths. Programs in which employees are offered "sweetened" retirement benefits to leave a firm earlier than planned are common in large companies.

As we have discussed, organizations have to be constantly prepared to exit and enter new lines of business, restructure, outsource, offshore, and sometimes downsize either because they have too many employees or employees with the wrong skill sets. Decisions about employee layoffs are usually based on seniority and/or performance. In some organizations, especially in Japanese firms, seniority is more likely to be the primary consideration. In other organizations, factors such as an employee's ability and productivity take precedence over seniority. In the case of unionized organizations, the criteria for determining who will be laid off are typically set forth in union agreements and based on seniority. Unions recognize seniority because they feel that their members deserve certain rights proportionate to the years they have invested in their jobs.

Employers often recognize the seniority of employees who are not unionized, though. But one disadvantage of doing so is that the less competent employees can end up receiving the same rewards and security as the more-competent employees. Also, the practice of using seniority as the basis for deciding which workers to lay off can inadvertently have a disparate impact on women and minority workers, who often have less seniority than other groups of workers.

When firms are downsizing, HR managers must ensure no laws are violated in the process, of which there are many. They range from laws designed to protect minorities and older employees from being unfairly targeted to laws requiring companies of a certain size laying off a certain number of employees to give them warning between 60 days to 6 months. Firms must also comply with government provisions, giving some workers who have been laid off and their families the right to temporary health care coverage at group rates. We will talk more about these laws in Chapter 13.

2.7 Step Six: Evaluation

LO 6

As an HR manager, how would you know whether or not your firm's overall strategy and HR strategy were being successfully implemented?

You probably know someone who graduated, went to work in a particular field, assessed their success (or lack of it) in that field, and then decided to do something else for a living. The same sort of reevaluation and assessment is an important function for businesses as well. At one level, it might seem that assessing a firm's effectiveness is the final step in the planning process. But it is also the first step. Planning is cyclical, of course, and while we have somewhat conveniently placed evaluation at the end of this chapter, the information it provides actually provides firms with inputs they need for the next cycle in the planning process.

To evaluate their performance, firms need to establish a set of "desired" objectives as well as the metrics they will use to monitor how well their organizations delivered against those objectives. The objectives can include achieving a certain level of productivity, revenue, profit, market share, market penetration, customer satisfaction, and so forth. For example, after Barnes and Noble saw lackluster sales for its Nook e-reader, the company reevaluated its strategy and began contemplating selling its Nook division for partnering with another company to produce it. Today it develops the tablets in conjunction with Samsung.

2.7a Evaluating a Firm's Strategic Alignment

This involves all aspects of the business, but in particular there needs to be a clear alignment between HR and the requirements of an organization's strategy. HR policies and practices need to achieve two types of fit: vertical and horizontal.[31]

Vertical Fit/Alignment

Vertical fit (or *vertical alignment*) focuses on the connection between the business's objectives and the major initiatives undertaken by HR. On the one hand, as we noted earlier, if a company's strategy focuses on achieving low cost, its HR policies and practices need to encourage employees to work more efficiently and be more productive. On the other hand, if the organization competes through innovation and new product development, then its HR policies and practices would be more aligned with the notion of fostering creativity and flexibility.

When ensuring alignment, firms have to ask themselves whether or not their capabilities, including those of its employees, are aligned with its value proposition. Most observers would agree that Tom Monahan, founder of Domino's, was able to change the pizza industry not because he created a better product but because he was able to offer a different value proposition—delivery in 30 minutes or the pizza was free—and then created the capability to "deliver" against that promise. Case Study 2 discusses Domino's alignment in more detail.

Horizontal Fit/Alignment

In addition to vertical alignment, or fit, managers need to ensure that their HR practices are all aligned with one another internally to establish a configuration that is mutually reinforcing. The entire range of the firm's HR practices—from its job design to staffing, training, performance appraisal, and compensation—need to focus on the *same* objectives. Too often, one HR practice will emphasize one objective, whereas another HR practice will emphasize another. Charles Schwab & Co. faced this situation. The company has a reputation in the financial services industry for developing a culture of teamwork that has been important to its strategy. However, when it changed its compensation strategy to provide more rewards to its high-performing brokers, the firm sent mixed signals to its employees. Which is more important: teamwork or individual high flyers?[32]

Figure 2.13 shows an example of how organizations can assess the horizontal fit of their HR practices. There are essentially three steps. First, managers need to identify the key workforce objectives they hope to achieve. The objectives might include loyalty, customer service, productivity, and creativity. Second, managers would identify each of the HR practices used to elicit or reinforce those workforce objectives (job design, staffing, training, appraisal, compensation, and so on). Third, managers would evaluate each HR practice on a scale of −5 (not supportive) to 5 (supportive). By tallying up the ratings across managers, organizations can get a very clear idea of which HR practices are working together to achieve the workforce objectives and which are not.

Keep in mind that horizontal fit is a necessary, but insufficient, cause of strategic alignment. A company could have nearly perfect alignment among its HR practices, and they still might not be aligned with the competitive strategy. For that reason, it is important for managers to assess both vertical and horizontal fit.

Strategic Alignment and the Balanced Scorecard

One of the tools for mapping a firm's strategy to ensure strategic alignment is the **balanced scorecard (BSC)**. Developed by Harvard professors Robert Kaplan and David Norton, the BSC is a framework that helps managers translate their firms' strategic goals into operational objectives. The model has four related cells: (1) financial, (2) customer, (3) processes, and (4) learning. The logic of the BSC is firmly rooted in human resources

balanced scorecard (BSC)
A measurement framework that helps managers translate strategic goals into operational objectives.

Figure 2.13   Assessing Horizontal Fit

WORKFORCE OBJECTIVES

ORGANIZATION		SALES PRODUCTIVITY	CUSTOMER SERVICE	MERCHANDISE INFORMATION	STOCK MAINTENANCE	TOTAL
Structure/Workflow						
	• Cross-functional teams	3	2	0	−1	4
	• Rotation (Depts.)	3	3	−1	−1	4
Staffing						
	• Test battery	2	2	1	1	6
	• Select for experience	5	0	2	2	12
Training						
	• Retail selling skills	4	5	1	1	11
Rewards						
	• Results appraisal	5	−4	−2	−5	−6
	• Individual incentives	5	−5	−3	−5	−8
Leadership						
	• Corporate	3	3	1	0	7
	• Store manager	4	2	2	2	10
Technologies						
	• Merchandise IS	5	2	5	1	13
	• Daily postings	4	−3	4	−1	4
		43/55	10/55	10/55	26/55	57/220

FUNCTIONAL COHESION

SYSTEM COHERENCE   26%

5 = Strongly supports the priority
0 = Neutral
−5 = Strongly counterproductive

management. People management and learning help organizations improve their internal processes and provide excellent customer service. Internal processes—product development, service, and the like—are critical for creating customer satisfaction and loyalty, and they are also important for ensuring productivity to contain costs for better financial performance. Customer value creation, in turn, drives up revenues, which enhances profitability.

Figure 2.14 shows how this might work at Starbucks. In each cell, Starbucks would identify the key metrics that help translate strategic goals to operational imperatives. For example, under customer metrics, Starbucks might look at percentage of repeat customers, number of new customers, growth rate, and so forth. Under people metrics, managers might measure the numbers of suggestions provided by employees, participation in the Starbucks stock sharing program, employee turnover, training hours spent, and the like. Each of these cells links vertically. People management issues such as rewards, training, and suggestions can be linked to efficient processes (brewing the perfect cup, delivering top-notch customer service, etc.). These processes then lead to better customer loyalty and growth. Growth and customer loyalty in turn lead to higher profitability and market value.

Figure 2.14 Building the Metrics Model

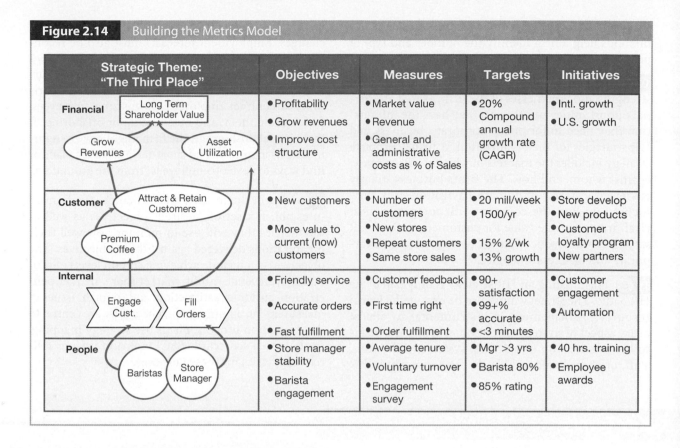

Summary

LO ① Strategic human resources management (SHRM) integrates strategic planning and HR planning. It can be thought of as the pattern of human resource deployments and activities that enable an organization to achieve its strategic goals. The firm's mission, vision, and values provide a perspective on where the company is headed and what the organization can become in the future. Ideally, they clarify the long-term direction of the company and its strategic intent.

LO ② Analyzing the firm's external environment is central to strategic planning. Benchmarking is the process of looking at your practices and performance and then comparing them to those of your competitors. Environmental scanning is the systematic monitoring of major external forces influencing the organization, including forces in the business environment and the competitive environment. Changes in the external environment have a direct impact on the way

organizations are run and people are managed. Some of these changes represent opportunities, and some of them represent real threats to the organization.

LO ③ Conducting an internal analysis to gauge the firm's strengths and weaknesses involves looking at a firm's core capabilities, its talent and composition in the firm, and the firm's corporate culture. An internal analysis enables strategic decision makers to assess the organization's workforce—its skills, cultural beliefs, and values.

An organization's success increasingly depends on the knowledge, skills, and abilities of employees, particularly as they help establish a set of core capabilities that distinguish an organization from its competitors. When employees' talents are valuable, rare, difficult to imitate, and organized, a firm can achieve a sustained competitive advantage through its people. HRP is a systematic process that involves forecasting the demand for labor, performing supply analysis, and balancing supply and demand considerations. Quantitative and qualitative methods help a firm identify the number and type of people needed to meet the organization's goals.

LO (4) After managers have analyzed the internal strengths and weaknesses of the firm, as well as external opportunities and threats, they have the information they need to formulate corporate, business, and HR strategies for the organization. A firm's corporate strategy includes the markets in which it will compete, against whom, and how. The firm's business strategy is viewed in terms of domain navigation. It is more focused on how the company will compete against rival firms to create value for customers. A firm's HR strategies and practices should be aligned with its corporate and business strategies.

LO (5) Formulating an HR strategy is only half of the HR battle. The strategy must also be executed. Human resources management is instrumental to almost every aspect of strategy execution, whether it pertains to the organization's structure, systems, style, skills, staff, or shared values. Like the firm as a whole, HR has to focus on ensuring agility when the environment changes. Employment forecasts must also be reconciled against the internal and the external supplies of labor the firm faces. This can include having current employees work overtime; hiring full-time, part-time, or contract employees; downsizing employees; furloughing them; and outsourcing or offshoring. If there is a labor shortage, the firm might have to reformulate its long-term and short-term strategic plans or find ways to develop employees "from the ground up."

LO (6) To evaluate their performance, firms need to establish a set of "desired" objectives as well as the metrics they will use to monitor how well their organizations delivered against those objectives. The objectives can include achieving certain levels of productivity, revenue, profit, market share, market penetration, customer satisfaction, and so forth. Issues of measurement, alignment, fit, and agility are central to the evaluation process. Firms use strategy mapping, the balanced scorecard (BSC) tool, and various HR-related metrics for these purposes.

Key Terms

balanced scorecard (BSC)	human resources planning (HRP)	strategic human resources management
benchmarking	management forecasts	strategic planning
business environment	Markov analysis	strategic vision
competitive environment	mission	succession planning
core capabilities	quality of fill	SWOT analysis
core values	replacement charts	talent reviews
cultural audits	skill inventories	trend analysis
environmental scanning	staffing tables	value creation
human capital readiness	stakeholders	

Discussion Questions

LO (1) Identify the three key elements of the human resources planning model and discuss the relationships among them.

LO (2) What external forces influence a firm's strategy?

LO (3) What criteria must be met if firms are to achieve a competitive advantage through their employees?

LO (4) Explain the difference between a firm's corporate strategy and business strategy. Why do firms need to look at both aspects?

LO (5) Why is it often difficult for a firm to match its strategy to HR deliverables?

LO (6) What steps does the firm need to take to execute its strategy and measure the results?

Customizing HR for Different Types of Human Capital

Part of strategic planning is mapping an organization's human capital. When we look at the strategic value of a person's skills as well as their uniqueness, we soon discover that organizations are comprised of different kinds of workers who have very different kinds of skills. Some are core knowledge workers; some are more traditional job-based employees; some are contract workers; and some are external partners. It is unlikely a firm would manage all of these employees the same way. There are differences in HR practices for different groups. That is not bad, but it makes the job of HR managers more difficult.

Assignment

The following are descriptions of three different employees. How would you characterize each worker? What role does each play when it comes to the organization's strategy?

Sobadia Bascomb is a highly talented computer programmer for Applied Software Solutions. She is among an elite set of engineers in the computer industry doing leading-edge work on advanced computer modeling. The firm's CEO, Bill Ding, believes the future of the company rests on the innovative work that Sobadia and her team are doing. He worries that someone might lure her away to work for them, so he wants to give her all the room she needs to grow and stay committed to the firm.

Calvin Duff is a salesperson on the retail side of the firm. He has daily contact with customers and is responsible for making sales and communicating with service personnel. Make no mistake: To many customers, Calvin and his coworkers are the "face" of the company. Always on the lookout for a better position, Calvin has thought about working for PeachTree Computing, Applied Software Solution's main competitor. Other salespeople have found that they can leave Applied Software Solutions and get "up to speed" easily at other firms. Their skills are very transferable, and the transition is not difficult. Bill Ding and other managers at the company recognize this fact, so they try to keep salespeople loyal and productive, recognizing that many of them do eventually leave.

Chandra Singh is a part-time administrative assistant for Applied Software Solutions. She handles routine typing and filing work for the company, particularly in peak periods in the summer and around the holidays. She usually works for a few weeks at a time and then takes time off. The executives at the company have considered either outsourcing her job to an agency or automating it through a new computer system. But for now things are steady.

CASE STUDY ❶ How a Strategy Change Led to Nike's Formation

Nike, the world's most famous athletic company, didn't start out by making Air Jordans. In fact, it didn't make shoes at all. It distributed them.

Nike actually began as company called Blue Ribbon. It was founded in 1964 by Phil Knight, a runner from Oregon, along with his former college track coach, Bill Bowerman. At the time, the running shoe market was dominated by the German firms Adidas and Puma. However, Knight and Bowerman had become intrigued by new lighter, lower-cost running shoes made in Japan. Bowerman had always tinkered with shoe designs to try to make his runners faster. Meanwhile, Knight had just earned an MBA from Stanford University and was looking for a way to combine what he loved—sports—with work. So, the two men each chipped in $500, and began importing and selling Tiger-brand shoes (now Asics) made by the Japanese company Onitsuka.

Blue Ribbon's start wasn't glamorous. Bowerman and Knight began by selling the shoes out of their cars at local track meets. But runners liked the new lighter shoes, and the company started earning a profit. Eventually the business did well enough it was able to hire some employees, most of whom were passionate runners like the owners.

For about a decade Blue Ribbon's strategy worked well. Business grew, and the company even opened its own store in Santa Monica, California. But by 1971, the firm was facing a crisis. Bowerman wanted Onitsuka to make a lighter shoe he had designed. Onitsuka wasn't interested. Moreover, Knight believed Onitsuka was looking for other distributors to cut Blue Ribbon out of the business.

What did Knight and Bowerman do? They designed their own shoe called "the Nike" and began selling it. Executives at Onitsuka were enraged by the move. They immediately stopped selling shoes to Blue Robbin and sued it to boot.

At that point, it looked like it might be the end of the road for Blue Ribbon. There wasn't much of a market for the Nike shoes yet. The company was still young and in debt, and a lawsuit would be expensive to fight.

Knight gave Blue Ribbon's employees the bad news. But instead of throwing in the towel, he laid out a new vision and mission for the firm: "This is the moment we've been waiting for," Knight recounts telling them in his bestselling book, *Shoe Dog*. "No more selling someone else's brand. No more working for someone else. Onitsuka has been holding us down for years. Their late deliveries, their mixed-up orders, their refusal to hear and implement our design ideas—who among us isn't sick of dealing with all that? . . . If we're going to succeed, or fail, we should do so on our own terms, with our own ideas—our own brand."

After the initial shock wore off, relief swept across Blue Ribbon's employees. Not only were they undaunted by the new mission, they were energized and excited about it. Their future lay in their own hands, and they would find a way to achieve it. Immediately they began formulating new strategies and plans.

Knight thinks the culture and agility of the company were major reasons why Nike became the success it is today. Most, if not all, of its employees were scrappy competitive types. "Each of us was willing to do whatever was necessary to win," he says. "And if 'whatever was necessary' fell outside our area of expertise, no problem. Not that any of us thought we wouldn't fail. In fact we had every expectation that we would. But when we did fail, we had faith we'd do it fast, learn from it, and be better for it . . . Taking a chance on people—you could argue that's what it's all been about."

Questions

1. Who is ultimately responsible for formulating a firm's strategy—its managers, employees, or both?

2. What strategy execution problems do you think Knight and Bowerman might have faced in their effort to make Nike successful?

Sources: Frank Kalman, "Nike, Phil Knight and The Power of Shared Purpose," *Talent Economy* (January 26, 2017), http://wwwtalenteconomy.com; Andy Gould, "Three Lessons for Entrepreneurs from Nike 'Shoe Dog' Phil Knight," *Motley Fool* (January 17, 2017), http://fool.com; Lara O'Reilly, "Eleven Things Hardly Anyone Knows about Nike," *Business Insider* (November 4, 2014), http://www.businessinsider.com.

CASE STUDY Domino's Tries to Get Its Strategic Recipe Right

Believe it or not, years ago it was normal for people to have wait an hour or more to get their pizzas delivered. But those were the years B.D.—before Domino's. Started by Tom Monahan and his brother in Ypsilanti, Michigan, in the 1960s, Domino's created a value proposition people were hungering for: pizza delivered in 30 minutes or less. Better yet, if a Domino's pizza *wasn't* delivered in 30 minutes, it was free. That was unheard of in the pizza business.

Monahan changed the pizza industry not because Domino's created a better product but because it was able to offer a different value proposition than anyone else was offering and align its people, processes, and systems to deliver against that promise. Domino's used assembly line–based systems and standardized processes to improve efficiency and reduce pizza preparation times. For example, it was the first to use conveyor-belt oven technology to ensure uniform temperatures and reduce baking times. Domino's also translated its strategy into HR deliverables by emphasizing and encouraging fast pizza-making and delivery. Annually the company holds a "World's Fastest Pizza Maker" competition in which its pizza makers compete for cash and other prizes.

As important as what Domino's did is what it did *not* do. Strategy is about making choices. Domino's did not focus on great pizza—it focused on fast pizza. It did not customize every order but prepared them all in advance. It didn't hire premiere pizza chefs who tossed pizza dough into the air to make lighter crusts. It didn't use the wood-fired stoves to give the pizza an old-world taste. And it didn't offer in-store dining.

Each of the ingredients in Monahan's formula was aligned around its value proposition of fast delivery—a strategy that worked well for Domino's for decades. This strategy and a franchise model helped the company grow by leaps and bounds. Today there are over 13,000 Domino's pizza stores, which are located in 80-plus countries around the world. India is currently the company's hottest market.

Over time, however, Domino's competitive environment changed. Other companies began delivering pizzas in about 30 minutes, and consumers began wanting more than fast pizza: They wanted good pizza. The problem was that Domino's wasn't delivering on that score. In taste tests, customers complained Domino's pizzas tasted like cardboard. At one point, the firms' customer-satisfaction scores in terms of its food and service were lower than any other pizza chain. Perhaps not surprisingly, the firm's stock price reflected as much.

To turn things around, the company had to rethink its value proposition. That included revamping its food. The company developed a new recipe for its pizza crusts; began using fresher, gourmet types of ingredients; and began offering new products, such as artisan pizzas, pasta, and desserts. It also remodeled stores and added in-store dining. But Domino's had to revamp its HR strategies and policies, too. One problem was employee turnover. Domino's turnover rate was 158 percent annually. In other words, for every employee hired during a year another 1.5 employees quit.

Domino's CEO at the time, David Brandon, wasn't convinced that higher pay for hourly-wage employees was the solution though. "If we could have increased everybody's pay 20 percent could we have moved the needle a little bit to buy some loyalty? Maybe, but that's not a long term solution." Moreover, because most of Domino's stores are individually owned rather than corporate owned, it is the individual owners of the stores who have to decide for themselves whether to increase hourly wages.

Instead, the company focused on the quality of store managers—choosing better ones, finding ways to retain good ones, and coaching them to train and motivate employees by being respectful and polite. It's store managers who cause employees to stick around—or not, said Rob Cecere, a regional manager for Domino's. Employees can go to McDonald's or Pizza Hut and make as much as they make at Domino's. "You've got to make sure they are happy to come to work for you," Cecere explained. Domino's also worked harder to promote a culture of "fun" via its World's Fastest Pizza competition and other initiatives.

Domino's chief strength still lies in its systems and technology though. The biggest department at the firm's headquarters in Ann Arbor, Michigan, is its technology department. The department has built novel applications over the years, such as an online ordering system that allows customers to "build" their pizzas online and track their preparation, cooking, and delivery times. Customers can also use a mobile app for ordering, an emoji to text a standard order, or simply tell "Dom," Domino's chatbot, what they want. In Australia and New Zealand, the company is experimenting with robot and drone delivery.

Has Domino's new recipe worked? By most accounts, yes. Turnover dropped by more than 100 percent following the initiative, and customer satisfaction scores jumped up, too. In 2016, Domino's sales growth was the best among the 25 largest restaurant chains in the United States. Its stock price has rocketed upward as well.

Still, strategy changes and their implementation are continually evolving challenges for firms, and Domino's is no exception. "We need to understand what's going on and create competitive advantage by being ahead of the curve," says the company's current CEO J. Patrick Doyle. For one, the company still faces issues with its HR piece of the puzzle and ensuring its strategy is aligned all the way down the food chain. Recently a group of franchise owners in New York agreed to pay $1.5 million to settle cases for minimum-wage and overtime violations.

Doyle says the firm *has* to start paying higher wages. Minimum-wage laws are rising in some states, and employers like Walmart and Target are raising their minimum wages. "The reality is the labor market is tightening up, and we've got to respond to that. It's getting harder to hire people," says Doyle. "We've got to do what the market demands to get the right people for our business," he says.

Will paying hourly-wage employees a little more buy Domino's a little more loyalty and prevent negative publicity for the company? And if so, would the costs have been worth the benefits? And who should incur these costs since most of the stores are privately owned? These questions are food for thought, ones that Domino's will have to resolve.

After all, even with the best technologies and systems, pizzas don't cook and deliver themselves. People do.

Questions

1. Explain how Domino's strategy differed from its competitors.

2. Has the firm been able to achieve a long-term strategic fit between its strategy and HR practices in your opinion? Why or why not?

Sources: Dave Buss, "What Matters to Domino's: Five Questions with CEO J. Patrick Doyle," *Brandchannel* (January 23, 2017), http://brandchannel.com; Kevin McCoy, "N.Y. Sues Domino's Pizza for Alleged Wage Theft," *USA Today* (May 24, 2016), http://www.usatoday.com; "Domino's Pizza Will Have To Raise Wages to Stay Competitive," *Reuters* (April 6, 2015), http://www.reuters.com; William James, David Kretzman, "Why Domino's Digital Component Is Important," *Motley Fool* (December 10, 2013), http://motleyfool.com; Erin White, "To Keep Employees, Dominos Decides It's Not All about Pay," *The Wall Street Journal* (February 17, 2005), http://online.wsj.com.

Notes and References

1. Chistopher Rees, Hasanah Johari, "'Senior Managers' Perceptions of the *HRM* Function during Times of 'Strategic Organizational Change,'" *Journal of Organizational Change Management* 23, no 2. (2010): 517.

2. Scott A. Snell, Mark Shadur, and Patrick M. Wright, "Human Resources Strategy: The Era of Our Ways," in M. A. Hitt, R. E. Freeman, and J. S. Harrison (eds.), *Handbook of Strategic Management* (Oxford, UK: Blackwell, 2002), 627–49; Patrick M. Wright, Benjamin Dunford, and Scott A. Snell, "Human Resources and the Resource-Based View of the Firm," *Journal of Management* 27, no. 6 (2002): 701–21; "What's Affecting HR Operations? Globalization, Sustainability, and Talent," *HR Focus* 84, no. 8 (August 2007): 8; Doris Sims, "Do You Know Where Your Talent Is?" *Training* 45, no. 1 (January 2008): 46–46.

3. "The Importance of HR," *HRFocus* 73, no. 3 (March 1996): 14; David Brown, "HR's Role in Business Strategy: Still a Lot of Work to Be Done," *Canadian HR Reporter* 14, no. 19 (November 5, 2001):1–20; "How Should the HR Dept. of 2004 Be Structured?" *Human Resource Department Management Report*, no. 3 (November 2003): 1.

4. Patrick Kiger, "Serious Progress in Strategic Workforce Planning," *Workforce Management* (July 1, 2010), http://workforce.com.

5. Bala Iyer, "Deconstructing Google," *Computerworld* 42, no. 15 (April 7, 2008): 32–33.

6. "Core Values and the Companies that Do Them Well, Grapper," *Grasslands: The Entrepreneurial Blog* (April 4, 2010), http://grasshopper.com.

7. Jay J. Jamrog and Miles H. Overholt, "Building a Strategic HR Function: Continuing the Evolution," *Human Resource Planning* 27, no. 1 (March 2004): 51; Gary L. Nielson, Karla L. Martin, and Elizabeth Powers, "The Secrets to Successful Strategy Execution," *Harvard Business Review* 86, no. 6 (June 2008):60–70.

8. Ann Zimmerman, "Dime a Dozen: Dollar Stores Pinched by Rapid Expansion," *WSJ Online* (February 4, 2013), http://www.wsjonline.com.

9. Hiroko Tabuchi, "In America's Heartland, Discussing Climate Change without Saying 'Climate Change,'" *New York Times* (January 28, 2017), https://www.nytimes.com.

10. Kelly Marchese, Siva Paramasivam, Michael Held, and Deloitte Consulting, "Bouncing Back: Supply Chain Risk Management Lessons from Post-Tsunami Japan," *Industry Week* (March 9, 2012), http://www.industryweek.com.

11. Paul Carsten, "Apple China Mobile Launch Could Spark Costly Subsidy War," *Reuters* (January 17, 2014), http:www.reuters.com.

12. Jan Alexander, "Virgin America's Guide to Not Screwing Up Customer Service," *BNET* (February 22, 2010), http://bnet.com.

13. John Gallagher, "Microsoft's Move Boosts Detroit's Credibility as Tech Hub," *Detroit Free Press* (February 3, 2017), http://www.freep.com.

14. For example, see U.S. Department of Labor, Bureau of Labor Statistics, *Geographic Profiles of Employment and Unemployment*. The data and information are accessible via the Office of Employment Projections home page at http://www.bls.gov/emp.

15. Ray Brillinger, "Best Practices: Human Resources Benchmarking," *Canadian HR Reporter* 14, no. 12 (June 18, 2001): 12; Chris Mahoney, "Benchmarking Your Way to Smarter Decisions," *Workforce* 79, no. 10 (October 2000): 100–103; Brian E. Becker and Mark A. Huselid, "Strategic Human

Resources Management: Where Do We Go from Here?" *Journal of Management* 32, no. 6 (January 2006): 898–925.

16. For more information on methods to identify a firm's core capabilities, see Khalid Hafeez, YanBing Zhang, and Naila Malak, "Core Competence for Sustainable Competitive Advantage: A Structured Methodology for Identifying Core Competence," *IEEE Transactions on Engineering Management* 49, no. 1 (February 2002): 28–35; J. B. Quinn, "The Intelligent Enterprise: A New Paradigm," *Academy of Management Executive* 6, no. 4 (2002): 48–63; Jane Wollman Rusoff, "Outsourced Solutions: Brokerage Firms Looking to Focus on Their Core Competencies Find the Most Value in a Resource-Rich Clearing Partner," *Research* 27, no. 11 (November 2004): 37–40.

17. Snell, Shadur, and Wright, "Human Resources Strategy," 627–49; Wright, Dunford, and Snell, "Human Resources and the Resource-Based View of the Firm," 701–21; David Collis and Cynthia Montgomery, "Competing on Resources," *Harvard Business Review* 86, no. 7/8 (July–August 2008): 140–150; Susan Cantrell, "The Work Force of One," *Wall Street Journal* 249, no. 140 (June 16, 2007): R10.

18. "'SAS Again Ranks No. 1 on FORTUNE Best Companies to Work For' List in America," *SAS.com* (January 20, 2011), http://www.sas.com.

19. Joseph F. Castellan and Susan S. Lightle, "Using Cultural Audits to Assess Tone at the Top," *CPA Journal* 75, no. 2 (February 2005): 6–11.

20. Patrick M. Wright, "Human Resource Strategy: Adapting to the Age of Globalization," SHRM Foundation.

21. Stephenie Overman, "Gearing Up for Tomorrow's Workforce," *HRFocus* 76, no. 2 (February 1999): 1, 15; Kathryn Tyler, "Evaluate Your Next Move," *HRMagazine* 46, no. 11 (November 2001): 66-71; Bill Leonard, "Turnover at the Top," *HRMagazine* 46, no. 5 (May 2001): 46–52.

22. Carolyn Hirschman, "Putting Forecasting in Focus," *HRMagazine* 52, no. 3 (March 2007): 44–49.

23. Leslie Kwoh, "Are Firms Neglecting Succession Planning?" *Wall Street Journal* (September 5, 2012), http://www.wsj.com.

24. Robert Kaplan and David Norton, *Strategy Maps: Converting Intangible Assets into Tangible Objectives* (Boston: Harvard Business School Press, 2006), Chapter.

25. John Huey, "Outlaw Flyboy CEOs," *Fortune* 142, no. 11 (November 13, 2000): 237–50; "Visions of the Future," *HumanResources* (January 2008): special section, 22.

26. Patrick Wright, "Human Resource Strategy: Adapting to the Age of Human Resources Management," SHRM Foundation (2008), http://www.shrm.org/foundation.

27. Scott A. Snell, Mark A. Shadur, and Patrick M. Wright, "Human Resources Strategy: The Era of Our Ways," *Center for Advanced Human Resource Studies* (November 1, 2000): working paper, 23–29.

28. R. Sanchez, "Strategic Flexibility in Product Competition," *Strategic Management Journal* 16 (1995): 135–59; Wright and Snell, "Toward a Unifying Framework," 756–72.

29. "Poll Shows Concern about Aging Workforce," *Credit Union Management* 32, no. 6 (January 2011): 36.

30. Patrick Kiger, "Serious Progress in Strategic Workforce Planning," *Workforce Management* (July 1, 2010), http://workforce.com.

31. Brian Becker, Mark Huselid, and Dave Ulrich, *The HR Scorecard: Linking People, Strategy, and Performance* (Cambridge, MA: Harvard Business School Press, 2001); see also Shari Caudron, "How HR Drives Profits," *Workforce* 80, no. 12 (December 2001): 26–31.

32. "A Singular Sensation for Schwab Brokers," *Businessweek* (January 24, 2002), http://www.businessweek.com.

Appendix

Calculating Employee Turnover and Absenteeism

Throughout this chapter, we have emphasized that HRP depends on having an accurate picture of both the supply of and the demand for employees. Two factors, employee turnover and absenteeism, have a direct impact on HR planning strategy and recruitment processes. In this appendix, we provide a detailed discussion of turnover and absenteeism, methods for measuring them, and suggestions for managing their impact.

A.1 Employee Turnover Rates

Employee turnover refers simply to the movement of employees out of an organization. It is often cited as one of the factors behind the failure of U.S. employee productivity rates to keep pace with those of foreign competitors. It is also one of the chief determinants of labor supply. Even if everything else about an organization stays the same, as employees turn over, its supply of labor goes down. This involves both direct and indirect costs to the organization.

A.1a Computing the Turnover Rate

The U.S. Department of Labor suggests the following formula for computing turnover rates:

$$\frac{\text{Number of separations during the month}}{\text{Total number of employees at midmonth}} \times 100$$

So, if there were 25 separations during a month and the total number of employees at midmonth was 500, the turnover rate would be:

$$\frac{25}{500} \times 100 = 5\,\text{percent}$$

Turnover rates are computed on a regular basis to compare specific units such as departments, divisions, and work groups. In many cases, comparisons are made with data provided by other organizations. The Bureau of Labor Statistics' *Job Openings and Labor Turnover Survey* is a very good source of comparative turnover data.[1]

Another method of computing the turnover rate is one that reflects only the avoidable separations (S). This rate is computed by subtracting unavoidable separations

(*US*)—for example, due to pregnancy, return to school, or death—from all separations. The formula for this method is as follows:

$$\frac{S-US}{M} \times 100 = T\,(\text{turnover rate})$$

where *M* represents the total number of employees at midmonth. For example, if there were 25 separations during a month, 5 of which were *US*, and the total number of employees at midmonth (*M*) was 500, the turnover rate would be:

$$\frac{25-5}{500} \times 100 = 4\,\text{percent}$$

A.1b Determining the Costs of Turnover

Replacing an employee is time consuming and expensive. Costs can generally be broken down into three categories: separation costs for the departing employee, replacement costs, and training costs for the new employee. These costs are conservatively estimated at two to three times the monthly salary of the departing employee, and they do not include indirect costs such as low productivity prior to quitting and lower morale and overtime for other employees because of the vacated job. Consequently, reducing turnover could result in significant savings to an organization. Highlights in HRM 4 details one organization's costs associated with the turnover of a single computer programmer. Note that the major expense is the cost involved in training a replacement.

A.2 Employee Absenteeism Rates

How frequently employees are absent from their work—the absenteeism rate—is also directly related to HR planning and recruitment. When employees miss work, the organization incurs direct costs of lost wages and decreased productivity. It is not uncommon for organizations to hire extra workers just to make up for the number of absences totaled across all employees. In addition to these direct costs, indirect costs may underlie excessive absenteeism. A certain amount of absenteeism is, of course, unavoidable. There will always be some who must be absent from work because of sickness, accidents, serious family problems, or other legitimate reasons. However, chronic absenteeism may signal deeper problems in the work environment.

A.2a Computing Absenteeism Rates

Managers should determine the extent of the absenteeism problem, if any, by maintaining individual and departmental attendance records and by computing absenteeism rates. Although there is no universally accepted definition of "absence" or a standard formula for computing absenteeism rates, the method most frequently used is that recommended by the U.S. Department of Labor.

$$\frac{\text{Number of worker}-\text{days lost through job absence during period}}{\text{Average number of employees 3 number of workdays}} \times 100$$

Costs Associated with the Turnover of One Computer Programmer

Turnover costs = Separation costs + Replacement costs + Training costs

Separation Costs

1. Exit interview = cost for salary and benefits of both interviewer and departing employee during the exit interview = $30 + $30 = $60

2. Administrative and record − keeping action = $30 Separation costs 5 = $60 + $30 = $90

Replacement Costs

1. Advertising for job opening = $2,500

2. Preemployment administrative functions and record-keeping action = $100

3. Selection interview = $250

4. Employment tests = $40

5. Meeting to discuss candidates(salary and benefits of managers while participating in meetings) = $250 Replacement costs = $2,500 + $100 + $250 + $40 + $250 = $3,140

Training Costs

1. Booklets, manuals, and reports = $50

2. Education = $240 / day for new employee's salary and benefits × 10 days of workshops, seminars, or courses = $2,400

3. One-to-one coaching = ($240 / day per new employee + $240 / day per staff coach or job expert) × 20 days of one-to-one coaching = $9,600

4. Salary and benefits of new employee until he or she gets "up to par" = $240 / day for salary and benefits × 20 days = $4,800

Training costs $50 + $2,400 + $9,600 + $4,800 = $16,850
Total turnover costs = $90 + $3,140 + $16,850 = $20,080

Sources: Adapted from the book *Turning Your Human Resources Department into a Profit Center* by Michael Mercer, PhD (Barrington, IL: Castlegate Publishers, Inc.). Copyright 2002 Michael Mercer. Reproduced with permission from Michael Mercer, PhD, http://www.DrMercer.com.

If 300 worker-days are lost through job absence during a month having 25 scheduled working days at an organization that employs 500 workers, the absenteeism rate for that month is:

$$\frac{300}{300 \times 25} \times 100 = 2.4 \text{ percent}$$

The U.S. Department of Labor defines job absence as the failure of employees to report to work when their schedules require it, whether or not such failure to report is excused. Scheduled vacations, holidays, and prearranged leaves of absence are not counted as job absence.

A.2b Comparing Absenteeism Data

The Bureau of Labor Statistics of the U.S. Department of Labor receives data on job absences from the Current Population Survey of Households conducted by the Bureau of the Census, and analyses of these data are published periodically. These analyses help identify problem areas—industries, occupations, or groups of workers with the highest incidence of absence or with rapidly increasing rates of absence. Comparison with other organizations may be made by referring to Bureau of Labor Statistics data reported in the *Monthly Labor Review*.

A.2c Costs of Absenteeism

The cost of each person hour lost to absenteeism is based on the hourly weighted average salary, costs of employee benefits, supervisory costs, and incidental costs. For example, XYZ Company, with 1,200 employees, has 78,000 person hours lost to absenteeism; the total absence cost is $560,886. When this figure is divided by 1,200 employees, the cost per employee is $467.41. (In this example, we are assuming the absent workers are paid. If absent workers are not paid, their salary figures are omitted from the computation.)

A.2d Absenteeism and HR Planning

While an employer may find that the overall absenteeism rate and costs are within an acceptable range, it is still advisable to study the statistics to determine whether there are patterns in the data. Rarely does absenteeism spread itself evenly across an organization. It is very likely that employees in one area (or occupational group) may have nearly perfect attendance records, while others in a different area may be absent frequently. By monitoring these differences, managers can assess where problems might exist and, more important, begin planning ways to resolve or improve the underlying causes. For example, incentives could be provided for perfect attendance. Alternatively, progressive discipline procedures might be used with employees having a record of recurring absenteeism.

By establishing a comprehensive absenteeism policy, Allen-Bradley (which is now a part of Rockwell Automation) cut absenteeism 83.5 percent in a 25-month period. This reduced the strain on labor costs and increased productivity.

Yuri_Arcurs/Getty Images

CHAPTER **3**

Equal Employment Opportunity and Human Resources Management

Learning Outcome

After studying this chapter, you should be able to

LO ❶ Describe the major equal employment opportunity (EEO) laws related to age, gender, religion, weight, and sexual orientation. Determine the employment practices they prohibit and the reason behind passage of EEO legislation. Describe what a bona fide occupational qualification is.

LO ❷ Explain how the Uniform Guidelines on Employee Selection Procedures were developed and how firms use them to ensure they are abiding by the law. Understand adverse impact and disparate treatment.

LO ❸ Understand Equal Employment Opportunity Commission (EEOC) record-keeping and posting requirements and describe how discrimination charges are processed by the EEOC.

LO ❹ Explain what affirmative action is and how companies today are seeing the value of voluntarily having diverse workforces.

O ne of the most important topics that must be discussed in any human resources management textbook is **equal employment opportunity (EEO)**. Equal employment opportunity, or the employment of individuals in a fair and nonbiased manner, commands the attention of the media, courts, legislators, HR managers, and their firms alike. In 2016, 91,503,412 private-sector workplace discrimination charges were filed with the U.S. **Equal Employment Opportunity Commission (EEOC)**, the federal agency that enforces the nation's fair employment laws.[1] The number of filings have gradually increased over the last 20 years, marking an increased importance for managers to know and comply with numerous EEO laws as the workforce becomes more diverse and multicultural.

When managers ignore or are unaware of fair employment laws, they and their firms run the risk of costly and time-consuming litigation, negative public attention, potentially lower sales, lower employee morale, and even damage to their own individual careers.[2] Because even unintentional discrimination can be illegal, supervisors need to be aware of their personal biases and how they can affect their dealings with their subordinates.[3] Employment discrimination is not only a legal issue, but also an emotional one. It concerns all individuals, regardless of their sex, race, religion, age, national origin, color, sexual orientation, physical condition, and position in an organization. Fortunately, it is a problem that can be minimized with good HR practices.

This chapter will help you better understand how to minimize employment discrimination and will also discuss the diversity efforts companies are actively pursuing

equal employment opportunity (EEO)

The treatment of individuals in all aspects of employment—hiring, promotion, training, etc.—in a fair and nonbiased manner.

Equal Employment Opportunity Commission (EEOC)

The EEOC's work consists of formulating EEO policy and approving all litigation involved in maintaining equal employment opportunity. The EEOC's guidelines are not federal law but administrative rules and regulations published in the *Federal Register*.

G-stockstudio/Shutterstock.com

The American Mustache Institute (AMI) has been working to alleviate facial hair discrimination in the United States.

as a way to gain a strategic edge. HR professionals agree that when all functions of HRM comply with the law, the organization becomes a fairer place to work and a more effective competitor.

LO 1

Have you ever felt discriminated against in the workplace? How about in school, by a teacher? How did it make you feel?

3.1 Historical Perspective of EEO Legislation

Equal employment opportunity as a national priority has emerged slowly in the United States. Three factors seem to have influenced the growth of EEO legislation: (1) changing attitudes toward employment discrimination; (2) published reports highlighting the economic problems and injustices experienced by minority workers; and (3) a growing body of disparate discrimination laws and regulations at different levels of government that legislators feel should be standardized. (See Figure 3.1). Although the United States has progressed substantially in improving business practices and public attitudes about discrimination, problems still persist.

3.1a Changing National Values

The United States was founded on the principles of individual merit, hard work, and equality. In spite of these values, employment discrimination has a long history in the United States. Organizations that claim to offer fair treatment to employees have intentionally or unintentionally engaged in discriminatory practices. As a result, laws have been passed to ensure equality and reward individual merit and hard work.

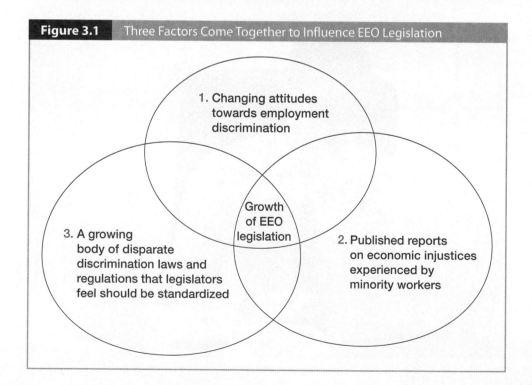

Figure 3.1   Three Factors Come Together to Influence EEO Legislation

1. Changing attitudes towards employment discrimination

Growth of EEO legislation

3. A growing body of disparate discrimination laws and regulations that legislators feel should be standardized

2. Published reports on economic injustices experienced by minority workers

Small Business Application

The Perils of Noncompliance

Owners and managers of growing small businesses should consider conducting routine HR compliance assessments, either annually or perhaps each time the company reaches another significant increase in employees, for example, from less than 5 to closer to 15 employees.

There are other occasions when a small firm should check its compliance as well. Eric A. Marks, a partner in charge of the Human Resources Consulting Practice at the New York accounting firm Marks Paneth & Shron, explains:

> Significant changes to the business, such as mergers; the retirement of senior managers; newly hired or promoted supervisors or managers who may lack HR experience; creation or revision of an employee handbook; changes in employee morale, turnover, attendance, or disciplinary problems; taking on government contracts where compliance requirements are often stricter; and major changes in state or federal regulations—any of

these are danger signs. They signal that the business has a fresh need to address compliance and make sure its house is in order.

In short, an HR compliance assessment reviews how well an employer is following employment, benefits, and safety laws. Fortunately, small-business owners do not have to remain in the danger zone. There are numerous HR consulting firms that not only can conduct a compliance assessment, but can also assist the owner with rectifying any noncompliant systems and procedures and train the company's managers and supervisors to maintain them. There are even HR compliance self-assessment forms available online. Help is only a mouse-click away.

Source: "New Risks to Small Businesses" *Marketwire* (February 28, 2011), http://www2.marketwire.com; "HR Compliance Assessment Overview," http://www.the-arnold-group.com/hr-assessment.cfm; "HR Challenges: Compliance," http://www.strategic-workplace-solutions.com/services/compliance.

Nonetheless, discrimination still persists. The Employment Non-Discrimination Act, or "ENDA," proposed by the U.S. Congress extends federal employment discrimination protection currently provided on race, religion, gender, national origin, age, and disability to include sexual orientation and gender identity.

3.1b Early Legal Developments

Litigation concerning discriminatory practices has been prevalent since the nineteenth century. In 1866, Congress passed the Civil Rights Act, which extended to all people the right to enjoy full and equal benefits of all laws, regardless of race. In 1933, Congress enacted the Unemployment Relief Act, which prohibited employment discrimination on account of race, color, or creed (religious beliefs). Then in 1941, President Franklin D. Roosevelt issued Executive Order 8802, which was to ensure that every American citizen, "regardless of race, creed, color, or national origin," would be guaranteed equal employment opportunities for workers employed by firms awarded World War II defense contracts. Over the next 20 years a variety of other legislative efforts were promoted to resolve inequities in employment practices.

Unfortunately, these early efforts did little to correct employment discrimination. First, nondiscrimination laws gave no enforcement powers to agencies. Laws did not specify what discriminatory practices or methods needed correction and employers were not required to comply with Equal Employment Opportunity legislation.

3.2 Government Regulation of Equal Employment Opportunity

Despite their shortcomings, the laws and executive orders discussed in the previous section laid the groundwork for a significant number of laws that have since been passed barring employment discrimination.

Part of the reason why it is so critical for managers and supervisors to understand and apply EEO laws is that employees act as agents of their employers. If a manager or supervisor violates the law, *both* she and her organization can face legal consequences. The organization cannot claim that it is not legally responsible for what the manager or supervisor did.

Figure 3.2 shows the various prohibited HR activities related to hiring, promoting, compensating employees, and so forth covered by EEO laws. If you think you already know what constitutes a legal or illegal employment practice, you might be surprised. Highlights in HRM 1 will test your current understanding of how equal employment opportunity laws are applied in the workplace.

Figure 3.2   Prohibited Discriminatory Employment Practices
It is illegal to discriminate in any aspect of employment, including:
• hiring and firing;
• compensation, assignment, or classification of employees;
• transfer, promotion, layoff, or recall;
• job advertisements;
• recruitment;
• testing;
• use of company facilities;
• training and apprenticeship programs;
• fringe benefits;
• pay, retirement plans, and disability leave; or
• other terms and conditions of employment.
Discriminatory practices under these laws also include:
• harassment on the basis of race, color, religion, sex, national origin, disability, genetic information, or age;
• retaliation against an individual for filing a charge of discrimination, participating in an investigation, or opposing discriminatory practices;
• employment decisions based on stereotypes or assumptions about the abilities, traits, or performance of individuals of a certain sex, race, age, religion, or ethnic group, or individuals with disabilities, or based on myths or assumptions about an individual's genetic information; and
• denying employment opportunities to a person because of marriage to, or association with, an individual of a particular race, religion, national origin, or an individual with a disability. Title VII also prohibits discrimination because of participation in schools or places of worship associated with a particular racial, ethnic, or religious group.

Test Your Knowledge of Equal Employment Opportunity Law

The following questions have been used as "icebreakers" by employers and consultants when training supervisors and managers in EEO legislation. What is your knowledge of EEO laws? Answers are found at the end of this chapter.

1. Two male employees tell a sexually explicit joke. The joke is overheard by a female employee who complains to her supervisor that this is sexual harassment. Is her complaint legitimate?
   _____Yes _____No

2. To be covered by Title VII of the Civil Rights Act, an employer must be engaged in interstate commerce and employ 25 or more employees.
   _____True _____False

3. People addicted to illegal drugs are classified as disabled under the Americans with Disabilities Act of 1990.
   _____Yes _____No

4. The Equal Pay Act of 1963 allows employers to pay different wages to men and women who are performing substantially similar work. What are the three defenses for paying a different wage?
   1. _____
   2. _____
   3. _____

5. A person applies for a job as a janitor at your company. During his interview with you, the person mentions that since birth he has sometimes experienced short periods of memory loss. Must you consider this individual a disabled person under the Americans with Disabilities Act of 1990?
   _____Yes _____No

6. On Friday afternoon, you tell Nancy Penley, a computer analyst, that she must work overtime the next day. She refuses, saying that Saturday is her regular religious holiday and she can't work. Do you have the legal right to order her to work on Saturday?
   _____Yes _____No

7. You have just told an applicant that she will not receive the job for which she applied. She claims that you denied her employment because of her age (she's 52). You claim she is not protected under the age discrimination law. Is your reasoning correct?
   _____Yes _____No

8. As an employer, you can select those applicants who are the most qualified in terms of education and experience.
   _____Yes _____No

9. As a manager, you have the legal right to mandate dates for pregnancy leaves.
   _____True _____False

10. State and local fair employment practice laws cover smaller employers not covered by federal legislation.
    _____True _____False

3.2a Major Federal Laws

Major federal EEO laws have been enacted to prevent discrimination against groups of workers most often affected by unfair employment practices. These groups are referred to as **protected classes**.[4] (See Figure 3.3).

Defined broadly, the classes include employees of a particular race, color, religion, national origin, sex, age, and those with physical or mental disabilities. Figure 3.4 lists the major and separate federal laws and their provisions governing equal employment opportunity.

protected classes
Individuals of a minority race, women, older people, and those with disabilities who are covered by federal laws on equal employment opportunity.

Equal Pay Act of 1963

The Equal Pay Act makes it illegal to discriminate against people in terms of the pay, employee benefits, and pension they earn based on their gender when they do equal work.[5] Jobs are considered "equal" when they require substantially the same skill, effort, and responsibility under similar working conditions and in the same establishment. However, a company does not violate the Equal Pay Act when the differences in the

Figure 3.3   Protected Classes of Employees

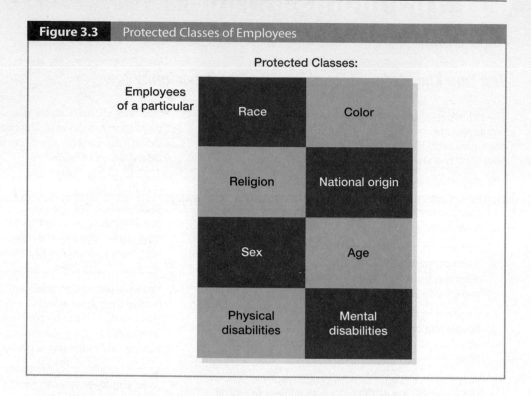

Protected Classes:

Employees of a particular

Race	Color
Religion	National origin
Sex	Age
Physical disabilities	Mental disabilities

wages it pays to men and women for equal work are based on seniority systems, merit considerations, or the workers' quantity or quality of production. Also, if a pay disparity between the sexes exists, employers cannot legally lower the wages of one gender to comply with the law; rather, they must raise the wages of the gender being underpaid.

Civil Rights Act of 1964

The Civil Rights Act of 1964 is a landmark law that addresses discrimination in society. Title VII of the act specifically bars employment discrimination in all HR activities, including hiring, training, promotion, transfers, pay, employee benefits, and other conditions of employment. Discrimination is prohibited on the basis of race, color, religion, sex, or national origin. Title VII of the Civil Rights Act also created the EEOC to administer the law in order to promote equal employment opportunity.

In response to the growing number of immigrant workers and workplace cultural and ethnic awareness, the EEOC has issued important guidelines on national origin discrimination.[6] A "national origin group" is defined as a group of people sharing a common language, culture, ancestry, and/or similar social characteristics. This definition includes people born in the United States who are not racial or ethnic minorities. Also prohibited under the act is discrimination based on pregnancy or a medical condition related to it or childbirth. The Civil Rights Act of 1964 covers a broad range of organizations. The law includes under its jurisdiction the following:

1. All private employers in interstate commerce who employ 15 or more employees for 20 or more weeks per year
2. State and local governments
3. Private and public employment agencies

Figure 3.4	Major Laws Affecting Equal Employment Opportunity
LAW	**PROVISIONS**
Equal Pay Act of 1963	Requires all employers covered by the Fair Labor Standards Act and others to provide equal pay for equal work, regardless of sex.
Title VII of Civil Rights Act of 1964 (amended in 1972, 1991, 1994, and 2009)	Prohibits discrimination in employment on the basis of race, color, religion, sex, or national origin; created the EEOC to enforce the provisions of Title VII.
Age Discrimination in Employment Act of 1967 (amended in 1986 and 1990)	Prohibits private and public employers from discriminating against people age 40 or older in any area of employment because of age; exceptions are permitted when age is a bona fide occupational qualification.
Equal Employment Opportunity Act of 1972	Amended Title VII of Civil Rights Act of 1964; strengthens the EEOC's enforcement powers and extends coverage of Title VII to government employees, employees in higher education, and other employers and employees.
Pregnancy Discrimination Act of 1978	Broadens the definition of sex discrimination to include pregnancy, childbirth, or related medical conditions; prohibits employers from discriminating against pregnant women in employment benefits if they are capable of performing their job duties.
Americans with Disabilities Act of 1990 (amended in 2008)	Prohibits discrimination in employment against people with physical or mental disabilities or the chronically ill; enjoins employers to make reasonable accommodation to the employment needs of the disabled; covers employers with 15 or more employees.
Civil Rights Act of 1991	Provides for compensatory and punitive damages and jury trials in cases involving intentional discrimination; requires employers to demonstrate that job practices are job-related and consistent with business necessity; extends coverage to U.S. citizens working for U.S. companies overseas.
Uniformed Services Employment and Reemployment Rights Act of 1994 (amended in 1998, 2004, and 2008)	Protects the employment rights of individuals who enter the military for short periods of service.
Don't Ask, Don't Tell Repeal Act of 2010	Bars discrimination against military personnel based on their sexual orientations.

4. Joint labor-management committees that govern apprenticeship or training programs
5. Labor unions having 15 or more members or employees
6. Public and private educational institutions
7. Foreign subsidiaries of U.S. organizations employing U.S. citizens

Certain employers are excluded from coverage of the Civil Rights Act. Broadly defined, these are (1) U.S. government–owned corporations; (2) bona fide, tax-exempt private clubs; (3) religious organizations employing people of a specific religion; and (4) organizations hiring Native Americans on or near a reservation.

Bona Fide Occupational Qualification. Under Title VII of the Civil Rights Act, employers are permitted limited exemptions from antidiscrimination regulations if the employment preferences are based on a bona fide occupational qualification. A **bona fide occupational qualification (BFOQ)** permits discrimination when employer

bona fide occupational qualification (BFOQ)
Suitable defense against a discrimination charge only when age, religion, sex, or national origin is an actual qualification for performing the job.

business necessity
A work-related practice that is necessary to the safe and efficient operation of an organization.

hiring preferences are a reasonable necessity for the normal operation of the business. Courts have ruled that a **business necessity** is a practice that is necessary for the safe and efficient operation of the organization.

However, a BFOQ is a suitable defense against a discrimination charge only when *age, religion, sex,* or *national origin* is an actual qualification for performing the job. (See Figures 3.5). For example, an older person could legitimately be excluded from consideration for employment as a model for teenage designer jeans. It is also reasonable to expect the Chicago Bears of the National Football League to hire male locker-room attendants or for Abercrombie and Fitch Clothing Store to employ females as models for women's fashions. Religion is a BFOQ in organizations that require employees to share a particular religious doctrine. National origin can also be a BFOQ if it is an actual qualification for a job. For example, to ensure the "authenticity" of the dining experience, an Asian restaurant could use the business-necessity defense to support its preference for hiring Asian American servers. The BFOQ exception does *not, however,* apply to discrimination based on race or color.

Religious Preference. Title VII of the Civil Rights Act prohibits employment discrimination based on a person's religion. Title VII does not require employers to grant complete religious freedom in employment situations, however. Employers need only make a *reasonable accommodation* for a current employee's or job applicant's religious observance or practice without incurring undue hardship in the conduct of the business. Managers or supervisors may have to accommodate an employee's religion in the specific areas of (1) holidays and observances (scheduling), (2) personal appearance (wearing beards, veils, or turbans), and (3) religious conduct on the job (missionary work among other employees).

What constitutes "reasonable accommodation" can be difficult to define. For example, in the 2012 case, *Porter v. City of Chicago,* the city of Chicago had tried to resolve scheduling conflicts with Latice Porter by offering an evening shift to appease her request for time off on Sundays for religious reasons. However, she wasn't interested in this option and didn't return to work. She was later fired for not fulfilling work responsibilities. She sued the city based on discrimination against her religion. The

Figure 3.5   BFOQ Bona Fide Occupational Qualification

Title VII of the Civil Rights Act requires employers to make reasonable accommodations for an employee's religious practices and observances.

City of Chicago won the case.[7] Reasonable accommodation doesn't mean an employer must accommodate at all costs, rather it is meant as a possible benefit to the employee.

Employer–employee cooperation and flexibility are often the key when it comes to employment accommodations, including those for religious reasons. The EEOC's position is not that firms need to quash religious expression in the workplace but to make a reasonable effort to accommodate people with different belief systems.

Amendments to the Civil Rights Act of 1964

Equal Employment Opportunity Act of 1972.   The Equal Employment Opportunity Act of 1972 amended the Civil Rights Act of 1964. Two important changes were made: (1) The act's coverage was broadened to include state and local governments and public and private educational institutions, and (2) the law strengthened the enforcement powers of the EEOC by allowing the agency itself to sue employers in court.

Civil Rights Act of 1991.   The Civil Rights Act of 1991 was enacted to allow employees who can prove they were intentionally discriminated against to seek compensatory monetary damages. Compensatory damages include money for emotional pain, suffering, mental anguish, and so forth.

The Civil Rights Act of 1991 also states that employees who are sent abroad to work for U.S.-based companies are protected by U.S. antidiscrimination legislation governing age and disability and Title VII of the Civil Rights Act of 1964.

Glass Ceiling Act of 1991.   The Glass Ceiling Act of 1991 was passed jointly with the Civil Rights Act of 1991. The "glass ceiling" represents an invisible barrier that prohibits protected class members from reaching top organizational positions. The act created the Glass Ceiling Commission to study and report on the status of and obstacles faced by minorities as they strive for top-level management jobs.

Lilly Ledbetter Fair Pay Act (2009). The Lilly Ledbetter Fair Pay Act states that the 180-day statute of limitations for filing an equal-pay lawsuit with EEOC resets with each new discriminatory paycheck an employee receives—not the date the employee received his or her first discriminatory paycheck as the U.S. Supreme Court had ruled. What this means is that employees can claim discrimination after years of getting unfair pay and demand to be compensated for the lost wages. Organizations therefore need to diligently and regularly examine their pay systems carefully to be sure they are equitable.

Age Discrimination in Employment Act of 1967

The Age Discrimination in Employment Act (ADEA) prohibits specific employers from discriminating against employees and applicants age 40 or older in any employment area. Employers affected are those with 20 or more employees; unions with 25 or more members; employment agencies; and federal, state, and local governments. Managers or supervisors discriminate against older employees if they:

- Exclude older workers from important work activities.
- Make negative changes in the performance evaluations of older employees.
- Deny older employees job-related education, career development, or promotional opportunities.
- Select younger job applicants over older, better-qualified candidates.
- Pressure older employees into taking early retirement or terminate them.
- Reduce the job duties and responsibilities of older employees.[8]

Exceptions to the law are permitted when age is a bona fide occupational qualification.

Amendments to the ADEA

The **Older Workers Benefit Protection Act of 1990** specifically prohibits employers from denying benefits to older employees except in limited circumstances. The law also allows employers to ask older employees to waive their legal rights under the ADEA in exchange for compensation such as severance packages or court settlements. As a result of the act, many firms that have downsized have been able to legally offer older employees early-retirement severance packages. However, to be valid, an ADEA waiver must be in writing, clear, and understandable, and the recipients need to be given a certain amount of time to consider the offer in the waiver.

Pregnancy Discrimination Act of 1978

The Pregnancy Discrimination Act amended the Civil Rights Act of 1964 by stating that pregnancy is a disability and that pregnant employees in covered organizations must be treated on an equal basis with employees having other medical conditions. Specifically, the Pregnancy Discrimination Act affects employee benefit programs including (1) hospitalization and major medical insurance, (2) temporary disability and salary continuation plans, and (3) sick leave policies.[9] The law also prohibits discrimination in the hiring, promotion, transfer, or termination of women because of pregnancy.

Americans with Disabilities Act of 1990

Congress in 1990 passed the Americans with Disabilities Act (ADA), which prohibits employers from discriminating against individuals with physical and mental disabilities and the chronically ill.[10] Disability discrimination charges from employees have doubled from 2005 to 2016, from 14,893 to 28,073.

The law defines a disability as "(a) a physical or mental impairment that substantially limits one or more of the major activities; (b) a record of such impairment; or (c) being regarded as having such an impairment." Note that the law also protects people "regarded" as having a disability—for example, individuals with disfiguring burns.

Not every mental or physical impairment is considered a disability under the law. For example, significant personality disorders are covered under the EEOC's "Enforcement Guidance on the Americans with Disabilities Act and Psychiatric Disabilities."[11] Covered personality disorders include schizophrenia, bipolar disorders, major affective disorders, personality disorders, and anxiety disorders. These impairments are characterized by aberrant behavior, self-defeating behavior, manipulation of others, and troublesome manners of behavior. However, mental impairments described as "adjustment disorders" or attributed to stress have generally not been subject to ADA coverage. Therefore, employees who claim to be "stressed" over marital problems, financial hardships, demands of the work environment, job duties, or harsh and unreasonable treatment from a supervisor would not be classified as disabled.

The act requires employers to make a reasonable accommodation for disabled people who are otherwise qualified to work, unless doing so would cause undue hardship to the employer.[12] "Undue hardship" refers to unusual work modifications or excessive expenses that might be incurred by an employer in providing an accommodation. **Reasonable accommodation** "includes making facilities accessible and usable to disabled persons, restructuring jobs, permitting part-time or modified work schedules, reassigning to a vacant position, changing equipment, and/or expense." An example of a reasonable accommodation case is that of *Minnihan v. Mediacom Communications* (2015). Minnihan had a seizure disorder that barred him from driving—an essential part of his job. Mediacom offered as many accommodations as possible, such as a nondriving job in another facility, contact information of an employee who could give Minnihan a ride to work, and information on public transportation. However, Minnihan didn't accept any of these suggestions and requested that Mediacom hire another employee to perform the driving portion of his job—but Mediacom rejected this idea. Mediacom was found to have provided reasonable accommodation.

Furthermore, employers cannot use selection procedures that screen out or tend to screen out disabled people unless the selection procedure "is shown to be job-related for the position in question and is consistent with business necessity" and acceptable job performance cannot be achieved through reasonable accommodation. Information and forms related to the health of employees must be kept confidential and separate from their regular personnel files.

reasonable accommodation
An attempt by employers to adjust, without undue hardship, the working conditions or schedules of employees with disabilities or religious preferences.

The ADA prohibits employers from discriminating against individuals regarded as having physical or mental disabilities.

ESB Professional/Shutterstock

Hiring disabled individuals is not only a legal mandate, it is also good business. Employers subject to the ADA and those who value the varied skills and abilities of the disabled approach the law as a proactive business requirement. Hiring the disabled emphasizes what these individuals *can* do rather than what they *cannot* do. Two of the most comprehensive studies conducted on the ADA show that the law has had a positive effect on both business outcomes and disabled employees. Conducted by the National Council on Disability (NCD), the studies reported positive gains regarding the ADA's four major goals: equal opportunity, full participation, independent living, and economic self-sufficiency for people with disabilities.[13] Figure 3.6 identifies specific ways to make the workplace more accessible to the disabled.

Amendments to the ADA

The **Americans with Disabilities Act Amendments Act** was enacted in 2008 in response to court rulings that had weakened the ADA. The ADAAA broadened the definition of what constitutes a disability. The new act makes it less likely a person will be denied protection because his or her condition does not seem severe enough or because it is improved by drugs, prosthetic devices, and so forth.

After the passage of the law, the EEOC filed a number of suits against companies including one that alleged that a longtime cashier with severe arthritis was denied a reasonable accommodation—a stool. The woman had used the stool for 7 years, but a new manager did not like the fact and had terminated her.[14]

Genetic Information Nondiscrimination Act of 2008

The Genetic Information Nondiscrimination Act (*GINA*) enacted in 2008 was passed to alleviate people's fears that their genetic information would be misused. Under Title II of the act, employers are prohibited from requesting, requiring, or purchasing the genetic information of workers or their family members. Employers that happen to possess genetic information as a result of health insurance records must keep the information confidential and separate from an employee's personnel files.[15]

Figure 3.6	Americans with Disabilities Act Suggestions for an Accessible Workplace

- Install easy-to-reach switches.
- Provide sloping sidewalks and entrances.
- Install wheelchair ramps.
- Reposition shelves for the easy reach of materials.
- Rearrange tables, chairs, vending machines, dispensers, and other furniture and fixtures.
- Widen doors and hallways.
- Add raised markings on control buttons.
- Provide designated accessible parking spaces.
- Install hand controls or manipulation devices.
- Provide flashing alarm lights.

- Remove turnstiles and revolving doors or provide alternative accessible paths.
- Install holding bars in toilet areas.
- Redesign toilet partitions to increase access space.
- Add paper cup dispensers at water fountains.
- Replace high-pile, low-density carpeting.
- Reposition telephones, water fountains, and other needed equipment.
- Add raised toilet seats.
- Provide a full-length bathroom mirror.

In 2016, this act was supported with the decision in the *EEOC v. Joy Mining Machinery* case, where the employer was denied the ability to make post-offer medical examinations in asking prospective employees if they had family medical history of tuberculosis, cancer, epilepsy, and heart disease.[16]

Uniformed Services Employment and Reemployment Rights Act of 1994 (USERRA)

The Uniformed Services Employment and Reemployment Rights Act of 1994 (USERRA) covers all military personnel, including National Guard members, reservists, and active-duty military personnel, who enlist either voluntarily or involuntarily during peace or wartime. Under this act, people who enter the military for a total of five years can return to their private-sector jobs without risk of loss of seniority or benefits.[17] The act protects against discrimination on the basis of military obligation in the areas of hiring, job retention, and advancement. The law does not require employers to pay the workers' wages while they are enlisted.

Amendments to the USERRA

In 2004, the USERRA was amended by the Veterans Benefits Improvement Act requiring employers to provide a notice of rights, benefits, and obligations of both employees and employers under USERRA.[18] For their part, service members must provide their employers advance notice of their military obligations in order to be protected by the reemployment rights statute.

3.2b Other Federal Laws and Executive Orders

Executive orders are used to provide equal employment opportunity to individuals employed by government contractors. Since many large employers—such as General Dynamics, Intel, Dell Computer, and Motorola—and numerous small companies have contracts with the federal government, managers are expected to know and comply with the provisions of executive orders and other laws. The federal laws and executive orders that apply to government agencies and government contractors are summarized in Figure 3.7.

Figure 3.7	EEO Rules Applicable to Federal Contractors and Agencies
LAW	**PROVISIONS**
Vocational Rehabilitation Act of 1973 (amended in 1974)	Prohibits federal contractors from discriminating against disabled individuals in any program or activity receiving federal financial assistance; requires federal contractors to develop affirmative action plans to hire and promote disabled people.
Executive Order 11246 (1965), as amended by Order 11375 (1966)	Prohibits employment discrimination based on race, color, religion, sex, or national origin by government contractors with contracts exceeding $10,000; requires contractors employing 50 or more workers to develop affirmative action plans when government contracts exceed $50,000 per year.
Executive Order 11478 (1969)	Obligates the federal government to ensure that all personnel actions affecting applicants for employment be free from discrimination based on race, color, religion, sex, or national origin.

Vocational Rehabilitation Act of 1973

The Vocational Rehabilitation Act was passed in 1973 and required private employers with federal contracts over $2,500 to take action to hire individuals with a mental or physical disability. Recipients of federal financial assistance, such as public and private colleges and universities, are also covered. In applying the safeguards of this law, the term **disabled individual** means "any person who (1) has a physical or mental impairment which substantially limits one or more of such person's major life activities, (2) has a record of such an impairment, or (3) is regarded as having such an impairment." Also, employment is not required when some aspect of the employee's disability prevents that person from carrying out essential parts of the job, nor is it required if the disabled person is not otherwise qualified.

In cases when people with contagious diseases are "otherwise qualified" to do their jobs, the law requires employers to make a reasonable accommodation to allow the disabled to perform their jobs.[19] Individuals with AIDS or HIV are also disabled within the meaning of the Rehabilitation Act. However, the Rehabilitation Act does not require employers to hire or retain a disabled person if he or she has a contagious disease that poses a direct threat to the health or safety of others and the individual cannot be accommodated.

disabled individual
Any person who (1) has a physical or mental impairment that substantially limits one or more of the person's major life activities, (2) has a record of such impairment, or (3) is regarded as having such an impairment.

Executive Order 11246

Federal agencies and government contractors with contracts of $10,000 or more must comply with the antidiscrimination provisions of Executive Order 11246. The order prohibits discrimination based on race, color, religion, sex, or national origin in all employment activities. Furthermore, it requires that government contractors or subcontractors having 50 or more employees with contracts in excess of $50,000 develop affirmative action plans; such plans will be discussed later in the chapter.

Don't Ask, Don't Tell Repeal Act of 2010. On September 20, 2011, the Don't Ask, Don't Tell Repeal Act was implemented to end the ban on gay, lesbian, or bisexual persons openly serving in the U.S. military.

3.2c Fair Employment Practice Laws

In addition to federal laws and executive orders, almost all states and many local governments have passed laws barring employment discrimination. Referred to as **fair employment practices (FEPs)**, these statutes are often more comprehensive than the federal laws.

fair employment practices (FEPs)
State and local laws governing equal employment opportunity that are often more comprehensive than federal laws and apply to small-business employers.

3.3 Other Equal Employment Opportunity Issues

Federal laws, executive orders, court cases, and state and local statutes provide the broad legal framework; and within these major laws, specific issues are of particular interest to supervisors and managers.

3.3a Sexual Harassment

sexual harassment
Unwelcome advances, requests for sexual favors, and other verbal or physical conduct of a sexual nature in the working environment.

Sexual harassment refers to unwelcome sexual advances, requests for sexual favors, and other verbal or physical harassment of a sexual nature. It can also include offensive remarks, vulgar or obscene gestures, language or comments, related to one's sex, an individuals body, or sexual activity. Both the victim and the harasser can be either female or male, and harassment can occur between individuals of the same or opposite sex. The harasser can be the victim's supervisor, a supervisor in another area, a coworker, or someone who is not an employee of the employer, such as a client or customer.[20]

The EEOC recognizes two forms of sexual harassment as being illegal under Title VII. The first, *quid pro quo harassment*, occurs when "submission to or rejection of sexual conduct is used as a basis for employment decisions."[21] This type of harassment involves a tangible or economic consequence, such as a demotion or loss of pay. If a supervisor promotes an employee only after the person agrees to an after-work date, the conduct is clearly illegal.

The second type of harassment, *hostile environment*, can occur when unwelcome sexual conduct "has the purpose or effect of unreasonably interfering with job performance or creating an intimidating, hostile, or offensive working environment."[22]

Dirty jokes, vulgar slang, nude pictures, swearing, and personal ridicule and insult create a hostile environment when an employee finds them offensive. Email, instant and text messages, and posts on social networking sites have become convenient ways for employees to sexually harass their coworkers electronically.

Via a questionnaire, it is possible to test the understanding of your employees about what is and what is not sexual harassment. Highlights in HRM 2 shows some sample questions firms can ask their employees to gauge their knowledge of the topic.

The EEOC considers an employer guilty of sexual harassment when the employer knew or should have known about the unlawful conduct and failed to remedy it or to take corrective action. Employers are also guilty of sexual harassment when they allow nonemployees (customers or salespeople) to sexually harass employees.[23] When charges of sexual harassment have been proved, victims forced out of their jobs can be awarded back pay, lost benefits, attorney's fees, and interest charges, and they may be reinstated in their jobs. Sexual harassment involving physical conduct can invite criminal charges, and punitive damages can be assessed against both the employer and the individual offender.[24]

Photographee.eu/Shutterstock

Sexual harassment includes any type of behavior, comments, gestures, and actions of a sexual nature that create a hostile work environment for an employee.

Questions Used to Audit Sexual Harassment in the Workplace

ACTIVITY	IS THIS SEXUAL HARASSMENT?			AWARE OF THIS BEHAVIOR IN THE ORGANIZATION?	
Employees post cartoons on bulletin boards containing sexually related material.	Yes	No	Uncertain	Yes	No
A male employee says to a female employee that she has beautiful eyes and hair.	Yes	No	Uncertain	Yes	No
A male manager habitually calls all female employees "sweetie" or "darling."	Yes	No	Uncertain	Yes	No
A manager fails to promote a female (male) employee for not granting sexual favors.	Yes	No	Uncertain	Yes	No
Male employees use vulgar language and tell sexual jokes that are overheard by, but not directed at, female employees.	Yes	No	Uncertain	Yes	No
A male employee leans and peers over the back of a female employee when she wears a low-cut dress.	Yes	No	Uncertain	Yes	No
A supervisor gives a female (male) subordinate a nice gift on her (his) birthday.	Yes	No	Uncertain	Yes	No
Two male employees share a sexually explicit magazine while observed by a female employee.	Yes	No	Uncertain	Yes	No
Female office workers are "rated" by male employees as they pass the men's desks.	Yes	No	Uncertain	Yes	No
Revealing female clothing is given as a gift at an office birthday party.	Yes	No	Uncertain	Yes	No
A sales representative from a supplier makes suggestive sexual remarks to a receptionist.	Yes	No	Uncertain	Yes	No

3.3b Sexual Orientation

Nearly half of U.S. states and some cities also have passed laws prohibiting sexual orientation discrimination in workplaces.[25] Although Title VII of the Civil Rights Act of 1964 lists "sex" as a protected class, currently no federal law bars discrimination based on one's sexual orientation. For lesbian, gay, bisexual, transgender, and queer (LGBTQ) employees who do not work for the federal government, protection from discrimination largely comes from fair employment practice laws passed at state and local levels. The laws vary regarding the protection afforded to the LGBTQ community and those who are covered under the laws. For example, in some states, public—but not private— sector employees are protected from discrimination based on their sexual orientation. Therefore, it becomes important for managers and supervisors to know and follow the legal rights of the LGBTQ community in their geographic area.[26] Figure 3.8 shows a list of states that have passed non-discrimination laws based on sexual orientation.

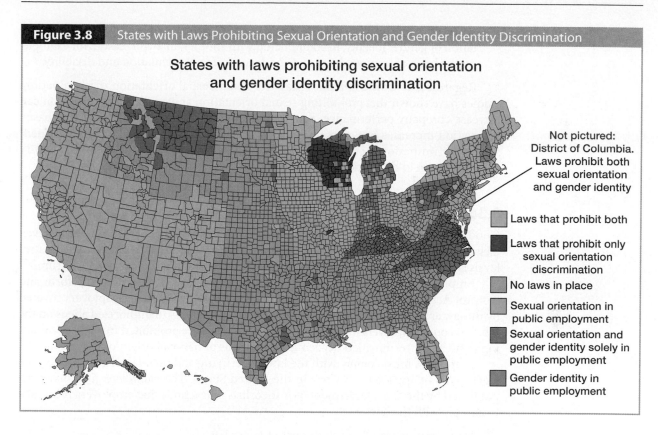

Figure 3.8 States with Laws Prohibiting Sexual Orientation and Gender Identity Discrimination

Regardless of any state or local laws, however, the EEOC interprets and enforces Title VII's prohibition of sex discrimination as forbidding any employment discrimination based on gender identity or sexual orientation.

The commission has obtained approximately $6.4 million in monetary relief for individuals, as well as numerous employer policy changes, in voluntary resolutions of LGBTQ discrimination charges under Title VII since data collection began in 2013. Some examples of LGBTQ-related claims that EEOC views as unlawful sex discrimination include:

- Failing to hire an applicant because she is *a transgender woman*.

- Firing an employee because he is planning or has made a *gender transition*.

- Denying an employee equal access to a common *restroom* corresponding to the employee's gender identity.

- Harassing an employee because of a gender transition, such as by intentionally and persistently *failing to use the name and gender pronoun that correspond to the gender identity with which the employee identifies*, and which the employee has communicated to management and employees.

- Denying an employee a promotion because of sexual orientation.

- Discriminating in *terms, conditions,* or *privileges of employment*, such as providing a lower salary to an employee because of sexual orientation, or denying spousal health insurance benefits to a female employee because her legal spouse is a woman, while providing spousal health insurance to a male employee whose legal spouse is a woman.

- *Harassing* an employee because of his or her sexual orientation, for example, by derogatory terms, sexually oriented comments, or disparaging remarks for associating with a person of the same or opposite sex.

- Discriminating against or harassing an employee because of his or her sexual orientation or gender identity, in combination with another unlawful reason, for example, on the basis of transgender status and race, or sexual orientation and disability.[27]

Regardless of how companies may feel about sexual orientation discrimination, studies have shown that prohibiting sexual orientation and gender discrimination can increase company performance. For example, one study points out that patent-based innovation increases by 8 percent in states after they adopt the federal Employment Non-Discrimination Act (ENDA) to ban sexual orientation and gender identity discrimination in the workplace.[28]

3.3c Immigration Reform and Control

Good employment is the magnet that attracts many people to the United States. However, illegal immigration is an issue of national concern at the federal, state, and local legislative levels and among employers, unions, civil rights groups, and, of course, Donald Trump.[29]

Employers must comply with the requirements of the Immigration Reform and Control Act (IRCA). The law has two employer mandates. First, all employers covered by the law are prohibited from knowingly hiring or retaining unauthorized aliens on the job.[30] Second, employers with four or more employees are prohibited from discriminating in hiring or termination decisions on the basis of national origin or citizenship.[31]

Employers must comply with the law by verifying and maintaining records on the legal rights of applicants to work in the United States. The *Handbook for Employers,* published by the U.S. Department of Justice, lists five actions that employers must take to comply with the law:

1. Have employees fill out their part of Form I-9.
2. Check documents establishing an employee's identity and eligibility to work.
3. Complete the employer's section of Form I-9.
4. Retain Form I-9 for at least three years.
5. Present Form I-9 for inspection to an Immigration and Naturalization Service officer or to a Department of Labor officer upon request.[32]

Employers with sizable contracts with the federal government must also use its E-Verification system. E-Verify is a system that provides an automated link to federal databases to help employers determine the legal eligibility of workers and the validity of their social security numbers. Employers that do not do business with the government can also use E-Verify.

Employers found to have violated the discrimination provisions of the Immigration Reform and Control Act will be ordered to cease the discriminatory practice. They may also be directed to hire, with or without backpay, individuals harmed by the discrimination and to pay a fine of up to $1,000 for each person discriminated against. Charges of discrimination based on national origin or citizenship are filed with the Office of Special Counsel in the Department of Justice.

3.3d Emerging Employment Discrimination Issues

Weight Discrimination

Some studies show that weight discrimination, especially against women, is not only increasing but has become almost as common as racial discrimination.[33] No federal laws prohibit weight discrimination, although the EEOC has said that morbid obesity is a

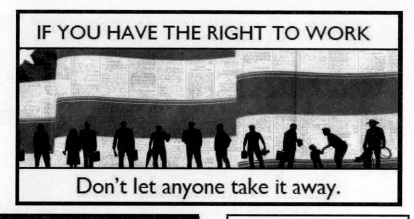

protected disability under the ADA. At some point it is not out of the realm of possibility that it could become a protected class.[34]

Attractiveness and Discrimination

There are no federal laws prohibiting discrimination in the workplace based on people's attractiveness, although it undoubtedly occurs. In a survey of hiring managers conducted by *Newsweek*, 57 percent of them said that qualified but unattractive job candidates would have a harder time landing a job.

Part of the problem of implementing a law making it legal to discriminate based on a person's appearance would be deciding who is unattractive enough to be protected by the law. Moreover, in some instances, good looks can be a BFOQ. The modeling business is one example.[35]

Caregivers and Discrimination

In 2007, the EEOC issued new enforcement guidelines to help prevent discrimination against workers with caregiving responsibilities. There are no federal statutes that prohibit discrimination based "solely" on a person being a caregiver. However, disparate

The EEOC provides guidelines to help prevent discrimination against caregivers.

g-stockstudio/Shutterstock

treatment arises when an employee with caregiving responsibilities is subjected to discrimination based on a protected characteristic under equal opportunity laws (such as sex, race, age).[36] The EEOC has outlined numerous scenarios it says could constitute discrimination against a caregiver. Denying women with young children an employment opportunity available to men with young children is an example. So is refusing to hire a worker who is a single parent of a child with a disability based on the assumption that caregiving responsibilities will make the worker unreliable.

LO 2

Following so many EEO laws might sound daunting. Would it help if you had some type of guideline when hiring a person to make sure you do not break any of these laws?

Uniform Guidelines on Employee Selection Procedures

A procedural document published in the Federal Register to help employers comply with federal regulations against discriminatory actions.

3.4 Uniform Guidelines on Employee Selection Procedures

Employers are often uncertain about the appropriateness of specific selection procedures, especially those related to testing and selection. To remedy this concern, the EEOC, along with three other government agencies, adopted the current **Uniform Guidelines on Employee Selection Procedures**.[37] The *Uniform Guidelines* is a very important procedural document for managers because it applies to employee selection procedures in the areas of hiring, retention, promotion, transfer, demotion, dismissal, and referral. It is designed to help employers, labor organizations, employment agencies, and licensing and certification boards comply with the requirements of federal laws prohibiting employment discrimination.

Validity

When using a test or other selection instrument to choose individuals for employment, employers must be able to prove that the selection instrument bears a direct relationship to success on the job. This proof is established through validation studies that show how related the test is to the job.

Adverse Impact and Disparate Treatment

For an applicant or employee to pursue a discrimination case successfully, the individual must establish that the employer's selection procedures resulted in an adverse impact on a protected class. **Adverse impact** refers to the unintentional rejection for employment, placement, or promotion of a significantly higher percentage of members of a protected class when compared with members of non-protected classes.[38] The *Uniform Guidelines* does not require an employer to conduct validity studies of its selection procedures when they have not resulted in adverse impact on a protected class. However, organizations that validate their selection procedures on a regular basis and use interviews, tests, and other procedures in such a manner so as to avoid adverse impact, will generally be in compliance and avoid costly litigation.

In EEO cases, it is important to distinguish between adverse impact and disparate treatment discrimination. Adverse impact cases deal with unintentional discrimination; **disparate treatment** cases involve instances of purposeful discrimination. Allowing men to apply for craft jobs, such as carpentry or electrical work, but denying this opportunity to women would also show disparate treatment. To win a disparate treatment case, the plaintiff must prove that the employer's actions intended to discriminate, which is often difficult.

There are two basic ways to show that adverse impact exists.

Adverse Rejection Rate, or Four-Fifths Rule. According to the *Uniform Guidelines*, a selection program has an adverse impact when the selection rate for any racial, ethnic, or sex class is less than four-fifths (or 80 percent) of the rate of the class with the highest selection rate. The EEOC has adopted the **four-fifths rule** as a rule of thumb to determine adverse impact in enforcement proceedings. The four-fifths rule is not a legal definition of discrimination; rather, it is a method by which the EEOC or any other enforcement agency monitors serious discrepancies in hiring, promotion, or other employment decisions. The appendix at the end of this chapter explains how adverse impact is determined and gives a realistic example of how the four-fifths rule is computed.

An alternative to the four-fifths rule, and one frequently used in discrimination lawsuits, is to conduct a standard deviation analysis of a firm's applicant data. The Supreme Court, in *Hazelwood School District v. United States*, set forth a standard deviation analysis that determines whether the difference between the expected selection rates for protected groups and the actual selection rates could be attributed to chance. If chance is eliminated for the lower selection rates of the protected class, it is assumed that the employer's selection technique has an adverse impact on the employment opportunities of that group.

Restricted Policy. Any evidence that an employer has a selection procedure that excludes members of a protected class, whether intentional or not, constitutes adverse impact. For example, hiring individuals who must meet a minimum height or appearance standard (at the expense of protected class members) is evidence of a restricted policy.

The benchmark case in employment selection procedures is *Griggs v. Duke Power Company* (1971). Willie Griggs, who was black, had applied for the position of coal handler with the Duke Power Company. His request for the position was denied because he was not a high school graduate, a requirement for the position. Griggs claimed the job standard was discriminatory because it did not relate to job success and because the standard had an adverse impact on a protected class. When employers use educational,

adverse impact
A concept that refers to the rejection of a significantly higher percentage of a protected class for employment, placement, or promotion when compared with the successful, nonprotected class.

disparate treatment
A situation in which protected class members receive unequal treatment or are evaluated by different standards.

four-fifths rule
A rule of thumb followed by the EEOC in determining adverse impact for use in enforcement proceedings.

physical, or intelligence standards as a basis for hiring or promotion, these must be absolutely necessary for job success.

Workforce Utilization Analysis

workforce utilization analysis

A process of classifying protected class members by number and by the type of job they hold within the organization.

As you have learned, employers must be aware of the impact their selection procedures have on protected class members. Part of this process involves analyzing the composition of their internal workforce when compared with their external labor market. The EEOC refers to this comparison as **workforce utilization analysis**. This concept simply compares an employer's workforce by race and sex for specific job categories against the surrounding labor market. The employer's relevant labor market is that area from which employees are drawn who have the skills needed to successfully perform the job. For example, if Squarespace, the website maker, is hiring computer technicians from a labor market composed of 10 percent black workers, 8 percent Hispanic workers, and 2 percent Native American workers, all of whom possess the qualifications for the job, the employer's internal workforce should reflect this racial composition. When this occurs, the employer's workforce is said to be *at parity* with the relevant labor market. If the employer's racial workforce composition is below external figures, then the protected class is said to be *underutilized*, and the employer should take steps to correct the imbalance.

3.5 Enforcing Equal Employment Opportunity Legislation

LO 3

Based on all these laws and regulations, wouldn't it be best for the company to not let employees know about them?

As the federal government's leading civil rights agency, the EEOC is responsible for ensuring that covered employers comply with equal employment opportunity legislation. The commission accomplishes this goal primarily by (1) issuing various employment guidelines and monitoring the employment practices of organizations and (2) protecting employee rights through the investigation and prosecution of discrimination charges.[39]

3.5a Record-Keeping and Posting Requirements

Organizations subject to Title VII are required by law to maintain specific employment records and reports. Those failing to comply with record-keeping and posting requirements or willfully falsifying records can incur penalties, including fines and imprisonment. See Highlights in HRM 3 for a recent example of one of the posters that companies are required by law to display in prominent places such as the cafeteria, by time clocks, or by the water cooler. It should be easier than finding Waldo in a *Where's Waldo* book. If not, then the EEOC could allow an employee to file a discrimination charge late (past the 180-day filing deadline).

3.5b Processing Discrimination Charges

charge form

A discrimination complaint filed with the EEOC by employees or job applicants.

Figure 3.9 summarizes the process of filing a discrimination charge with the EEOC.[40] (Note that the process is slightly different for federal employees and job applicants.) Employees or job applicants who believe they have been discriminated against first file a discrimination complaint, or **charge form**, with the EEOC. The charge must be filed

EEOC Poster Supplement for 2016

"EEO is the Law" Poster Supplement
Employers Holding Federal Contracts or Subcontracts Section Revisions

The Executive Order 11246 section is revised as follows:

RACE, COLOR, RELIGION, SEX, SEXUAL ORIENTATION, GENDER IDENTITY, NATIONAL ORIGIN

Executive Order 11246, as amended, prohibits employment discrimination based on race, color, religion, sex, sexual orientation, gender identity, or national origin, and requires affirmative action to ensure equality of opportunity in all aspects of employment.

PAY SECRECY

Executive Order 11246, as amended, protects applicants and employees from discrimination based on inquiring about, disclosing, or discussing their compensation or the compensation of other applicants or employees.

The Individuals with Disabilities section is revised as follows:

INDIVIDUALS WITH DISABILITIES

Section 503 of the Rehabilitation Act of 1973, as amended, protects qualified individuals with disabilities from discrimination in hiring, promotion, discharge, pay, fringe benefits, job training, classification, referral, and other aspects of employment. Disability discrimination includes not making reasonable accommodation to the known physical or mental limitations of an otherwise qualified individual with a disability who is an applicant or employee, barring undue hardship to the employer. Section 503 also requires that Federal contractors take affirmative action to employ and advance in employment qualified individuals with disabilities at all levels of employment, including the executive level.

The Vietnam Era, Special Disabled Veterans section is revised as follows:

PROTECTED VETERANS

The Vietnam Era Veterans' Readjustment Assistance Act of 1974, as amended, 38 U.S.C. 4212, prohibits employment discrimination against, and requires affirmative action to recruit, employ, and advance in employment, disabled veterans, recently separated veterans (i.e., within three years of discharge or release from active duty), active duty wartime or campaign badge veterans, or Armed Forces service medal veterans.

Mandatory Supplement to EEOC P/E-1(Revised 11/09) "EEO is the Law" Poster.

If you believe that you have experienced discrimination contact OFCCP: 1-800-397-6251 | TTY 1-877-889-5627 | www.dol.gov.

within 180 days of the alleged unlawful practice occurring.[41] The processing of a charge includes notifying the employer that a charge of employment discrimination has been filed. See Figure 3.9 to understand how to file a charge of employment discrimination. Employers will receive a copy of the charge within 10 days of it being filed. Both parties, the plaintiff (employee) and the defendant (organization), must be prepared to support their beliefs or actions.

Retaliation

Managers and supervisors must not retaliate against individuals who invoke their legal rights to file charges or to support other employees during EEOC proceedings.[42] Retaliation can include any punitive action taken against employees who elect to exercise their legal rights before any EEO agency.[43] These actions can include terminating employees, giving them unjustified negative appraisals, subjecting them to more supervision, demoting them, and reducing their salaries and work responsibilities, and transferring to a less desirable job.[44] Of course, employees are not excused from continuing to perform their jobs or follow their company's legitimate workplace rules just because they have filed a complaint with the EEOC or opposed discrimination.

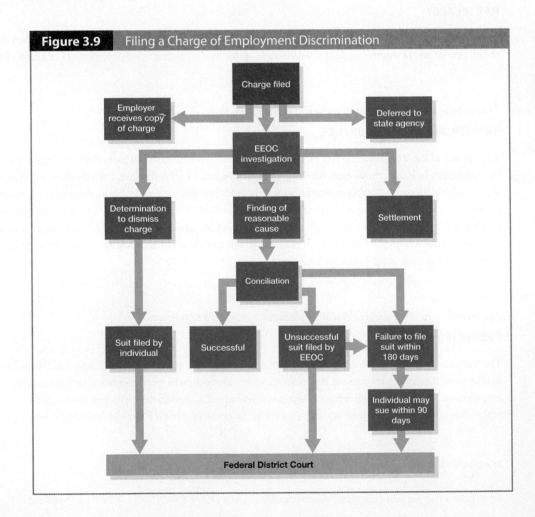

Figure 3.9   Filing a Charge of Employment Discrimination

3.5c Preventing Discrimination Charges

Both large and small employers understand that the foundation to preventing any form of discrimination is having a comprehensive EEO policy. Employers that do not have an EEO policy are legally vulnerable. Antidiscrimination policy statements must be inclusive; they must cover all applicable laws and EEOC guidelines and contain practical illustrations of specific inappropriate behavior. For the policy to have value, it must be widely disseminated to managers, supervisors, and all non-managerial employees. A complete policy will include specific sanctions for those found guilty of discriminatory behavior.[45]

Since managers and supervisors are key to preventing and correcting discrimination, they, in particular, must be trained to understand employee rights and managerial obligations.[46] A comprehensive training program will include (1) the prohibitions covered in the various EEO statutes and executive orders, (2) guidance on how to respond to complaints of discrimination, (3) procedures for investigating complaints (see Chapter 13), and (4) suggestions for remedying inappropriate behavior. Perhaps the ultimate key to preventing employment discrimination is for managers and supervisors to create an organizational climate in which the principles of dignity, respect, and the acceptance of a diverse workforce are the norm and therefore expected.

3.6 Affirmative Action and Diversity Management

Equal employment opportunity legislation requires managers to provide the same opportunities to all job applicants and employees regardless of race, color, religion, sex, national origin, or age. **Affirmative action** goes beyond not discriminating among employees. Affirmative action occurs when employers take proactive steps to help reverse the impact of past discrimination against minorities. Employers with voluntary affirmative action programs actively encourage employment diversity, post job opportunities with minority agencies, remove unnecessary barriers to employment, and offer comprehensive training and mentoring to protected class members.

So what happens when affirmative action becomes controversial? Students at the University of Texas at Austin in 2016 illustrated the controversy through an affirmative action bake sale. Depending on your race or gender, you were charged a different amount to buy a pastry. View this clip to see the controversy: https://www.youtube.com/watch?v=dUR_MCdnUAo. Based on this clip, what is your own take on affirmative action within college?

Employers establish affirmative action programs for several reasons. Affirmative action programs are required by the OFCCP for employers with federal contracts greater than $50,000. The OFCCP provides regulations and suggestions for establishing affirmative action plans. Specifically, employers must (1) provide an organizational profile that graphically illustrates their workforce demographics (see workforce utilization analysis previously discussed), (2) establish goals and timetables for employment of underutilized protected classes, (3) develop actions and plans to reduce underutilization, including initiating proactive recruitment and selection methods, and (4) monitor progress of the entire affirmative action program.

LO 4

What effect, if any, do you think ending affirmative action programs in the United States have on the diversity and competitiveness of U.S. businesses?

affirmative action
A policy that goes beyond equal employment opportunity by requiring organizations to comply with the law and correct any past discriminatory practices by increasing the numbers of minorities and women in specific positions.

Courts will sometimes mandate employers that have been found guilty of past discrimination to establish affirmative action programs, particularly when the discrimination has been pervasive and a long-held organizational practice. A court-ordered program, often implemented through a *consent decree* between the court and employer, will require the setting of hiring and promotional goals along with stated timetables for compliance. When the requirements of the consent decree are met, the employer is no longer bound by the court order.

Sometimes employers voluntarily develop their own affirmative action programs to ensure that protected class members receive fair treatment in all aspects of employment. For example, some companies employ chief diversity officers. A **chief diversity officer (CDO)** is a top executive responsible for the implementation of a firm's diversity efforts. For example, in 2016 Salesforce, Dropbox, Pinterest, and Twitter all hired a chief diversity officer, following the footsteps of tech giants like Google, Microsoft, and Facebook. Today, about one in five Fortune 1000 companies have a CDO. A number of studies have demonstrated how a diverse workforce drives up a company's revenue.[47] In fact, one study has shown that having a diverse set of leaders can improve a company's likelihood of improving market share by 45 percent. As HR professionals readily note, the success of any voluntary affirmative action program or diversity effort largely depends on the support given to it by senior managers and supervisors at all organization levels.[48] The EEOC recommends that organizations developing affirmative action programs follow specific steps, as shown in Highlights in HRM 4.

One of the drawbacks of implementing an affirmative action program is that an employer can be accused of **reverse discrimination**, or giving preference to members of protected classes to the extent that unprotected individuals believe they are suffering from discrimination. When these charges occur, organizations encounter a "catch-22" as they are caught between attempting to correct past discriminatory practices and handling present complaints from unprotected members alleging that HR policies are unfair.

chief diversity officer (CDO)
A top executive responsible for implementing a firm's diversity efforts.

reverse discrimination
The act of giving preference to members of protected classes to the extent that unprotected individuals believe they are suffering discrimination.

3.6a Court Decisions

In the 1970s, regarding two leading cases of reverse discrimination, *University of California Regents v. Bakke* and *United States Steelworkers of America v. Weber*,[49] the Supreme Court ruled that applicants must be evaluated on an individual basis and race can be one factor used in the evaluation process as long as other competitive factors are considered. The Court stated that affirmative action programs were not illegal per se as long as rigid quota systems were not specified for different protected classes. Also, voluntary affirmative action programs are permissible where they attempt to eliminate racial imbalances in traditionally segregated job categories.

The judicial support for affirmative action programs has eroded over the decades, however. During the mid-1990s, federal courts increasingly restricted the use of race and ethnicity in awarding scholarships, determining college admissions, making layoff decisions, selecting employees, promoting employees, and awarding government contracts. Then in 2009, the Supreme Court heard *Ricci vs. DeStafano*, a lawsuit brought against the City of New Haven, Connecticut, by 19 city firefighters. The firefighters alleged that the city discriminated against them by invalidating a test for a promotion because no black firefighters had passed it with a score high enough to warrant promotion. The firefighters, 17 of whom are white and 2 of whom are Hispanic, claimed they were denied the promotions because of their race.

Basic Steps in Developing an Effective Affirmative Action Program

Filing a Charge of Employment Discrimination

1. Issue a written equal employment opportunity policy and an affirmative action commitment statement.
2. Publicize the policy and the organization's affirmative action commitment.
3. Appoint a top official within the organization to direct and implement the program.
4. Survey minority and female employment by department and job classification.
5. Develop goals and timetables to improve utilization of minorities and women in each area in which underutilization has been identified.
6. Develop and implement specific programs to achieve goals.
7. Establish an internal audit and reporting system to monitor and evaluate progress in each aspect of the program.
8. Develop supportive in-house and community programs.

Source: U.S. Equal Employment Opportunity Commission.

In a split decision, the Court ruled in the firefighters' favor. The ruling didn't question the fire department's efforts to ensure minorities were fairly promoted. However, it said throwing out the test midstream (which, incidentally, had been designed by an outside consulting firm to be nondiscriminatory) was unfair to those who had passed it. In its ruling, the Court said: "once that process has been established and employers have made clear their selection criteria, they may not then invalidate the test results, thus upsetting an employee's legitimate expectation not to be judged on the basis of race."

The ruling underscores the importance of designing careful selection procedures as well as following them once they are designed. It also shows how tricky it can be to implement an affirmative action program.[50]

One of the ways companies can foster diversity within their organizations is by getting employees to talk about their differences. For example, the Mallon Group Training and Management has developed a series of Know Me games that enable participants of different cultures, races, sexual orientations, and so forth to explore issues of diversity together.

Rawpixel.com/Shutterstock

3.6b Beyond Affirmative Action: Leveraging Diversity

The future of affirmative action might not rest in judicial decisions or laws, but in managers' attitudes and voluntary actions to make the workplace fairer and more competitive. Managers who embrace a diverse workforce know individual employee differences and the contributions made by people of varied abilities are one way to develop a competitive advantage. For example, some studies have found that companies with more progressive nondiscrimination policies outperform competing firms that lack them.[51] As more companies expand around the globe either physically or on the Web, they are recognizing that they need to employ diverse people with different talents to better understand and compete in various markets abroad.

According to Martin Davidson, a professor and researcher at the Darden School of Business at the University of Virginia, strategically leveraging employee's differences means seeing not only the more obvious differences between people, such as their ethnic backgrounds, sexes, ages, religions, and so forth, but how they think, learn, work, and interact with each other. How do they use their time? How do they solve problems? Why do some people "think outside of the box," whereas others do not? What is it about the experiences, mindsets, and talents of different groups of people that can be utilized in a strategic way?

The steps toward leveraging people's differences involves seeing, understanding, and valuing them, as shown in the model in Figure 3.10. Highlights in HRM 5 shows the actual activities individuals and organizations can take to facilitate each of these steps. We will discuss more about diversity in Chapter 5 and throughout this textbook.

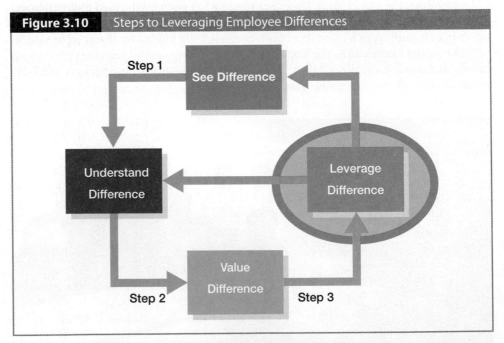

Figure 3.10   Steps to Leveraging Employee Differences

Step 1 — See Difference

Step 2 — Understand Difference

Step 3 — Value Difference

Leverage Difference

Source: Martin N. Davidson, *The End of Diversity as We Know It: Why Diversity Efforts Fail and How Leveraging Difference Can Succeed* (San Francisco: Berrett-Kohler Press, 2011).

Embracing Diversity and Leveraging Employee Differences

Practices for Individuals

Seeing

- Openly acknowledge that relevant differences are common.
- Address points of conflict. Observe while remaining silent.

Understanding

- Seek sources of information that bring understanding about the differences.
- Acquire data through listening, asking questions, and sharing your story.
- Involve people who are different from you in your network.

Valuing

- Avoid being overly careful in dealing with differences.
- Accept that there will be conflict and discomfort that require perseverance.
- Use data to develop a new perspective.

Practices for Organizations

Seeing

- Openly address tension among members. Encourage members to avoid secrecy.

Understanding

- Seek sources of information that bring understanding about the differences.
- Gather data through surveys and other techniques. Establish inclusive structures.

Valuing

- Reward members for engaging in activities that address and diminish differences.
- Hold employees accountable for employing new behaviors. Actively seek diversity when recruiting.

Source: Adapted from Martin N. Davidson, *The End of Diversity as We Know It: Why Diversity Efforts Fail and How Leveraging Difference Can Succeed.* (San Francisco: Berrett-Kohler Press, forthcoming, 2011).

Summary

LO 1 Government reports show that the wages and job opportunities of minorities typically lag behind those for white males. EEOC was originally set up to ensure fair employment practices regardless of race, gender, or age. Being fair requires knowing the legal aspects of the employment relationship, including the laws and various executive orders mentioned in this chapter. Other areas that have more recently become a concern include discrimination based on disabilities, sexual orientation, weight, appearance, or status as a caregiver.

LO 2 The *Uniform Guidelines on Employee Selection Procedures* is designed to help employers comply with federal bans against employment practices that discriminate on the basis of race, color, religion, gender, or national origin. The *Uniform Guidelines* provides employers with a framework for making legally enforceable employment decisions. Employers must be able to show that their selection procedures are valid when it comes to predicting a person's job performance.

LO 3 To ensure that organizations comply with antidiscrimination legislation, the EEOC was established to monitor employers' actions. Employers subject to federal laws must maintain certain records and report certain employment statistics where mandated. Employees or applicants for employment who believe they have been discriminated against may file a discrimination complaint (a charge form) with the EEOC. If an agreement is not reached, the EEOC may elect to sue the employer in federal court. Figure 3.9 illustrates the steps in filing a discrimination charge.

LO ④ Affirmative action goes beyond providing equal employment opportunities to employees. Firms with federal contracts and firms that have been found guilty of past discrimination can be required to utilize affirmative action programs. This is accomplished by employing protected classes for jobs in which they are underrepresented. The employer's goal is to have a balanced internal workforce representative of the employer's relevant labor market. The future of affirmative action might not rest in judicial decisions or laws but in the efforts of managers to voluntary embrace and foster diversity. Differences of all sorts among people are ubiquitous in the workforce. Managers need to leverage these differences because they can be the source of organizational strength.

Key Terms

adverse impact

affirmative action

bona fide occupational
    qualification (BFOQ)

business necessity

charge form

chief diversity officer (CDO)

disabled individual

disparate treatment

equal employment opportunity

Equal Employment Opportunity
    Commission (EEOC)

fair employment practices (FEPs)

four-fifths rule

protected classes

reasonable accommodation

reverse discrimination

sexual harassment

workforce utilization analysis

Uniform Guidelines on Employee
    Selection Procedures

Discussion Questions

LO ① EEO legislation was prompted by significant social events. List those events and describe how they influenced the passage of various EEO laws. Cite and describe the major federal laws and court decisions that affect the employment process of both large and small organizations. After receiving several complaints of sexual harassment, the HR department of a city library decided to establish a sexual harassment policy. What should be included in the policy? How should it be implemented?

LO ② What is the *Uniform Guidelines on Employee Selection Procedures?* To whom do the guidelines apply? What do they cover? Joe Alverez has filed a complaint with the EEO alleging that his employer, Universal Mortgage Company, promotes more whites than Hispanics into managerial positions. Explain the statistical methods used by the EEOC to investigate this adverse impact claim.

LO ③ Understand how the EEOC affects companies and what you must do as a manager to appropriately respond to the administrative rules and regulations published in the *Federal Register.*

As a marketing manager, you have recently turned down Nancy Conrad for a position as sales supervisor. Nancy believes the denial was due to her gender, and she has filed a sex discrimination charge with the EEOC. Explain the steps the EEOC will use to process the charge; include Nancy's options during the process.

LO ④ Affirmative action is both a legal and emotional issue affecting employees and employers. Develop as many arguments as you can both supporting and opposing affirmative action as an employer policy. If you were asked to implement such a program, what steps would you follow?

CASE STUDY **1** Going to the Dogs

Let's admit it: With very few exceptions, we all love dogs. We love to be with our dogs, and our dogs love to be with us. So it is only natural, then, to want to keep our dogs with us as much as possible, even when we go to work. Pet Sitters International thinks this is such a good idea that they have instituted "Take Your Dog to Work Day," a once-a-year event designed to raise awareness of the benefits of dog ownership and to encourage pet adoption.

But maybe you would like something a bit more regular, like having the option to bring Fido to work every day? According to a survey by the American Pet Products Manufacturers Association, it should not be too hard to find an opportunity since nearly one in five companies already allows pets in the workplace. You can even find a list of employers that allow canines at work on DogFriendly.com. Fans of the dogs-at-the-office policy say it increases employee morale and decreases stress.

Before we go too far with this idea, however, perhaps we should take note of some arguments against bringing dogs to work. First, some HR experts like Ethan Winning have cautioned that dogs can be messy, placing an unfair burden on employers to clean up afterwards. Dogs can also be a distraction, and other employees may be allergic or otherwise disturbed by them. And what happens when two or more employees bring their dogs to work on the same day, and Fido and Fifi don't want to play nice?

Of course, some people actually need to bring their dogs to work, which is why the Americans with Disabilities Act permits the use of "service animals" to assist those with disabilities. For example, seeing-eye dogs are allowed to accompany blind individuals at work. The EEOC guideline is reasonable since guide dogs are necessary to blind individuals, and furthermore, guide dogs are trained not to be a nuisance.

It can be challenging, however, for employers to know where to draw the line. Take the case of Elizabeth Booth, a quadriplegic hired by Case Services Corporation as an accountant in the billing department. Booth, who uses a wheelchair for mobility, has trained her small, well-behaved dog to pick up small items that Booth has dropped. Along with a formal request to be allowed to bring her dog to work to assist her, Booth submitted to her employer a letter from her doctor stating that the dog would also help relieve Booth's stress. When Case Services's HR director denied the request, Booth immediately filed a discrimination charge with the EEOC, claiming the company did not provide a reasonable accommodation to her disability or her health needs.

When it comes to establishing a pet policy, as is so often the case, balancing the employer's needs and responsibilities with the employees' needs and wants presents something of a dilemma.

Questions

1. What is your position on this issue? Provide two or three reasons to support your argument.

2. If you were an HR manager of a company, what pet policy would you set and how would you implement it?

3. How would you decide the case of Elizabeth Booth, and which laws would you base your decision on? Explain.

Sources: James J. McDonald, Jr., "Take Your Dog to Work Every Day," *Employee Relations Law Journal* 32, no. 3 (Winter 2006): 86; "Has Your Organization Gone to the Dogs?" http://www.hrwebcafe .com/2007/06/has_your_organization_gone_to.html; Ethan A. Winning, "Pets at the Corporate Zoo," http://www.ewin.com/arch/pets .htm; "About Take Your Dog to Work Day," http://www.takeyourdog .com/About/; "Take Your Dog to Work Every Day," http://www .dogfriendly.com/server/general/workplace/.

HRM Experience

Sexual Harassment: A Frank Discussion

Over the past decade, the problem of sexual harassment has captured the attention of all managers and employees. While it is widely known that sexual harassment is both unethical and illegal, the incidents of sexual harassment continue to plague business. Unfortunately, when these cases arise, they cause morale problems among employees, embarrassment to the organization, and costly legal damages. Consequently, all managers and supervisors play a central role in preventing sexual harassment complaints. It is important that managers understand the definition of sexual harassment, who is covered by sexual harassment guidelines, and how to prevent its occurrence. This skill-building exercise will provide you with knowledge in each of these areas.

Assignment

1. Working in teams of female and male members, develop a list of behaviors that could be classified as quid pro quo harassment or hostile environment. Explore the possibility that some sexual harassing behaviors might be viewed differently by female and male employees. Give examples.
2. Many sexual harassment incidents go unreported. Fully discuss why this can occur and what might be done to reduce this problem.
3. The cornerstone to addressing sexual harassment is achieving organizational awareness through training. Develop a sexual harassment training program for a company of 250 employees that covers, at a minimum, the following: (1) who should attend the training sessions, (2) the content outline for the training program (the list of materials your team wants to teach), (3) specific examples to illustrate the training materials, and (4) how to investigate sexual harassment complaints.
4. This chapter will assist you with this assignment. You can obtain additional materials from EEOC offices and from various HR magazines.
5. Be prepared to present your training outline to other class members.

CASE STUDY Misplaced Affections: Discharge for Sexual Harassment

Peter Lewiston was terminated on July 15, 2017, by the governing board of the Pine Circle Unified School District (PCUSD) for violation of the district's sexual harassment policy. Prior to Lewiston's termination he was a senior maintenance employee with an above-average work record who had worked for the PCUSD for 11 years. He had been a widower since 2012 and was described by his coworkers as a friendly, outgoing, but lonely individual. Beverly Gilbury was a fifth-grade teacher working in the district's Advanced Learning Program. She was 28 years old and married and had worked for PCUSD for 6 years. At the time of the incidents, Lewiston and Gilbury both worked at the Simpson Elementary School, where their relationship was described as "cooperative." The following sequence of events was reported separately by Lewiston and Gilbury during the district's investigation of this sexual harassment case.

Gilbury reported that her relationship with Lewiston began to change during the last month of the 2016–2017 school year. She believed that Lewiston was paying her more attention and that his behavior was "out of the ordinary" and "sometimes weird." He began spending more time in her classroom talking with the children and with her. At the time she did not say anything to Lewiston because "I didn't want to hurt his feelings since he is a nice, lonely, older man." However, on May 25, when Lewiston told Gilbury that he was "very fond" of her and that she had "very beautiful eyes," she replied, "Remember, Peter, we're just friends." For the remainder of the school year, there was little contact between them; however, when they did see each other, Lewiston seemed "overly friendly" to her.

June 7, 2017. On the first day of summer school, Gilbury returned to school to find a dozen roses and a card from Lewiston. The card read, "Please forgive me for thinking you could like me. I played the big fool. Yours always, P.L." Later in the day Lewiston asked Gilbury to lunch. She replied, "It's been a long time since anyone sent me roses, but I can't go to lunch. We need to remain just friends." Gilbury told another teacher that she was uncomfortable about receiving the roses and card and that Lewiston would not leave her alone. She expressed concern that Lewiston might get "more romantic" with her.

June 8, 2017. Gilbury arrived at school to find another card from Lewiston. Inside was a handwritten note that read, "I hope you can someday return my affections for you. I need you so much." Later in the day, Lewiston again asked her to lunch, and she declined, saying, "I'm a happily married woman." At the close of the school day, when Gilbury went to her car, Lewiston suddenly appeared. He asked to explain himself but Gilbury became agitated and shouted, "I have to leave right now." Lewiston reached inside the car, supposedly to pat her shoulder, but touched her head instead. She believed he meant to stroke her hair. He stated that he was only trying to calm her down. She drove away, very upset.

June 9, 2017. Gilbury received another card and a lengthy letter from Lewiston, stating that he was wrong in trying to develop a relationship with her and he hoped they could still remain friends. He wished her all happiness with her family and job.

June 11, 2017. Gilbury obtained from the Western Justice Court an injunction prohibiting sexual harassment by Lewiston. Shortly thereafter Lewiston appealed the injunction. A notice was mailed to Gilbury giving the dates of the appeal hearing. The notice stated in part, "If you fail to appear, the injunction may be vacated and the petition dismissed." Gilbury failed to appear at the hearing, and the injunction was set aside. Additionally, on June 11 she had filed with the district's EEOC officer a sexual harassment complaint against Lewiston. After the investigation, the district concluded that Lewiston's actions created an "extremely sexually hostile" environment for Gilbury. The investigative report recommended dismissal based upon the grievous conduct of Lewiston and the initial injunction granted by the Justice Court.

Questions

1. Evaluate the conduct of Peter Lewiston against the EEOC's definition of sexual harassment.

2. Should the intent or motive behind Lewiston's conduct be considered when deciding sexual harassment activities? Explain.

3. If you were the district's EEOC officer, what would you conclude? What disciplinary action, if any, would you take?

Sources: This case is adapted from an actual arbitration hearing conducted by George Bohlander. The background information is factual. All names and dates are fictitious.

Answers to Highlights in HRM 1

1. Yes
2. False
3. No
4. Merit, seniority, incentive pay plans
5. Yes
6. Yes, if no reasonable accommodation can be made
7. No
8. Yes, except if under a court order
9. False
10. True

Notes and References

1. U.S. Equal Employment Opportunity Commission, "Charge Statistics: FY 1997 Through FY 2016," USA.gov (March 7, 2017), https://www.eeoc.gov/eeoc/statistics/enforcement/charges.cfm.

2. J. B. Becton, J. B. Gilstrap, and M. Forsyth, "Preventing and Correcting Workplace Harassment: Guidelines for Employers," *Business Horizons 60*, no. 1 (2017): 101–111; Darla Mercado, "Morgan Stanley Settles $46 Million Discrimination Suit," Workforce.com (October 16, 2007), http://www.workforce.com/articles/morgan-stanley-settles-46-million-discrimination-suit.

3. Michael Orey, "White Men Can't Help It," *Business Week* (May 15, 2006): 54.

4. For a practical overview of EEO law, see David J. Walsh, *Employment Law for Human Resource Practice*, 3rd ed. (Mason, OH: South-Western, 2010).

5. Dennis Cauchon, "Gender Pay Gap Is Smallest on Record," *USA Today* (September 14, 2010), http://www.usatoday.com.

6. For information on national origin discrimination, go to http://www.justice.gov/crt/publications/natorigin2.php.

7. *Porter v. City of Chicago*, No. 11-2006 (7th Cir. 2012 [March 7, 2017]), http://law.justia.com/cases/federal/appellate-courts/ca7/11-2006/11-2006-2012-11-08.html.

8. Lynn D. Lieber, "As Average Age of Workforce Increases, Age Discrimination Verdicts Rise," *Employment Relations Today* 34, no. 1 (Spring 2007): 105.

9. Maria Greco Danaher, "Include Pregnancy Leave in Pension Credit," *HR Magazine* 52, no. 11 (November 2007): 98.

10. United States Department of Justice Civil Rights Division, "The Americans with Disabilities Act of 1990 and Revised ADA Regulations Implementing Title II and Title III," ADA.gov (Jan 2014), http://www.ada.gov/2010_regs.htm.

11. U.S. Equal Employment Opportunity Commission, "EEOC Enforcement Guidance on the Americans with Disabilities Act and Psychiatric Disabilities," EEOC (1997; January 2014), http://www.eeoc.gov/policy/docs/psych.html.

12. Jonathan R. Mook, "Accommodation Paradigm Shifts," *HR Magazine* 52, no. 1 (January 2007): 115; see also, James J. McDonald, Jr., "Take Your Dog to Work Everyday," *Employee Relations Law Journal* 32, no. 3 (Winter 2006): 86.

13. Bill Leonard, "Studies: ADA Makes Business Better," *HR Magazine* 52, no. 10 (October 2007): 22.

14. "Broadening the Coverage of the ADA: The 2008 Amendments to the Americans with Disabilities Act," *INSIGHT into Diversity* (November 2010): 32–35.

15. "Genetic Information Nondiscrimination Act: A Primer on Title II," *Venulex Legal Summaries* (Winter 2010): special section, 1.

16. "Joy Mining Machinery Settles EEOC Genetic Information Non-Discrimination Act Lawsuit," US Equal Employment Opportunity Commission, https://www.eeoc.gov/eeoc/newsroom/release/1-7-16.cfm.

17. Gary L. Tidwell, Daniel A. Rice, and Gary Kropkowski, "Employer and Employee Obligations and Rights under the Uniformed Services Employment and Reemployment Rights Act," *Business Horizons* 52, no. 3, (May 2009): 243–250, DOI: 10.1016/j.bushor.2009.01.003. Find additional information on the law at the USERRA Advisor at the Department of Labor's website, http://www.dol.gov/claws.

18. Veterans Benefits Improvement Act of 2004, Public Law 108–454 (December 20, 2004).

19. As currently defined, an "otherwise qualified" employee is one who can perform the "essential functions" of the job under consideration.

20. *Oncale v. Sundowner Offshore Services, Inc.* 72 PED 45, 175; WL 88039 (U.S. 11998), http://www.eeoc.gov/laws/types/sexual_harassment.cfm.

21. *Guidelines on Discrimination Because of Sex*, 29 C.F.R. Sec. 1604.11(a) (1955).

22. *Guidelines on Discrimination*, Sec. 1605.11(a).

23. Jeffrey I.Chasen, "Discrimination and Harassment in the Workplace: Five Essential Strategies for Smarter Risk Management," *Risk Institute. PERI* (January 2014), http://www.riskinstitute.org/.

24. Margaret Bryant, "Harassment Lawsuits and Lessons," *Security Management* 60, no. 4 (April 2006): 50.

25. Laura G. Barron, "Sexual Orientation Employment: Anti-Discrimination Legislation and Hiring Discrimination and Prejudice," *Academy of Management Annual Meeting Proceedings* (2009): 1.

26. "What You Should Know about EEOC and the Enforcement Protections for LGBT Workers," U.S. Equal Employment Opportunity Commission (March 7, 2017), https://www.eeoc.gov/eeoc/newsroom/wysk/enforcement_protections_lgbt_workers.cfm. The EEOC has ruled that transgender and transsexual individuals are not covered by Title VII of the Civil Rights Act. According to the EEOC, gender only applies to one's sex at the time of birth and not to one's sexual orientation. See Jon D. Bible, "In a Class by Themselves: The Legal Status of Employee Appearance Policies Under Title VII after *Jespersen v. Harrah's Operating Co.*," *Employee Relations Law Journal* 32, no. 4 (Spring 2007): 3. See also, Stan Malos, "Appearance-Based Sex Discrimination and Stereotyping in the Workplace: Whose Conduct Should We Regulate?" *Employee Responsibilities and Rights Journal* 19, no. 2 (June 2007): 95.

27. What You Should Know about EEOC and the Enforcement "Protections for LGBT Workers," U.S. Equal Employment Opportunity Commission (March 7, 2017), https://www.eeoc.gov/eeoc/newsroom/wysk/enforcement_protections_lgbt_workers.cfm.

28. Huasheng Gao and Wei Zhang, "Non-Discrimination Laws Make U.S. States More Innovative," *Harvard Business Review* (August 17, 2016).

29. Ali Vitali, "President Trump Signs New Immigration Executive Order," *NBC News* (March 6, 2017); Mark Schoeff, "DHS Rule Rankles Employer Groups," *Workforce Management* 86, no. 14 (August 20, 2007): 1.

30. 8 U.S.C.A. § 1324a (a) (1), (2) (2005).

31. 8 U.S.C.A. § 1324B (1) (2005).

32. U.S. Department of Justice, Immigration and Naturalization Service, *Handbook for Employers: Instructions for Completing Form I* (Washington, D.C.: U.S. Government Printing Office, 2005).

33. Jacqueline Howard. "Weight Bias Is Bigger Problem than You May Think, Experts Say," *CNN.com*; Svetlana Shkolnikova, "Weight Discrimination Could Be as Common as Racial Discrimination," *USA Today* (May 28, 2008), http://www.usatoday.com.

34. Donna Ballman, "Is Weight Discrimination At Work Illegal?" *AOL Jobs* (November 6, 2012), http://jobs.aol.com/articles/2012/11/06/is-weight-discrimination-illegal/.

35. Enbar Toledano, "May the Best (Looking) Man Win: The Unconscious Role of Attractiveness in Employment Decisions," *Cornell (University) HR Review* (February 14, 2013), http://www.cornellhrreview.org.

36. Gerald E. Calvasina, Richard V. Calvasina, and Eugene J. Calvasina, "Caregiver Responsibility Discrimination and EEOC Guidelines," *Journal of Legal, Ethical & Regulatory Issues* 13, no. 2 (June 2010): 1–2.

37. The guidelines themselves and examples of their application can be found at www.uniformguidelines.com.

38. *Uniform Guidelines*, Sec. 40. Adverse impact need not be considered for groups that constitute less than 2 percent of the relevant labor force.

39. The primary website for the EEOC is http://www.eeoc.gov. This website contains a wealth of information about the EEOC, including the agency's history and administration, how discrimination charges are filed and processed, training and outreach programs, litigation statistics, and various pamphlets and posters offered free of charge to interested parties.

40. Howard S. Lavin and Elizabeth E. DiMichele, "The Time for Filing Charges of Discrimination: The Supreme Court's Decision and Its Aftermath," *Employee Relations Law Journal* 33, no. 3 (Winter 2007): 113; see also, Reynolds Holding, "Stumble on the Bench," *Time* (June 18, 2007): 56.

41. The time period is 300 days in states in which the charge is deferred to a state agency.

42. David Sherwyn, Zev Eigen, and Gregg Gilman, "Retaliation: The Fastest Growing Discrimination Claim," *Cornell Hotel and Restaurant Administration Quarterly* 47, no. 4 (November 2006): 350.

43. Rebecca M. Archer and Stephen T. Lanctot, "Are Your Hands Tied? A Practical Look at Employee Claims of Retaliation," *Employee Relations Law Journal* 33, no. 1 (Summer 2007): 53; see also, Mary Price Birk, "Walking on Eggshells—Avoiding Retaliation Claims When the Employee Does Not Leave," *Employee Relations Law Journal* 32, no. 3 (Winter 2006): 10; and Martin K. LaPointe, "The Supreme Court Sets the Standard for Title VII Retaliation Claims: Burlington Northern and *Santa Fe Railway v. White*," *Labor Law Journal* 57, no. 4 (Winter 2006): 205.

44. Jathan Janove, "Retaliation Nation," *HR Magazine* 51, no. 10 (October 2006): 62.

45. Heather J. Broadwater, "Preventing Workplace Sexual Harassment," *Rural Telecommunications* 25, no. 5 (September /October 2006): 34.

46. Michael W. Johnson, "Harassment and Discrimination Prevention Training," *Labor Law Journal* 55, no. 2 (Summer 2004): 119.

47. Alison DeNisco, "Does Your Company Need a Chief Diversity Officer?" *TechRepublic* (September 28, 2016).

48. Voluntary Diversity Plans Can Lead to Risk," *HR Focus* 84, no. 6 (June 2007): 2.

49. *University of California Regents v. Bakke*, 438 U.S. 265 (1978) and *United Steelworkers of America v. Weber*, 443, U.S. 193 (1979).

50. Daniel A. Biddle and Richard E. Biddle, "*Ricci v. Destefano*: New Opportunities for Employers to Correct Disparate Impact," *Labor Law Journal* 61, no. 3 (Fall 2010): 123–41.

51. Peng Wang and Joshua L. Schwarz, "Stock Price Reactions to GLBT Nondiscrimination Policies," *Human Resource Management* 49, no. 2 (March–April 2010): 195.

Determining Adverse Impact

A.1 The Four-Fifths Rule

Employers can determine adverse impact by using the method outlined in the interpretive manual for the *Uniform Guidelines on Employee Selection Procedures*.

1. Calculate the rate of selection for each group (divide the number of people selected from a group by the number of total applicants from that group).
2. Observe which group has the highest selection.
3. Calculate the impact ratios by comparing the selection rate for each group with that of the highest group (divide the selection rate for a group by the selection rate for the highest group).
4. Observe whether the selection rate for any group is substantially less (usually less than four-fifths, or 80 percent) than the selection rate for the highest group. If it is, adverse impact is indicated in most circumstances.

Example

	Job Applicants	Number Hired	Selection Rate Percent Hired
Step A	Whites 100	52	52 / 100 = 52%
	Blacks 50	14	14 / 50 = 28%
Step B	The group with the highest selection rate is whites, 52%.		
Step C	Divide the black selection rate (28%) by the white selection rate (52%). The black rate is 53.8% of the white rate.		
Step D	Since 53.8% is less than four-fifths, or 80%, adverse impact is indicated.		

Source: Adoption of Questions and Answers to Clarify and Provide a Common Interpretation of the *Uniform Guidelines on Employee Selection Procedures, Federal Register* 44, no. 43 (March 2, 1979): 11998.

CHAPTER **4**

Job Analysis and Job Design

Learning Outcomes

After studying this chapter, you should be able to

LO 1 Explain what a job analysis is and how it is used in conjunction with a firm's HRM functions.

LO 2 Explain how the information for a job analysis typically is collected and incorporated into various sections of a job's description.

LO 3 Provide examples illustrating the various factors that must be taken into account when designing a job, including what motivates employees.

LO 4 Describe the different group techniques and types of work schedules used to broaden a firm's job functions and maximize the contributions of employees.

job
An activity people do
for which they get paid,
particularly as part of the
trade or occupation they
occupy.

Organizations exist because people can accomplish more together than they can on their own. However, the actions of an organization need to be coordinated, and each person within it needs to do those things he or she does best. This coordination is typically achieved by creating individual jobs. A **job** can be defined as an activity people do for which they get paid, particularly as part of the trade or occupation they occupy. But how exactly should the work be divided, and which people should do which tasks or jobs. These are questions businesspeople such as Henry Ford and scientific management researchers such as Frederick Winslow Taylor sought to answer at least a century ago, and ones managers still ask today.

The answers to the questions about what jobs an organization should have stem from a firm's strategy. What good or service does the firm intend to provide and how much of it? What does the firm believe its competitive advantage is? Is the company trying to capture market share based on a new product it has developed? A lower-priced product? A higher-quality product? How and where will the product will be produced, and distributed, and with what technology? What types of people and skills will be needed to accomplish these tasks and how should they be organized?

A *workflow analysis* can help a company answer these questions. A *workflow analysis* helps a firm determine the best processes, types, and mix of jobs, and how they should ideally be organized to execute the firm's mission. For example, both Apple and Lenovo make computers. However, Apple focuses on producing innovative products, whereas Lenovo has traditionally focused on producing low-priced products. As a result, how the companies are organized, their workflows, and numbers and types of jobs differ in significant ways. To develop and improve their workflows, large organizations often hire outside business analysts and operations management specialists who work in conjunction with the firm's top managers and HR personnel to do so. The resulting workflow analysis outlines the division of labor among employees, the degree to which they are specialized, to whom they report to, and that person's authority, or span of control over his or her subordinates.

However, as the competitive environment changes, these elements have to change as well. Formerly Lenovo had a typical hierarchical organizational structure. (Recall from your introduction to business and management classes that tall organizational structures are characterized by many managerial levels with narrow spans of control and jobs that are narrowly focused.) That structure worked well for the firm's PC business, but to remain competitive, the company needed to improve its innovation capabilities and expand its product lineup to attract new types of customers.

So, a few years ago, Lenovo flattened its organization by dividing its PC-focused division into four separate business units: PCs, mobiles devices, servers and storage, and cloud computing systems. It also divided countries into emerging and mature markets and developed different strategies and personnel for each. Today, not only is Lenovo the biggest seller of PCs in the world, it also sells more mobile phones in China than any other company, including Apple.

What will workflows and jobs look like in the near future? The biggest game changer is likely to be automation. Virtually all companies must compete on price, at least to some extent. And in the long run, automating repetitive tasks is cheaper than hiring people to do them. Amazon.com has developed a grocery store that allows people to walk in, load up their groceries, automatically pay for them, and leave without going through a checkout stand. In Japan, conveyor belts deliver sushi to customers almost as soon as they click on a menu to choose their selections. Computer chips in the plates sense when entrées have been chosen and the customer's bill gets tallied up based on what they grab. U.S. restaurants are automating, too.

And it's not just service jobs that are being replaced. In the oil and gas industry, thousands of workers who drilled and monitored wells have been replaced by robots and electronic equipment and sensors. "Pretty soon every rig will have just one worker and one robot," says Eustasio Velazquez, a 44-year-old oil field worker who recently lost his job. Oil companies are hiring smaller numbers of high-tech workers, such as engineers, data scientists, and mathematicians, who often work in mission-control-like centers. Twenty-five-year old Andre Nel, a mechanical engineer with a computer science background, is one of them. In addition to designing systems and software for his petroleum company, Nel can monitor the maintenance history and production trends of thousands of wells with just the click of a mouse.[1]

4.1 What Is a Job Analysis and How Does It Affect Human Resources Management?

LO 1
Are there any HR functions not affected by the job analysis process? If so, what are they?

Think about an organization you worked for or a job or position you have held. Did you ever think about ways to make the organization's workflow better? If so, you were doing an informal work analysis. Likewise, did you analyze the tasks you were doing and conclude they should be done by someone else or vice versa? If so, you were doing an informal analysis of your job. A **job analysis** is the systematic process of collecting information about all of the parameters of a job—its basic responsibilities, the behaviors, skills, and the physical and mental requirements of the people who do it.

A job analysis should also outline the tools needed to do the job, the environment and times at which it needs to be done, with whom it needs to be done, and the outcome or performance level it should produce.[2] Normally, a manager or an HR manager such as a job analyst is responsible for collecting the information for a job analysis. These people rely on the cooperation of employees and their supervisors to gather the information needed for the analysis of jobs.

How does a job analysis help facilitate a firm's human resources efforts? As Figure 4.1 shows, the information in a job analysis is crucial to a number of HRM functions, including the following:

job analysis
The process of obtaining information about a job by determining its duties, tasks, or activities.

- **Strategic HR planning.** A job analysis is used to examine a company's organizational structure and strategically position it for the future. Does the firm have the right numbers and types of jobs and skills needed to cover the scope of its activities

Figure 4.1	Job Analysis: The Cornerstone of HRM Functions	
Alignment of:	**Job Description (TDRs)**	**Job Specification (KSAOs)**
• HR Strategy and Planning	Nature of structure and work to achieve business results and goals	Supply and demand of labor, number and kinds of people needed to fill open positions
• Workflow Analysis and Job Design	Sequencing or grouping of related jobs, and the nature of interdependence	Enriching or expanding jobs to develop and motivate employees further
• Recruitment and Selection	Posting advertisements, etc. of jobs to fill and the nature of responsibilities	Hiring criteria for evaluating candidates who apply for open positions
• Performance Appraisal Process	Setting goals, duties, and activities that define the desired performance	Attributes and demonstrated qualities used to assess performance and give feedback
• Compensation and Benefits	Job evaluation of the job in terms of responsibilities and working conditions	Job evaluation of the skills, effort required, etc. that are rewarded
• Legal Compliance	Equal employment requirements	Fair treatment and valid employment practices

now and in the future? In addition, are the jobs aligned with one another, or do their purposes or duties conflict with one another? Are there tasks that need to be done in the organization that are not clearly assigned to a particular job? Conducting a job analysis helps ensure alignment.

- **Workflow analysis and job design.** The information generated by a job analysis can be used to analyze a company's work processes—that is, how work is done. Would rearranging an organization's workflow or jobs help a company better compete? Can the nature of the jobs be redesigned to improve the firm's performance?

- **Recruitment and selection.** Some of the information provided in a job analysis is contained in job advertisements. The information and qualifications provide a basis for attracting qualified applicants and discourageing unqualified ones.

- **Training and development.** Any discrepancies between the abilities of jobholders and a firm's job descriptions provide clues about the training jobholders need to succeed and advance into different jobs as well as the training the firm needs to provide.

- **Performance appraisal and compensation.** A job analysis provides the criteria for evaluating what constitutes a good performance versus a poor performance; the firm can then take steps to improve the latter.

- **Compensation management.** Conducting a job analysis helps HR managers figure out the relative worth of positions so the compensation for them is fair and equitable, and employees want to remain with the firm rather than search for other jobs.

- **Legal compliance.** If the criteria used to hire and evaluate employees are not job related, employers are more likely to find themselves being accused of discrimination. In decades past, before firms regularly analyzed jobs, non-job-related criteria were prevalent: For example, laborers were often required to have high school diplomas; plumbers, electricians, and machinists were sometimes required to be male. As you learned in Chapter 3, these kinds of job specifications are discriminatory.

4.1a Major Parts of the Job Analysis

Let's look at the two major pieces of information that come out of a job analysis:

1. A **job description**, which is a written document that describes the overall purpose of the job, and tasks, duties, and responsibilities, or what human resources personnel refer to as TDRs, and the qualifications needed to do it. The following is an excerpt of the purpose and TDRs for a firefighter's position posted by the city of Del Mar, California.

   Purpose

   Responds to emergency calls to protect life and property; participates in training, drill and independent study activities; participates in the maintenance of fire department apparatus, equipment and facilities; performs various staff support assignments; and performs related work as assigned.

   Tasks, Duties, and Responsibilities

   - Responds to a wide variety of emergency alarms, such as structural and environmental fires, traffic accidents, natural gas leaks, medical emergencies, and hazardous material spills.
   - Provides first-responder medical emergency response at the basic life support level, including initial patient and situation assessment, cardiopulmonary resuscitation and trauma emergency medical care; prepares patients and assists paramedics in advanced life support emergency medical care.

2. **Job specifications**, or qualifications, which are a part of the written job description and outline the specific knowledge, skills, abilities, and other attributes (often referred to as KSAOs) required of the person performing the job. *Knowledge* refers to what you know. Your education is an example of knowledge. For example, some cities require firefighters to be certified paramedics. Other cities don't. *Skills* are things you have learned to do. If you're a firefighter, that experience could include knowing how to make minor repairs to fire equipment. *Abilities* are your innate aptitudes. You don't have to be taught them or learn them on a job. Examples for a firefighter would include the ability to lift firefighting equipment and stay calm during an emergency. *Other attributes* refer to your personality, values, and so on. Helpfulness and the predisposition toward teamwork are examples of "other attributes" firefighters need.

Are you thinking you want to go into human resources management? If so, Highlights in HRM 2 later in the chaper will give you an idea of what a job description for an entry-level position in this field would look like. Note that a job description isn't necessarily the information you would see in a job posting, which is used for advertising. The job description in Highlights in HRM 2 is an internal document used by the firm and HR personnel for their planning and staffing needs. For example, note that the job analyst who compiled the information and the date the job was analyzed are included at the top of the document. We will take a closer look at the parts of the document later in the chapter.

job description
A statement of the tasks, duties, and responsibilities of a job to be performed.

job specifications
A statement of the specific knowledge, skills, and abilities of a person who is to perform a job needs.

Answer the questions in Highlights in HRM 1 based on the job you currently hold or most recently held. Then organize the information into the various job sections of a job description.

4.2 Sources of Job Analysis Information

You have learned that a job analysis is an important HR building block. What you are probably wondering now is how a person does one. The first step is to collect information needed to analyze jobs. The most common methods of collecting this information are interviews, questionnaires, observation, and diaries.

- *Interviews.* A job analyst or supervisor interviews individual employees and their managers about the parameters of the job. Highlights in HRM 1 shows the types of questions asked as part of job analysis interviews. When a job is particularly complex, firms sometimes interview a panel of *subject matter experts* (*SMEs*). SMEs are job experts who actually do the job or train and supervise others to do the job.

- *Questionnaires.* The job analyst or supervisor circulates standard questionnaires for jobholders to fill out individually. The forms contain questions similar to those asked in an interview.

- *Observation.* The job analyst or supervisor learns about the job by observing and recording the activities associated with it on a standardized form.

- *Diaries.* Jobholders are asked to keep diaries of their work activities for an entire work cycle. The diaries are normally filled out at specific times of the work shift (such as every half hour or hour) and maintained for a 2- to 4-week period.

Job analysis software and templates available on the Web have greatly facilitated the job analysis process. They normally contain task statements that can apply to many different jobs. Managers and employees select those statements that best describe the job under review, indicating the importance of the task to the job.

Figure 4.2 shows the job analysis process. It includes how the information to be analyzed is collected and feeds back into the HRM functions we discussed in Figure 4.1.

4.2a Controlling the Accuracy of the Job Data Collected

When interviewing employees or reviewing their questionnaires, a job analyst should look for any responses that contradict other facts or impressions he or she has received about the job. Sometimes employees exaggerate the difficulty of their positions to inflate their egos and their paychecks.[3] Inflating a job's responsibilities can also occur unintentionally. For example, people who have been in their jobs for a long time and are good at them sometimes mistakenly believe that the skills needed for their jobs are higher than they really are. As one job analyst noted, "When in doubt about the accuracy of employee responses, always double-check the data with others."[4] In other words, collect information from a representative sample of individuals doing the same job, not just one or two jobholders. Also, once a job analysis is done, it should be checked for accuracy by the jobholders and their managers.[5]

4.2b Other Sources of Job Analysis Information

Do managers and job analysts have to start from scratch when it comes to designing questionnaires to gather job information and analyzing it? No, not necessarily, even if a position is a new one. Several different quantitative job analysis approaches already exist. Each has its own advantages and disadvantages.[6] Five of the more popular methods are the functional job analysis, the position analysis system, the critical incident method, a task inventory analysis, and a competency-based job analysis.

Job Analysis Interview Questions

The following are examples of interview questions HR professionals use to gather information for a job analysis.

1. Job's purpose
   - What work do you essentially do? What is the job's overall purpose?
   - How do you see your work contributing to the overall mission or purpose of the organization, now and in the future?

2. Job's duties
   - Describe your duties in terms of what they are, how you do them, how often you perform them, and how long they each take.
   - Does the job have to be done in the way you were trained to do it, or do you see ways to improve it?
   - Are you performing duties not presently included in your job description? Describe them.
   - Are the instructions you receive from your supervisor clear and consistent with your job description?

3. Job criteria and results
   - Have work standards for the job been established (errors allowed, time taken for a particular task, etc.)? If so, what are they?
   - Describe the successful completion and/or end results of the job.

4. Background and knowledge
   - What personal attributes are needed to be successful in this position?
   - Describe the level, degree, and breadth of knowledge required for this position.
   - Indicate the education, certification, and license requirements for the job.

5. Training
   - Describe the orientation you received when you first began this job and its effectiveness.
   - What sort of on-the-job training and training period is needed for the position?
   - What tools, equipment, or other resources are needed to train people for this position?
   - What assessment tests are needed to determine if someone is competent in this position?

6. Abilities required
   - Do you use special software tools, equipment, or machines? If so, list them.
   - What manual skills are needed to operate the machines, tools, and equipment to do the job?
   - What reasoning or problem-solving ability must you have?
   - Are any supervisory or managing abilities required?
   - What physical abilities such as strength, coordination, or visual acuity must you have?

7. Working conditions
   - Describe your working conditions.
   - Describe the frequency and degree to which you encounter working conditions such as these: contact with hazardous materials, strenuous physical labor, cramped quarters, moving objects, vibration, and inadequate ventilation.

8. Authority
   - What is the job's level of authority, and to whom are you accountable?
   - What kinds of independent action are you allowed to take?

9. Responsibilities
   - Are you responsible for any confidential material? If so, describe how you handle it.
   - Are you responsible for any money or things of monetary value? If so, describe how you handle it.

10. Evaluation and compensation
    - In what ways and how often is your performance evaluated and feedback provided?
    - What criteria do you think should be used in the evaluation process?
    - Considering your level of productivity and the skill level required to fulfill your responsibilities, do you think you are compensated adequately?
    - Describe the criteria that should be used to determine the compensation for the position: responsibilities, skills, experience, knowledge, work environment, safety hazards, and so forth.

Sources: Michael G. Aamodt, *Industrial/Organizational Psychology: An Applied Approach*, 7th ed. (Mason, OH: Cengage Learning, 2012); David Ngo, "Job Analysis Questions," (March 3, 2011), http://www.humanresources.hrvinet.com; "Job Analysis: Overview," HR Guide to the Internet, http://www.job-analysis.net/G000.htm; "Job Analysis: Asking Questions," Department for Business Innovation & Skills, http://www.bis.gov.uk.

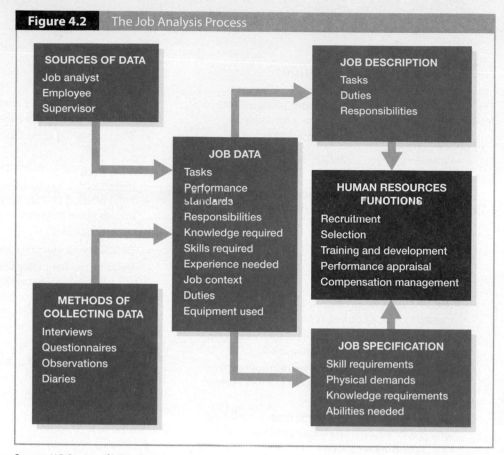

Figure 4.2   The Job Analysis Process

SOURCES OF DATA
Job analyst
Employee
Supervisor

JOB DATA
Tasks
Performance standards
Responsibilities
Knowledge required
Skills required
Experience needed
Job context
Duties
Equipment used

METHODS OF COLLECTING DATA
Interviews
Questionnaires
Observations
Diaries

JOB DESCRIPTION
Tasks
Duties
Responsibilities

HUMAN RESOURCES FUNCTIONS
Recruitment
Selection
Training and development
Performance appraisal
Compensation management

JOB SPECIFICATION
Skill requirements
Physical demands
Knowledge requirements
Abilities needed

Source: U.S. Bureau of Labor Statistics

Functional Job Analysis System

functional job analysis (FJA)

A job analysis approach that utilizes an inventory of the various types of work activities that can constitute any job.

Developed by the U.S. Training and Employment Service, the **functional job analysis (FJA)** approach utilizes an inventory of the various types of work activities that can constitute any job. Basic activities called worker functions are used to describe what workers do with regard to "information, people, and things" as part of this system. For example, when it comes to people, the basic functions of a job might include coordinating and supervising them. Each job function is assigned a percentage in terms of its importance to the job. For example, supervising might be 75 percent of the job.

The U.S. Department of Labor has a comprehensive occupation-information website called O*NET Online that contains thousands of free job descriptions that can help match people's interests and abilities with occupations as well as serve as a starting point for analyzing a job. The jobs on the site are classified into broader functional areas, from entry level to advanced, and across various specialties and contain comprehensive information about the tasks, tools and technology, KSAOs, education, interests, works styles, wages, and employment outlook associated with the jobs. Free job analysis questionnaires can be downloaded from O*NET. Although they are generic, they can be customized and used to collect occupational information from jobholders and their managers.

The Position Analysis Questionnaire System

The **position analysis questionnaire (PAQ)**, which identifies approximately 300 different worker tasks, has been widely used for decades to collect and analyze job information. The PAQ seeks to determine the degree to which the different tasks are involved in doing a particular job. The results obtained with the PAQ are quantitative and can be statistically analyzed. Although a PAQ tends to be accurate, it requires a person to have a high level of reading ability.[7] To obtain the best results, it should be administered to employees by a job analyst rather than having the employees complete the questionnaire alone. Also, the questionnaire isn't free. Firms must pay for it.

position analysis questionnaire (PAQ)
A questionnaire that identifies approximately 300 different tasks to determine the degree to which each is involved in doing a job.

The Critical Incident Method

The objective of the **critical incident method** is to identify both desirable and undesirable behaviors that resulted in either a very good outcome or a very bad outcome on the job. For example, a job analyst might ask a company's customer service employees to describe incidents that led to either a good or bad outcome with a customer. The following are examples of questions that might be asked:

critical incident method
A job analysis method used to identify both desirable and undesirable behaviors that resulted in either a very good outcome or a very bad outome on the job.

- What happened?
- How did the incident happen?
- Did the incident have a good or bad outcome?
- What led to the outcome?
- What actions were effective or ineffective?
- What would you do differently if the situation occurred again?

The information, which can be collected through interviews or surveys, helps pinpoint important behaviors for a job analysis. Figure 4.3 illustrates the critical incident. The incidents in the middle of the figure are associated with neutral outcomes. Most of the outcomes will fall into this area. The incidents on the ends of the figure are good and bad outcomes. Relatively fewer of the incidents will occur in these areas. Nonetheless, examining them is important because they can reveal critical job behaviors.

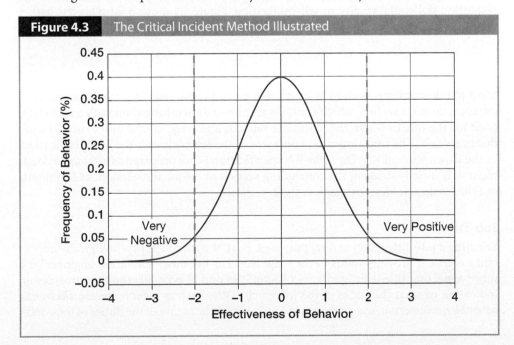

Figure 4.3 The Critical Incident Method Illustrated

task inventory analysis
An organization-specific list of tasks and their descriptions used as a basis to identify components of jobs.

Task Inventory Analysis

The **task inventory analysis** method was pioneered by the U.S. Air Force. Unlike the PAQ, which uses a standardized form to analyze jobs in different organizations, a task inventory questionnaire can be tailored for a specific organization. With the help of employees and their managers, a list of tasks and their descriptions for different jobs are developed and then rated based on how important they are. The goal is to produce a comprehensive list of task statements applicable to all jobs. Task statements then are listed on a task inventory survey form to be completed by the person analyzing the job under review. A task statement might be: "Monitors current supplies to maintain stock levels." The job analysis would also note the importance of the task, frequency of occurrence, and time spent on the task to the successful completion of the job.

Competency-Based Approach

The approaches to job analysis we have discussed so far focus on the tasks employees do, but not what they are capable of doing. The following statement by two HR professionals highlights this concern: "Typically, job analysis looks at how a job is currently done. But the ever-changing business market makes it difficult to keep a job analysis up-to-date. Also, companies are asking employees to do more, so there is a question of whether 'jobs' as we know them are obsolete." The risk is that in a dynamic environment where job demands rapidly change, obsolete job analysis information will hinder an organization's ability to adapt to change.

When organizations operate in a fast-moving environment, managers often adopt a competency-based approach to job analysis.[8] This job analysis method relies on building job profiles that look at not only the responsibilities and activities of jobs a worker does currently but the competencies or capabilities he or she needs to do them well and to adapt to new job challenges. *How* the work is done (and therefore can be improved) becomes more of the focus than just *what* work is done.[9]

The objective is to identify key competencies for the organization's success. Competencies can be identified through focus groups, surveys, or interviews and might include such things as interpersonal communication skills, decision-making ability, conflict resolution skills, adaptability, or self-motivation. Figure 4.4 shows a form used to gather information for a competency-based job analysis.

4.2c Parts of a Job Description

Most job descriptions contain at least three parts: (1) the job's title and location; (2) a job identification section, which contains administration information such a numerical code for the job, to whom the jobholder reports, and wage information; and (3) a job duties section. The other important outcome of the job analysis is the job specification, or the description of KSAOs. If the job specification is not prepared as a separate document, it is usually stated in the concluding section of the job description, as Highlights in HRM 2 shows. Next, let's look at these sections.

Job Title

Selecting a job's title serves several purposes. First, the job title is psychologically important because it provides status to the employee. For instance, "sanitation engineer" is a more appealing title than "garbage collector." Second, if possible, the title provides an indication of what the duties of the job entail. Titles such as *meat inspector, electronics assembler, salesperson*, and *engineer* obviously hint at the nature of the duties of these jobs.

Figure 4.4	Form Used to Gather Information for a Competency-Based Job Analysis

Part B: Skill Matrix in a Dejobbed Organization

Job Title: XYZ

8	8	8	8	8	8
7	7	7	7	7	7
6	6	6	6	6	6
5	5	5	5	5	5
4	4	4	4	4	4
3	3	3	3	3	3
2	2	2	2	2	2
1	1	1	1	1	1
Technical Expertise	Communication & Interpersonal Ability	Business Acumen & Decision Making	Leadership & Guidance	Planning & Organizing	Initiative & Problem Solving

➤ The numbers in the matrix describe each skill level. For example, for technical expertise (1) might read: basic knowledge of handling machine, while (8) might read: conducts and supervises complex tasks requiring advanced knowledge of a range of skills.
➤ The shaded boxes indicate the minimum level of skill required in each skill category for the position XYZ.
➤ The jobholder is required to move from the minimum level to higher levels. The appraisal and rewards are tied to this movement.

Source: Feza Tabassum Azmi, "Job Descriptions to Job Fluidity: Treading the Dejobbing Path," *EBS Review*, no. 23 (2007): 8. Reprinted by permission.

The job title also should indicate the level of the job in the organization. For example, the title *junior engineer* implies that this job occupies a lower level than that of *senior engineer*.

Job Identification Section

The job identification section usually follows the job title. It includes such items as the department and location of the job, the person to whom the jobholder reports, and the date the job description was last revised. Sometimes it also contains a payroll or code number, the number of employees performing the job, the number of employees in the department where the job is located, and the code assigned to the job using the O*NET system. A "Purpose" statement usually appears at the bottom of this section and distinguishes the job from other jobs in the organization—something the job title might fail to do. Working conditions may also be listed.

Tasks, Duties, and Responsibilities Section

Statements covering job duties are typically arranged in order of their importance. Sometimes the statements indicate the percentage of time devoted to each duty. The Civil Rights Act of 1991, the American with Disabilities Act (ADA), and landmark court rulings require employers to show that the job criteria they use to select employees for a particular position are valid and relate specifically to the duties for that job. Moreover, the duties must be *essential functions* for success on the job. For example, if the job requires the jobholder to categorize materials or memorize stock codes, these requirements should be stated within the job description. Criteria that are vague or not job related are increasingly and successfully challenged.

An Example of a Job Description

Title: Employment Assistant

Job Identification

Division:	Southern Division
Department:	Human Resources
Job Analyst:	Antonio Flores
Date Analyzed:	1/3/18
Wage Category:	Exempt
Report to:	HR Manager
Job Code:	1117
Date Verified:	1/17/18

Purpose

Performs professional human resources work in the areas of employee recruitment and selection, testing, orientation, transfers, and maintenance of employee human resources files. May handle special assignments and projects related to EEO/affirmative action, employee grievances, training, or classification and compensation. Works under general supervision. Incumbent exercises initiative and independent judgment in the performance of assigned tasks.

Working Conditions: This job is done in a professional office environment with the use of equipment such as laptop computers, photocopiers, and smartphones. Working hours are Monday through Friday, 8:30 a.m. to 5:00 p.m. Evening, weekend work, and travel may be required occasionally.

Tasks, Duties, and Responsibilities

1. Maintains a daily working relationship with division managers on human resource matters, including recruitment concerns, retention or release of probationary employees, and discipline or discharge of permanent employees. (25%)

2. Schedules and conducts personal interviews to determine applicants' suitability for employment. Includes reviewing applications and resumes. Supervises the administration of the applicant testing program.

Responsible for developing or improving testing instruments and procedures. (20%)

3. Presents orientation program to all new employees. Reviews and develops all materials and procedures for the orientation program. (15%)

4. Coordinates the division job posting and transfer program. Establishes job posting procedures. Responsible for reviewing transfer applications, arranging transfer interviews, and determining effective transfer dates. (10%)

5. Distributes new or revised human resource policies and procedures to all employees and managers through email, the company's intranet, meetings, memorandums, or personal contact. (10%)

6. Prepares recruitment literature and job advertisements. (10%)

7. Performs related duties as assigned by the human resources manager. (10%)

Job Specifications

- Four-year college or university degree with major course work in human resources management, business administration, or industrial psychology; OR a combination of experience, education, and training equivalent to a 4-year college degree in human resources management.

- Detailed knowledge of the principles of employee selection and assignment of personnel.

- Ability to express ideas clearly in both written and oral communications.

- Ability to independently plan and organize one's own activities.

- Knowledge of HRIS applications desirable.

Physical Requirements: The employee is regularly required to talk and hear. Occasionally the employee is required to stand, walk, sit, and use hands and figures to control objects. Occasional lifting or movement of office products and supplies, up to 10 pounds is required.

Job Specifications Section

Typically, a job specifications section covers two areas of qualifications: (1) the skills required to perform the job and (2) the job's physical demands. Skills relevant to a job include the education, experience, and specialized training it requires, and the personal traits or abilities and manual dexterities it requires. To comply with EEOC requirements, the physical demands of a job should refer to how much walking, standing, reaching, lifting, bending, or talking must be done on the job. Recall from Chapter 3 that an organization is legally required to make a reasonable accommodation for disabled individuals who would be able to do the functions if they were accommodated. The condition of the physical work environment and the hazards an employee might encounter in the position are also among the physical demands of a job.

The job specifications section should also include interpersonal skills if a competency-based job analysis approach is used. For example, behavioral competencies might include the ability to make decisions based on incomplete information, handle multiple tasks, and resolve conflicts.

4.2d Writing Clear and Specific Job Descriptions

Several problems are frequently associated with job descriptions, including the following:

1. If they are poorly written, using vague rather than specific terms, they provide little guidance to the jobholder.
2. They are sometimes not updated as job duties or specifications change.
3. They may violate the law or union agreements and lead to employee greivances.
4. They can limit the scope of activities of the jobholder, reducing an organization's flexibility.

When writing a job description, keep the items on it direct and simply worded. Unnecessary words or phrases should be eliminated. The term "occasionally" is used to describe duties that are performed once in a while. The term "may" is used in connection with duties performed only by some workers on the job.

To help alleviate the problem of employees claiming that a task "is not my job," organizations often include language in their job descriptions stating that the jobholder will perform "other duties" as needed. Notice that the job duties section in Highlights in HRM 2 contains the following language: *Performs related duties as assigned by the human resources manager.*

4.3 Job Design

Job design, which is an outgrowth of job analysis, focuses on reconfiguring jobs to capture the talents of employees, improve their work satisfaction, and enhance an organization's performance.[10] Companies such as Harley-Davidson and Banner Health are among the many firms that have revamped their jobs to eliminate unnecessary job tasks and find better ways of doing work. As Figure 4.5 shows, four basic approaches can be used to design jobs. Top-down approaches (industrial engineering and ergonomics) focus on the tasks of a job and how they can be done better. Bottom-up approaches (enrichment and empowerment) are more person focused. The idea behind these two approaches is to design jobs so that the people doing them are more motivated to do them well. Motivating people is especially important when you consider the fact that

LO 3

Can a firm's managers control the process of job crafting? What challenges does it present for them?

job design

An outgrowth of job analysis that improves jobs through technological and human considerations in order to enhance organization efficiency and employee job satisfaction.

people—not machines—are the most strategic asset companies have today. However, all four approaches need to be considered when designing a single job.

industrial engineering
A field of study concerned with analyzing work methods and establishing time standards.

Industrial engineering, a top-down job design approach, is the study of work to determine which, if any, elements of work can be modified, combined, rearranged, or eliminated to reduce the time needed to complete the work cycle. Time standards are then established by recording the time required to complete each element in the work cycle, using a stopwatch or work-sampling technique. Industrial engineering dramatically changed how people worked around the beginning of the twentieth century and for decades to come, and continues to do so today. For example, consider the jobs done by pit crews in NASCAR races. It used to be that the members of NASCAR pit crews were mechanics who worked at the races on weekends. Changing the tires on a vehicle took about 30 seconds. Today, pit crews need to change the tires in under 12 seconds for teams to win. The jobs are now done by former athletes who are stronger and faster, work out, and watch tapes to speed up the 70-plus moves they need to make during a pit stop.[11]

4.3a Ergonomics

ergonomics
The process of studying and designing easy-to-use equipment and systems so the physical well-being of employees isn't compromised and work gets done more efficiently.

Ergonomics, a top-down approach in Figure 4.5, is the process of studying and designing equipment and systems that are easy and efficient for employees to use so that their physical well-being isn't compromised and work gets done more efficiently in the organization. In other words, in contrast to industrial engineering, which focuses on time and efficiency, ergonomics focuses on the well-being of workers so as to improve efficiency. Factors such as the climate employees work in, the temperatures of facilities, noise and lighting conditions, and the length of schedules and fatigue factors are examined. UPS developed an ergonomic simulator to help train its drivers to walk on ice without injuring themselves.[12] Even just sitting for long periods of time like office

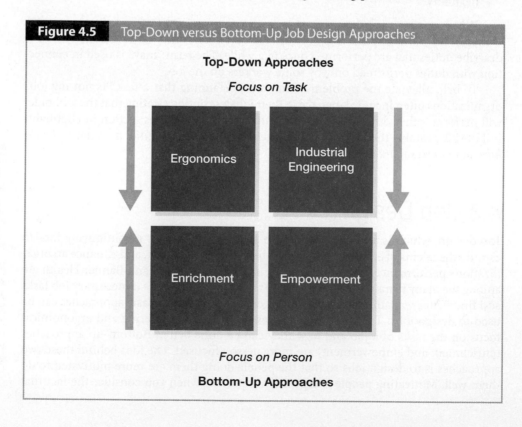

| **Figure 4.5** | Top-Down versus Bottom-Up Job Design Approaches |

Top-Down Approaches

Focus on Task

Ergonomics

Industrial Engineering

Enrichment

Empowerment

Focus on Person

Bottom-Up Approaches

Although not inexpensive, standing desks and treadmills can improve a workplace's ergonomics.

iStock.com/Jacob Ammentorp Lund

workers do can be hazardous to one's health. Doing so slows down a person's metabolism and can lead to diabetes and heart problems. Standing desks and treadmill desks have been developed to help alleviate this problem.

Ergonomics efforts need not be that complicated though. They can be as simple as rearranging the flow of work so workers need to take fewer steps or organizing items so they are within easier reach of workers. Part of ergonomics involves looking at the design of equipment and the physical abilities of the different operators who use it. That could include lowering shelves so female workers are more easily able to reach items or redesigning hand controls to make them easier for women use. Or it could include encouraging employees to wear fitness trackers that electronically prompt them to move around after sitting for long periods of time. Fitbit Inc. has contracted with more than a thousand firms, including Target, IBM, and Gonzaga University, to outfit their employees with Fitbit trackers.[13] Ergonomics will be discussed in more detail in Chapter 12.

4.3b Enrichment

Would you find it motivating if your supervisor timed to the minute each of the tasks associated with your job and then asked you to meet those times? Probably not. Such an approach would get mind-numbing. After a while, you would begin to feel like a machine. In an effort to counter the motivational problems that occur when workers do standardized, repetitive tasks, researchers began proposing theories they believed could improve both the efficiency of organizations and the job satisfaction of employees.[14]

Any effort that makes work more rewarding or satisfying by adding more variety and meaning to a job is called **job enrichment**. Job enrichment was pioneered by Frederick Herzberg in the 1960s.[15] Its goal is to enrich a job so that it is *intrinsically motivating* to employees versus *extrinsically motivating*. Extrinsic motivators are external rewards such as money and bonuses. But most employers want their employees to do more than just work for a paycheck. When people are intrinsically motivated they take pride in their work and want to do a good job because it's interesting and they feel they are making a difference by doing it.

job enrichment
Enhancing a job by adding more meaningful tasks and duties to make the work more rewarding or satisfying.

job characteristics model

A job design theory that purports that three psychological states (experiencing meaningfulness of the work performed, responsibility for work outcomes, and knowing the results of the work performed) result in a jobholder's improved work performance, internal motivation, and lower absenteeism and turnover.

The **job characteristics model** is a more recent theory proposed by Richard Hackman and Greg Oldham.[16] According to this model, the following three psychological states of a jobholder result in improved work performance, internal motivation, and lower absenteeism and turnover:

1. Experiencing the meaningfulness of the work performed
2. Experiencing responsibility for work outcomes
3. Knowing the results of the work performed.[17]

Hackman and Oldham believe that five core job dimensions produce the three psychological states. The five job characteristics are as follows as well as illustrated in Figure 4.6:

1. *Skill variety.* The degree to which a job includes a variety of activities, which demand the use of a number of different skills and talents by the jobholder.
2. *Task identity.* The degree to which a jobholder is able to complete a whole and identifiable piece of work—that is, do a job from beginning to end with a visible outcome.

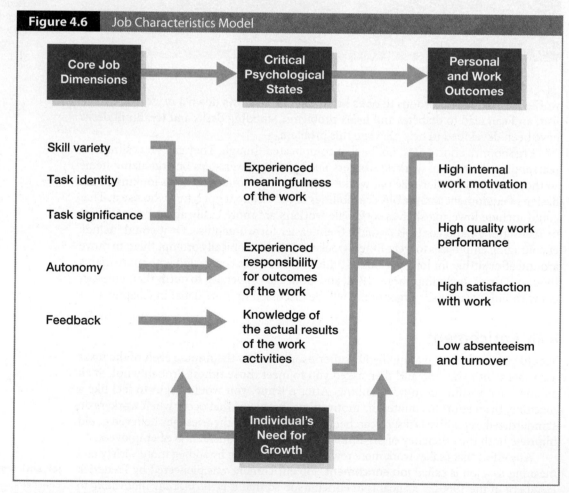

Figure 4.6   Job Characteristics Model

Source: Richard Hackman and Greg R. Oldham, "Motivation through the Design of Work: Test of a Theory," *Organizational Behavior and Human Performance* 16, no. 2 (August 1976).

3. *Task significance.* The degree to which the job has a substantial impact on the lives or work of other people in one's organization or elsewhere.

4. *Autonomy.* The degree to which the job provides a person the freedom and discretion to schedule his or her work and determine how to do it.

5. *Feedback.* The degree to which a person is given direct and clear information about the effectiveness of his or her job performance.

Other techniques to enrich jobs include job enlargement and job rotation. **Job enlargement** is the process of adding a greater variety of tasks to a job. Maytag, IBM, and AT&T are some of the firms that have used job enlargement to motivate their employees.[18] **Job rotation** is a process whereby employees rotate in and out of different jobs.

job enlargement
The process of adding a greater variety of tasks to a job.

Job enlargement and job rotation help prevent the boredom people experience where they perform narrow, specialized jobs. Rotating people in and out of different jobs can also help employees who do repetitive physical tasks avoid health problems and on-the-job injuries. For instance, after a number of hours on his feet, a drugstore cashier might move to the store's photo department and process photos while sitting down.

job rotation
The process whereby employees rotate in and out of different jobs.

Empowerment

The techniques we have described are ones in which managers change the jobs of employees. A less-structured method is to allow employees to initiate their own job changes through the concept of empowerment. **Employee empowerment** encourages workers to become innovators and managers of their own work, and it involves them in their jobs in ways that give them more control and autonomous decision-making capabilities.

employee empowerment
Giving employees the power to initiate change, thereby encouraging them to take charge of what they do.

AT&T and Dick's Sporting Goods are companies that have decentralized their work units and allowed decisions to be made by employees who are directly involved in the production of the products or services being delivered.[19] The objective is to develop jobs and basic work units that are adaptable enough to thrive in a world of high-velocity change. The cosmetics maker Avon empowered its minority managers to improve the sales and service the company offers in inner-city markets. Grounded in the belief that minority managers better understand the culture of inner-city residents, Avon turned unprofitable markets into highly profitable ones. See Highlights in HRM 3 for more examples of employee empowerment.

Employee empowerment succeeds when the culture of an organization is open and receptive to change.[20] Workers with innovative ideas need to be encouraged to explore new paths and take reasonable risks at reasonable costs. An empowered environment is created when curiosity is as highly regarded as technical expertise. Employees also must have access to a wide range of information within their firms and be held accountable for the results of their empowerment.

Employee empowerment won't work without the support of an organization's senior managers though. They set the tone of the organization. If they are honest, confident, trusting, receptive to new ideas, and respect employees as partners in the organization's success, it's more likely the firm will be able to empower its employees.

Closely related to employee empowerment is workplace democracy. *Workplace democracy* is the utilization of democratic principles such as voting and debate to give employees more say on how an organization is run and the direction it will take. The

Empowered Employees Achieve Results

By empowering their employees, Home Depot, Walmart, Cigna HealthCare, Costco, AutoZone, Disney, and Applebee's have reduced costs, successfully modified products, and created new ones.

- Kraft Foods employees at the company's Sussex, Wisconsin, food plant redesigned their work, which increased the plant's productivity, reduced its overhead, and cut assembly times.

- Employees at Ford Motor Company's assembly plant in Wayne, Michigan, saved $115,000 a year on protective gloves used to handle sheet metal and glass. The group figured out how to have the gloves washed so they could be used more than once.

- Home Depot's Special Project Support Teams (SPST) improved the company's business and information services. Employees with a wide range of backgrounds and skills collaborated to address a variety of strategic and tactical business needs.

- The American Airlines "Rainbow Team" of employees brought in $192 million in annual revenue by targeting the gay community.

grocer Whole Foods allows its employees to vote on issues both large and small. W.L. Gore & Associates, which makes Gore-Tex fabric, surgical, aerospace, and other products, asked its employees to help choose its current CEO. But like empowerment initiatives, with workplace democracy, managers have to be willing to give up some decision-making authority.[21]

Another type of empowerment technique that occurs at the individual level is job crafting. According to Amy Wrzesniewski at the Yale School of Management, **job crafting** is a naturally occurring phenomenon whereby employees mold their tasks to better fit their individual strengths, passions, and motives.[22] Dorothy Galvez, an administrative assistant at the W. P. Carey School of Business at Arizona State University is an example. Galvez found a way to make her job more meaningful by doing a lot more than traditional administrative work. She expanded her role by planning college activities and events, preparing special college reports, and serving as the dean's representative at college and business events.

job crafting
A naturally occurring phenomenon whereby employees mold their tasks to fit their individual strengths, passions, and motives better.

To help spark innovation at Microsoft, the company created "Microsoft Garage" by renovating an older building. The building has whiteboards, 60 touchscreen monitors, comfortable chairs, 3D printers, laser cutters, and other gadgets. The goal is to encourage employees as well as people from the community to hang out and to tinker at Microsoft on their own time like they would their own garages at home.

Source: http://www.microsoft.com/en-us/news/stories/garage/index.html

"The Garage allowed us to have our own startup within Microsoft"

One study found that employees who are proactive like Galvez are more likely to job craft.[23] But whether their managers want them to or not, employees of all types often reshape their jobs, Wrzesniewski says. And in many cases, job crafting results in significantly more employee engagement, which we briefly discussed in Chapter 1. **Employee engagement** is a situation in which workers are enthusiastic and immersed in their work to the degree that it improves the performance of their companies.

employee engagement
A situation in which workers are enthusiastic and immersed in their work to the degree that it improves the performance of their companies.

4.4 Employee Teams and Flexible Work Schedules

Do you enjoy working teams? If not, you might want to work on learning how to enjoy the arrangement. Increasingly, teams are how work gets done in organizations. There's a sense among firms that the traditional ways of organizing are too rigid for today's dynamic marketplace and that they don't meet employees' needs. In addition, companies are seeing advantages of tinkering with and redesigning work schedules to make them more flexible, and adding flexibility to where employees can work.

LO 4

Describe the types of teams you have worked in. Were some more successful than others? If so, why? How might what you have learned from being a team member be applied in an HR context?

4.4a Employee Teams

An **employee team** can be defined as a group of employees working together toward a common purpose, in which members have complementary skills, members' work is mutually dependent, and the group has discretion over tasks performed. Organizations of all types—Federal Express, Trek Bikes, Calvin Klein, and Lucasfilm, the producer of the *Star Wars* and *Indiana Jones* films—are using employee teams to solve unique and complex problems and improve the collaboration among workers and their morale.[24] Even the U.S. Army has turned to teams. Early on in the Iraq war, the army's hierarchical structure hindered its operations. General Stanley McChrystal's solution was to learn something from the insurgents the army was fighting: decentralize authority to self-organizing teams.[25]

Part of the reason why employee teams exist is that employees, not managers, are closest to the work that's actually being done in an organization. Thus, they are often in a better position to see how the work can be done better. Teamwork also can result in synergy. Synergy occurs when the interaction and outcome of team members is greater than the sum of their individual efforts.[26] Synergy in teams does not automatically happen, though. Figure 4.7 lists the behaviors that can help a team develop synergy.

Teams can operate in a variety of structures, each with different strategic purposes or functional activities. Figure 4.8 describes common team forms. They include cross-functional teams, project teams, self-directed teams, task-force teams, process-improvement teams, and virtual teams. Self-directed teams are often championed as being the highest form of teams. Also called *autonomous work groups, self-managed teams,* or *high-performance teams,* they consist of groups of employees who are accountable for an entire work process or segment that delivers a product or service to an internal or external customer. For example, in a manufacturing environment, a team might be responsible for a whole product such as a computer screen or a clearly defined segment of the production process, such as the building of an engine for a passenger car. Similarly, in a service environment, a team is usually responsible for an entire group of products and services. Or a team might be responsible for serving clients in one particular geographical area.

employee team
A group of employees working together toward a common purpose, in which members have complementary skills, members' work is mutually dependent, and the group has discretion over tasks performed.

Figure 4.7	Synergistic Team Characteristics

Team synergy is heightened when team members engage in the following behaviors.
- *Support*. The team exhibits an atmosphere of inclusion. All team members speak up and feel free to offer constructive comments.
- *Listening and Clarification*. Members honestly listen to others and seek clarification on discussion points. The team members summarize discussions held.
- *Disagreement*. Disagreements are seen as natural and are expected. The members' comments are nonjudgmental and focus on factual issues rather than personality differences.
- *Consensus*. The team's members reach agreements through consensus. Proposals that are acceptable to all team members are adopted, even if they are not the first choice of some of the individual members. Common ground among ideas is sought.
- *Acceptance*. The team members value one another as individuals. They recognize that each person brings a valuable mix of skills and abilities to the team.
- *Quality*. Each team member is committed to excellence. There is emphasis on continuous improvement and attention to detail.

Figure 4.8	Forms of Employee Teams

Cross-Functional Team. A group staffed with a mix of employees from an organization's marketing, production, engineering departments, and so forth and is formed to accomplish a specific objective.

Project Team. A group formed specifically to design a new product or service. The members are assigned by their managers on the basis of their ability to contribute to the team's success. The group normally disbands after the task is completed.

Self-Directed Team. Groups of highly trained individuals performing a set of interdependent job tasks within a natural work unit. The team members rely on consensus-type decision-making to perform their work duties, solve problems, or deal with internal or external customers.

Task Force Team. A group formed by management to immediately resolve a major problem.

Process-Improvement Team. A group made up of experienced people from different departments or functions. The group is charged with improving quality, decreasing waste, or enhancing the productivity of processes that affect all departments or functions. The members are normally appointed by management.

Virtual Team. A team that utilizes telecommunications technology to link team members who are geographically dispersed—often worldwide across cultures and across time zones.

Typical team functions include setting work schedules, dealing directly with external customers, training team members, setting performance targets, budgeting, inventory management, and purchasing equipment or services. To operate efficiently, team members generally acquire multiple skills so that they are able to perform a variety of tasks as part of the team. Job rotation is also often used in work teams so members can trade off doing different tasks as needed.

dejobbing

Refers to a process of structuring organizations not around jobs but around projects that are constantly changing.

Closely associated with teams is dejobbing. **Dejobbing** refers to a process of structuring organizations not around jobs but around projects that are constantly changing and have different team members. In a dejobbed organization, a skills matrix like the one shown in Figure 4.4 is likely to be used instead of a traditional job description that defines specific work. Hackman and Oldham predict that this type of organizational structure will be the norm in the future.[27]

To be sure, it is hard to imagine a world without jobs. Nonetheless, dejobbed organizations do exist. There are no bosses at W.L. Gore or traditional jobs *per se*. All employees are hired as "associates" and assigned to "sponsors" in the functional groups in which they work. The structure has helped create a culture of innovation within the company that has repeatedly landed it on *Fortune* magazine's annual list of the U.S. "100 Best Companies to Work For." Zappos, the online shoe seller, is an extreme example of dejobbing. A few years ago the company did away with all of its hierarchical structures. There are no jobs, no bosses, or sponsors at the company. Case Study 1 at the end of the chapter explains what Zappos did and how well it's working.

Virtual Teams

Virtual teams utilize telecommunications technology to link team members who are geographically dispersed—often worldwide across cultures and across time zones. The technology virtual teams use includes wikis, document sharing platforms such as Google Docs, online chat and instant messaging, web- and videoconferencing, and electronic calendar systems, to name a few. People and firms working virtually in hundreds of countries worldwide helped design the U.S. Defense Department's latest and greatest fighter jet, the F-35. Microsoft used a virtual team of top scientists around the world to improve the functionality of the Windows 10 Cortana product.[28]

virtual teams
Teams that utilize telecommunications technology to link team members who are geographically dispersed— often worldwide across cultures and across time zones.

Virtual teams do not have to work for just one organization, though. Many virtual teams consist of members from different organizations. For example, to improve workflows in supply chains, it is not uncommon for manufacturers to have their employees team up with the employees of their suppliers and the employees of the retailers who buy the manufacturers' products.

Although virtual teams have many benefits, they are not without their problems.[29] They include language and cultural barriers, unclear objectives, time conflicts due to diverse geographical locations, and members' ability to work in a collaborative setting.[30] NASA encountered an extreme problem of this type when it lost a $125 million space probe as a result of its team members around the world using different units of measurement—the English system versus the metric system.

Navi Radjou, an expert in network innovations, notes, "One problem with distributing work is that you lose the intimacy of talking things through at the local café." To help virtual teams "gel," more companies are beginning to use online collaborative meeting spaces that allow the members of a team to share photos of themselves, their bios, links to the social media sites they frequent, and engage with one another via private chat. Go-To-Meeting and iMeet are examples of online meeting spaces designed to create more intimacy among team members. At Nokia, team members are encouraged to

Online services such as Skype and iMeet allow virtual workers to get better acquainted with one another and have face-to-face conversations across any distance.

vectorfusionart/Shutterstock

Small Business Application

Building Teams in the Small Business Environment

Specialization and employees solely dedicated to well-defined tasks may work well in large corporations, but small businesses can't really afford that luxury. In an entrepreneurial business setting, employees typically wear multiple hats. They need to understand what their coworkers do and how they do it so that the business can always continue to function, regardless of the circumstances. That's why a team environment—where a small number of employees are cross-trained to perform a variety of roles—is an ideal strategy for the small-business owner.

In some ways, establishing a team environment within a small business may be easier because it's so obvious how individuals are contributing to the whole—a key component of success in team building. Adds human resources and management development consultant Susan M. Heathfield, "Fostering teamwork is creating a work culture that values collaboration. In a teamwork environment, people understand and believe that thinking, planning, decisions, and actions are better when done cooperatively." To nurture this kind of environment, Heathfield recommends holding regular discussions about collaboration and its purpose, recognizing and rewarding teamwork both publicly and privately, and finding ways to build some fun into team activities in addition to doing the hard work.

Of course, a successful team starts with an effective leader. Some teams have a single leader while others are structured so that members take turns leading. Business strategist Rick Johnson says that team managers need to know how to communicate expectations clearly, how to avoid micromanaging, and how to build confidence in team members, which empowers them to perform well. This means team leaders will need to learn how to act as facilitators. "Coaching is a skill set that should be required training for all managers to improve team management," adds Johnson.

Craig Wagganer, a speaker and trainer who specializes in team building, has developed an easy-to-remember method for effectively leading teams, which he calls the CARE method. He suggests that team leaders:

- Consider each team member's strengths, goals, and relationship to the team. A good leader will not only capitalize on what the team member has to offer, the leader will help the member realize his or her potential.
- Appreciate each team member's gifts and contributions, and express that appreciation often.
- Respect differences among team members so that conflicts can be resolved fairly and impersonally and mistakes can be handled with grace, not blame.
- Encourage team members, individually and as a group, in their efforts.

Wagganer goes on to describe the ripple effect of a healthy team environment under expert leadership: "When the heart of each team member is encouraged first by the team leader, then the team will be poised to cheer on each other. It starts at the top. And when a person feels encouraged, their outlook changes and becomes one of enthusiasm for the cause and excitement for the team making a positive difference and being successful in its endeavors." That kind of optimism goes a long way in the small business environment.

Sources: Stephane Kasriel "Three Team-Building Secrets of Successful Small-Business Owners," *Entreprenuer* (May 2, 2016), https://www.entrepreneur.com; "Building a High-Performance Sales Team," *Atlanta Journal-Constitution* (January 30, 2014), http://ajc.com; Chuck Stinnett, *Evansville Courier Press* (February 26, 2011), http://www.courierpress.com; Rick Johnson, "The Six Principles of Effective Team Management," www.teambuildingtips.com; Susan M. Heathfield, "How to Build a Teamwork Culture," http://humanresources.about.com; Craig Wagganer, "Team Building Starts with Team Member Building," www.leadershipinstitute.com.

network online and to share their pictures and personal biographies. Gathering the members of a team together, especially when the team is first launched and at intervals, can also help a team build trust among the members and "gel."

Facilitating Teams

Regardless of the structure or purpose of the team, the following characteristics have been identified with successful teams:

- A commitment to shared goals and objectives
- Motivated and energetic team members

- Open and honest communication
- Shared leadership
- Clear role assignments
- A climate of cooperation, collaboration, trust, and accountability
- The recognition of conflict and its positive resolution

Unfortunately, not all teams succeed or operate at their full potential. Richard Hackman (who helped develop the job characteristics model discussed earlier in the chapter) once said, "I have no question that when you have a team, the possibility exists that it will generate magic, producing something extraordinary … But don't count on it."[31] Power struggles, uncertainty about the roles members should play, a lack of resources, conflicts of interest, and personality differences are common team problems. Another difficulty with work teams is that they alter the traditional manager–employee relationship. Managers sometimes feel threatened by the growing power of the team and the reduced power of management.

Organizations can help prevent some of the problems a team experiences. First the firm should determine when and when not a team is needed. It's not unusual for teams to be assembled for tasks that could be better done by individuals working alone or working separately and collaborating only occasionally with one another. To determine whether a team is appropriate, researcher Jeffrey Polzer suggests firms do a *process analysis* to evaluate the work by looking at its complexity and the interdependence of the tasks that need to be done. Complex tasks include projects that are large, uncertain, and for which there are no standard procedures for completing. Interdependent tasks require people to rely closely on one another to execute. Teams are ideal for projects that are *both* highly complex and require a high degree of interdependence.[32]

Once it's been determined a team is a needed, a company can help it succeed by designing the compensation so that the team's members individually and jointly work for its achievements and have the members undergo team training. Complete training for the team would cover the importance of skills in (1) team leadership, (2) mission/goal setting, (3) how to conduct meetings, (4) team decision-making, (5) conflict resolution, (6) effective communication, and (7) diversity awareness.[33] In addition, research shows that teams are more effective when they initially establish "ground rules" for how they should operate and their members should behave. HRM Experience, at the end of the chapter, presents an exercise to set team ground rules.

4.4b Flexible Work Schedules

Employers sometimes depart from the traditional workday or workweek to improve their productivity and the morale of their employees by giving them more control over the hours they work.[34] Fifty-five percent of companies recently survey by the Society for Human Resources offer their employees flexible working options.[35] As we explained earlier in the book, flexible work schedules can be used to attract and retain employees when a company is facing tough times or is unable to offer the benefits or pay a competitor would. In one survey, 42 percent of employers who were unable to provide raises to their employees said they were willing to offer them flexible hours instead.[36] The more common flexible work schedules are the compressed workweek, flextime, job sharing, and telecommuting.

Flextime

Flextime, or flexible working hours, give employees the option of choosing daily starting and quitting times, provided they work a certain number of hours per day or week. With flextime, employees are given considerable latitude in scheduling their work. Often there

flextime
Flexible working hours that give employees the option of choosing daily starting and quitting times, provided that they work a set number of hours per day or week.

is a "core period" during the morning and afternoon when all employees are required to be on the job.

Flextime provides both employees and employers with several advantages. By allowing employees greater flexibility in work scheduling, employers can reduce some of the traditional causes of tardiness and absenteeism.[37] Employees can adjust their work to accommodate their particular lifestyles and, in doing so, gain greater job satisfaction. Employees can also schedule their working hours for the time of day when they are most productive. In addition, variations in arrival and departure times can help reduce traffic congestion at the peak commuting hours, so employees spend less time on the road.

Younger workers in particular want flexibility on the job. A lack of it was making it difficult for PricewaterhouseCoopers, a Big-4 accounting firm, to retain millennials, especially during the busy tax auditing season. So, the company implemented a program that encourages employees to customize their schedules to avoid burnout. Kathie Lingle, national director of work/life at KPMG, a competing Big-4 accounting firm, says flextime is the number-one driver of retention for her firm.[38]

Besides being a good employee recruiting and retention tool, flextime allows organizations that want to improve their service to customers or clients to extend their operating hours. CenturyLink, a telecommunications company, uses flextime to keep its business offices open for customers who cannot get there during the day. Research demonstrates that flextime can have a positive impact on the performance measures of reliability, quality, and quantity of the employee's work.

There are some disadvantages to flextime. First, it is not suited to some jobs, such as those that require specific workstations to be staffed at all times. Second, it can create problems for managers trying to supervise and schedule meetings with employees who aren't onsite when they are. To keep in closer touch with employees when they are working offsite, some firms utilize work-oriented social media tools such as Slack, Yammer, and Workplace by Facebook.

Compressed Workweek

A compressed workweek is one in which the number of days in the workweek is shortened by lengthening the number of hours worked per day. So, for example, employees might work 10 hours a day for 4 days a week. Or, they might work 80 hours over 9 days and take 1 day off every other week.

Compressed workweeks have been shown to reduce absenteeism and make recruiting and retaining employees easier.[39] Many workers like the arrangement because it lengthens their weekends and decreases the time and money they spend getting ready for work and commuting back and forth to it. The major disadvantage of the compressed workweek involves federal laws regarding overtime. The Fair Labor Standards Act has stringent rules requiring the payment of overtime to nonsupervisory employees who work more than 40 hours a week. (See Chapter 9.) Another disadvantage of the compressed workweek is that it can increase the stress employees experience because long workdays can be exhausting.

Job Sharing

job sharing
An arrangement whereby two part-time employees do a job normally held by one full-time employee.

An arrangement whereby two part-time employees do a job normally held by one full-time employee is called **job sharing**. People who have families or want to work part time, and older workers who want to phase into retirement by shortening their workweeks, often find job sharing desirable.[40] After her doctor warned that the stress of her 100-mile round-trip daily commute could shorten her life, Mary Kaye Stuart decided to pursue a job-sharing situation. "I had been wanting more balance in my life, and this was the answer," says Stuart, 63, an account executive in Austin, Texas.[41] Job sharing can also reduce layoffs in hard economic times. Companies with job sharing programs include Sprint, American Express, and Kaiser Permanente, one of the nation's largest health organizations.

Telecommuting

Globalization and technology are drastically changing how we do our jobs and the offices we do them in. **Telecommuting** is the use of smartphones, tablets, personal computers, and other communications technology to do work traditionally done in the workplace.[42] Telecommuting, which is also referred to as *working from home* or *remote working*, is increasing. It is fairly prevalent in states like California, where commute times are long.

telecommuting
The use of personal computers, networks, and other communications technology to do work in the home that is traditionally done in the workplace.

A survey by the Hudson Group, a global consulting firm, found that most workers believe that telecommuting at least some of the time is the ideal work situation. Telecommuting may also reduce stress. According to a study conducted by the University of Wisconsin–Milwaukee, employees who telecommute are more satisfied with their jobs because they experience fewer interruptions and less office politics.[43] However, telecommuters often end up working a few more hours per week than people who don't telecommute.[44]

How does telecommuting help firms? The better work-life balance employees experience can help firms attract and retain valuable employees who otherwise might quit. Telecommuting can also dramatically lower a firm's real estate costs by reducing the amount of office space it needs and restructuring it. At a major publishing company in Boston, employees telecommute on a regular basis. No one is assigned a cube or office. Instead, open arrangement desks and other spaces allow employees to sit where they want when they come to the office. Community areas with couches, small meeting rooms, and a food court are places employees can congregate.

Not all employees have the self-discipline to work alone at home, however. In addition, collaboration and communication within an organization can suffer because employees are not interacting face to face with one another on a regular basis. For reasons such as these, some companies require employees to work at least a couple of days of week in the office.[45] Other companies, including large ones such as Yahoo, IBM, and Best Buy, have curtailed the practice altogether. Case Study 2 at the end of this chapter explains why. Figure 4.9 presents suggestions for establishing a successful telecommuting program.

Figure 4.9	Keys for Successful Telecommuting

- *Determine the Jobs Suitable for Telecommuting.* Jobs that require face-to-face contact with customers or the use of specialized equipment, or require a physical presence, such as security guards aren't candidates. Also, determine eligibility criteria to assess who is or who is not eligible to telecommute based on their types of jobs or collective bargaining agreements, for example.
- *Establish formalized telecommuting guidelines.* The guidelines could cover hours of availability, office reporting periods, performance expectations, and weekly progress reports or email updates.
- *Identify the equipment.* The equipment needed for telecommuting should be specified. What equipment is the firm providing? What equipment is the teleworker providing? Who provides technical assistance in the event of equipment disruption?
- *Keep telecommuters informed.* Physical separation can make telecommuters feel isolated and invisible. Department and staff updates, including telecommuters on project teams, requiring their attendance at meetings, and "chat room" discussions can keep telecommuters "in the loop."
- *Recognize when telecommuting is not working.* State in telecommuting policies that the arrangement can be terminated when it no longer serves the company's needs or if the employee's performance declines.

Sources: Barbara Hemphill, "Telecommuting Productivity," *Occupational Health and Safety* 73, no. 3 (March 2004): 16; U.S. Office of Personnel Management, "Guide to Telework in the Federal Government" (April 2011), I.D. No.: ES/WLW-04-11, http://www.telework.gov.

Summary

LO 1 A job analysis is the systematic process of collecting information about all of the parameters of a job—its basic responsibilities, the behaviors, skills, and the physical and mental requirements of the people who do it. A job analysis should also outline the tools needed to do the job, the environment and times at which it needs to done, with whom it needs to be done, and the outcome or performance level it should produce. The information a job analysis collects serves many HRM functions, including a firm's workflow and design of jobs, its legal compliance efforts, and the recruitment, selection, training and development, performance appraisal, and compensation of employees. To comply with the law, human resources decisions must be based on criteria objectively collected by analyzing the requirements of each job.

LO 2 Job analysis information can be gathered in several ways—via interviews, questionnaires, observations, and diaries. Other more quantitative approaches include the U.S. Department of Labor's job analysis system, the Position Analysis Questionnaire system, the critical incident method, a task inventory analysis, and a competency-based analysis. The format of job descriptions varies widely, often reflecting the needs of the organization and the expertise of the writer. At a minimum, job descriptions should contain a job title, a job identification section, the purpose of the job, the tasks, duties, and responsibilities of the job, and the job's specifications (KSAOs). Job descriptions should be written in clear and specific terms with consideration given to their legal implications.

LO 3 Job design, which is an outgrowth of job analysis, focuses on restructuring jobs in order to capture the talents of employees, improve their work satisfaction, and an organization's performance. Top-down job design techniques such as industrial engineering and ergonomics focus more on tasks; bottom-down techniques such as enrichment and empowerment focus more on workers and how to motivate them to do their jobs better. In the job characteristics model, five job factors affect employees' satisfaction: job skill variety, task identity, task significance, autonomy, and feedback. All factors should be built into jobs, since each factor affects the psychological state of employees.

LO 4 Increasingly, firms are using employee teams to solve unique and complex problems, enhance the collaboration among workers, improve their morale and performance, and make the most of a firm's scarce resources. An employee team is a group of individuals working together toward a common purpose, in which members have complementary skills, members' work is mutually dependent, and the group has discretion over the tasks it performs. The types of teams commonly used are cross-functional teams, project teams, self-directed teams, task-force teams, process-improvement teams, and virtual teams. Employers sometimes depart from the traditional workday or workweek to improve their productivity and the morale of their employees by giving them more control over the hours they work. Compressed workweeks, flextime, job sharing, and telecommuting allow employees to adjust their work periods to accommodate their particular lifestyles.

Key Terms

critical incident method

dejobbing

employee empowerment

employee engagement

employee team

ergonomics

flextime

functional job analysis (FJA)

industrial engineering

job

job analysis

job characteristics model

job crafting

job description

job design

job enlargement

job enrichment

job rotation

job sharing

job specification

position analysis questionnaire (PAQ)

task inventory analysis

telecommuting

virtual teams

HRM Experience

Establishing Ground Rules for a Team's Success

Ground rules—or team norms—are agreed-on formal rules that guide the behavior of a team's members, including how they want to be treated and agree to treat others. Ground rules help teams maintain order, promote positive behavior, and can be used to correct undesirable actions.

Assignment

1. Divide your class into teams.
2. Using the list below, have each team member *silently* select 10 behaviors they believe are most critical for a team's success. The first list of 10 behaviors (each person's A list) should consist of those most important for group conduct. The second list of 10 behaviors (each person's B list) should consist of those that are desirable.
3. Next, have the members of your team select a final list of 10 behaviors from both lists. These will become your team's ground rules. The items can be modified or combined to meet your team's specific needs.

Behaviors List

While working in our team, individuals should:

1. Do their fair share of the work.
2. Check to ensure that everyone clearly understands what is to be done.
3. Encourage planning, including short-range agendas as well as long-range goals.
4. Encourage open and candid opinions about issues.
5. Listen willingly and carefully to other people's ideas, even if those people have a different viewpoint.
6. Prepare thoroughly before meetings.
7. Make team members feel at ease during discussions.
8. Encourage members to ask questions when they do not clearly understand tasks or procedures.
9. Outline the pros and cons of decisions faced by the team.
10. Follow through on task assignments.
11. Help other members when they need assistance.
12. Treat all team members as equals.
13. Paraphrase or restate what someone else says in order to check its meaning.
14. Openly voice opinions and share ideas.
15. Be flexible in arranging meeting schedules.
16. Compliment others for things they have said or done.
17. Be willing to meet whenever it is necessary to discuss a problem.
18. Bring conflicts to the attention of the team and deal with them directly.
19. Express enthusiasm about what the team is doing.
20. Encourage budgeting of the team's time.
21. At the end of a meeting, have members restate their own responsibilities to check for agreement.
22. Be serious about the team's work.
23. Arrive on time for regularly scheduled meetings.
24. Be willing to listen to other team members' ideas.
25. Get the team's approval on important matters before proceeding.

Discussion Questions

LO 1 Assume you are the general manager of a service department. How might formally written job requirements help you manage your work unit?

LO 2 Discuss the various ways in which a job analysis can be completed. Compare and contrast these methods, noting the pros or cons of each.

LO 3 Why is employee motivation such an important aspect of designing today's jobs? The job characteristics model has five components—skill variety, task identity, task significance, autonomy, and feedback. Provide an example of how each component can be used to improve an organization and the job of an employee. (Suggestion: Consider your present or a recent job to answer this question.)

LO 4 Figure 4.8 shows the different forms of employee teams. Provide an example of where each type of team can be used. How do teams create synergy?

CASE STUDY The Zappos Experiment

There are many different ways in which firms can organize themselves: There are flat organizations and there are tall organizations. There are organizations structured by products, divisions, and geography. But one thing nearly all structures have in common is a chain of command, or hierarchy.

Do companies have to set up that way? Tony Hsieh doesn't think so. Hsieh is the CEO of Zappos, the online seller of shoes. Hsieh is a guy who thinks outside of the box. When he started Zappos in 1999, no one was selling shoes online. It seemed like a crazy idea—you can't try on shoes online to see if they fit. But Zappos made the business work by offering good product, free shipping and returns, and great customer service.

Hsieh believes it's not just the Zappos business model that has led to its success. Employees and their satisfaction are, too. To keep workers happy and passionate about their jobs, the company offers top-of-the-line and unusual perks: Good pay, free health care, and employees can bring their dogs to work if they are well socialized. Quirky celebrations and parties are the norm at the company, which routinely makes Fortune's "Best Places to Work" List.

Happy Zapponians and a booming business weren't enough for Hsieh though. He had noticed that most companies on the Fortune 500 list in 1955 were no longer on it today. In fact, many of them no longer existed.

Hisieh figured it was because as firms grow, they become slow and lose touch with their customers. Executives at the top make the decisions, but they don't really understand what customers want, how products can be improved, or have a lot ideas for transforming the business. Lower-level employees—the people closest to the work— often do, but their suggestions rarely make it up the food chain. He didn't want that to happen at Zappos.

So what did Hsieh do? In 2014, he instituted a new type of self-management system. There are no managers at Zappos anymore. Everyone is an equal, and no one can tell anyone else what to do.

Employees at Zappos don't have job titles. They have "roles" and their coworkers are their "partners." They work together in "circles" (or teams) of their choosing. The members of a circle meet regularly to talk about improvements and ideas. A "chit chat" is held at the beginning of each meeting. Everyone is required to speak, which ensures even the quietest employee is heard. A software system then tracks the circle's goals and who agreed to do what and when. "Really what we're trying to do is turn each employee into a mini entrepreneur who has the ability to sense ideas and do something about it," says John Bunch, who oversees the Zappos self governing system.

There are also no performance appraisals at Zappos. If you're doing a poor job, your coworkers will let you know. Each employee gets 100 "people points" to distribute to the members in their circles. If an employee doesn't get enough points, the person may get booted from a circle—like contestants get voted off of the island in *Survivor*. And if the person has no circle to work in, he or she is out of job. Pay raises are based on new skills a person develops, a system called "badging." For example, a person might earn a badge for Java coding or merchandising.

If ditching the old corporate structure for something new sounds simple, it turned out to be anything but that for Zappos. First, there were all kinds of rules and meetings required to set up the system: "Tactical" meetings focused on the workflows, and "governance" meetings focused on hashing out processes and eliminating roadblocks. Second, employees had trouble understanding the new system and weren't sure what they were supposed to be doing. Former managers felt diminished. They no longer had any power or status, and they never would. So much for having climbed the corporate ladder. Writer/editor Roger Hodge referred to the new Zappos organizational structure as "a radical experiment … to end the office workplace as we know it."

Hsieh knew the transition wouldn't be easy, so he offered employees who didn't like the new system a buyout, which amounted to about 5 months' pay. Eighteen percent of the workforce, or 1,600 employees, took it. Another 15 percent or so quit later. Morale fell, and Zappos dropped off of Fortune's "Best Companies to Work for List" for the first time in its history.

Does Hshieh have any regrets about implementing such a radical change at an already successful company? No, although he admits he was surprised how hard it was for people to leave their bureaucratic baggage behind. "In retrospect, I would have probably ripped off the Band-Aid sooner," he says.

Employees say Zappos is running more smoothly now and that things improved after their coworkers who didn't like the system left. The company also implemented a program to better screen and prepare new employees to manage themselves. And reportedly the firm's profit margins are holding up.

Derek Noel, an employee with Zappos, says the new system has let his ideas be heard and allowed him to take on a more substantive role in the company. "My worst day at Zappos is still better than my best day anywhere else," he says. "I can't imagine going back to traditional hierarchy anymore."

Discussion Questions

1. Is a self-managing organization a good idea? Why or why not?
2. Could Zappos have done anything to make the transition to the new system smoother? If so, what?

Sources: Zack Guzman, "Zappos CEO Tony Hsieh on Getting Rid of Managers: What I Wish I'd Done Differently," *CNBC* (September 13, 2016), http://www.cnbc.com; Yuki Noguchi, "Zappos: A Workplace Where No One and Everyone Is the Boss," *NPR* (July 21, 2015), http://npr.org; Jennifer Reingold, "How a Radical Shift Left Zappos Reeling," *Fortune* (March 4, 2017), http://fortune.com; Camille Sweeney and Josh Gosfied, "No Managers Required: How Zappos Ditched the Old Corporate Structure for Something New," *Fast Company* (January 6, 2014), https://www.fastcompany.com.

CASE STUDY ② Are Firms Moving Away from Telecommuting?

Telecommuting has been on the rise for years. According to the Bureau of Labor Statistics, about a quarter of workers do all or some of their work at home. And about 40 percent of people who hold management, business, financial operations, and professional jobs do. Sixty-eight percent of workers say that they expect to work remotely in the future.

But not all firms are jumping on the telecommuting bandwagon. In fact, some firms are jumping off it. In 2013, Marissa Mayer, who at the time had just been named Yahoo's new CEO, ended telecommuting at the struggling Internet-search company. Yahoo's decision surprised people because telecommuting is prevalent in high-tech industries, particularly in Silicon Valley, where Yahoo is located. How could the firm hope to compete for employees in the area if it ended telecommuting? One tech news outlet called it "the worst decision Marissa Mayer has made in her tenure as Yahoo CEO."

Yahoo had been struggling. It's likely that Mayer thought some synergy was being lost by telecommuting because it left fewer Yahoo employees communicating face to face with one another. Mayer had also learned that many of Yahoo's telecommuters weren't logged onto Yahoo's intranet when they were supposed to be and that the company's offices were nearly empty on Fridays.

The memo Yahoo sent its employees announcing telecommuting would be discontinued read: *It is critical that we are all present in our offices. Some of the best decisions and insights come from hallway and cafeteria discussions, meeting new people and impromptu team meetings.*

Shortly after Yahoo ended telecommuting, Best Buy and Hewlett-Packard did the same. More recently, Honeywell and IBM ended the practice, citing the same reasons as Yahoo: Being in the office fosters teamwork and idea sharing. The move by IBM was particularly surprising because the company was an early champion of telecommuting. It published studies on the practice and persuaded its clients that its benefits more than made up for the loss of in-person interaction. The company also developed software to facilitate communications with remote workers.

One thing notable about the companies was that they were all facing tough competitive challenges when they ended telecommuting. Some employees suspected their employers were just trying to coerce them to quit so they wouldn't have to downsize them. However, there may be a less sinister reason: The CEOs who ended remote working may not think it's necessarily a bad practice, but that a firm's HR and other policies can't be set in stone. In other words, firms have to tailor their HR strategies and the design of jobs to meet the conditions they are facing.

Cassidy Solis, a workplace flexibility program specialist with the Society for Human Resource Management, agrees. "It depends on the business's circumstances," Solis says. "And telecommuting is not the only flex work arrangement that an employer can offer."

Solis notes that shortly after ending telecommuting, Yahoo began offering employees generous amounts of time off and more parental leave. "The beauty of a flexible work arrangement is that it matches both the employees' and the employer's needs," she says. And although the company won't comment on it, Yahoo has begun allowing employees to work offsite again. Time and changing conditions will tell whether Best Buy, Hewlett-Packard, IBM, and Honeywell do the same.

Discussion Questions

1. How can a firm know when it's a good idea to implement telecommuting or not?

2. Can you think of any other pros and cons related to telecommuting that aren't mentioned in this case?

Sources: Erika Morphy and Noreen Seebacher, "IBM Reportedly Ends Remote Working as Layoff Rumors Grow," *CMS Wire* (February 15, 2017), http://www.cmswire.com; Laura Shin, "Work from Home in 2017," *Forbes* (January 31, 2017), http://forbes.com; Dee DePass, "Honeywell Ends Telecommuting Option," *Star Tribune* (October 21, 2016), http://startribune.com; James Surowiecki, "Face Time," *The New Yorker* (March 18, 2103), http://www.newyorker.com; Chris Isidore and Paul Steinhauser, "Americans Say Telecommuting Works," *CNNMoney* (March 14, 2013), http://money.cnn.com; "Best Buy Copies Yahoo, Reigns in Telecommuting," *USA Today* (March 6, 2013), http://www.usatoday.com; John Challenger, "Yahoo's Telecommuting Ban Shows Mayer Is Working," *MarketWatch* (March 4, 2013), http://www.marketwatch.com.

Notes and References

1. Anna M. Tinsely, "Jobs Are Left Behind as Texas Oil Fields Turn to Automation," *Fort Worth Star-Telegram* (February 21, 2017): 1A.

2. Rehman Safdar, Ajmal Waheed, and Khattak Hamid Rafiq, "Impact of Job Analysis on Job Performance: Analysis of a Hypothesized Model," *Journal of Diversity Management* 5, no. 2 (Summer 2010): 17–36.

3. Fredenick P. Morgeson, Kelly Delaney-Klinger, Melinda S. Mayfield, Philip Ferrara, and Michael A. Campion, "Self-Presentation Processes in Job Analysis: A Field Experiment Investigating Inflation in Abilities, Tasks, and Competencies," *Journal of Applied Psychology* 89, no. 4 (August 2004): 674.

4. Interview with job analyst Carol Tucker, Mesa, Arizona, (May 10, 2006).

5. Angela R. Connell and Satris S. Culbertons, "Eye of the Beholder: Does What Is Important About a Job Depend on Who Is Asked?" *Academy of Management Perspectives* 24, no. 2 (May 2010): 83.

6. A detailed description of different job analysis techniques is beyond the scope of this text. For those interested in more comprehensive information or job analysis tools, see Michael T. Bannick, Edward L. Levine, and Frederick P. Morgeson, *Job and Work Analysis: Methods, Research, and Applications for Human Resource Management*, 2nd ed. (Thousand Oaks, CA: Sage, 2007).

7. V. S. Rama Rao, "Quantitative Job Analysis Techniques," *The Cite Man Network* (March 4, 2011), http://www.citeman.com.

8. Piers Steel and John Kammeyer-Mueller, "Using a Meta-Analytic Perspective to Enhance Job Component Validation," *Personnel Psychology* 62, no. 3 (2009): 533.

9. Eric Klas, Alexandros Papalexandris, George Ioannou, and Gregory Prastacos, "From Task-Based to Competency-Based," *Personnel Review* 39, no. 3 (2010): 325–346, DOI: 10.1108/0048348101103052.

10. Gensheng Liu, Rachna Shah, and Roger G. Schroeder, "Linking Work Design to Mass Customization: A Socio-technical Systems Perspective," *Decision Sciences* 37, no. 4 (November 2006): 519; Nicolai J. Foss, Dana B. Minbaeva, Torben Pedersen, and Mia Reinholt, "Encouraging Knowledge Sharing among Employees: How Job Design Matters," *Human Resource Management* 48, no. 5 (2009): 871.

11. Jay Heizer and Barry Render, *Operations Management*, 11th ed. (Upper Saddle River, NJ, Pearson: 2013), 396.

12. Ibid.

13. Christina Farr, "How Fitbit Became the Next Big Thing in Corporate Wellness," *Fast Company* (April 18, 2016), http://fastcompany.com.

14. Pooja Garg and Renu Rastogi, "New Models of Job Design: Motivating Employees' Performance," *The Journal of Management Development* 25, no. 6 (2006): 572.

15. Narasimhaiah Gorla, Ravi Chinta, and Tam Wai Chu, "An Enhanced Business Process Re-engineering Model for Supply Chain Management and a Case Study," *Journal of Information Technology Case and Application Research* 9, no. 2 (2007): 5.

16. For the original article on the job characteristics model, see J. Richard Hackman and Greg R. Oldham, "Motivation through the Design of Work: Test of a Theory," *Organizational Behavior and Human Performance* 16, no. 2 (August 1976): 250–79.

17. Jed DeVaro, Robert Li, and Dana Brookshire, "Analyzing the Job Characteristics Model: New Support from a Cross-Section of Establishments," *The International Journal of Human Resource Management* 18, no. 6 (June 2007): 986.

18. O. C. Ferrell, Geoffrey Hirt, and Linda Ferrell, *Introduction to Business* (Burr Ridge, IL: McGraw-Hill, 2008), 309.

19. For Herzberg's important article on job enrichment, see Frederick Herzberg, "One More Time: How Do You Motivate Employees?" *Harvard Business Review* 46, no. 2 (January–February 1968): 53–62.

20. To come

21. Rachel Emma Silverman, "Workplace Democracy Catches On," *Wall Street Journal* (March 28, 2016): B5.

22. To come

23. Judith Plomp, Maria Tims, Svetlana Khapova, Paul Jansen, and Arnold Baker, "Proactive Personality and Well-Being: The Mediating Role of Job Crafting and Career Competencies," *Academy of Management Proceedings* (January 2016), DOI: 10.5465/AMBPP.2016.11411abstract.

24. Feza Tabassum Azmi, "Job Descriptions to Job Fluidity: Treading the Dejobbing Path," *EBS Review* 2, no. 23 (2007): 8.

25. "Team Spirit," *The Economist* (March 19, 2016), http://www.economist.com.

26. Brian Hindo, "The Empire Strikes at Silos," *Business Week* (August 20, 2007): 63.

27. Leigh Thompson, "Improving the Creativity of Organizational Work Groups," *Academy of Management Executive* 17, no. 1 (February 2003): 96.

28. Matt Weinberger, "How the Forgetfulness of One of Microsoft's Top Scientists Inspired a Killer New Feature for Windows 10," *Business Insider* (February 9, 2017), http://www.businessinsider.com.

29. Laura A. Hambley, Thomas A. O'Neil, and Theresa J. B. Klien, "Virtual Team Leadership: The Effects of Leadership Style and Communication Medium on Team Interaction Styles and Outcomes," *Organizational Behavior and Human Decision Processes* 103, no. 1 (May 2007): 1.

30. Interview with Paulette Tichenor, Arizona State University, Tempe, Arizona, (January 18, 2007).

31. "Team Spirit," *The Economist* (March 19, 2016), http://www.economist.com.

32. Jeffrey T. Holzer, *Leading Teams* (HBS 9-403-094) (Cambridge, MA:Harvard Business School), 1–23.

33. Jay F. Nunamaker Jr., Bruce A. Reinig, and Robert O. Briggs, "Principles for Effective Virtual Teamwork," *Communications of the ACM* 52, no. 4 (2009): 113; Stephen B. Knouse, "Building Task Cohesion to Bring Teams Together," *Quality Progress* 40, no. 3 (March 2007): 49.

34. Michelle Conlin, "Smashing the Clock," *Businessweek* (December 11, 2006): 60.

35. Mark Fadden, "Workplace Trends," *Fort Worth Star-Telegram* (February 19, 2017): E1.

36. "Employers Willing to Negotiate Salary," *OfficePro* 7, no. 1 (2011): 4.

37. Rita Zeidner, "Bending with the Times," *HR Magazine* 53, no. 7 (July 2008): 10.

38. Mark Fadden, "Workplace Trends", *Fort Worth Star-Telegram* (February 19, 2017): E1.

39. Lori L. Wadsworth and Rex L. Facer, "Work–Family Balance and Alternative Work Schedules," *Public Personnel Management* 45, no. 4 (December 2016): 42; Kathy Gurchiek, "Good News for Moms Reconsidering Work," *HR Magazine* 51, no. 7 (August 2006): 39.

40. "Have You Considered Job Sharing as a Retention Tool?" *HR Focus* 83, no. 9 (September 2006): 10.

41. Vivian Wagner, "Take This Job and Share It," *AARP* (January 27, 2017), www.aarp.org.

42. http://www.wikipedip.org/wiki/telecommuting.

43. Wendell Joice, "Implementing Telework: The Technology Issue," *Public Manager* 36, no. 2 (Summer 2007): 64.

44. Megan Scudellari, "The Downsides of Telecommuting," *Boston Globe* (February 10, 2017), http://bostonglobe.com.

CHAPTER **5**

Expanding the Talent Pool: Recruitment and Careers

Learning Outcomes

After studying this chapter, you should be able to

LO ① Describe how a firm's strategy affects its recruiting efforts, and outline the elements that are part of a strategic recruiting strategy.

LO ② Describe the methods firms use to recruit externally and internally.

LO ③ List some of the ways firms can improve their recruiting and the metrics they use to do so.

LO ④ Explain how career management programs integrate the needs of individual employees and their organizations.

LO ⑤ Explain why diverse recruitment and career development activities are important to companies.

In this chapter, we will discuss the many strategies and techniques organizations use both internally and externally to recruit the talent they need. The competition for top talent requires firms not only to look for talented pools of employees but also to figure out what they want, determine how to develop relationships with them, and establish the firm as an employer of choice. In this chapter, we will also discuss the approaches organizations take toward helping employees manage their careers. This is important because, unlike physical assets, human assets (employees) can decide to leave the firm. Finally, at the end of the chapter, we devote special attention to the recruitment and career development of diverse employees.

5.1 Business Strategies and Their Link to Strategic Recruiting

LO **1**

This section describes some of the major factors that can affect a firm's recruiting. What other factors might play a role? Hint: Refer to Chapter 1.

Suppose you're an entrepreneur trying to capitalize on the next "big idea." You have developed a strategic vision for your firm, analyzed its workflows, and determined the jobs you will need and how many of them. Now where do you begin to look for talent?

The decisions you make about talent—regardless of whether they pertain to recruiting, transferring, promoting, developing, or deploying people—need to be considered within the context of your business's strategies and priorities. Consider the decision to outsource and offshore work: Most American clothing makers have outsourced or offshored work because labor costs are cheaper outside the United States. (Nearly all of the clothing purchased in the United States today is imported. Just check your clothing labels.) But that's not the strategy Round House Workwear, based in Oklahoma, and All American Clothing, based in Ohio, have pursued. These companies have managed to carve out a niche by selling products with the "Made in America" label to appeal to people who see it as a sign of prestige or national pride. The point of this story is that recruiters always have to consider the firm's strategy.

5.1a Elements of a Recruiting Strategy

Figure 5.1 shows the various elements a firm has to consider as part of its recruitment strategy. The elements include the strength of the firm's employment "brand," the types of positions the company is recruiting for, where it needs them, when it needs them, and who is responsible for doing the recruiting and making the recruiting decision. We will talk about each of these factors next.

Note that at any given time a firm might need to use multiple recruiting strategies. Moreover, a strategy that works for one firm or one job might not work for another firm (or job). For example, an engineering firm might place a premium on finding highly qualified applicants, whereas an amusement park ramping up for a new season might place a premium on hiring quickly. Recruiting strategies and their effectiveness can change over time as well. As a result, firms need to continuously examine their recruiting efforts and refine them. So, for example, if the engineering firm landed a huge construction contract, being able to hire engineers quickly could become a priority.

Figure 5.1   Elements of a Recruitment Strategy

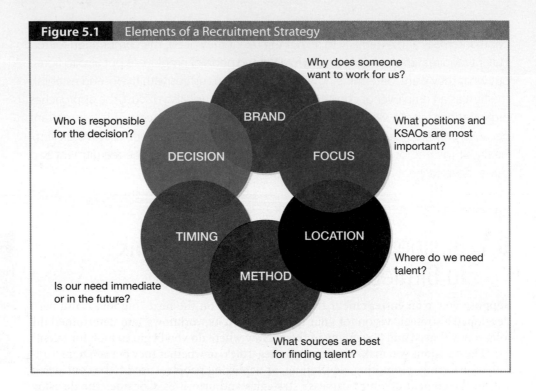

Brand: How Do We Attract Talent?

Whomever and wherever a firm is recruiting, it wants to be *the* employer of choice to attract and hire top candidates before its competitors do. Branding can help organizations do this. **Branding** refers to a company's efforts to help existing and prospective workers understand why it is a desirable place to work as opposed to its competitors. A LinkedIn survey found that the hiring costs for firms with strong employer brands are two times lower than the hiring costs of firms with weaker employer brand rankings. Companies with strong employer brands also experienced less turnover.[1]

So how does a company "burnish" its employment brand? One way is to think of applicants as consumers and focus on what they want in terms of jobs and careers as opposed to what an organization has to "sell" them, says Diane Delich, with the Kansas City, Missouri-based recruiting company Executive Pursuits. Delich advises companies to listen to and reach out to applicants just like they do consumers. In fact, some firms make their customers their employers. A high percentage of the people the Container Store recruits are customers who like doing business with the storage-solution company. "Basically we have mini human resources departments in each of our stores. We challenge each of our 4,000 employees to be recruiters and refer us to great people," says the Container Store's Director of Recruiting Karyn Maynard.[2]

Another way is by reaching out to people via social networks. Firms are creating pages on websites like LinkedIn, Facebook, and Google+ to promote their organizations and careers they have to offer. The sites allow recruiters to strike up conversations with potential applicants on those pages and give them a preview of what it is like to work for their firms. Writing blogs and articles for industry publications is another way.

branding
A company's efforts to help existing and prospective workers understand why it is a desirable place to work.

lukeslobster [Follow]

1,801 posts **39.1k** followers **1,758** following

lukeslobster Traceable, Sustainable Seafood. Roots in Maine with shacks in NYC, DC, Philly, Chicago, Boston, Las Vegas, Maine, and Miami. #tastethesource
www.lukeslobster.com/location/market-east

Luke's Lobster Holding LLC

Luke's Lobster uses social networking to promote its brand.

Using the Internet and social networks is an inexpensive way to brand and recruit. The strategy can be particularly effective for small companies that can't afford to pay for a lot of job advertising to promote their firms and attract candidates. Luke's Lobster, a chain that began as a small restaurant in New York City, uses all the social media tools it can—Facebook, LinkedIn, YouTube, Twitter, Tumblr, Pinterest, and Vimeo—to post photos and videos about the restaurant and its employees and make announcements about specials, contests, and job openings. This has made it easy to recruit great employees, each of whom are featured in colorful profiles on the company's website. We will talk more about social networks as a recruiting tool later in the chapter.

In the global arena, branding can be enormously helpful because locals are often unfamiliar with foreign firms. In India, the firms people work for are very important to applicants and their families. U.S. firms often set up "storefronts" in major Indian cities to promote their employment brands. Candidates can walk in and chat with company representatives about what these firms do and the kinds of opportunities they offer.

Online games are good branding and recruiting tool as well. Barclays Investment Bank has a free online stock-trading game that uses real-time market data. More than 4,500 people, mostly college students, have played the game, and about 8 percent of them have applied for jobs with the company.[3] Philanthropic activities can help burnish a company's employer brand, too, especially among Generation Z and millennial employees, who want more out of life than just a job and a paycheck. The accounting firm Deloitte sponsors volunteer spring-break programs for undergraduate students, who work alongside the firms' employees to help communities in need. Highlights in HRM 1 shows how Marriott lives up to its brand in order to recruit talent.

Focus: What Types of Positions Are Needed?

As you learned from Chapter 2, a major responsibility of human resources managers is knowing what jobs a firm needs now and in the future as well as the KSAOs required for those jobs. Given those needs, the condition of the labor market can have a big effect on a firm's recruiting plans. During periods of high unemployment, an organization might be able to maintain an adequate supply of qualified candidates by accepting unsolicited

Marriott's Recruitment Principles: Living Up to the Employment Brand

1. **Build the Employment Brand.** Marriott attracts employees the same way it attracts customers. Just as consumers buy experiences, not just products, potential employees are looking for a great work experience when they shop for jobs. As the company's founder, J. W. Marriott, put it: "For more than 70 years, we've lived by a simple motto: If we take care of our associates, they'll take care of our guests."

2. **Get It Right the First Time.** Marriott "hires friendly" and "trains technical." It is better to hire people with "the spirit to serve" and train them to work than hire people who know business and try to teach them to enjoy serving guests. Marriott hires cooks who love to cook and housekeepers who love to clean. They have learned that this approach works both for delivering excellent service and for retaining their employees.

3. **Money Is a Big Thing, But…** The top concern of Marriott associates is total compensation. But intangible factors taken together, such as work-life balance, leadership quality, opportunity for advancement, work environment, and training, far outweigh money in their decisions to stay or leave. From flexible schedules to tailored benefit packages and development opportunities, Marriott has built systems to address nonmonetary factors.

4. **A Caring Workplace Is a Bottom-Line Issue.** When employees come to work, they feel safe, secure, and welcome. Managers are accountable for associate satisfaction ratings and for turnover rates. Every day, associates in each of Marriott's full-service hotels participate in a 15-minute meeting to review basic values such as respect and encourage associates to raise their personal concerns. They take the time to celebrate birthdays and anniversaries. Practices such as these build loyalty among associates and repeat business from customers.

5. **Promote from Within.** More than 50 percent of Marriott's current managers have been promoted from within. All associates are given the opportunity to advance as far as their abilities will carry them. Elevating employees who have continually served the company to positions of leadership helps Marriott pass on the soul of its business—its corporate culture—from one generation to the next.

Sources: J. W. Marriott, "Competitive Strength," *Executive Excellence* 18, no. 4 (April 2001): 3–4; J. W. Marriott, "Our Competitive Strength: Human Capital," *Executive Speeches* 15, no. 5 (April/May 2001): 18–21.

---

internal labor markets
Labor markets in which workers are hired into entry-level jobs and higher-level jobs are filled from within.

résumés and applications and from internal labor markets. **Internal labor markets** are associated with "promotion within" policies, where workers are hired into entry-level jobs and higher-level jobs are filled from within.[4] By contrast, a tight labor market (one with low unemployment) might force the employer to advertise heavily and/or seek assistance from recruiting and employment agencies. Keep in mind that the actual labor market a company faces depends upon the industry in which the firm operates and the types of positions it is seeking to fill. In one industry, the supply of qualified individuals might be plentiful for a particular position. In another industry, they may not be.

Location: Where Do We Need the Talent, and Where Will We Find It?
The two primary locations in which to find candidates are those internal to the firm (internal candidates) and those external to the firm (external candidates), each of which are recruited somewhat differently.

Internal versus External Recruiting Markets. Recruiting internally is generally easier, faster, and less expensive. However, not all positions can be filled internally. Jobs that require specialized training and experience cannot always be easily filled from within and may need to be filled from the outside. This is especially common in small organizations in which the existing talent pool is limited. Moreover, in rapidly changing industries there may not be time for a company's employees to develop completely new skill sets. Consequently, hiring from the outside makes sense.

Applicants hired externally can also be a source of new ideas and creativity, and may bring with them the latest knowledge acquired from their previous employers. It is not uncommon for firms to attempt to gain secrets from their competitors by hiring away their employees. Amazon.com was sued by Walmart, which accused the online retailer of hiring away employees who had in-depth knowledge about Walmart's sophisticated inventory systems. Tesla Motors sued a former employee for allegedly stealing its self-driving car technology and trying recruit dozens of the company's engineers for a startup firm.[5]

Some applicants bring more than knowledge to their new employers. They bring revenue. Talented salespeople, doctors, accountants, lawyers, and hairdressers are examples. When these people leave their organizations, their clients often go with them. Recruiting externally in this case makes sense. Reaching an employer's diversity goals is another factor that can lead a firm to recruit externally.

Regional Recruiting Markets. Have you ever noticed that competing firms are often located in the same areas? Oil and gas companies are plentiful in the Houston area. Film and television companies are clustered around Los Angeles. This is not a coincidence. These "business clusters" occur because the resources these firms need—both human and natural—are located in some areas and not others. Many manufacturers have located to the South because lower-cost labor is plentiful there and unions are less prevalent than they are in the North. Likewise, because nearby Stanford University has one of the top computer science schools in the country, high-tech companies have flocked to Silicon Valley in California.[6]

Global Recruiting Markets. To stay apace of their competitors and expand their operations around the world, companies not only look globally for goods and services, but also for labor. Firms aren't doing this just to save on labor costs. They are doing it to attract the best talent wherever it may be. Firms in countries such as China and India have heated up the competition for talent to staff the growing high-tech industries in these nations. It is not just technical positions firms are trying to fill either. It is lower-skilled positions, too. Resorts and vacation areas, and cruise lines are among the businesses that frequently have trouble finding employees to staff their operations and must hire globally.

Recruiting abroad can be very complicated, however. In addition to having to deal with a myriad of local, national, and international laws, as well as visas and work permits, employers also have to take into account the different labor costs, preemployment and compensation practices, and cultural differences associated with the countries in which they are recruiting. In volatile areas of the world, security is a concern. Recruiting globally is likely to become even more difficult as U.S. immigration laws tighten. To help them navigate challenges such as these, many companies utilize firms such as Genpact and Robert Half International, which specialize in global recruiting.

Timing: When Do We Need the Talent?

You have probably heard the saying "Timing is everything." This is especially true for recruiters. HR professionals shouldn't just engage in recruiting when a position comes open. Instead, they need to understand their firm's business strategies, the talent the company currently has by studying succession plans and what it will need in the future, and then translate these into ongoing recruiting plans. Is the firm rapidly expanding? If so, how many positions will be needed and in what areas? How many applicants will need to be recruited to result in a single hire? If a firm waits too long to hire, its competitors may capitalize on emerging business opportunities before it can.

In addition, HR managers have to consider which jobs have the biggest impact on the firm's financial results and prioritize filling them. It may be possible for a firm to leave an administrative position unfilled for a few months by assigning some of the job's duties to other people. By contrast, leaving open a salesperson's position in a sales territory that generates a lot of revenue and is highly competitive could take a serious toll on a company's revenues.

Timing also comes into play in terms of the recruiting process. Some jobs, such as the job of an administrative assistant, can be advertised and filled relatively quickly. Other jobs, such as a search for a CEO, can take months. These factors have to be taken into consideration when recruiting and moving applicants through the various hiring stages.

Method: How Do We Find the Talent?

Firms use different methods to try to recruit different types of people for different jobs. The methods also change over time as technology changes and the sources of candidates change. Recruitment ads on the Internet and social media sites like LinkedIn have replaced the bulk of print advertisements.

UPS needs to recruit more than 50,000 temporary workers to help deliver the millions of extra packages the company ships during the holiday season. Using mobile apps the company reached a broader talent pool. City youths who used to have to go to a library or school to search for UPS jobs and fill out forms once they were hired can now do so on their mobile devices.

Decision: Who Does the Recruiting and Makes the Final Hiring Decision?

The size of an organization often affects who performs the recruitment function. Most large firms have full-time, in-house HR recruiters. In smaller organizations, the recruiting might be done by an HR generalist. If the organization has no HR function, managers and supervisors recruit their own employees. At companies such as Macy's and Williams-Sonoma, the members of work teams help select new employees for their groups.

recruiting process outsourcing (RPO)

The practice of outsourcing an organization's recruiting function to an outside firm.

Organizations that want to focus on their core functions, including small businesses that lack time or HR personnel, sometimes outsource their recruiting functions to outside firms. This practice is known as **recruiting process outsourcing (RPO)**. Organizations also sometimes use RPO providers when they need to hire a lot of employees or hire employees quickly. RPO providers can also be useful when a firm has had trouble finding suitable candidates in the past or needs a different way to tap different talent pools, perhaps to find more diverse candidates.

Regardless of who does the recruiting, they must have a good understanding of the knowledge, skills, abilities, experiences, and other characteristics required for the job and be personable, enthusiastic, and competent. Recruiters can often enhance the perceived attractiveness of a job and an organization—or detract from it. They are often a major reason why applicants select one organization over another.

5.2 External and Internal Recruiting Methods

When you graduate, what sources do you expect to use to search for a job? Conversely, what is the best source, or method, a firm should use to find talented people like you to hire? In essence, these two questions are really different sides of the same coin. Employers are searching for the right employees and the right places to find them. Conversely, people searching for work are looking for the best companies they can find and ways to connect with them.

5.2a External Recruiting Methods

Figure 5.2 shows the major external recruitment methods. The "active" and "passive" labels indicate that some methods take more effort on the part of the applicant and/or the recruiting firm than others. The sources from which employers recruit externally will vary with the type of position to be filled. A computer programmer, for example, is not likely to be recruited from the same source as a machine operator. Trade schools can be a good source of applicants for entry-level positions. Firms also keep detailed statistics by job type on the sources from which their employees are hired. This helps human resource managers make better decisions about the places to begin recruiting when different job openings arise. We will talk more about recruiting statistics later in the chapter.

Advertisements

Advertising job openings on websites, social media, and in newspapers and trade journals is a common way to attract candidates. But help-wanted signs, billboards, and even Craigslist are sometimes used. In countries in which literacy rates are low, radio and television ads can be more effective. Amazon.com places ads on bus stop benches

LO 2
Sometimes firms do not post internal openings for which anyone may apply. Instead, they select someone to promote. Why might a firm do this and what drawbacks could result?

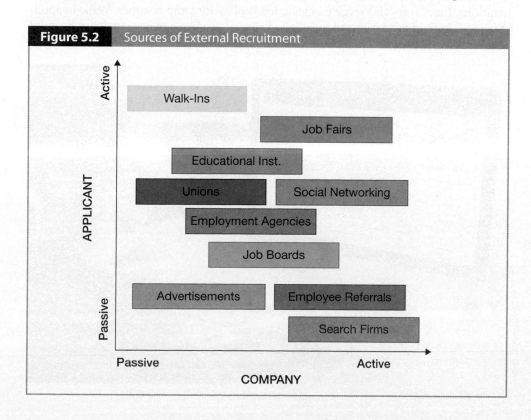

Figure 5.2   Sources of External Recruitment

- Walk-Ins
- Job Fairs
- Educational Inst.
- Unions
- Social Networking
- Employment Agencies
- Job Boards
- Advertisements
- Employee Referrals
- Search Firms

APPLICANT (Active / Passive)

COMPANY (Passive / Active)

to alert prospective applicants to job openings at its distributions center. Job postings that include videos describing the firm and the positions it offers are particularly effective. According to the job website CareerBuilder, ads such as these get viewed more frequently and generate significantly more applicants.[7]

Advertising has the advantage of reaching a large audience of possible applicants. However, some degree of selectivity can be achieved by choosing among the sources to use. Professional and trade journals, blogs, the professional social networking groups on LinkedIn, and the publications of unions and various fraternal or nonprofit organizations will attract different types of candidates than help-wanted signs, for example.

Preparing recruiting advertisements not only is time consuming; it requires creativity in terms of developing their design and message content. Well-designed advertisements highlight the major assets of the position while showing the responsiveness of the organization to the job, career, and lifestyle needs of applicants. Among the information typically included in advertisements is that the recruiting organization is an equal opportunity employer. Advertisements also need to be written so as to attract diverse candidates and avoid bias. For example, because it can discourage good candidates, experts on HR diversity advise firms to delete from their job descriptions (and postings) wording such as "degree from a top-tier school required."

Also, there appears to be a correlation between the accuracy and completeness of information provided in job advertisements and an organization's recruitment success. The more information disclosed, the better. However, even when a job opening is described thoroughly in an advertisement, many unqualified applicants will still apply. Later in the chapter we will talk about how firms go about screening the many applications they get.

Walk-Ins and Unsolicited Applications and Résumés

Walk-in jobseekers looking for jobs that pay hourly wages are common in smaller organizations. Employers also receive unsolicited applications and résumés. Walk-in applicants and individuals who send unsolicited résumés to firms may or may not be good

Textio is a Web-based product that checks job posting for bias. You paste in a post, and the software suggests how to rephrase it to attract more diverse candidates.

Rawpixel.com/Shutterstock

prospects for employment. However, they are a source that should not be ignored. In fact, it is often believed that individuals who contact employers on their own initiative will be better employees than those recruited through advertisements.

Any person contacting an organization for a job should be treated with courtesy and respect. SkipTheDishes, a chain that delivers restaurant food to people's businesses and homes, found this out the hard way: In 2017, a candidate who had interviewed with the company politely emailed her interviewer to find out what the job's hourly wage and benefits were. She was essentially told her questions were inappropriate and her second interview was cancelled as a result. People on Twitter expressed anger after the candidate posted the exchange. The CEO publicly apologized and offered to reschedule the interview.[8] The moral of this story is that hiring is no longer a one-way street: Companies are realizing they need to improve the "candidate experience," which is the idea that to attract candidates (and customers), they need to make the recruiting process a positive experience for people, whether they get hired or not. Not doing so directly harms a company's brand.

The Internet

Looking on the Internet is the most commonly used search tactic by jobseekers and recruiters to connect with one another. Both companies and applicants find the approach cheaper, faster, and potentially more effective. There are tens of thousands of independent job boards on the Web. Widely used jobs boards include Monster, CareerBuilder, Indeed, GlassDoor and Google for Jobs. Staffing experts say it is also a good idea to post your firm's jobs at free association and trade group sites, where your specific talent pool is most likely to congregate.[9]

Specialty Internet recruiting sites such as Medzilla (for the pharmaceutical industry), AMFMJobs (for radio personnel), and JobsInLogistics (for supply-chain jobs) are common, too. "Niche job boards are particularly useful for cutting through the clutter and finding talent for hard-to-fill roles, specialized positions, specific industries—or to tap into unique candidate audiences, such as military veterans," says Susan Vitale, the chief marketing officer at Matawan, a N.J.-based recruitment software provider.[10] Of course, most large companies post job openings on their own corporate websites, usually under a "careers" link, along with information about the benefits of working for their firms.

Other companies are taking Internet recruiting to a whole new level. Instead of recruiters trying to figure out where to place individual ads and when to take them down, they are using big data, robots, and software to do the job. Appcast is software that trolls the Internet looking for candidates who are well suited for positions based on the interests they express, where they go on the Web, and whether or not they appear to be looking for jobs. Job ads then appear on their screens—just like ads for products do when you are shopping online. The software recruiting company FirstJob has developed a chatbot named "Mya" to help recruit candidates for jobs. Mya converses with candidates online to encourage them to apply—or not to apply—for certain jobs, reviews their applications, and can even schedule interviews with them, among other things.[11]

Social Media

As we indicated, to help establish their employer brands as well as recruit talent, firms are utilizing social media websites, where they can create company pages, post and advertise jobs, showcase their company's attractive features, and join groups that target certain types of professionals. Potential applicants can then "follow" companies they are interested in working for. The online shoe seller Zappos no longer accepts résumés. Instead, it uses social media to recruit applicants. By using social media, recruiters at UPS say they were able to access a new applicant pool—namely, millennials—and significantly increase the number of them applying with the company. UPS engages them with conversations with other UPS employees and unscripted "day in the life" videos of employees and interviews with senior managers explaining how they first started with the company and possible career paths.[12]

LinkedIn has become the social media site of choice for recruiters—so much so that it's disrupting the market for job boards, advertisers, recruitment service firms, and recruitment software companies. For a subscription fee, firms can use LinkedIn Recruiter to search its 400-million-plus member database for talented passive jobseekers. Passive jobseekers are people who are not looking for jobs but could be persuaded to take new ones given the right opportunity. Software developers such as TalentBin and ZoomInfo have created applications that search the Web for passive job candidates based on information they post on industry blogs, social networking sites, and so forth.

Facebook has made it easier to find passive jobseekers, as well. Recruiters can create job postings targeted at certain types of people's newsfeeds and contact them via Messenger if they want. Those who are interested in the job can simply click on the "Apply Now" button, and their applications are automatically populated with information from their Facebook profiles.[13]

A potential drawback of using social media, and the Internet in general, is that some groups of people, including older adults and people with less than a high school education, are less likely to go online. A study by the Kessler Foundation and National Organization on Disability (NOD) found that only a little over half of adults with disabilities go online. As a result, relying too heavily on electronic recruiting could hurt a company's diversity efforts.[14]

passive jobseekers
People who are not looking for jobs but could be persuaded to take new ones given the right opportunity.

Mobile Recruiting

mobile recruiting
The process of recruiting candidates via their mobile devices.

Mobile recruiting is the process of recruiting candidates via their mobile devices. People around the world are glued to their mobile phones. For this reason, whatever social networking or Internet platform an organization uses should have a mobile application tied to it that people can use to search for jobs and apply for them.

Recruiters are also using text messages, sometimes to announce job openings and to communicate information about interview schedules and speed up the recruitment process. Text messages work well because they are inexpensive, easy to send, and fast. Plus, because most people have their mobile devices on all of the time, they get the messages immediately instead of having to launch applications on their phones to get to a site such as Facebook or LinkedIn.

Job Fairs

Job fairs can be a good way to cast a wide net for diverse applicants in a certain region. At a job fair companies and their recruiters set up booths, meet with prospective applicants, and exchange employment information. Often the fairs are industry specific.

Although job fairs often attract a lot of applicants, many of them might not be qualified. Another problem is that they only attract applicants in the regional area in which they are held.

virtual job fair
Job fairs conducted online.

One way to get around the latter problem is to hold an online virtual job fair and use networks such as LinkedIn, Facebook, and Twitter to inform potential candidates about it. During a virtual job fair, recruiters man "virtual booths" online, where they provide links to their career resources, collect résumés, and talk with candidates via online chat functions and webcams. Holding a virtual job fair can also be cost effective for both recruiters and attendees because they do not have to pay travel costs.

Some larger companies, such as Procter & Gamble, host virtual fairs on their own websites. Others, including Boeing and Citigroup, join virtual job fairs hosted by other companies such as the job board Monster and Unicruit.com, which is a company that hosts virtual job fairs designed to attract new graduates.[15]

Employee Referrals

The recruitment efforts of an organization can be greatly aided when its employees refer potential candidates. In fact, word-of-mouth recommendations are the way most job positions are filled. (Apparently there is truth to the phrase "It is not what you know, but who you know.") A number of studies have found that employee referrals are the best source of applicants. Referred employees have much higher retention rates than employees who are not referred and are hired in less than half the time as other candidates, one study found.

Research shows that once hired, applicants referred by an employee tend to remain with the organization longer, as well.[16] Some firms have created referral pages on their intranets to make it easier for employees to refer candidates and to track their progress through the hiring process.[17] Highlights in HRM 2 shows some additional ways firms can encourage employee referrals.

There are some negative factors associated with employee referrals and profiles, though. They include the possibility of corporate "inbreeding." Because employees and the people they refer tend to have similar backgrounds, firms that rely heavily on referrals may intentionally or unintentionally screen out, and thereby discriminate against, protected classes. In 2016, the U.S. Labor Department sued Plantir, a Silicon Valley data-mining company, for not hiring enough Asians. It wasn't that Plantir had intentionally discriminated against Asians; it had simply relied too heavily on applicants its employees had referred, most of whom weren't Asian.

Some researchers have found that inbreeding occurs gradually as part of a three-stage trend: According to the attraction–selection–attrition (ASA) model, in the first stage (attraction) people with values similar to an organization are attracted to it and become employees. In the second stage (selection), these employees then choose applicants similar to themselves. In the final stage (attrition) employees who do not fit in leave. The result is an ultra-homogenized organization.[18] One way to remedy the problem is by offering employees larger referral bonuses for underrepresented groups. Intel was able to increase the portion of women in its workforce this way.[19]

Nepotism, which is the preference for hiring the relatives of employees, can invite charges of favoritism. Various anti-nepotism laws exist at the local, state, and federal levels. However, in other cultures, including Asia and the Middle East, nepotism is the norm, and hiring managers need to be aware of it. But even in the United States, nepotism gets mixed reviews, in part because family members are in an ideal position to pass job knowledge and skills on to one another. Many corporate dynasties (Ford Motor Company and the Rockefeller Foundation among them) have been built on nepotism. Labor unions would not have flourished without it. In recent years, a number of law firms and universities have dropped restrictions against hiring spouses on the basis that they are prejudicial.[20]

nepotism
A preference for hiring the relatives of current employees.

Making Employee Referral Programs Work

- Educate employees about the kinds of people the organization wants to hire.
- Acknowledge referrals promptly. Not doing so makes employees feel as if their suggestions are poor ones or are being ignored. Let the candidate and the referring employee know right away when a referral has entered the system.
- Reward employees with something they value such as bonuses and recognition within the company for referrals. Small rewards can be given for candidates that meet the company's requirements but are not selected and larger rewards for successful matches. Consider offering larger rewards for referrals that improve a firm's diversity.

- Give employees the right tools. Make it easy for employees to post or tweet information about job openings to their online network of associates.
- Measure results after the program is implemented and study them in terms of the volume of referrals, qualifications of candidates, and success of new hires on the job.

Sources: Stephen V. Burks, Bo Cowgill, Mitchell Hoffman, and Michael Housman, "The Value of Hiring through Employee Referrals," *Quarterly Journal of Economics* 130, no. 2 (February 2015): 805–39; "How a Talent Management Plan Can Anchor Your Company's Future," *HR Focus* 81, no. 10 (October 2004): 7–10; Susan M. Heathfield, "You Can Inspire Great Employee Referrals," http://humanresources.about.com; John Sullivan, "Advanced Employee Referral Programs—Best Practices You Need to Copy," www.drjohnsullivan.com.

Re-recruiting

re-recruiting

The process of keeping track of and maintaining relationships with former employees to see if they would be willing to return to the firm.

Re-recruiting is the process of keeping track of and maintaining relationships with former employees to see if they would be willing to return to the firm. Former employees that return to their former firms are sometimes referred to as "boomerang" employees. At the accounting and consulting firm Deloitte, over 75,000 former employees are kept track of via an online alumni network. Alumni networks are often hosted on Facebook and LinkedIn or on the employees' former firms' websites.

Re-recruiting is an attractive option for recruiters. They don't have to sift through scores of résumés to find qualified applicants and have a better idea of how boomerang employees will perform. Boomerang employees also tend to have better retention rates.[21]

Executive Search Firms

In contrast to public and private employment agencies, which help jobseekers find the right job, executive search firms (often called "headhunters") help employers find the right person for a job. Firms such as Korn Ferry International, N2Growth, and Heidrick & Struggles are top recruiting firms for executives. Executive search firms do not advertise in the media for job candidates, nor do they accept a fee from the individual being placed. The fees charged by search firms can range anywhere from 25 to 40 percent of the annual salary for the position to be filled. A large number of CEOs are hired with the help of executive search firms. However, newer data suggest that CEOs who are promoted from within their organizations actually outperform those hired from the outside.

Educational Institutions

Educational institutions typically are a source of young applicants with formal training but little full-time work experience. High schools are often a source of employees for clerical and blue-collar jobs. Community colleges, with their various types of specialized training, can provide candidates for technical jobs. These institutions can also be a source of applicants for a variety of white-collar jobs, including those in the sales and retail fields and some management trainee jobs. For technical and managerial positions, companies generally look to colleges and universities. Campus recruiting is a win–win for companies that need talent and schools trying to place students.

Rather than recruiting students from dozens of schools, which can be expensive, more companies are targeting smaller numbers of colleges and forming closer partnerships with them. Employees guest lecture at the schools and develop relationships with instructors, who then recommend students for jobs. Some companies are sending their CEOs to campus because they have found that it puts a "face" on the company and attracts more applicants.[22] Figure 5.3 shows some of the steps firms can take to strengthen their on-campus recruiting relationships.

Work-Study Programs and Internships. To attract high-demand graduates, in addition to offering higher pay, firms sometimes use work-study (co-op) programs and offer low-interest loans for promising recruits, scholarships, and internships. Internships can be a great way for firms to "try out" college students who want to work in their fields and for students to decide if they want to work for an organization long term.

However, many internships are not as successful as they should be because the sponsoring firms haven't thought through how to effectively utilize their interns. This can lead to bored interns who can, in turn, become disillusioned about their fields. Highlights in HRM 3 shows steps companies can take to ensure their internships are successful.

Firms also have to be careful about whether or not their internships should be paid. In recent years, interns have sued companies for wages claiming they did the work of employees and should have been compensated as such or were promised full-time jobs once their internships were over but were not hired. Figure 5.4 shows the criteria that must be met if an intern is not to be paid, according to the U.S. Department of Labor.

Professional Associations and Labor Unions

Many professional associations and societies offer a placement service to members as one of their benefits. For the mutual benefit of employers and job seekers, placement centers are usually included at the national meetings of professional associations. The

---

Figure 5.3	Steps for Strengthening a Firm's On-Campus Recruiting Relationships

- Invite professors and advisers to visit your office and take them to lunch.
- Invite them to bring a student group to the office.
- Send electronic press releases to students and bring them up to date on the firm's latest news and innovations.
- Provide guest speakers for classes.
- Conduct mock interviews, especially in years when not interviewing for full-time or internship positions.
- Provide scholarships to students.
- Attend the campus career fair, even when the firm is not going to be hiring, so that its name becomes known by the faculty and students.
- Offer job-shadowing programs for students.

Sources: Bruce Busta, D'Arcy Becker, and Jane P. Saly, "Effective Campus Recruiting: The Faculty Perspective," *CPA Journal* 77, no. 7 (July 2007): 62–65; Deborah J. Sessions, "Recruiting Made Easy," *Journal of Accountancy* 201, no. 5 (May 2006): 31–34.

Making Your Internship Program a Success

- Build relationships with colleges and universities. Let the career advisors at these schools know what you are looking for and what you have to offer the interns on an ongoing basis.
- Make it clear the type of candidate you're looking for—for example, the required GPA, preferred or required major, specific skills, attributes, and other experience.
- Develop a work-learning plan for each intern. Give interns actual work related to their majors.
- Create an internship handbook or website that includes information on intern orientation, mentoring, executive engagement, project work, and cross-functional activity opportunities. Provide this to all of the supervisors and mentors in the program as well as the interns.
- Set up a system for providing interns with feedback on their performance, preferably at the midpoint of their internship and again at the conclusion.
- Survey interns and conduct interviews with them after their internships to find out what went well and what could be improved.

Sources: Michelle Bradford, "Follow Practical Advice to Limit Legal Challenges Regarding Internship Programs," *Campus Legal Advisor* 16, no. 5 (2016): 6; "Getting the Most from Internship Programs," *Supply Chain Management Review* 13, no. 8 (2009): 34; Audrey Watters, "5 Tips for Creating an Internship Program for Your Startup," www.readwriteweb.com; Jean Scheid, "Designing Internship Programs," www.brighthub.com; Penny Loretto, "Developing an Internship Program," http://internships.about.com.

Society for Human Resource Management (SHRM), for example, helps employers and prospective HR employees come together.

Labor unions have been a principal source of applicants for blue-collar and some professional jobs. Some unions, such as those in the maritime and construction industries, maintain hiring halls that can provide a supply of applicants, particularly for short-term needs. Unions also offer their members training and in some cases apprenticeship programs, making these organizations a good source of candidates.

Public Employment Agencies

Each of the 50 U.S. states maintains an employment agency that administers its unemployment insurance program. The agencies work with employers to post their openings in online job banks such as America's Job Exchange and America's Career InfoNet (ACINet) and match unemployed qualified workers to the jobs so they can

Figure 5.4	Unpaid Internship Guidelines

1. The internship, even though it includes actual operation of the facilities of the employer, is similar to training that would be given in an educational environment.
2. The internship experience is for the benefit of the intern.
3. The intern does not displace regular employees but works under close supervision of existing staff.
4. The employer that provides the training derives no immediate advantage from the activities of the intern, and on occasion its operations may actually be impeded.
5. The intern is not necessarily entitled to a job at the conclusion of the internship.
6. The employer and the intern understand that the intern is not entitled to wages for the time spent in the internship.

apply for them. In addition to matching unemployed applicants with job openings, public employment agencies sometimes assist employers with apprenticeship programs, employment testing, job analysis, evaluation programs, and community wage surveys.

Private Employment Agencies

Private employment agencies are companies that, for a fee, match people with full-time jobs. The fee may be paid by the employer, the jobseeker, or both. It is not uncommon for private employment agencies to charge an employer a 25 to 30 percent fee, based on the position's annual salary, if the employer hires an applicant found by the agency.

Private employment agencies often specialize in serving specific occupational or geographic areas. When recruiting abroad, companies frequently use local employment agencies because they understand a country's culture, labor market, and better how to recruit workers there. Companies also sometimes use private employment agencies when they are trying to recruit many people or when they have had trouble in the past recruiting enough applicants, finding applicants with the right skills, finding diverse applicants, or finding the time or personnel needed to recruit, screen, and hire applicants.

Staffing Agencies

Staffing agencies are firms that hire and place workers in temporary positions. Adecco, ManpowerGroup, and Kelly Services are among the major U.S. staffing agencies. "Temps" are typically used for short-term assignments or to help when managers cannot justify hiring a full-time employee, such as for vacation fill-ins, for peak work periods, or during an employee's pregnancy leave or sick leave. A firm contracts with a staffing agency, and the employees hired are paid by the staffing agency itself and are available to work for multiple organizations.

Temps give organizations added flexibility because they can be used when needed. In addition, the employment costs of temporaries are often lower than those of permanent employees because temps are not provided with benefits and can be let go without the firm having to file unemployment insurance claims. Many temporary employees are eventually hired full time. Temping allows them and the firms they contract with to try one another out before a permanent commitment is made.

One concern related to using temps is that they have less of an incentive to be loyal to an employer and its clients or to go the extra mile to help a company achieve success. Instead of hiring temps, the Hilton hotel chain sends full-time employees from one hotel to another to address temporary spikes in demand. This strategy not only makes efficient use of the hotel chain's staff but also has helped it to develop an agile workforce.[23]

Independent Contractors

Independent contractors are workers who are self-employed and do project work on a contract basis for organizations. Often these workers are referred to as "freelancers" because they are "free" to work for multiple organizations on multiple projects at the same time. Independent contractors can be found on freelance job boards, staffing agencies, and websites such as elance.com. Former and retired employees who want to work on a freelance basis are also a good source of independent contractors for a firm because they are familiar with its business, its personnel, and how work gets done in the organization. Employers face similar concerns with contractors as they do temporary workers. Some experts believe the national security leaks the United States has

independent contractors
Workers who are self-employed and do project work on a contract basis for different organizations.

experienced were due to the fact that leakers like Edward Snowden were independent contractors and not actual employees of the agencies they worked for. Consequently, they were less loyal to the agencies.

As with temps, a firm can use independent contractors as needed, and they don't receive benefits. In addition, companies don't pay social security, unemployment, or workers' compensation taxes when they hire independent contractors. The independent contractors must pay these taxes themselves. However, numerous companies, including Lowe's, Lufthansa, Microsoft, and FedEx, have been fined millions of dollars for misclassifying permanent workers as independent contractors in an effort to cut employment-related costs. To prevent such abuses, Congress and the U.S. Department of Labor have established criteria companies should follow when deciding how to characterize their workers. Highlights in HRM 4 offers some guidance firms can use to make this determination.

However, the U.S. Supreme Court has ruled that there is no single test to determine whether an employee is an independent contractor or not. To avoid any hint of impropriety, companies are increasingly requiring independent contractors to sign up with staffing agencies and then hiring the contractors through them.

Employee Leasing

employee leasing
The process of dismissing employees who are then hired by a leasing company (which handles all HR-related activities) and contracting with that company to lease back the employees.

Employee leasing by professional employer organizations (PEOs) has grown rapidly since the passage of the Tax Equity and Fiscal Responsibility Act of 1982. As we explained in Chapter 1, more than 150,000 businesses and roughly 3 million U.S. workers are involved in PEO arrangements, according to the National Association of Professional Employer Organizations (NAPEO). Basically, a PEO—typically a larger company—takes over the management of a smaller company's HR tasks and becomes a coemployer to its employees. The PEO performs all the HR duties of an employer—recruiting, background checks, hiring, payroll, performance appraisal, benefits administration, and other day-to-day HR activities—and in return is paid a placement fee of normally 4 to 8 percent of payroll cost plus 9 to 20 percent of gross wages. Unlike temporary agencies, which supply workers only for limited periods, employee leasing companies place their employees with subscribers on a permanent basis.

Because PEOs can coemploy a large number of people working at many different companies, they can provide employees with benefits such as 401(k) and health plans that small companies cannot afford. (The average client of a PEO is a business with 19 employees.) The Society of Human Resources Management reports that companies with fewer than 50 employees can save anywhere from $5,000 to $50,000 in time and labor costs annually by hiring a PEO.[24]

5.2b Internal Recruiting Methods

Most companies try initially to fill job vacancies above the entry-level position through promotions and transfers. Internal candidates are readily available, get up to speed faster, and there is less uncertainty about how they will perform. You also do not have to run advertisements to find them, which can be costly.

By filling vacancies internally, an organization can capitalize on the investment it has made in recruiting, selecting, training, and developing its current employees. Promoting employees rewards them for their past performance and encourages them

Is a Worker an Independent Contractor—or Not?

Signs of independent contractor status include a person who:

- Is free from direct supervision and control
- Has an established business
- Keeps a place of business and invests in facilities, equipment, and supplies
- Pays his or her own expenses
- Assumes the risk for profits or losses
- Sets his or her own schedule
- Sets or negotiates his or her own pay rate

- Offers services to other businesses (competitive or noncompetitive)
- Is free to refuse work offers
- May choose to hire help
- Carries insurance
- Advertises in the electronic and/or print media
- Uses business cards, stationery, and billheads

Source: Adapted from "Independent Contractor," New York Department of Labor, http://www.labor.ny.gov.

to continue their efforts. This can improve morale within the organization and support a culture of employee engagement. Promotion-from-within policies at Marriott, Nordstrom's, Nucor Steel, and Whole Foods have contributed to the companies' overall growth and success.[25]

However, at least one research study has found that managers often hire external candidates rather than promote their current employees because they have a tendency to overvalue unfamiliar candidates and undervalue known ones.[26] This may be because the managers are not yet as familiar with the external candidates' flaws as they are with internal candidates' flaws. At other times, extremely good employees are prevented from being promoted to other departments because their current managers are reluctant to lose them.

Research by Matthew Bidwell suggests that internal candidates are likely to outperform external candidates. Bidwell looked at seven years of data and 5,300 employees in different jobs in the financial industry. Even though external hires got paid nearly 20 percent more, they received significantly lower marks on their performance reviews for their first two years on the job. External hires were also 61 percent more likely to be fired. In addition, the productivity of business units and groups with a new hire suffered because it took time for the groups to help the new employees learn their jobs and become proficient at them.[27]

When qualified employees are passed over for external candidates (often whom they are asked to train), a firm's current employees can become disillusioned to the point where they begin looking elsewhere for jobs, even when the external candidates hired end up being very qualified for their positions. Employee surveys and other research show that a lack of career advancement is a major reason why people quit their jobs.[28]

When experienced employees leave an organization they take with them years of corporate knowhow that is hard to replace. Some signs that the firm needs to work harder at grooming internal talent are shown in Figure 5.5. To lessen the chances of losing top performers, some managers actively identify "at risk" employees and take steps to retain these people.

Figure 5.5	Warning Signs of a Weak Talent "Bench"

1. It takes a long time to fill key positions.
2. Key positions can be filled only by hiring from the outside.
3. Key positions cannot be filled with confidence in the abilities of those chosen for them.
4. Replacements for positions often are unsuccessful in performing their new duties.
5. Promotions are made on the basis of whim, favoritism, or nepotism.

Sources: Adapted from William Rothwell, *Effective Succession Planning* (New York: AMACOM, 2000); Victor Lipman, "Why Employee Development Is Important, Neglected, and Can Cost You Talent," *Forbes* (January 29, 2013), https://www.forbes.com.

Internal Job Postings

Internal job postings are a quick way to find qualified employees interested in a position. A small business might simply post a notice on a bulletin board in its break room. Larger companies generally post their openings on their intranet sites. The intranets of some companies alert employees about jobs in which they may be interested. As a position becomes available, a list of employees interested in that position is retrieved, and the records of these employees are reviewed to select possible candidates for interviews. The employees can be electronically notified about interview schedules and track their progress electronically through the various hiring stages.[29]

Identifying Talent through Performance Appraisals

nine-box grid
A comparative diagram that includes appraisal and assessment data to allow managers to easily see an employee's actual and potential performance.

Successful performers are often good candidates for a promotion. Identifying and developing all employees is a role that all managers should take seriously. A tool called a **nine-box grid** is helping firms such as General Electric, Novartis, and others do this. The grid helps managers by compiling appraisal and assessment data into a single visual reference so they can see both an employee's actual performance and potential performance. This can then help managers determine what the developmental needs of the employee are and what the person's next steps within the organization might be. Figure 5.6 is an example of a nine-box grid.

Skills Inventories and Replacement Charts

Recall from Chapter 2 that firms utilize talent reviews, or strategic meetings, to determine if a company has the human resources it needs to compete in the future. The chapter also discussed skills inventories, which help track an employee's education, past work experience, vocational interests, specific abilities and skills, compensation history, and job tenure to see how they can best be used. Procter & Gamble and HSBC are among the firms that track their employees this way to locate capable employees who can be recruited to fill open positions. Along with skill inventories, replacement charts are an important tool for succession planning. At GE, for every position at or above a director level, two or three people are usually identified who can easily step in when the current jobholder moves on.[30]

As we also discussed in Chapter 2, more firms are electronically capturing the qualifications of each of their employees. Companies such as Oracle and SAP have developed automated staffing and skills management software that allow an organization to rapidly screen its entire workforce to locate suitable candidates to fill an internal opening. The data can also be used to predict the career paths of employees and to anticipate when and where promotion opportunities might arise.[31]

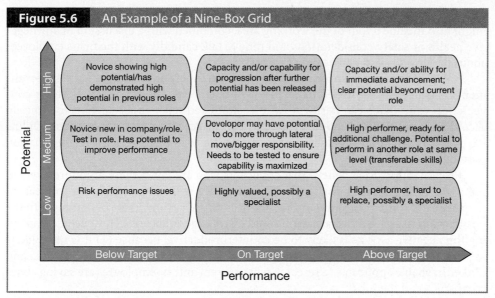

Figure 5.6   An Example of a Nine-Box Grid

Source: © RapidBI.com 2000–2008

5.3 Improving the Effectiveness of Recruiting

How can a firm improve its effectiveness when it comes to recruiting? First, recruiters need an accurate job analysis. What skills and abilities are they truly recruiting for? Have they been precisely defined? Firms often neglect to update their job descriptions, which in turn results in job postings that aren't accurate and the wrong candidates applying for jobs. Second, line managers and employees need to be intimately involved in the process. Without their input, the hiring process is far more likely to fail. Third, a job-starting date that works for both the organization and the potential new hire needs to be established. Fourth, after the person has been hired, the firm should conduct a "debrief" and identify any lessons learned to improve the recruiting process.

Other questions a firm needs to ask itself are the following: How well is a company doing when it comes to recruiting talent from all sources? Are some sources more effective than others? Have the firm's recruiters been able to hire enough employees to meet the company's needs, including key personnel? Are the recruiters slow or fast when it comes to filling positions? Are line managers happy with the process and the quality of the people hired? Are the people who have been hired happy with their jobs and likely to remain with the firm and advance in the organization? HR managers have many tools available to them to gauge their efforts and improve their recruiting. Let's now look at a few of them.

5.3a Using Realistic Job Previews

One way organizations may be able to increase the effectiveness of their recruitment efforts is to provide job applicants with a **realistic job preview (RJP)**. An RJP informs applicants about all aspects of the job, including both its desirable and undesirable

realistic job preview (RJP)

Informing applicants about all aspects of the job, including both its desirable and undesirable facets.

facets. In contrast, a typical job preview presents the job in only positive terms. The RJP might also include a tour of the working area, combined with a discussion of any negative health or safety considerations and time to talk candidly with the firm's employees about the upsides and downsides of the job.

Boeing posts video versions of its RJPs on YouTube. SunTrust Banks cut its recruitment costs in half and upped its retention of tellers with an online RJP. At their convenience, candidates can perform various simulated teller tasks, such as looking up account information and entering customer data, to see if they might like the job. Online job previews can help candidates get a better feel for the work than a written description provides.[32]

Proponents of RJPs believe that applicants who are given them are more likely to remain on the job and be successful because they will experience fewer unpleasant surprises. Yet some companies avoid RJPs because they worry that presenting both the positive and negative aspects of a job could discourage applicants. However, downplaying the negative aspects is likely to be counterproductive, because (1) it is more likely to result in turnover, and (2) postings on social media sites such as Glassdoor and LinkedIn enable applicants to research what current and ex-employees are saying about companies and the jobs.

5.3b Surveys and Employee Profiles

employee profiles
A profile of a worker developed by studying an organization's top performers to recruit similar types of people.

Another way to improve a company's recruiting is to survey managers about how satisfied they are with the process. Are managers happy with the time it takes to hire new employees, the degree to which they need to be involved in the process, and the overall quality of the people recruited? Why or why not? To find ways to reach out to and recruit the right kinds of candidates some companies develop **employee profiles** by surveying their top performers about what they like to do, what events they attend, what websites they visit, and how they like to be contacted and recruited. New hires can also be surveyed to see how satisfied they are. Last, candidates who turned down jobs often can provide valuable information about why they did not accept the firm's offer.

5.3c Recruiting Metrics

As we explained earlier in the chapter, recruiters should keep statistics on the sources from which candidates are recruited and hired as well as the costs of each source. The time it takes to recruit various employees from various sources as well as the quality of employees are other statistics recruiters collect and study. Doing so helps them understand which recruiting sources work best for different employees, which allows them to find better employees faster and at a lower cost. The following are some of the metrics used.

Time to Fill

time-to-fill
Metrics that refer to the number of days from when a job opening is approved to the date a person accepts the job and begins it.

The **time-to-fill** metrics refer to the number of days from when a job opening is approved to the date a person accepts and/or begins the job. Figure 5.7 shows how time-to-fill metrics are calculated. Generally speaking, lower time-to-fill statistics are better. However, a trade-off has to be made between the time to fill a position and the quality of the candidates needed for the position.

Figure 5.7	Time-to-Fill Calculations				
Position	Date Position Approved	Date Offer Accepted	Date Started Work	Selection Time	Time to Start
Engineer	10/10/18	11/30/18	12/15/18	51	15
Marketing Manager	10/11/18	11/24/18	12/16/18	44	22
Salesperson	10/12/18	11/13/18	11/20/18	32	7
Administrative Assistant	10/13/18	11/7/18	11/14/18	25	7
Clerk	10/13/18	10/30/18	11/14/18	17	15
Averages				**33.8**	**13.2**

Quality of Fill

Hiring quality employees is also a primary concern of recruiters. Firms have attempted to develop a **quality-of-fill** metric that measures how well new hires have gotten "up to speed," are performing, and their retention levels. The quality-of-fill metric can be calculated as follows:

$$\text{Quality of fill} = (PR + HP + HR) \div N$$

where

PR = Average job performance rating of new hires

HP = Percentage of new hires reaching acceptable productivity within acceptable timeframe

HR = Percentage of new hires retained after 1 year

N = Number of performance indicators

Example:

PR = Average 3.5 on a 5.0 scale = 70%

HP = of 100 new hires, 75 are meeting acceptable productivity levels = 75%

HP = 80% of new hires have been retained

N = 3

$$\text{Quality of fill} = (70 + 75 + 80) \div 3 = 75\%$$

Yield Ratio

Yield ratios help indicate which recruitment sources are most effective at producing qualified job candidates. A **yield ratio** is the percentage of applicants from a particular source that make it to the next stage in the selection process. For example, if 100 résumés

quality-of-fill

A metric that measures how well new hires have gotten "up to speed," are performing, and their retention levels.

yield ratio

The percentage of applicants from a particular source that make it to the next stage in the selection process.

were obtained from an employment agency and 17 of the applicants submitting those résumés were invited for an onsite interview, the yield ratio for that agency would be 17 percent (17 ÷ 100).

Yield ratios help firms determine which sources produce the most qualified applicants. Yield ratios can also be used to determine how many total applicants a firm typically needs to attract and advance to different stages in the hiring process to fill different jobs.

Acceptance Rate

acceptance rate
The percentage of applicants who accept a firm's jobs after being offered them.

The **acceptance rate** is the percentage of applicants who accept a firm's jobs after being offered them. So, if over the course of a year a firm offers 100 applicants jobs, 90 of whom accept them, the firm's acceptance rate is 90 percent. A firm can track its acceptance rate for the company overall or particular jobs. Normally, high acceptance rates are better.

If a firm has lower acceptance rates or declining acceptance rates, the firm and its HR personnel must determine why employees are declining offers. Is the pay not competitive? Does the firm have a problem with its branding? Are its recruiters, managers, and employees doing a good job of "selling" the firm to potential applicants? Is the firm looking toward the right sources to recruit applicants? If acceptance rates are low, a firm may want to consider hiring a private employment agency to help improve its recruiting.

Cost of Recruitment

The average cost of recruiting a new hire can be computed rather simply. The firm's total recruiting costs from all sources—including advertising, travel expenses, referral bonuses, and so on—are summed up and then divided by the number of people hired:

Total recruiting costs ÷ Number of people hired = Average recruiting cost per hire

The same calculation can be used to determine the cost of recruiting from a single source, such as employee referrals. To calculate this metric, the firm would divide the total referral bonuses it paid employees by the number of people hired. So, if the firm spent $10,000 on referral bonuses and hired 40 people in a given year, the average cost of recruitment in terms of referral bonuses paid that year would be:

$$10,000 \div 40 = \$250 \text{ per hire}$$

applicant tracking system (ATS)
A system recruiters use to post job openings, screen résumés and uploaded profiles, contact via email potential candidates for interviews, and track the time, costs, and other metrics related to hiring people.

When combined with information about yield ratios, these calculations can provide valuable information to managers about the usefulness of different approaches and sources of recruitment. For example, although ads and employee referrals may both yield qualified applicants, managers may find that referral bonuses are a more economical alternative.

An **applicant tracking system (ATS)** enables recruiters to electronically post job openings, screen the uploaded profiles and/or the résumés of applicants, rank them, and contact them via email for interviews. An ATS also tracks the sources of applicants—from the various websites they use to apply for jobs and how far they got in the process—and the time and costs related to hiring people. Looking at this data can help recruiters fine-tune where and how they are recruiting.[33]

Rather than employing an ATS, Google has used reams of data and analytics to figure out why it was having problems recruiting diverse candidates, particularly women engineers. The company also developed an algorithm to predict which candidates have the highest probability of succeeding once hired. Spokespeople for Google say the company is determined to bring the same level of rigor to personnel decisions as it does its engineering decisions.[34] Moreover, Google isn't waiting for great candidates to come for it. It's a search-engine company after all. The company is using machine learning and big data to suggest opportunities at Google aligned to a jobseeker's skill sets and interests.[35]

5.3d Retention: How Do We Keep Our Talent?

The flipside of recruiting is retaining employees. You've burnished your brand and enticed people to join your organization. But what will make them remain with your firm? Turnover drags down morale among a firm's staff and takes a toll on productivity. Replacing employees is extremely costly and time consuming. Yet a recent Dale Carnegie Training study estimated that nearly a quarter of U.S. employees are planning to look for new jobs in the coming year, and 15 percent are already doing so.[36]

Why are so many employees planning to leave their jobs? And, what, if anything, can be done about it? Many managers believe employees leave their organizations for better pay and benefits they can't match. Google offers employees free massages and rides back and forth to work. Some organizations are attracting and retaining employees by offering them student-loan repayment assistance. The insurer Aetna is one of them. Aetna will match $2,000 per year of an employee's payments, for up to $10,000 total. Programs such as these are helping companies retain Generation Z and millennial workers, who tend to switch employers frequently.

But for many firms, especially smaller ones, matching pay and benefits such as these isn't possible. Perks that don't cost a lot can go a long way toward retaining employees though. Flextime, telecommuting, relaxed dress codes or no dress codes, summer hours, and modest performance bonuses are examples. Requiring employees to shut off their mobile phones after hours is another work-life balance perk firms are increasingly giving their employees.

However, contrary to what managers believe, factors other than pay and benefits are usually what prompt employees to quit: They quit their jobs because they think their input isn't valued, they were a poor fit for the job in the first place, or they have too few growth and advancement opportunities.

The Carnegie study found that leadership is the key reason for turnover. Supervisors have to demonstrate interest in and empathy toward their employees but too few do. Supervisors also need to help employees grow and develop, a topic that's discussed in the next section.

Some firms conduct "stay" interviews with longtime employees to determine why they have remained with the firm for as long as they have. What do they like about it, and what needs improving? Human resource managers can then use that information to develop retention strategies.

LO 4

Why should both employees and their employers be concerned about career management programs?

5.4 Career Management: Developing Talent over Time

As a manager or owner of firm, why might you want to help employees develop their careers over time when you can just hire people in from the outside as you need them, especially since they can quit their jobs at any time? Too often firms do just that. Their career development and recruiting are reactive processes they engage in periodically when a position needs to be filled.

Proactive companies see career development and recruiting functions as strategic imperatives and, therefore, as an ongoing process designed to maximize the talents of their employees and retain them. These companies study their firms' strategies in conjunction with their organizational charts, job analysis information, and external factors such as the labor market and the competition, and then recruit proactively and continually. At the Container Store, which regularly tops *Fortune*'s "100 Best Companies to Work For," store managers spend a couple of hours a week identifying potentially good candidates for future potential openings.

Regardless of the source from which employees are recruited—internally or externally—managers play a key role in expanding the talent pools of firms. Good managers "grow" talent by listening to their employees' aspirations, act as coaches, identify their strengths and areas for improvement, and offer them continual feedback. Good managers also ensure employees receive training, self-assessment tools, and information about the organization and possible career paths within it. As you have learned, internal recruiting is highly effective. It also builds loyalty between firms and their employees, something that seems to be in short supply in today's transaction-based labor market.

Figure 5.8 shows the steps in the career management process. For example, to plan their careers, employees need organizational information—information that strategic planning, forecasting, succession planning, and skills inventories can provide. Similarly, as they obtain information themselves and use it to plan their careers, employees need to know what the career paths within their organizations are and how managers view their performance.

5.4a The Goal: Matching the Needs of the Organization to the Needs of Employees

A career development program should be viewed as a dynamic process that matches the needs of the organization with the needs of employees as those needs change. Each party has a distinct role to play in the process.

The Employee's Role

Because having a successful career involves creating your own career path—not just following a path that has been established by the organization—employees need to take an active role in planning their careers, especially in light of how fast the world of work is changing. This includes identifying their knowledge, skills, abilities, interests, and values and seeking out information about career options in conjunction with their managers. Managers can help with the process by offering their subordinates continual feedback about their performance and providing them with self-assessment tools, training, and information about the organization and possible career paths within it. General Motors, for example, has prepared a career development guide that groups jobs by fields of work such as engineering, manufacturing, communications, data processing, financial, HR,

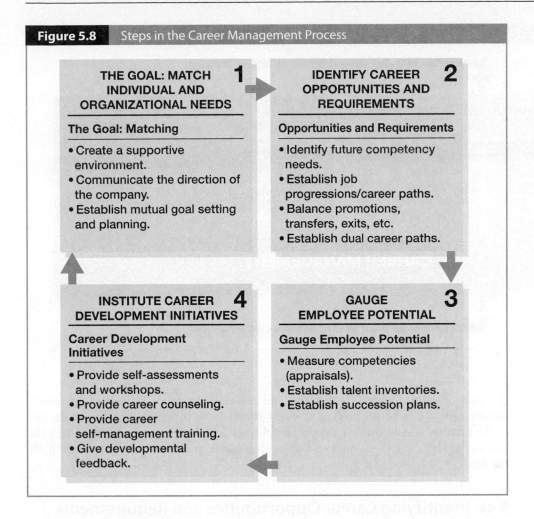

Figure 5.8   Steps in the Career Management Process

THE GOAL: MATCH INDIVIDUAL AND ORGANIZATIONAL NEEDS   1

The Goal: Matching

- Create a supportive environment.
- Communicate the direction of the company.
- Establish mutual goal setting and planning.

IDENTIFY CAREER OPPORTUNITIES AND REQUIREMENTS   2

Opportunities and Requirements

- Identify future competency needs.
- Establish job progressions/career paths.
- Balance promotions, transfers, exits, etc.
- Establish dual career paths.

INSTITUTE CAREER DEVELOPMENT INITIATIVES   4

Career Development Initiatives

- Provide self-assessments and workshops.
- Provide career counseling.
- Provide career self-management training.
- Give developmental feedback.

GAUGE EMPLOYEE POTENTIAL   3

Gauge Employee Potential

- Measure competencies (appraisals).
- Establish talent inventories.
- Establish succession plans.

and scientific. These categories give employees an understanding of the career possibilities in the various fields and logical ways to move from one area into another.

The Organization's Role: Establishing a Favorable Career Development Climate

Ideally, senior line managers and HR department managers should work together to design and implement a career development system that reflects the goals and culture of the organization. Says Karyn Maynard of the Container Store: "There is constant, consistent communication with management on growth opportunities. Rather than follow one career path, the company works to leverage employees' talents for new and different roles, as well as giving them as much exposure as possible to other positions and responsibilities in the company to ensure they're challenged."[37]

Blending the Goals of Individual Employees with the Goals of the Organization

As Figure 5.9 shows, the organization's goals and needs should be linked with the individual career needs of its employees in a way that improves the effectiveness of workers and their satisfaction as well as achieves the firm's strategic objectives. For example, if

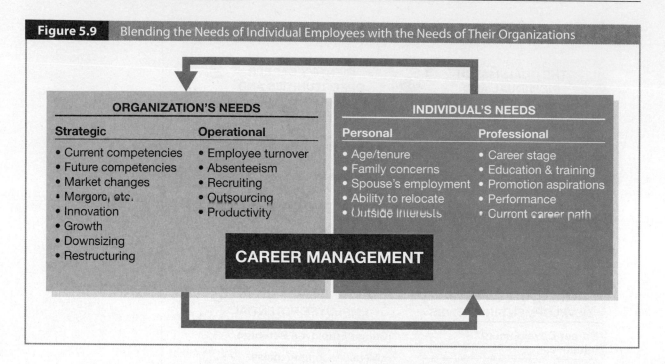

Figure 5.9   Blending the Needs of Individual Employees with the Needs of Their Organizations

the technology of a business is changing and new skills are needed, will the firm retrain its employees to meet this need or hire new talent? Is there growth, stability, or decline in the number of employees needed? If employees don't have a good understanding the goals of their firms, they could end up setting career goals that are a poor match for the firm.

5.4b Identifying Career Opportunities and Requirements

To identify career opportunities and requirements managers have to continually analyze the competencies required for jobs, progression among related jobs, and supply of ready (and potential) talent available to fill those jobs. In Chapter 4, we discussed a variety of ways this can be done, such as via questionnaires and interviews. Informal discussion with different groups, such as new employees, managers, longtime employees, minority employees, and technical and professional employees, is another way. Identifying the needs and problems of these groups provides the starting point for the organization's career development efforts.

Begin with a Competency Analysis

In Chapter 4, we also discussed how firms analyze jobs carefully to identify and assign weights to the knowledge and skills that each one requires. The system one major retailer uses measures three basic competencies for each job: knowhow, problem-solving, and accountability. Knowhow is broken down into three types of job knowledge: technical, managerial, and human relations. Problem-solving and accountability also have several dimensions. Scores for each of these three major competencies are assigned to each job, and a total value is computed for each job. This information is then used to make certain that a transfer to a different job provides an employee with the following experiences:

(1) an increase in at least one skill area on each new assignment, (2) an increase of at least 10 percent in total points on each new assignment, and (3) assignments in several different functional areas.[38]

Identify Job Progressions and Career Paths

Once the skill demands of jobs are identified and weighted according to their importance, it is then possible to plan **job progressions**. A new employee with no experience is typically assigned to a "starting job." After a period of time in that job, the employee can be promoted to one that requires more knowledge and/or skill. While most organizations concentrate on developing job progressions for managerial, professional, and technical jobs, progressions can and should be developed for all categories of jobs.

Job progressions then can serve as a basis for developing **career paths**—the lines of advancement within an organization—for individuals. Figure 5.10 illustrates a typical advancement for an HR associate for a large multinational corporation.

Career development and planning systems were once primarily focused on promotions. However, in today's flatter organizations and more dynamic work environment, an individual's career advancement can move along several different paths via promotions, transfers, demotions, and even exits. A **promotion** is a change of assignment to a job at a higher level in the organization. The new job normally provides an increase in pay and status and demands more skill or carries more responsibility. To retain employees and improve their promotability, many larger firms offer to reimburse employees for getting advanced degrees and remaining with the company for a certain period of time. "Corporate universities"—special facilities where employees receive training—are also utilized. (We will talk more about these programs in Chapter 7.)

In flatter organizations, there are fewer promotional opportunities, so many individuals find career advancement through lateral moves. A **transfer** occurs when an employee is placed in another job for which the duties, responsibilities, status, and pay and benefits

job progressions
The hierarchy of jobs a new employee might experience, ranging from a starting job to jobs that successively require more knowledge and/ or skill.

career paths
Lines of advancement in an occupational field within an organization.

promotion
A change of assignment to a job at a higher level in the organization.

transfer
The placement of an employee in another job for which the duties, responsibilities, status, and pay and benefits are approximately equal to those of the previous job the person held.

Figure 5.10 Typical Line of Advancement in HR Management

				Vice president, HR
			Corporate HR director	
		Corporate HR manager	Division HR director	
		Asst. division HR director		
	Regional HR manager	Plant HR manager		
	Asst. plant HR manager			
Regional HR associate	HR supervisor			
HR associate				

Career Path of Jeff Bezos, Founder of Amazon.com

1986—Graduated from Princeton University with a B.S. in electrical engineering and computer science

1986—Hired by Fitel, a telecommunications and information technology firm that created software for tracking international stock trades

1988—Hired by Bankers Trust, Co., a financial firm that specialized in risk management utilizing new sophisticated computer systems

1990—Promoted to vice president

1990—Hired by D.E. Shaw, an investment and hedge fund company

1992—Promoted to senior vice president

1995—Founded Amazon.com

---

are approximately equal to those of the previous job he or she held (although as an incentive to make a transfer, organizations sometimes offer transferred employees small pay increases). Individuals who look forward to change or want a chance to learn more about their organizations and obtain different skills often seek out transfers. Frequently these employees do so to augment their skills so they will be more promotable in the future.

A transfer sometimes requires the employee to change work group, workplace, work shift, or organizational unit; it may even necessitate moving to another geographic area. Thus, transfers make it possible for an organization to place its employees in jobs where there is a greater need for their services and where they can acquire new knowledge and skills.

demotion
A downward transfer that moves an individual into a lower-level job that can provide developmental opportunities.

A downward transfer, or **demotion**, moves an individual into a lower-level job that can provide developmental opportunities. Although a demotion is ordinarily considered unfavorable, some individuals actually may request it to return to their "technical roots." Engineers and computer programmers who get promoted to managers but end up missing their former jobs are examples. It is also not uncommon for organizations to appoint temporary leaders (especially in team environments) to positions with the understanding that they will eventually return to their former jobs.

Transfers, promotions, and demotions require individuals to adjust to new job demands and usually to a different work environment. A transfer that involves moving to a new location within the United States or abroad requires the person to not only adapt to a new work environment but to new living conditions. Employees with families have the added responsibility of helping family members adjust to the new living arrangements. Even though some employers provide all types of relocation services—including covering moving expenses, help selling a home, and providing cultural orientation and language training—there is always some loss in the employee's productivity during the relocation process. Pretransfer training, whether it's related to job skills or to the lifestyle changes required is one of the most effective ways to reduce lost productivity.

Of course, many employees choose to exit their organizations as part of their career development. When a person's career opportunities within a firm are limited and his or her skills are in demand externally, the best career options could be for the individual to switch companies or to work as a freelancer, consultant, or entrepreneur. Although some employees leave voluntarily, other employees are forced to leave. Larger organizations often provide **outplacement services** to help terminated employees find jobs elsewhere.

outplacement services
Services provided by organizations to help terminated employees find a new job.

Rather than laying off employees if it can help it, Scripps Health, a California-based hospital group, has created a career center for workers who might otherwise lose their jobs.[39]

(See Case Study 1 at the end of the chapter.) However, even with the best career planning, it is almost impossible for people to have perfect certainty about where their careers are going. People change over time, and because of that, their needs and interests change. Moreover, successful career paths often do not proceed in a lockstep manner. As Highlights in HRM 5 mentions, before founding Amazon.com, Jeff Bezos spent a number of years in the financial industry. In terms of their career advancements, many people note that they were either "in the right place at the right time" or carved out entirely new career paths for themselves.

Track Employees' Career Stages

A person's knowledge, skills, abilities, and attitudes as well as career aspirations change with age and maturity. The challenges and frustrations people face at the same stages in their careers are remarkably similar. A model describing these stages is shown in Figure 5.11. The stages are (1) preparation for work, (2) organizational entry, (3) early career, (4) midcareer, and (5) late career. The typical age range and the major tasks of each stage are also presented in the figure.

The first stage—preparation for work—encompasses the period prior to entering an organization, often extending until age 25. It is a period in which individuals must acquire the knowledge, abilities, and skills they need to compete in the marketplace. The second stage, typically from ages 18 to 25, is devoted to soliciting job offers and selecting

Figure 5.11	Stages of Career Development

Stage 5: Late Career (ages 55–retirement):

Continue to improve one's productivity, mentor other employees, and prepare for retirement.

Stage 4: Midcareer (ages 40–55):

Reappraise early career and early adulthood goals, reaffirm or modify goals, continue to improve one's productivity, and mentor other employees.

Stage 3: Early Career (ages 25–40):

Learn job, learn organizational rules and norms, fit into chosen occupation and organization, increase competence, pursue goals.

Stage 2: Organizational Entry (ages 18–25):

Obtain job offer(s) from desired organization(s), select appropriate job based on complete and accurate information.

Stage 1: Preparation for Work (ages 0–25):

Develop occupational self-image, assess alternative occupations, develop initial occupational choice, pursue necessary education.

Small Business Application

Small Companies Often Offer Big Rewards

Many new grads and seasoned professionals alike are choosing to work for less-than-500-employee firms because of the many advantages they offer, and smaller firms are welcoming these workers with open arms. For midterm and advanced career professionals, a smaller company often means jumping straight into the limelight. The change is rejuvenating because they find themselves taking on more diverse responsibilities, getting involved in new arenas, and seeing more clearly how their own efforts impact the company's results. "You are more likely to be listened to, and to feel that you are an important part of the company and that your ideas really matter," says Lindsey Pollak, a management expert of next-generation career trends. That's what happened to Mike Barnes, a logistics executive who went to work at Halton Co., a construction equipment provider in Portland, Oregon. Barnes says the closer connection to the mission of the business gave him a level of job satisfaction he had not felt in a long time.

However, employees who opt for working in a small firm cannot expect to find everything they might get in a larger corporation. Tighter budgets mean smaller companies sometimes cannot afford to pay salaries equal to those of big firms, and they often cannot provide the support systems or perks, like generous expense accounts, hefty bonuses, and company-paid smartphones. But many small employers provide alluring trade-offs such as shorter workweeks, less travel, and work-life balance incentives, including telecommuting and flextime.

Where people decide to work really comes down to determining how they are going to meet their career and life goals. Notes management author and analyst Tony Jacowski, "Your choice of organization should be based on the quality of work experience you will gain rather than the size of the organization."

Sources: Michael Mazzeo, Paul Oyer, and Scott Schaefer, "What Small Businesses Do Better than Corporate America," *Fortune* (June 10, 2014), http://www.fortune.com; Sarah E. Needleman, "Moving to a Small Company Can Lead to Big Rewards," *Wall Street Journal* (March 5, 2008), http://online.wsj.com; Lindsey Pollak, "The Advantages of Working for a Small Company," http://www.lindseypollak.com; Tony Jacowski, "Benefits of Working in a Small Company vs a Corporation," http://ezinearticles.com; Jacqueline Parks, "The Benefits of Working for a Small Business," http://www.associatedcontent.com.

appropriate jobs. During this period, a person might also be involved in preparing for work. The next three stages entail fitting into a chosen occupation and organization(s), modifying one's goals, continuing to improve one's productivity, helping groom other employees, and finally preparing for retirement.

Offer Different Career Paths

As we have indicated, one of the ironies of organizations is that people in technical careers—successful engineers, scientists, and so on—are often promoted right out of their area of specialization into management. Instead of doing what they are good at, they end up in jobs they aren't well suited for or don't enjoy.

The solution has been to develop *dual career paths*, or tracks, that provide for progression in special areas such as information technology, finance, marketing, and engineering, with compensation that is comparable to that received by managers at different levels. As we explained in Chapter 2, Microsoft offers software engineers both a management-focused and technical-specialist career track and allows them to move back and forth between the two.

Fast-track programs are another way to give employees exposure to different types of jobs, particularly younger employees with high potential who seek meaningful training assignments whom a firm is trying to retain. In fast-track programs, "HIPOs" (high-potential employees) progress rapidly through a number of managerial positions designed to expose them to different functions within the organization. GE has an intensive two-year program of this type. Employees in the program might, for example, spend a number of months in the company's energy division in Atlanta, its aviation division in Cincinnati, and in Brazil working for GE's oil and gas division.

However, proactive companies try to make the most of *all* of their talent rather than just high-potential employees. It's not uncommon for an employee to do poorly in one position but be an excellent fit for another, or an employee who is burned out to be reinvigorated by a different job role.

One way to help rank-and-file employees learn new skills, identify new roles they might aim for in the future, and retain them is by allowing them to exchange or swap jobs. Virgin America and PricewaterhouseCoopers have programs that allow flight attendants and junior staffers, respectively, to swap jobs with their counterparts in the United States and Australia. BNSF Railway allows employees to switch jobs in different areas and in different locales. The swaps are referred to as "career development moves."[40]

5.4c Career Development Initiatives

Workers today are not waiting to get laid off. They are taking charge of planning their career paths and getting the skills and development they need to go from one job (and employer) to the next. Employers who understand this trend can take preemptive action by having career conversations with employees and implementing career management programs to prevent them from leaving. Next, let's look at some of them.[41]

Career Counseling

A key part of developing your talent pool is talking to your employees about their current job activities and performance, personal and career interests and goals, personal skills, and suitable career development objectives. This can be provided by HR staff members, managers and supervisors, or outside consultants. Often it is done as part of the performance appraisals. Once the conversation has begun, how those goals can be achieved and fit in with the organization's goals can be discussed and a career "action" plan for the employees established. The telecommunications company Verizon has rolled out a program whereby career advisors counsel employees one on one and hold periodic webinars and workshops about the career and education opportunities the company offers. The firm also has an online career center with careers maps to help employees chart possible job progressions.[42]

Some organizations have instituted "career self-management" programs to help employees learn to continuously gather feedback and information about themselves and their careers. Employees typically undertake self-assessments to increase their awareness of their own career attitudes and values and attend workshops. In addition, they are encouraged to widen their viewpoint beyond the next company promotion to broader opportunities in the marketplace, attend conferences, and develop good long-term relationships with their bosses and colleagues. General Electric has developed an extensive set of career development programs to help employees explore life issues that affect career decisions.[43]

Mentoring Programs

People often mention coworkers who positively influenced them early on in their careers. Individuals who coach, advise, and encourage employees of a lesser rank are called **mentors**. Millennials consistently say they want coaching and feedback. When Deloitte surveyed millennials, it found the ones who planned to stay with their employers more than 5 years were twice as likely to have a mentor as those who did not.[44]

mentors
Individuals who coach, advise, and encourage employees of a lesser rank.

Myths about Mentors

- *Mentors exist only for career development.* Sometimes the mentor focuses on formal career development. Sometimes the mentor is teacher, counselor, and friend.

- *You need only one mentor.* We can have multiple mentors in our lives. Different mentors provide different things.

- *Mentoring is a one-way process.* Learning flows both ways. The mentor often learns from the protégé, so the growth is reciprocal.

- *A mentor has to be older than the protégé.* Age does not matter. Experience and wisdom matter.

- A mentor has to be the same gender and race as the protégé. Seek mentors who are different from you.

- *Mentor relationships just happen.* Being in the right place at the right time can help, but don't be afraid to actively seek a mentor.

- *High-profile people make the best mentors.* Prestige and success can help, but good mentors are people who challenge you according to your needs, readiness, and aspirations.

- *Once a mentor, always a mentor.* Over time, the mentor should let the protégé go his or her own way but maintain contact. The relationship changes over time.

reverse mentoring
A program whereby younger employees are called on to mentor older employees and executives about social media trends, new technology, and marketplace trends.

Mentors need not be more senior employees, however. **Reverse mentoring** is a program whereby younger employees are called on to mentor older employees and executives about social media trends, new technology, and marketplace trends. Hewlett-Packard, Cisco, and the advertising agency Ogilvy & Mather are among the companies that have implemented reverse mentoring. Spencer Osborn, an executive with Ogilvy and Mather, said his younger mentors helped him jazz up his Twitter posts, which had a reputation for being boring. At Cisco, when the word got out that some executives had younger mentors, other executives wanted mentors, too. Reverse mentoring programs help younger employees feel valued and "heard" and can increase their retention.[45]

Mentoring relationships don't have to be formal though. Informal mentoring goes on daily within every type of organization. Generally, the mentor initiates the relationship, but sometimes an employee will approach a potential mentor for advice. Most mentoring relationships develop over time on an informal basis. They frequently end that way, too. A study of 15 high-ranking executive women found that although many of them lacked formal mentors, they had successfully engaged in a kind of "360-degree" networking: The women made it a point to form and maintain relationships with people above, below, and at the same level as themselves, which helped advance their careers.[46] Highlights in HRM 6 shows some of the myths about mentoring relations. Highlights in HRM 7 shows how, as an employee you can take the initiative to form a relationship with a mentor, even if your firm doesn't have a formal mentoring program.

Not surprisingly, mentoring and networking are being done electronically. "A lot of our people work virtually, and [electronic] mentoring can erase geographic and business-unit borders," explained one IBM manager.[47] At Rockwell Collins, a communication and aviation electronics company, nearly 6,000 employees utilize an e-mentoring software solution. The software can connect to a firm's existing talent management software, gauge competency gaps, and match mentors and mentees based upon their knowledge and learning needs.[48]

Establishing a Relationship with a Mentor

1. *Research the person's background.* The more you know about your potential mentor, the easier it will be to approach him or her and establish a relationship that will work for both of you.

2. *Make contact with the person.* Introduce yourself or have a mutual friend or acquaintance do it. Alternately, get involved with your potential mentor in business settings. That will help the mentor see your skills in action.

3. *Request help on a particular matter.* Let the mentor know that you admire him or her, and ask for help in that arena. For example, you might say, "You're good at dealing with customers. Would it be ok if I came to you for advice on my customers from time to time?"

4. *Consider what you can offer in exchange.* Mentoring is a two-way street. If you can do something for your potential mentor then, by all means, tell him or her.

5. *Arrange a meeting.* Prepare a list of questions for the meeting. Listen closely.

6. *Follow up.* Try some of your potential mentor's suggestions and share the results. *Ask to meet on an ongoing basis.* Express appreciation and suggest that you meet with your mentor regularly, or ask permission to get help on an ad hoc basis.

Sources: Mattia Martin and Dario Cavenago, *International Journal of Training & Development* 21, no. 1 (March 2017), 18–34; Jeff Barbian, "The Road Best Traveled," *Training* 39, no. 5 (May 2002): 38–42; Kathleen Barton, "Will You Mentor Me?" *Training and Development* 56, no. 5 (May 2002): 90–92.

Tuition Assistance Programs

Large corporations often offer their employees tuition assistance to help them further their careers if they take courses related to the firms' businesses. For example, managers or would-be managers might be reimbursed for taking postgraduate classes such as MBA courses or other courses related to their professional development. The terms of the programs vary as do the amounts employees are reimbursed annually. Sometimes the amount of reimbursement depends on the grade an employee earns in class. Companies often require employees who are reimbursed for courses to remain with their firms for a certain amount of time after completing the courses.

Career Plateau Initiatives

Career plateaus are common obstacles in the career development of employees. A **career plateau** is a situation in which, for either organizational or personal reasons, the probability of moving up the career ladder is low. There are three types of plateaus: structural, content, and life. A *structural plateau* marks the end of promotions. A *content plateau* occurs when a person has learned a job too well and is bored with day-to-day activities. A *life plateau* is more profound and may feel like a midlife crisis. People who experience life plateaus often have allowed work or some other major factor to become the most significant aspect of their lives, and they experience a loss of identity and self-esteem when they are no longer advancing in their careers. Figure 5.12 lists some probing questions managers can ask themselves if they think their employees are experiencing a career plateau.

Organizations can help individuals cope with plateaus by providing them with opportunities for lateral growth or allowing them to choose their own assignments when opportunities for advancement do not exist. Companies with international divisions

career plateau
A situation in which for either organizational or personal reasons the probability of moving up the career ladder is low.

Figure 5.12	Career Plateau Questions

"No" answers may indicate an employee is facing a career plateau.
1. Does the employee accept high visibility assignments
2. Has the employee continued to advance his or her education, both formal and vocational?
3. Is the employee recognized by leaders in the organization, routinely promoted, and rewarded?
4. Does the employee get high performance ratings and larger-than-normal raises?
5. Does the employee have a career plan with measurable objectives that has been updated recently?

Source: John Rosche, "Who's Managing Your Career?" *Contract Management* 44, no. 2 (February 2004): 20–22.

sabbatical
An extended period of time in which an employee leaves an organization to pursue other activities and later returns to his or her job.

can encourage employees to take assignments abroad to expand their horizons, lead philanthropic and volunteer activities for their firms, or take sabbaticals. A **sabbatical** is an extended period of time during which an employee leaves an organization to pursue other activities before returning to the firm. A sabbatical can help prevent employee burnout and increase a person's loyalty to a company. Some but not all sabbaticals are paid. About 20 percent of companies on Fortune's "100 Best Companies to Work For" list offer paid sabbaticals. Some smaller companies do, too. The convenience-store chain QuickTrip does for employees with 20 years of service.[49] That might sound like a long time to wait, but due its great employment practices, many QuickTrip employees end up working for the firm for decades.

LO 5

How are the career challenges of minorities both similar to and different from those of women in your opinion?

5.5 Developing a Diverse Talent Pool

As an employer, would you like to hire people who are extremely loyal to your firm and likely to remain with it? Are their groups of employees you might have overlooked who could help you grow your business? Firms look to diverse talent not only for these reasons but to meet their legal obligations to provide equal employment opportunities. Employers often develop formal EEO/affirmative action policies to recruit and promote members of protected classes so that their representation at all levels within the organization approximates their proportionate numbers in the labor market.

However, the reasons to develop a diverse talent pool are not merely legal ones—not by a long shot. Today, ethnic minorities represent approximately 30 percent of the total U.S. population. In 2060, they are expected to comprise 60 percent of the population. These groups have a growing amount of buying power. Some researchers predict that companies that fail to diversify their talent pools will have a hard time identifying with their target customers and competing with firms that do. But perhaps most importantly, as companies face tougher competition in the United States and abroad, they will need all the leadership, productivity, innovation, and creativity the talent pool has to offer. A diverse talent pool increases the range of human capital available to the firm.

5.5a Women

Women make up a little under half of the total U.S. labor force and are the largest of the protected classes. A major employment obstacle for women, both skilled and unskilled, is the stereotyped thinking that persists within our society. Women traditionally have been at a disadvantage because they have not been part of the so-called "good old boys' network." That network is an informal one of interpersonal relationships that has traditionally provided a way for senior (male) members of the organization to pass along news of advancement opportunities and other career tips to junior (male) members as well as to recommend them.

In the past, women were not as likely as men to have professional training and preparation for entrance or advancement into management positions. But that's not the case today. Now, three of five U.S. college graduates are women, and according to the U.S. Census Bureau, more women hold bachelor's degrees than do men. Women also hold 51.5 percent of management, professional, and related positions. At IBM, scores of women run $100-million-plus divisions.

Still, the entire picture is not necessarily a rosy one. Women still make less than men, on average, and sometimes feel as if the workplace is a "man's world," and the proportion of women in top echelons of management, although growing, still remains extremely low.[50] In 2017, only 29 of the companies in the Fortune 500 were run by women. But that is 26 more than there were in 2000. Although these data suggest that there has been some progress, there is much left to do to break the "glass ceiling."

Eliminating Women's Barriers to Advancement

Glass ceiling audits are conducted by the U.S. Department of Labor to identify practices that appear to hinder the upward mobility of both qualified women and minorities. Black women in particular are at risk of not being promoted relative to other groups, say labor economists.

Organizations are increasingly conducting their own glass ceiling audits prior to government review to avoid fines and externally imposed corrective action. These audits can document any ceilings and the reasons they exist. Self-audits are one step toward tapping the potential of a diversified workforce. Following the largest class-action suit ever brought in the United States, Walmart began conducting self-audits. The company now has certain promotion goals for women and minorities. For example, if 40 percent of the qualified people who apply for assistant store manager positions are women, 40 percent of those hired should be women. JCPenney created advisory teams to help increase the representation of women and minorities at the senior management level and to find ways to make the company's affirmative action plan more effective. Each team is composed of 16 to 18 management associates. Firms are establishing professional groups within their organizations to help minorities, including women, connect with one another and combat their difficulty in advancing in organizations. At BNSF Railway, a women's network serves as a system for encouraging and fostering women's career development and for sharing information, experiences, and insights. Women in lower levels of the company are mentored by women at higher levels. Corporate officers are invited to regularly scheduled network meetings to discuss such matters as planning, development, and company performance. Minorities and women are also breaking through the glass ceiling by starting their own businesses. As one entrepreneur put it, "It's not hard to break through the glass ceiling when you own it."

Pete Marovich/Bloomberg /Getty Images

Mary Barra broke through many barriers on her way to becoming the CEO of GM.

Accommodating Families

One of the major problems women have faced is balancing their careers with their families. This is particularly true of single mothers, who are a growing segment of the population. Women with young children often experience conflict between their responsibility to the children and their duty to the employer. If the conflict becomes too painful, they may decide to forgo their careers, at least temporarily, and leave their jobs.

In recent years, many employers, including AFLAC, SunTrust Banks, Quaker Oats Company, Abbott Labs, Bristol-Myers Squibb, IBM, and the accounting firm KPMG, have launched programs mutually advantageous to the career-oriented woman and the employer. The programs, which include alternative career paths, extended leave, flextime, job sharing, and telecommuting, provide new ways to balance career and family. AFLAC offers families hot take-home meals at their onsite cafeterias to ease the burden of employees' having to prepare dinner after leaving the office for the day. The company also subsidizes babysitting for parents on Saturday nights so they can spend some free time together.[51] These efforts are paying off. Both IBM and KPMG, for example, report that their programs have helped them retain and increase their numbers of women workers.

Retaining employees who are part of dual-career couples can also be a challenge, especially if an employee needs to be relocated or travel extensively. To help make the transition easier, organizations now offer job-finding assistance for spouses of employees who are relocated, including payment of fees charged by employment agencies, job counseling firms, and executive search firms.

Organizations are also developing networking relationships with other employers to find jobs for the spouses of their relocating employees. These networks can provide a way to "share the wealth and talent" in a community while simultaneously assisting in the recruitment efforts of the participating organizations.[52]

Relocating dual-career couples to foreign facilities is a major issue that international employers face. Fewer employees are willing to relocate without assistance for their spouses. Many employers have developed effective approaches for integrating the various allowances typically paid for overseas assignments when husband and wife work for the same employer. Far more complex are the problems that arise when couples work for two different employers. The problems associated with overseas assignments of dual-career couples will be examined in greater detail in Chapter 15.

5.5b Minorities

Since the passage of the Civil Rights Act of 1964, many members of minority groups have substantially improved their economic well-being. However, for many minorities, employment opportunities still remain limited because of educational and societal disadvantages. The unemployment rates for minority youths are particularly high.

Black Collegian Online and Diversity Employers are two online job boards aimed at minority jobseekers and companies that want to hire them. Facebook and LinkedIn have functions that allow recruiters to create targeted advertising campaigns designed to reach diverse groups. Community action agencies, civil rights organizations, and church groups within communities can help recruiters reach inner-city residents.

Internships are another way in which organizations are building relationships with prospective minority employees. *The Chicago Tribune* offers a newsroom training program for aspiring minority journalists who want to work as news reporters. ABC, NBC, CBS, and Fox networks work with the Emma L. Bowen Foundation to provide internships, college scholarships, and postgraduate employment for minorities. The defense contractor Lockheed Martin teamed up with Operation Enterprise, the American Management Association's summer program for high school and college students, to offer 10-week paid internships to students of America's historically black colleges and universities.[53]

Like with women's networks, larger firms often have networks, or groups, minorities can join to help them advance their careers. General Electric's African-American Forum (AAF) began informally but has grown into a major initiative.[54] The company also has forum networks for employees who are Asian and Pacific Americans, women, Hispanics, gays, lesbians, bisexuals, and transgenders. Highlights in HRM 8 shows how to design a tailored approach to diversity planning.

5.5c People Who Are Disabled

If someone told HR managers where they could find millions of working-age people who are proven problem-solvers, provide a tax benefit for their companies, and have higher retention rates than average employees, they likely would ask: "What's the catch?" Not only is there no catch, but such a group of potential employees also currently exists. The group is those individuals with disabilities.[55]

According to the U.S. Census Bureau, more than 50 million Americans of working age have a disability. Currently, about 18 percent of disabled workers are unemployed, according to the Bureau of Labor Statistics.[56] Of those who do not work, most would like to. They often aren't working because employers mistakenly believe there are no jobs they might be able to do.

The Job Accommodation Network (JAN), sponsored by the U.S. Department of Labor, is a site that connects disabled jobseekers with employers. JAN also provides

Tips for Enhancing a Firm's Diversity

- Ascertain whether diversity is adequately represented in the firm's workforce by comparing company data to the statistics on diversity within the general workforce in the region. Diversity data within a firm should be broken down and measured across various specific categories, such as management, customer service, accounting, and so forth.

- Clearly define the goals of the diversity recruitment and retention program, and ensure managers at all levels understand its significance and support its motives.

- Understand demographic changes in the workforce.

- Build long-term relationships with minority organizations, colleges, and other strategic resources.

- Become the employer of choice for a diverse workforce by developing a diversity-friendly corporate culture and fostering a culturally sensitive work environment. Showcase the fact with a diversity statement on social media and your website. Include diversity stats and photos, and testimonial videos of minority employees at various levels.

- Establish a presence among minority communities by participating in job fairs, targeting recruitment advertising to minority publications such as Diversity Inc., and monitoring websites where résumés of diverse individuals are more likely to be found.

- Use internal employee resource groups. Demonstrate the organization's commitment to diversity by making it a formal part of the employee referral program.

- Train hiring managers to ensure diverse applicants are not discounted in the interviewing process because they are different.

- Measure the efficacy of these recruitment efforts, and use the results to improve the program.

Sources: Condensed from Patricia Digh, "Getting People in the Pool: Diversity Recruitment That Works," *HR Magazine* 44, no. 10 (October 1999): 94–98; Sungjoo Choi, "Workforce Diversity and Job Satisfaction of the Majority and the Minority," *Review of Public Personnel Administration* 37, no. 1 (March 2017): 84–107; John Sullivan and Sally Baack, "Diversity Recruiting Is a Failure: It's Time to Raise the Bar," http://www.multiculturaladvantage.com; Aaron Green, "Diversity Recruiting: Getting It Right," http://www.boston.com.

information about how to accommodate different types of disabilities in the workplace. According to data from the U.S. Department of Labor's Office of Disability Employment, 15 percent of accommodations cost nothing; 51 percent cost between $1 and $500; 12 percent cost between $501 and $1,000; and 22 percent cost more than $1,000.[57] Many managers are unaware of how low cost most accommodations can be overall.

IBM hired its first disabled employee in 1914. This is not surprising, since the company makes software and other products that help eliminate workplace barriers for individuals with disabilities. IBM's viewpoint is that no employee should be overlooked because of a disability, thinking he or she may be the person to develop the next generation of hardware or software from which the company will profit. Several of the company's researchers have a hearing impairment; they are responsible for world-class work with innovations such as voice recognition technology.

IBM also participates in mentoring and internships for people with disabilties. The Workforce Recruitment Program for College Students with Disabilities (WRP) is one internship organization. WRP puts together profiles of thousands of college students and recent graduates seeking summer internships or permanent employment nationwide with federal agencies. These profiles are then made available free of charge to business owners. Similarly, the American Association for the Advancement of Science has a program called Entry Point, which has placed hundreds of science and engineering students with disabilities in internships in the public and private sectors.

5.5d Veterans

The federal government requires firms that do business with it to hire a certain percentage of workers who are veterans. But firms aren't recruiting military personnel just because they do business with the government and have to, but because it's good business. AT&T, Starbucks, Amazon, Capital One, and Lowe's are among the many companies that have found veterans to be a valuable source of candidates. Employers say veterans have a good work ethic, are disciplined, follow the chain of command, and make good decisions in different situations, such as mission types of operations. According to a study by CareerBuilder.com, 65 percent of employers said, given the choice between two equally qualified applicants, they are more likely to hire the veteran.[58]

Numerous websites are dedicated to recruiting veterans. They include Veterans4Hire, veteranrecruiting.com, and Milicruit.com. Milicruit holds virtual job fairs, which can help vets apply for jobs while they are still enlisted, if they are disabled, or otherwise are unable to travel to a regular job fair. Contacting and forming a relationship with a military base is another way. Most military bases have career centers for people leaving the military. These are often the first place military personnel turn to when they are transitioning into civilian lives. The U.S. Department of Labor's VETS program is another good source. VETS has local veterans' employment representatives across the country dedicated to increasing the employment of former military members.[59]

5.5e Older Employees

A growing number of people over 65 are continuing to work—a trend that is likely to increase as more babyboomers retire.[60] The move has come both as a result of changing workforce demographics, rising health care costs, and babyboomers spending down their retirement savings.

Stephen Brashear/Getty Images

During annual meetings of shareholders in 2017, Starbucks announced a new goal to hire 25,000 veterans by 2025.

Why should a company hire older workers? For one, because they have proven employment experience, are reliable, and are more likely to remain with a firm than job hop. They are also an excellent recruitment source to staff part-time and full-time positions that are otherwise hard to fill. Independent contracting or consulting, on-call work (such as substitute nursing or teaching), and temporary work in administrative or IT roles are examples. Some retirees return or stay in the workforce at the request of their employers, who cannot afford to lose the knowledge accumulated by longtime employees or their reliable work habits that have a positive effect on the entire work group.

But even though age discrimination is illegal, it is still a problem. Managers wonder whether older employees are adaptable enough to learn new processes and technologies. Younger workers are more likely to get interviews than older people, studies have shown. To counter problems such as these, the AARP, the advocacy group for retired people, offers virtual job fairs and online videos to help its members assess, brush up on, and learn new tech skills. The organization also partners with firms that recruit older workers and offer them flexible work schedules and health benefits. The Home Depot, Staples, and Toys "R" Us are some of the firms featured on the site. The AARP will even pay an older worker's wages and workers-compensation costs as part of a "try before you hire" program it has with companies. After a trial period of working for a company, the firm can decide whether or not it wants to hire the worker.

Summary

LO ① The decisions a company makes about talent need to be considered within the context of the business's strategies: What types of positions are needed; where the talent is needed and where can it be found; the strength of the firm's employment "brand"; how the talent can be attracted; and who will recruit the talent and make the final hiring decision. Which internal and external sources and methods are used in recruiting will depend on the strategy and goals of the organization, conditions of the labor market, and specifications of the jobs to be filled.

LO ② Outside candidates are recruited when internal talent is lacking or a firm wants to hire employees with expertise from other organizations for competitive reasons and to prevent the inbreeding of ideas within their organization. To help meet a firm's EEO requirement and diversify its talent pools, firms also look externally for candidates. Advertisements, the Internet, social networks, mobile recruiting, employment agencies, tapping educational institutions and professional associations, and re-recruiting are among the many ways firms recruit external candidates.

Employers usually find it advantageous to use internal promotions and transfers to fill as many openings as possible above the entry level. Doing so is faster, less expensive, and more likely to result in a successful hire. It also builds loyalty among workers. Internal job postings, performance appraisals, skills inventories, and replacement charts are ways in which firms identify internal talent.

LO ③ HR managers have many tools available to them to gauge their efforts and improve their recruiting. Using realistic job reviews, surveying managers and applicants about the process, and examining metrics such as the cost per hire, time to fill a position, yield ratios, and acceptance rates are some of the ways in which firms evaluate their recruiting efforts. An applicant tracking system (ATS) can help a firm automatically track and calculate many of these statistics. The flipside of recruiting is retaining employees. Pay and benefits are important, but nonmonetary aspects, such as the support of one's supervisor and the ability to further one's career in an organization, can ultimately lead to an employee's retention.

LO ④ Identifying and developing talent is a responsibility of all managers. A career development program is a dynamic process that should integrate the career goals of employees with the goals of the organization. Job opportunities can be identified by studying jobs and determining the knowledge and skills each one requires. Once that is accomplished, key jobs can be identified, and job progressions can be planned. These progressions can then serve as a basis for developing the career paths of employees. Employees need to be made aware of the organization's philosophy and its goals; otherwise they will not know how their goals match those of the organization. Firms can "grow" their internal talent by offering employees different career paths and programs, counseling them about their careers, establishing mentoring and tuition assistance programs, and helping them overcome career plateaus.

LO 5 The first step toward facilitating the career development of women is to eliminate barriers to their advancement. Creating professional networks for women, providing them with managerial training and mentors, and accommodating families have been found to be effective ways to facilitate women's career development.

A diversified workforce is composed of many different groups, an important segment of which is minority groups. Many organizations have special programs such as internships that provide minority groups with hands-on experience as well as special training opportunities. Other groups that require the attention of management are the disabled, veterans, older workers, and dual-career couples, who often need flexible working options.

Key Terms

acceptance rate

applicant tracking system (ATS)

branding

career paths

career plateau

demotion

employee leasing

employee profile

independent contractors

internal labor market

job progressions

mentors

mobile recruiting

nepotism

nine-box grid

outplacement services

passive jobseekers

promotion

quality of fill

realistic job preview (RJP)

recruiting process outsourcing (RPO)

re-recruiting

reverse mentoring

sabbatical

time to fill

transfer

virtual job fair

yield ratio

Discussion Questions

LO 1 Name some companies with whom you have done business. Then discuss how you view their employer brands. Would you want to work for them or not? How might these firms improve their employer brands?

LO 2 Think of a new type of business you would like to start up or manage. Which sources would you use to recruit employees who could help you make it a success?

LO 3 Explain how realistic job previews (RJPs) operate. As a manager or business owner, would you use them?

LO 4 How can a career management program help an organization forced to downsize its operations?

LO 5 What barriers to career advancement do women and minorities face?

Career Management

Do successful people plan their careers in advance and then work toward their goals in a logical and sequential way? Or does a career occur as a result of a person's preparedness, insight, and taking advantages of opportunities as they arise?

Assignment

1. Form teams of four to six members. Identify three different people to interview about their careers. One person should be in the early stages of his or her career, one should be in midcareer, and one should be in the final stages of his or her career.

2. Ask each person to identify his or her career goals and how they have changed or are expected to change over time.

3. Ask each person to describe the sequence of events that led to where he or she is.

4. Ask each person what (if anything) he or she would do differently. Ask what advice he or she has for you about how to approach your career.

CASE STUDY A Lifecycle Approach to Talent

To build a workforce that can respond to the health-care industry's rapid transformation, Scripps Health, in San Diego, accommodates the needs of employees at the beginning, middle, and later stages in their careers. The result is higher morale and impeccable performance. "One-size-fits-all HR practices don't work when you want a diverse, knowledge-based workforce," says Victor Buzachero, corporate senior vice president for innovation, human resources, and performance management. "Originally many HR practices were designed primarily to be consistent and to avoid legal issues. Today our focus is on HR practices that engage people and encourage a higher contribution."

For example, Scripps has implemented daily "huddles," where workers can offer input and affect decisions—something especially prized by millennial employees. "In the past workers wanted a supervisor who acted like a "boss." Buzachero say, "Today they want a supervisor who acts like a coach, and we're educating our supervisors to be strong coaches."

In one program, seasoned nurses are trained to mentor recent nursing graduates to improve their critical-thinking skills; as a result, the graduates indicate they feel more prepared for their role. Scripps currently offers over 1,870 skills-building, leadership training, and continuing education units.

Scripps also encourages movement across the organization to remain a career destination for talent mid-career. For example, workers in medical surgical units can receive 26 weeks of training to shift into areas where skilled workers are in short supply, such as operating rooms.

Also, traditional retirement packages that max out at age 60 can encourage these experienced workers to leave, even if they want to continue working. Scripps lets retirement plans continue to grow past age 65, while allowing staged retirement programs such as job sharing. "One of our most successful clinical nursing units is managed by two women who job share," Buzachero says. "If we didn't offer that kind of flexibility, they may have gone somewhere else."

This lifeycle approach creates a diverse workforce able to address the healthcare industry's mandate to improve outcomes while cutting costs. "As patients ask for more and more from us, we need a workforce with all-encompassing view and innovative approach, Buzachero says. "But we can only build a highly skilled, varied workforce if we satisfy the many career needs of a varied workforce."

Questions

1. In what ways does the Scripps lifecycle approach lead to a more diverse workforce?

2. Why are managers increasingly being encouraged to act as coaches? Do you see any problems with a manager acting as both a coach and a supervisor?

Source: Scripps Health.

CASE STUDY Homegrown Talent: Mary Barra Rises to GM's Top Post

When Mary Barra was a kid, she used to hang out in the garage with her dad tinkering on cars. Little did her father, a lifelong die-maker for GM's Pontiac division, know that his daughter would one day become the CEO of the company and the first woman ever to lead a major U.S. car manufacturer. But that's what happened in 2013. Barra was unanimously chosen by the board members of General Motors to lead the company—a decision employees cheered when they heard about it over the loudspeakers at corporate headquarters. Maybe they cheered because unlike GM's previous two CEOs, Barra was one of them. Having worked in multiple departments at GM since she was 18, she knows the car business through and through. "There's nobody with more years of honest 'car guy' credentials than she has," says Ross Gordon in the Ross School of Business at the University of Michigan.

Barra, who grew up in a Detroit suburb, initially began working for GM in the 1980s as part of a work-study program. In this program, which is also referred to as a co-op program, students alternate working full time (for pay) and going to college. She earned an undergraduate degree in electrical engineering and GM later sent her to Stanford, where she got an MBA. During her career she has rotated through various positions at GM. Besides working in engineering and design, she managed one GM's manufacturing plants and most recently was the senior vice president for global product development and quality control. Under her watch, the company has rolled out successful models that have helped bring the company back out of bankruptcy during the latest economic recession.

Barra has a reputation for getting results. Not only does she know cars, she knows people and how to manage them. When an updated version of the Chevy Malibu floundered because of design and other problems, she mobilized a team of employees and found a way to fix the Malibu in record time. Her great people management skills might explain why when GM was going through bankruptcy, she was put in charge of human resources for GM, an area she had never worked in before. GM hoped putting her in the job would prevent key talent from heading for the exits during the bankruptcy process. It did and GM bounced back. In 2016, GM sold more than 10 million vehicles worldwide, and its net income exceeded $9 billion. GM's Chevy Volt was named North American Car of the Year in 2017, and the company announced a partnership to develop on-demand, self-driving vehicles in conjunction with the ride-sharing company Lyft. In short, the company is on a roll.

Sue Meisinger, formerly the president and CEO of the Society of Human Resources Management, says that Barra's being named CEO underscores the importance of HR personnel working in and understanding different areas of their firms. "If you're interested in a career path that extends beyond HR, you need to have experience in multiple facets of the business," Meisinger says. She notes that for many HR professionals, their crowning achievement is to be the head of HR. Barra's rise to CEO, however, will have many of these professionals shifting their career goals.

Questions

1. Mary Barra's father worked at General Motors. Was her hiring an example of nepotism? If you were a business owner, would you want to hire relatives of your employees? What would the pros and cons of doing so be?

2. What role did Mary Barra play in advancing her career? What role did GM play in "growing" her career?

Sources: Tom Beaman, "CEO Mary Barra Revs Things Up at General Motors," *Costco Connection* 32, no 4 (April 2017): 45. Dee Ann Durbin and Tom Krisher, "Barra Inherits a Stronger GM," Associated Press (December 29, 2013), www.ap.org; Dee Ann Durbin and Tom Krisher, "GM Picks Woman CEO," Associated Press (December 29, 2013), www.ap.org; Chris Woodyard, "Who Is Mary Barra, the Next CEO of GM?" *USA Today* (December 10, 2013), www.usatoday.com; Mary Pyrillis, "Mary Barra, General Motors' Next CEO Breaks Ground for Women and HR," *Workforce* (December 11, 2013), http://www.workforce.com.

Notes and References

1. R. Bruab and David G. Allen, "Third Party Employment Branding: Human Capital Inflows and Outflows following 'Best Places to Work' Certifications," *Academy of Management Journal* 59, no. 1 (2016): 90–112.

2. Blake Landua, "The Uncontained Culture of the Container Store," *Human Resources IQ* (March 6, 2008), http://www.humanresources.iqu.com.

3. Sarah E. Needleman, "Play This Game and Win a Job," *Wall Street Journal* (March 14, 2016): R2.

4. Damali Curry Edwards, "People and Technology: A Winning Recruiting Combination," *Career Planning and Adult Development Journal* 32 no. 3 (2016): 45; Edward P. Lazear, Paul Oyer, Internal and External Labor Markets: A Personnel Economics Approach, *NBER* (Working paper, 2003), http://www.nber.org/papers/w10192.

5. Debbie Mack, "P&G Fights to Protect Its Bounty," *Corporate Legal Times* 13, no. 135 (February 2003): 64; Alexandria Sage, "Tesla Sues Ex-Autopilot Head over Recruiting," *Reuters* (January 27, 2017), http://reuters.com.

6. Jeff Tanner and Mary Anne Raymond, *Principles of Marketing* (Washington, DC: FlatWorld Knowledge, 2016): 79.

7. Kazim Ladimeji "Five Ways to Significantly Increase Recruiting Effectiveness," *Recruiter* (September 28, 2012), https://www.recruiter.com.

8. Lauren Krugel, "SkipTheDishes Apologies, Offers to Reschedule Interview," *Canadian Press* (March 14, 2017), http://www.thecanadianpress.com.

9. Henry S. Faber, Dan Silverman, and Till Von Wachter, "Determinants of Callbacks to Job Applications: An Audit Study," *The American Economic Review* 106 no. 5 (2016): 314–18; Douglas P. Shuit, "Monster Board Games," *Workforce Management* 82, no. 2 (November 2003): 37–42; Joe Dysart, "New Directions in Internet Recruiting," *Contractor Magazine* 53, no. 7 (July 2006): 33–36.

10. Roy Maurer, "Niche Job Boards Muscle into Recruiting Marketplace," SHRM (February 24, 2017), https://www.shrm.org.

11. Allan Schweyer, "Robots in Recruiting: The Implications of AI on Talent Acquisition," Webinar, 2017, http://info.appcast.io.

12. Mike Vangel, "Social Recruitment Delivers Results for UPS," *Talent Management* (August 13, 2013), http://www.talentmgt.com.

13. John E. Dunn, "Facebook's New Job Service Sparks Privacy Fears," *Naked Security* (February 20, 2017), https://nakedsecurity.sophos.com.

14. Monica Anderson and Andrew Perri, "13% of Americans Don't Use the Internet. Who Are They?" *Pew Research* (September 7, 2016); http://www.pewresearch.org.

15. Emily Glazer, "Virtual Fairs Offer Real Jobs," *Wall Street Journal* (October 31, 2011): B9.

16. Kazim Ladimeji, "Five Ways to Significantly Increase Recruiting Effectiveness," *Recruiter* (September 28, 2012), https://www.recruiter.com.

17. Stephen V. Burks et al., "The Value of Hiring through Employee Referrals," *The Quarterly Journal of Economics* (2015): qjv010; Jennifer Salopek, "Employee Referrals Remain a Recruiter's Best Friend," *Workforce Management* (December 2010), http://www.workforce.com.

18. Sara Stockman and Greet Van Hoye, "Rewarding Employee Referrals: Effects on Organizational Attractiveness," *9th Dutch HRM Network Conference*, 2016; Jennifer Taylor Arnold, "Employee Referrals at a Keystroke," *HRMagazine* 51, no. 10 (October 2006): 82–88; VictoriaFurnes, "The New Frontier," *Personnel Today* (January 22, 2008): 13–16.

19. Greg Patrick Haudek, "A Longitudinal Test of the Attraction-Selection-Attrition Model," *ETD Collection for Wayne State University* (January 1, 2001), Paper AAI3010091, http://digitalcommons.wayne.edu.

20. Joshua Brustein, "Plantir Case Draws Attention to Discriminatory Potential of Referral Programs," *Blooomerg* (September 28, 2017), https://www.bloomberg.com.

21. Joanne B. Ciulla, "In Praise of Nepotism?" *Business Ethics Quarterly* 15, no. 1 (January 2005): 153–61; Richard Reeve and Gavin Sheridan, "Nepotism: Is It Back?" *New Statesman* 135 (September 29, 2003): 22–25.

22. Abbie J Shipp et al. "Gone Today but Here Tomorrow: Extending the Unfolding Model of Turnover to Consider Boomerang Employees," *Personnel Psychology* 67, no. 2 (2014): 421–462; Melissa Korn, "Boomerang Employees," *Wall Street Journal*

Online (October 24, 2011), http://wjsonline.com; Madeline Laurano, "Best Practices in Re-Recruiting Top Talent," *Bersin & Associates* (blog), (August 6, 2009), http://www.bersin.com.

23. Rachel Feintzeigm "CEOs Head Back to School," *Wall Street Journal* (February 2, 2017): B4.

24. Paul Benjamin Lowry and David Wilson, "Creating Agile Organizations through IT," *The Journal of Strategic Information Systems* 25 no. 3 (2016): 211–26; Ed Frauenheim, "Companies Focus Their Attention on Flexibility," *Workforce Management* (February 2011): 3–4.

25. Chris Pentilla, "Got It Covered: If You Can't Afford to Offer Employee Benefits on Your Own, Why Not Join Forces with a PEO?" *Entrepreneur* 32, no. 2 (February 2004): 66–68; Bill Leonard, "Small Firms Prepare for Aging Workforce," *HR Magazine* 53, no. 5 (May 2008): 32.

26. Robert Rodriguez, "Filling the HR Pipeline," *HR Magazine* 49, no. 9 (September 2004): 78–84; James W. Walker, "Perspectives," *Human Resource Planning* 25, no. 1 (2002): 12–14.

27. "Heading for the Fast Track: New Studies Examine Who Gets Promoted and Why," *Knowledge@Wharton* (August 10, 2005), http//www. knowledge.wharton.upenn.edu.

28. Matthew Bidwell, "Paying More to Get Less: Specific Skills, Matching, and the Effects of External Hiring versus Internal Promotion," *Administrative Science Quarterly* (2011): 369–407.

29. Pamela Tate, "Calling on Career Development," *Talent Management* (January 7, 2014), http://www.talentmgt.com.

30. Pandey Smita and Mishra Sarika, "Analysis of the Pros and Cons of Online Recruitment Methods in India," *International Journal of Engineering and Management Sciences* 6, no. 2 (2015): 65–67; The Pros and Cons of Online Recruiting," *HR Focus* 81 (April 2004): S2.

31. Matthew Bidwell and J.R. Keller, "Within or Without? How Firms Combine Internal and External Labor Markets to Fill Jobs," *Academy of Management Journal* 57, no. 4 (2014): 1035–1055; Stanely Ragalevsky, "CEO Succession: Five Best Practices for Internal Candidates," *Community Banker* 17, no. 2 (February 2008): 24–25.

32. "How to Implement an Effective Process for a New HR Management System," *HR Focus* 82, no. 1 (January 2005): 3–4; Connie Winkler, "Job Tryouts Go Virtual," *HR Magazine* 51, no. 9 (September 2006): 131–134.

33. Connie Winkler, "Job Tryouts Go Virtual."

34. Colin Lee, "The Potential of Computer-aided Applicant Pre-screening," *RSM Discovery-Management Knowledge* 26, no. 2 (2016): 21–22; "Applicant Tracking System," *SearchCIO.com* (March 18, 2011), http://searchcio.techtarget.com.

35. BruceFecheyr-Lippens, Bill Schaninger, and Karen Tanner, "Power to the New People Analytics," *McKinsey Quarterly* 51, no. 1 (2015): 61–63; John Sullivan, "How Google Is Using People Analytics to Completely Reinvent HR," *TLNT* (February 26, 2013), http://www.tlnt.com.

36. Sunil Bagai, "Google Brings Machine Learning to the Staffing Industry," *B2C* (November 18, 2016), http://www.business2community.com.

37. "Dale Carnegie Training Global Leadership Study: USA 2016," http://www.dalecarnegie.com.

38. Blake Landau, "The Uncontained Culture of the Container Store," *Human Resources IQ* (March 6, 2008), http://www.human resourcesiq.com.

39. Jos Akkermans et al. "It's All about CareerSKILLS," *Human Resource Management* 54, no. 4 (2015): 533–551; Peg O'Herron and Peggy Simonsen, "Career Development Gets a Charge at Sears Credit," *Personnel Journal* 74, no. 5 (May 1995): 103–06; see also Jules Abend, "Behind the Scenes at: Sears," *Bobbin* 39, no. 11 (June 1998): 22–26; Shari Caudron, "The De-Jobbing of America," *Industry Week* 243, no. 16 (September 5, 1994): 30–36; Edward E. Lawler III, "From Job-Based to Competency-Based Organizations," *Journal of Organizational Behavior* 15, no. 1 (January 1994): 3–15; Douglas T. Hall, "Accelerate Executive Development—At Your Peril!" *Career Development International* 4, no. 4 (1999): 237–239.

40. Erika Fry, "An Ex-Cop Comes to the Rescue," *Fortune* (March 18, 2013): 38.

41. "Coworkers Get a Chance to Change Places," *Wall Street Journal* (February 21, 2012), http://online.wsj.com.

42. Hank Boyer, "Emerging Trends in Career Management," LinkedIn (February 2, 2016), https://www.linkedin.com.

43. Tate, "Calling on Career Development."

44. Elaine Farndale et al., "Balancing Individual and Organizational Goals in Global Talent Management," *Journal of World Business* 49, no. 2 (2014): 204–214; "How a Talent Management Plan Can Anchor Your Company's Future," *HR Focus* 81, no. 10 (October 2004): 7–10; "Heading for the Fast Track? New Studies Examine Who Gets Promoted and Why," *Knowledge@ Wharton* (August 10, 2005), http://knowledge.wharton.upenn.edu.

45. Dona Dezube, "How a Workplace Mentoring Program Can Benefit Your Company," *Tampa Bay Times* (January 18, 2017), http://www.tampabay.com.

46. Leslie Kwoh, "Reverse Mentoring Cracks Workplace," *Wall Street Journal* (November 28, 2011): B7.

47. Tory Paez, "My Friend, My Mentor: The Benefits of Peer Mentoring in the Workplace," *Catalyst* (2016); Suzanne C. de Janasz, Shery E. Sullivan, and Vicki Whiting, "Mentor Networks and Career Success: Lessons for Turbulent Times," *Academy of Management Executive* 17, no. 4 (November 2003): 78–92; Kate Walsh and Judith Gordon, "Creating an Individual Work Identity," *Human Resource Management Review* 18, no. 1 (March 2008): 46–61.

48. Jos Akkermans et al., "It's All about CareerSKILLS," *Human Resource Management* 54 no. 4 (2015): 533–51; Larry Cambron, "Career Development Pays," *Far Eastern Economic Review* 164, no. 42 (October 25, 2001): 83.

49. Kevin Jimmy, "A Dimensional Study on Employee Mentoring and Coaching Management," *Scholedge International Journal of Management & Development* 2, no. 5 (2015): 64–67; Laura M. Francis, "The Shifting Shape of Mentoring," *Training & Development* (September 2009), http://www.astd.org.

50. Sheryl Smolkin, "Sabbaticals Said to Reduce Burnout, Improve Worker Loyalty," *Benefit News* (May 17, 2016), http://www.benefitnews.com.

51. Heidi Hartmann, Jeffrey Hayes, and Jennifer Clark, "How Equal Pay for Working Women Would Reduce Poverty and Grow the American Economy" (Washington, DC: Institute for Women's Policy Research, Briefing paper IWPR# C411, January 10, 2014); Hope Yen, "Women Gain Ground against Salary Disparity," *Fort Worth Star-Telegram* (December 11, 2103): 6A.

52. Eunmi Chang, Hyun Chin, and Jieun Ye, "Organizational Work-Family Culture and Working Mothers' Affective Commitment," *Human Resource Management* 53, no. 5 (2014): 683–700; Alison Stein Wellner, "Welcoming Back Mom," *HR Magazine* 49, no. 6 (June 2004): 76–83; "Mothers' Labor Force Participation," *Monthly Labor Review* 137, no. 5 (May 2004): 2; Brian Braiker and Anna Kuchment, "Just Do Not Call Me Mr. Mom," *Newsweek* 150, no. 15 (October 8, 2007): 52–55; Melissa Fletcher, "Working Moms Fully in Favor of Going Part-Time," *Fort Worth Star-Telegram* (August 30, 2007): E1, 9.

53. Courtney R. Masterson and Jenny M. Hoobler, "Care and Career: A Family Identity-Based Typology of Dual-Earner Couples," *Journal of Organizational Behavior* 36, no. 1 (2015): 75–93; Janice Rosenberg, "Dual Career Couples Face Expensive Choices," Bankrate.com (July 2, 2007); Erin White, "Help Increases for Partners of Relocated Workers," *Wall Street Journal* 251, no. 70 (March 25, 2008): D4.

54. "Recruiting Minorities," *Black Enterprise* 35, no. 6 (January 2005): 53; Debbie Smith, "Building a New Diversity Road Map," *Multichannel News* 25, no. 38 (September 20, 2004): 82.

55. Yeung, "Finders Keepers," 42–44; Janny Scott, "Nearly Half of Black Men Found Jobless," *The New York Times* (February 28, 2004), B1; Sylvia Ann Hewlett, Carolyn Buck Luce, and Cornel West, "Leadership in Your Midst," *Harvard Business Review* 83, no. 11 (November 2005): 74–82.

56. Kathleen C. Brannen and Terrence M. Begley, "The Americans with Disabilities Act: What It Means to Small Business Owners," *Journal of Small Business Strategy* 6, no. 1 (2015): 79–92; Joe Mullich, "Hiring without Limits," *Workforce Management* 83, no. 6 (June 1, 2004): 53–60; Julie Hotchkiss, "Growing Part-Time Employment among Workers with Disabilities," *Economic Review* 89, no. 3 (July 2004): 25–42; "Entry Point Interns Top 400 in Seventh Year," *Science* 301, no. 5637 (August 29, 2003): 1195; Kelly Butler, "Ten Million Ways to Fill the Talent Gap," *Employee Benefit News* 21, no. 3 (March 2007): 22–24.

57. "Persons with a Disability: Labor Force Characteristics Summary," U.S. Bureau of Labor Statistics (June 21, 2016), https://www.bls.gov; Sam Hananel, "New Rules Boost Hiring of Vets, Disabled," Associated Press (August 28, 2013), http://www.ap.org.

58. Nabanita Datta Gupta, Mona Larsen, and Lars Stage Thomsen, "Do Wage Subsidies for Disabled Workers Reduce Their Nonemployment?" *IZA Journal of Labor Policy* 4 no. 1 (2015): 10; "As ADA Turns 20, Harris Interactive Survey Finds Lifestyle and Economic Gaps Still Remain between Americans with and without Disabilities," Kessler Foundation and National Organization on Disability (press release), July 26, 2010.

59. Gregg Zoroya, "Wanted: Military Vets for Good Management Jobs," *USA Today* (March 6, 2013), http://www.usatoday.com.

60. Kimberly Curry Hall et al., "Connecting Veterans and Employers" (2015); Jessica Miller-Merrell, "How to Recruit Veterans," *GlassDoor* (June 20, 2013), http://glassdoor.com.

61. Christopher Reynolds, "Boomers, Act II," *American Demographics* 27, no. 8 (October 2004): 10–12; TheresaMinton-Eversole, "Senate Forum Explores Ways to Keep Aging Workforce Working," *HR Magazine* 48, no. 10 (October 2003): 30; Carly Foster, "Rehiring Retirees among 2008's Top Recruiting Trends," *Employee Benefit News* (January 8, 2008): 5.

Appendix

Personal Career Development

Because you are likely to spend more time working during your life than doing anything else, it makes sense to plan your career. Although organizations can be a positive force in the career development process, the primary responsibility for your career is yours.

A.1 Developing Personal Skills and Competencies

Planning for a career involves more than simply acquiring specific job knowledge and skills. You must also develop other skills to be successful as an employee. To succeed as a manager, you must achieve still higher-level skills in the areas of communication, time management, self-motivation, interpersonal relationships, and leadership. Highlights in HRM 9 shows the competencies candidates "must have" today to successfully embark on a career in any field.

A.2 Choosing a Career

People often have to do a lot of searching and changing of jobs before they find a career that suits them. Counselors at colleges and universities, as well as those in private practice, help individuals evaluate their aptitudes, abilities, interests, and values as they relate to selecting careers. Placement offices and continuing education centers also offer career planning assistance.

Critical to your career planning is determining the long-term opportunities and salaries in the occupational fields you are considering. Most job-related websites, including Monster, CareerBuilder, Indeed, and LinkedIn contain free information about careers and wages. Government sources include O*Net OnLine, America's Career InfoNet, and Career Outlook.

A.3 Self-Evaluation

Successful career development depends in part on an individual's ability to conduct an accurate self-evaluation. When you are doing a self-evaluation, you need to consider factors that are personally significant to you. What activities do you like to do? Do you

"Must Have" Career Competencies

The following are "must have" career competencies according to the National Association of Colleges and Employers.

- **Critical Thinking/Problem Solving:** Exercise sound reasoning to analyze issues, make decisions, and overcome problems. The individual is able to obtain, interpret, and use knowledge, facts, and data in this process, and may demonstrate originality and inventiveness.

- **Oral/Written Communications:** Articulate thoughts and ideas clearly and effectively in written and oral forms to persons inside and outside of the organization. The individual has public speaking skills; is able to express ideas to others; and can write/edit memos, letters, and complex technical reports clearly and effectively.

- **Teamwork/Collaboration:** Build collaborative relationships with colleagues and customers representing diverse cultures, races, ages, genders, religions, lifestyles, and viewpoints. The individual is able to work within a team structure, and can negotiate and manage conflict.

- **Digital Technology:** Leverage existing digital technologies ethically and efficiently to solve problems, complete tasks, and accomplish goals. The individual demonstrates effective adaptability to new and emerging technologies.

- **Leadership:** Leverage the strengths of others to achieve common goals, and use interpersonal skills to coach and develop others. The individual is able to assess and manage his/her emotions and those of others; use empathetic skills to guide and motivate; and organize, prioritize, and delegate work.

- **Professionalism/Work Ethic:** Demonstrate personal accountability and effective work habits (e.g., punctuality, working productively with others, and time workload management), and understand the impact of nonverbal communication on professional work image. The individual demonstrates integrity and ethical behavior, acts responsibly with the interests of the larger community in mind, and is able to learn from his/her mistakes.

- **Career Management:** Identify and articulate one's skills, strengths, knowledge, and experiences relevant to the position desired and career goals, and identify areas necessary for professional growth. The individual is able to navigate and explore job options, understands and can take the steps necessary to pursue opportunities, and understands how to self-advocate for opportunities in the workplace.

- **Global/Intercultural Fluency:** Value, respect, and learn from diverse cultures, races, ages, genders, sexual orientations, and religions. The individual demonstrates openness, inclusiveness, sensitivity, and the ability to interact respectfully with all people and understand individuals' differences.

---

like working alone or with other people? Do you like technical work or creative work? Do you think you would like working in an office, or would you prefer another setting? What have you always dreamed of doing?

A.3a Interest Inventories

Psychologists who specialize in career counseling typically administer a battery of tests. The *Strong Interest Inventory*, developed by E. K. Strong Jr., was among the first of the interest tests.[1] Strong found people's interests vary from occupation to occupation. Strong's assessment tool can help you learn the degree to which your interests correspond with those of successful people in a wide range of occupations. Another inventory that measures both interests and skills is the *Campbell Interest and Skill Survey*

(CISS). Occupations are identified with advice about whether each of the occupations should be "pursued," "explored," or "avoided" by the person who took the test. Both tests can be taken online for a fee. About.com has a number of free self-assessments as do other sites such as MyPlan.com, CareerPath, and LiveCareer. The *O*Net Interest Profiler* is a free online interest assessment tool offered by the U.S. Department of Labor.

Note, however, that people have taken interest and skills inventories that dissuaded them from their chosen careers, pursued them anyway, and have become extremely successful. If you find yourself in such a situation, do not be discouraged about your career choice. Consider exploring the career further via internships, informational interviews, and job shadowing (discussed next). Also, keep in mind that most people change careers multiple times during their lives. If your first choice of a career is not what you hoped it would be, you are always free to pursue another.

A.3b Informational Interviews, Job Shadowing, and Internships

An **informational interview** is a conversation you have with someone in an occupation that you are interested in. You invite the person to lunch or for coffee and ask the individual what the job is really like—the good and the bad, qualifications needed, the outlook for the career, and so forth. Most people are flattered to be asked to provide career information and like to talk about what they do. However, make it clear that you are not soliciting the person for a job—just seeking information.

Job shadowing is the process of observing someone in his or her own work environment to better understand what he or she does. Generally this is done for a few hours to a halfday. The website Virtualjobshadow.com provides videos of professionals in approximately 100 different careers who explain their jobs. The site also contains information about the earnings and outlook of professions, educational requirements, and a search function that lists colleges that offer degrees for specific professions. People who sign up for the site can also ask a professional questions they might have. As we explained earlier in this chapter, internships can be a great way to experience a particular field of work, as is volunteering. Check with your college advisor and career placement center to find opportunities such as these.

Networking is a way to find out not only about different professions but different employers you might be interested in working for. Some of the best places to network include:

- Social media websites
- Your college alumni association or career office networking lists
- Your own extended family
- Your friends' parents and other family members
- Your professors, advisors, coaches, tutors, and clergy
- Your former bosses and your friends' and family members' bosses
- Members of clubs, religious groups, and other organizations to which you belong
- All of the organizations near where you live or go to school[2]

informational interview
A conversation you have with someone in a career you are interested in to gather information about it.

job shadowing
The process of observing someone in his or her work environment to see if the job is of interest to you.

A.4 Choosing an Employer

Once you've made a career choice, even if only tentatively, the next major step is deciding which employer you think you might want to work for and where. Numerous company directories containing information about privately and publicly held companies are available. Hoovers.com is one online source, as is Vault.com. Corporate websites are another source. Often under the "Investors" or "Media" tabs you can find press releases issued by the companies in which you are interested. The releases often highlight the initiatives companies are pursuing and the directions in which they are taking their business. You can also sign up for Google Alerts to get news on companies you are researching. Knowing something about an employer and industry can give you a competitive edge in terms of getting an interview, landing a job, and negotiating a good salary.

Once you have landed an interview, you have the opportunity to learn more about an employer, including the type of people who work there, its corporate culture, benefits, and so forth. If you are offered a job with the firm, a website such as Salary.com can help you determine whether the firm's offer is acceptable to you. CNNMoney.com's cost of living calculator, titled "How far will my salary go in another city?" can help you figure out whether it is monetarily feasible to relocate for a job. Highlights in HRM 10 shows the questions you should ask yourself before you accept a job offer with a particular company.

A.5 Consider the Boundaryless Career

A generation ago, career success was synonymous with ascending a corporate hierarchy over the course of a lifetime spent in a single firm. Today, however, individuals pursuing *boundaryless careers* prefer to see themselves as self-directed "free agents" who develop a portfolio of employment opportunities by proactively moving from employer to employer, simultaneously developing and utilizing their marketable skills. Employees pursuing boundaryless careers develop their human capital along dimensions of industry and occupational knowledge. That is, they may be experts in computer programming or have great insights into trends in the banking industry. In contrast, individuals pursuing more traditional careers develop their knowledge in ways specific to a given firm.

Alternately, you might want to become an entrepreneur. Being an **entrepreneur**—one who starts, organizes, manages, and assumes responsibility for a business or other enterprise—offers a personal challenge that many individuals prefer over being an employee.[3]

entrepreneur
One who starts, organizes, manages, and assumes responsibility for a business or other enterprise.

A.6 Keeping Your Career in Perspective

For most people, work is a primary factor in the overall quality of their lives. Nevertheless, it is advisable to keep one's career in perspective so that other important areas of life are not neglected.

Questions to Ask Yourself Before You Accept a Job

- Have I been offered a fair salary? Is it comparable to what other people in the same position are making and work with my budget?
- What is the benefit package and when am I eligible for it?
- Do I like my potential boss? Does he or she seem like someone with whom I can have a good working relationship?
- Do I like my potential coworkers?

- Will I be comfortable in this office environment?
- Is the corporate culture in line with my own values, attitudes, and goals?
- Am I genuinely excited about the job?
- Can I handle the commute to this job?

Sources: Liz Ryan, "Five Questions to Ask before You Accept a Job Offer," *Forbes* (January 1, 2015), https://www.forbes.com; Dawn Rosenberg McKay, About.com, © 2007 About.com, Inc., a part of the New York Times Company. All rights reserved.,

A.6a Developing Off-the-Job Interests

How satisfied you are with your life is a product of many forces. When people complain about not having a good work-life balance, often the problem is not too much work but too little "life."[4] Some of the more important ingredients of "life" are physical health, emotional well-being, harmonious interpersonal relationships, financial security, freedom from too much stress, and achievement of one's goals. While a career can provide some of the satisfaction that one needs, most people find it necessary to turn to interests and activities outside their career. Off-the-job activities not only provide a respite from daily work responsibilities but also offer satisfaction in areas unrelated to work. With that said, it is up to you to decide what is important to you and how to spend your work and off-the-job time. Your life is yours to live, and it is shorter than you think.

A.6b Balancing Marital and/or Family Life

As we have said, the one event that often poses the greatest threat to a family is relocation. Families often experience conflicts between the desire to advance the careers of different parents and settling down in one place. If an employee is experiencing ambiguity and/or conflict with his or her work role, a low level of supervisory support, or disappointment due to unfulfilled work expectations, this can affect his or her family life as well. Other conflicts include work-life balance problems, such the need to spend time with a person's family members and to care for children, aging elders, or a spouse. The different employment patterns in a family and dissimilarity in a couple's career orientations can take a toll on employees.

A number of employers are doing more today to help their employees cope with these problems via alternative work options. Employees are also actively looking for companies that have family-friendly policies. *Working Mother* magazine annually publishes a survey of the 100 top companies in the United States for working parents. Understand that "to be a success in the business world takes hard work, long hours, persistent effort, and constant attention. To be a success in marriage takes hard work, long hours, persistent effort, and constant attention. The problem is giving each its due and not shortchanging the other."[5]

A.6c Planning for Retirement

Although you might be many years from retirement, it is never too early to plan for it. In your 20s, you will want to begin a savings plan and start paying off your student loans. As you get older, your goals will probably change. Perhaps you will want to buy a home, and you will need money for a down payment. Regardless of what stage of your life you are in, you should never neglect saving for your retirement throughout your working years. A small sum of money saved early, compounded with interest over years, can amount to millions of dollars. But if you wait until later, you will have to save a lot of money for it to amount to as much.

Your employer can help you with some aspects of retirement planning by providing you with information about tax-advantaged employer and individual savings plans. But although employer-sponsored preretirement programs can be helpful (as we will see in Chapter 11), planning for your own retirement is up to you. Do you want to travel or live in another state or country? What kind of retirement does your spouse envision? How much money will all of this require?

Your employer will not be able to answer these questions. However, by reading about the subject of retirement and taking it seriously while you are young, you will be able to answer these questions yourself. Planning early will help you set the stage for a healthy and satisfying retirement as free as possible from worries—especially worries that could have been avoided or minimized had you taken a few easy steps earlier in life.

Key Terms

entrepreneur   informational interview   job shadowing

Notes and References

1. E.K. Strong Jr., of Stanford University, was active in the measurement of interests from the early 1920s until his death in 1963. Since then his work has been carried on by the staff of the Measurement Research Center, University of Minnesota. The Strong Interest Inventory is distributed by Consulting Psychologists Press, Inc., to qualified people under an exclusive license from the publisher, Stanford University Press.

2. Carol Carter, *Keys to Business Communication* (Upper Saddle River, NJ: Pearson, 2012), Chapter 15.

3. Julie Rose, "The New Risk Takers," *Fortune Small Business* 12, no. 2 (March 2002): 28–34; Jack Howard, "Balancing Conflicts of Interest When Employing Spouses," *Employee Responsibilities & Rights* 20, no. 1 (March 2008): 29–43.

4. Jamie Eckle, "Randall Craig," *Computerworld* 42, no. 26 (June 23, 2008): 36.

5. Maria Malik et al., "The Role of Work Life Balance in Job Satisfaction and Job Benefit," *Journal of Applied Business Research* 30, no. 6 (2014): 1627; Christopher Caggiano, "Married … with Companies," Inc. 17, no. 6 (May 1995): 68–76; Sue Shellenbarger, "Sustaining a Marriage When Job Demands Seem to Be Endless," *The Wall Street Journal* (December 8, 1999): B1; Johan A. Turner, "Work Options for Older Americans: Employee Benefits for the Era of Living Longer," *Benefits Quarterly* 24, no. 3, (2008): 20–25.

CHAPTER 6

Employee Selection

Learning Outcomes

After studying this chapter, you should be able to

LO 1 Explain what the objectives of the employee selection process are, its steps, and why the information gathered during the process must be reliable and valid.

LO 2 Describe the tools used to screen applicants, the types of employment interviews and methods to administer them, and the post-interview screening tools firms use.

LO 3 Compare the value of different types of employment tests and how their validity and reliability are assessed.

LO 4 Explain how firms evaluate the information they collect on candidates and the decision strategies they use to select employees.

Regardless of whether a company is large or small, it wants to hire the best and the brightest employees. In addition, equal employment opportunity legislation, court decisions, and the *Uniform Guidelines* (discussed in Chapter 3) make it critical for the selection process to be done well: One group of researchers found that employers lose approximately 90 percent of all hiring discrimination suits, and the average payout per case is $1.5 million. The bottom line is good selection decisions make a difference. So do bad ones.[1]

LO ①

Managers often understand employees' jobs well. But how important do you think it is for them to understand the job selection process to make good employment decisions?

selection

The process of choosing individuals who are qualified to fill existing or projected job openings

6.1 Overview of the Selection Process

Suppose you have started a small business, and a number of people have expressed interest in working for you. Now you have to pick the right employees and avoid the wrong ones. But how should this be done? And what happens if it is not done correctly?

Selection is the process of choosing individuals who are qualified to fill existing or projected job openings. Figure 6.1 shows that the overall goal of selection is to maximize "hits" and avoid "misses." Hits are accurate predictions, and misses are inaccurate ones. The cost of one type of miss would be the expense of hiring an employee who turns out to be unsuccessful. The cost of the other type of miss is an opportunity cost—someone who could have done a great job but did not get the chance to do so.

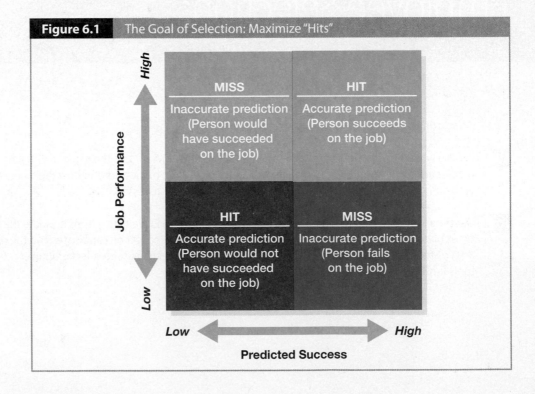

Figure 6.1   The Goal of Selection: Maximize "Hits"

6.1a Begin with a Job Analysis

Job specifications help identify the competencies employees need for success—the knowledge, skills, abilities, and other factors (KSAOs) that lead to superior performance. Managers then use selection methods such as interviews, references, and preemployment tests to measure applicants' KSAOs against the competencies required for the job. Complete and clear job specifications help interviewers differentiate between qualified and unqualified applicants and reduce the effect of an interviewer's biases and prejudices. Applicants whose KSAOs are well matched to the jobs they are hired for are also found to perform better and be more satisfied.[2]

Ordinarily, line managers are well acquainted with the skills, physical demands, and other characteristics of the jobs in their organizations. Interviewers and members of the HR department who participate in the selection process should become familiar with the jobs and competencies needed to perform them as well. In addition to the requirements of the job, many organizations, including Morgan Stanley, Merck, Southwest Airlines, and Starbucks, also try to hire individuals who match their values and cultures. Recall from Chapter 2 that this process is referred to as values-based hiring. Zappos and Salesforce.com are firms that give their employees the power to veto candidates they don't think will fit in with their cultures. In contrast, Facebook discourages hiring for cultural fit because it can result in a lack of diversity.[3]

6.1b Steps in the Selection Process

The steps in the selection process and their sequence will vary, not only with the organization, but also with the type of job being filled. Each step should be evaluated in terms of its contribution to the process. The steps that typically make up the selection process are shown in Figure 6.2. Not all applicants will go through all of these steps. Some will be rejected after the preliminary interview, others after taking tests, and so on.

As Figure 6.2 shows, organizations gather information about applicants in a number of ways: via résumés, applications, interviews, tests, medical examinations, and background and other checks. For an internal candidate not all of these steps may be needed. The person might need to submit a résumé and go through an interview but not necessarily a background investigation. However, some experts say it is a good idea to treat internal and external candidates the same way because it helps ensure no special treatment was given to any one candidate, and the best person for the job is chosen.

6.1c Obtaining Reliable and Valid Information

Regardless of whether a position is filled internally or externally, the information gathered about candidates must be reliable and valid. **Reliability** occurs when an interview, test, or other selection procedure results in consistent information about a candidate when repeated. A test that produces vastly different scores for individuals when administered to these same people a few days apart is unreliable. Likewise, unless an interviewer judges the capabilities of an applicant to be the same today as yesterday, the interviewer's judgments are unreliable (i.e., unstable). *Interrater reliability*—agreement among two or more raters—is one measure of a method's consistency. Reliability also refers to the extent to which two or more methods (e.g., interviews and tests) yield similar results or are consistent with one another.

reliability
The degree to which an interview, test, or other selection procedures result in consistent information about a candidate

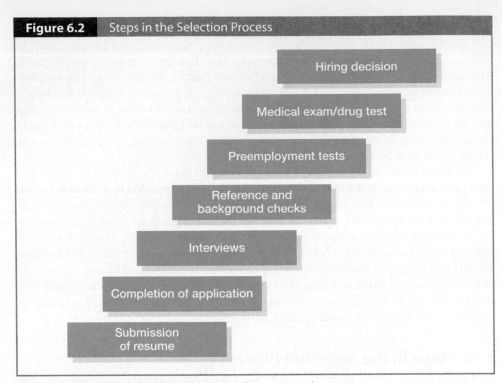

Figure 6.2   Steps in the Selection Process

Note: Steps may vary. An applicant may be rejected after any step in the process.

validity
The degree to which a test or selection procedure actually measures or predicts a person's ability to do a job

Validity refers to the degree to which a test or selection procedure actually predicts how well a person performs on the job. EEOC regulations require selection procedures to be valid. Like a new medicine, a selection procedure must be validated before it is used.[4]

6.2 Initial Screening

LO 2
Many employers do Internet searches to turn up information on job candidates. Can you see any problem related to doing so?

As an employer, would you want to interview all applicants who applied for one of your jobs? Probably not. Doing so would be very time consuming, and because time is money, it would be very expensive. Instead you would first want to screen out people who aren't qualified for the job. Next, let's look at the tools you can use to do this.

6.2a Initial Screening Methods

Employers use many different pieces of information to try to determine if an applicant will be successful on the job. The initial information tools for screening candidates include résumés, cover letters, the Internet, phone screening, and application forms.

Cover Letters and Résumés

Résumés and cover letters continue to be used to assess applicants, especially for salaried positions. Generally, these documents are reviewed first with an eye toward who can be eliminated because they do not have the skills, abilities, education, or experience outlined in the job description for the application. Did the applicant submit a thoughtful cover letter? Or is he or she simply "spamming" companies with résumés? A lack of a cover letter could be one way of eliminating applicants.

Was the cover letter well written? Well-written cover letters are important if a requirement of the job is having good written communication skills, which is the case for many jobs. For example, if a person who applied for an online customer service job that includes writing chat messages to customers submitted a cover letter with numerous typos, this could be grounds for passing over the person. Good writing skills might be less important for a person who works as a Walmart greeter. Good verbal or interpersonal skills might suffice for this position.

Evaluating résumés can be a subjective process. Evaluators often have a difficult time applying a set of consistent standards across multiple candidates or they consistently apply standards that are irrelevant to success on the job. The fact that there is no set format for writing résumés—that they vary from person to person—make them difficult for people to screen as well. Bias can also enter the process. One research study found that qualified applicants with black-sounding names had to send out 15 résumés to get an interview, whereas candidates with white-sounding names only had to send out 10.[5]

Developing clear evaluation criteria and a structured way to review résumés can help make the process less subjective. Using an assessment grid like the one shown in Figure 6.3 to take some of the guesswork out of the process. Job description criteria are placed in the left-hand column of the grid, and candidates are then ranked based on a scale as to whether the skills outlined in their résumés and cover letters match the job. The totals for the candidates are then compared.

Figure 6.3	Application/Résumé Assessment Grid			

Rate each candidate on a scale of 1–5, with 5 being the highest rating.

Quantitative requirements	Applicant A	Applicant B	Applicant C	Applicant D
Business degree and/or MBA	5			
Two years' managerial experience	5			
Ability to develop strategies	2			
Ability to manage budgets	2			
Qualitative requirements				
Demonstrated interpersonal skills	4			
Demonstrated coaching and development skills	4			
Ability to manage diverse teams and work with other departments	4			
Flexibility	3			
Writing and verbal skills	4			
Presentation skills	4			
Level of integrity	4			
Totals	**41**			

The downside of manually screening and assessing cover letters is that firm can get hundreds of them for a single position. As you learned in Chapter 5, some companies use software such as applicant tracking systems to screen résumés. For example, a hiring manager or human resources representative will specify the educational and experience levels a job requires and keywords that indicate experience. The software then scans the résumés collected for that position, pulls a list of qualified candidates, and ranks them according to how closely they match the job criteria. Some of the systems also prescreen people who submit résumés by first asking them to take a short questionnaire to determine how qualified they are. Résumé screening software isn't perfect, though.[6] Case Study 2 at the end of the chapter takes a closer look at the pros and cons of résumé screening.

Internet Checks

According to a survey by the website CareerBuilder, about 60 percent of employers research candidates using the Internet and social media sites, a practice that's grown exponentially.[7] However, doing so can be problematic for a number of reasons:

1. It can be difficult to verify the authenticity of information posted online (i.e., did the candidate really post the information, or did someone else?) and easy to confuse an applicant with someone else who has the same name, which could result in a lawsuit. Some federal courts have ruled that employers *must ensure* the information they collect online is verified by multiple sources.

2. Much of the information people post online isn't job related. For example, recruiters need to ensure they don't screen out applicants because they discovered they smoke or drink alcohol or engage in other activities that are not job related and are, in fact, legal.[8]

3. Third, scouring the Internet and social media sites can inadvertently lead to discrimination against members of protected classes.[9]

Another CareerBuilder survey found the biggest factor influencing an employer's decision not to hire an applicant was provocative photos on social media, an issue that is more likely to affect women than men. Religious discrimination can be a problem, too. Researchers at Carnegie Mellon University found that applicants whose online profiles indicated they were Muslim were less likely to get called for interviews than Christian applicants.[10]

Companies are still in the process of developing policies related to social media and Internet searches—that is, what information should be searched for and when, how it should be documented, and by whom. To avoid discrimination, most HR experts advise firms to not conduct any searches until after an applicant has been interviewed, and to use the same search process for all candidates. Candidates should also be told during their interviews that their public (not private) online profiles may be checked. Not all applicants realize the checking occurs and could feel their privacy is violated without such notice. At a minimum, advance notice gives candidates a chance to review and edit their profiles or make them private, if they want.

video résumés
Short video clips that highlight applicants' qualifications beyond what they can communicate on their résumés

Phone and Video Screening

Short phone interviews, or screening interviews, are often conducted, many times by HR personnel, to narrow down the field and save managers time by eliminating candidates who are not likely to be hired. Video is being used to prescreen applicants as well. To give employers a "preview" of themselves, some candidates post **video résumés** on YouTube and include links to them in their résumés and LinkedIn profiles.[11] Video résumés are short video clips that highlight applicants' qualifications beyond what they can communicate via their résumés and cover letters. The videos allow employers to see how well they present themselves and decide whether they should be interviewed.

However, not all employers accept video resumes, and there is a concern they can result in employers screening people based on their looks, sexes, or ethnicities rather than their qualifications. To eliminate bias and recruit more diverse workforces, some companies actually strip out names and photos from résumés before reviewing them. The recruiting software Hired does this automatically. Mehul Patel, the CEO of Hired, says he can envision a day when virtual reality programs disguise the appearances and voices of candidates, forcing recruiters and interviewers to focus on their experience and skills.[12]

Application Forms

Application forms provide a fairly quick and systematic means of obtaining a variety of information about the applicant, such as whether the applicant meets the minimum requirements for experience, education, and so on. Even when applicants come armed with elaborate résumés, they should complete application forms because it is a way to gather consistent information about candidates. People, even those in high positions, frequently exaggerate their qualifications on their résumés and omit unflattering information. George O'Leary had to resign as head football coach at Notre Dame after falsely claiming he had played football at New Hampshire and had a master's degree from New York University. Radio Shack CEO David Edmondson was forced to resign after claiming on his résumé that he had earned college degrees in theology and psychology. Not only had he not graduated, but the college he attended did not even offer a psychology degree.[13]

Far fewer people lie on application forms relative to their résumés, a survey by the job board CareerBuilder found. Most forms require an applicant to sign a statement verifying the information on the form is true and granting the employer the right to terminate the candidate's employment if any of the information is found to be false.[14]

However, the EEOC and the courts have found that many questions on application forms discriminate against women and minorities and often are not job related. Highlights in HRM 1 offers firms some guidelines about the types of questions that should and should not be asked on an application form if a firm wants to stay out of court.

Because of differences in state laws, organizations operating in more than one state will find it difficult to develop one form that can be used nationally. For example, roughly half of U.S. states and more than 150 cities have banned boxes applicants must check about their criminal history because it can adversely affect minorities. Although it's not a federal mandate, the EEOC supports "banning the box" because it helps ex-offenders reenter the workforce instead of being sidelined for life.[15] When the boxes are present, virtually anyone with even a minor conviction that may have occurred years ago will get screened out.

That doesn't mean a company can't check a candidate's criminal record later in the hiring process for job-related reasons, though. If someone applying for a bookkeeper's job was recently convicted of embezzlement, a firm needs to be able to check that. Some state laws require firms to delay asking about an applicant's criminal history until after an interview or provisional offer has been made to the candidate.

What to Include—and Not to Include—on a Job Application Form

- *Application date.* This helps managers know when the form was completed and gives them an idea of the time limit (e.g., one year) that the form should be on file.
- *Educational background.* Include blanks for high school, college, and post-college attendance—but not the dates attended, since that can be connected with age.
- *Experience.* Virtually any questions that focus on work experience related to the job are permissible.
- *Arrests and criminal convictions.* Don't ask questions about arrests. Questions about convictions and guilty pleadings can be problematic if they are not related to the job. Some states prohibit conviction questions, and the EEOC has indicated that they can have a disparate impact on African American and Hispanic workers.
- *Marital status and dependents.* Don't ask questions about marital status or whether a person has dependents or children.
- *National origin.* Don't ask questions about an applicant's national origin. However, it is acceptable to ask whether the person is legally prevented from working in the United States.
- *References.* Most applications include blanks for the names, addresses, and phone numbers of references provided by applicants.

- *Disabilities.* Don't ask applicants questions designed to elicit information about the existence, nature, or severity of a disability. Inquiries about the ability of the person to perform job functions, however, are acceptable. Under the most recent guidelines issued by the EEOC, employers can ask whether an applicant needs reasonable accommodation *if the disability is obvious or if* the applicant has voluntarily disclosed the disability.

Disclaimers

- *EEOC and at-will statements.* State on the application form that the firm does not discriminate and is an EEOC employer. If your state allows it, the form should state that all employees are hired *at will.* This gives both employer and employee the right to end the employment relationship at any time without reason.
- *Reference checks.* Include language that gives the hiring firm the right to contact the applicants' previous employers listed on the form and their résumés.
- *Employment testing.* List any tests the applicant may have to take and ask the applicant to sign the application consenting to their use.
- *Information falsification.* Notify applicants that any falsification of the information they provide could result in their disqualification or termination should they be hired.

6.3 Employment Interviews

Even though they are plagued by subjectivity and have shown to be poor predictors of performance, employment interviews are almost always utilized in the selection process. As Figure 6.4 shows, situational factors and candidate characteristics, such as a person's race and sex, can affect the perceptions of an interviewer and ultimately the interview's outcome. Nonetheless, firms continue to use interviews because (1) they are practical when there are only a small number of applicants; (2) they serve other purposes, such as public relations; and (3) interviewers trust their judgments when it comes to making decisions about which candidates to choose. Even a limited understanding of the variables in Figure 6.4 and periodic training have been shown to dramatically improve the effectiveness of interviewers, however.[16]

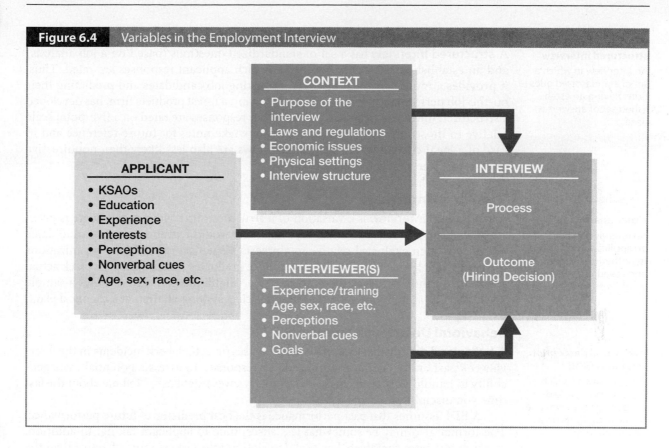

Figure 6.4 Variables in the Employment Interview

CONTEXT
- Purpose of the interview
- Laws and regulations
- Economic issues
- Physical settings
- Interview structure

APPLICANT
- KSAOs
- Education
- Experience
- Interests
- Perceptions
- Nonverbal cues
- Age, sex, race, etc.

INTERVIEWER(S)
- Experience/training
- Age, sex, race, etc.
- Perceptions
- Nonverbal cues
- Goals

INTERVIEW

Process

Outcome
(Hiring Decision)

6.3a Types of Interviews

Interviewing methods differ in several ways. In highly structured interviews, the interviewer determines the course that the interview will follow as each question is asked. In a structured interview the applicant plays a larger role in determining the course the discussion will take. Next, let's look at the different types of interviews from the least structured to the most structured. Note that different types of interview styles and questions they utilize can be mixed and matched to yield a more complete picture of candidates.

Nondirective Interviews

In a **nondirective interview**, the interviewer asks broad, open-ended questions—such as "Tell me more about your experiences on your last job" —and allows the applicant to talk freely with a minimum of interruption. The freedom afforded to the applicant helps uncover information a candidate might not disclose during more structured questioning. However, because the applicant determines the course of the interview, the information gathered on one applicant can be vastly different from the information gathered on another. Thus, the reliability and validity of these interviews are not likely to be as great.

nondirective interview
An interview in which the applicant is allowed the maximum amount of freedom in determining the course of the discussion, while the interviewer carefully refrains from influencing the applicant's remarks

Structured Interviews

structured interview
An interview in which a set of standardized questions having an established set of answers is used

A **structured interview** has a set of standardized questions (based on a job analysis) and an established set of answers against which applicant responses are rated. Thus, it provides a more consistent basis for evaluating job candidates and predicting their on-the-job performance. Weyerhaeuser Company, a forest products firm, has developed a structured interviewing process. Candidates' responses are rated on a five-point scale relative to those answers, and the interviewers take notes for future reference and in case of a legal challenge. Structured interviews are also less likely than nondirective interviews to be attacked in court.[17]

Situational Interviews

situational interview
An interview in which an applicant is given a hypothetical incident and asked how he or she would respond to it

A **situational interview** is a variation of a structured interview. A candidate is given a hypothetical incident and asked how he or she would respond to it. The candidate's response is then evaluated relative to a preestablished standard. Many organizations use situational interviews to select new college graduates because they may lack actual situations in the workplace they can describe. Highlights in HRM 2 shows a sample question from a situational interview used to select systems analysts at a chemical plant.

Behavioral Description Interviews

behavioral description interview (BDI)
An interview in which an applicant is asked questions about what he or she actually did in a given situation

A **behavioral description interview (BDI)** focuses on actual work incidents in the interviewee's past and what the applicant did in response. To assess a potential manager's ability to handle a problem employee, an interviewer might ask, "Tell me about the last time you disciplined an employee."

A BDI assumes that past performance is the best predictor of future performance. The format also may be somewhat less susceptible to applicant faking. In addition, research indicates that the behavioral description interview is more effective than the situational interview for hiring higher-level positions such as general managers and executives.[18]

Sequential and Panel Interviews

sequential interview
A format in which a candidate is interviewed by multiple people, one right after another

A **sequential interview** is one in which a candidate is interviewed by multiple people, one right after another. Sequential interviews are very common. They allow different interviewers who have a vested interest in the candidate's success to meet and evaluate the person one-on-one. The interviewers later get together and compare their assessments of the candidates.

panel interview
An interview in which a board of interviewers questions and observes a single candidate

In a **panel interview**, the candidate meets with a group of interviewers who each take turns asking questions. After the interview, the interviewers pool their observations and their scores of the candidate. Because these interviews involve input from multiple people, they tend to be more reliable and accepted as fair by candidates. If the panels are composed of a diverse group of interviewers, there is some evidence that hiring discrimination is minimized.[19] A panel interview also results in a shorter decision-making period than if each applicant has to be interviewed by each interviewer separately.

6.3b Methods for Administering Interviews

Most interviews take place in person. However, they can be administered in other ways to broaden the talent pool and make interviewing easier, faster, and less costly.

Sample Situational Interview Question

Question:

It is the night before your scheduled vacation. You are all packed and ready to go. Just before you get into bed, you receive a call from the plant. A problem has arisen that only you can handle. You are asked to come in to take care of things. What would you do in this situation?

Record Answer:

_____
_____
_____

Scoring Guide:

Good: "I would go in to work and make certain that everything is OK. Then I would go on vacation."
Good: "There are no problems that *only* I can handle. I would make certain that someone qualified was there to handle things."
Fair: "I would try to find someone else to deal with the problem."
Poor: "I would go on vacation."

Video and Phone Interviews

In an independent study of 500 HR managers at U.S. companies, 6 in 10 said their firms often conduct **video interviews** via webcams and services such as Skype.[20] Video interviews are convenient, low cost, and make it easier to interview people in different geographic areas, thereby expanding the talent pool. However, a study by DeGroote School of Business at McMaster University in Ontario, Canada, found that candidates interviewed via video came across as less likable. Some candidates may be more comfortable on camera or using the technology than other candidates. The researchers suggested

video interviews
Interviews conducted via videoconferencing or over the Web

LDprod/Shutterstock

Video interviews make it easy and cost-effective to interview candidates from different geographic areas.

Hiring Managers Reveal Mistakes Candidates Make during Job Interviews

The following are some memorable blunders that have caused managers to not hire candidates.

- "The candidate spoke no English, so he brought his mother to translate for him during the interview. It was for a customer-service position."
- "She kept telling me about her marital problems."
- "The candidate knew nothing about the job being offered or our organization."
- "One guy ate a sandwich."
- "The candidate asked me to hurry up because she left her child in the car."

- "He told me the only reason he was here was because his mother wanted him to get a job. He was 37."
- "One candidate did not wear shoes to the interview."
- "Body odor so bad I had to excuse myself midinterview and put lip gloss in my nose in order to get through the rest."
- "One guy asked if we drug-tested and if we gave advance notice (we are a drug treatment facility)."

Sources: CareerBuilder.com, *Reader's Digest*.

---

that at a minimum all candidates be treated the same in terms of the methods by which they are interviewed.[21]

Phone interviews can be effective and actually help expand a company's pool of talent as well. Via phone, Pacific Islands Club, a resort in Guam, is able to recruit people from around the world who want to work for the resort. After a successful phone interview, Rebecca Cummings, a young graduate living in the United States, went to work for the resort as an activities director. A face-to-face interview would have been cost prohibitive.[22]

Computer-Administered (Automated) Interviews

Nike, Safeway Cigna Insurance, and Pinkerton Security are among the many companies that have used computer-assisted, or automated, interviews to gather information as well as compare candidates. In a **computer-administered (automated) interview**, the questions are administered to applicants via a computer. The interviews can be conducted at a firm's facilities, using kiosks, via phone, or online. A drawback of computer-administered interviews is that recruiters and managers can't immediately ask candidates follow-up questions based on their answers. Consequently, organizations use automated interviews mainly as a complement to, rather than as a replacement for, live interviews. Automated interviews can also be perceived as impersonal.[23]

When the grocer Giant Eagle needed to hire 1,000 employees, it utilized computer-administered interviews at a Pittsburgh-area convention center. People who passed them were then led to group interviews, where HR personnel worked with as many as 20 applicants at a time. [24] Some firms use automated video interviewing services like HireVue and VidCruiter.com. Applicants are invited to interview by email, given passwords to log onto the sites, and questions to answer, which are then recorded by their webcams and sent to the hiring firm. HireVue uses machine learning to analyze the video, audio, and language metrics in the interviews and then rank candidates based on previous top and bottom performers.

computer-administered (automated) interview
Interviews in which the questions are administered to applicants via computers. The interviews can be conducted at a firm's facilities, using kiosks, online, or via phone

6.3c Diversity Management: Could Your Questions Get You into Legal Trouble?

What questions should be or should not be asked in an interview? The EEOC discourages direct or indirect questions related to race, color, age, religion, sex, sexual orientation, national origin, caregiver status, and other factors we talked about in Chapter 3. Some questions that interviewers once felt free to ask are now problematic. Asking women (or men) if they are married or have children are examples. Several states have fair employment practice laws that are more restrictive than federal legislation. In general, if a question is job related, is asked of everyone, and does not discriminate against a certain class of applicants, it is likely to be acceptable.

Employers should provide their interviewers with instructions on how to avoid potentially discriminatory questions in their interviews. The examples of appropriate and inappropriate questions shown in Highlights in HRM 4 can serve as guidelines for application forms as well as preemployment interviews. Complete guidelines can be developed from current information available from district and regional EEOC offices and from state fair-employment practice offices.

6.4 Post-Interview Screening

After a candidate has been interviewed and appears to be a good potential new hire, information about the person's previous employment as well as other information provided by the applicant is investigated.

6.4a Reference Checks

Organizations check the references of employees in a number of ways. Phone checks are fast and make it easy for references to elaborate on a candidate. Prescient InfoTech, a software development company in Fairfax, Virginia, first calls references to establish contact and then emails them a two-page questionnaire, asking them to numerically rank the applicant's various job-related attributes. There is room at the end of the questionnaire for comments and recommendations.

The most reliable information usually comes from supervisors, who are in the best position to report on an applicant's work habits and performance. Verification related to an applicant's job title, duties, and pay level from a former employer's HR office is also very helpful. Highlights in HRM 5 includes a list of helpful questions to ask about candidates when checking their references.[25]

Prior to checking a candidate's references, the candidate must complete forms permitting information to be solicited from former employers and other reference sources. Even with these safeguards, organizations are often reluctant to put into writing an evaluation of a former employee for fear of being sued by the person. Many employers will only verify former employees' employment dates and positions. Even firms that have refused to give an employee a recommendation have found themselves sued. Other firms have been sued for knowing a former employee posed a danger to others but failing to disclose it. Recognizing this predicament, a number of states have enacted statutes offering protection from liability for employers who give references in good faith.[26]

Appropriate and Inappropriate Interview Questions

	APPROPRIATE QUESTIONS	INAPPROPRIATE QUESTIONS
National origin	What is your name? Have you ever worked under a different name? Do you speak any foreign languages that may be pertinent to this job?	What is the origin of your name? What is your ancestry?
Age	Are you over 18? If hired, can you prove your age?	How old are you? What is your date of birth?
Gender	(Say nothing unless it involves a bona fide occupational qualification.)	Are you a man or a woman?
Race	(Say nothing.)	What is your race?
Disabilities	Do you have any disabilities that may inhibit your job performance? Are you willing to take a physical exam if the job requires it?	Do you have any physical defects? When was your last physical?
Height and weight	(Not appropriate unless it is a bona fide occupational qualification.)	How tall are you? How much do you weigh?
Residence	What is your address? How long have you lived there?	What are the names and relationships of those with whom you live?
Religion	(You may inform a person of the required work schedule.)	What church do you go to?
Military record	Did you have any military education/experience pertinent to this job?	What type of discharge did you receive?
Education and experience	Where did you go to school? What is your prior work experience? Why did you leave? What is your salary history?	Is that a church-affiliated school? When did you graduate?
Criminal record	Have you ever been convicted of a crime? (May not be appropriate unless not being convicted is a bona fide occupational qualification.)	Have you ever been arrested?
Citizenship	Do you have a legal right to work in the United States?	Are you a U.S. citizen?
Marital/family status	What is the name, address, and telephone number of a person we may contact in case of an emergency?	Are you married, divorced, single? Do you prefer Miss, Mrs., or Ms.? Do you have any children? How old are they?

negligent hiring
The failure of an organization to discover, via due diligence, that an employee it hired had the propensity to do harm to others

6.4b Background Checks

Background investigations, which require the consent of applicants, have become standard procedure for many companies. Moreover, state courts have ruled that companies can be held liable for **negligent hiring** if they fail to do adequate background checks. Federal law requires comprehensive background checks for all child care providers, for example. It also prohibits convicted felons from engaging in financial and

Sample Reference-Checking Questions

- What is your relationship to the applicant? Are you the person's supervisor, peer, or subordinate?
- What were the start and end dates of the applicant's employment?
- What were the applicant's title and responsibilities?
- In what areas did the applicant excel?
- What unique, or exceptional, talents does the applicant have?
- In what areas did the applicant need improvement?
- What was the applicant's biggest accomplishment at your organization?
- How well does the applicant communicate with and get along with others?
- How does the applicant deal with conflicts and stress?

- To what extent is the applicant driven to succeed?
- Was the applicant punctual?
- For what reason did the applicant leave your organization?
- Would you rehire the applicant?
- Are there any serious problems with the applicant we should know about?
- Is there any additional information about the applicant you would like to share with me?

Sources: "Four Reasons Why You Should Always Check References," *Human Resources Today* (December 29, 2015), http://www.humanresourcestoday.com; Alison Doyle, "Reference Check Questions," About.com (March 24, 2011), http://www.about.com; Carolyn Hirschman, "The Whole Truth," *HRMagazine* 45, no. 6 (June 2000): 86–72.

---

security-oriented transactions. According to the Society of Human Resources Management, companies are increasingly background-checking contingent workers given the growth of the "gig" economy. Uber and Lyft drivers are examples. Some employers, but certainly not all, rescreen their employees when they change jobs within their companies.

Among the checks are social security verification, past employment, education, and certification and license verification. A number of other checks can be conducted if they pertain to the job for which one is being hired. They include a driving-record check (for jobs involving driving), a credit check (for money-handling jobs), a military records check, and criminal records check.

To run background checks, firms must obtain clear and conspicuous written consent from applicants beforehand (usually on a separate form). Applicants must also be told if the information uncovered is going to be used to deny their employment; they must be given a copy of the report(s), the right to dispute it (them), and time to do so. This is important because it's not uncommon for background checks to be inaccurate or even include information about the wrong applicant.[27] To comply with various laws, many companies hire firms that specialize in background checks to conduct them for them or use the Department of Homeland Security's free e-Verify system.

Criminal Records Checks

According to the Society of Human Resources Management, most major firms check candidates' backgrounds for criminal records. However, as we have indicated, the EEOC has found that they can have a disparate impact on black and Hispanic workers, who, relative to other groups of people, have higher conviction and incarceration rates.

If criminal histories are taken into account, employers must also consider the nature of the job. For example, it may make sense to disqualify an applicant convicted of theft for a clerk's position, but not drunk driving. Even if the person were convicted of theft, the EEOC requires the employer to consider mitigating factors such as the individual's age at the time of conviction, how long ago it occurred, whether the person has been successfully rehabilitated, or has worked successfully in the same type of work following the conviction.[28]

Credit Checks

Credit checks used to be conducted primarily to screen applicants who handled money, such as banking employees. However, the number of companies conducting credit check tests has risen—even though the evidence is mixed as to whether there is a clear correlation between good employees and good credit scores.[29] Too often credit checks are used when they are not really needed, and candidates tend to view them as invasive and question their job relatedness. Eight of ten companies surveyed by the Society of Human Resources have gone ahead and hired job candidates with negative credit scores.[30]

Credit checks can also adversely affect qualified applicants who have been unemployed for long periods of time or faced bankruptcies or home foreclosures—problems that became more common among workers during the last recession. The EEOC has also warned employers that credit checks can have an adverse impact on some protected groups. For reasons such as these, a number of states, including Washington, California, Connecticut, Maryland, Illinois, and Hawaii, prohibit credit checks; many other states and U.S. lawmakers are considering similar action.

6.5 Preemployment Tests

LO 3

Personality tests, like other tests used in employee selection, have been under attack for several decades. Why do you think some applicants find personality tests objectionable? On what basis could their use for selection purposes be justified?

preemployment test
An objective and standardized test used to gauge a person's knowledge, skills, abilities, and other characteristics (KSAOs) relative to other individuals

What if you have narrowed down the list of candidates you're considering hiring but still can't decide among them? Is there a test you could use that would tell you which ones would perform better than the others? That's what people have wondered for years, hence the development of preemployment tests.

A **preemployment test** is an objective and standardized device used to gauge a person's KSAOs relative to other individuals.[31] Not all companies conduct preemployment tests, but many do. One of the drawbacks of preemployment tests is that they create the potential for legal challenges by applicants claiming the tests they took were discriminatory. FedEx used to administer a basic skills test for the purposes of promoting employees, but it dropped the test following a lawsuit that alleged it was discriminatory.

The cost, time, and ease of administering and scoring the tests must also be considered. For some jobs, the costs of testing may outweigh the benefits. There is also some evidence that the more tests that are required, the higher the likelihood of a lawsuit, and the more important it is for companies to demonstrate their reliability and validity in their procedures.[32]

It is a test developer's responsibility to ensure it meets accepted standards of validity and reliability.[33] The data about a test's reliability are ordinarily presented in the manual for the test. However, a firm should not just take a developer's word that its tests are reliable and valid. One source of information about commercially available tests—the *Mental Measurements Yearbook (MMY)*—contains descriptive information plus critical reviews by experts of various types of tests. The firm should also check to be sure the test was professionally validated in compliance with the Uniform Guidelines on Employee Selection Procedures, that it has been vetted for disparate impact, and that it has not been contested in court or by the EEOC.

Small Business Application

Adding Structure to the Employee Selection Process in Small Businesses

How do small businesses go about selecting employees to work at their firms? Not very systematically, some human resources professionals and researchers say. "All too often, employees are relatives or friends that lack the basic skills to augment the organization's ability to be profitable/successful," says an executive who coaches other businesspeople to help them achieve superior results.

Sometimes a small firm will make poor selections because it is anxious to get someone hired when the firm is short staffed. But if the wrong person is hired, that only compounds the problem. Another pitfall is being too confident about the right "type" of person for the job, which can cause hiring managers to make snap judgments about candidates based on casual conversations, before examining the candidates' qualifications for the job. Properly vetting candidates not only can lead to better employees, but can also help a company defend itself should it be accused of discriminatory practices. And at least one research study has found that the use of formal recruitment and selection techniques gives employees a positive perception of their firms and their bosses and results in greater loyalty to their organizations.

Adding structure to the selection process doesn't have to be difficult. You can map out the qualifications for the job on a form similar to the one shown in Figure 6.3. Then develop a series of open-ended and situational questions designed to elicit information about the candidate's job knowledge, conscientiousness, interest in the work, and how well his or her personality squares with the job.

Once you have the questions drafted, ask the same questions of all candidates. Last, embezzlement and theft can be particularly devastating to small businesses, so *do* run background checks on employees and check their references, even if you know the candidates. You might be surprised by what you find.

Sources: Robert N. Lussier and Joel Corman, "There Are Few Differences between Successful and Failed Small Businesses," *Journal of Small Business Strategy* 6, no. 1 (2015): 21–34; "Selecting the Best," *Elitefts* (November 9, 2010), http://www.elitefts.com/; Barbara Reda and Linda Dyer, "Finding Employees and Keeping Them: Predicting Loyalty in the Small Business," *Journal of Small Business & Entrepreneurship* 23, no. 3 (2010): 445.

Keep in mind that even if a test is reliable and valid for positions in other organizations, it might not be reliable and valid for the positions in your organization because they may be somewhat different. Managers therefore need to do a thorough job analysis to determine the skills candidates actually need to be tested for and eliminate any unnecessary or duplicate tests.

6.5a Types of Tests

We will talk more about what the EEOC demands as far as the validity of preemployment tests goes later in this section. First let's look at the different types of preemployment tests.

Job Knowledge Tests

Job knowledge tests are achievement tests designed to measure people's level of understanding, or knowledge, about a particular job. The Uniform CPA Examination used to license certified public accountants is one such test. Most civil service examinations, for example, are used to determine whether an applicant possesses the information and understanding to do the job without further training.[34] Job knowledge tests are also used by the U.S. Armed Forces.

Work Sample Tests

Work sample tests, or job sample tests, require the applicant to perform tasks that are actually a part of the work required on the job. Examples include a map-reading test for traffic control officers, a lathe test for machine operators, and a test to determine if an administrative assistant understands Microsoft Office. Computer simulations are sometimes used, particularly when testing a candidate might prove dangerous. Anyone who wants to become a pilot in the armed services and fly multimillion-dollar jets, for example, must undergo this type of testing. (Case Study 1 looks at different simulations firms are using.) Like job knowledge tests, when work sample tests are constructed from a carefully developed outline that experts agree includes the major job functions, the tests are considered effective, reliable, valid, and fair.[35]

Assessment Center Tests

assessment center test

A process by which managerial candidates are evaluated at an assessment center as they participate in a series of situations that resemble what they might need to handle on the job

An **assessment center test** is used to evaluate candidates, often as a group, as they participate in a series of situations that resemble what they might be called on to handle on the job. Some assessment centers, which are where the tests are professionally conducted, take a "day in the life" approach. Candidates "report to work" at the assessment center and receive the usual steady diet of emails and other interruptions, meet with various role-players who play different characters, and handle manufactured events while they are observed and recorded.[36] Because they are costly, assessment centers are often used to select managers and executives.

Cognitive Ability Tests

Cognitive ability tests measure mental capabilities such as general intelligence, verbal fluency, numerical ability, and reasoning ability. The Scholastic Aptitude Test (SAT) and Graduate Management Aptitude Test (GMAT) are examples. The Wonderlic Personnel Test is a cognitive ability test also used by many organizations, including the National Football League. Figure 6.5 shows some items that could be used to measure different cognitive abilities.

Although cognitive ability tests can be developed to measure very specialized areas such as reading comprehension and spatial relations, many experts believe that the validity

With jobs that require specific skills, it is quite common for employers to ask candidates to demonstrate their abilities through work sample tests.

fizkes/Shutterstock

Figure 6.5	Examples of Questions on a Cognitive Ability Test

Verbal	1. What is the meaning of the word "surreptitious"?
	a. covert c. lively
	b. winding d. sweet
Quantitative	2. Divide 50 by 0.5 and add 5. What is the result?
	a. 25 c. 95
	b. 30 d. 105
Reasoning	3. _____ is to *boat* as *snow* is to _____.
	a. Sail, ski c. Water, ski
	b. Water, winter d. Engine, water
Mechanical	4. If gear A and gear C are both turning counterclockwise, what is happening to gear B?
	a. It is turning counterclockwise. c. It remains stationary.
	b. It is turning clockwise. d. The whole system will jam.

Answers: 1. a, 2. d, 3. c, 4. b

of cognitive ability tests simply reflects their connection to general intelligence. Past studies of general intelligence, such as IQ, have shown to be good predictors of performance across a wide variety of jobs. However, newer studies suggest that this may be more of a perception in Western cultures, and that choosing people with the highest IQs might not always lead to hiring the best candidates.[37] Cognitive ability tests also have to be job related and carefully validated. Ford Motor Co. settled a $1.6 million case with the EEOC for having implemented a cognitive ability test that had a disparate impact on black applicants.

Biographical Data (Biodata) Tests

Biographical data tests (biodata tests) collect biographical information about candidates who has shown to correlate with on-the-job success. Candidates are questioned about events and behaviors that reflect attitudes, experiences, interests, skills, and abilities. Typically the questions relate to events that have occurred in a person's life and ask what the person typically did in those situations. The idea is that past behavior is the best predictor of future behavior. For example, a question on a biodata test might ask, "How do you handle stressful situations?" or "How often have you put aside tasks to complete another, more difficult assignment?" Test takers choose one of several predetermined alternatives to best match their past behavior and experiences. Because it costs about $100,000 to train an air-traffic controller, in 2014, the Federal Aviation Administration (FAA) instituted a biodata test to identify people who can handle the high-stress, high-stakes work without quitting.[38]

A response to a single biodata question is of little value. Rather, it is the pattern of responses across several different situations that give biographical data the power to predict future behavior on the job. Although biodata tests have been found to be good predictors of on-the-job success, they are sophisticated and must be professionally developed and validated. Another drawback is that the questions might not appear to be clearly related to the job being tested for, so applicants might question the test's validity. So many people with aviation experience failed the FAA test that it came under fire. The personal nature of biodata questions can also lead applicants to believe the tests invade their privacy.[39]

Personality and Interest Inventories

During the 1990s, testing by the U.S. Army found that cognitive ability tests were the best predictors of how well soldiers were able to acquire job knowledge and, ultimately, of their technical proficiencies. But personality tests were the better predictors of their motivation, such as their leadership efforts and propensity to adhere to rules. Years of research show that five dimensions can summarize personality traits. The "Big Five" factors are as follows:

1. *Extroversion*—the degree to which someone is talkative, sociable, active, aggressive, and excitable.

2. *Agreeableness*—the degree to which someone is trusting, amiable, generous, tolerant, honest, cooperative, and flexible.

3. *Conscientiousness*—the degree to which someone is dependable and organized and perseveres in tasks.

4. *Neuroticism*—the degree to which someone is secure, calm, independent, and autonomous.

5. *Openness to experience*—the degree to which someone is intellectual, philosophical, insightful, creative, artistic, and curious.[40]

Well-known personality tests include the California Psychological Inventory (CPI); the 180-question Caliper test, whose users range from FedEx to the Chicago Cubs; and the Predictive Index, which complies with EEOC guidelines.

Although there is some evidence to show that personality tests can help predict how well a person will perform on the job, historically the connection between the two has been quite low. There is also some concern that the tests can easily be "faked" by applicants trying to give hiring firms the answers they think they want to hear. Personality tests can also be problematic if they inadvertently discriminate against individuals who would otherwise perform effectively, which is why several states severely restrict their usage.[41] In addition, personality tests that reveal anything about a person's mental impairment or a psychological condition, even inadvertently, violate the Americans with Disabilities Act. Rather than being used to make hiring decisions, personality and interest inventories may be most useful for helping people with their occupational selection and career planning.

Polygraph Tests

The polygraph, or lie detector, is a device that measures the changes in breathing, blood pressure, and pulse of a person who is being questioned. Questions typically cover such items as whether a person uses drugs, has stolen from an employer, or has committed a serious undetected crime. The growing swell of objections to the use of polygraphs in employment situations culminated in the passage of the federal Employee Polygraph Protection Act of 1988. The act generally prohibits using lie detectors for prehire screening and random testing of a firm's current employees and applies to all private employers except pharmaceutical companies and security service firms.[42] Federal, state, and local governments can use polygraphs to screen applicants, but normally they are used only for law-enforcement personnel and high-security CIA- and FBI-type jobs.

Honesty and Integrity Tests

In response to the restrictions imposed by the Employee Polygraph Protection Act, employers have begun using honesty and integrity tests. The questions that might appear on an integrity test include the following:

- How likely would you be to report a coworker you discovered was stealing office supplies?
- Should an employee who lied on the application be fired if the falsification is uncovered?

Kansas-based Payless ShoeSource used an honesty test that reduced employee theft by 20 percent, the company claims.[43]

Although some studies have shown that honesty tests are valid for predicting job performance as well as a wide range of disruptive behaviors such as theft, disciplinary problems, and absenteeism, other studies have questioned their validity.[44] It is possible that the tests "work" not because they predict behavior but because they deter less-than-honest applicants from joining a company. Evolv, an assessment company, is one of a number of firms attempting to improve the accuracy of honesty and integrity tests by using big data and other analysis technology in the process.[45]

Physical Ability Tests

For some jobs, employers need to assess a person's physical abilities. Particularly for demanding and potentially dangerous jobs such as those held by firefighters and police officers, physical abilities such as strength and endurance tend to be good predictors not only of performance but also of accidents and injuries.[46]

Like other organizations, the Marine Corp has had to ensure its physical abilities tests are job related.

Source: http://www.marinecorpstimes.com/article/20140127/NEWS/301270047/
Marine-Corps-struggles-challenge-making-women-do-pullups

Physical ability tests must be used cautiously as well. In the past, requirements for physical characteristics such as strength, agility, height, and weight were often determined by an employer's unvalidated notion of what should be required. This often put women and disabled job applicants at a disadvantage. After a Dial Corp. plant in Fort Madison, Iowa, began using a strength test, the company was sued. Prior to the test's use, nearly 50 percent of the people hired at the plant were women. Once the test was implemented, the percentage dropped dramatically. An appeals court ruled the test had a disparate impact on women because, although injuries at the plant fell, they only did so after the company instituted new safety rules, which happened years before the strength test was implemented.[47] Because of situations such as these, physical requirements have been questioned and modified so as to represent typical job demands.

Medical Examinations

A medical examination is one of the later steps in the selection process because the law prohibits it being administered to an applicant before he or she has been made a conditional employment offer and agreed to undergo it. A medical examination can only be given to ensure that the health of an applicant is fit for duty.[48] The Americans with Disabilities Act limits the types of medical inquiries and examinations employers may use and states that all exams must be directly related to the requirements of the job. Furthermore, the ADA prohibits companies from screening out a prospective employee because he or she has an elevated risk of on-the-job injury or a medical condition that could be aggravated because of job demands.

Drug Tests

In the United Sates, not only do employers have the right to use drug tests to screen candidates who use illegal substances, but roughly half of them do. Different states have different laws regarding drug testing. In some states, drug tests can only be given to candidates after they have been extended job offers conditional upon their passing the tests. A candidate can refuse to take the test, but that is tantamount to turning down the job.[49] As with other background checks, candidates must be given the results of the tests and the right to dispute them.

However, some studies have failed to show that drug testing makes the workplace safer or leads to improvements in the performance of workers. Relatively few applicants test positive for drugs (about 4 percent). In fact, legal drugs such as alcohol and prescription painkillers such as opioids appear to create more problems than illegal drugs in the workplace.[50] Marijuana is legal for recreational use in a number of states, which complicates the use of what drugs can be tested for, and it can be medically prescribed. It is also not uncommon for "false positives" to occur—that is, for a test to mistakenly show someone has used illegal drugs when he or she hasn't. Over-the-counter drugs can lead to false positives.

For reasons such as these and because candidates view them as invasive, some companies no longer conduct drug tests on job candidates. Or should a candidate fail a drug test, they allow the candidate to retake it to ensure its accuracy. Other companies say drug testing has saved them thousands of dollars in workers' compensation and other costs. The weight of the evidence suggests that testing is most appropriate for high-risk and safety-critical positions and those required by state and federal laws.

The U.S. Department of Labor suggests that if a company wants to implement drug testing, it seek legal advice and follow the testing standards federal agencies follow—namely, the procedures established by the Substance Abuse and Mental Health Services Administration (SAMHSA). Of course, not testing job candidates for drugs doesn't mean firms can't continue to have drug-free workplace policies requiring employees to come to work sober.

6.5b Determining the Validity of Tests

The *Uniform Guidelines* (see Chapter 3) recognizes and accepts different approaches to validating tests (and selection procedures in general): criterion-related validity, content validity, and construct validity.

Criterion-Related Validity

The extent to which a test significantly correlates with important work behaviors is known as **criterion-related validity**. How well a person performs on a test, for example, is compared with his or her actual production records, supervisor's ratings, training outcomes, and other measures of on-the-job success. Sales figures are commonly used for sales jobs. In production jobs, the quantity and quality of output are likely to be the best indicators of job success.

There are two types of criterion-related validity: concurrent and predictive. **Concurrent validity** is the extent to which the test scores of a firm's current employees correlate with their job performance. To test concurrent validity, a firm obtains data from its current employees at about the same time that test scores (or other predictor information) are obtained. For example, a supervisor would rate a group of clerical employees on the quantity and quality of their performance. These employees would then be given a clerical aptitude test, and their scores would be compared with the supervisor's ratings to determine the degree of relationship between them. Establishing the concurrent validity of a test prior to administering it to candidates can be quick and convenient because the firm has employees readily available to take the test. The drawback of this approach is that current employees have a great deal more experience, so their scores may not be comparable to candidates' scores.

Predictive validity involves testing candidates and obtaining criterion data after the individuals have been hired and on the job for a period of time. For example, candidates would be given clerical aptitude tests, which would then be filed away for later study. After the individuals have been on the job for several months, supervisors (who should not know the employees' test scores) are asked to rate them on the quality and quantity of their performance. The test scores are then compared with the supervisors' ratings. If the scores and supervisor's ratings are in line with one another, the test has predictive validity and can be used to test subsequent job candidates. Obviously this approach to testing will take longer to develop than the concurrent approach.

Regardless of the method used, cross-validation is essential. **Cross-validation** is a process in which a test or battery of tests is administered to a different sample of people (drawn from the same population) for the purpose of verifying the results obtained from the original validation study. One way to measure a test's validity is to administer it to an organization's current employees and create a benchmark score to which candidates' scores can be compared. This is what FedEx has agreed to do before administering any new tests.

Correlation methods are generally used to determine the relationship between predictor information such as test scores and criterion data. The correlation scatterplots in Figure 6.6 illustrate the difference between a selection test with zero validity (A) and one with high validity (B). Each dot represents a person.

criterion-related validity
The extent to which a selection tool predicts, or significantly correlates with, important work behaviors

concurrent validity
The extent to which the test scores of current employees correlate with their job performance

predictive validity
The extent to which candidates' test scores match criterion data obtained from them after they have been hired and on the job for a period of time

cross-validation
Verifying the results obtained from a validation study by administering a test or test battery to a different sample (drawn from the same population)

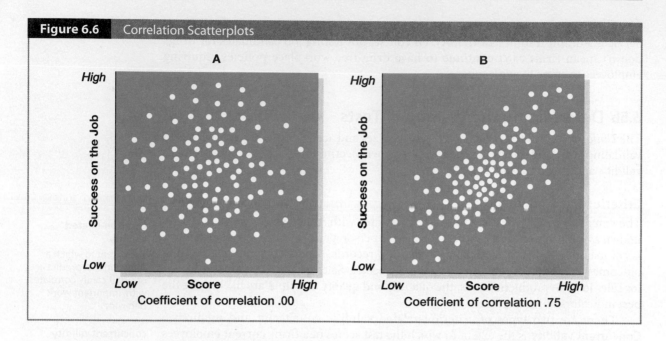

Figure 6.6   Correlation Scatterplots

Note that in scatterplot A, there is no relationship between test scores and success on the job; in other words, the validity is zero. In scatterplot B, those who score low on the test tend to have low success on the job, whereas those who score high on the test tend to have high success on the job, indicating high validity. In actual practice, we would apply a statistical formula to the data to obtain a coefficient of correlation referred to as a *validity coefficient*. Correlation coefficients range from 0.00, denoting a complete absence of relationship, to +1.00 and to –1.00, indicating a perfect positive and perfect negative relationship, respectively.

Combining two or more procedures such as an interview or a test can improve the validity of a firm's selection process. The higher the overall validity is, the greater the chances are of hiring individuals who will be the better performers.

Content Validity

content validity

The extent to which a selection instrument, such as a test, adequately samples the knowledge and skills needed to do a particular job

When it is not feasible to use the criterion-related approach, often because of limited samples of employees or applicants are available for testing, the content method is used. **Content validity** is assumed to exist when a test adequately samples the knowledge and skills a person needs to do a particular job. The closer the content of the selection instrument is to actual work samples or behaviors, the greater its content validity is. For example, a test for accountants has high content validity when it requires applicants to solve accounting problems representative of those found on the job. Asking an accountant to lift a 60-pound box, however, is a selection procedure that has content validity only if the job description indicates that accountants must be able to meet this requirement.

Content validity is the most direct and least complicated type of validity to assess. It is generally used to evaluate the job knowledge and skill tests. Unlike the criterion-related method, content validity is not expressed as a correlation. Instead, an index is computed (from the evaluations of an expert panel) that indicates the relationship between the content of the test items and a person's performance on the job.[51] Although content validity does have its limitations, it has made a positive contribution to job analysis procedures and the role expert judgments play in sampling and scoring procedures.

Construct Validity

The extent to which a test measures a theoretical construct, or trait, is known as **construct validity**. Typical constructs are intelligence, mechanical comprehension, and anxiety. They are in effect broad, general categories of human functions that are based on the measurement of many discrete behaviors. For example, the Bennett Mechanical Comprehension Test consists of a wide variety of tasks that measure the construct of mechanical comprehension.

Measuring construct validity requires showing that the psychological trait is related to a satisfactory job performance and that the test accurately measures the psychological trait. There is a lack of literature covering this concept as it relates to employment practices, probably because it is difficult and expensive to validate a construct and to show how it is job related.[52]

As you can tell from this discussion, developing valid selection procedures, especially selection tests, can be complicated and require expertise. Employers should ensure that tests and selection procedures are not adopted casually. If a selection procedure screens out a protected group, the employer should determine whether there is an equally effective alternative selection procedure that has less adverse impact and, if so, adopt the alternative procedure. Because valid custom tests are more defensible in court if applicants challenge them, many large organizations that subject applicants to multiple tests hire outside vendors with industrial-organizational psychologists on staff to help them develop selection procedures.

construct validity
The extent to which a selection tool measures a theoretical construct or trait

6.6 Reaching a Selection Decision

You now have a wealth of information about the candidates who want to work for you. How do you weigh it all so as to make a final decision? Next, we'll take a look at the various approaches you might use.

6.6a Summarizing Information about Applicants

Once you have gathered relevant information about multiple applicants, you have to systematically organize and evaluate it. Summary forms and checklists such as the one shown in Figure 6.7 can be used to ensure that all of the pertinent information about applicants has been included. Fundamentally, an employer is interested in what an applicant can do and will do. Evaluating candidates on the basis of information you have assembled should focus on these two factors, as Figure 6.8 shows. The "can-do" factors include a candidate's knowledge and skills, as well as the aptitude (potential) for acquiring new knowledge and skills. The "will-do" factors include the candidate's motivation, interests, and other personality characteristics. Both factors are essential to successful performance on the job. The employee who has the ability (can do) but is not motivated to use it (will not do) is little better than the employee who lacks the necessary ability.

LO 4
How have your skills, knowledge, aptitudes, and motivation affected the types of jobs you have applied for in the past or how well you did a particular job?

Figure 6.7	Candidate Evaluation Form

Position:
Candidate Name:
Interviewer Name:
Interview Date:

Complete the comments section as you interview the candidate. After the interview, circle your ratings for each section, and then add them together for a final score. The ratings scale is as follows:

RATINGS SCALE

1. Negligible or doesn't meet requirements
2. More needed
3. Adequate
4. Exceeds requirements

Education
Comments:
Rating: _____

Experience
Comments:
Rating: _____

Job Knowledge
Comments:
Rating: _____

Job Skills
Comments:

Interest in Position
Comments:
Rating:

Problem Solving Ability
Comments:
Rating: _____

Communication Skills
Comments:
Rating: _____

Leadership Skills
Comments:
Rating: _____

_____ TOTAL POINTS

Rater's Recommendation:

Figure 6.8	"Can-Do" and "Will-Do" Factors in Selection Decisions

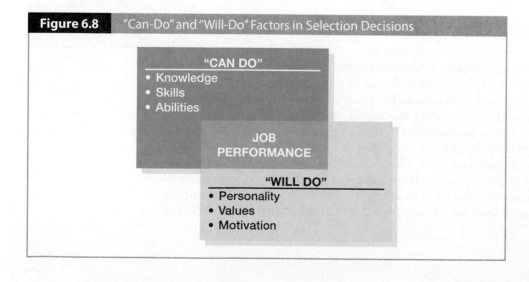

It is much easier to measure what individuals can do than what they will do. The can-do factors are readily evident from test scores and verified information. What the individual will do can only be inferred. Employers can use the responses to interview and application form questions and references to obtain information for making inferences about what an individual will do.

6.6b Decision-Making Strategy

The strategy used to make personnel decisions for one type of job, such as a manager, will differ from those used to make decisions for other types of job, such as a clerk or technician. Although many factors have to be considered, the following are some of the questions firms must consider when deciding on whom to hire:

1. Should the individuals be hired according to their highest potential or according to the needs of the organization?
2. At what grade or wage level should the individual be hired?
3. Should the selection be based on finding an ideal employee to match the job currently open, or should a candidate's potential for advancement in the organization be considered?
4. Should individuals who are not qualified but trainable be considered?
5. Should overqualified individuals be considered?
6. What effect will the decision have on the firm's affirmative action plans and diversity goals?

In addition to these factors, a firm must decide which selection approach to use: the clinical (personal judgment) approach or the statistical approach, which are discussed next.

Clinical Approach

Using the clinical approach, those making the selection decision review all the data on the applicants. Then, on the basis of their understanding of the job and the individuals who have been successful in that job, they make a decision. Different evaluators will make different decisions about an applicant when they use the clinical approach because each of them will make different judgments about the applicant's strengths and weaknesses. Unfortunately, personal biases and stereotypes are frequently covered up by what appear to be rational reasons for either accepting or rejecting a candidate. The clinical approach can also lead to a homogenous workforce because, as you learned in Chapter 5, according to the attraction–selection–attrition (ASA) model, people are often tempted to hire applicants like themselves.

Statistical Approach

The statistical approach to decision making is more objective. It involves identifying the most valid predictors and weighting them using statistical methods such as multiple regression.[53] Quantified data such as scores or ratings from interviews, tests, and other procedures are then combined according to their weighted value. Individuals with the highest combined scores are selected. Compared to the clinical approach, the statistical approach has shown to be superior in a wide variety of situations.

With a strictly statistical approach, a candidate's high score on one predictor (such as a cognitive ability test) will make up for a low score on another predictor (such as

compensatory model

A selection decision model in which a high score in one area can make up for a low score in another area

multiple cutoff model

A selection decision model that requires an applicant to achieve some minimum level of proficiency on all selection dimensions

multiple hurdle model

A selection decision model in which only the applicants with the highest scores at an initial test stage go on to subsequent stages

the interview). For this reason, this model is a **compensatory model**. However, it is frequently important for applicants to achieve some minimum level of proficiency on *all* selection dimensions. When this is the case, a **multiple cutoff model** can be used in which only those candidates who score above the minimum cutoff on all dimensions are considered. A selection from that subset of candidates is then made.[54]

A variation of the multiple cutoff model is the **multiple hurdle model**. After candidates go through an initial evaluation stage, those who score well advance to the next stage. The process continues through several stages (hurdles) before a final decision is made. This approach is especially useful when either the testing or training procedures are lengthy and expensive.

Each of the statistical approaches requires that a decision be made about where the cutoff lies—that point in the distribution of scores above which a person should be considered and below which the person should be rejected. The score that the applicant must achieve is the cutoff score. Depending on the labor supply and diversity and antidiscrimination considerations, it may be necessary to lower or raise the cutoff score.

The effects of raising and lowering the cutoff score are illustrated in Figure 6.9. Each dot in the center of the figure represents the relationship between the test score

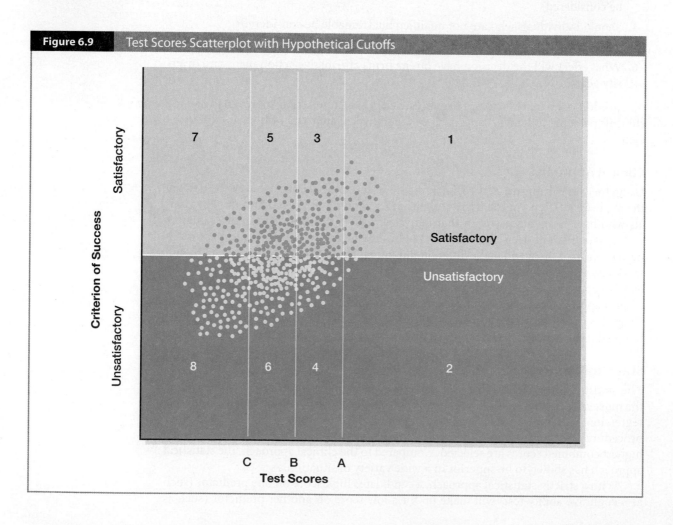

Figure 6.9   Test Scores Scatterplot with Hypothetical Cutoffs

(or a weighted combination of test scores) and the criterion of success for one individual. The elliptical pattern of the dots indicates the test has a fairly high validity. Note that the high-scoring individuals are concentrated in the satisfactory job success category, whereas the low-scoring individuals are concentrated in the unsatisfactory category.

If the cutoff score is set at A, only the individuals represented by areas 1 and 2 will be accepted. Nearly all of them will be successful. If more employees are needed, the cutoff score can be lowered to point B. In this case, a larger number of potential failures will be accepted, as shown in quadrants 2 and 4. Even if the cutoff is lowered to C, the total number of satisfactory individuals selected (represented by the dots in areas 1, 3, and 5) exceeds the total number selected who are unsatisfactory (areas 2, 4, and 6). Thus, the test serves to maximize the selection of probable successes and to minimize the selection of probable failures. This is all we can hope for in terms of predicting on-the-job success: the probability of selecting a greater proportion of individuals who will be successful rather than unsuccessful.

A related factor helps ensure the best qualified people are selected: having an adequate number of candidates from which to make a selection. This factor is typically expressed in terms of a **selection ratio**, which is the ratio of the number of applicants to be selected to the total number of applicants. A ratio of 0.10, for example, means that 10 percent of the applicants will be selected. A ratio of 0.90 means that 90 percent will be selected. If the selection ratio is low, only the most promising applicants will be hired. When the ratio is high, very little selectivity will be possible because even applicants with mediocre abilities will have to be hired to fill the firm's vacancies. When this is the situation, a firm's managers can fall prey to what some experts call the "desperation bias"—choosing someone because you are in a pinch. It is a common problem among managers because of the many time and operating constraints they face.

selection ratio
The number of applicants compared with the number of people to be hired

6.6c Final Decision

In large organizations, managers or supervisors usually make the final decision about whom to hire, and communicate it to the human resources department. HR personnel then notify the candidate about the decision and make a job offer. The HR department should confirm the details of the job, working arrangements, hours, wages, and so on and specify a deadline by which the applicant must reach a decision. If, at this point, findings from the medical examination or drug test are not yet available, an offer is often made contingent on the applicant passing the examination. This information can be verbally communicated initially. It is commonplace to first contact candidates by phone to inform them of the offer. The offer should then be put in writing, generally in a letter to the candidate.

The process of notifying internal candidates is slightly different. Generally, the hiring manager contacts the candidates personally and informs them of the decision. However, it is still important to put the offer in writing if an internal candidate is chosen so there is no ambiguity or dispute about its terms.

Rejecting both internal candidates and external candidates is a difficult task, but rejecting internal candidates can be particularly tricky. Most internal candidates seeking a promotion are valuable employees their firms would rather not lose. The manager delivering the bad news should explain to the employee that the person who got the job has skills more closely aligned with the firm's needs but that the process has given the organization a better understanding of her or his background when future job openings arise. The manager should also explain that the decision was made in a systematic way based on objective criteria but that it was nonetheless a hard one to make.[55]

Last, organizations should not fail to notify candidates who are not chosen for the position. This happens too often with both internal candidates and external candidates. It is not uncommon for external candidates to be customers of the firms to which they apply. Not letting them know about the employment decision can jeopardize that relationship. The same is true for internal candidates. One employee lamented that after applying internally for a job, no one contacted him or the other candidates to tell them they did not get the job. They only learned about it after a manager sent out an email about the new hire. "After 10-plus years of working for the company, I felt I deserved better treatment than that," says the employee.

Summary

LO 1 The employee selection process should start with a job analysis. The steps in the selection process and their sequence will vary, not only with the organization, but also with the type and level of jobs to be filled. The employee selection process should provide reliable and valid information about applicants so that their qualifications can be carefully matched with the job's specifications. The information that is obtained should be clearly job related, predict success on the job, and be free from discrimination. Reliability refers to the consistency of test scores over time and across measures. Validity refers to what a test or other selection procedure is supposed to measure and how well it actually measures it.

LO 2 Initial applicant screening tools include résumés and cover letters, application forms, references, Internet checks and phone screening, and sometimes short electronic questionnaires. Despite problems with its validity, the employment interview remains central to the selection process. Depending on the type of job, applicants could be interviewed by one person, members of a work team, or other individuals in the organization. Structured interviews have been found to be better predictors of the performance of job applicants than nonstructured interviews. Some interviews are situational and can focus on hypothetical situations or actual behavioral descriptions of a candidate's previous work experiences. Most interviews are conducted in person, but they can also be conducted via video,

phone, or administered by a computer (automated). Post-interview screening tools include reference and background checks, including criminal, drug, and credit checks.

LO 3 Preemployment tests are more objective than interviews and can give managers a fuller sense of the capabilities of different candidates. A wide range of tests exist. Cognitive ability tests are especially valuable for assessing verbal, quantitative, and reasoning abilities. Personality and interest-inventory tests are perhaps best used for placement or career development. Job knowledge and work sample tests are achievement tests that are useful for determining whether a candidate can perform the duties of the job without further training. Physical ability tests can be used to prevent accidents and injuries, particularly for physically demanding work. However, they must not be used if they have a disparate impact on candidates in protected classes. Medical examinations and drug tests should only be administered after a conditional offer of employment has been made. A test's validity can be assessed in terms of whether the measurement is based on a job specification (content validity), whether test scores correlate with performance criteria (predictive validity), and whether the test accurately measures what it purports to measure (construct validity).

LO 4 In the process of making decisions, all "can-do" and "will-do" factors should be assembled and weighted systematically so that the final decision can be based on a composite of the most reliable and valid information. Although the clinical approach to decision making is used more than the statistical approach, the former lacks the accuracy of the latter. Compensatory models allow a candidate's high score on one predictor to make up for a low score on another. When the multiple cutoff model is used, only those candidates who score above a minimum cutoff level remain in the running. A variation of the multiple cutoff is the multiple hurdle model, which involves several stages and cutoff levels. Organizations should not fail to notify candidates who are not chosen for jobs. Those who are chosen should receive their offers in writing so the terms are clearly agreed upon and be given a time limit to either accept or reject the offer.

Key Terms

assessment center test

behavioral description interview (BDI)

compensatory model

computer-administered (automated) interview

concurrent validity

construct validity

content validity

criterion-related validity

cross-validation

multiple cutoff model

multiple hurdle model

negligent hiring

nondirective interview

panel interview

predictive validity

preemployment test

reliability

selection

selection ratio

sequential interview

situational interview

structured interview

validity

video interviews

video résumés

Discussion Questions

LO 1 Is there a "best" employment process stepwise? What steps must come first and last?

LO 2 Compare briefly the major types of employment interviews described in this chapter. Which type would you prefer to conduct? Why?

LO 3 What characteristics do job knowledge and job sample tests have that often make them more acceptable to candidates than other types of tests?

LO 4 What is meant by the term *criterion* as it is used in personnel selection? Give some examples of criteria used for jobs with which you are familiar.

Designing Selection Criteria and Methods

Making hiring decisions is important but difficult. Without good information, managers have almost no chance of making the right choice. They may as well randomly choose a candidate.

The information-gathering process begins with a sound understanding of the job: the tasks, duties, and responsibilities associated with it, and the knowledge, skills, and abilities needed to do it. A job analysis should be done to make certain that all managers have assembled all of the information they need to ensure a good person–job fit. However, this information may not be enough. Other information about the company's values and philosophy are likely to be required to ensure that a good person–organization fit results.

Assignment

1. Working in teams of four to six individuals, choose a job with which you are familiar and identify the KSAOs needed to do it well.

2. Next, identify how you would evaluate candidates with these qualities. What tools would you use (applications, interviews, cognitive or ability tests, work samples, etc.) and why? Justify the cost and time required to conduct each.

3. After you have identified your selection criteria and methods, do a "reality check" in a real organization. Interview a manager who employs someone in that job. For example, if the job you selected is salesperson, go to a local business to learn how they select individuals for sales jobs. Compare what you thought would be a good selection approach with what you learned from the company you visited.

4. Identify the reasons for any discrepancies between your approach and theirs. Which approach do you think is better?

CASE STUDY **1**   Job Candidate Assessment Tests Go Virtual

A growing number of preemployment tests simulate a job's functions and are being conducted via computer or on the Web. You can liken them to video games but within a work setting. Toyota, Starbucks, the paint maker Sherwin Williams, and numerous financial firms such as SunTrust Banks, KeyBank, and National City Bank have successfully used virtual job simulations to assess applicants.

At Toyota, applicants participating in simulations read dials and gauges, spot safety problems, and use their ability to solve problems as well as their general ability to learn as assessed. The candidates can see and hear about the job they're applying for from current Toyota employees. National City Bank has used virtual assessments to test call-center candidates and branch manager candidates. Call-center candidates are given customer-service problems to solve, and branch manager candidates go through a simulation that assesses their ability to foster relationships with clients and make personnel decisions.

The virtual assessments tools, which are produced by companies such as Shaker Consulting Group, Profiles International, and others, do not come cheap. But although they can cost tens of thousands of dollars, larger companies that can afford them are saying they are worth it. The benefits? Better qualified candidates, faster recruiting, and lower turnover among employees hired. KeyBank says that by using virtual testing tools, it realized savings of more than $1.75 million per year due to lower turnover.

Candidates also seem to like the assessments because they provide a more realistic job preview and make them feel like they are being chosen for jobs on more than just their personalities or how they performed during an interview. "It was a very insightful experience that made you think about what exactly you like and dislike in the workplace and if you really enjoy helping customers and have patience to do so," says one candidate tested for a customer service job.

It is not just younger candidates who play a lot of video games who like the tests. Older candidates do as well. "We haven't seen any adverse impact," says Ken Troyan, chief staffing officer for SunTrust Banks. "There's some mythology—if you will—about older people not being computer-savvy, and that's just not so." One study found that the simulations also tend to result in less of a gap between minority and white candidates than when paper-and-pencil tests are used.

A handful of software companies have developed games that don't mirror work tasks but actual video games you would play for fun. "Bomba Blitz" and "Meta Maze" are two mobile games developed by the preemployment-testing company Knack. According to Knack, the games utilize behavioral neuroscience and big data—in this case, the game scores and decision-making traits of thousands of different types of workers—to match people with jobs.

HR experts warn that companies need to be sure they aren't simply buying glitzy simulations that don't translate well to the jobs for which they are hiring. Games like those produced by Knack are just now starting to be used, and firms generally aren't solely relying on them to make hiring decisions. Also, the tools could potentially eliminate candidates who have

trouble with simulations, games, or computers but might make good employees. You should still use the U.S. Department of Labor's "whole person approach" to hiring, says one HR professional. The whole person approach factors in the results of a variety of accepted tests along with prior actual performance and interview results to get the most complete picture of an employee or candidate.

Questions

1. What do you think are the prime advantages and disadvantages of "virtual tryouts"?

2. Do you think there would be any EEOC concerns regarding this system?

3. Do you think virtual job tryouts might be better suited for some jobs than others? If so, which ones?

Sources: Sarah Needleman, "Play This Game and Win a Job!" *Wall Street Journal* (March 14, 2016): R2; Karen Vilardo, "KeyBank's Success with the 'Virtual Job Tryout,'" *Journal of Corporate Recruiting Leadership* 5, no. 4 (May 2010): 24; Ira S. Wolfe and "Success Performance Solutions," *The Total View Newsletter* (May 12, 2010); Connie Winkle, "HR Technology: Job Tryouts Go Virtual," *HR Magazine* (September 1, 2006), http://www.shrm.org/; Gina Ruiz, "Job Candidate Assessment Tests Go Virtual," *Workforce Management Online* (January 2008), http://www.workforce.com; "Clients and Case Studies," *Shaker Consulting Group* (March 27, 2011), http://www.shakercg.com.

CASE STUDY ❷ Pros and Cons of Cleaning Up the "Resu-mess"

HR and hiring managers often find themselves swamped by résumés because they are so easy to send with a click of a button. Some large retailers can get a million or more résumés a year. Even small businesses get flooded with them. When Raising Cain, a Louisiana-based fast-food chain, opened an office in Dallas, the firm needed to hire 35 people. It received 10,000 résumés and had to hire an outside firm to help sort through them.

Applicant tracking systems and résumé screening software are helping harried HR personnel, managers, and business owners cope with the problem. After résumés are screened and reviewed, interviews can be scheduled automatically using a firm's email system and electronic calendar, and job offers sent to candidates to sign electronically and return. Many job boards have résumé screening capabilities and

algorithms to recommend candidates similar to the way Amazon.com recommends products based on what a person has purchased in the past.

Not all HR professionals are fans of résumé screening software, however. Managers tend to use huge numbers of key words so that very few applicants can make it past the screen. Different kinds of software can have different kinds of glitches. The software might not read certain types of fonts or reject a résumé of a good candidate if it contains a single typo. Unqualified applicants have learned to "pepper" their résumés with a job's keywords to get past résumé-screening software.

Peter Cappelli, a University of Pennsylvania professor, has written a book called *Why Good People Can't Get Jobs.* Cappelli relates an incident in which an HR manager put his own résumé through his company's screening process and got rejected. In another instance, an engineering firm received more than 25,000 résumés for a job but none of the candidates made it past electronic screening.

There is also a lack of the human touch and judgment in the process. Résumé-screening software can't easily pick up on candidates' "soft" skills, such as a person's ability to interact well with other people. And managers don't end up seeing interesting résumés—résumés from people who have different skills or life experiences that would translate well to the job. Consequently, a lot of people who would make excellent employees never get a glance.

Some recruiters have found ways to avoid the downsides of automatic résumé screening altogether. Kevin Mercuri, president of Propheta Communications, a public relations firm in New York City, got tired of being swamped by résumés. Now when he needs to recruit personnel, he posts a message about job openings on his LinkedIn page. "I get people vouching for each applicant, so I don't have to spend hours sorting through résumés," he says.

Questions

1. What impact do you think résumé screening tools are having on HR departments? What about line managers? Would you use the software to screen résumés?

2. How might the drawbacks associated with résumé screening software be addressed?

Sources: Ryan Craig, "Blame Bad Applicant Tracing for the Soft Skills Shortage at Your Company," *TechCrunch* (March 5, 2017), https://techcrunch.com; Dave Wessel, "Software Raises the Bar for Hiring," *Wall Street Journal* (May 31, 2012), http://online.wsj.com; Darren Dahl, "Tapping the Talent Pool … without Drowning in Resumes," *Inc.* 31 no. 3 (April 2009): 122; Anne Kadet, "Did You Get My Résumé?" *Smart Money* (February 27, 2009), http://www.smartmoney.com; Drew Robb, "Screening for Speedier Selection," *HR Magazine* 49, no. 9 (September 2004): 143–147.

Notes and References

1. Philip L. Roth et al., "Social Media in Employee-Selection-Related Decisions a Research Agenda for Uncharted Territory," *Journal of Management* (2013), 0149206313503018; Kate Z. Williams, Meline M. Schaffer, and Lauren E. Ellis, "Legal Risk in Selection: An Analysis of Processes and Tools," *Journal of Business & Psychology* 28, no. 4 (December 2013), DOI: 10.1007/s10869-013-9299-4.

2. Misty L. Loughry, Matthew W. Ohland, and D. Dewayne Moore, "Development of a Theory-Based Assessment of Team Member Effectiveness," *Educational & Psychological Measurement* 67, no. 3 (June 2007): 505–524; Patrick D. Converse, Fredrick L. Oswald, Michael A. Gillespie, Kevin A. Field, and Elizabeth B. Bizot, "Matching Individual to Occupations Using Abilities and the O*NET," *Personnel Psychology* 57, no. 2 (Summer 2004): 451–488.

3. Rachel Feintzeig, "Cultural Fit Plays Role in Hiring," *Wall Street Journal* (October 12, 2006), https://www.wsj.com.

4. Joe Williams, "Bringing the Human Touch to Recruitment," *Bloomberg Businessweek* (January 24, 2011), http://bx.businessweek.com.

5. Mary-Kathryn Zachary, "Discrimination without Intent," *Supervision* 64, no. 5 (May 2003): 23–29; Neal Schmitt, William Rogers, David Chan, Lori Sheppard, and Danielle Jennings, "Adverse Impact and Predictive Efficiency of Various Predictor Combinations," *Journal of Applied Psychology* 82, no. 5 (October 1997): 719–730.

6. Gary N. Burns et al., "Effects of Applicant Personality on Resume Evaluations," *Journal of Business and Psychology* 29, no. 4 (2014): 573–591; Michael Luo, "'Whitening' the Résumé,"

New York Times (December 5, 2009), http://www.nytimes.com.

7. Roy Mauer, "Know Before You Hire: 2017 Employment Screening Trends," *Society of Human Resources Management* (January 25, 2017), https://www.shrm.org.

8. Op cit.

9. Alexander Reicher, "The Background of Our Bing: Internet Background Checks in the Hiring Process," *Berkeley Technology Law Journal* 28, no. 1 (Spring 2013): 115–153.

10. Jennifer Valentino DeVries, "Bosses May Use Social Media to Discriminate against Job Seekers," *Wall Street Journal* (November 20, 2013), https://www.wsj.com.

11. Lisa Takeuchi Cullen, "It's a Wrap: You're Hired," *Time* (February 22, 2007, http://time.com.

12. Hanna Kuchler, "Silicon Valley Tactics for Waging War on Biases in the Workplace" (March 7, 2017), https://www.ft.com.

13. "A New Assistant at Georgia Tech Made False Claims," *The New York Times* (January 29, 2002), D7; Stephanie Armour, "Security Checks Worry Workers; Padded Résumés Could Be Exposed," *USA Today* (June 19, 2002): B1.

14. Scott Bennet, *The Elements of Résumé Style: Essential Rules for Writing Résumés and Cover Letters that Work.* (AMACOM, 2014); "Busted," *Training Development* 60, no. 12 (December 2006): 19; Pamela Babock, "Spotting Lies," *HRMagazine* 48, no. 10 (October 2003): 46–51; Tammy Prater and Sara Bliss Kiser, "Lies, Lies, and More Lies," *A.A.M. Advance Management Journal* 67, no. 2 (Spring 2002): 9–14.

15. Max Mihelich, "Check on Background Checks," Workforce.com (September 23, 2013), http://www.workforce.com.

16. Amy Maingault, John Sweeney, and Naomi Cossack, "Interviewing, Management Training, Strikes," *HRMagazine* 52, no. 6 (June 2007): 43; James Bassett, "Stop, Thief!" *Gifts & Decorative Accessories* 104, no. 1 (January 2003): 130–134; Richard A. Posthuma, Frederick Morgeson, and Michael Campion, "Beyond Employment Interview Validity: A Comprehensive Narrative Review of Recent Research and Trends over Time," *Personnel Psychology* 55, no. 1 (Spring 2002): 1–8.

17. Robert Gatewood, Hubert S. Feild, and Murray Barrick, *Human Resource Selection* (Nelson Education, 2015); Yen-Chun Chen, Wei-Chi Tsai, and Changya Hu, "The Influences of Interviewer-Related and Situational Factors on Interviewer Reactions to High Structured Job Interviews," *International Journal of Human Resource Management* 19, no. 6 (June 2008): 1056–1071; Jesus F. Salgado and Silvia Moscoso, "Comprehensive Meta-Analysis of the Construct Validity of the Employment Interview," *European Journal of Work and Organizational Psychology* 11, no. 3 (September 2002): 299–325.

18. Julia Levashina et al., "The Structured Employment Interview: Narrative and Quantitative Review of the Research Literature," *Personnel Psychology* 67, no. 1 (2014): 241–293; Allen Huffcutt, Jeff Weekley, Willi Wiesner, Timothy Degroot, and Casey Jones, "Comparison of Situational and Behavior Description Interview Questions for Higher-Level Positions," *Personnel Psychology* 54, no. 3 (Autumn 2001): 619–644.

19. Allen I. Huffcutt, Satoris S. Culbertson, and William S. Weyhrauch, "Employment Interview Reliability", *International Journal of Selection and Assessment* 21, no. 3 (2013): 264–76; Peter Herriot, "Assessment by Groups: Can Value Be Added?" *European Journal of Work & Organizational Psychology* 12, no. 2 (June 2003): 131–146; Salgado and Moscoso, "Comprehensive Meta-Analysis", Amelia J. Prewett-Livingston, John G. Veres III, Hubert S. Field, and Philip M. Lewis, "Effects of Race on Interview Ratings in a Situational Panel Interview," *Journal of Applied Psychology* 81, no. 2 (April 1996).

20. Delroy L. Paulhus et al., "Self-Presentation Style in Job Interviews, "*Journal of Applied Social Psychology* 43, no. 10 (2013): 2042–59; "Survey: Six in Ten Companies Conduct Video Job Interviews," *PR Newswire* (August 30, 2012), http://www.prnewswire.com.

21. Julia Thomas, "Video Killed the Interview Star," *DeGroote School of Business* (July 29, 2013), http://www.degroote.mcmaster.ca.

22. Carol Carter, *Keys to Business Communication* (Upper Saddle River, NJ: Pearson, 2012): Chapter 15.

23. Darren Dahl, "Tapping the Talent Pool…without Drowning in Resumés," *Inc.* 31, no. 3 (April 2009): 122.

24. Joe Smydo, "Giant Eagle Job Fairs Attract Hundreds," *Pittsburgh Post-Gazette* (September 21, 2014), http://www.post-gazette.com.

25. Jack Welch and Suzy Welch, "Hiring Is Hard Work," *Business Week Online*, no. 4091 (July 7, 2008): n.p.; Michele V. Rafter, "Candidates for Jobs in High Places Sit for Tests That Size Up Their Mettle," *Workforce Management* 83, no. 5 (May 2004): 70–73.

26. Kira Vermond, "References Done Right," *Profit* 26, no. 2 (May 2007): 101; Kathleen Samey, "A Not-So-Perfect Fit," *Adweek* 44, no. 47 (December 1, 2003): 34; Ann Fisher, "How Can We Be Sure We're Not Hiring a Bunch of Shady Liars?" *Fortune* 147, no. 10 (May 26, 2003).

27. "New Employee Privacy Rights in Oregon and Washington," *Venulex Legal Summaries* (2007 Q3): 1–4; Barry J. Nadell, "The Cut of His Jib Doesn't Jibe," *Security Management* 48, no. 9 (September 2004): 108–114.

28. Will Dobbie et al., *Bad Credit, No Problem?* (National Bureau of Economic Research, 2016): w22711; Mary-Kathryn, "Labor Law for Supervisors," *Supervision* 67, no. 2 (February 2006): 22–23; "Some Job-Screening Tactics May Be Illegal," *Fort Worth Star-Telegram* (August 12, 2010): 5A; Katherine Erdel, "Changes May Prompt Review of Background Check Policies," *Corporate Counsel Guide* 24 (2014): 12B–13B.

29. Marsha Nielsen and Kristine Kuhn, "Late Payments and Leery Applicants: Credit Checks as a Selection Test," *Employee Responsibilities & Rights Journal* 21, no. 2 (June 2009): 115.

30. Beth Braverman, "Employers Running Credit Checks on Job Applicants Must Tread Carefully," *CreditCards.com* (July 25, 2016), http://www.creditcards.com.

31. Elizabeth D. MacGillivray, Juanita H. Beecher, and Diedre M. Golden, "Employment Testing: The New Hot Button Issue for Federal Agencies—and Other Legal Developments," *Global Business & Organizational Excellence* 27, no. 3 (March-April 2008): 68–78.

32. "EEOC Clarifies the Definition of Who Is an 'Applicant' in the Context of Internet Recruiting and Hiring," *Fair Employment Practices Guidelines*, no. 587 (April 1, 2004): 3–13; Kathryn Tyler, "Put Applicants' Skills to the Test," *HRMagazine* 45, no. 1 (January 2000): 74–80.

33. Standards that testing programs should meet are described in *Standards for Educational and Psychological Tests* (Washington, DC: American Psychological Association, 1999).

34. Hershey H. Friedman, Linda Weiser Friedman, and Chaya Leverton, "Increase Diversity to Boost Creativity and Enhance Problem Solving," *Psychosociological Issues in Human Resource Management* 4, no. 2 (2016): 7–33; John Bret Becton, Hubert S. Feild, William F. Giles, and Allison Jones-Farmer, "Racial Differences in Promotion Candidate Performance and Reactions to Selection Procedures: A Field Study in a Diverse Top-Management Context," *Journal of Organizational Behavior* 29, no. 3 (April 2008): 265–285.

35. Rachel Suff, "Testing the Water: Using Work Sampling for Selection," *IRS Employment Review*, no. 802 (June 18, 2004): 44–49; Leonard D. Goodstein and Alan D. Davidson, "Hiring the Right Stuff: Using Competency-Based Selection," *Compensation & Benefits Management* 14, no. 3 (Summer 1998): 1–10.

36. Stuart Crandell, "Assessment Centers in Talent Management: Strategies, Use, and Value," *Talent Management* (January 7, 2008), http://www.talentmgt.com.

37. Ken Richardson and Sarah H. Norgate, "Does IQ Really Predict Job Performance?" *Applied Development Science*

19, no. 3 (2011): 153–69; Matthew Night, "Does IQ Predict Performance at Work?" *CNN* (February 28, 2011), http://edition.cnn.com; Noelle Murphy, "Testing the Waters: Employers' Use of Selection Assessments," *IRS Employment Review* 852 (August 4, 2006): 42–48.

38. Candice Rudd, "FAA's Bid to Expand Air Traffic Hiring Pool Hits Turbulence," *Newsday* (April 24, 2016), http://www.newsday.com.

39. "Biographical Data (Biodata) Tests," *Personnel Selection and Resource Center* (Washington DC: U.S. Office of Personnel Management, 2011), http://apps.opm.gov.

40. Jesús F. Salgado and Gabriel Táuriz, "The Five-Factor Model, Forced-Choice Personality Inventories and Performance," *European Journal of Work and Organizational Psychology* 23, no. 1 (2014): 3–30; Timothy Judge and Joyce Bono, "Five-Factor Model of Personality and Transformational Leadership," *Journal of Applied Psychology* 85, no. 5 (October 2000): 751–765; J. Michael Crant and Thomas S. Bateman, "Charismatic Leadership Viewed from Above: The Impact of Proactive Personality," *Journal of Organizational Behavior* 21, no. 1 (February 2000): 63–75.

41. Jason L. Huang et al., "Personality and Adaptive Performance at Work," *Journal of Applied Psychology* 99, no. 1 (2014): 162; Frederick P. Morgeson, Michael A. Campion, Robert L. Dipboye, John R. Hollenbeck, Kevin Murphy, and Neal Schmitt, "Reconsidering the Use of Personality Tests in Personnel Selection Contexts," *Personnel Psychology* 60, no. 3 (Autumn 2007): 683–729; Gregory Hurtz and John Donovan, "Personality and Job Performance: The Big Five Revisited," *Journal of Applied Psychology* 85, no. 6 (December 2000): 869–879.

42. Julie Furr Youngman, "The Use and Abuse of Pre-Employment Personality Tests," *Business Horizons* (2017); Lawrence Peikes and Meghan D. Burns, "Polygraph Test Request Unlawful," *HRMagazine* 50, no. 7 (July 2005): 110; "Pretext for Discrimination: How to Avoid Looking Like a Liar," *Fair Employment Practices Guidelines*, no. 592 (September 1, 2004): 1–3; Gillian Flynn, Diane D. Hatch, and James E. Hall, "Know the Background of Background Checks," *Workforce* 81, no. 9 (September 2002): 96–98.

43. "If the Shoe Fits," *Security Management* 40, no. 2 (February 1996): 11; Michelle Cottle, "Job Testing: Multiple Choices," *The New York Times* (September 5, 1999): 3, 10.

44. Taya R. Cohen et al., "Moral Character in the Workplace," *Journal of Personality and Social Psychology* 107, no. 5 (2014): 943; Thomas J. Ryan, "Nerves of Steal," *SGB* 37, no. 6 (June 2004): 8–10; D. S. Ones, C. Viswesvaran, and F. L. Schmidt, "Comprehensive Meta-Analysis of Integrity Test Validities: Findings and Implications for Personnel Selection and Theories of Job Performance," *Journal of Applied Psychology* 78 (August 1993): 679–703.

45. Steve Lorh, "Big Data, Trying to Build Better Workers," *New York Times* (April 20, 2013), http://www.nytimes.com.

46. Paul Zielbauer, "Small Changes Could Improve Police Hiring, Panel Says," *The New York Times* (January 7, 1999): 8; Lynn McFarland and Ann Marie Ryan, "Variance in Faking across Noncognitive Measures," *Journal of Applied Psychology* 85, no. 5 (October 2000): 812–21.

47. Robert Gatewood, Hubert S. Feild, and Murray Barrick, *Human Resource Selection* (Nelson Education, 2015); Maria Greco Danaher, "Strength Test Falls," *HRMagazine* 52, no. 2 (February 2007): 115–116; M.S. Sothmann, D.L. Gebhardt, T.A. Baker, G.M. Kastello, and V.A. Sheppard, "Performance Requirements of Physically Strenuous Occupations: Validating Minimum Standards for Muscular Strength," *Ergonomics* 47, no. 8 (June 22, 2004): 864.

48. Kenneth G. Dau-Schmidt, Matt Finkin, and Robert Covington, *Legal Protection for the Individual Employee* (West Academic, 2016); Michael Adams, Ben Van Houten, Robert Klara, and Elizabeth Bernstein, "Access Denied?" *Restaurant Business* 98, no. 2 (January 15, 1999): 36–48; "Medical Screening: Are Employers Going Too Far?" *Employee Benefit Plan Review* 53, no. 11 (May 1999): 42–43.

49. "News Briefs," *Security Director's Report* 13, no. 18 (August 2013): 6.

50. Ibid.

51. Philip Bobko, Philip L. Roth, and Maury A. Buster, "The Usefulness of Unit Weights in Creating Composite Scores: A Literature Review, Application to Content Validity, and Meta-Analysis," *Organizational Research Methods* 10, no. 4 (October 2007): 689–709.

52. Deniz S. Ones, Chockalingam Viswesvaran, and Frank L Schmidt, "No New Terrain: Reliability and Construct Validity of Job Performance Ratings," *Industrial & Organizational Psychology* 1, no. 2 (June 2008): 174–79; D. Brent Smith and Lill Ellingson, "Substance versus Style: A New Look at Social Desirability in Motivating Contexts," *Journal of Applied Psychology* 87, no. 2 (April 2002): 211–219; Ken Craik, et al., "Explorations of Construct Validity in a Combined Managerial and Personality Assessment Programme," *Journal of Occupational and Organizational Psychology* 75, no. 2 (June 2002): 171–193.

53. Multiple regression is a statistical method for evaluating the magnitude of effects of more than one independent variable (e.g., selection predictors) on a dependent variable (e.g., job performance) using principles of correlation and regression.

54. Patricia M. Buhler, "Managing in the New Millennium," *Supervision* 68, no. 11 (November 2007): 17–20; Ann Marie Ryan, Joshua Sacco, Lynn McFarland, and David Kriska, "Applicant Self-Selection: Correlates of Withdrawal from a Multiple Hurdle Process," *Journal of Applied Psychology* 85, no. 2 (April 2000): 163–179.

55. "Considering and Evaluating Internal Candidates for Senior-Level Nonprofit Positions," *Bridgestar* (March 27, 2011), http://www.bridgestar.org.

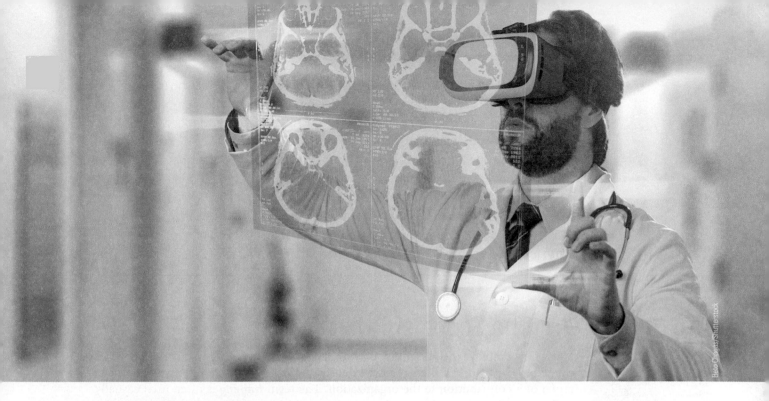

CHAPTER **7**

Training and Development

Learning Outcomes

After studying this chapter, you should be able to

LO ① Discuss the scope of training and development and its strategic aspects.

LO ② Describe how a training needs assessment should be done.

LO ③ Describe the factors that must be taken into account when designing a training program.

LO ④ Identify the types of training-delivery methods organizations use.

LO ⑤ Explain how the effectiveness of training programs are evaluated, and describe some of the additional training programs conducted by firms.

Workplace training used to be rather boxlike. It focused on teaching employees to do particular activities—operate machines, process work, and so forth. However, as the workplace has shifted from "touch labor" to "knowledge workers" (see Chapter 1), the focus of training has shifted as well. Companies are realizing that workers need not only operational knowhow but also superior job expertise; knowledge about competitive, industry, and technological trends; and the ability to continually learn and utilize new information. These characteristics better help an organization adapt and innovate to compete far more effectively in today's fast-paced global business world. Because training plays a central role in nurturing, strengthening, and expanding the capabilities of a firm in this way, it has become part of the backbone of strategic management.

LO 1

What aspects of training plans do you think are strategic, and how are these plans similar or dissimilar to the college and career plans you have created for yourself?

7.1 The Scope of Training

Many new employees come equipped with most of the knowledge, skills, and abilities needed to start work. Others require extensive training before they are ready to make much of a contribution to the organization. The term *training* is often used casually to describe almost any effort initiated by an organization to foster learning among its members. However, many experts distinguish between *training*, which tends to be more narrowly focused and oriented toward short-term performance concerns, and *development*, which, as you learned in Chapter 5, tends to be oriented more toward broadening an individual's skills for future responsibilities. The two terms tend to be combined into a single phrase—*training and development*—to recognize the combination of activities organizations use to increase the knowledge and skills of employees.

Research shows that an organization's revenues and overall profitability are positively correlated to the amount of training it gives its employees. According to *Training* magazine's ongoing industry report, U.S. businesses provide each of their employees between 35 and 55 hours, on average, of training annually.[1] By contrast, the 100 best U.S. companies to work for, as cited by *Fortune* magazine, provide their employees with approximately double that amount of training and sometimes even more. New employees hired by the Ritz Carlton hotel chain get over 300 hours of training. The greatest proportion of training is spent on rank-and-file employees and supervisors.

It's not unusual for large corporations to have their own "universities" where they train their employees and future managers. Hamburger University, operated by McDonald's Corporation near Chicago, is probably the best known corporate university. General Electric has a 53-acre training campus north of New York City, where about 10,000

Hamburger University, located at headquarters in Oak Brook, Illinois, is McDonald's management training center.

Qilai Shen/Getty Images

people attend classes each year. The Campbell's Soup Company operates Campbell University, which has a 2-year program focused on personal leadership development for both aspiring and seasoned managers.

So how much does all of this corporate training cost? About $70 billion annually. That's a significant amount of money, so firms want to ensure it's well spent.

U.S. businesses spend nearly four times as much on informal instruction as they do formal instruction, however. The informal instruction ranges from simple, on-the-job instruction to sophisticated skills training conducted on multimillion-dollar simulators. Other types of training include regular training given to new hires, customer service and communication-skills training, and compliance training—training employees must receive as a result of various legal mandates, such as EEO requirements or OSHA requirements. Airline attendants must undergo mandatory safety training designated by the Federal Aviation Administration. Train crews must annually undergo training mandated by the Federal Railroad Administration.

7.1a A Strategic Approach to Training

Managers should keep a close eye on their firm's goals and strategies and orient their training accordingly. Is it the firm's goal to develop new product lines? If so, how should this goal affect its training initiatives? Is the firm trying to lower its costs of production so it can utilize a low-cost strategy to capture new business? If so, are there training initiatives that can be undertaken to deliver on this strategy?

Unfortunately, some organizations fail to make the connection between training and an organization's goals. Instead, they do whatever the competition is doing or what is the latest trend. As a result, training programs are often misdirected, poorly designed, and inadequately evaluated—not to mention a waste of money. One, not all of a firm's strategic initiatives can be accomplished with training. Two, not all training programs—no matter how widely they are adopted by other organizations—will be a strategic imperative for your firm.

Because business conditions change rapidly, as does technology, keeping abreast of the types of training a firm's employees need to remain competitive can be a challenge. If employees consistently fail to achieve their productivity objectives, this might be a signal that training is needed. Likewise, if organizations receive an excessive number of customer complaints, this, too, might suggest a firm's training is inadequate. Larger firms typically have **chief learning officers**, who are high-ranking executives responsible for ensuring a company's training is timely, well designed, and focused on the firm's strategic issues.

chief learning officers
A high-ranking executive responsible for fostering employee learning and development within the firm

To ensure a firm's training and development investment has the maximum impact possible, a strategic and systematic approach should be used that involves four phases:

1. A needs assessment based on the firm's competitive objectives: What training does the firm really need?
2. Program design: Given those needs, how should the training program best designed or structured?
3. Implementation: How should the program be delivered—that is, by what method?
4. Evaluation: How can the firm tell if the training program is really working?

Figure 7.1 presents these elements. We will use it as a framework for organizing the material in this chapter.

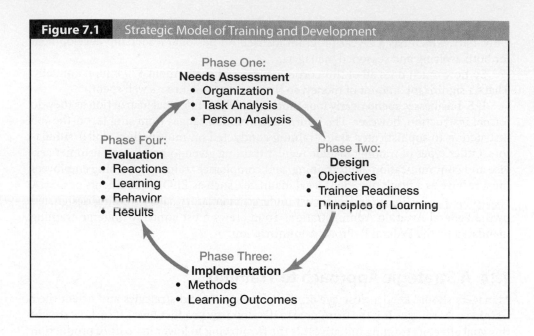

Figure 7.1 Strategic Model of Training and Development

Phase One:
Needs Assessment
- Organization
- Task Analysis
- Person Analysis

Phase Two:
Design
- Objectives
- Trainee Readiness
- Principles of Learning

Phase Three:
Implementation
- Methods
- Learning Outcomes

Phase Four:
Evaluation
- Reactions
- Learning
- Behavior
- Results

LO **2**

If you were launching a new business, what factors would you look at to do a training-needs assessment for the organization?

7.2 Phase 1: Conducting the Needs Assessment

If you own or manage a business, how would you figure out what types of training your employees need and how much of it? The following are some of the most common types of training employees are given. "Hard skills" refer to the tangible and teachable skills needed to do a job. Learning to operate a machine is an example. "Soft skills" refer to subjective skills that are harder to measure, requiring more discretion or judgment, but equally valuable in the workplace. Working well with other people is an example of a soft skill.

Hard-Skills Training

- On-the-job training for new hires
- Basic skills training
- Budgeting and accounting training
- Machinery operating training
- IT/computer training
- Customer service training
- Compliance (regulations) training

Soft-Skills Training

- Ethics training
- Diversity training
- Leadership training
- Communications training
- Team training
- Time management training
- Interpersonal skills training

To determine what type of training your firm needs, you must conduct a training needs assessment. However, a study conducted a few years ago by the American Society for Training and Development found that organizations conduct needs assessments less than 50 percent of the time. This situation has improved somewhat, in part because tighter training budgets have forced firms to ensure that their training is well aligned with their objectives. Being able to quickly assess the training your employees need is especially important for small businesses that may not have the time or resources to do lengthy needs assessment analyses. Doing a needs assessment does not need to be a laborious task, as this chapter's small-business feature shows.[2] As Figure 7.2 shows, a needs assessment consists of three parts: an organization analysis, a task analysis, and a person analysis. Each of these steps will be discussed next.

7.2a Organization Analysis

An **organization analysis** is an examination of a firm's environment, goals, strategies, performance, and resources so as to determine what training it should do. For this purpose, HR personnel typically collect data such as information on the quality of a firm's goods or services, its absenteeism, turnover, and number of accidents. The availability of potential replacements and the time required to train them are important factors in organization analysis. Other issues include technological change, innovation, globalization, quality and process improvement, mergers and acquisition, and restructuring—all of which necessitate training. Why? Because they frequently require employees and managers to take on new roles and responsibilities and adjust to new cultures and ways of doing business.

organization analysis
An examination of an organization's environment, goals, strategies, performance, and resources so as to determine what training it should do

Economic and public policy issues influence corporate training needs as well. For example, terrorist and cyber attacks continue to change the training that airport and airline workers need, as well as police, IT and transportation employees, nuclear power plant employees, and even security staff at theme parks.[3] Finally, trends in the workforce itself affect a firm's training needs. As older workers near retirement, younger workers need the training and knowledge to take their place.

Conducting an organization analysis also involves examining a firm's resources—technological, financial, and human—available to conduct the training. HR departments are under constant pressure to make the most of their training dollars. When budgets are tight, training and development are usually the first programs to be cut. Companies such as Darden Restaurants, Ford, and Merck have used information technology to significantly cut their training budgets. Other companies outsource their training programs, or at least part of them, to external firms to cut costs or to take advantage of

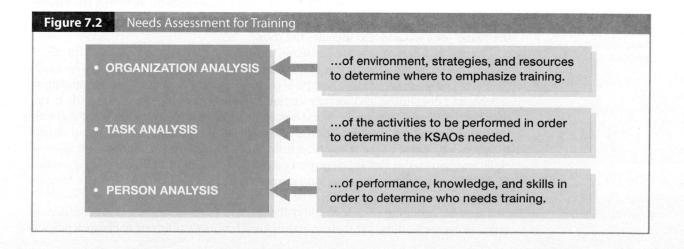

Figure 7.2   Needs Assessment for Training

- **ORGANIZATION ANALYSIS** ←— ...of environment, strategies, and resources to determine where to emphasize training.

- **TASK ANALYSIS** ←— ...of the activities to be performed in order to determine the KSAOs needed.

- **PERSON ANALYSIS** ←— ...of performance, knowledge, and skills in order to determine who needs training.

Small Business Application

A Small Business's Guide to Quickly Assessing Its Training Needs

Do environmental scanning. Continually look at what is going on in your industry and organization to anticipate upcoming training needs. Enlist the help of employees and managers in the process. Question managers about their strategic goals and their impact on the organization, and gear your analysis accordingly.

Do internal scanning. Determine what skills are most important to acquire in terms of your organization's current and future needs. Which ones will provide the biggest payback?

Gather organizational data. Performance data for your firm (such as errors, sales, and customer complaints) and staffing data (such as turnover and absenteeism) can be very helpful as a starting point.

Develop a plan. Once the training need has been identified, identify various ways to deliver it and consider the costs and benefits of each. Determine what kind of growth or other measure is a reasonable result of the training.

Utilize state and local government programs. Many state and local governments have programs to help small businesses train their employees. For example, the Texas Workforce Commission will pay small businesses in Texas up to $1,800 annually in tuition and fees for each new full-time employee hired and trained at a local college. (For a current employee, the program covers tuition and fees up to $900 annually.)

Make the needs-assessment process ongoing. Repeat these activities as your business needs change.

Sources: Patti Greene, "Five Affordable and Effective Ways Small Business Owners Could Better Train Employees," *Forbes* (October 21, 2016), https://www.forbes.com; "TWC Launches Small Busin.ess Employee Training Program," *Your Houston News* (November 20, 2010), http://www.yourhoustonnews.com; "Employee Training Tips," D&B.com, http://small-business.dnb.com; Ron Zemke, "How to Do a Needs Assessment When You Think You Don't Have Time," *Training* 35, no. 3 (March 1998): 38–44.

---

expertise the firm lacks. Other organizations purchase "off the shelf" course materials developed by training companies rather than develop their own. Another trend is for companies to partner with firms in their supply chains to jointly train their employees more cost effectively.[4]

7.2b Task Analysis

task analysis

The process of determining a training program's content by studying the tasks and duties a job involves

The second step in training-needs assessment is task analysis. A **task analysis** involves reviewing the job description and KSAOs of a particular position, including the specific actions and behaviors required to do it. In other words, a task analysis goes beyond just the "what" of a job and also includes the "how."

If the job is new or jobs are changing, the first step in a task analysis is to list all the tasks or duties included in the job. The second step is to list the steps the employee needs to take to complete each task. The type of performance for each task (i.e., manipulation, speech, and discrimination), along with the skills and knowledge necessary to do it, can then be identified. For example, in the task of taking a chest X-ray, a radiologist correctly positions the patient (manipulation), gives special instructions (speech), and checks the proper distance of the X-ray tube from the patient (discrimination). The types of skills and knowledge that trainees need can be determined by observing and questioning skilled jobholders or by reviewing job descriptions. This information helps trainers select program content and choose the most effective training methods.

Jobs are changing so quickly today that instead of focusing on a fixed sequence of tasks, firms are finding that their employees need more flexible sets of competencies to adapt. A **competency assessment** focuses on the sets of skills and knowledge employees need to be successful, particularly for decision-oriented and knowledge-intensive jobs. A competency assessment goes beyond simply describing the traits employees must have to successfully perform the work. It also captures elements of how those traits should be used within an organization's context and culture. That might include the motivation levels of employees, their interpersonal skills, and so on. "It's easy for top performers to become experts in a certain niche, but 'talent factories' focus on creating generalists," explains one HR consultant. "To get the most from talented employees, they should know how to handle a wide range of functions."[5]

Instead of offering a laundry list of training plans as it used to, Amway has established job competencies for its employees around the world. The competencies denote the particular skills each employee needs for his or her job and a training "road map" to get them there.[6] Highlights in HRM 1 shows an example of a partial competency assessment tool used for evaluating a manager.

competency assessment
An analysis of the sets of skills and knowledge needed for decision-oriented and knowledge-intensive jobs

7.2c Person Analysis

A **person analysis** is the process of determining which employees require training and, equally important, which do not. This helps organizations avoid providing all employees training when some do not need it. In addition, a person analysis helps managers determine what prospective trainees are able to do currently so that the programs can be designed to provide training that will benefit them.

Performance appraisal information can also be used to conduct a person analysis. However, although performance appraisals might reveal which employees are not meeting the firm's expectations, for example, they typically do not reveal why. If the performance is due to ability problems, training is likely to be a good solution. If the performance is due to poor motivation or factors outside an employee's control, training might not be the answer. Conducting a deeper performance diagnosis is discussed in Chapter 8 on performance appraisals. Ultimately, managers have to sit down with employees to talk about areas for improvement so that they can jointly determine the training or other approaches that will have maximum benefit.[7] A person analysis along with appraisal information can also be used to determine the training someone needs for a new position, a promotion, or to take on new responsibilities.

person analysis
The process of determining the specific individuals who need training in an organization

7.3 Phase 2: Designing the Training Program

Once you have assessed your firm's training needs, the next step is to design the training program. Experts believe that the design of training programs should focus on at least four related issues: (1) the training's instructional objectives, (2) readiness of trainees and their motivation, (3) principles of learning, and (4) characteristics of instructors.

LO **3**
What has your college experience taught you about how people learn that can be applied to the workplace?

7.3a Developing Instructional Objectives

After conducting organization, task, and person analyses, managers should have a more complete picture of their firms' training needs. On the basis of this information, they can more formally state the desired outcomes of training via written **instructional objectives**, which describe the skills or knowledge to be acquired and/or the attitudes to be changed. The learning objectives at the beginning of this chapter are examples of instructional objectives.

instructional objectives
The desired outcomes of a training program

A Competency Assessment for a Managerial Position

For each item, select the number that best describes the manager's characteristics. For items that do not apply, select **NA** (not applicable). For other items for which you lack sufficient observations or documentary evidence, select **DK** (don't know).

4 – Exemplary

3 – Proficient

2 – Progressing

1 – Needs Assistance

NA – Not Applicable

DK – Don't Know

Competency 1: Behaves professionally and encourages other staff members to do likewise.

4 3 2 1 NA DK

Evidence:_____

Competency 2: Behaves ethically and encourages staff members to do likewise.

4 3 2 1 NA DK

Evidence:_____

Competency 3: Uses a variety of modes of communication and conveys information fully and clearly.

4 3 2 1 NA DK

Evidence:_____

Competency 4: Seeks input from all levels and demonstrates fairness and consistency.

4 3 2 1 NA DK

Evidence:_____

Competency 5: Engages in an open style of management and is open to criticism from supervisors and subordinates.

4 3 2 1 NA DK

Evidence:_____

Competency 6: Searches for and embraces innovative solutions to improve department's programs and products.

4 3 2 1 NA DK

Evidence:_____

The objectives should be performance centered. Performance-centered objectives typically include precise terms, such as "to calculate," "to repair," "to adjust," "to construct," "to assemble," and "to classify."[8] For example, the stated objective for one training program might be, "Employees trained in team methods will be able to perform the different jobs of their team members within six months."

7.3b Assessing the Readiness and Motivation of Trainees

Two preconditions for learning affect the success of those who are to receive training: readiness and motivation. *Trainee readiness* refers to whether or not the experience and knowledge of trainees have made them ready to absorb the training. Do they have the background knowledge and the skills necessary to absorb what will be presented?

It is often desirable to group individuals according to their readiness, as determined by test scores or other assessment information, and to provide alternative types of instruction for those who need it. The receptiveness and readiness of participants in training programs can be increased by having them complete questionnaires about why they are attending training and what they hope to accomplish as a result of it.

The other precondition for learning is *trainee motivation*. The organization needs to help employees understand the link between the effort they put into training and the payoff. Why is the training important? What will happen if it does not occur? Moreover, what is in it for the individual employee? By focusing on the trainees themselves, managers can create a training environment that is conducive to learning. Unless they are nearing retirement, most employees are motivated by training if it can help them perform better, advance their careers, or both.

7.3c Incorporating the Principles of Learning

What makes some types of training more effective than others? Training has to build a bridge between employees and the organization. One important step in this transition is giving full consideration to the psychological principles of learning—that is, the characteristics of training programs that help employees grasp new material, make sense of it in their own lives, and transfer it back to their jobs. All things considered, training programs are likely to be more effective if they incorporate the principles of learning shown in Figure 7.3.

Figure 7.3   Principles of Learning

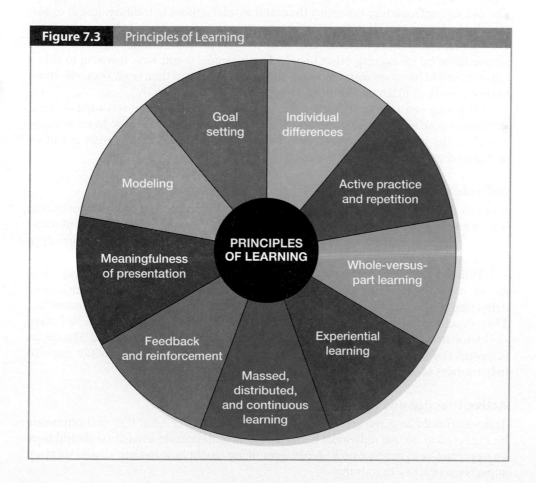

Goal Setting

In some cases, goal setting can simply take the form of a "road map" of the course or program, its objectives, and its learning points.[9] When trainers take the time to explain the training's goals and objectives to trainees—or when trainees are encouraged to set goals on their own—the level of interest, understanding, motivation, and effort directed toward the training is likely to increase. Allowing employees to undergo training in areas that they want to pursue can be very motivating, as can enlisting employees to train other employees with the information they learn. Who in an organization does not want to be called upon for their expertise?

Meaningfulness of Presentation

Trainees will be better able to learn new information if it is presented using terminology they can understand and the training is connected with things already familiar to them. This is the reason why trainers frequently use colorful examples to which trainees can relate. The examples make the material meaningful. In addition, material should be arranged so that each experience builds on preceding ones. In this way, trainees are able to integrate the experiences into a usable pattern of knowledge and skills.

Modeling

The old saying "A picture is worth a thousand words" applies to training. Just as examples increase the meaningfulness of factual material or new knowledge in a training environment, modeling increases the salience of behavioral training. In other words, people learn by mimicking other people. For example, if you were learning to ride a horse, it would be much easier to watch someone do it—and then try it yourself—than to read a book or listen to a lecture and hope you can do it right.[10]

Modeling can take many forms. Real-life demonstrations and recorded demonstrations, visual aids, pictures, and drawings can get the message across. In some cases, modeling the wrong behavior can even be helpful if it shows trainees what not to do and then clarifies the right behavior.

Individual Learning Differences

People learn at different rates and in different ways. Visual learners absorb information best through pictures, diagrams, and demonstrations. Verbal learners absorb information best through spoken or written words. Similarly, some learners who do horribly in large lecture settings excel in small discussion groups.

Trainers can help accommodate different learning styles in a variety of ways. The key is to avoid delivering the material in only one way. So, for example, instead of delivering a monologue, trainers should incorporate variety into their presentations. They should use visual aids, encourage the participation of learners by including them in demonstrations, and ask them questions about their own experiences. Hands-on activities and breaking large groups into smaller groups for specific activities can also help trainers accommodate different learning styles.[11]

Active Practice and Repetition

Trainees should be given frequent opportunities to practice what they will ultimately be expected to do. An individual being taught how to operate a machine should have an opportunity to practice on it. A manager being taught how to train should be given supervised practice in training.

Practice causes behaviors to become second nature. For example, when you first learned to drive a car, you focused a great deal on the mechanics: "Where are my hands, where are my feet, and how fast am I going?" As you practiced driving, you began to think less about the mechanics and more about the road, the weather, and the traffic. Other forms of learning are no different—by practicing, a trainee can forget about distinct behaviors and concentrate on the subtleties of how they are used.

Experiential Learning

Experiential learning refers to the process of learning by experience or "doing," often outside the classroom and without traditional ready-made learning content. Experiential learning might sound like hands-on learning, which can be a part of experiential learning, but it is more than that. It involves not only engaging in an activity, but reflecting on it, critically analyzing it—and potentially improving upon it—and then applying it in new situations or settings. Benjamin Franklin once said, "Tell me and I forget, teach me and I remember, involve me and I will learn." Experiential learning corresponds to the "involve me and I will learn" part of Franklin's statement. Simulations, games, and special assignments, which we will discuss later in the chapter, fall into the category of experiential learning.

> **experiential learning**
> The process of learning by "doing," reflecting on it, critically analyzing it, and applying it in new situations or settings

Whole-versus-Part Learning

Most jobs and tasks can be broken down into parts that lend themselves to further analysis. Learning to sell a product is an example. The process can essentially be broken down into a few discrete steps: finding customer opportunities; uncovering a prospective customer's needs by learning the proper questions to ask him or her; presenting the firm's product in a way that meets those needs; and finally, learning how and when to ask the customer to buy the product (closing the deal). If the task can be broken down successfully, it probably should be to facilitate learning; otherwise, it should probably be taught as a unit.

Programmed instruction, which is also referred to as *self-paced learning*, is often used to break down learning into sequences for employees to learn at their own pace. After being presented with a small segment of information, the trainee is required to answer a question, either by writing in a response or selecting one on a computer. If the response is correct, the trainee is presented with the next step (or screen) in the material. If the response is incorrect, further explanatory information is given, and the trainee is told to try again.

Massed, Distributed, and Continuous Learning

Another factor that determines the effectiveness of training is the amount of time devoted to practice in one session. Should trainees be given training in five 2-hour periods or in ten 1-hour periods? It has been found in most cases that spacing out the training will result in faster learning and longer retention. This is the principle of *distributed learning*. Rather than a serious of events, *continuous learning* is an ongoing process whereby employees are continually acquiring new skills and knowledge via training, observing more experienced workers, and asking for help from others when they need it.

A person's training progress, measured in terms of either mistakes or successes, can be plotted on a learning curve like the one in Figure 7.4. In many learning situations, there are times when progress does not occur. Such periods show up on the curve as a fairly straight horizontal line called a *plateau*. A plateau can occur because of reduced motivation or because a person gets discouraged when he or she does not always perform a new task as well as hoped. It is a natural phenomenon, and learners usually experience a spontaneous recovery later, as Figure 7.4 shows.

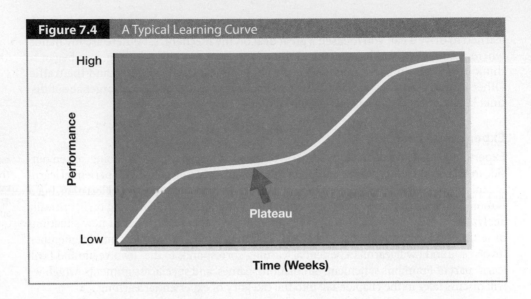

Figure 7.4   A Typical Learning Curve

Feedback and Reinforcement

Can any learning occur without feedback? Some feedback comes from trainees themselves via self-monitoring, whereas other feedback comes from trainers, fellow trainees, and the like. Feedback can help individuals focus on what they are doing right and what they are doing wrong. Think about when you first learned how to throw a baseball, ride a bicycle, or swim. Someone, perhaps a parent, told you what you were doing right and what things to correct. As you corrected those things, you perhaps got better.

As a follow-up to training or as part of the training itself, managers can use relatively simple rewards to discourage undesired behaviors and encourage and maintain desired behaviors. Doing so is a form of behavior modification. **Behavior modification** operates on the principle that behavior that is rewarded, or positively reinforced, will occur more frequently, whereas behavior that is penalized or unrewarded will decrease in frequency. The retailer Nordstroms has found that nothing more than words of encouragement and feedback are needed to strengthen employee behaviors. This approach is often used in smaller companies that don't have particularly formal or sophisticated rewards systems. However, more tangible rewards such as prizes, awards, and ceremonies can help reinforce desirable behaviors.

Encouragement is most effective when it is given immediately after a trainee successfully accomplishes a certain task. This is why some employers, including Nordstroms and Whole Foods, have instituted **spot rewards** programs, which award employees "on the spot" when they do something particularly well during training or on the job. The awards can consist of cash, gift cards, time off, or anything else employees value.

behavior modification
A technique that operates on the principle that behavior that is rewarded, or positively reinforced, will be exhibited more frequently in the future, whereas behavior that is penalized or unrewarded will decrease in frequency

spot rewards
Programs that award employees on the spot when they do something particularly well during training or on the job

7.3d Characteristics of Instructors

The success of any training effort will depend in large part on the teaching skills and personal characteristics of the people doing the training. What separates good trainers from mediocre ones? Often a good trainer is one who shows a little more effort or demonstrates more instructional preparation. However, training is also influenced by the trainer's personal manner and characteristics such as his or her knowledge of the subject, enthusiasm and sincerity, interest in trainees, sense of humor, ability to communicate clearly, and willingness to provide individual assistance to trainees. Because they can have a huge impact on the workforce, organizations should reward managers who are excellent trainers. Too often managers are not recognized for their contributions to this important aspect of HRM.

7.4 Phase 3: Implementing the Training Program—Training Delivery Methods

LO 4

What training methods have you personally experienced? Which were most effective in your opinion, and why?

Have you ever sat through a less-than-great training session and thought to yourself, "There has got to be a better way to get this material across"? Perhaps what was lacking was the right training method. Choosing the right one depends on the KSAOs to be learned. To organize our discussion of various training methods, we have placed them along the learning continuum shown in Figure 7.5—from learning that is very reactive and passive to learning that is very active. For example, if the material is mostly factual or designed to create a shift in employee attitudes, methods such as lecture, classroom, or online instruction may be fine. However, if the training involves a large behavioral or skill component, more hands-on methods such as on-the-job training or a special job assignment are likely to work better.[12] In other words, the method should be matched to the learning outcome you are trying to achieve.

Keep in mind that many of the methods are used to train both nonmanagers and managers, although some are more used predominantly for one group than the other. In addition, multiple training methods are often used in conjunction with different types of learners. Using multiple methods is referred to as blended learning. As Figure 7.6 shows, traditional classroom instruction delivered by lecturers continues to be the number-one

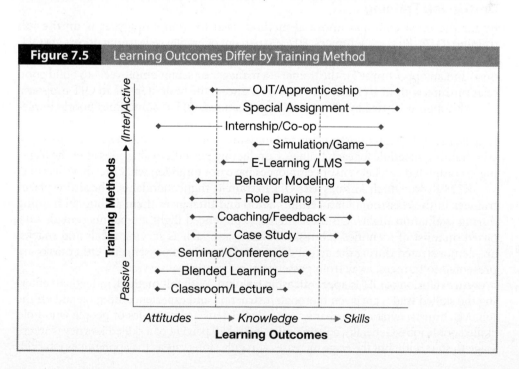

Figure 7.5 Learning Outcomes Differ by Training Method

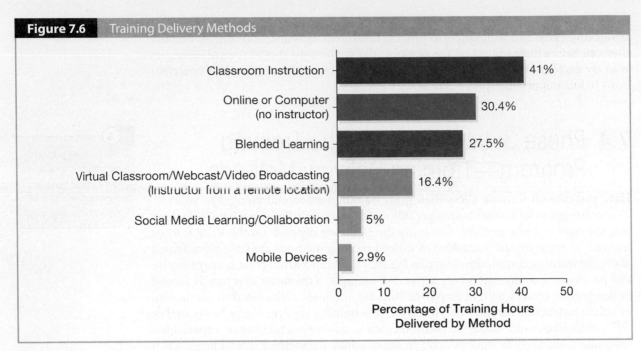

Figure 7.6 Training Delivery Methods

Source: Adapted from "2016 Training Industry Report," *Training* (November–December 2016): 36.

training delivery method for formally training employees. However, its popularity has been steadily dropping relative to electronic-based methods, which we will discuss shortly.

On-the-Job Training

on-the-job training (OJT)

A method by which employees are given hands-on experience with instructions from their supervisor or other trainer

By far the most common informal method used to train employees is **on-the-job training (OJT)**. By some estimates, 80 to 90 percent of employee learning occurs via OJT. OJT has the advantage of providing hands-on experience under normal working conditions and an opportunity for the trainer—a manager or senior employee—to build good relationships with new employees. Figure 7.7 shows the basic steps of an OJT program.

Although it is used by all types of organizations, OJT is sometimes poorly implemented because of its informal nature. To overcome these problems, training experts suggest firms develop realistic goals and measures for the training as well as plan a specific training schedule for each trainee. Conducting periodic evaluations after the training is completed can help ensure employees have not forgotten what they have learned.

KLM Royal Dutch Airlines uses OJT to train its flight attendants. The airline places trainees in the classroom for a certain period and then gives them additional training during evaluation flights. On these flights, experienced flight attendants provide OJT based on a list of identified job tasks. Some tasks, such as serving meals and snacks, are demonstrated during the actual delivery of services to passengers. Other tasks are presented to trainees, away from passengers, between meal service.[13]

apprenticeship training

A system of training in which a worker entering the skilled trades is given thorough instruction and experience, both on and off the job, in the practical and theoretical aspects of the work

An extension of OJT is **apprenticeship training**. With this method, individuals entering the skilled trades are given thorough instruction and experience, both on and off the job. Machinists, aviation mechanics, and electricians are examples of people who hold skilled-trade jobs. Generally, an apprentice is paid 50 percent of a skilled journey worker's wage to start with, but the wage increases at regular intervals as the apprentice's job skills

| **Figure 7.7** | The PROPER Way to Do On-the-Job Training |

P **Prepare.** Decide what employees need to be taught. Identify the best sequence or steps of the training. Decide how best to demonstrate these steps. Have materials, resources, and equipment ready.

R **Reassure.** Put each employee at ease. Learn about his or her prior experience, and adjust accordingly. Try to get the employee interested, relaxed, and motivated to learn.

O **Orient.** Show the employee the correct way to do the job. Explain why it is done this way. Discuss how it relates to other jobs. Let him or her ask lots of questions.

P **Perform.** When employees are ready, let them try the job themselves. Give them an opportunity to practice the job and guide them through rough spots. Provide help and assistance at first, then less as they continue.

E **Evaluate.** Check the employees' performance, and question them on how, why, when, and where they should do something. Correct errors; repeat instructions.

R **Reinforce and Review.** Provide praise and encouragement, and give feedback about how the employee is doing. Continue the conversation and express confidence in his or her doing the job.

Source: Scott Snell, University of Virginia.

increase. When the apprentice successfully completes the apprenticeship, he or she becomes a certified journey-level worker earning full pay.[14] Case Study 2 at the end of the chapter explains how Whirlpool Corporation is utilizing apprenticeships to hire new employees.

Apprenticeship programs originated in Europe centuries ago and are still used extensively there. In the United States, tens of thousands of organizations have registered their programs with the U.S. Department of Labor's Office of Apprenticeships and state agencies. There are apprenticeships available in a wide range of industries, including construction and manufacturing and the telecommunications, arts, and health fields.

Special Assignments

Special job assignments (discussed in Chapter 5) involve assigning trainees, who are often but not always on managerial tracks, to different jobs in different areas of a firm, often in different regions and countries. In some cases, they are groomed by other managers in *understudy assignments* to do important job functions. Job rotation and lateral transfers also provide trainees with a variety of hands-on work experiences. Special projects, task forces, and *junior boards* give trainees an opportunity to study an organization's challenges, make decisions about them, discuss what aspects of the projects went right and wrong, and plan and work on new initiatives.

Cooperative Training, Internships, and Governmental Training

Similar to apprenticeships, **cooperative training** programs combine practical on-the-job experience with formal classes. For example, a student might alternate work at an organization for one semester (for pay) and then go to school the next semester. Many

cooperative training
A training program that combines practical on-the-job experience with formal educational classes

Apprenticeships are a good way to recruit and train employees.

© runzelkorn/Shutterstock.com

organizations, including Fannie Mae, General Motors, Burger King, Champion International, Cray, Inc., and the insurance company UNUM, have invested millions of dollars in educational cooperative training programs in conjunction with high schools and colleges.

Internship programs, which we discussed in Chapter 5, are jointly sponsored by colleges, universities, and a variety of organizations. The programs offer students the chance to get real-world experience while finding out how they will perform in work organizations. Organizations benefit by getting student-employees with new ideas, energy, and eagerness to accomplish their assignments. Some universities and community colleges allow students to earn college credits for successfully completing internships.

The federal government and various state governments work together with private employers to sponsor training programs for new and current employees at career centers nationwide that take place at American Job Centers, which are also known as "Career One Stop" centers, or "Workforce Development" centers. The centers help workers find jobs, help employers find qualified workers, and provide job training and other employment services all under one roof (hence the name One Stop). 3M, Honeywell, and General Mills are just a few of the companies involved in the One Stop program.[15]

Simulations

Simulations are used when it is either impractical or unwise to train employees on the actual equipment used on the job. An obvious example is training employees to operate aircraft, spacecraft, and other highly technical and expensive equipment. Southwest Airlines has 10 full-motion 737 flight simulators at its training center adjacent to Southwest's headquarters at Dallas's Love Field. During each 4-hour training situation in a simulator, a flight crew faces more abnormal flight situations than it would in a lifetime. The Federal Aviation Administration developed a simulator to dramatically speed up the training of air traffic controllers, a process that used to take as long as 5 years. Variables such as wind speed, precipitation, and the number of airplanes to be guided can be adjusted on the simulator to test the ability of trainees.

The distinction between simulators like the cockpits at Southwest Airlines that move/jostle flight crews about and computer-based simulations has blurred. To train its forklift operators, the aluminum company Alcoa uses a computer simulation called Safedock. In the simulation, trainees perform common tasks such as moving loads from one end of a loading area to the other. If a trainee makes a wrong move, he or she instantly sees the consequences: The forklift might end up driving off the dock or crashing into another forklift.[16] Medical students and doctors are putting on virtual reality headsets to train for different types of trauma care, too.[17]

Simulations can also be used to help employees and managers make tactical decisions. Marriott International has a computer program called Business Acumen to train

Arterra/Getty Images

Pilots are trained with flight simulators to help them make the right decision for critical situations without the risk.

its managers on the finer points of hotel operation. The program simulates hotel operation scenarios such as budgetary decisions.[18] The Federal Emergency Management Agency has used simulations to help managers better respond to crises. In one computer simulation, a chemical cloud engulfs a city, and managers attempt to respond dynamically to the various problems it creates.

Games

Games are becoming more popular for training purpose, a phenomenon that's being referred to as to the "gamification" of learning. Sometimes the games resemble actual tasks done in the workplace. At other times, the games communicate principles that can be transferred to the job. Because games have a competitive component and are fun, trainers have found people are more likely to want to engage with them as well as remember what they learned from them. Generation Zers and millennials tend to like them. To train its retail employees, many of whom are younger, Bloomingdales uses games they can load on a wide variety of devices and play during slow times on the job. Employees report that the games have given them more confidence in their selling skills and increased their desire to participate in corporate training.[19]

Games (and simulations) do not always require a computer, however. Motorola developed a noncomputer-based simulation called "Equal Employment Opportunity: It's Your Job" to teach the basic principles of equal employment opportunity to managers. Trainees get caught up in the competitive spirit of the game and at the same time absorb and remember government regulations. They also become aware of how their own daily decisions affect their employer's compliance with these regulations.

E-Learning

The training methods we just discussed are evolving into what trainers today refer to as e-learning. **E-learning** covers a wide variety of electronic applications such as Web and computer-based training (CBT), and social networks. It includes the delivery of

e-learning
Learning that takes place via electronic media

Virtual reality headsets are being used to train people in different occupations, including people in medical occupations.

iStockphoto.com/yoh4nn

learning management system (LMS)

Online system that provides a variety of assessment, communication, teaching, and learning opportunities

content via the Internet, intranets and extranets, mobile devices, DVDs, podcasts, and "virtual classrooms" found in the gaming platform Second Life.[20] E-learning need not be expensive. Many e-learning training programs use existing applications employees are familiar with such as PowerPoint, Word, Adobe Acrobat, and audio and video files that can be easily uploaded and viewed or listened to online using computers and mobile devices.

Increasingly, e-learning involves the use of a **learning management system (LMS)**, which combines a company's e-learning, employee assessment tools, and other training functions into one electronic tool, often custom built for the firm by software vendors. Using the software, managers can assess the skills of employees, register them for courses, deliver interactive learning modules directly to employees' desktops when they need or want them, evaluate and track their progress, and determine when they are ready to be promoted.

A major advantage of e-learning is that it allows the firm to bring training to employees, which is generally more efficient and cost effective than the other way around. The nuclear power plant industry is a case in point: Nuclear power plant training is frequent and time consuming. For workers just to remove their protective gear and commute to a separate training venue can take an hour or more. One nuclear power company that switched to e-learning reported that it saved nearly $1 million and 10,000 employee-hours in a single year by doing so.[21]

just-in-time training

Electronic training delivered to trainees when and where they need it to do their jobs

Just-in-Time Training and Microlearning E-learning also allows companies to offer individual training to employees exactly when and where they need it, which is referred to as **just-in-time training**. Just-in-time training helps alleviate the boredom trainees experience during full-blown training courses, and employees are more likely to retain the information when they can immediately put it to use.

Microsoft has created hundreds of short audio and video clips the company's sales professionals can download onto their mobile devices as they need them. Long training courses pulled people away from making sales, and with so many products continually being launched, it was difficult for them to keep up to date if they had to take frequent training sessions. Also, employees didn't remember the training if they could not put it to use immediately.[22]

To be sure, shorter training sessions are definitely a growing trend. Duolingo is one of a number of e-learning companies that offers microlearning training sessions. **Microlearning** refers to training sessions that take place in very short timeframes, usually 5 minutes or less. Between rides, Uber drivers in Colombia, Brazil, and Mexico can use the Duolingo app to improve their English-language skills. When the drivers complete a certain number of lessons, they are allowed to provide rides to English-speaking riders.[23] Microlearning and just-in-time training are examples of distributed learning rather than mass learning.

microlearning
Training sessions that take place in a very short timeframe, usually 5 minutes or less

MOOCs Recall from Chapter 1 that a MOOC is an online course anyone can take. Although they were initially used in academia, MOOCs are now being used by businesses. To help its client companies find web developers with coding experience, the recruiting company Aquent launched a MOOC. Thousands of people signed up for a coding course Aquent hosted. A couple of hundred went on to get jobs.[24]

Rather than developing their own MOOCs, Bank of America, Qualcomm, and other firms are assigning employees content aligned to their training in already-existing MOOCs. There are literally thousands of MOOCs. Udacity, edX, Coursera, and Khan Academy are some of the major MOOC providers.

Like other types of online learning, the lack of contact with other people can be a problem for some learners. Some MOOCs allow students to have classroom discussions virtually with other people. Others include application assignments and projects. Still others allow instructors to record audio comments or videos about what's going on in the course each week, which can help keep learners engaged.[25]

Social Media About 5 percent of the training hours delivered to employees involve social media sites, such as blogs and wikis (sites where people can post information as they can on Wikipedia).[26] When U.S. soldiers were having problems using a grenade launcher, a unit commander posted a question on one of the Army's internal social media sites. Shortly thereafter, someone who had experienced a similar problem posted a simple solution. The Cheesecake Factory restaurant chain trains employees by letting them upload and share video snippets on job-related topics, including how best to prepare certain foods and provide good customer service.[27]

Workplace by Facebook and Yammer are two corporate social media tools firms can use, but even a basic community page on LinkedIn or Facebook will work: A trainer can set up a page to provide information about an upcoming training session, post materials for it, and engage participants by allowing them to ask questions, volunteer answers, and collaborate with one another before and after the session.[28]

Behavior Modeling

Behavior modeling is a learning approach in which work behaviors are modeled, or demonstrated, and trainees are asked to mimic them. Behavior modeling consists of four basic components:

behavior modeling
A learning approach in which work behaviors are modeled, or demonstrated, and trainees are asked to mimic them

1. *Learning points.* For example, the learning points might describe the skill, why it's important for trainees to learn, and when it should be utilized.

2. *Modeling.* Participants might view a video in which a manager deals with an employee in an effort to improve his or her performance. The manager would model how specifically to deal with the situation and demonstrate the learning points.

3. *Practice.* Trainees then practice the behaviors modeled.

4. *Feedback and reinforcement.* The trainer and other trainees reinforce the behavior with praise, approval, encouragement, and attention. Digitally recording the sessions can also be very instructive.

Behavior modeling seems to work, according to various studies. Military training is a classic example of how behavior modeling can work. Drill sergeants model the behavior expected of new recruits, who, in turn, by emulating them, develop discipline and confidence.[29]

Role-Playing

Role-playing consists of playing the roles of others, often a supervisor and a subordinate who are facing a particular problem, such as a disagreement or a performance problem. Role-playing is used not only for managers, but also to train salespeople to question customers to understand their needs for goods and services. Health care professionals also use role-playing to learn to question patients and be empathetic and sensitive to their concerns. Virgin America uses role-playing exercises to help employees lean how to deal with irate or unruly passengers.

Computer programs that simulate role-playing have also been developed. Virtual Leader, a product by SimuLearn, is one such program: Management trainees interact with animated "employees"—some of whom are more cooperative than others. The trainees are then given feedback as to how well they applied their managerial skills to each situation.

Coaching

Coaching consists of a continuing flow of instructions, comments, and suggestions from the manager to a subordinate. Coaching is more than just a flow of instruction though. It is a flow of encouragement and support meant to help people not just do their jobs right and get ahead but become leaders.

Part of coaching involves talking to one's employees about what their goals are and being excited about their achieving those goals, even if it means good employees will ultimately leave your department and you will have to replace them with new ones and begin the process anew. Once a manager understands the employee's goals, the manager can design ways to help them grow their skills by taking on new leadership responsibilities, training and mentoring other employees, spearheading projects, and then providing the individual with performance feedback on.[30]

One way to coach employees being groomed as managers is to allow them to participate in managers' staff meetings. This can help them become more familiar with the problems and events occurring outside their immediate areas and how they are handled by exposing them to the ideas and thinking of other managers. Note, however, that coaching is important for all employees to receive—not just employees who are on managerial tracks. Many top managers as well as rank-and-file employees say that without coaching they would never have accomplished for their organizations what they might have.

Case Studies

A particularly useful method used in classroom learning situations is the case study. The FBI's Integrated Case Scenario method is used as part of a multiweek training program for all new FBI agents. Using documented examples, case-study participants learn how to analyze (take apart) and synthesize (put together) facts, become conscious of the many variables on which management decisions are based, and, in general, improve their decision-making skills.[31] Figure 7.8 provides a set of guidelines for when and how to conduct case studies.

Seminars and Conferences

Seminars and conferences, like classroom instruction, are useful for bringing groups of people together for training and development. Seminars and conferences can be used to communicate ideas, policies, or procedures, but they are also good for raising points of debate and discussing issues (usually with the help of a qualified leader) that have no set answers or resolutions. For this reason, seminars and conferences are often used when change is an organization's goal.

Outside seminars and conferences are often conducted jointly with universities and consulting firms. Associations and third-party organizations, such as the American Management Association, the Conference Board, and the Center for Creative Leadership, also offer many different types of management seminars. The construction and mining equipment manufacturer Caterpillar is one company that, in conjunction with an outside consulting firm, has developed a training program to groom new managers so it would have enough of them to effectively run the company in the coming decade. Caterpillar began with a series of high-level meetings and strategy sessions. Out of those meetings 11 characteristics were identified that the company seeks in its managers and leaders.

Classroom (Lecture) Instruction

You might wonder why firms use classroom training when so many other interactive (often electronic) methods are available. Some of the advantages of classroom instruction relate to motivation and attendance. Have you ever taken a self-paced course that lacked a classroom setting? If so, you might have had a hard time completing it. As one professor put it, "When it comes to learning, just getting to class is half the battle." In addition, if a trainee experiences problems, a live instructor is generally in the best position to help the trainee.

Classroom training need not necessarily take place in a classroom per se. Electronic Data Systems uses videoconferencing to train its employees wherever they are in the world rather than having them travel to one location. The company conducted a "coaching skills for leaders" program for 1,500 managers in 41 countries via videoconferencing.

Figure 7.8	Case Studies

When Using Case Studies ...

- Decide which goals can best be achieved by using case studies.
- Identify available cases that might work or consider writing your own.
- Set up the activity—including the case material, the room or place, and the schedule.
- Give all participants a chance to take part in the discussions and activities and try to keep the groups small.
- Bridge the gap between the theories presented in case studies and how they can actually be put into practice in your organization.

Source: Adapted from Albert A. Einsiedel Jr., "Case Studies: Indispensable Tools for Trainers," *Training and Development* (August 1995): 50–53.

Blended Learning

blended learning

The use of both in-person classroom learning and online learning

Blended learning is the use of both in-person classroom learning and online learning. Blended learning is effective because different people learn better in different ways, and it breaks up the tedium of a single learning technique. For example, to instruct flight crew trainees, airlines play actual cockpit audio recorded on airplanes involved in accidents. After listening to the recordings, the trainees discuss the behavior of the crew during the crisis. Recordings of trainees themselves can also be used. Golf and tennis coaches frequently record their students to let them see their mistakes and then provide them with verbal instructions for improvement. Figure 7.6 shows blended learning is the third most common way firms deliver training to their employees.

LO 5

To what extent do firms need to utilize additional training programs? Does it depend on the type of firm or the types of employees who need training?

7.5 Additional Training and Development Programs

In addition to training to address the demands of a particular job, many employers develop training programs to meet the special needs of employees. In this final section, we summarize some of these programs, including orientation training and onboarding, basic skills training, team training, cross-training, and ethics and diversity training. Intercultural training will be covered in Chapter 15.

7.5a Orientation and Onboarding

orientation

The formal process of familiarizing new employees with the organization, their jobs, and their work units

Orientation is the formal process of familiarizing new employees with the organization, their jobs, and their work units. Like training, which emphasizes the *what* and the *how*, orientation often stresses the *why*. It outlines the organization's philosophy and is designed to influence employee attitudes about their role and work they will be doing.

An organization's HR department ordinarily is responsible for coordinating orientation activities and providing new employees with information about their conditions of employment, pay, benefits, and other areas not directly under a supervisor's direction. Those responsible for conducting the orientation often use checklists so no aspect of the orientation is overlooked. The checklist would include such things as (1) an introduction to other employees, (2) an outline of training, (3) attendance, conduct, and appearance expectations, (4) the conditions of employment, such as hours and pay periods, (5) an explanation of job duties, standards, and appraisal criteria, (6) safety regulations, (7) a list of the chain of command, and (8) an explanation of the organization's purpose and strategic goals. Highlights in HRM 3 shows the types of materials new hires can be given and the various steps that can ease their transition into the workplace.[32] To be sure no materials are forgotten, companies often post orientation materials on their intranets and then provide new hires with passwords to access the sites.

Some organizations combine orientation programs with computer-based training. Macys cut its orientation training time in half this way, orienting 2,500 new employees in just 6 weeks. New hires at SumTotal Systems, an e-learning company based in Bellevue, Washington, go online for virtual tours of the company's various departments with introductions to company leaders sprinkled throughout. Of course, these types of programs *supplement*—but do not replace—the value of face-to-face orientations.[33]

onboarding

The process of systematically socializing new employees to help them get "on board" with an organization

Onboarding is the process of systematically socializing new employees to help them get "on board" with an organization. Onboarding goes beyond just orienting new employees to their new environment. It brings them into the organization's fold so that

Checklist for Orienting New Employees

Orientation Items

- Welcome information outlining the company background's, corporate vision, and mission statement
- Map of the facility, including parking information
- Computer passwords, security cards, and parking decals
- Current organizational chart
- Information about where to find the firm's corporate news, intranet sites, and bulletin boards
- Phone numbers, email addresses, and locations of key personnel and help desk personnel
- A copy of the employee's specific job goals and job description
- Lists of unique terms in the industry, company, and job

- Training class schedules
- Safety and emergency procedures
- The organization's policy handbook, including the firm's EEOC policies, office hours, dress code, vacation, and email and Internet rules
- List of employee benefits, including insurance plans
- Holiday schedule

Follow-Up Activities

- Ensure that employee has completed the required paperwork, including benefit enrollment forms
- Revisit the employee's performance standards
- Schedule the employee's first performance appraisal meeting

they truly feel as if they are a part of it. This is important because new hires are at a high risk of quitting.

Many new hires quit their jobs not because they can't handle the job tasks but because they are going through culture shock within the new organization. When new employees quit soon after being hired, companies are then forced to begin recruiting, interviewing, and screening candidates all over again. The best recruiting and selection processes are therefore of little value if a firm is not able to retain the people it hires.

To help new hires avoid culture shock, some companies make videos and podcasts available to them before they even begin work. The mission and goals of an organization, a mini-tour of its facilities, and interviews with current employees talking about what they like about the organization are featured. Executives are often featured as well, which helps new hires develop an early understanding of who's who in the organization.

In some firms, experienced coworkers serve as volunteer "sponsors," or buddies, for incoming employees. In addition to providing them with practical help they are an important source of information about the culture of the organization, different workgroups, and what is expected of employees. These relationships help with the socialization of new employees and contribute significantly to their long-term success within the organization. PepsiCo has a buddy system for new hires. The company's Barcelona unit created a YouTube video explaining where they need to go on their first day and what to expect. They also get a set of written information, and a box of PepsiCo chips and sodas as a welcome gift.

Southwest Airlines approaches onboarding as a welcoming party. "It was so much fun and so informative," remarked one eager new employee after Southwest's onboarding process.[34] New employees always start on Fridays at CityMax.com, a build-your-own-website service in Vancouver, British Columbia. On Fridays, people are in a better mood, more relaxed, and are more willing to spend time getting to know new hires.[35]

7.5b Basic Skills Training

Remedial, or basic skills, training for adults has grown to be a full-blown educational industry on which businesses now spend billions of dollars annually. A report by the National Endowment for the Arts recently concluded that employers ranked the lack of reading and writing skills as the top deficiencies in new hires. Although literacy levels today are similar to what they were in 1970, the economy has changed drastically since then. Most U.S. workers today need to be able to read and analyze complex, often very technical material to succeed. Recently the Pew Research Center conducted a survey of young people between the ages of 18 and 34 and found that most of them felt they lacked the education and training to get ahead, a situation exacerbated by the high cost of college. "Jobs that don't have much in the way of skills have moved out of the United States or are not living-wage jobs," says Timothy Shanahan, a professor of urban education and reading at the University of Illinois at Chicago. The basic skills employees need in addition to reading, writing, and computing include speaking, listening, problem-solving, working in teams, and leading other people.[36]

Smith & Wesson, Hewlett-Packard, Motorola, and the City of Phoenix instituted basic skills assessment programs to teach reading, math, and communication skills to employees who show some level of deficiency. Ford, Polaroid, United Technologies, and AT&T are among the many companies who now offer remedial courses to their employees, many of which are conducted in-house.

The National Institute for Literacy connects employers, learners, volunteers, social service providers, and others with literacy programs in all 50 states and U.S. territories. Employees and employers need only go to the institute's online directory and type in their locations to find the literacy help centers nearest them. A number of states offer businesses tax credits for conducting remedial training (and other types of training) for their employees.[37]

Recognizing that the skills gap is increasing, colleges and companies have begun teaming up to bridge the gap. For example, Pierce College, a 2-year college in California (which had previously concentrated on preparing students for 4-year colleges), now provides remedial instruction to employees at the offices of more than 30 companies in the San Fernando Valley area, where the college is located.

To implement a successful program in basic and remedial skills, managers should do the following:

1. Explain to employees why and how the training will help them in their jobs.
2. Relate the training to the employees' goals.
3. Respect and consider participants' experiences and use them as a resource.
4. Use a task-centered or problem-centered approach so that participants learn by doing.
5. Give employees feedback on their progress toward meeting their learning objectives.

7.5c Team Training

As we discussed earlier in the book, organizations rely on teams to help them attain their strategic and operational goals. Whether the team is an aircrew, a research team, or a manufacturing or service unit, the contributions of the individual members of the team are not only a function of the KSAOs of each individual but also of the interaction of the team members. The teamwork behaviors of effective teams are shown in Figure 7.9. Team training focused on team roles, group dynamics, and problem-solving provides skills needed to function effectively as a team.[38]

Games are often used in team training as is adventure-based learning. **Adventure-based learning** is the use of adventures, such as games, trust activities and problem-solving initiatives for the personal and social development of participants.[39] Combine the TV shows *The Amazing Race* and *Survivor* with corporate training, and you will get an idea of what adventure-based learning is. Adventure-based learning is a type of experiential learning (learning by experience). Facebook, Google, Reebok, Coca-Cola, and Dell are among the companies that have utilized adventure-learning for team-building purposes.

How effective is the adventure-based learning method? It depends. "The most creative way to teach valuable lessons of leadership and communication is to engage employees in an unexpected activity that is carefully designed and backed by parallels to real-life situations," says Chad Michael, the founder of AdVenture Games, a San Diego company that provides corporate training. "If the team building activity does not come with lessons learned and a creative way to instill valuable skill sets, the investment is no more effective than an afternoon at the park."

adventure-based learning
The use of adventures, such as games, trust activities, and problem-solving initiatives, for the personal and social development of participants

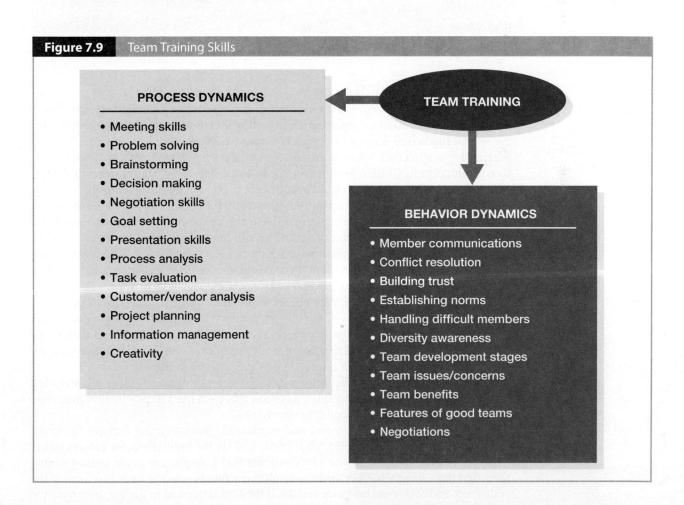

Figure 7.9   Team Training Skills

TEAM TRAINING

PROCESS DYNAMICS
- Meeting skills
- Problem solving
- Brainstorming
- Decision making
- Negotiation skills
- Goal setting
- Presentation skills
- Process analysis
- Task evaluation
- Customer/vendor analysis
- Project planning
- Information management
- Creativity

BEHAVIOR DYNAMICS
- Member communications
- Conflict resolution
- Building trust
- Establishing norms
- Handling difficult members
- Diversity awareness
- Team development stages
- Team issues/concerns
- Team benefits
- Features of good teams
- Negotiations

AdVenture Games is a San Diego-based company that provides companies with adventure-based games. The games are designed to improve employees' strategic leadership and creativity, among other things.

iStock.com/Blulz60

7.5d Cross-Training

cross-training

The process of training employees to do multiple jobs within an organization

Closely related to team training is **cross-training**. Cross-trained employees learn how to do different jobs within an organization as well as their own. Part of the motivation for cross-training is that it gives firms flexible capacity. Workers can be shifted when and where they are needed. Cross-training represents a shift from Henry Ford's assembly line production to flexible production. Coca-Cola's Fountain Manufacturing Operation (which makes the syrup for Coke and Diet Coke) developed team training for its manufacturing employees. The program focuses on three skill categories: (1) technical, (2) interpersonal, and (3) team action. The technical component, called Four-Deep Training, requires each individual to learn four different jobs to allow for team flexibility.

Some companies have used cross-training to keep their workers and plants in the United States versus offshoring them. Pace Worldwide, a Maryland-based company that sells soldering equipment, watched all of its competitors move offshore. To compete with its low-cost rivals abroad, Pace grouped workers into teams and trained each team to build an entire product as well as different products. "Some of the people could only do certain things, and if they had no work, they would just sit and wait," said one Pace manager. "Now they have ownership of it all." Employees have an incentive to learn because their hourly wages get bumped up as they master more skills.

Now Pace builds products to meet actual customer demand rather than storing inventory, which is more costly, and it has been able to shorten its production times and move its operations into one building versus two.

By keeping workers interested and motivated, cross-training can cut turnover, increase productivity, pare down labor costs, and lay the foundation for careers rather than dead-end jobs. At Boston's The Gourmet Pizza, employees begin cross-training their first day on the job. They cycle through every function in the back and front of the restaurant and then plot their own course. If they are interested in the bar, they have the opportunity to work there in various positions; those who want to become managers or franchise owners learn the entire operation, a process that takes 8 to 12 months.[40] In addition to making them more productive, research shows that cross-training gives employees the "big picture," making them more creative and better problem-solvers.[41]

7.5e Ethics Training

Ethics training became more prevalent in companies following a number of high-profile corporate scandals in the early 2000. Corporate scandals are, of course, not new to the twenty-first century. The most common forms of ethics violations, such as harassment, health and safety, and wage-and-hour violations, are related to employment laws.

Government contractors and subcontractors with contracts that last for 120 days or more and are more than $5 million are required by law to have business ethics codes and compliance policies and procedures. Other organizations are not legally required to. However, in the event of a violation, those that have "effective programs to prevent and detect violations of law" will face reduced penalties under U.S. federal sentencing guidelines.

Workers who are responsible for areas that expose them to ethical lapses are likely to require special training. Employees who do the purchasing for their firms are one example. Likewise, some firms offer special training to their overseas personnel who work in countries in which corruption and bribery are prevalent. (We will talk more about bribery in Chapter 15, which covers international topics.) Bringing in an outside expert trained in ethics or values-based management can be helpful as can surveying employees, managers, and sometimes even customers about what they believe the ethical state of their companies are and where improvements could be made. Other efforts a firm can take to ensure employees at all levels are behaving ethically and legally include establishing toll-free ethics hotlines and secure email addresses where employees can confidentially report violations they have noticed.

Some firms have **chief ethics officers**—high-ranking managers directly responsible for fostering the ethical climate within their firms and ensuring compliance. The Business Roundtable Institute for Corporate Ethics, the Ethics Resource Center, and Ethics & Compliance Officer Association are some additional sources human resource managers can turn to in order to develop ethics training programs. Keep in mind, however, that employees take their cues from top managers and mirror their behavior. If these people don't behave ethically, no ethics training program within a company can be effective.

chief ethics officers
A high-ranking manager directly responsible for fostering the ethical climate within the firm

7.5f Diversity and Inclusion Training

Diversity training programs were designed in response to an increase in globalization, an awareness of the varied demographics of the workforce, challenges of affirmative action, dynamics of stereotyping, changing values of the workforce, and potential competitive payoffs from bringing different people together for a common purpose. There are basically three types of diversity training: (1) awareness building, which helps employees appreciate the benefits of diversity; (2) training to prevent discrimination, harassment, and associated lawsuits, which for some firms is a major reason why they conduct them; and (3) skill building, which provides employees with the KSAOs necessary for working with people who are different from them with regard to race, gender, and age.[42]

The San Francisco 49ers football team underwent diversity training after Lindsey McLean, a retired gay trainer with the team, admitted publicly that he was gay and that he had endured taunts and humiliation from players at times during his 24 years with the 49ers. "We're trying to create an environment where we can talk about these things and eliminate the problems and violence that can take place and help them understand that they can create an environment that people can work in, even if they are different," said one 49ers manager.[43]

The effectiveness of diversity training has come to be debated, however. A comprehensive review of 31 years of data from 830 midsize to large U.S. workplaces found that following diversity training even fewer minorities and women were being promoted into management at firms. But that does not necessarily mean that diversity training in and of itself has led to fewer promotions for women and minorities. Moreover, not all diversity training was ineffective, the review found. Rather, it showed that mandatory programs—solely avoiding liability in discrimination lawsuits—were the problem. When diversity training is voluntary and undertaken to increase awareness of the problem and advance a company's business goals, it can be quite effective.[44] This is one of the reasons why companies are increasingly focusing on *inclusion*. An inclusive workplace is one in which people are treated fairly and with respect, and are supported and encouraged to participate in all aspects of the organization.

7.6 Phase 4: Evaluating the Training Program

How can you figure out whether the training program you conducted was successful? A variety of methods are available to assess the extent to which a firm's training programs improve learning, affect behavior on the job, and impact the bottom-line performance of an organization. Figure 7.10 shows that four basic criteria are available to evaluate training: (1) reactions, (2) learning, (3) behavior, and (4) results. Some of these criteria are easier to measure than others, but each is important in that it provides different information about the success of the training. The combination of these criteria can give a total picture of a training program to help managers decide where problem areas lie, what to change about the program, and whether to continue it.

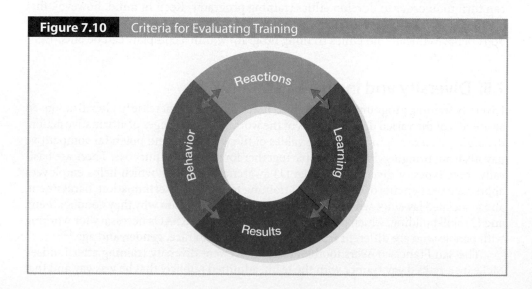

Figure 7.10   Criteria for Evaluating Training

7.6a Criterion 1: Reactions

One of the simplest approaches to evaluating a training program is to assess participants' reactions to it. In addition to indicating whether they enjoyed the training, they can give insights into the content and techniques they found most useful. They can critique the instructors, suggest ways to improve the training, and indicate whether or not it should be continued.

However, positive reactions to a training session are no guarantee it has been successful. It may be easy to collect glowing comments from trainees, but as gratifying as this information is, it may not be useful to the organization unless it translates into tangible, improved on-the-job performance based on the firm's strategic goals. Reaction measures should not stop with assessing the training's entertainment value.[45]

7.6b Criterion 2: Learning

Beyond what participants *think* about the training, did they actually learn anything? Testing the knowledge and skills of trainees before and after a training program will help determine their improvement. The skill and knowledge levels of employees who have undergone a training program can also be compared to employees who have not. Federal Express took this approach. The company studied 20 van drivers who attended a weeklong new hire training program. The company then compared the performance of these drivers with a control group of 20 drivers who had received only OTJ training. FedEx found that the drivers who had been formally trained made fewer package processing errors, saving the company about $500 per trained driver.[46]

7.6c Criterion 3: Behavior

The **transfer of training** refers to how well employees apply what they have learned to their jobs. There are several ways to assess the transfer of learned skills back to the job. At Xerox, trainers observe trainees once they return to their regular positions, interview the trainees' managers about their progress later on, and examine their post-training performance appraisals.

You might be surprised to learn that much of what is learned in a training program never gets used back on the job. To maximize the transfer of training, managers and trainers can take several approaches:

1. *Feature identical elements.* Have conditions in the training program come as close as possible to those on the job. For example, instead of verbally explaining a manufacturing process, it is better to demonstrate it on a factory floor.

2. *Focus on general principles, if necessary.* When jobs change or the work environment cannot be matched exactly, trainers often stress the general principles behind the training rather than focusing on rote behavior. This approach helps trainees learn how to apply the main learning points to varying conditions on the job.

3. *Establish a climate for transfer.* In some cases, trained behavior is not implemented because old approaches and routines are still reinforced by people within the organization. To prevent this kind of problem, firms need to encourage their managers to embrace the strategic changes their organizations are seeking to implement and reinforce and reward trainees for applying the new skills or knowledge.

transfer of training
The effective application of principles learned to what is required on the job

4. *Give employees transfer strategies.* Particularly in settings that are not conducive to transfer, managers should provide trainees with strategies and tactics for dealing with their transfer environment. One approach, called *relapse prevention (RP)*, teaches individuals how to anticipate and cope with the inevitable setbacks they will encounter back on the job—that is, a relapse into former behaviors.[47]

7.6d Criterion 4: Results, or Return on Investment (ROI)

Human resource managers are under pressure from top managers to show that their training programs produce bottom-line results.[48] Most organizations today measure their training in terms of its return on investment (ROI), which is also sometimes referred to as the *utility* the firm gets for its training dollars. A company's ROI refers to the benefits it derives from training compared to what it costs.

The benefits can include higher revenues generated, increased productivity, improved quality, lower costs, more satisfied customers, higher job satisfaction, lower employee turnover, and greater innovation. To put a dollar value on these benefits, HR managers use various types of data such as sales data, human resources and financial data, and employee survey and control group data gathered from various sources within the organization.

To put a dollar value on the firm's training costs, the company calculates the direct costs of the programs (materials, software, employee travel and meals, meeting site costs, equipment, trainers' salaries or fees, etc.) as well as the indirect costs of the programs (participants' salaries and the productivity they lose while they are attending the training).

Recall that benchmarking is the practice of comparing data and statistics from your operations, such as training, against those of recognized leaders in your industry. The American Society of Training has developed training benchmarks from hundreds of different companies to which other firms can compare the data on their training costs, staffing, administration, design, development, and delivery of training programs. Benchmarks such as these can help organizations evaluate their current and future training programs. Highlights in HRM 3 shows several aspects of training that can be benchmarked.

As e-learning continues to change training, the benchmarks for it are changing as well. Measures such as the extent to which learning content has been accessed, downloaded, and the ratings given it by users are likely to become new measures of how well a firm's training programs are working.[49]

Some HR experts think managers can get overly preoccupied with ROI calculations and benchmarking. Why? Because often the benefits of training can be intangible or take a long time to appear. Measuring participants' reactions can be done immediately, of course. However, measuring improved employee skills, customer satisfaction, and so forth can take somewhat longer, and factors other than training can also affect these measures. Finally, the development of groundbreaking new products or processes can also be sparked by training but take years to develop, making them hard to attribute to training. Developments such as these nonetheless can transform organizations.

The key to improving a training program's effectiveness is continually evaluating it. The information generated by the evaluations then feeds back into Phase 1 of the training process, as shown in Figure 7.1. By tying the training closely to key performance metrics and then measuring the training's impact against them, a firm will be in a better position to improve its programs over time.[50]

Benchmarking HR Training

MEASUREMENT	HOW TO CALCULATE
Percent of payroll spent on training	Total training expenditures ÷ total payroll
Training dollars spent per employee	Total training expenditures ÷ total employees served
Average training hours per employee	Total number of training hours (hours × participants) ÷ total employees trained
Percent of employees trained per year	Total number of employees receiving training ÷ total employee population
HRD staff per 1,000 employees	Number of human resource development staff ÷ total employee population × 1,000
Cost savings as a ratio of training	Total savings in scrap or waste ÷ dollars invested expenses in training
Profits per employee per year	Total yearly gross profits ÷ total number of employees
Training costs per student hour	Total costs of training ÷ total number of hours of training

Summary

LO 1 The types of training given employees range from simple, on-the-job instruction to sophisticated skills training conducted on multimillion-dollar simulators. Training programs cover a broad range of subjects and involve personnel at all levels. The goal of training is to contribute to an organization's overall strategic goals. To be effective, training programs need to be developed systematically. This approach consists of four phases: (1) needs assessment, (2) program design, (3) implementation, and (4) evaluation.

LO 2 The needs assessment phase begins with an organization analysis. Managers must establish a context for training by deciding where training is needed, how it connects with their firms' strategic goals, and how their companies' resources can best be used in terms of training. A task analysis is used to identify the knowledge, skills, and abilities employees need. A person analysis is used to identify which people need training.

LO 3 When designing a training program, managers need to consider the two preconditions for learning: the readiness and motivation of trainees. In addition, the principles of learning should be considered to create an environment that is conducive to learning. These principles include goal setting, the meaningfulness of presentation, modeling, individual differences, active practice and repetition, experiential learning, whole-versus-part learning, massed, distributed, and continuous learning, and feedback and reinforcement.

LO 4 A wide variety of methods are available to train personnel. On-the-job training is one of the most commonly used methods. Apprenticeship training and internships are especially effective. On-the-job experiences include coaching, understudy assignments, job rotation, lateral transfers, project and committee assignments, and staff meetings. Off-the-job experiences include analysis of case studies, role-playing, and behavior modeling.

Classroom training is still the most popular way to train employees. However, e-learning methods, such as simulations, games, just-in-time learning, microlearning, and social media are rapidly becoming more popular. Using multiple methods, or what is called blended learning, has been found to be most effective.

LO 5 Employers develop different training programs for various purposes. Orientation training allows new hires to more quickly acquire the knowledge, skills, and attitudes that increase the probabilities of their success within the organization. Onboarding programs help new hires feel like they truly are a part of a firm. This is important because new hires are at a high risk of quitting. Basic skills training, team and cross-training, ethics training, and diversity training are other programs commonly conducted by organizations.

LO 6 The effectiveness of training can be evaluated on several criteria: participants' reactions, the amount of learning they have acquired, their behavioral changes on the job, and bottom-line results such as the program's return on investment. The transfer of training is measured via examination of the degree to which trained skills are demonstrated back on the job. Benchmarking and utility analysis help evaluate the impact of training and provide the information for further needs assessment.

Key Terms

adventure-based learning

apprenticeship training

behavior modeling

behavior modification

blended learning

chief ethics officer

chief learning officers

competency assessment

cooperative training

cross-training

e-learning

experiential learning

instructional objectives

just-in-time training

learning management system (LMS)

microlearning

on-the-job training (OJT)

onboarding

organization analysis

orientation

person analysis

spot rewards

task analysis

transfer of training

Discussion Questions

LO 1 What economic, social, and political forces have made employee training even more important today than it was in the past?

LO 2 What analyses should be done to determine the training needs of an organization? After the needs are determined, what is the next step?

LO 3 Which principles of learning do you see demonstrated in your own classes? In what ways might you bring other principles into them?

LO 4 Suppose that you are the manager of an accounts receivable unit in a large company.

You are switching to a new system of billing and record-keeping and need to train your three supervisors and 28 employees in the new procedures. What training method(s) would you use? Why?

LO 5 Participants in a training course are often asked to evaluate the course by means of a questionnaire. What are the pros and cons of this approach? Are there better ways of evaluating a course?

HRM Experience

Training and Learning Principles

Even though it is not difficult to do so, a surprising number of training programs don't explicitly incorporate the principles of learning (goal setting, modeling, individual differences, and feedback). To prove incorporating them is not difficult to do, complete the following assignment for building a paper airplane.

Assignment

1. Form teams of four to six members. Identify someone on the team who knows how to make a paper airplane. That person will be the trainer.

2. Identify someone who will be the observer/recorder. That person will not participate in the training but will write down how many (and how effectively) principles of learning are used in the instruction:

   a. Goal setting
   b. Modeling
   c. Meaningfulness
   d. Individual differences
   e. Whole versus part learning
   f. Mass versus distributed learning
   g. Active practice
   h. Feedback
   i. Experiential learning

3. Give the trainer 10 to 15 minutes to train the group in making a paper airplane. The observer/recorder will keep notes of effective and ineffective training techniques (demonstrated learning principles).

4. Have someone from each team—not the trainer—volunteer to come before the class for a friendly competition. The instructor will give each team member 2 minutes to make a paper airplane. Then, just for fun, they can compete by seeing which one flies the farthest. (No wagering, please.)

5. To finish the exercise, the observers/recorders will lead a discussion of the learning principles that were demonstrated. If the principles were incorporated for this activity, discuss why they might not be incorporated in other training settings.

CASE STUDY ① Whirlpool Mixes Up Its Managerial Training: Closed-Looped Method Brings Learning Full Circle

Most Americans are familiar with Whirlpool. Whirlpool, which is based in Benton Harbor, Michigan, and has been in business for more than century, is perhaps best known for the washers and dryers it makes. But the company also makes refrigerators, freezers, and cooking appliances that it sells under various other brand names around the world (Amana, Maytag, KitchenAid, and Roper are some of them).

During the last economic recession appliance sales plummeted, and Whirlpool was forced to lay off thousands of workers. Although budgets were being slashed, Whirlpool needed to develop managers who could lead the company through the downturn as well as provide training that would have a measurable impact at a lower cost.

Previously Whirlpool University, the company's 100-acre learning division located at its corporate headquarters, had used mainly classroom learning. The university now has a learning management system and conducts online training. A series of 30-minute modules are used to help familiarize and onboard new hires. In addition, Whirlpool now takes a "closed-loop" approach to training. Instead of just doing popular types of training other companies were doing, it surveys managers to find out what types of training Whirlpool truly needed and what types it didn't and then designs training programs based on those specific needs.

Because they are central to the training and development of their employees and in the best position to

273

observe and coach rank-and-file employees, to train managers, Whirlpool utilizes a 12-month-long inter-mittent training program called Leading People. The program consists of blended learning, including pre-work modules managers do online, followed by class-room training, business projects, and seminars with top managers. A manager's direct reports provide an initial baseline assessment of his or her skills, and then the manager is assessed again following the training. James Crawford, in Whirlpool's Chicago division, said the training helped him become a better leader. "It helped me pinpoint weak spots in my leadership prac-tices and then gave me a strategy for turning those weaknesses into strengths," Crawford says. The man-agers are later surveyed as to how well the training is working and what can be done to improve it. In other words, there is a feedback system in place, hence the "closed-loop" moniker. That way, the design, delivery, and redesign of the training is a continuous circle and constantly being improved over time.

The closed-loop feedback system has helped Whirlpool continue to assess and alter its train-ing to adapt to new conditions. For example, today Whirlpool isn't laying off employees; it's trying to hire more of them as its older workers retire. To attract

millennials, the company has partnered with high school and colleges to offer an onsite apprenticeship program called "Work, Earn, and Learn." In 2017, Whirlpool's CEO, Jeff Fettig, was one of a number of corporate executives who met with President Don-ald Trump to talk about saving American jobs and encourage the support of vocational training for the high-tech skills manufacturers today need. "The jobs are there, but the skills are not," said one executive at the meeting.

Questions

1. Why are a needs assessment and ongoing training important for firms like Whirlpool to conduct?

2. How do you think Whirlpool's training strategy will need to change in the future?

Source: Greg Sowinski, "Manufacturers Prep to Replace Retiring Work-force," *LimaOhio.com* (March 5, 2017), http://limaohio.com; Christopher S. Rugaber, "U.S. Factory CEOs to Trump: Jobs Exist; Skills Don't," *Chicago Tri-bune* (February 24, 2017), http://www.chicagotribune.com; Garry Kranz, "Whirlpool Adopts E-Learning for Leadership," *Workforce* (November 14, 2012), http://www.workforce.com; Tamara Patrick, "Unleashing a Learn-ing Partnership with Managers," *ATD* (August 16, 2012), http://www.astd .org; Tamara Patrick, "Whirlpool University Re-Invents in the Face of the Recession," *Management Innovation Exchange* (September 16, 2011), http://www .managementexchange.com.

CASE STUDY ② Loews Hotels: Training for Four-Diamond Service and More

Most people expect to receive great service at four-diamond hotels. But that's not good enough for Loews. The New York–based hotel chain, which has proper-ties in 16 cities across the United States and Canada, tries to "wow" every one of its guests with high-quality accommodations, impressive surroundings, personal-ized service, and thoughtful amenities for a luxurious experience.

A key element of success at Loews is the exten-sive training it provides its employees. Whether they work at the front desk, as housekeepers, accountants, or marketing managers, they learn about the big-picture goals of the company and how the quality of service differentiates one company from another in the hotel business. "The key is to train *all* depart-ments of your organization to be customer-centric," says Jon Tisch, the company's co-chairman. "Thinking

about customers can't be left to marketing and sales alone. Manufacturing, R&D, strategy, management, all have to be focused on the needs and desires of the customer."

Customer-facing employees at Loews undergo classroom training, including role-playing and simu-lations to learn how to deal with customers. "Living Loews," a 2-day training program, teaches employ-ees not only the finer points of etiquette but how to really sell the Loews experience—even when things go wrong. "We're all human, so mistakes can hap-pen," Tisch explains. "But when they do, we train our coworkers to impress our guests with an extraordinary recovery that we hope they'll remember even more."

Training sessions such as "Green" training, "Loews Meeting Experience," "Loews Pool Concierge" program, "Spa 101," and the "YouFirst" guest loyalty program ensure that customers of all types who use the hotel's various services get top-notch service.

The training does not end with the sessions, though. Once it is over, training managers go out on the front lines to do spot checks and offer feedback to employees to make sure the training really "sticks." A train-the-trainer program and other managerial workshops such as "Communicating Loews" help managers promote the hotel brand and inspire their employees to do so as well. A comprehensive executive training program covers topics ranging from communication and salesmanship to public speaking and presentation skills.

Loews also tries to "grow" its own talent. Most training managers, for example, are promoted from line-level jobs or from operations, so they know the company's processes and culture firsthand. The company also has a tuition assistance program.

To recruit undergraduates, Loews offers paid summer internships. Interns work in a variety of areas such as the rooms division, food and beverage department, sales and marketing, and human resources. Each intern is assigned a mentor and given opportunities to network by attending operational meetings. At the conclusion of their internships they complete a report on their experience. Successive year internships give them exposure to additional functional areas, project work, supervisory experience, and ultimately the opportunity to join the company's management training program.

So successful is the training at Loews that even trainers are impressed. Douglas Kennedy, the founder and president of the Kennedy Training Network, which specializes in hospitality training, says he was knocked out by his experience while conducting training at Loews's various properties. Kennedy says he's gotten very spoiled during his overnight stays at Loews hotels: "I'm sure it will be a rude awakening next month when I return to staying in more typical upscale hotels."

Questions

1. How do the training programs at Loews relate to the company's business strategy?

2. Why does the company encourage its employees to focus on the customers' needs versus other metrics?

Sources: Amy Bertrand, "Luxury Hotel Trends to Watch," *St. Louis Today* (February 4, 2014), http://www.stltoday.com; Jill Busch "Training Reveals Rankings for 2011 Top 125," *Training Magazine* (February 8, 2011), http://www.trainingmag.com; Ann LaGreca, "Loews Hotels CEO Jonathan Tisch on the Essence of Customer Service: Experience, Service and Quality," *Knowledge@Emory* (July 11, 2007), http://knowledge.emory.edu; "Loews Hotels Named Among 'Top 125' by Training Magazine," *Hotel and Motel Management* (March 9, 2009), http://www.hospitalityworldnetwork.com; Holly Dolezalek, "We Train to Please" *Training* 45, no. 3 (March–April 2008): 34–35.

Notes and References

1. "2016 Training Industry Report," *Training* (November–December 2016): 31.

2. Peter Franks, Stephen Hay, and Tim Mavin, "Can Competency-Based Training Fly?: An Overview of Key Issues for AB Onitio Pilot Training," *International Journal of Training Research* 12, no. 2 (2014): 132–47; Lori Freifeld, "Best of the Best," *Training* 45, no. 2 (February 2008): 8; David Dubois and William Rothwell, "Competency-Based or a Traditional Approach to Training?" *Training and Development* 58, no. 4 (April 2004): 46–59; see also Irwin L. Goldstein and J. Kevin Ford, *Training in Organizations: Needs Assessment, Development and Evaluation*, 4th ed. (Belmont, CA: Wadsworth, 2002). For the classic citation on needs assessment, see William McGehee and Paul W. Thayer, *Training in Business and Industry* (New York: John Wiley and Sons, 1961).

3. Mackenzie Adams and Maged Makramalla, "Cybersecurity Skills Training: An Attacker-Centric Gamified Approach," *Technology Innovation Management Review.* 5, no. 1 (2015); Liam Lahey, "RFIDs Touted as Standard for Airport Security," *Computing Canada* 28, no. 13 (June 21, 2002): 21; Caroline Wilson, "Ensuring a Smooth Ride," *Security Management* 46, no. 8 (August 2002): 92.

4. Laurie Bassi and Daniel McMurrer, "How's Your Return on People?" *Harvard Business Review* 8, no. 3 (March 2004): 18; Tracy Mauro, "Helping Organizations Build Community," *Training and Development* 56, no. 2 (February 2002): 25–29.

5. Sanghamitra Chaudhuri and Kenneth R. Bartlett, "The Relationship Between Training Outsourcing and Employee Commitment to Organization," *Human Resource Development International* 17, no. 2 (2014): 145–163; Brad Long, "Strategic Human Resource Management and the Worker's Experience,"

Journal of Individual Employment Rights 12, no. 3 (2007): 265–282; "E-Learning and Teleconferencing Join Needs Assessment to Control Training Costs," *Managing Training & Development*, no. 3 (December 2003): 1; Thomas Gainey, Brian Klaas, and Darla Moore, "Outsourcing the Training Function: Results from the Field," *Human Resource Planning* 25, no. 1 (2002): 16; Sarah Fister Gale, "Creative Training: Doing More with Less," *Workforce* 80, no. 10 (October 2001): 82–88.

6. Peter Franks, Stephen Hay, and Tim Mavin, "Can Competency-Based Training Fly?"; Scott A. Yorkovich, Gregory S. Waddell, and Robert K. Gerwig, "Competency-based Assessment Systems: Encouragement Toward a More Holistic Approach," *Proceedings of the Northeast Business & Economics Association* (2007): 77–81; Patty Davis, Jennifer Naughton, and William Rothwell, "New Roles and New Competencies for the Profession: Are You Ready for the Next Generation," *Training and Development* 58, no. 4 (April 2004): 26–38; David Dubois and William Rothwell, "Competency-Based or a Traditional Approach to Training?" *Training and Development* 58, no. 4 (April 2004): 46–59.

7. Allison S. Gabriel et al., "The Supervisor Feedback Environment Is Empowering, But Not all the Time: Feedback Orientation as a Critical Moderator," *Journal of Occupational and Organizational Psychology* 87, no. 3 (2014): 487–506; Gary Kranz, "Special Report: More to Learn," *Workforce Management* (January 2011), http://www.workforce.com/.

8. Nima Jafari Navimipour and Batool Zareie, "A Model for Assessing the Impact of E-learning Systems on Employees' Satisfaction," *Computers in Human Behavior* 53 (2015): 475–485; Thomas Hoffman, "Motivation: These IT Leaders Keep Staffers Upbeat during Lean Times by Targeting What Drives Them: Technology and Training," *Computerworld* 38, no. 1 (January 5, 2004): 39; Elwood Holton, Reid Bates, and Sharon Naquin, "Large-Scale Performance-Driven Training Needs Assessment: A Case Study," *Public Personnel Management* 29, no. 2 (Summer 2000): 249–267.

9. Alice Hsiaw, "Goal-Setting and Self-Control," *Journal of Economic Theory* 148, no. 2 (2013): 601–626; Debbie Schachter, "How to Set Performance Goals: Employee Reviews Are More Than Annual Critiques," *Information Outlook* 8, no. 9 (September 2004): 26–30; "Burger Olympics," *Training* 41, no. 7 (July 2004): 20; Jason A. Colquitt and Marcia J. Simmering, "Conscientiousness, Goal Orientation, and Motivation to Learn during the Learning Process: A Longitudinal Study," *Journal of Applied Psychology* 83, no. 4 (August 1998): 654–665.

10. Leroy Hannes et al., "Mindfulness, Authentic Functioning, and Work Engagement: A Growth Modeling Approach," *Journal of Vocational Behavior* 82 no. 3 (2013): 238–247; Annette Towler and Robert Dipboye, "Effects of Trainer Expressiveness, Organization, and Trainee Goal Orientation on Training Outcomes," *Journal of Applied Psychology* 86, no. 4 (August 2001): 664–673; Steve Kozlowski, Stanley

Gully, Kenneth Brown, and Eduardo Salas, "Effects of Training Goals and Goal Orientation Traits on Multidimensional Training Outcomes and Performance Adaptability," *Organizational Behavior and Human Decision Processes* 85, no. 1 (May 2001): 1–31.

11. The classics by Albert Bandura include *Social Foundations of Thought and Action: A Social Cognitive Theory* (Englewood Cliffs, NJ: Prentice Hall, 1986) and *A Social Learning Theory* (Englewood Cliffs, NJ: Prentice Hall, 1977); see also Melesa Altizer Bolt, Larry Killough, and Hian Chye Koh, "Testing the Interaction Effects of Task Complexity in Computer Training Using the Social Cognitive Model," *Decision Sciences* 32, no. 1 (Winter 2001): 1020; Rose M. Marra et al., "Why Problem-based Learning Works," *Journal on Excellence in College Teaching* 25, no. 3/4 (2014): 221–238; Susan Pedersen and Min Liu, "The Transfer of Problem-Solving Skills from a Problem-Based Learning Environment: The Effect of Modeling an Expert's Cognitive Processes," *Journal of Research on Technology in Education* 35, no. 2 (Winter 2002): 303–321.

12. Chadwick Reese and Debra Hunter, "What about the Middle Man? The Impact of Middle Level Managers on Organizational Learning," *Journal of Management* 4, no. 1 (2016): 17–25; Joe M. Ricks, Jacqueline A. Williams, and William A. Weeks, "Sales Trainer Roles, Competencies, Skills, and Behaviors: A Case Study," *Industrial Marketing Management* 37, no. 5 (July 2008): 593–609; John L. Bennett, "Trainers as Leaders of Learning," *Training and Development* 55, no. 3 (March 2001): 42–45; Ruth Palombo Weiss, "Deconstructing Trainers' Self-Image," *Training and Development* 55, no. 12 (December 2001): 34–39.

13. Josep-Maria Batalla-Busquets and Carmen Pacheco-Bernal, "On-the-Job e-Learning: Workers' Attitudes and Perceptions," *The International Review of Research in Open and Distributed Learning* 14, no. 1 (2013): 40–64; "Eight Steps to Better On-the-Job Training," *HRFocus* 80, no. 7 (July 2003): 11; Alison Booth, Yu-Fu Chen, and Gylfi Zoega, "Hiring and Firing: A Tale of Two Thresholds," *Journal of Labor Economics* 20, no. 2 (April 2002): 217–48.

14. Information found on the Apprenticeship page, Spokane Community College website (February 9, 2005), http://www.scc.spokane.edu/tech/apprent.

15. Yeonsoo Kim, "Use of Career One Stop and Career Network in US," *Talent Management Monthly* 121 (2015): 83; "Workforce Investment Act: One-Stop Centers Implemented Strategies to Strengthen Services and Partnerships, but More Research and Information Sharing Is Needed," *General Accounting Office Reports & Testimony* 2003, no. 7 (July 2003).

16. Dominic Gorecky, Mohamed Khamis, and Katharina Mura, "Introduction and Establishment of Virtual Training in the Factory of the Future," *International Journal of Computer Integrated Manufacturing* 30, no. 1 (2017): 182–90; Sarah Fister Gale, "Virtual Training with Real Results," *Workforce Management* (December 2008), http://www.workforce.com.

17. Joanne Viviano, "Ohio Doctors Employ Virtual Reality to train for Trauma Care," *Columbus Dispatch* (March 26, 2017), http://www.dispatch.com; "Soup to Nuts: Simulator Manufacturing Is a Lucrative but Risky Business, Which Is Why Market Leader CAE Has Tapped into the More Stable World of Flight Training," *Air Transport World* 40, no. 5 (May 2003): 69–71; "SimsSir: Modeling and Simulation Are Leading the Assault on New Learning Technologies That Are Winning Favor with the U.S. Military," *Training and Development* 57, no. 10 (October 2003): 46–52.

18. Erika Darling et al., "Effective Game-Based Training at the Point of Need," in *Advances in Human Factors, Business Management, Training and Education* (New York: Springer International Publishing, 2017): 677–685; Adam Kirby "Guest Service Is Fun and Games," *Hotels* 42, no. 5 (May 2008): 71–72; Dan Heilman, "Putting Games to Work: Game-Based Training Is Shaping Up to Be One of This Generation's Primary Teaching Tools, in Business and Elsewhere," *Computer User* 22, no. 2 (February 2004): 14–16.

19. Judy Mottl, "Bloomingdales, Altar'd State Share Associate Training Success Stores," *Retail Customer Experience* (February 28, 2017), https://www.retailcustomerexperience.com.

20. Anjali Bal et al., "Second Best in Second Life: Teaching Marketing Cases in a Virtual World Environment," *Proceedings of the 2010 Academy of Marketing Science (AMS) Annual Conference*, Springer International Publishing, 2015; Aili McConnon, "The Games Managers Play," *BusinessWeek* (June 25, 2007): 12.

21. Phil Britt, *"E-Learning on the Rise in the Classroom: Companies Move Content Online: Cisco Systems'* Employees and Partners Routinely Watch Videos on the Internet," *EContent* 27, no. 11 (November 2004): 36–41; Heather Johnson, "The Whole Picture: When It Comes to Finding Out How Employees Feel about Training, Many Companies Fail to Get a Clear Picture," *Training* 47, no. 7 (July 2004): 30–35.

22. Ravi Rajputh et al., "Interactive Materials Development Using the Rapid e-Learning Method—Examples from the Field" (2016); "What to Do Now That Training Is Becoming a Major HR Force," *HRFocus* (February 2005): 5–6; Tammy Galvin, "The Delivery," *Training* 38, no. 10 (October 2001): 66–72; Kenneth G. Brown, "Using Computers to Deliver Training: Which Employees Learn and Why?" *Personnel Psychology* 54, no. 2 (Summer 2001): 271–296; Bill Roberts, "E-Learning New Twist on CBT," *HRMagazine* 46, no. 4 (April 2001): 99–106.

23. Lara Kolodny, "A New Way to Train Workers, One Small Bite at a Time," *Wall Street Journal* (May 13, 2016), https://www.wsj.com.

24. Garry Kranz, "Online Learning Gets Massive, Open," *Workforce Management* (August 13, 2013), http://www.workforce.com.

25. David Ong et al., "Reducing Employee Learning and Development Costs: The Use of Massive Open Online Courses (MOOC)," *Development and Learning in Organizations:* *An International Journal* 30, no. 5 (2016): 18–21; Geoffrey Fowler, "An Early Report Card e-ln MOOCs," *Wall Street Journal* (October 8, 2013), http://online.wsj.com.

26. "2016 Training Industry Report" *Training* (November-December 2016): 31.

27. "Learning 2.0: Improving Workforce Productivity," *Workforce Management* (April 2010), http://www.workforce.com.

28. Bill Leonard, "Social Media Can Enhance Employee Learning," *HR Today* (May 20, 2015), https://www.shrm.org.

29. T.L. Stanley, "Be a Good Role Model for Your Employees," *Supervision* 65, no. 5 (January 2004): 5–8; Gary May and William Kahnweiler, "The Effect of a Mastery Practice Design on Learning and Transfer in Behavior Modeling Training," *Personnel Psychology* 53, no. 2 (Summer 2000): 353–73.

30. Jason J. Dahling et al., "Does Coaching Matter? A Multilevel Model Linking Managerial Coaching Skill and Frequency to Sales Goal Attainment," *Personnel Psychology* (2015); Avery Augustine, "How to Coach Your Really Good Employees," *Forbes* (January 22, 2014), http://www.forbes.com.

31. Amir Elnaga and Amen Imran, "The Effect of Training on Employee Performance," *European Journal of Business and Management* 5, no. 4 (2013): 137–47; Chris Whitcomb, "Scenario-Based Training to the F.B.I.," *Training and Development* 53, no. 6 (June 1999): 42–46; Anne Hoag, Dale Brickley, and Joanne Cawley, "Media Management Education and the Case Method," *Journalism and Mass Communication Educator* 55, no. 4 (Winter 2001): 49–59.

32. M. Srimannarayana, "Designing New Employee Orientation Programs an Empirical Study," *Indian Journal of Industrial Relations* 51, no. 4 (2016): 620–33; Mike Frost, "Creative New Employee Orientation Programs," *HRMagazine* 47, no. 8 (August 2002): 120–121; Marilyn Moats Kennedy, "Setting the Right Tone, Right Away," *Across the Board* 36, no. 4 (April 1999): 51–52.

33. Vurain Tabvuma, Yannis Georgellis, and Thomas Lange, "Orientation Training and Job Satisfaction: A Sector and Gender Analysis," *Human Resource Management* 54, no. 2 (2015): 303–321; Emmanuella Plakoyiannaki, Nikolaos Tzokas, Pavlos Dimitratos, and Michael Saren, "How Critical Is Employee Orientation for Customer Relationship Management? Insights from a Case Study," *Journal of Management Studies* 45, no. 2 (March 2008): 268–93.

34. Kathryn Tyler, "Take New Employee Orientation off the Back Burner," *HRMagazine* 43, no. 6 (May 1998): 49–57; Noel Tichy, "No Ordinary Boot Camp," *Harvard Business Review* 79, no. 4 (April 2001): 63–70.

35. Gail B. Caldwell and Cam Caldwell, "Ten Classic Onboarding Errors–Violations of the HRM-Employee Relationship," *Business and Management Research* 5, no. 4 (2016): 47; Leigh Buchanan, "How to Make New Hires Feel at Home," *Inc.* (June 8, 2010), http://www.inc.com.

36. "Corporate America Can't Write," *Work & Family Newsbrief* (January 2005): 4; Matt Bolch, "School at Work," *Training* 39,

no. 2 (February 2002); Slav Kanyba, "Community Colleges React to Job-Training Request," *San Fernando Valley Business Journal* 9, no. 2 (June 7, 2004): 1–2.

37. Michael A. Verespej, "The Education Difference," *Industry Week* 245, no. 9 (May 6, 1996): 11–14; Richard D. Zalman, "The Basics of In-House Skills Training," *HRMagazine* 34, no. 2 (February 1990): 74–78; Ron Zemke, "Workplace Illiteracy—Shall We Overcome?" *Training* 26, no. 6 (June 1989): 33–39.

38. "Behavior-Based Sales Team Training Produces a 56% Increase in Revenues," *Managing Training & Development* (April 2004): 1.

39. Marg Cosgriff, "Walking Our Talk: Adventure-Based Learning and Physical Education," *Journal of Physical Education, New Zealand* 33, no. 2 (September 2000): 90.

40. J.K. Winch, X Cai, and G.L. Vairaktarakis, "Cyclic Job Scheduling in Paced Assembly Lines with Cross-Trained Workers," *International Journal of Production Research* 45, no. 4 (February 2, 2007): 803–28; Lisa Bertagnoli, "The Ten-Minute Manager's Guide to …Cross-Training Staff," *Restaurants & Institutions* 114, no. 18 (August 15, 2004): 26–28; Wallace J. Hopp and Mark P. Van Oyen, "Agile Workforce Evaluation: A Framework for Cross-Training and Coordination," *IIE Transactions* 36, no. 10 (October 2004): 919–941.

41. Tomislav Hernaus, Matej Černe, and Miha Škerlavaj, "Going the Extra Mile: Cross-Training, Relational Job Design, and Extra-Role Behavior of High-Skilled and Low-Skilled Workers," *International HRM Workshop* (2016); Lorraine Mirabella, "Productivity Gains in Maryland Mean Less Hiring But More Job Cross-Training," *The Baltimore Sun (via Knight-Ridder/Tribune Business News)* (April 17, 2004).

42. Gary Stern, "Small Slights Bring Big Problems," *Workforce* 81, no. 8 (August 2002): 17.

43. "49ers Decide to Add Diversity to Training Camp," *The New York Times* (July 8, 20014): D3.

44. Shankar Vedantam "Most Diversity Training Ineffective, Study Finds, *Washington Post* (January 19, 2008), http://www.washingtonpost.com.

45. Jolyn Gelens et al., "Talent Management and Organizational Justice: Employee Reactions to High Potential Identification," *Human Resource Management Journal* 24, no. 2 (2014): 159–175; Heather Johnson, "The Whole Picture: When It Comes to Finding Out How Employees Feel about Training,

Many Companies Fail to Get a Clear Picture," *Training* 47, no. 7 (July 2004): 30–35; Martin Delahoussaye, "Show Me the Results," *Training* 39, no. 3 (March 2002): 28–29; Reinout van Brakel, "Why ROI Isn't Enough," *Training and Development* 56, no. 6 (June 2002): 72–74.

46. "Dissatisfaction with Job Training Contributes to Low Job Satisfaction," *Managing Training & Development* (November 2003): 8; James Pershing and Jana Pershing, "Ineffective Reaction Evaluation," *Human Resource Development Quarterly* 12, no. 1 (Spring 2001): 73–90.

47. Anna Grohmann and Simone Kauffeld, "Evaluating Training Programs: Development and Correlates of the Questionnaire for Professional Training Evaluation," *International Journal of Training and Development* 17, no. 2 (2013): 135–55; Andreas Putra, "Evaluating Training Programs: An Exploratory Study of Transfer of Learning onto the Job at Hotel A and Hotel B, Sydney, Australia," *Journal of Hospitality and Tourism Management* 11, no. 1 (April 2004): 77–78.

48. Delahoussaye, "Show Me the Results," 28–29; van Brakel, "Why ROI Isn't Enough," 72–74.

49. Richard J. Wagner and Robert J. Weigand, "Can the Value of Training Be Measured? A Simplified Approach to Evaluating Training," *The Health Care Manager* 23, no. 1 (January–March 2004): 71–79; van Brakel, "Why ROI Isn't Enough," 72–74; Sarah Fister Gale, "Measuring the ROI of E-Learning," *Workforce* 81, no. 8 (August 2002): 74–77; Earl Honeycutt, Kiran Karande, Ashraf Attia, and Steven Maurer, "A Utility-Based Framework for Evaluating the Financial Impact of Sales Force Training Programs," *Journal of Personal Selling and Sales Management* 21, no. 3 (Summer 2001): 229–38.

50. Bradford S. Bell et al., "100 Years of Training and Development Research: What We Know and Where We Should Go" (2017); "Three Quick and Easy Ways to Gauge Your Training Outcomes," *IOMA's Report on Managing Training & Development* (January 2005): 4–5; "Use This Eight-Step Process to Predict the ROI of Your Training Programs," *IOMA's Human Resource Department Management Report* (December 2004): 4–5; Ellen Drost, Colette Frayne, Keven Lowe, and J. Michael Geringer, "Benchmarking Training and Development Practices: A Multi-Country Comparative Analysis," *Human Resource Management* 41, no. 1 (Spring 2002): 67–86; Daniel McMurrer, Mark Van Buren, and William Woodwell, "Making the Commitment."

CHAPTER **8**

Performance Management

Learning Outcomes

After studying this chapter, you should be able to

LO ① Explain what performance management is and how the establishment of goals, ongoing performance feedback, and the evaluation process are part of it.

LO ② Describe the different sources of performance-management information.

LO ③ Explain the various methods used to evaluate the performance of employees.

LO ④ Outline the characteristics of effective performance review meetings and feedback sessions and ways in which the performance of employees can be improved.

LO ①

Does your school have a performance management system in place to help students succeed? If so, how do you think the system might be similar or different to performance management systems in the workplace?

performance management

The process of creating a work environment in which people can perform to the best of their abilities

performance reviews

A process in which a manager evaluates an employee's performance relative to the requirements of his or her job and uses the information to show the person where improvements can be made and how

8.1 Performance Management Systems

We have discussed some of the ways that you as a manager can acquire top-notch employees and train and develop them. But how do you know if your efforts are really paying off in terms of what the employees are contributing once they are on the job?

Performance management is the process of creating a work environment in which people can perform to the best of their abilities in order to meet a company's goals. It is an entire work system that flows from a company's goals. Figure 8.1 shows the elements of a performance management process.

Performance reviews are the result of a process by which a manager evaluates an employee's performance relative to the requirements of his or her job, the goals set with his or her manager, and then uses the information to show the person where improvements can be made and how. The reviews are a tool organizations can use to develop employees. Performance reviews are also referred to as *performance appraisals* and *performance evaluations*.

Typically performance reviews are delivered annually, biannually, or sometimes on a quarterly basis. However, firms are finding that more frequent short reviews that provide employees with feedback regularly are more effective. At RoundPegg, a hiring startup that develops social applications, all employees have quarterly reviews, or "feedback sessions," that last just 20 minutes. "My job here isn't just to make sure everyone is crossing their T's and dotting their I's," says Brent Daily, RoundPegg's cofounder and chief operating officer. "My job is to remove the obstacles they face and allow them to do what they do best."[1]

In Figure 8.1, the performance review is just part of the performance management process. Aligning the goals of employees with those of the firm, providing workers with continual on-the-job feedback, and encouraging and rewarding them for a job done well are critical, too.

You might compare a performance review to taking a test in college. Do tests motivate you? Do they make you want to truly excel, or do you just want to get through them? Now compare your test-taking experience with an experience in which your instructor talked to you about your career plans, complimented you on your performance, and offered you suggestions for improving it. That probably motivated you more.

We hope you can see the analogy we are making. Employers have to look at how well you are doing on the job, just as your university has to test you to be sure you graduate with the qualifications people in society expect. But your performance in either scenario consists of so much more than that. This is why organizations need to look at the performance management system as a whole, to motivate and foster the growth of employees so they can contribute the maximum value to the firm. Reviews are simply a logical extension of the day-to-day performance management process, not the end goal.[2]

8.1a The Purposes of Performance Management

Figure 8.2 shows the other two most common purposes of performance management programs—*developmental* and *administrative*. Next, let's look at each purpose.

Developmental Purposes

A performance management system gives managers a concrete framework they can use to gather information about the performance of employees, provide them with feedback, and discuss their goals and how they align with the organization's goals. The goal is to

| Figure 8.1 | Steps in the Performance Management Process |

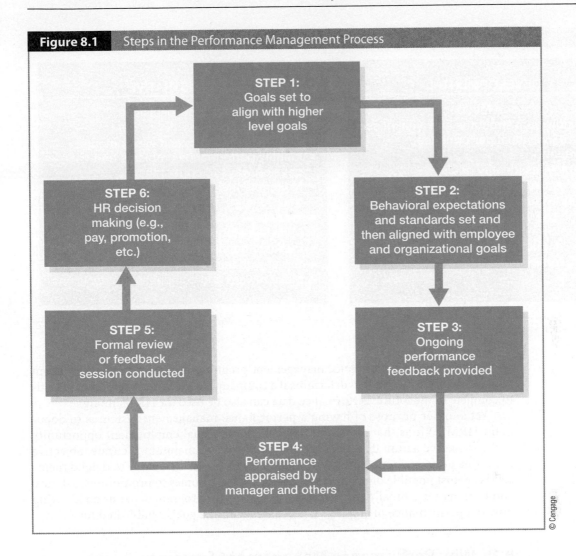

© Cengage

build on a person's strengths, eliminate potential weaknesses, and further his or her career while improving the performance of the organization as well. By taking a developmental approach to the performance management process, managers help employees understand that the feedback they are getting is designed to improve their future competencies and further their careers, and are not being conducted simply to judge them. Companies such as GE and Microsoft are among the organizations that have redesigned their performance management programs to focus more on ongoing employee feedback, support, development, and learning. The idea is to shift the role of manager from that of "judge" to one of "coach."[3]

Administrative Purposes

Performance management programs provide input that can be used for the entire range of HRM activities, such as determining the relative worth of jobs, recruiting criteria, validating selection tests, promotions, transfers, layoffs, and pay decisions. "Pay-for-performance" systems—basing employees' pay on their achievements—is found in all types of organizations. Studies have shown employees who earn performance-based pay

Figure 8.2 Purposes of a Performance Review

DEVELOPMENTAL

- Provide performance feedback
- Identify individual strengths and weaknesses
- Recognize individual performance achievements
- Help employees identify goals
- Evaluate goal achievement of employees
- Identify individual training needs
- Determine organizational training needs
- Allow employees to discuss concerns
- Improve communication
- Provide a forum for leaders to help employees

ADMINISTRATIVE

- Document personnel decisions
- Promote employees
- Determine transfers and assignments
- Identify performance problems and develop ways to correct them
- Make retention, termination, and layoff decisions
- Validate selection criteria
- Meet legal requirements
- Evaluate training programs/progress
- Assist with human resources planning
- Make reward and compensation decisions

are more satisfied.[4] Performance management programs also provide input for talent reviews: strategic meetings to determine if a company has the human resources it needs to compete in the future. Performance data can also be used for HR planning.

Yet another purpose of having a performance management system is to document HRM actions that can result in legal action. Equal employment opportunity and affirmative action directives require employers to maintain accurate, objective employee performance records. Without them, firms will be unable to defend themselves against possible discrimination charges when it comes to promotions, salaries, and terminations. Finally, the success of the entire HR program depends on knowing how the performance of employees compares with the goals established for them.

8.1b Why Performance Management Systems Sometimes Fail

Performance reviews often fall short of their potential. But why? According to a survey by the Society for Human Resource Management, only half of HR professionals say annual performance reviews are an accurate appraisal of an employee's performance. Forty-nine percent believe their firms' performance-review process needs to be reevaluated.[5] Employees and managers alike often dread appraisals, and complain that they are time consuming and ineffective.

Many people fault the formal review process. They believe it discourages teamwork by focusing on workers' individual achievements rather than what their teams or firms accomplish. (Who gets the best rating and the biggest raise? Who does not?) Others contend that reviews are useful only at the extremes—for highly effective or highly ineffective employees—and are not as useful for the majority of employees in the middle. Other people point out that reviews often focus on short-term achievements rather than long-term improvement and learning. Still others complain that the only feedback they get is during formal reviews, or they aren't done at all. This can especially be a problem in small businesses, as this chapter's small business feature shows. A more complete list of the reasons why formal reviews fail is shown in Figure 8.3.

Figure 8.3	Let Me Count the Ways … Reasons Why Performance Reviews Can Fail

- Inadequate preparation on the part of the manager.
- The employee is not given clear objectives at the beginning of performance period.
- The manager may not be able to observe performance or have all the information.
- The performance standards may not be clear.
- Inconsistent ratings among supervisors or other raters.
- Manager rates employee's personality rather than performance.
- The halo effect, contrast effect, or some other perceptual bias.
- Inappropriate time span for review (either too short or too long).
- Overemphasis on uncharacteristic performance.
- Inflated ratings because managers do not want to deal with "bad news."
- Subjective or vague language in written reviews.
- Organizational politics or personal relationships cloud judgments.
- No thorough discussion of causes of performance problems.
- Manager may not be trained at evaluation or giving feedback.
- No follow-up and coaching after the review.

Sources: Patricia Evres, "Problems to Avoid during Performance Evaluations," *Air Conditioning, Heating & Refrigeration News* 216, no. 16 (August 19, 2002): 24–26; Clinton Longnecker and Dennis Gioia, "The Politics of Executive Appraisals," *Journal of Compensation and Benefits* 10, no. 2 (1994): 5–11; "Seven Deadly Sins of Performance Appraisals," *Supervisory Management* 39, no. 1 (1994): 7–8.

Small Business Application

Does a Small Business Need to Formally Evaluate Its Employees?

So now you have your own business. That means you can dispense with those pesky, time-consuming performance reviews everyone dreads, right? You never liked them as an employee. In fact, maybe they helped solidify your desire to work for yourself. Why would you like them any more as a manager, entrepreneur, or small business owner?

Do not be so fast to dump formal performance reviews. Without them, you might end up "flying blind" when it comes to some important performance metrics. "In a small business in particular, the performance review is like a dashboard—it gives you all kinds of gauges about quality, job knowledge, and customer service," says Robert Chanin, the director of client services for the Alcott HR Group. "If there isn't any gauge, you don't know if your business is doing well or not."

By contrast, put a good performance management system in place and the sky is the limit, says Barrie Gross, a human resources expert and employment law attorney. "They're one of the tools businesses can use to get employees more involved, increase their motivation, and help them achieve success," Gross explains. Evaluating your employees also lets them know they are not just human cogs in the production process—that you care about them, their involvement in the firm, and their

personal goals. This can help a small business retain its top employees rather than losing them to big companies where they are often treated more impersonally. The feedback can be verbal, if the reviews are for development purposes only. However, if the reviews are used in conjunction with raises and promotions, they should be written in order to provide a firm with greater legal protection.

Small businesses can utilize off-the-shelf systems consisting of either printed forms or software. Featherlight and Halogen's Performance product are two web-based systems. Generally, a manager can customize the review forms by selecting elements from a list of attributes and behaviors that describe on-the-job success for a position.

Performance reviews are not about the forms, though. They are a two-way discussion. In addition to your employees learning about how they can improve their performance, the reviews can help you learn how to improve yours.

Sources: Leanne Hoaglund-Smith, "Small Business Roles and Responsibilities, Require Clarity, Documentation," *Chicago Tribune* (February 10, 2017), http://www.chicagotribune.com; Amy Linn, "Boost Performance with Performance Reviews," *Small Business Review*, http://smallbusinessreview.com; David Javitch, "How to Survive Employee Appraisals," Entreprenur.com, http://www.entreprenur.com.

For reasons such as these, a substantial number of organizations, including Adobe Systems, the Gap, Microsoft, GE, and IBM have abolished their performance reviews in favor of continuous feedback and coaching.[6] Adobe has an ongoing "check-in" system employees and their managers use to give each other feedback. Written reviews aren't requried.[7] (See Case Study 1 at the end of the chapter.) But although many people have predicted that formal performance reviews will one day be obsolete, firms continue to use them, often for legal reasons such as justifying promotions and pay decisions.

LO ②

Do you think as an employee you would be in a good position to appraise your boss? What aspects of his or her performance might you be in a good position to appraise?

8.2 Developing an Effective Performance Management System

A firm's HR department ordinarily has the primary responsibility for overseeing and coordinating its performance management system. However, managers from the company's operating departments must also be actively involved, particularly when it comes to helping establish the objectives for the program, ensure they are aligned with a company's strategic goals, and actually translate to on-the-job efforts.

Employees are more likely to accept and be satisfied with a performance management system when they have the chance to participate in its development. Asking experienced employees to help identify important job behaviors and SMART goals also helps ensure the system accounts for all of the tasks that need to be done in an organization, especially when major changes in the firm and its jobs are taking place.[8]

8.2a What Are the Performance Standards?

SMART goals

Goals that are specific, measurable, achievable, realistic, and time-based

Performance standards should be based on job-related requirements derived from a job analysis and reflected in an employee's job description and job specifications. Establishing SMART goals can be very helpful for this purpose. **SMART goals** are goals that

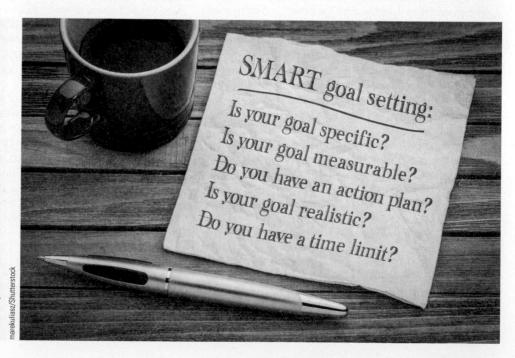

SMART goals can help improve the performance of employees as well as remove the vagueness and subjectivity of performance reviews.

marekuliasz/Shutterstock

SMART goal setting:
Is your goal specific?
Is your goal measurable?
Do you have an action plan?
Is your goal realistic?
Do you have a time limit?

are **s**pecific, **m**easurable, **a**ttainable, **r**ealistic, and **t**ime-based—hence, the abbreviation *SMART*. Realistic and specific performance standards that are actually attainable in a certain amount of time (given the firm's current resources and employee's abilities), measurable, and written down communicate precise information to employees. For example, "the ability and willingness to handle customer orders" is not as good a performance standard as "all customer orders will be filled in 4 hours with a 98 percent accuracy rate in 2019." When the standard is expressed in specific, measurable terms, comparing an employee's performance against it results in more accurate feedback. The ultimate goal is to create effective goals that will work for your employees, says Gary Foster, customized training program manager at Minnesota's Ridgewater College. "It's not an easy task; it's not a short task, but it can be done."[9]

As Figure 8.4 shows, there are four basic elements that must be considered when establishing performance standards: strategic relevance, criterion deficiency, criterion contamination, and reliability.

Strategic Relevance

Strategic relevance refers to the extent to which the performance standards relate to the strategic objectives of the organization. For example, if an organization has established a standard that "95 percent of all customer complaints are to be resolved in one day," then it is relevant for the firm's customer service representatives to be held to this standard when evaluated. Companies such as 3M and Buckman Laboratories have strategic objectives to the effect that a certain percent of their sales are to be generated from recently developed products. These objectives are then translated into performance standards for their employees. General Motors and Whirlpool's strategic objectives include cost, quality, and speed, and the two companies have developed metrics to identify and compare their performance around the world on these measures. A strategy-driven review process also provides the documentation HR managers require to justify training expenses needed to close any gaps between employees' current skills and those they will need in the future to execute the firm's strategy. Moreover, because they provide

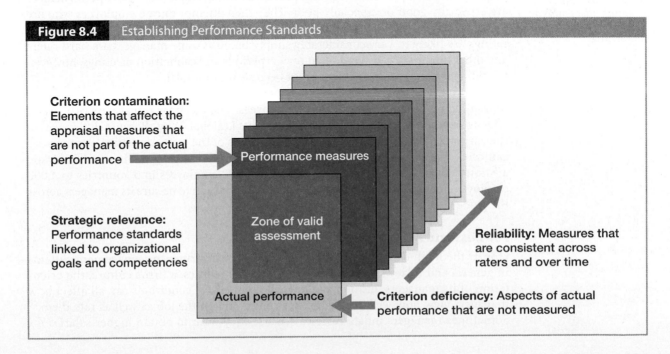

Figure 8.4   Establishing Performance Standards

Criterion contamination: Elements that affect the appraisal measures that are not part of the actual performance

Performance measures

Strategic relevance: Performance standards linked to organizational goals and competencies

Zone of valid assessment

Actual performance

Reliability: Measures that are consistent across raters and over time

Criterion deficiency: Aspects of actual performance that are not measured evidence of a person's performance, review metrics based on a firm's strategy are more defensible in court.[10]

Criterion Deficiency

The performance standards should capture the entire range of an employee's performance. When they focus on a single criterion (such as sales revenues) to the exclusion of other important but less quantifiable performance dimensions (such as customer service), then the performance management system is said to suffer from criterion deficiency.[11]

Criterion Contamination

Just as performance criteria can be deficient, they can also be contaminated. There are factors outside an employee's control that can influence his or her performance. A comparison of performance of production workers, for example, should not be contaminated by the fact that some work with newer machines than others do. A comparison of the performance of traveling salespeople should not be contaminated by the fact that territories differ in terms of their sales potential.[12]

Reliability

As we discussed in Chapter 6, reliability refers to the stability or consistency of a standard or the extent to which individuals tend to maintain a certain level of performance over time. Reliability can be measured by correlating two sets of ratings made by a single rater or by two different raters. For example, two managers would rate the same individual. Their ratings would then be compared to determine interrater reliability.

calibration

A process whereby managers meet to discuss the performance of individual employees to ensure their employee reviews are in line with one another

To make sure managers are rating employees consistently, some companies use a process called **calibration**. During calibration meetings, a group of supervisors, led by their managers and facilitated by an HR professional, discuss the performance of individual employees to ensure all managers apply similar standards to all of the firm's employees. The supervisors begin the process by rating employees whose performances are especially good or especially poor. They then attempt to rate employees who are more in the middle and try to achieve a consensus on their performance. Initially, the ratings are likely to vary considerably simply because some managers are hard raters and others are not. Over subsequent review periods and calibration meetings, however, the ratings should begin to converge, or become more similar.

As we will discuss, calibration meetings can be particularly helpful when it comes to training new managers to appraise employees. The meetings can also be very useful after a merger or acquisition—especially one that is global. Why? Because differences in the corporate cultures and performance standards of the formerly separate companies can cause the same employees to be rated quite differently. When Lawson Software, a Minnesota-headquartered firm, grew from 1,400 employees in 3 countries to 4,000 employees in 30 countries, it successfully used calibration to be sure its managers across the globe were assessing employees accurately.[13]

Fairness and Acceptability

One of the main concerns employees have about performance management systems in general and reviews is fairness. Organizational politics, a firm's culture, the orientation of its managers, history, and current competitive conditions can all affect how managers view how well their employees are doing on the job as well as rate them.[14] Sometimes managers inflate reviews because they want to obtain higher salaries for their employees or because higher ratings for their subordinates make them look good as supervisors.

Even when reviews are supposed to be confidential, employees often have a keen sense about whether the process is fair or not, or at least they think they do. Employees who believe the system is unfair are likely to consider the process a waste of time or feel frustrated and cynical. As we discussed earlier in the section on developing a management performance system, if employees are allowed input as to what constitutes a good performance and how the performance management system operates, they are more likely to believe it's fair, and the program is more likely to be successful.

Acceptability relates to how hard or difficult it is to administer and use the performance management system. If using it is time consuming or difficult, or if it's hard to see how it's really helping the organization, the system is likely to fail.

8.2b Do Your Performance Reviews Comply with the Law?

Performance reviews must meet certain legal requirements, just like selection procedures must.[15] Carefully defined and measurable performance standards are required. In one landmark case, the U.S. Supreme Court found that employees had been ranked against a vague standard, open to each supervisor's own interpretation.[16] The decision prompted organizations to try to eliminate vagueness of descriptions for attitudes, cooperation, dependability, initiative, and leadership. For example, the trait "dependability" can be made much less vague if it is spelled out in terms of employee tardiness and/or unexcused absences.

Other court decisions indicate that employers might face legal challenges when reviews indicate an employee's performance is acceptable or above average but then the person is later passed over for promotion, disciplined for poor performance, discharged, or laid off from the organization. In another U.S. Supreme Court case, an employee claimed she was terminated because the company she worked for said she had a poor attitude. The problem? Her reviews stated that she was "a pleasure to work with and handles herself in a professional manner," and that she "hit the ground running in eastern and is doing an excellent job for that department. The staff in eastern is enjoying her presence." The court ruled in her favor.[17]

Other companies have faced legal battles because their performance reviews discriminated against older workers, minorities, and women. A researcher who studied 250 reviews of high-achieving tech workers found that women received far more critical reviews than men.[18]

So, from a legal perspective, performance reviews can be a double-edged sword. You need them to help employees perform better and document your actions as a manager, but if they are poorly done or inaccurate, or you don't make decisions based on them, you can find yourself in legal trouble. To avoid problems such as these, performance reviews should meet the following legal guidelines:

- Performance ratings must be job related, with performance standards developed through a job analysis. Only evaluate those areas that are necessary for effective job performance.

- Employees must be provided with clear, written job standards in advance of their reviews so they understand what they need to do to get top ratings.

- Managers who conduct the reviews must be able to observe the behavior they are rating. This implies having measurable standards with which to compare employee behavior.

- Do not allow performance problems to continue unchecked. Document problems when they occur and refer to them in employees' reviews. This information may prove decisive should an employee take legal action. Supervisors should be trained to use review forms correctly and apply the review standards when making judgments.

- A firm's HR department should review the evaluations to see if minority groups are being adversely impacted.

- The reviews should be discussed openly with employees and counseling or corrective guidance offered to help poor performers improve their performance. Be open to the possibility that employees could be transferred to other positions that better suit their abilities.

- An appeals procedure should be established to enable employees to express their disagreement with the evaluations.[19]

HR professionals should also review the supervisors' review comments that could indicate the firm is not complying with the law. Consider the following comments: "Ted was absent for several weeks in 2017, which adversely affected operations." If some of Ted's absences were taken in conjunction with the Family Medical Leave Act, the comment could be used in court to show Ted was deprived of his right to take leave under the act without being retaliated against.[20] Having reviews examined by a supervisor's superior can also reduce the chance of biased reviews and evaluations that could be legally problematic.

8.2c Sources of Performance Review Information

Given the complexity of today's jobs, it's unrealistic to presume that one person can fully observe and evaluate an employee's performance. At IBM, employees are regularly reviewed by a broad cross section of the company's leaders, not just their immediate bosses. As Figure 8.5 shows, the raters can include supervisors, peers, team members, employees themselves, their subordinates, customers, vendors, and suppliers.

Figure 8.5	Alternative Sources of Reviews

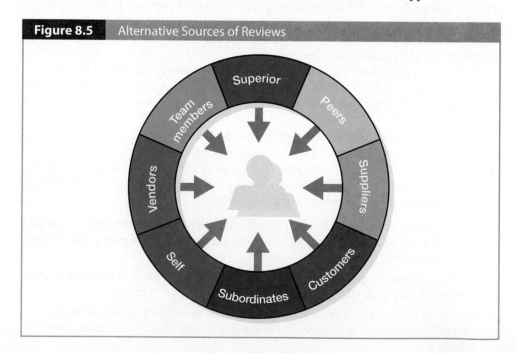

Manager/Supervisor

The **manager and/or supervisor evaluation** has traditionally been used to evaluate the performance of employees. Supervisors are in the best position to perform this function, although it may not always be possible for them to do so. Managers with many subordinates often complain they don't have time to fully observe the performance of each of them. The managers must then rely on the employees' performance records. If reliable and valid measures are not available, the review is likely to be less than accurate as a result. (Recall our earlier discussion of criterion deficiency and criterion contamination.) In addition, research has shown that the ratings managers give employees they have known for less than 1 year are less reliable, which can be a drawback of relying solely on information from managers.[21]

> **manager and/or supervisor evaluation**
> A performance evaluation done by an employee's manager and often reviewed by a manager one level higher

The Employee

In many firms, employees are asked to provide feedback on self-evaluation forms. A **self-evaluation** can increase an employee's involvement in the review process and get the employee thinking about his or her strengths and weaknesses. In other words, self-evaluations serve as a catalyst for discussion. The employee and his or her manager then discuss the employee's job performance and agree on a final evaluation.

It's not uncommon for employees to present themselves highly favorably in self-evaluations or believe they will give them more influence over their performance ratings. If that expectation is not met, an employee can become frustrated. For this reason, self-evaluations are often best used for developmental purposes rather than for administrative decisions.[22]

> **self-evaluation**
> A performance evaluation done by the employee being evaluated, generally on an evaluation form completed by the employee prior to the evaluation meeting

Subordinates

Subordinate evaluations have been used by both large and small organizations to give managers feedback on how their subordinates view them.[23] Subordinates are in a good position to provide feedback to their managers because they are in frequent contact with their superiors and occupy a unique position from which to observe many performance-related behaviors, such as their leadership ability, ability to delegate, employee supportiveness, and so on. The information gathered is often used for developmental rather than administrative purposes. Evidence suggests that when managers heed the advice of their subordinates, their own performance can improve substantially. To avoid any problems with retaliation, subordinate evaluations should be submitted anonymously and the results combined in a single report. The manager's supervisor then uses the information as part of the person's final evaluation.[24]

> **subordinate evaluation**
> A performance evaluation of a superior by an employee, which is often used for developmental rather than for administrative purposes

Peers

Individuals of equal rank who work together are increasingly asked to evaluate each other using a **peer evaluation**. With peer evaluations, coworkers complete a review on the employee. The information is then usually combined and given to the employee's supervisor for use in the person's final evaluation. One advantage of peer evaluations is that they can sometimes provide more accurate and valid information about employees. Supervisors often see employees putting their best foot forward. Those who work together on a regular basis may see a more realistic picture. Peers can readily identify the leadership and interpersonal skills of their coworkers along with their other strengths and weaknesses. For example, a superior asked to rate a patrol officer on a dimension such as "dealing with the public" might not have had much opportunity to observe it. Fellow officers, on the other hand, likely would have.

> **peer evaluation**
> A performance evaluation done by one's fellow employees, generally on forms compiled into a single profile for use in the evaluation meeting conducted by the employee's manager

For employees who have trouble confronting their coworkers about problems, the reviews provide a forum in which to address issues and resolve conflicts. They also provide an opportunity to hand out praise.[25] However, peer evaluations alone should not be used to make administrative decisions related to salaries, bonuses, promotions, and other major decisions about an employee. They should also be kept confidential, so interpersonal rivalries or hurt feelings don't result among coworkers. Instead of listing individual comments and ratings from an employee's peers, the ratings should be tallied to arrive at a composite score, and the comments summarized by the worker's supervisor.

Team Members

team evaluation

A performance evaluation that recognizes team accomplishments rather than individual performance

An extension of the peer evaluation is the **team evaluation**. In a team setting, it may be nearly impossible to distinguish one individual's contribution. To address this issue, organizations such as Google, Boeing, and Apple have used team evaluations to evaluate the performance of their teams as a whole.[26] These companies believe that team evaluations can help break down barriers between individual employees and encourage a joint effort on their part.

Frequently, the system is complemented by the use of team incentives or group variable pay (see Chapters 10 and 16). When Apple developed the iOS 10 (operating system), team rewards were used. No one member of the 600-person team could receive an exceptional performance review unless the entire team did.[27]

Customers

customer evaluation

A performance evaluation that includes evaluations from both a firm's external and internal customers

Customer evaluations are another source of performance review information. FedEx, Best Buy, and Isuzu are among the companies that have utilized external customers to provide feedback for their employees' evaluations. Other companies survey their vendors and suppliers as part of the review process. By including the firm's business partners in the performance reviews, managers hope to produce more objective reviews, more effective employees, more satisfied customers, and a better business performance.[28]

In contrast to external customers, internal customers include anyone inside the organization who depends on an employee's work output. For example, managers who rely on the HR department for selecting and training employees would be candidates for conducting internal customer evaluations of employees in the department or the department as a whole. For both developmental and administrative purposes, internal customers can provide extremely useful feedback about the value added by an employee or team of employees.

8.2d Putting It All Together: 360-Degree Evaluations

360-degree evaluation

A performance evaluation done by different people who interact with the employee, generally on forms compiled into a single document for use in the evaluation meeting conducted by the employee's manager

Companies such as Intel, Morgan Stanley, and Disney are among the many organizations that have used a multiple-rater approach—or **360-degree evaluation**—that combines various sources of performance review information.[29] Jobs are multifaceted, and different people see different things. As the name implies, 360-degree feedback is intended to provide employees with as accurate a view of their performance as possible by getting input from all angles: supervisors, peers, subordinates, customers, and the like. The information is then compiled into a single document, which is synthesized by the employee's manager as part of the overall evaluation. Figure 8.6 shows a list of the advantages and disadvantages of a 360-degree review.

Figure 8.6	Pros and Cons of 360-Degree Reviews

PROS

- The system is more comprehensive because feedback is gathered from multiple perspectives.
- It may lessen bias and prejudice since feedback comes from more people, not one individual.
- The feedback from peers and others may improve an employees' self-development.

CONS

- The system is complex in combining all the responses.
- The feedback can be intimidating and cause resentment if employees feel the respondents have "ganged up" on them.
- There may be conflicting opinions, though they may all be accurate from the respective standpoints.
- Raters must undergo some training.
- Employees may collude or "game" the system by giving invalid evaluations to one another.
- Raters may not feel accountable if their reviews are anonymous.

Sources: Compiled from David A. Waldman, Leanne E. Atwater, and David Antonioni, "Has 360-Degree Feedback Gone Amok?" *Academy of Management Executive* 12, no. 2 (May 1998): 86–94; Bruce Pfau, Ira Kay, Kenneth Nowak, and Jai Ghorpade, "Does 360-Degree Feedback Negatively Affect Company Performance?" *HRMagazine* 47, no. 6 (June 2002): 54–59; Maury Peiperl, "Getting 360-Degree Feedback Right," *Harvard Business Review* 79, no. 1 (January 2001): 142–147; Joyce E. Bono and Amy E. Colbert, "Understanding Responses to Multi-Source Feedback: The Role of Core Self-Evaluations," *Personnel Psychology* 58, no. 1 (Spring 2005): 171–205.

8.2e Training Appraisers

Training appraisers can vastly improve the performance review process. A weakness of many performance review programs is that raters are not adequately trained for the task, and so the feedback they provide their subordinates is not as accurate or useful as it might be, or is actually destructive According to one HR manager: "What's not important is the (review) form or the (measuring) scale. What's important is that managers can objectively observe people's performance and objectively give feedback on that performance." Nonetheless, in a survey of 55 HR managers from medium and large companies, more than half said their companies did either little or no assessment of how well their supervisors do reviews.[30] In addition to providing supervisors with training, firms should make accurately evaluating and developing their subordinates a standard by which the supervisors themselves will be evaluated.

Establishing a Review Plan

A training program for raters is most effective when it follows a systematic process that begins by explaining the objectives of the firm's performance management system and its philosophy on reviews. For example, the rater needs to know the purpose for which the review is to be used. Using the review for compensation decisions rather than development purposes can affect how the rater evaluates the employee, and it may change the rater's opinion of how the review form should be completed. The mechanics of the rating system should also be explained, including how managers keep performance records and review them, how frequently the reviews are to be conducted, who will conduct them, what the standards of performance are, and how to go about preparing for reviews. In addition, evaluation training should alert raters to the weaknesses and problems of reviews so they can be avoided.

Eliminating Rating Errors

Eliminating the subjective errors made by managers in the rating process is an extremely important part of evaluating the performance of an employee. The "halo error," discussed in Chapter 6 when we looked at selecting employees, can occur during the review process if raters do not have carefully developed descriptions of the employee behaviors being rated. The "horn error" is the opposite of the halo effect. It occurs when a manager focuses on one negative aspect about an employee and generalizes it into an overall poor rating. A personality conflict between a manager and his or her employees increases the probability of the horn effect, which can lead to a high level of frustration on the employee's part if it is not corrected.[31]

Distributional Errors. A *distributional rating error* occurs when a single rating is skewed toward an entire group of employees. For example, raters who are reluctant to assign either extremely high or extremely low ratings commit the **error of central tendency**. In this case, all employees are rated about average. It is also common for some raters to give unusually high or low ratings. For example, a manager might erroneously assert, "All my employees are excellent" or "None of my people are good enough." These beliefs give rise to what is called **leniency or strictness error**.[32]

One way to reduce distributional errors is to explain to raters that when you are looking at large groups of employees, you should generally expect to find significant differences among them. Using clearly defined characteristics or dimensions of performance and providing meaningful descriptions of behavior on the scale, known as "anchors," can help raters determine how individual employees should be rated. Another approach is to require ratings to conform to a **forced distribution**, which is also sometimes referred to as *forced ranking*. Managers appraising employees under a forced distribution system are required to place a certain percentage of employees into various performance categories. For example, a firm may require that 10 percent of ratings be poor (or excellent). This is similar to the requirement in some schools that instructors

error of central tendency

A performance rating error in which all employees are rated about average

leniency or strictness error

A performance rating error in which the appraiser tends to give employees either unusually high or unusually low ratings

forced distribution

A performance ranking system whereby raters are required to place a certain percentage of employees into various performance categories

Performance evaluation programs are most effective when managers have been properly trained to adequately observe and give feedback to their employees.

Andrey_Popov/Shutterstock

grade on a curve. A variation of this is *peer ranking*, whereby employees in a work group are ranked against one another from best to worst. The rankings are then used to determine pay raises. Some companies go so far as to terminate low-ranking employees. As you can probably tell, ranking systems can be controversial and divisive.

Although forced distribution and peer ranking may solve leniency and strictness errors, they can create other rating errors—particularly if most employees are performing above the standard, in the middle, or below the standard. Similarly, with peer ranking, three employees all performing nearly at the same level would have to be ranked one, two, and three. That process creates a misleading picture of how well the individuals are performing, which in turn affect their pay, promotability, and so forth. Moreover, if the system has a disparate impact on a legally protected group, such as a minority or older employees, it can result—and has resulted—in discrimination lawsuits. GE, which pioneered forced ranking, found this out firsthand. Other companies, including Ford, Goodyear, and Microsoft, abandoned their forced ranking systems after lawsuits, lower morale, decreased teamwork, and destructive employee competition ensued following their use. Eventually even GE discontinued the practice. The company now has a mobile app employees and managers can use to request feedback and provide each other with performance-related comments.[33] In addition, not all corporate cultures are conducive to forced ranking systems. For example, at Starbucks, which fosters a corporate climate based on teamwork, using a forced ranking system would probably be counterproductive.

Because teamwork is so important in organizations today, companies are starting to use crowdsourcing as part of their performance management systems. In an HR context, *crowdsourcing* involves continually gathering feedback, compliments, and suggestions from the different people who work with an employee using "social recognition" software and mobile apps. (You can think of the applications as being somewhat analogous to "liking" something someone posts on Facebook.) Achievers and Globoforce are two such brands. Hey Taco and Growbot are two crowdsourcing add-ons that can be used with the popular chat platform Slack. When employees are recognized by other workers for doing a good job, they get points that translate into monetary and other rewards, such as time off or gift cards. 3M, the Marriott and Starwood hotel chains, and the pharmaceutical company Eli Lilly are using this type of software.

To track the performance of its sales agents and motive them, the Home Shopping Network (HSN) uses a game module that enables agents to earn badges of increasing difficulty that reflect their performance.[34] Badgeville is a performance-management game Samsung and the accounting firm Deloitte have used to motivate their call center representatives and salespeople. The games make attaining one's performance goals more fun. Digital "leaderboards" that show at a glance who is "winning" in various areas spark competition without hampering teamwork.

Temporal Errors. Some rating errors are *temporal* in that the performance review is biased either favorably or unfavorably depending on the way performance information is selected, evaluated, and organized by the rater over time. For example, when the evaluation is based largely on the employee's recent behavior, good or bad, the rater has committed the **recency error**. Managers who give higher ratings because they believe an employee is "showing improvement" may unwittingly be committing recency error. Having the rater routinely document employee accomplishments and failures throughout the whole review period can minimize the recency error. One way for managers to do this is by keeping a diary or a log.

Contrast Error. A **contrast error** occurs when an employee's review is biased either upward or downward because of another employee's performance. For example, an

recency error
A performance rating error in which the evaluation is based largely on the employee's most recent behavior rather than on behavior throughout the evaluation period

contrast error
A performance rating error in which an employee's review is biased either upward or downward because of comparison with another employee just previously evaluated

Achievers.com, http://www.achievers.com/solutions/employee-recognition#/images/4

A dashboard in Achievers allows managers to see which employees are being recognized by other people for their contributions.

average employee may appear very productive when compared with a poor performer. However, that same employee could appear unproductive when compared with a star performer. Contrast errors are most likely when raters are required to rank employees in order from the best to the poorest.[35]

similar-to-me error

A performance rating error in which an appraiser inflates the review of an employee because of a mutual personal connection

Similar-to-Me Error. The **similar-to-me error** occurs when a supervisor inflates the reviews of people with whom they have something in common. For example, if both the manager and the employee are from the same state or went to the same schools, the manager may unwittingly have a more favorable impression of the employee. The similar-to-me error can be powerful, and when the similarity is based on race, religion, gender, or some other protected category, it can result in discrimination.

Furthermore, raters should be aware of any stereotypes they may hold toward particular groups. For example, one study found that men who experience conflicts between family and work received lower overall performance ratings than men who did not experience such conflicts. Women, on the other hand, were judged no differently whether they experienced family–work conflicts or not.[36]

Holding "mock" calibration meetings can help trainers improve the accuracy of their ratings. The training can pay off, particularly when participants have the opportunity to (1) observe other managers making errors, (2) actively participate in discovering their own errors, and (3) practice job-related tasks to reduce the errors they tend to make.[37] Google, which often conducts performance reviews with input from employee groups, has compiled a "cognitive biases" list for employees to refer to as they discuss ratings.[38] Other companies, including the consulting firm Accenture and the software developer SAP, are experimenting with *machine learning* to collect data on employees' work and analyze it to get an unbiased picture of a person's performance.[39] Machine learning is a type of artificial intelligence that allows computers to discover new insights in data without being programmed where to look for it.[40]

Feedback Training

A training program for raters should provide some pointers managers can use to provide performance feedback to employees on an ongoing basis and during formal reviews and feedback sessions. During formal reviews in particular, many managers are as nervous about giving feedback as employees are about receiving it. Oftentimes they just want them to be over. When this happens managers do not engage employees in much of a conversation during the reviews, which is a major drawback.

Managers need to understand that employees want to know how they are doing and how they can improve. They are less eager to be appraised or judged. This is why it is important for their managers to provide them with ongoing feedback and not just "dump on them" during a review. If an employee is doing something wrong, waiting for a formal evaluation later in the year to communicate that information is the wrong approach. The person needs to be corrected immediately.

Even when appraising an outstanding employee, managers often are reluctant to evaluate an employee's performance. Sometimes it is as simple as the manager lacks the skills to execute an effective performance review session; sometimes there is never enough money to recognize even the top performer. So reviews are postponed or handled poorly, and the result is that even the organization's best performers are left frustrated, angry, disillusioned, and demotivated.

Conflicting purposes of the review can also hamper the effectiveness of the feedback employees receive. For example, if a review program is used to determine an employee's future pay and at the same time to motivate the person to perform better, the two purposes can end up conflicting with one another. Often when salary decisions are discussed during a performance review, they tend to become the dominant topic of conversation, and managers spend a lot of time justifying their pay decisions. As a result, ways to improve the employee's future job performance get less discussion.

Feedback training should cover at least three basic areas: (1) communicating effectively so as to gain the employee's support, (2) diagnosing the root causes of performance problems, and (3) setting goals and objectives for the employee to achieve in conjunction with the feedback. A checklist like the one in Highlights in HRM 1 can be used to help supervisors prepare for performance review meetings.

8.3 Performance Review Methods

Now that you understand more about performance management, the question is, How do you go about measuring, or appraising, it? Performance review methods can be broadly classified as measuring traits, behaviors, or results. Trait approaches based on people's characteristics continue to be used despite their subjectivity. Behavioral approaches provide more action-oriented information to employees and may be best for development. The results-oriented approach has become more popular because it focuses on the measurable contributions that employees make to the organization.

LO 3

As an employee, would you rather be evaluated on your personal traits or characteristics, your on-the-job behaviors, or the results you get? Would it depend upon the job you were doing?

Supervisor's Checklist for a Formal Performance Review Meeting

Scheduling

1. Schedule the meeting and notify the employee 10 days to 2 weeks in advance.
2. Ask the employee to prepare for the session by reviewing his or her performance, job objectives, and development goals.

Preparing

1. Review the performance documentation collected throughout the year. Concentrate on work patterns that have developed.
2. Be prepared to give specific examples of above- or below-average performance.
3. If the performance meets or exceeds expectations, discuss this and ways to reinforce it. When the performance falls short of expectations, determine what changes need to be made.

4. After the review is written, set it aside for a few days and then review it again.

Conducting the Review

1. Select a private location that is comfortable and free of distractions.
2. Discuss each area of performance one at a time and address both the employee's strengths and shortcomings in that area.
3. Be specific and descriptive, not general and judgmental. Report occurrences rather than evaluating them.
4. Discuss your differences and resolve them.
5. Jointly discuss and design plans for taking corrective action if necessary as well as plans for growth and development.
6. Maintain a professional and supportive approach to the discussion.

8.3a Trait Methods

Trait approaches are designed to measure the extent to which an employee possesses certain characteristics—such as dependability, reactivity, initiative, and leadership—that are viewed as important for the job and the organization in general. Trait methods became popular because they are easy to develop. However, if not designed carefully on the basis of job analysis, trait evaluations can be notoriously biased and subjective.

graphic rating scale method

A trait approach to performance rating whereby each employee is rated according to a scale of characteristics

Graphic Rating Scales

In the **graphic rating scale method**, each trait or characteristic to be rated is represented by a scale on which a rater indicates the degree to which an employee possesses that trait or characteristic. An example of this type of scale is shown in Highlights in HRM 2. In HRM 2, the dimensions are defined briefly, and some attempt is made to define the points on the scale. Defining them precisely helps reduce subjectivity.[41]

mixed-standard scale method

A trait approach to performance rating similar to other scale methods but based on a comparison with (better than, equal to, or worse than) a standard

Mixed-Standard Scales

Rather than evaluating traits according to a single scale, with a **mixed-standard scale method**, the rater is given three specific randomly sequenced descriptions of each trait: superior, average, and inferior. As Highlights in HRM 3 shows, supervisors evaluate employees by indicating whether their performance is better than, equal to, or worse than the standard for each behavior.

A Graphic Rating Scale with Comments

Appraise employee's performance in PRESENT ASSIGNMENT. Check (✔) most appropriate square. Appraisers are *urged to freely use* the "Remarks" sections for significant comments descriptive of the individual.

1. KNOWLEDGE OF WORK:
Understanding of all phases of his/her work and related matters

Needs instruction or guidance		Has required knowledge of own and related work		Has exceptional knowledge of own and related work
□	□	□	✔	□

Remarks: *Is particularly good on gas engines.*

2. INITIATIVE:
Ability to originate or develop ideas and to get things started

Lacks imagination		Meets necessary requirements		Unusually resourceful
□	✔	□	□	□

Remarks: *Has good ideas when asked for an opinion, but otherwise will not offer them. Somewhat lacking in self-confidence.*

3. APPLICATION:
Attention and application to his/her work

Wastes time Needs close supervision		Steady and willing worker		Exceptionally industrious
□	□	✔	□	□

Remarks: *Accepts new jobs when assigned.*

4. QUALITY OF WORK:
Thoroughness, neatness, and accuracy of work

Needs improvement		Regularly meets recognized standards		Consistently maintains highest quality
□	□	□	✔	□

Remarks: *The work he turns out is always of the highest possible quality.*

5. VOLUME OF WORK:
Quantity of acceptable work

Should be increased		Regularly meets recognized standards		Unusually high output
□	□	✔	□	□

Remarks: *Would be higher if he did not spend so much time checking and rechecking his work.*

Forced-Choice Method

The **forced-choice method** requires the rater to choose from statements, often in pairs, that appear equally favorable or equally unfavorable but are designed to distinguish between successful and unsuccessful performance. For example, forced-choice pairs might include the following:

1. _____ (a) Works hard   _____ (b) Works quickly
2. _____ (a) Shows initiative   _____ (b) Is responsive to customers
3. _____ (a) Work is reliable   _____ (b) Performance is good

The rater then selects one statement from the pair without knowing *which* statement correctly describes successful job behavior. Because it's not immediately clear which response results in a higher rating, less bias results.

forced-choice method

A trait approach to performance rating that requires the rater to choose from statements designed to distinguish between successful and unsuccessful performance

297

Example of a Mixed-Standard Scale

DIRECTIONS: Indicate whether the individual's performance is above (1), equal to (0), or lower than (2) each of the following standards.

1. _____ Employee uses good judgment when addressing problems and provides workable alternatives; however, at times does not take actions to prevent problems. (*medium PROBLEM-SOLVING*)

2. _____ Employee lacks supervisory skills; frequently handles employees poorly and is at times argumentative. (*low LEADERSHIP*)

3. _____ Employee is extremely cooperative; can be expected to take the lead in developing cooperation among employees; completes job tasks with a positive attitude. (*high COOPERATION*)

4. _____ Employee has effective supervision skills; encourages productivity, quality, and employee development. (*medium LEADERSHIP*)

5. _____ Employee normally displays an argumentative or defensive attitude toward fellow employees and job assignments. (*low COOPERATION*)

6. _____ Employee is generally agreeable but becomes argumentative at times when given job assignments; cooperates with other employees as expected. (*medium COOPERATION*)

7. _____ Employee is not good at solving problems; uses poor judgment and does not anticipate potential difficulties. (*low PROBLEM-SOLVING*)

8. _____ Employee anticipates potential problems and provides creative, proactive alternative solutions; has good attention to follow-up. (*high PROBLEM-SOLVING*)

9. _____ Employee displays skilled direction, effectively coordinates unit activities, is generally a dynamic leader, and motivates employees to high performance. (*high LEADERSHIP*)

Essay Method

essay method
A trait approach to performance rating that requires the rater to write a statement describing an employee's behavior

The **essay method** requires the rater to write a description of the employee's performance and make recommendations for his or her development. Often the method is combined with other rating methods because it provides additional descriptive information about an employee's performance that can't be described with a rating scale. Essays also provide an excellent opportunity for supervisors to point out the unique characteristics of employees, including their promotability, special talents, skills, strengths, and weaknesses. A limitation of the essay method is that it can be subjective.

8.3b Behavioral Methods

As you have learned, trait-oriented performance reviews can be vague and subjective. In contrast, behavioral methods specifically describe which actions should (were or were not) be exhibited on the job. Let's look at some behavioral methods.

Critical Incident Method

Recall from Chapter 4 that a critical incident occurs when employee behavior results in unusual success or failure. The manager keeps a log or diary for each employee throughout the review period and notes specific critical incidents related to how well they perform. The critical incident method can also help a manager counsel employees when they are having performance problems. It also increases the objectivity of the review by requiring the rater to use job performance criteria to justify the ratings.[42]

Behavioral Checklist Method

The behavioral checklist method requires the rater to check statements on a list that describe characteristics of the employee's behavior. A checklist developed for salespeople who sell electronic products might include the following:

- Questions customers about their needs.
- Identifies products that meet customers' needs.
- Keeps abreast of new developments in technology.
- Processes orders correctly.

Behaviorally Anchored Rating Scale

A **behaviorally anchored rating scale (BARS)** consists of a series of five to ten vertical scales—one for each important dimension of performance. These dimensions are "anchored" by behaviors identified through a critical incident job analysis. The critical incidents are placed along the scale and are assigned point values according to the opinions of experts. A BARS for a job dimension for firefighters is shown in the upper portion of Highlights in HRM 4.

A BARS is typically developed by a committee that includes both subordinates and managers. Employee participation can lead to greater acceptance of the performance review process and of the performance measures that it uses. The procedures followed in developing a BARS also result in scales that have a high degree of content validity.

behaviorally anchored rating scale (BARS)
A behavioral approach to performance rating that consists of a series of vertical scales, one for each important dimension of job performance

Behavior Observation Scale

A **behavior observation scale (BOS)** is similar to a BARS in that they are both based on critical incidents. However, the lower portion of Highlights in HRM 4 shows that rather than asking the evaluator to choose the most representative behavioral anchor, a BOS is designed to measure how frequently each of the behaviors has been observed.

behavior observation scale (BOS)
A behavioral approach to performance rating that measures the frequency of observed behavior

8.3c Results Methods

Rather than looking at employees' traits or on-the-job behaviors, many organizations evaluate employees' accomplishments—such as the sales and output results they achieve. Employees are responsible for their outcomes along with discretion over the way they accomplish them (within limits). Advocates of results-based reviews argue that they are more objective and empowering for employees.

Sales, Productivity, and Quality Measures

Salespeople are evaluated on the revenue they bring in. Production workers are evaluated on the number of units they produce and perhaps the scrap rate or number of defects detected in their work. Executives are frequently evaluated on the basis of a company's profits or growth rate. Each of these measures directly links what employees accomplish to results that benefit the organization. In this way, results-based reviews can directly align an employee and an organization's goals.

BARS and BOS Examples

Example of a BARS for Firefighters

FIREFIGHTING STRATEGY: Knowledge of Fire Characteristics. This area of performance assesses the ability of a firefighter to understand fire characteristics to develop the best strategy for fighting a fire.

HIGH	7	—Finds the fire when no one else can
	6	—Correctly assesses the best point of entry for fighting fire
	5	—Uses the type of smoke as indicator of type of fire
AVERAGE	4	—Understands basic hydraulics
	3	—Cannot tell the type of fire by observing the color of flame
	2	—Cannot identify the location of the fire
LOW	1	—Will not change the firefighting strategy in spite of flashbacks and other signs that accelerants are present

Source: Adapted from Landy, Jacobs, and Associates. Reprinted with permission.

Sample Items from Behavior Observation Scales

For each behavior observed, use the following scale:

5 represents *almost always*	95–100% of the time
4 represents *frequently*	85–94% of the time
3 represents *sometimes*	75–84% of the time
2 represents *seldom*	65–74% of the time
1 represents *almost never*	0–64% of the time

SALES PRODUCTIVITY	NEVER				ALWAYS
1. Reviews individual productivity results with manager	1	2	3	4	5
2. Suggests to peers ways of building sales	1	2	3	4	5
3. Uncovers specific needs for each contact	1	2	3	4	5
4. Keeps account plans updated	1	2	3	4	5
5. Follows up on customer leads	1	2	3	4	5

But there are some problems with results-based reviews. For jobs that are more service oriented, it is not enough to simply look at production or sales figures. Factors such as cooperation, adaptability, initiative, and concern for human relations are important to the job success of employees, too. If these factors are important job standards, they should be added to the evaluation review. Thus, to be realistic, both the results and the methods or processes used to achieve them should be considered.[43]

Management by Objectives

management by objectives (MBO)

A philosophy of management that rates the performance of employees based on their achievement of goals set mutually by them and their managers

One method that attempts to overcome some of the limitations of results-based reviews is **management by objectives (MBO)**. Employees establish objectives (such as production costs, sales per product, quality standards, and profits) by consulting with their managers and are then evaluated based on their meeting those objectives.[44] An MBO system (Figure 8.7) consists of a cycle that begins with setting the organization's common goals and objectives and ultimately returns to that step. The system acts as a goal-setting process whereby objectives are established for the organization (Step 1), departments (Step 2), and individual managers and employees (Step 3).

As Figure 8.7 shows, employees help establish specific goals, but those goals are based on a broad statement of an employee's responsibilities prepared by the person's

Figure 8.7	Performance Review under an MBO Program

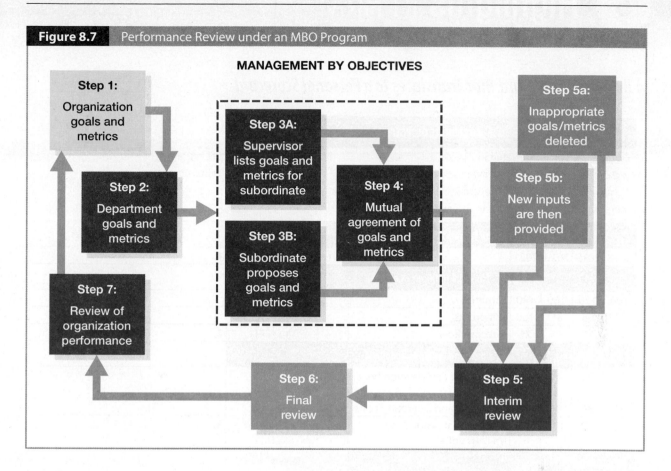

MANAGEMENT BY OBJECTIVES

supervisor. The employee-established goals are then discussed with the supervisor and jointly reviewed and modified until both parties are satisfied with them (Step 4). The goal statements are accompanied by a detailed account of the actions the employee proposes to take to reach the goals and how they will be measured (the metrics).

During periodic reviews, the progress the employee makes toward the goals is then assessed (Step 5). The goals and metrics may be changed at this time as new or additional information is received. After a period of time, the employee does a self-evaluation and documents what he or she has accomplished. The person and his or her manager then jointly review and discuss the self-evaluation (Step 6). The final step (Step 7) is reviewing the connection between the employee's performance and the organization's. Notice how the steps in an MBO program are similar to the steps in Figure 8.1 at the beginning of the chapter but are more specific.

The Balanced Scorecard

The balanced scorecard (BSC), which we first discussed in Chapter 2, can be used to appraise individual employees, teams, business units, and the corporation itself. A BSC review takes into account four related categories: (1) financial measures, (2) customer measures, (3) process measures, and (4) learning measures. Highlights in HRM 5 shows how a balanced scorecard in the financial category translates to a personal scorecard for an employee. The corporation's financial objectives have already been spelled out on the top of the scorecard. Then the various business unit targets are added, followed by

A Balanced Scorecard that Translates to a Personal Scorecard

CORPORATE OBJECTIVES

- Double our corporate value in 7 years.
- Increase our earnings by an average of 20% per year.
- Achieve an internal rate of return 2% above the cost of capital.
- Increase production by 20% in the next decade.

❏ Corporate
❏ Business Unit
❏ Team/Individual

Corporate Targets and Business-Unit Targets									Team/Individual Objectives
2018	2019	2020	2021		2014	2015	2016	2017	**1.**
Financial (millions of dollars)									
100	120	160	180	Earnings					
35	55	85	100	Net profits					
15	35	65	75	Net cash flow					**2.**
Operating (millions of dollars)									
35	35	40	50	Production and development costs					
30	30	35	30	Overhead and operating costs					
100	105	108	110	Total annual production (million units)					**3.**
Team/Individual Measures					**Targets**				
1.									
2.									**4.**
3.									
4.									

Source: Adapted from Robert Kaplan and David Norton, "Using the Balanced Scorecard as a Strategic Management System," *Harvard Business Review* (January–February 1996): 75–85.

the target objectives of the firm's teams and individual employees. The scorecard helps an employee see clearly how his or her performance ties in to the overall performance of the firm.

The BSC review method is similar to an MBO system in that it translates broad corporate goals into divisional, departmental, team, and individual goals in a cascading way. This ensures that implementing the firm's strategy becomes "everyone's" job.

8.3d Which Performance Review Method Should You Use?

Figure 8.8 lists some of the strengths and weaknesses of trait, behavior, and results approaches to appraising employees. Although traditionally researchers and HR managers believed that the more sophisticated and time-consuming methods offer more

Figure 8.8 A Summary of Various Review Methods

	ADVANTAGES	DISADVANTAGES
Trait Method	1. Are inexpensive to develop 2. Use meaningful dimensions 3. Are easy to use	1. Have a high potential for rating errors 2. Are not useful for employee counseling 3. Are not useful for allocating rewards 4. Are not useful for promotion decisions
Behavioral Methods	1. Use specific performance dimensions 2. Are acceptable to employees and superiors 3. Are useful for providing feedback 4. Are fair for reward and promotion decisions	1. Can be time consuming to develop/use 2. Can be costly to develop 3. Have some potential for rating error
Results Methods	1. Have less subjectivity bias 2. Are acceptable to employees and superiors 3. Link individual performance to organizational performance 4. Encourage mutual goal setting 5. Are good for reward and promotion decisions	1. Are time consuming to develop/use 2. May encourage a short-term perspective 3. May use contaminated criteria 4. May use deficient criteria

useful information, that view has been called into question. Even a simple system, when used properly, can initiate a discussion between managers and employees that genuinely leads to a better performance. Says Ronald Gross, an industrial psychologist and human resources consultant: "I've seen many systems fail miserably because they're too complex, too time-consuming, and too burdensome. I've never seen a system fail because it was too simple."[45]

The accounting firm Deloitte uses a form with only four measures that it administers quarterly. For example, one measure asks evaluators to use a five-point scale to answer the following question: "Given what I know of this person's performance, I would always want him or her on my team."[46] One way to assess whether an organization's review system is effective is by doing an annual, or at least periodic, audit of the process using a survey instrument that both managers and employees complete on a periodic basis. This should give HR a better sense of whether the review process is improving.

8.4 Performance Review Meetings and Feedback Sessions

After you have evaluated how well your employees are doing using one or more review methods, how should you begin to present the information to them in a review meeting or feedback session? The format for the meeting or session will be determined in large part by its purpose, type of performance management system used, and organization of a firm's review form. A formal performance evaluation should be scheduled far enough in advance to allow the subordinate and manager to prepare for the discussion. Usually 10 days to 2 weeks is a sufficient amount of lead time.

Sometimes discussing an employee's past performance and future development goals can make for a meeting or feedback session that is too long. It can also be difficult for a supervisor to perform the role of both evaluator and counselor in the same review

LO 4

As a manager, how might you get an employee who is reluctant to talk during a review to share his or her thoughts?

period. Dividing the meeting into two sessions, one for the performance review and the other for the employee's growth plans, can be helpful.

8.4a Types of Performance Review Meetings and Feedback Sessions

There are three basic types of formats for providing feedback during a performance review meeting or feedback session: tell-and-sell, tell-and-listen, and problem-solving. No one format is best for every review session. Rather, managers can use one or more of the formats depending on the purpose of the session, the topic being discussed, and the receptiveness of the employee.

- **Tell-and-Sell**. The skills required in the tell-and-sell format include the ability to persuade an employee to change his or her behavior in a certain way. This requires a manager to skillfully use motivational and persuasive techniques to try to change the behavior. But because there is less communication on the part of the employee with this format, it is less than ideal when used for this purpose. However, the tell-and-sell format may be used if other formats haven't worked, the employee is resistant to change, or the employee is reluctant to participate in the discussion.

- **Tell-and-Listen**. In the tell-and-listen format, the appraiser or supervisor communicates the strong and weak points of an employee's job performance during the first part of the session. During the second part of the session, the employee's feelings about the review are thoroughly explored. The tell-and-listen method gives both managers and employees the opportunity to release and iron out any frustrating feelings they might have.

- **Problem-Solving**. This format is the most proactive. Listening, accepting, and responding to feelings are essential elements of it. However, the format goes beyond an interest in the employee's feelings. It seeks to obtain the employees' buy-in for a mutually agreed-upon way to overcome obstacles and actually improve the person's actual performance. One of the ways in which a problem-solving format is accomplished is by beginning with the employee's self-evaluation. That way, the manager and employee can compare where they agree and disagree, and focus on problem-solving instead of the manager trying to convince the employee he or she is right.

8.4b Conducting the Performance Review Meeting or Feedback Session

There are no hard-and-fast rules for how to conduct a review, but the guidelines that follow can increase the willingness of employees to accept feedback, discuss their performance and improve it, and increase their overall satisfaction with the feedback process.

Ask for a Self-Evaluation

Research shows that employees are more satisfied and view review systems as more fair when they have input into the process. A self-evaluation can be used to discuss areas in which the manager and the employee have reached different conclusions—not so much to resolve the "truth" as to work toward the resolution of problems. A self-evaluation also ensures that the employee knows against what criteria he or she is being evaluated, eliminating any potential surprises.

Invite Participation

Communication is a two-way street. Most experts advise supervisors to encourage their employees to speak freely and listen closely to what they have to say. The more likely an employee is an active participant in the discussion, the more likely it is that any root causes and obstacles to his or her performance will be uncovered and constructive ideas for improvement developed. In addition, research suggests that an employee's ability to participate in the discussion is strongly related to the person's satisfaction with the feedback delivered, the extent to which the person believes it is fair and useful, and the desire to improve his or her performance. As a rule of thumb, supervisors should spend only about 30 to 35 percent of the time talking. They should spend the rest of the time listening to the information their employees volunteer and their responses to questions.

Express Appreciation

Because praise is a powerful motivator and employees are seeking positive feedback, it is frequently beneficial to start the session by expressing appreciation for what the employee has done well. Surprisingly, not all supervisors actually think to do this. They should. A performance review is the perfect time to tell people they are valued, top performers in particular, so they feel encouraged and motivated to continue to come to work day after day and remain with the firm.

Starting the meeting by talking about what the employee is doing well will also make the person less defensive and more likely to talk about aspects of the job that are not going so well. Don't, however, deliberately "sandwich" positive statements followed by negative ones, which are then followed by positive statements. If you do, the individual will be less likely to take the praise seriously and view it instead as a way to soften the bad news. Furthermore, if employees are given feedback on their performance on a regular basis, there will be no need to sandwich bad news between good news.

Be Supportive and Demonstrate That You Care

One of the better techniques for engaging an employee is for the manager to ask: "What can I do to help?" Employees frequently attribute performance problems to either real or perceived obstacles (such as bureaucratic procedures or inadequate resources). By being open and supportive, the manager conveys to the employee that he or she will try to eliminate roadblocks and will work with the employee to achieve a higher standard of performance. Good managers also demonstrate during reviews and on the job that not only do they support their employees work efforts and ways to improve them, they care about them personally and want to help them get what they want out of life. No one wants to be just a "cog in the machine."

Minimize Criticism

Even the most stoic employees can absorb only so much criticism before they start to get defensive. If an employee has many areas in need of improvement, managers should focus on the issues that are most problematic or most important to the job. In other words, criticism should be given in small doses.

Some tips for using criticism constructively include the following:

- *Consider whether it's really necessary.* Sometimes a manager's frustration with a performance problem is little more than "letting off steam." Be sure that the criticism focuses on a recurrent problem or a consistent pattern of behavior over which the employee has control.

- *Consider the person's ability to handle it.* Everyone handles criticism differently. Some people are able to handle it well. Others react very negatively to even the slightest criticism.
- *Be specific and don't exaggerate.* Sometimes we overstate problems in order to be convincing or to demonstrate our concern. Try to keep criticism simple, factual, and to the point. Avoid using terms such as *always, completely,* and *never.*
- *Watch your timing.* Properly timed criticism can often mean the difference between success and failure. Even good criticism given late in the day, for example, can touch a raw nerve if the employee is tired. Take a break or save it for another day.
- *Make improvement your goal.* It's hard to change a person's behavior with a single conversation, so "laying it on the line" is not probably a good idea. Instead of getting into a "blame game" in which both manager and employee enter into a potentially endless discussion of why a situation has occurred, focus on the problem and come up with a solution to it.[47]

Establish Goals

The final step is establishing goals for the next performance-management cycle. Jointly establishing goals and then revisiting and revising them at the end of the cycle is a critical part of the review process. Revisiting goals during a performance review also emphasizes the ongoing nature of the process.

Because one of the major purposes of the review meeting or feedback session is to improve an employee's future performance, his or her manager should focus the person's attention on the future rather than the past:

- Emphasize strengths on which the employee can build rather than weaknesses to overcome.
- Drop unproductive tasks.
- Limit improvement plans to a few important items that can be accomplished within a reasonable period of time and spell out how they will be achieved. The plans might include a list of resources, contact information for people who can help the employee achieve the goals, and timetables for following up to ensure they are met.
- Highlight how both the employee and firm will excel if the goals are achieved.

Follow Up Day to Day

Often both managers and employees are frequently happy to finish formal performance reviews and file away the review form. As we have emphasized, a better approach is to have informal talks periodically to follow up on the issues that were discussed. This puts managers in more of a coaching role versus that of a judge.

For example, as a sales manager, should you wait to appraise your employees once or twice a year? Probably not. Most likely you would want to monitor their sales on a weekly and monthly basis. Has a particular salesperson met his or her customer-contact numbers this week? Why or why not? Is the salesperson closing deals with the people he or she does contact? If at the 6-month mark, the salesperson isn't making his or her goals, how can you help the person if you haven't provided the individual with ongoing feedback? The lack of sales will be hard to make up at this point.

It's not just salespeople who need continual feedback. All types of employees can benefit from ongoing performance conversations with their managers. "Millennials and Gen Z-ers don't want hierarchy, formal feedback processes and appraisals," says Nicholas Greschner, the Canadian director of human resources for the consulting firm Accenture.

"They demand real-time, in-person feedback, forward-looking conversations and support to grow their careers."[48] Once the manager and employees have a series of discussions, there is an ebb and flow of ideas, some with the potential to serve as catalysts for improvement within the company.[49] The ultimate purpose is to better both parties.

Providing employees with feedback on a continuous basis also helps them know where they stand if and when they receive formal reviews. As a result, the anxiety they experience is often alleviated, and a more meaningful conversation with them and their supervisors can take place. If employees are surprised by their reviews, it is probably safe to say that their supervisors have not been providing them much ongoing feedback.

8.4c Improving Performance

What if one of your employees is performing poorly? What can you do to help the person perform better? This requires some diagnosis of the situation. But although performance management systems can often tell us who is not performing well, they typically cannot reveal why.

Identifying the Sources of Ineffective Performance

A person's performance is a function of several factors, but perhaps it can be boiled down to three primary concerns: ability, motivation, and environment. Each individual has a unique pattern of strengths and weaknesses that play a part. But talented employees with low motivation are not likely to succeed. In addition, other factors in the work environment—or even in the external environment, which includes personal, family, and community concerns—can affect a person's performance either positively or negatively. To diagnose a poor performance managers should focus on these three interactive elements. Figure 8.9 provides a better picture of how these three factors (ability, motivation, and environment) can influence people's performance.

As Figure 8.10 shows, if an employee's performance is not up to standards, the cause could be a skill problem (a lack of knowledge, abilities, or technical competencies), an effort problem (a lack of motivation to get the job done), or some problem in the external conditions of work (poor economic conditions, worker shortages due to downsizing, difficult sales territories, etc.). Problems in any one of these areas could cause the person's performance to suffer.

Too often, however, managers assume that poor performance is due first to lack of ability, second to poor motivation, and third to external conditions an employee faces. Ironically, research also suggests that we tend to draw exactly the opposite conclusion about our

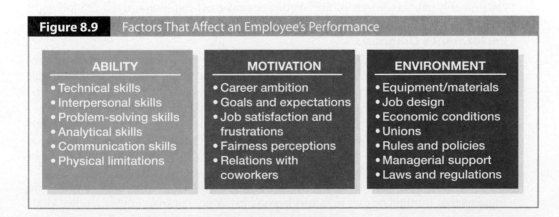

Figure 8.9	Factors That Affect an Employee's Performance

ABILITY	MOTIVATION	ENVIRONMENT
• Technical skills	• Career ambition	• Equipment/materials
• Interpersonal skills	• Goals and expectations	• Job design
• Problem-solving skills	• Job satisfaction and frustrations	• Economic conditions
• Analytical skills	• Fairness perceptions	• Unions
• Communication skills	• Relations with coworkers	• Rules and policies
• Physical limitations		• Managerial support
		• Laws and regulations

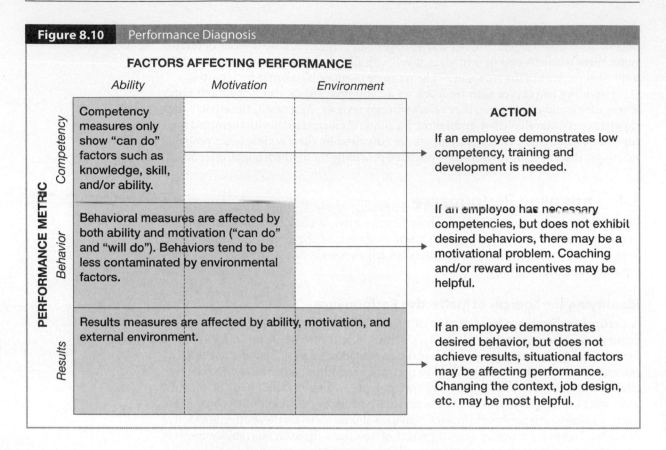

Figure 8.10   Performance Diagnosis

FACTORS AFFECTING PERFORMANCE

	Ability	Motivation	Environment	ACTION
Competency	Competency measures only show "can do" factors such as knowledge, skill, and/or ability.			If an employee demonstrates low competency, training and development is needed.
Behavior	Behavioral measures are affected by both ability and motivation ("can do" and "will do"). Behaviors tend to be less contaminated by environmental factors.			If an employee has necessary competencies, but does not exhibit desired behaviors, there may be a motivational problem. Coaching and/or reward incentives may be helpful.
Results	Results measures are affected by ability, motivation, and external environment.			If an employee demonstrates desired behavior, but does not achieve results, situational factors may be affecting performance. Changing the context, job design, etc. may be most helpful.

PERFORMANCE METRIC (vertical label)

own performance. We first attribute poor performance to external constraints such as bad luck or factors out of our control. If the problem is internal, then we typically attribute it to temporary factors such as low motivation or energy ("I had a bad day"). Only as a last resort are we likely to admit our poor performance might be due to our abilities or lack of them.

This difference in opinion between the two parties can result in a negative feedback cycle if it's not handled properly. A manager who assumes an employee isn't motivated or not capable may begin to treat the person differently (perhaps by supervising the individual too closely or watching for the employee's next mistake). This is likely to decrease the employee's motivation and result in a lower performance level by the person. Seeing this might confirm the manager's initial belief that the employee does not "measure up." As you can probably tell, this "set-up-to-fail" syndrome can be self-fulfilling and self-reinforcing.[50]

Performance Diagnosis

So what can be done to diagnose the *real* reasons for poor performance? More specifically, how can managers identify the root causes and get to work on a solution that improves performance? By comparing different performance measures, managers can begin to get an idea of the underlying causes of performance problems.

For example, as Figure 8.10 shows, results measures cannot distinguish between ability, motivation, and the situational determinants of performance. So if someone is not achieving the desired results, it could be due to one or more of these factors. In contrast, behavioral measures are less affected by external constraints. So if someone is demonstrating all the desired behaviors but is not achieving the desired results, logic suggests that it might be due to factors beyond his or her control. Similarly, other kinds of diagnoses are possible by comparing still other measures of performance. Only by correctly diagnosing the causes of performance problems can managers—and employees—hope to improve them.

Managing Ineffective Performance

Once the sources of performance problems are known, a course of action can be planned. This might involve providing training in areas that would increase the knowledge and skills the employee needs to perform effectively. A transfer to another job or department might give an employee a chance to become a more effective member of the organization. In other instances, different ways to motivate the individual might have to be found. Sometimes underperformers simply do not understand exactly what is expected of them. However, once their responsibilities are clarified, they are in a position to take the corrective actions needed to improve their performance.

Focus on Changing the Behavior, Not the Person

A bad performance on the part of an employee is likely to make his or her supervisor's job harder. As hard as it might be to do, the supervisor has to try to separate the employee from the behavior—it is not the employee who is bad but his or her actions exhibited on the job. One way to communicate this to employees is to not make suggestions about personal traits they should change but instead to suggest more acceptable ways of performing. For example, instead of focusing on a person's "unreliability," a manager might focus on the fact that the employee "has been late to work seven times this month." It is difficult for employees to change who they are; it is usually much easier for them to change how they act.

If the ineffective performance persists, it may be necessary to transfer the employee, take disciplinary action, or discharge the person from the organization. Not only is the ineffective behavior likely affecting the manager and the organization as a whole, but it is also probably affecting the person's coworkers. Whatever action is taken, however, should be done legally, fairly, and with an understanding of the feelings of the individual involved. A new manager is likely to need training in this area because it is one of the most difficult aspects of supervising people.

Summary

LO 1 Performance management is the process of creating a work environment in which people can perform to the best of their abilities to meet a company's goals. Performance reviews and feedback sessions, which are used for administrative and development purposes, are the result of a process in which a manager meets with and evaluates an employee's performance relative to the requirements of his or her job and uses the information to show the person where improvements could be made and why. The reviews are just part of the performance management process, however. Aligning the goals of employees with that of the firm, providing employees with continual on-the-job feedback, and rewarding them are critical as well.

Although some firms believe performance reviews are ineffective and no longer use them, most organizations continue to do so. The ultimate success or failure of a performance review program depends on the philosophy underlying it, its connection with the firm's business goals, and the attitudes and skills of those responsible for its administration.

LO 2 Information about how well employees are performing can be derived from a variety of sources, including the employee, his or her supervisor, peers, customers, suppliers, and subordinates. Using multiple sources is frequently a good idea because different individuals see different facets of an employee's performance.

Performance management systems must comply with the law and, like selections tests, be job related, valid and reliable, and free from criterion deficiency and contamination. Employees must understand their performance standards in advance, and appraisers must be able to observe job performance, be trained, and have an appeals procedure established. Some companies hold calibration meetings to compare the behavior of employees and ensure their managers are accurately evaluating their performance.

LO 3 Several methods can be used to gauge the performance of employees. These include trait approaches (such as graphic rating scales, mixed-standard scales, forced-choice forms, and essays), behavioral methods (such as critical incident ratings, checklists, BARS, and BOS), and results methods (MBO). The choice of method depends on the purpose of the review. Trait methods are simple to develop and complete, but they are more subjective and less useful for providing feedback. Behavioral methods provide more specific information for giving feedback but can be time consuming and costly to develop. Results methods are more objective and can link an employee's performance to the organization as a whole. However, they may encourage a short-term perspective (such as meeting annual goals) and may not encourage subtle yet important aspects of performance.

LO 4 Although there are various approaches to review meetings, research suggests that employee participation and goal setting lead to higher satisfaction and improved performance. Discussing problems with employees, showing support for them, minimizing criticism, and rewarding them when they perform well are critical. During the meeting, performance deficiencies can be discussed and plans for improvement can be made.

Key Terms

behavior observation scale (BOS)	forced distribution	performance management
behaviorally anchored rating scale (BARS)	graphic rating scale method	recency error
	leniency or strictness error	self-evaluation
calibration	management by objectives (MBO)	similar-to-me error
contrast error	manager and/or supervisor evaluation	SMART goals
customer evaluations		subordinate evaluation
error of central tendency	mixed-standard scale method	team evaluation
essay method	peer evaluation	360-degree evaluation
forced-choice method	performance review	

Discussion Questions

LO 1 Describe how the performance management process is linked to employee selection, training, and development.

LO 2 What sources could be used to evaluate the performance of people working in the following jobs?

   a. Sales representative
   b. Robotics engineer
   c. Director of nursing in a hospital
   d. HR manager
   e. Air traffic controller

LO 3 Three types of review meetings are described in this chapter.

   a. What different skills are required for each? What reactions can one expect from using these different skills?
   b. How can a manager develop the skills needed to conduct a problem-solving type of meeting?
   c. Which method do you feel is the least desirable? Why?

LO 4 Discuss how you would go about diagnosing an employee's performance problems. List several factors to consider.

HRM Experience

Performance Diagnosis

Managing the performance of employees is a vital—yet delicate—responsibility. One of the toughest aspects of performance management is assessing why someone is not performing well. Although it may be easy to spot who is not performing well, it is not always easy to diagnose the underlying causes of the person's poor performance (such as their motivation, ability, and external constraints). But without a correct diagnosis, it is nearly impossible to fix the problem. Managers also need to coach employees to improve their performance.

Assignment

The following are descriptions of three different employees. Describe what the potential causes of poor performance for each of the following employees might be and solutions that could enhance the person's performance.

1. *Carl Spackler* is the assistant greenskeeper at Bushwood Country Club. Over the past few months, members have been complaining that gophers are destroying the course and digging holes in the greens. Although Carl has been working evenings and weekends to address the situation, the problem persists. Unfortunately, his boss is interested only in results, and because the gophers are still there, he contends that Carl is not doing his job. He has accused Carl of "slacking off" and threatened his job.

2. *Clark Griswold* works in research and development for a chemical company that makes nonnutritive food additives. His most recent assignment has been the development of a nonnutritive aerosol cooking spray, but the project is way behind schedule and seems to be going nowhere. CEO Frank Shirley is decidedly upset and has threatened that if things do not improve, he will suspend bonuses again this year, as he did last year. Clark feels dejected because without the bonus he will not be able to make a down payment on the family's swimming pool.

3. *Tommy Callahan Jr.* recently graduated from college after 7 years and returned home to Sandusky, Ohio. His father, Big Tom Callahan, the owner of Callahan Motors, offers Tommy a job in the auto parts factory that makes brake pads. The factory is in severe danger of going under unless sales of the company's new brake pads increase dramatically. Tommy must go on the road with Richard (Big Tom's right-hand man) in a last-ditch effort to save the company. But Tommy proves to be unfocused, inexperienced, and lacking in confidence. Sales call after sales call he meets with rejection, even when the prospect looks promising. Customers express some concern about a warranty on the brake pads, but Richard believes that Tommy's inexperience and awkward approach are the big problems.

CASE STUDY 1   Adobe Ditches Formal Performance Reviews—And Wants to Help Other Companies Do So Too

As we explained in the chapter, an increasing number of companies are no longer conducting formal performance reviews. However, most still do. In a recent survey of 1,500 U.S. office workers, 88 percent of them reported receiving formal written reviews—often with rankings—usually on an annual basis.

The survey, which was conducted by Adobe Systems, the maker of Acrobat, Photoshop, and Flash software, also revealed the following bad news about formal performance reviews:

- More than half of office workers feel that formal performance reviews have no impact on how they

do their jobs (59 percent) and are a needless HR requirement (58 percent).

- Eighty percent of office workers would prefer feedback in the moment rather than a progress review after a certain number of months.

- Performance reviews are extremely stressful for both managers and employees. Rankings and ratings create competition among employees and result in even more stress.

- A surprisingly large number of workers, both male and female, reported actually crying after a performance review and either looked for another job or quit their jobs shortly afterward.

- Nearly two-thirds of millennials (61 percent) would switch jobs to a company with no formal performance reviews even if the pay and job level were the same.

For reasons such as these, Adobe stopped doing formal reviews in 2012. The effort to ditch them began somewhat haphazardly: Donna Morris, then a senior vice-president of human resources for Adobe, believed the firm's 360 employee reviews and ranking process was too complex, bureaucratic, and ate up massive amounts of time for which the company saw little or no return. She also believed they created barriers to teamwork and innovation because being ranked for compensation seemed to pit employees against one another.

The problem was something Morris had been thinking about at Adobe's offices in India while being interviewed for a major business publication in the country. The reporter conducting the interview asked Morris what new cutting-edge HR practices Adobe was implementing. Suffering from jetlag, offhandedly she responded: "We plan to abolish the annual performance review format."

Quickly Morris's announcement made headlines. There was just one problem with it: She had only been contemplating ending formal performance reviews. She hadn't actually cleared the idea with her CEO. Needless to say, when she got back to Adobe's office in the United States, she had some explaining to do.

Morris wrote her case for ending performance reviews and posted it on the company's intranet. She encouraged employees and managers to examine Adobe's current review practice to figure out how to improve it, which they subsequently did. What they discovered was troubling. Adobe's managers were spending in excess of 80,000 hours annually on the reviews. Worse yet, feeling demoralized by their reviews and rankings, a high number of Adobe employees quit after having them. That was making it

hard for Adobe to retain talent, especially because it's located in Silicon Valley, where the demand for tech employees is high.

Instead of formal performance reviews, today Adobe employees have periodic "check-ins" with their managers who offer them feedback, help with on-the-job problems, and ideas for their growth and development. No written review is required.

So does the new check-in system work? Yes. In surveys, employees say the check-ins make performance conversations easier, and less stressful, and that they get better feedback. Voluntary turnover has dropped dramatically.

In fact, Adobe believes its check-in system works so well it is helping other companies adopt it—for free. No software purchase necessary. The company has posted information about the system and all of its associated documents available on its pubic website. Among the items posted are worksheets and discussion guides for managers and employees and FAQs (frequently asked questions) about how the check-in process works and how to implement it.

"We love talking to other companies who are considering a move away from structured performance reviews, and many have adopted some form of check-in already," says Morris. "Now we want to make it easier to share our experience with people who are exploring a model like this—whether they're in technology or a totally different industry."

Questions

1. Why did Adobe need a new performance management system? What drawbacks might there be to the company's check-ins?

2. Are formal performance reviews always bad? Why or why not?

Sources: David Burkus, "How Adobe Scrapped Its Performance Review System and Why It Worked," *Forbes* (June 1, 2016); Kate Samuelson, "Twenty-five Percent of Men Cry after a Progress Review, Study Shows," *Forbes* (January 13, 2017); "Adobe Study into Performance Reviews Shows Office Workers Waste Time and Tears," *Which-50*, https://which-50.com; "About Adobe Check-in," Adobe.com (April 2, 2017).

CASE STUDY ❷   "Project Oxygen" Resuscitates Google's Poor-Performing Bosses

When it comes to gathering data and analyzing it to build new and better products, few companies do it as well as Google. Recently Google decided to use its info-tech expertise to answer an important question: Since people make the difference between good and great companies, could a data-driven, analytical approach be used to improve Google's human resources management function? Such an approach worked for Billy Beane, so surely it could work for Google, couldn't it? Recall from Chapter 1 that Beane, the manager of the Oakland A's, dramatically improved players and the team using data and statistics. (Actor Brad Pitt dramatized Beane's efforts in the movie *Moneyball*.)

One thing Google wanted to know was if it could "build" better bosses. Why? Because despite the many job perks Google's workers get, the company's employee turnover rate was surprisingly high. It's been said that the number 1 reason people leave their jobs is because of their bosses. Could this be true at Google? And if so, could the behaviors of good bosses be pinpointed and used to improve the performance of not-so-good bosses? The researchers at Google wanted to find out. They also wanted to answer these questions using data from their own organization to find out precisely what would work for Google rather than other organizations.

To answers these questions, a team of 25-plus Google researchers and scientists began studying the company's supervisors using their performance reviews, surveys from their employees, interviews, and observations of their behaviors. Over 10,000 observations were collected on 100 variables to determine how well the supervisors were performing. Initially, not all supervisors were thrilled to be evaluated by their subordinates and "put under the microscope." Consequently, the effort took some "selling" to Google's top management. The fact that the researchers could point to dramatic differences in the overall ratings employees gave different managers and that some teams performed much better than others helped fuel the fire to get "Project Oxygen" off the ground. (Presumably a good boss gives you room to breathe, whereas a bad boss can suck the life right out of you, hence the project's name.)

Once concluded, Project Oxygen yielded a wealth of information, some which mirrored conventional wisdom and some which did not: Teams with higher-rated managers performed better, the employees in them were happier, and they stayed with the company longer. Their managers had more impact on how the employees felt about their jobs than any other factor. However, it turned out that best bosses weren't the ones with the greatest technical expertise, as Google had anticipated. Instead they were those who are even tempered, help their employees think through problems without micromanaging them, and care about them as people. Google then used the information it gathered to implement training and coaching programs to quickly improve the managerial skills of its worst performing managers.

Specifically, Google identified eight behaviors you should engage in if you want to be a good boss—at least at Google:

1. Be a good coach.
2. Empower your team and don't micromanage.
3. Express interest in team members' success and personal well-being.
4. Be productive and results oriented.
5. Be a good communicator and listen to your team.
6. Help your employees with career development.
7. Have a clear vision and strategy for the team.
8. Have key technical skills so you can help advise the team.

Questions

1. Why isn't having the greatest amount of technical expertise the key to being a good supervisor at Google?
2. Does Google's research on the performance of its managers surprise you? Why or why not?

Sources: Brad Hall, "Google's Project Oxygen Pumps Fresh Air into Management," *TheStreet* (February 11, 2014), https://www.thestreet.com; Adam Bryant, "Google's Quest to Build a Better Boss," *New York Times* (March 12, 2011), http://www.nytimes.com; Meghan Casserly, "Google's Failed Quest to Find Managers Are Evil, and Why You Should Care," *Forbes* (July 17, 2103), http://www.forbes.com; Judith Aquino, "Eight Traits of Stellar Managers as Defined by Googlers," *Business Insider* (March 15, 2011), http://www.businessinsider.com.

Notes and References

1. Ladan Nikravan, "A Needed Change: Make Reviews Pro-active, Not Reactive," *Forbes* (September 29, 2013), http://forbes.com.

2. Susan Scherreik, "Your Performance Review: Make It Perform," *Businessweek*, no. 3762 (December 17, 2001): 139; Dick Grote, "Performance Evaluations: Is It Time for a Makeover?" *HRFocus* 77, no. 11 (November 2000): 6–7; "Employers Need to Do a Better Job of Performance Management," *Managing Training & Development* (April 2003): 8; Christopher D. Lee, "Feedback, Not Appraisal," *HRMagazine* 51, no. 11 (November 2006): 111–114; R. L. Cardy and B. Leonard, *Performance Management: Concepts, Skills, and Exercises* (Armonk NY: M. E. Sharpe, Inc., 2011).

3. Jason J. Dahling, et al., "Does Coaching Matter?" *Personnel Psychology* (2015); Donna Doldwasser, "Me a Trainer?" *Training* 38, no. 4 (April 2001): 60–66; Rebecca Ganzel, "Mike Carter," *Training* 38, no. 7 (July 2001): 28–30; Carla Joinson, "Making Sure Employees Measure Up," *HRMagazine* 46, no. 3 (March 2001): 36–41; Morton D. Rosenbaum, "Gratitude Adjustment: When a Pat on the Back Isn't Enough," *Meetings & Conventions* 39, no. 7 (June 2004): 20; James W. Smither, Manuel London, and Richard R. Reilly, "Does Performance Improve Following Multisource Feedback?" *Personnel Psychology* 58, no. 1 (Spring 2005): 33–67.

4. Janet Wiscombe, "Can Pay for Performance Really Work?" *Workforce* 80, no. 8 (August 2001): 28–34; Charlotte Garvey, "Meaningful Tokens of Appreciation: Cash Awards Aren't the Only Way to Motivate Your Workforce," *HRMagazine* 49, no. 8 (August 2004): 101–106; Lisa D. Sprenkle, "Forced Ranking: A Good Thing for Business?" Workforce.com.

5. Heather R. Huhman, "Five Ways HR Technology Can Improve Performance Reviews," *Entrepreneur* (July 23, 2014), https://www.entrepreneur.com; Don Pontefract, "Only 55 Percent of Employees Feel as Though Performance Management Appraisals Are Effective," *Forbes* (March 31, 2015), https://www.forbes.com; Drew Robb, "Building a Better Workforce: Performance Management Software Can Help You Identify and Develop High-Performing Workers," *HRMagazine* 49, no. 10 (October 2004): 86–93.

6. Sunnie Giles, "Turning Performance Reviews into a Vehicle for Radical Innovation," *Forbes* (March 28, 2017), https://www.forbes.com; Jonathan A. Segal, "86 Your Appraisal Process?" *HRMagazine* 45, no. 10 (October 2000): 199–206; Barry Witcher and Rosie Butterworth, "Honshin Kanri: How Xerox Manages," *Long-Range Planning* 32, no. 3 (June 1999): 323–332.

7. Jeff Kauflin, "Hate Performance Reviews? Good News? They're Getting Shorter and Simpler," *Forbes* (March 9, 2017), http:// https://www.forbes.com.

8. David Javitch, "How to Survive Employee Appraisals," Entrepreneur.com (April 23, 2011), http://www.entrepreneur.com.

9. Juliana Thill, "Set Goals to Get Results," Crow River Media (April 5, 2017), http://www.crowrivermedia.com.

10. Mahmoud Javidmehr and Mehrdad Ebrahimpour, "Performance Appraisal Bias and Errors: The Influences and Consequences," *International Journal of Organizational Leadership* 4, no. 3 (2015): 286; Doug Cederblom, "From Performance Appraisal to Performance Management: One Agency's Experience," *Public Personnel Management* 31, no. 2 (Summer 2002): 131–140; "Anonymous 360-Feedback Drives Vauxhall Strategy," *Personnel Today* (August 19, 2003): 16; Cindy Romaine, "Staying Relevant: Competencies and Employee Reviews," *Information Outlook* 8, no. 7 (April 2004): 21–25; Jerry K. Palmer and James M. Loveland, "The Influence of Group Discussion on Performance Judgments: Rating Accuracy, Contrast Effects, and Halo," *Journal of Psychology* 142, no. 2 (March 2008): 117–130; "When Promotions Are on the Line, Follow Your Criteria and Beware Supervisor Bias," *HR Specialist: Ohio Employment Law* 3, no. 12 (December 2009): 2.

11. Jason D. Shaw and Nina Gupta, "Let the Evidence Speak Again! Financial Incentives Are More Effective than We Thought," *Human Resource Management Journal* 25, no. 3 (2015): 281–293; "Job Complexity, Performance, and Well-Being: When Does Supplies-Values Fit Matter?" *Personnel Psychology* 57, no. 4 (Winter 2004): 847–880.

12. Joel Lefkowitz, "The Role of Interpersonal Affective Regard in Supervisory Performance Ratings: A Literature Review and Proposed Causal Model," *Journal of Occupational and Organizational Psychology* 73, no. 1 (March 2000): 67–85; Scott Highhouse, "Assessing the Candidate as a Whole: A Historical and Critical Analysis of Individual Psychological Assessment for Personnel Decision Making," *Personnel Psychology* 55, no. 2 (Summer 2002): 363–397.

13. Joanne Sammer, "Calibrating Consistency," *HRMagazine* 53, no. 1 (January 2008): 73–75; Jennie Sumelius, et al., "What Determines Employee Perceptions of HRM Process Features?" *Human Resource Management* 53, no. 4 (2014): 569–592.

14. Silva Karkoulian, Guy Assaker, and Rob Hallak, "An Empirical Study of 360-degree Feedback, Organizational Justice, and Firm Sustainability," *Journal of Business Research* 69, no. 5 (2016): 1862–1867; Kathryn Bartol, Cathy Durham, and June Poon, "Influence of Performance Evaluation Rating Segmentation on Motivation and Fairness Perceptions," *Journal of Applied Psychology* 86, no. 6 (December 2001): 1106–1119; Anne P. Hubbell, "Motivating Factors: Perceptions of Justice and Their Relationship with Managerial and Organizational Trust," *Communication Studies* 56, no. 1 (March 2005): 47; Rebecca M. Chory-Assad, "Room for Improvement," *Training* 40, no. 11 (December 2003): 18–20; Deanna M. Merritt, "Appraising the Performance Appraisal," *Supervision* 68, no. 4 (April 2007): 3–5.

15. *Brito v. Zia Company*, 478 F.2d 1200 (10th Cir. 1973); Treena L. Gillespie and Richard O. Parry, "Fuel for Litigation? Links between Procedural Justice and Multisource Feedback," *Journal of Managerial Issues* 18, no. 4 (Winter 2006): 530–546; Suzanne Tsacoumis and Michelle Davis King, "Litigation Driven Human Resource Management Changes," *Advancing Human Resource Project Management* (2014): 48–72.

16. *Albemarle Paper Company v. Moody*, 422 U.S. 405 (1975); Terry Gillen, "Appraisal: When Best Practice Is Bad Practice," *People Management* 11, no. 19 (September 29, 2005): 58.

17. Ladan Nikravan, "It's Not Just About Performance: Time to Think Differently," *Forbes* (September 29, 2013), http://www.forbes.com.

18. Kieran Snyder, "High Achieving Men and Women Are Described Differently in Reviews," *Fortune* (August 26, 2014), http://fortune.com.

19. Gillian Flynn, "Getting Performance Reviews Right," *Workforce* 80, no. 5 (May 2001): 76–78; David C. Martin, Kathryn M. Bartol, and Patrick E. Kehoe, "The Legal Ramifications of Performance Appraisal: The Growing Significance," *Public Personnel Management* 29, no. 3 (Fall 2000): 381; Deanna M. Merritt, "Appraising the Performance Appraisal," *Supervision* 68, no. 4 (April 2007): 3–5; Kevin R. Murphy, "Perspectives on the Relationship between Job Performance and Ratings of Job Performance," *Industrial & Organizational Psychology* (June 2008): 197–205; Cindy Miller, "Performance Appraisals in a Legal Context," *HR Info* (July 8, 2008), http://cindymiller.wordpress.com/.

20. Suzanne Tsacoumis and Michelle Davis King, "Litigation Driven Human Resource Management Changes," *Advancing Human Resource Project Management* (2014): 48–72; "Loose Lips Lose Lawsuits: Screen Performance Reviews for FMLA Comments," *Business Management Daily* (August 31, 2010), http://www.businessmanagementdaily.com.

21. Silva Karkoulian, Guy Assaker, and Rob Hallak, "An Empirical Study of 360-degree Feedback, Organizational Justice, and Firm Sustainability," *Journal of Business Research* 69, no. 5 (2016): 1862–1867; Joan Brett and Leanne Atwater, "360-Degree Feedback: Accuracy, Reactions, and Perceptions of Usefulness," *Journal of Applied Psychology* 86, no. 5 (October 2001): 930–942; Bruce Pfau, Ira Kay, Kenneth Nowak, and Jai Ghorpade, "Does 360-Degree Feedback Negatively Affect Company Performance?" *HRMagazine* 47, no. 6 (June 2002): 54–59; Maury Peiperl, "Getting 360-Degree Feedback Right," *Harvard Business Review* 79, no. 1 (January 2001): 142–147; Robert Gandossy and Tina Kao, "Talent Wars: Out of Mind, Out of Practice," *Human Resource Planning* 27, no. 4 (December 2004): 15–20; Nima Jafari Navimipouret, et al., "Expert Cloud: A Cloud-Based Framework to Share the Knowledge and Skills of Human Resources," *Computers in Human Behavior* 46 (2015): 57–74.

22. Corey E. Miller and Carl L. Thornton, "How Accurate Are Your Performance Appraisals?" *Public Personnel Management* (Summer 2006): 153–162; Edward J. Inderrieden, Robert E. Allen, and Timothy J. Keaveny, "Managerial Discretion in the Use of Self-Ratings in an Appraisal System: The Antecedents and Consequences," *Journal of Managerial Issues* 16, no. 4 (Winter 2004): 460–484.

23. Michael C. Campion, Emily D. Campion, and Michael A. Campion, "Improvements in Performance Management through the Use of 360 Feedback," *Industrial and Organizational Psychology* 8, no. 1 (2015): 85–93; Jeffrey Seglin, "Reviewing Your Boss," *Fortune* 143, no. 12 (June 11, 2001): 248; Ann Harrington, "Workers of the World, Rate Your Boss!" *Fortune* 142, no. 6 (September 18, 2000): 340–342; Robert Thompson, "Management Lite: Less Control, More Innovation," *HRMagazine* 44, no. 8 (August 1999): 10.

24. Brett and Atwater, "360-Degree Feedback," 930–942; Paula Silva and Henry L. Tosi, "Determinants of the Anonymity of the CEO Evaluation Process," *Journal of Managerial Issues* 16, no. 1 (Spring 2004): 87–103.

25. Angelo S. DeNisi and Kevin R. Murphy, "Performance Appraisal and Performance Management: 100 Years of Progress?" (2017); John Drexler Jr., Terry Beehr, and Thomas Stetz, "Peer Appraisals: Differentiation of Individual Performance on Group Tasks," *Human Resource Management* 40, no. 4 (Winter 2001): 333–345.

26. Tammy L. Rapp, et al., "The Role of Team Goal Monitoring in the Curvilinear Relationship between Team Efficacy and Team Performance," *Journal of Applied Psychology* 99, no. 5 (2014): 976; Scott and Einstein, "Strategic Performance Appraisal in Team-Based Organizations," 107–116; Debbie Kibbe and Jill Casner-Lotto, "Ralston Foods: From Greenfield to Maturity in a Team-Based Plant," *Journal of Organizational Excellence* 21, no. 3 (Summer 2002): 57–67; Simon Taggar and Mitchell Neubert, "The Impact of Poor Performers on Team Outcomes: An Empirical Examination of Attribution Theory," *Personnel Psychology* 57, no. 4 (Winter 2004): 935–969.

27. Stephanie Vozza, "Why Employees at Apple and Google Are More Productive," *FastCompany* (March 13, 2017), https://www.fastcompany.com.

28. Michael Cohn, "Best Buy Beefs Up Customer Value at the Call Center," *Internet World* 8, no. 6 (June 2002): 42–43; Joe Kohn, "Isuzu Has IDEA for Boosting Sales," *Automotive News* 76, no. 5973 (March 4, 2002): 41; D. L. Radcliff, "A New Paradigm of Feedback," *Executive Excellence* 19, no. 4 (April 2002): 20; Neeraj Bharadwaj and Anne Roggeveen, "The Impact of Offshored and Outsourced Call Service Centers on Customer Appraisals," *Marketing Letters* 19, no. 1 (January 2008): 13–23.

29. Kenneth M. Nowack, "360 Feedback: From Insight to Improvement," *Public Manager* 44, no. 2 (2015): 20; Pfau, Kay, Nowak, and Ghorpade, "Does 360-Degree Feedback Negatively Affect Company Performance?" 54–59; Peiperl, "Getting 360-Degree Feedback Right," 142–147; Jack Kondrasuk and Matt Graybill, "From Paper to Computer," *The Human Resource Professional* 13, no. 6 (November–December 2000): 18–19.

30. Seymour Adler, et al., "Getting Rid of Performance Ratings: Genius or Folly? A Debate," *Industrial and Organizational Psychology* 9, no. 2 (2016): 219–252; Gary E. Roberts, "Perspectives on Enduring and Emerging Issues in Performance Appraisal," *Public Personnel Management* 27, no. 3 (Fall 1998): 301–320; William Hubbartt, "Bring Performance Appraisal Training to Life," *HRMagazine* 40, no. 5 (May 1995): 166, 168; Filip Lievens, "Assessor Training Strategies and Their Effects on Accuracy, Interrater Reliability, and Discriminant Validity," *Journal of Applied Psychology* 86, no. 2 (April 2001): 255–264; Dick Grote, "Performance Appraisals: Solving Tough Challenges," *HRMagazine* 45, no. 7 (July 2000): 145–150; Leslie A. Weatherly, "Performance Management: Getting It Right from the Start," *HRMagazine* 49, no. 3 (March 2004): S1-S12.

31. E. Deepa, R. Palaniswamy, and S. Kuppusamy, "Effect of Performance Appraisal System in Organizational Commitment, Job Satisfaction and Productivity," *Journal of Contemporary Management Research* 8, no. 1 (2014): 72; Gary P. Latham and Kenneth N. Wexley, *Increasing Productivity through Performance Appraisal*, 2nd ed. (Reading, MA: Addison-Wesley, 1994), 137.

32. Jeffrey R. Spence and Lisa M. Keeping, "The Road to Performance Ratings Is Paved with Intentions," *Organizational Psychology Review* 3, no. 4 (2013): 360–383; Lefkowitz, "The Role of Interpersonal Affective Regard in Supervisory Performance Ratings," 67–85; Edwin Arnold and Marcia Pulich, "Personality Conflicts and Objectivity in Appraising Performance," *The Health Care Manager* 22, no. 3 (July–September 2003): 227; Krista Uggersly and Lorne M. Suksy, "Using Frame-of-Reference Training to Understand the Implications of Rater Idiosyncrasy for Rating Accuracy," *Journal of Applied Psychology* 93, no. 3 (May 2008): 711–719.

33. "Times Are Changing: The Future of Performance Management and Reviews," Business.com (February 22, 2017), https://www.business.com; Christopher Bartlett and Andrew McLean, "GE's Talent Machine," *Harvard Business School* (2006), Case # 9-304-049.

34. "HSN Enhances Employee Engagement with Nice Performance Management," *BusinessWire* (March 8, 2017), http://www.businesswire.com.

35. Sue H. Moon, Steven E. Scullen, and Gary P. Latham, "Precarious Curve Ahead: The Effects of Forced Distribution Rating Systems on Job Performance," *Human Resource Management Review* 26, no. 2 (2016): 166–179; Gail Johnson, "Forced Ranking: The Good, the Bad, and the Alternative," *Training* 41, no. 5 (May 2004): 24–31; Christine A. Amalfe and Eileen Quinn Steiner, "Forced Ranking Systems: Yesterday's Legal Target?" *New Jersey Law Journal* (March 28, 2005); Jessica Marquez, "Is GE'S Ranking System Broken?" *Workforce Management* 86, no. 12 (June 25, 2007): 1–3.

36. Andrew Li, Jessica Bagger, and Russell Cropanzano, "The Impact of Stereotypes and Supervisor Perceptions of Employee Work–Family Conflict on Job Performance Ratings," *Human Relations* 70, no. 1 (2017): 119–145; Adam B. Butler and Amie Skattebo, "What Is Acceptable for Women May Not Be for Men: The Effect of Family Conflicts with Work on Job-Performance Ratings," *Journal of Occupational and Organizational Psychology* 77, no. 4 (December 2004): 553–564; Cheri Ostroff, Leanne E. Atwater, and Barbara J. Feinberg, "Understanding Self-Other Agreement: A Look at Rater and Ratee Characteristics, Context, and Outcomes," *Personnel Psychology* 57, no. 1 (Summer 2004): 333–337; Mike Schraeder and Jim Simpson, "How Similarity and Liking Affect Performance Appraisals," *Journal for Quality & Participation* 29, no. 1 (Spring 2006): 34–40.

37. Lisa Keeping and Paul Levy, "Performance Appraisal Reaction: Measurement, Modeling, and Method Bias," *Journal of Applied Psychology* 85, no. 5 (October 2000): 708–723.

38. Adam Bryant, "Google's Quest to Build a Better Boss," *New York Times* (March 12, 2011), http://www.nytimes.com.

39. Braveteta Hassell, "Machine Learning Could Mean a Lot for People Management," *Chief Learning Officer* (November 30, 2016), http://www.clomedia.com.

40. "Machine Learning: What It Is and Why It's Important," SAS .com (April 2, 2017), https://www.sas.com.

41. Kristina E. Chirico, M. Ronald Buckley, Anthony R. Wheeler, Jeffrey D. Facteau, H. John Bernardin, and Danielle S. Beu, "A Note on the Need for True Scores in Frame-of-Reference (FOR) Training Research," *Journal of Managerial Issues* 16, no. 3 (Fall 2004): 382–398; Christopher D. Lee, "Feedback, Not Appraisal," *HRMagazine* 51, no. 11 (November 2006): 111–114.

42. Patrick Kampkötter, "Performance Appraisals and Job Satisfaction," *The International Journal of Human Resource Management* (2016): 1–25; Stephen C. Behrenbrinker, "Conducting Productive Performance Evaluations in the Assessor's Office," *Assessment Journal* 2, no. 5 (September–October 1995): 48–54; Aharon Tziner, Christine Joanis, and Kevin Murphy, "A Comparison of Three Methods of Performance Appraisal with Regard to Goal Properties, Goal Perception, and Rate Satisfaction," *Group & Organization Management* 25, no. 2 (June 2000): 175–190.

43. Daniel Bachrach, Elliot Bendoly, and Philip Podsakoff, "Attributions of the 'Causes' of Group Performance as an Alternative Explanation of the Relationship between Organizational Citizenship Behavior and Organizational Performance," *Journal of Applied Psychology* 86, no. 6 (December 2001): 1285–1293; Susan Leandri, "Measures That Matter: How to Fine-Tune Your Performance Measures," *Journal for Quality and Participation* 24, no. 1 (Spring 2001): 39–41.

44. Peter F. Drucker, *The Practice of Management* (New York: Harper & Brothers, 1954), reissued by HarperCollins in 1993; Janice S. Miller, "High Tech and High Performance: Managing Appraisal in the Information Age," *Journal of Labor Research* 24, no. 3 (Summer 2003): 409–425.

45. Deloris McGee Wanguri, "A Review, an Integration, and a Critique of Cross-Disciplinary Research on Performance Appraisals, Evaluations, and Feedback," *Journal of Business Communications* 32, no. 3 (July 1995): 267–293; Tziner, Joanis, and Murphy, "A Comparison of Three Methods of Performance Appraisal," 175–190; "Good Appraisal Is Simple, Happens Often, Experts Say"; Joanna Haworth, "Measuring Performance," *Nursing Management—UK* 15, no. 3 (June 2008): 22–28.

46. Jeff Kauflin, "Hate Performance Reviews? Good News? They're Getting Shorter and Simpler," *Forbes* (March 9, 2017), http:// https://www.forbes.com.

47. Kwok Leung, Steven Su, and Michael Morris, "When Is Criticism Not Constructive? The Roles of Fairness Perceptions and Dispositional Attributions in Employee Acceptance of Critical Supervisory Feedback," *Human Relations* 54, no. 9 (September 2001): 1155–1187; Ted Pollock, "Make Your Criticism Pay Off," *Electric Light & Power* 81, no. 1 (January 2003): 31; "Five Ways to Tackle Poor Performers," *Law Office Management & Administration Report* 6, no. 12 (December 2006): 9.

48. Virginia Galt, "Is It Time to Retire the Employee Ranking System?" *Globe and Mail* (March 10, 2017), http://www.theglobeandmail.com.

49. "Focus on Success," *Aftermarket Business* 115, no. 2 (February 2005): 1.

50. Helen Wilkie, "The Tricky Art of Criticism," *HRMagazine* 49, no. 12 (December 2004): 77–83.

CHAPTER **9**

Managing Compensation

Learning Outcomes

After studying this chapter, you should be able to

LO 1 Distinguish a strategic compensation program from one that is non-strategic.

LO 2 Determine how to design pay systems.

LO 3 Estimate whether or not a pay system is consistent within the firm as well as comparable to industry standards and government laws.

LO 4 Design a compensation scorecard.

Compensation is a way to increase employee loyalty and to decrease the likelihood that employees will be hired away by competitors. It reflects a strategic move on the part of the company to show that its employees are the most important component for success.[1] So why focus on compensation to retain talent? Why not hire employees who will be more loyal? Why not improve the training programs or evaluation systems? The answer is simple: Compensation is directly linked to an employee's livelihood. Employees can receive stellar training, copious growth opportunities, and be completely satisfied with their work and environment, but they will not show up to work if there is no paycheck in return.

9.1 What Is Compensation?

Compensation consists of three main components: *direct compensation* encompasses employee wages and salaries, incentives, bonuses, and commissions; *indirect compensation* comprises the many benefits supplied by employers; and *nonfinancial compensation* includes employee recognition programs, rewarding jobs, organizational support, work environment, and flexible work hours to accommodate personal needs (see Figure 9.1).

Figure 9.1	Compensation Components

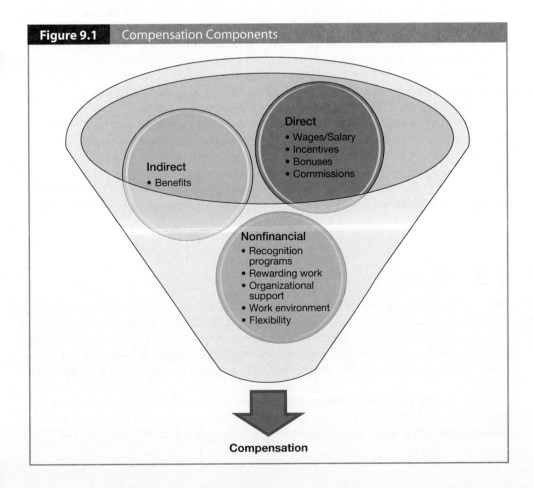

Indirect
• Benefits

Direct
• Wages/Salary
• Incentives
• Bonuses
• Commissions

Nonfinancial
• Recognition programs
• Rewarding work
• Organizational support
• Work environment
• Flexibility

Compensation

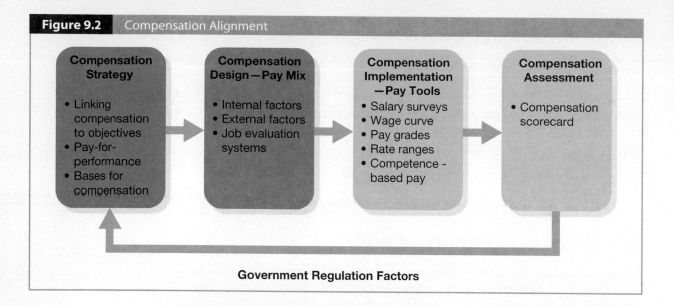

Figure 9.2   Compensation Alignment

Compensation Strategy
- Linking compensation to objectives
- Pay-for-performance
- Bases for compensation

Compensation Design—Pay Mix
- Internal factors
- External factors
- Job evaluation systems

Compensation Implementation —Pay Tools
- Salary surveys
- Wage curve
- Pay grades
- Rate ranges
- Competence - based pay

Compensation Assessment
- Compensation scorecard

Government Regulation Factors

The way these three components of compensation are allocated sends a message to the employees about what management believes is important and the types of activities it encourages.[2] However, for an employer, compensation constitutes a sizable operating cost. Ravin Jesuthasan, compensation specialist at Towers Perrin, notes, "Labor costs are a significant portion of expenses for any organization and a very substantial portion for some, but companies continue to spend on pay programs without any evidence of business relevance."[3] This means that compensation should be managed strategically to ensure that costs are kept down while employee motivation and performance are kept up. Achieving such a balance is no easy task.

In this chapter, we will help you learn how to strategically align the three aspects of compensation with an organization's objectives, design a pay mix based on the compensation strategy, implement the mix using a series of pay tools, and assess the compensation system using a scorecard. We will also discuss how government regulation might influence these decisions about compensation (see Figure 9.2 for details). In Chapter 10, we will review financial incentive plans for employees. Employee benefits that are part of the total compensation package are discussed in Chapter 11.

LO 1

Should compensation systems differ depending upon the company's objectives?

9.2 Strategic Compensation

What is strategic compensation? Simply stated, it is the compensation of employees in ways that enhance motivation and growth, while at the same time aligning their efforts with the objectives of the organization. Strategic compensation has redefined the role and perceived contribution of compensation. No longer merely a "cost of doing business," when used strategically, compensation becomes a tool to secure a competitive advantage.

Developing a compensation strategy requires that the organizational objectives are first analyzed. What does the company want to be known for? What are its growth projections? What are its core competencies? Once you figure this out, you can then decide what types of behaviors and skills will be rewarded. By rewarding specific skills and behaviors, you demonstrate that you are willing to pay for performance and not just for showing up to work. Then, as part of your strategy you need to decide on the compensation base most appropriate for the types of jobs in your company. For example, you might want to pay a sales representative based more on commission and a manager more on a yearly salary.

Strategic compensation goes beyond determining the appropriate market rates to pay employees, although market rates are one element of compensation planning. Strategic compensation should also purposefully link compensation to the organization's mission and general business objectives. For example, while a company's decision to increase base pay for all its employees is a strategic move to be more competitive with market rates, companies should also recognize that base pay is not everything. For example, one product development manager stated, "I could be making much more than I'm getting at Google, but I chose Google because of the flexibility to grow and work on exciting new products … plus, where else can you get a chef making you breakfast, lunch, and dinner anytime you want?"[4] In this regard, Google has not only aligned its compensation strategy with the external market, it has also aligned it with its desire to be a flexible and innovative company that capitalizes on the creativity of its people. Commenting on the importance of strategic compensation to organizational success, compensation specialists Gerald Ledford and Elizabeth Hawk note, "Companies throughout the economy have begun to rethink their compensation systems in search for competitive advantage."

Additionally, strategic compensation serves to mesh the monetary payments made to employees with other HR initiatives, such as recruitment, selection, training, retention, and performance appraisal. For example, starting pay can make a difference in whether or not someone will apply for the job. A compensation specialist speaking to one of the authors noted, "The linkage of pay levels to labor markets is a strategic policy issue because it serves to attract or retain valued employees while affecting the organization's relative payroll budget." For example, colleges such as University of Arkansas, Fayetteville; Bridgewater State University, Monroe College; and Brown Mackie College know that they cannot attract or retain qualified professors unless their pay strategy is linked to competitive market rates.

Many fast-food restaurants, such as Burger King, Taco Bell, and Blimpie's—traditionally low-wage employers—have needed to raise their starting wages to attract a sufficient number of job applicants to meet staffing requirements. If pay rates are high, it creates a large applicant pool from which organizations raise their selection standards and hire better-qualified employees. This in turn can reduce employer training costs. When employees perform at exceptional levels, their performance appraisals may justify an increased pay rate. For these reasons and others, an organization should develop a formal program to manage employee compensation. Step one of this program is to develop a compensation strategy that is linked to the organization's objectives.

9.2a Linking Compensation to Organizational Objectives

In a radical reconsidering of compensation strategy, Zappos has moved toward paying employees based on their skills rather than their position. This move came from an ongoing transition from a traditional management structure to a holacracy, a system where work is organized around roles rather than titles and employees report to teams instead of individual supervisors. When this transition was completed, Zappos began using a system of badges to represent roles rather than job titles to determine compensation. Employees are free to earn badges as they wish, with a chance to earn more and plot a unique path in the company. The idea behind the badges is similar to leveling up in a video game—Zappos CEO Tony Hsieh is hoping the badge-based compensation system will encourage employees to focus on building skills rather than climbing a corporate latter and to explore different aspects of the company, rather than adhering to a strict hierarchy of roles. This idea is in line with some of Zappos basic cultural values, such as pursuing growth and learning; being adventurous, creative, and open-minded; and embracing and driving change."[5]

The new compensation landscape requires that managers be more strategic about their compensation decisions. Managers must first and foremost understand the strategic objectives of the organization in relation to the industry in which it operates. Next, they need to move away from paying for a specific position or job title to rewarding employees on the basis of their individual competencies or work contributions to the organizational objectives, similar to the Zappos emerging pay strategy. In fact, a sample of Fortune 500 companies headquartered in America, Europe, and Asia showed that pay for performance that is linked to organizational objectives is a primary component of most compensation systems.[6]

As part of linking compensation systems to company objectives, managers need to consider what kinds of compensation create value. Managers are asking questions such as: "How will this pay program help to retain and motivate valued employees?" and "Does the benefit or pay practice affect the administrative cost?" If a component of the compensation package—whether benefits, base pay, incentives, or other—doesn't advance either the employee or the organization, it should be removed from the compensation program.[7] It is not uncommon for organizations to establish very specific goals for linking their organizational objectives to their compensation program.[8] Formalized compensation goals serve as guidelines for managers to ensure that wage and benefit policies achieve their intended purpose.

The #Fightfor15 movement on Twitter and in the streets, many Americans advocated a minimum wage increase of $15 per hour.

FREDERIC J. BROWN/Getty Images

For instance, tech companies such as Google, Oracle, Twitter, LinkedIn, and MoneyDesktop (MX) have adopted what is known as an Objectives and Key Results (OKR) system to tie compensation to objectives. The OKR system originally came from Intel and represents a simple way of linking compensation to performance. Here's how it works:

1. Set up an *objective* for your team and the individuals within the team. Your objective should be definitive and measurable. For instance, don't say, "I want my website to be faster." Say, "I want my website to be 30 percent more efficient."

2. Set up a number of *key results* that are quantifiable that your team and each member of the team must complete by a specific time period.

To be successful at the OKR system, you need to have an annual checkup with quarterly check-ins. The check-ins should be at the team level, at the manager level, and at the individual team member level. They all work together to keep the company on track toward its objectives. At Google, all OKRs are public from Larry Page on down. Posting the OKRs helps people know what everyone is working on.[9]

While not all companies tie OKRs to compensation, if you do there are a few things you must remember:

1. Clarify expectations. If you intend to reward contributors who go above and beyond to complete their objectives, you must first identify the criteria for outstanding performance versus just completing your OKRs on time.

2. Balance aspirational with operational. Some OKRs can be big stretch goals while others can be simply operational. Once you've determined how many of the goals were stretch from stuff that needed to be done, you can determine a ratio and increase people's performance based on work that they did that was a stretch.

3. Consider additional performance factors. Hitting your objectives demonstrates hard work, but they do not cover everything that should be rewarded. For example, you may want to reward people for developing their skills, attitude and professionalism, and the difficulty of the OKRs.

4. Drive collaboration, not competition. One of the biggest dangers that comes from rewarding people based on reaching their OKRs is that they may focus too much on their individual OKRs at the expense of those of a team or group. So you might want to provide bonuses or pay raises based on a combination of individual-level and group-level OKRs.[10]

9.2b The Pay-for-Performance Standard

In a study from the Institute for Corporate Productivity, researchers found that nearly half of the high-performing organizations surveyed recognized their long-term competitive advantage came from motivating and rewarding their top talent.[11]

The **pay-for-performance standard** in these companies serves to raise productivity and lower labor costs in today's competitive economic environment, which will be discussed in more depth in Chapter 10.

The term "pay-for-performance" refers to a wide range of compensation options, including merit-based pay, bonuses, salary commissions, job and pay banding, team/group incentives, and various gainsharing programs. (Gainsharing plans are discussed in Chapter 10.) Each of these compensation systems seeks to differentiate between the

pay-for-performance standard
A standard by which managers tie compensation to employee effort and performance

pay of average performers and that of outstanding performers. The Bridges to Excellence program seeks to increase performance of health care professionals by switching to a pay-for-performance system. Rather than using a traditional salary-based compensation strategy, doctors are rewarded based on quality of care rather than quantity, thus increasing motivation and performance. Now, more than half of health care organizations utilize some form of pay-for-performance, and studies have even shown that doctors on pay-for-performance plans have improved performance, better patient health, and reduced cost of care.[12]

Motivating Employees through Compensation

Pay constitutes a quantitative measure of an employee's relative worth. For most employees, pay has a direct bearing not only on perceived fairness, but also on the status and recognition they may be able to achieve both on and off the job. Because pay represents a reward received in exchange for an employee's contributions, it is essential, according to the equity theory, that the pay be equitable in terms of those contributions. It is essential also that an employee's pay be equitable in terms of what other employees are receiving for their contributions.

Pay Equity

Simply defined, equity embraces the concept of fairness. Equity theory, also referred to as *distributive fairness,* is a motivation theory that explains how people respond to situations in which they feel they have received less (or more) than they deserve.[13]

For employees, **pay equity** is achieved when the compensation received is equal to the value of the work performed. There are three kinds of pay equity:

pay equity
An employee's perception that compensation received is equal to the value of the work performed

1. External equity—people in similar jobs compare themselves to what others are making in different organizations.

2. Internal equity—people compare themselves to peers in different jobs in the same organization.

3. Individual equity—people compare themselves to others in their organization with the same job.

Research clearly demonstrates that employees' perceptions of pay equity, or inequity, can have dramatic effects on their motivation for both work behavior and productivity. Managers must, therefore, develop strategic pay practices that are both internally and externally equitable.

Expectancy Theory and Pay

Another tool to help determine your compensation strategy is expectancy theory. The expectancy theory of motivation predicts that one's level of motivation depends on the attractiveness of the rewards sought and the probability of obtaining those rewards.[14] Expectancy theory holds that employees should exert greater work effort if they have reason to expect that it will result in a reward that is valued.[15] To motivate this effort, the value of any monetary reward should be attractive. Employees also must believe that good performance is valued by their employer and will result in their receiving the expected reward.

Figure 9.3 shows the relationship between pay-for-performance and the expectancy theory of motivation. The model predicts, first, that high effort will lead to high performance (expectancy). For example, if an employee believes she has the skills and abilities

| Figure 9.3 | Pay-for-Performance and Expectancy Theory |

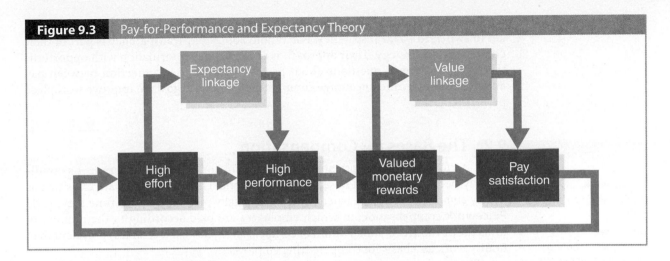

to perform her job and if she works hard (effort), then her performance will improve or be high. Second, high performance should result in rewards that are appreciated by the employee (valued). Elements of the compensation package are said to have *instrumentality* when an employee's high performance leads to monetary rewards that are valued. As previously stated, pay for performance leads to a feeling of pay satisfaction, and this feeling should reinforce one's high level of effort.

Thus, how employees view compensation can be an important factor in determining the motivational value of compensation. Furthermore, the effective communication of pay information together with an organizational environment that elicits employee trust in management can contribute to employees' having more accurate perceptions of their pay. The perceptions employees develop concerning their pay are influenced by the accuracy of their knowledge and understanding of the compensation program's strategic objectives.

Pay Secrecy

Misperceptions by employees concerning the equity of their pay and its relationship to performance can be created by secrecy about the pay that others receive. Secrecy can generate distrust in the compensation system, reduce employee motivation, and inhibit organizational effectiveness. Yet pay secrecy seems to be an accepted practice in many organizations. A U.S. survey found that about half of all workers, women and men, say they work in a place where discussions of pay are "either discouraged or prohibited and/or could lead to punishment."[16]

There are a few reasons why management refuses to divulge salary information. Managers may want to reduce conflict between people about their pay, especially if an employee makes less than someone they consider an inferior.[17] Secrecy can also cover up inequalities in internal pay structure, such as in the epic employment discrimination case *Ledbetter v. Goodyear Tire & Rubber Co.* In the case, the plaintiff may have found out that she was being paid less than men doing the same job and remedied the problem much earlier if she had been allowed to ask about other workers' pay.

Now it is harder for managers to maintain pay secrecy among employees with Internet salary survey data such as Glassdoor. Ready access to free online salary surveys gives employees an approximate idea of how their salary compares to others nationally or locally, which has been encouraging companies like Whole Foods Market to switch to pay transparency. For Whole Foods, pay transparency is part of their compensation strategy. Their approach is to release pay information with opportunities to ask managers questions about pay, understand the connection between pay and performance, and encourage competition and create goals to improve workplace performance.

9.2c The Bases for Compensation

Work performed in most private, public, and not-for-profit organizations has traditionally been compensated based on **hourly work**. These employees are classified as *hourly employees*, or wage earners, and are normally paid only for the time they work. **Piecework** compensation, in which employees are paid according to the number of units they produce, is another kind of compensation, though it is far less prevalent than hourly work as a basis for compensating employees.

Those whose compensation is computed on the basis of weekly, biweekly, or monthly pay periods are classified as *salaried employees*. Salaried employees, unlike hourly employees, are generally paid the same for each pay period, even though they occasionally may work more hours or fewer than the regular number of hours in a period. They also usually receive certain benefits not provided to hourly employees.

Another basis for compensation centers on whether employees are classified as *nonexempt* or *exempt* under the Fair Labor Standards Act (FLSA).[17] **Nonexempt employees** are covered by the act and must be paid at a rate of one and a half times their *regular* pay rate for time worked in excess of 40 hours in their workweek. Most hourly workers employed in interstate commerce are considered nonexempt workers under the FLSA. Employees not covered by the overtime provision of the FLSA are classified as **exempt employees**. The U.S. Department of Labor (DOL) considers employees as exempt when their primary duty includes "the exercise of discretion and independent judgment with respect to matters of significance."[18] This includes managers, supervisors, and a large number of white-collar employees. There are other classifications for exemption, so employers should check the exact terms and conditions of exemption before classifying employees as either exempt or nonexempt. (see "Exemption from Overtime Provisions" in Figure 9.4).

To help in these types of decisions, larger companies will often use compensation consultants. A study showed that about 86 percent of large U.S. companies use a compensation consultant to help them with their compensation strategy and pay mix.[19]

9.3 Compensation Design—The Pay Mix

An employee may ask, "How is my pay determined?" In practice, a combination of *internal* and *external* factors can directly or indirectly influence the rates at which employees are paid. The interaction of these factors constitutes the pay mix, as shown in Figure 9.5. For example, the area pay rate for administrative assistants might be $11.50 per hour. However, one employer may elect to pay its administrative assistants $14.25 per hour because of their excellent performance. The influence of government legislation on the pay mix will be discussed later in the chapter.

hourly work
Work paid on an hourly basis

piecework
Work paid according to the number of units produced

nonexempt employees
Employees covered by the overtime provisions of the Fair Labor Standards Act

exempt employees
Employees not covered by the overtime provisions of the Fair Labor Standards Act

LO 2
Say you get hired making $10 per hour. What most helps you determine if that is an appropriate amount?

Figure 9.4	Six Excluded Employee Groups

Category	Job Duties Required
Executive	Primary duty must be managing the enterprise, or managing a customarily recognized department or subdivision of the enterprise; must customarily and regularly direct the work of at least two or more other full-time employees or their equivalent; and must have the authority to hire or fire other employees, or the employee's suggestions and recommendations as to the hiring, firing, advancement, promotion, or any other change of status of other employees must be given particular weight.
Administrative	Primary duty must be the performance of office or non-manual work directly related to the management or general business operations of the employer or the employer's customers; and includes the exercise of discretion and independent judgment with respect to matters of significance.
Learned	Primary duty must be the performance of work requiring advanced knowledge, defined as work which is predominantly intellectual in character and which includes work requiring the consistent exercise of discretion and judgment; the advanced knowledge must be in a field of science or learning; and the advanced knowledge must be customarily acquired by a prolonged course of specialized intellectual instruction.
Creative	Primary duty must be the performance of work requiring invention, imagination, originality, or talent in a recognized field of artistic or creative endeavor.
Computer	Must be employed as a computer systems analyst, computer programmer, software engineer or other similarly skilled worker in the computer field. The primary duty must consist of (1) the application of systems analysis techniques and procedures, including consulting with users, to determine hardware, software or system functional specifications; (2) the design, development, documentation, analysis, creation, testing, or modification of computer systems or programs, including prototypes, based on and related to user or system design specifications; (3) the design, documentation, testing, creation, or modification of computer programs related to machine operating systems; or (4) a combination of the aforementioned duties, the performance of which requires the same level of skills.
Outside Sales	Primary duty must be making sales (as defined in the FLSA), or obtaining orders or contracts for services or for the use of facilities for which a consideration will be paid by the client or customer; and must be customarily and regularly engaged away from the employer's place or places of business.
Highly Compensated	The regulations contain a special rule for "highly-compensated" workers who are paid total annual compensation of $100,000 or more. A highly-compensated employee is deemed exempt under Section 13(a)(1) if the employee earns total annual compensation of $100,000 or more, which includes at least $455 per week paid on a salary basis; the employee's primary duty includes performing office or non-manual work; and the employee customarily and regularly performs at least one of the exempt duties or responsibilities of an exempt executive, administrative, or professional employee.
Other	Teachers are exempt if their primary duty is teaching, tutoring, instructing or lecturing in the activity of imparting knowledge, and if they are employed and engaged in this activity as a teacher in an educational establishment. Practice of Law or Medicine: An employee holding a valid license or certificate permitting the practice of law or medicine is exempt if the employee is actually engaged in such a practice. An employee who holds the requisite academic degree for the general practice of medicine is also exempt if he or she is engaged in an internship or resident program for the profession.

Source: Adapted from Vicki M. Lambert, "The top three FLSA violations and how to avoid them," ADP, 2008.

9.3a Internal Factors

The internal factors that influence pay rates are the organization's compensation strategy, the worth of a job, an employee's relative worth in meeting job requirements, and an employer's ability to pay.

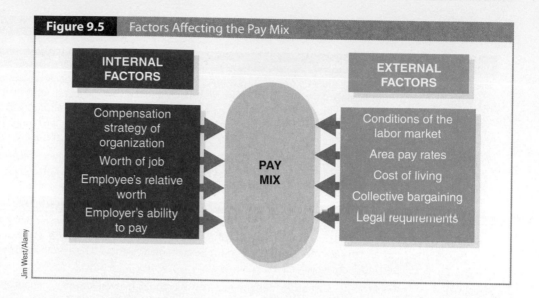

Figure 9.5   Factors Affecting the Pay Mix

INTERNAL FACTORS

- Compensation strategy of organization
- Worth of job
- Employee's relative worth
- Employer's ability to pay

PAY MIX

EXTERNAL FACTORS

- Conditions of the labor market
- Area pay rates
- Cost of living
- Collective bargaining
- Legal requirements

Jim West/Alamy

Compensation Strategy

Highlights in HRM 1 illustrates the compensation strategies of two organizations, Tri Star Performance and Preventive Health Care. The strategy of Preventive Health Care is to be an industry pay leader, while Tri Star Performance seeks to be pay competitive. Both employers strive to promote a compensation policy that is internally fair.

Tri Star Performance and Preventive Health Care, like other employers, will establish numerous compensation objectives that affect the pay employees receive. At a minimum, both large and small employers should set pay policies reflecting (1) the internal wage relationship among jobs and skill levels, (2) the external competition, or an employer's pay position relative to what competitors are paying, (3) a policy of rewarding employee performance, and (4) administrative decisions concerning elements of the pay system such as overtime premiums, payment periods, and short- or long-term incentives.

Worth of a Job

Organizations without a formal compensation program generally base the worth of jobs on the subjective opinions of people familiar with the jobs. In such instances, pay rates may be influenced heavily by the labor market or, in the case of unionized employers, by collective bargaining. Organizations with formal compensation programs, however, are more likely to rely on a system of *job evaluation* to aid in rate determination. (This topic will be covered later in the chapter under pay structure.) Job evaluation can assist the organization in maintaining some degree of control over its pay structure, even when rates are subjected to collective bargaining. The use of job evaluation is widespread in both the public and the private sectors. The cities of Chicago and Miami use job evaluation in establishing pay structures, as do Google, Goldman Sachs, and GM. The jobs covered most frequently by job evaluation are clerical, technical, and various blue-collar groups, as well as managerial and top executive positions.

In today's competitive environment, compensation professionals believe that the worth of a job should be based on more than market prices or job evaluation programs.

Rather, a job's value should be based on *the total value* delivered to the organization. That is, some jobs may simply be more important to organizational success than others regardless of how they are internally evaluated.[20] Valuing work not only properly enables organizations to price "important" jobs effectively, but also provides insight into how a job relates to the organization's objectives and can attract and retain the right talent to drive organizational performance.[21]

Employee's Relative Worth

In both hourly and salary jobs, employee performance can be recognized and rewarded through promotion and with various incentive systems. (The incentive systems used most often will be discussed in Chapter 10.) Superior performance can also be rewarded by granting merit raises on the basis of steps within a rate range established for a job class. If merit raises are to have their intended value, however, they must be determined by an effective performance appraisal system that differentiates between employees who deserve the raises and those who do not. This system, moreover, must provide a visible and credible relationship between performance and any raises received. Unfortunately, too many so-called merit systems provide for raises to be granted automatically. As a result, employees tend to be rewarded more for merely being present than for being productive on the job.

Employer's Ability to Pay

Pay levels are limited by earned profits and other financial resources available to employers. Competition and recessions can force prices down and reduce the income from which compensation payments are derived. In such situations, employers have little choice but to reduce wages and/or lay off employees or, even worse, to go out of business. This is especially true for small businesses. In a survey of small businesses about performance and financial decisions, half of the respondents stated that the reason they

Several factors should be taken into consideration when determining how much a worker like this one should be paid.

Frances Roberts/Alamy

Comparison of Compensation Strategies

Compensation strategies and objectives can differ widely across large and small employers as well as across employers in the private and public sectors. Here are the compensation strategies at Tri Star Performance and Preventive Health Care.

Tri Star Performance

- Promote pay-for-performance practices
- Pay market-competitive compensation
- Achieve internal and external pay equity
- Achieve simplicity in compensation programs
- Strive for employee commitment and a collaborative work environment
- Promote gender fairness in pay and benefits
- Comply with all governmental compensation regulations
- Minimize increased fixed costs

Preventive Health Care

- Be a pay leader in the health care industry
- Promote open and understandable pay practices
- Ensure fair employee treatment
- Offer benefits promoting individual employee needs
- Offer compensation rewarding employee creativity and achievements
- Offer compensation to foster the strategic mission of the organization
- Obtain employee input when developing compensation practices
- Emphasize performance through variable pay and stock options

didn't hire more employees is because of high wages and benefit costs, and almost a third cited the uncertain economic climate.[22]

Furthermore, an organization's ability to pay is determined in part by the productivity of its employees. This productivity is a result not only of employee performance, but of the amount of capital the organization has invested in labor-saving equipment. Generally, increases in capital investment reduce the number of employees required to perform the work and increase an employer's ability to provide higher pay for employees.

9.3b External Factors

The major external factors that influence pay rates include labor market conditions, area pay rates, cost of living, collective bargaining if the employer is unionized, and legal requirements. The legal requirements of compensation will be discussed later in the chapter.

Labor Market Conditions

The labor market reflects the forces of supply and demand for qualified labor within an area. These forces help influence the pay rates required to recruit or retain competent employees. It must be recognized, however, that counterforces can reduce the full impact of supply and demand on the labor market. The economic power of unions, for example, may prevent employers from lowering pay rates even when unemployment is high among union members. Government regulations also may prevent an employer from paying at a market rate less than an established minimum.

Area Pay Rates

A formal pay structure should provide rates that are in line with those being paid by other employers for comparable jobs within the area. Data pertaining to area pay rates may be obtained from local wage surveys. Wage survey data may be obtained from a variety of sources, including the American Management Association, Administrative Management Society, U.S. Department of Labor, and Federal Reserve Banks. Smaller employers such as the Woodsmith Corporation and Golden State Container use government surveys to establish rates of pay for new and senior employees. Many organizations, such as the City of Atlanta, Delta Airlines, and Progress Energy, conduct their own surveys. Others engage in a cooperative exchange of wage information or rely on various professional associations for these data. A high percentage of wage data surveys are inexpensive—less than $100—and are therefore available to all employers, regardless of size.

Wage surveys (discussed fully later in the chapter) serve the important function of providing external pay equity between the surveying organization and other organizations competing for labor in the surrounding labor market. Importantly, data from area wage surveys can be used to prevent the rates for jobs from drifting too far above or below those of other employers in the region.

Small Business Application

Compensation for Small Businesses

Big business can woo job candidates by offering comprehensive compensation packages that include stock options, consistent pay raises, security, and sometimes even a Starbucks in the lobby. While small businesses cannot offer these things, they can offer more customized pay packages to deal with employees' individual needs. For example, not having a complex and bureaucratic compensation system means a small company can more readily adjust its employees' wages to match those of the external market. If the small business is private, there are many opportunities to attract and retain top talent by padding lower salaries with stock in the company. By offering shares of a private company as a form of compensation, small, private companies can offer the possibility for its employees to make larger sums of money in the future. Offering shares or options to buy shares as a form of compensation can be extremely attractive, as employees can make a lot of money when their young company finally goes public and is sold on the stock market. For example, when Snap, owner of Snapchat, became a public company in 2017, hundreds of the employees who were with the company early on made enough to become instant millionaires.[23]

Following is a list of specific things small businesses can do to compete with the compensation packages of big business:

1. **Tailor the pay mix to individual employee needs and wants.** For example, one employee may value greater bonus opportunities than base pay, while another may want the money the company would spend on health insurance to be paid in salary.

2. **Provide stock options in high-growth environments.** Potential employees will find the opportunity to be part of a high-growth company as an exciting and potentially lucrative risk.

3. **Provide faster promotions.** Express how the smallness of your company allows people to move into new and exciting positions quickly, without the bureaucratic red tape found in big business.

4. **Provide frequent contact to top management.** Not being able to interact with and receive mentoring from top management is a major concern for young talent. Smaller companies are able to offer more of these types of growth opportunities than larger competitors.

5. **Provide a greater sense of personal involvement.** One of the advantages of a small company is that they can treat their employees like family. In an age of depersonalized billion-dollar companies, a sense of belongingness, where you know the company cares about you, can go a long way in compensating for lower pay.

Cost of Living

consumer price index (CPI)

A measure of the average change in prices over time in a fixed "market basket" of goods and services

Because of inflation, compensation rates have to be adjusted upward periodically to help employees maintain their purchasing power. Employers make these changes with the help of the **consumer price index (CPI)**. The CPI is a measure of the average change in prices over time in a fixed "market basket" of goods and services. The Bureau of Labor Statistics collects price information on a monthly basis and calculates the CPI for the nation as a whole and various U.S. city averages.

CPI figures can have important consequences for organizational morale and productivity. Granting wages based largely on "cost-of-living" figures will not inspire higher employee performance because pay is unrelated to individual performance and may cause valued employees to leave the organization. Furthermore, should cost-of-living increases be discontinued, managers can expect disgruntled employees who may be less likely to receive merit raises.

escalator clauses

Clauses in labor agreements that provide for quarterly cost-of-living adjustments in wages, basing the adjustments on changes in the consumer price index

Employees who work under a union contract may receive wage increases through **escalator clauses** found in their labor agreement. These clauses provide for cost-of-living adjustments (COLA) in wages based on changes in the CPI. The most common adjustments are 1 percent per hour for each 0.3- or 0.4-point change in the CPI. COLAs are favored by unions during particularly high periods of inflation.

Collective Bargaining

real wages

Wage increases larger than rises in the consumer price index, that is, the real earning power of wages

One of the primary functions of a labor union is to bargain collectively over conditions of employment, the most important of which is compensation.[24] The union's goal in each new agreement is to achieve increases in **real wages**—wage increases larger than the increase in the CPI—thereby improving the purchasing power and standard of living of its members.

Employee wages may be based in part on how much money people in that area need for day-to-day living.

Stokkete/Shutterstock

9.4 Job Evaluation Systems

As we discussed earlier, one important component of the pay mix is the worth of the job. Organizations formally determine the value of jobs through the process of job evaluation. **Job evaluation** is the systematic process of determining the *relative* worth of jobs to establish which jobs should be paid more than others within the organization and therefore helps establish internal equity between various jobs. The relative worth of a job may be determined by comparing it with others within the organization or by comparing it with a scale that has been constructed for this purpose.

job evaluation
A systematic process of determining the relative worth of jobs to establish which jobs should be paid more than others within an organization

Three traditional methods of comparison provide the basis for the principal systems of job evaluation:

1. Rank the value of jobs from highest to lowest.
2. Classify jobs so they can be benchmarked internally and externally.
3. Award points to each job based on its link to organizational objectives.

Such a job valuation system can prove effective not only in designing employee compensation, but in determining whether a job can be contracted to a local or offshore company—a major decision that should always take into account the value of the job. For example, Delta Airlines brought back more than 4,500 customer service jobs from overseas to the United States. They reported that "customers weren't happy with the service they got from operators based [overseas]." We will begin by discussing the simpler nonquantitative approaches and conclude by reviewing the more popular quantitative system and work evaluation. Regardless of the methodology used, it is important to remember that all job evaluation methods require varying degrees of managerial judgment. Also, those involved in evaluating jobs must consider the impact of the Americans with Disabilities Act on the process (see Chapter 3).

9.4a Job Ranking System

The simplest and oldest system of job evaluation is the **job ranking system**, which ranks jobs on the basis of their relative worth. Job ranking can be done by a single individual knowledgeable about all jobs or by a committee comprising of management and employee representatives. For one technique, the ranker(s) arranges cards, one for each job with a list of their duties and responsibilities, in order of the importance of the jobs.

job ranking system
The simplest and oldest system of job evaluation by which jobs are arrayed on the basis of their relative worth

The basic disadvantage of the job ranking system is that it is not a very precise measure of each job's worth, can only be used on a small number of jobs, and only indicates the relative importance of the job, not the differences in the degree of importance that may exist between jobs. Its simplicity, however, makes it ideal for use by small businesses.

9.4b Job Classification System

job classification system
A system of job evaluation in which jobs are classified and grouped according to a series of predetermined wage grades

In the **job classification system**, jobs are classified and grouped according to a series of predetermined grades. Successive grades require increasing amounts of job responsibility, skill, knowledge, ability, or other factors selected to compare jobs, and is widely used by municipal and state governments.[24] For example, Grade GS-1 from the federal government grade descriptions reads as follows:

> GS-1 includes those classes of positions the duties of which are to perform, under immediate supervision, with little or no latitude for the exercise of independent judgment (A) the simplest routine work in office, business, or fiscal operations; or (B) elementary work of a subordinate technical character in a professional, scientific, or technical field.

The descriptions of each of the job classes constitute the scale against which the specifications for the various jobs are compared. Managers then evaluate jobs by comparing job descriptions with the different wage grades to "slot" the job into the appropriate grade. While this system has the advantage of simplicity as well, the point system is more precise.

9.4c Point System

point system

A quantitative job evaluation procedure that determines the relative value of a job by the total points assigned to it

The **point system** is a quantitative job evaluation procedure that determines a job's relative value by calculating the total points assigned to it.[25] The principal advantage of the point system is that it provides a more refined basis for making judgments than either the ranking or classification system and thereby can produce results that are more valid and less easy to manipulate. It has been successfully used by high-visibility organizations such as Digital Equipment Company, Met Life, Johnson Wax, Prudential Financial, TransAmerica, and many other public and private organizations, large and small. Although point systems are rather complicated to establish, once in place they are relatively simple to understand and use.

The point system permits jobs to be evaluated quantitatively on the basis of factors or elements—commonly called *compensable factors*—that constitute the job.[26] Some compensable factors might include fiscal accountability, leadership, teamwork, and project accountability. The number of compensable factors an organization uses depends on the nature of the organization and the jobs to be evaluated. Once selected, compensable factors will be assigned weights according to their relative importance to the organization. For example, if responsibility is considered extremely important to the organization's objectives, it could be assigned a weight of 40 percent. Next, each factor will be divided into a number of degrees. Degrees represent different levels of difficulty associated with each factor.

The Point Manual

The point system requires the use of a *point manual*. The point manual is, in effect, a handbook that contains a description of the compensable factors and the degrees to which these factors may exist within the jobs. The point value assigned to a job represents the sum of the numerical degree values of each compensable factor that the job possesses.

Using the Point Manual

Job evaluation under the point system is accomplished by comparing the job descriptions and job specifications, factor by factor, against the various factor-degree descriptions contained in the manual. Each factor within the job being evaluated is then assigned the number of points specified in the manual. When the points for each factor have been determined from the manual, the total point value for the job as a whole can be calculated.

9.4d Work Valuation

Work valuation is a relatively new job evaluation system championed to meet the demands of a dynamic business environment. The cornerstone for **work valuation** is that work should be valued relative to the business goals of the organization rather than by an internally applied point-factor job evaluation system.[28] As noted by one compensation specialist, "Valuing work properly enables organizations to not only price individual jobs effectively, but provides insight into how jobs relate to overall organizational goals and objectives and how roles ultimately contribute to organizational success."[29] Additionally, work valuation serves to direct compensation dollars to the type of work pivotal to organizational goals.

work valuation
A job evaluation system that seeks to measure a job's worth through its value to the organization

9.4e Job Evaluation for Management Positions

Because management positions are more difficult to evaluate and involve certain demands not found in jobs at the lower levels, some organizations do not attempt to include them in their job evaluation programs for hourly employees. Rather, they employ either a standardized (purchased) program or customize a point method to fit their particular jobs. However, regardless of the approach adopted, point plans for executive and managerial employees operate similarly to those for other groups of employees.

One of the better-known standardized job evaluation programs for evaluating executive, managerial, and professional positions is the **Hay profile method**, developed by Edward N. Hay.

The three puzzle pieces that constitute the evaluation in the "profile" are knowledge (or knowhow), mental activity (or problem-solving), and accountability

Hay profile method
A job evaluation technique using three factors—knowledge, mental activity, and accountability—to evaluate executive and managerial positions

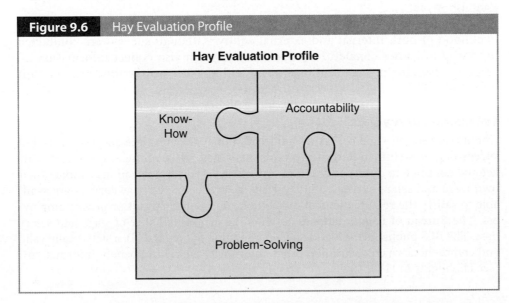

| **Figure 9.6** | Hay Evaluation Profile |

Hay Evaluation Profile

Know-How

Accountability

Problem-Solving

(Figure 9.6). These factors represent the most important aspects of all executive and managerial positions. The profile for each position is developed by determining the percentage value to be assigned to each of the three factors. Jobs are then ranked on the basis of each factor, and point values that make up the profile are assigned to each job on the basis of the percentage-value level at which the job is ranked.

LO 3
As an HR manager, what resources can you use to determine if pay is appropriate?

9.5 Compensation Implementation—Pay Tools

Compensation design systems, such as job evaluations, provide for internal equity and serve as the basis for pay rate determination. They do not in themselves determine the pay rate. The evaluated worth of each job in terms of its rank, class, points, or monetary worth must be implemented into an hourly, daily, weekly, or monthly pay rate. To appropriately implement compensation, specific tools must be incorporated. The primary compensation tool used to set pay is the wage and salary survey.

9.5a Wage and Salary Surveys

wage and salary survey
A survey of the wages paid to employees of other employers in the surveying organization's relevant labor market

The **wage and salary survey** is a survey of the wages paid by employers in an organization's relevant labor market—local, regional, or national—depending on the job. The labor market is frequently defined as the area from which employers obtain certain types of workers. The labor market for office personnel would be local, whereas the labor market for engineers would be national and even global. It is the wage and salary survey that permits an organization to maintain external equity—that is, to pay its employees wages equivalent to the wages similar employees earn in other establishments.

When job evaluation and wage survey data are used jointly, they link the likelihood of both internal and external equity. Although surveys are conducted primarily to gather competitive wage data, they can also collect information on employee benefits or organizational pay practices (such as overtime rates or shift differentials).

Collecting Survey Data

Conducting surveys and collecting information may take up time and resources, but survey data lets Human Resource professionals stay aware of the employment market and continue to attract and retrain top talent.[30] Many organizations conduct their own wage and salary surveys, and a variety of "preconducted" pay surveys are available to satisfy the requirements of most public and not-for-profit or private employers. The Bureau of Labor Statistics (BLS) is the major publisher of wage and salary data. The BLS publishes the National Compensation Survey (NCS), a statistically valid and comprehensive compensation program of wage, salary, and benefit information[31] (see Highlights in HRM 2).

Bureau of Labor Statistics National Compensation Survey

NCS data are used by managers and compensation specialists in large and small organizations to answer such questions as the following:

- How much must I pay accountants in Atlanta, Georgia?
- Is a 3-percent benefits increase comparable to that of other employers in the manufacturing industry?
- Is vision coverage a prevalent benefit among large employers in the Northeast?
- How have wage costs changed over the past year?

How the NCS Survey Works

The National Compensation Survey is an area-based survey. Wage and benefit data are collected from a predetermined set of 154 metropolitan and nonmetropolitan areas through the 50 states and the District of Columbia to represent the United States. Compensation information is collected from such diverse locations as Knoxville, Tennessee; Pittsburgh, Pennsylvania; Reno, Nevada; and Richland-Kennewick-Pasco, Washington. All areas are selected to produce regional estimates for nine broad geographic divisions and four broad regions.

Within each area, a scientific sample of establishments represents all area establishments. An "establishment" is a single physical location, such as a plant, warehouse, corporate office, or retail outlet. State and local government offices are also included in the survey.

Once an establishment has been chosen for inclusion in the survey, a BLS economist selects occupations within that establishment to represent all occupations in the establishment. The BLS limits the selection to a small number of occupations to reduce the survey burden for employers. Data are collected for all incumbents in a selected occupation.

The selected occupations are then classified based on the Census Bureau's occupation classification system. The census classification categorizes approximately 450 individual occupations into 10 major groupings such as sales, professional specialty, technical and machine operators, assemblers, and inspectors. For the occupations selected, wage and benefit data are collected. Items included in the collection of wages are time-based payments, piece rates, commissions, hazard pay, and other items directly related to the work being performed. A variety of benefit data are collected, including paid vacations, paid holidays, paid sick leave, shift differentials, and nonproduction bonuses.

Salary Surveys

Wage and benefits survey data can be found on numerous websites. The previously mentioned National Compensation Survey is an example. Also readily available are commercial products such as those offered at Salary.com or Glassdoor. Other, less well-known places to find salary information include the Salary Wizard, Comp Analyst, and Survey Finder. Survey Finder has a database of hundreds of compensation surveys offered by more than 50 independent vendors. Managers and compensation specialists can search for applicable surveys for either purchase or participation.[31]

The race for free salary data is currently being won by Glassdoor. It was not originally built, however, for companies to discover how to pay their employees. Rather, Glassdoor provided a safe platform where people could anonymously share information about their pay and company in return for free information about other companies and salaries. Glassdoor now provides a platform where you can view salary information, company reviews, and job postings. You can even figure out who the top paying companies are and target your search accordingly. For example, in 2017

Glassdoor collects salary data from employees who anonymously volunteer salary information and comments about employers in return for access to salary and company information about other companies.

Glassdoor.com

Personalized

Receive a custom salary estimate based on your title, company, location and experience.

Private

Glassdoor is committed to your privacy. Your market value is only shared with you.

Comprehensive

We calculate your worth using millions of salaries and current job openings relevant to you.

Glassdoor listed the 25 highest paying companies in the United States. Looks like consulting and technology companies may be the way to go… if you're interested in high pay.

1. A.T. Kearney
- Median Total Compensation: $167,534
- Median Base Salary: $143,620
- Industry: Consulting

2. Strategy&
- Median Total Compensation: $160,000
- Median Base Salary: $147,000
- Industry: Consulting

3. Juniper Networks
- Median Total Compensation: $157,000
- Median Base Salary: $135,000
- Industry: Technology

4. McKinsey & Company
- Median Total Compensation: $155,000
- Median Base Salary: $135,000
- Industry: Consulting

5. Google
- Median Total Compensation: $153,750
- Median Base Salary: $123,331
- Industry: Technology

6. VMware
- Median Total Compensation: $152,133
- Median Base Salary: $130,000
- Industry: Technology

7. Amazon Lab126
- Median Total Compensation: $150,100
- Median Base Salary: $138,700
- Industry: Technology

8. Boston Consulting Group
- Median Total Compensation: $150,020
- Median Base Salary: $147,000
- Industry: Consulting

9. Guidewire
   - Median Total Compensation: $150,020
   - Median Base Salary: $135,000
   - Industry: Technology

10. Cadence Design Systems
    - Median Total Compensation: $150,010
    - Median Base Salary: $140,000
    - Industry: Technology

11. Visa
    - Median Total Compensation: $150,000
    - Median Base Salary: $130,000
    - Industry: Finance

12. Facebook
    - Median Total Compensation: $150,000
    - Median Base Salary: $127,406
    - Industry: Technology

13. Twitter
    - Median Total Compensation: $150,000
    - Median Base Salary: $133,000
    - Industry: Technology

14. Box
    - Median Total Compensation: $150,000
    - Median Base Salary: $130,000
    - Industry: Technology

15. Walmart eCommerce
    - Median Total Compensation: $149,000
    - Median Base Salary: $126,000
    - Industry: Technology

16. SAP
    - Median Total Compensation: $148,431
    - Median Base Salary: $120,000
    - Industry: Technology

17. Synopsys
    - Median Total Compensation: $148,000
    - Median Base Salary: $130,000
    - Industry: Technology

18. Altera
    - Median Total Compensation: $147,000
    - Median Base Salary: $134,000
    - Industry: Technology

19. LinkedIn
    - Median Total Compensation: $145,000
    - Median Base Salary: $120,000
    - Industry: Technology

20. Cloudera
    - Median Total Compensation: $145,000
    - Median Base Salary: $129,500
    - Industry: Technology

21. Salesforce
    - Median Total Compensation: $143,750
    - Median Base Salary: $120,000
    - Industry: Technology

22. Microsoft
    - Median Total Compensation: $141,000
    - Median Base Salary: $125,000
    - Industry: Technology

23. F5 Networks
    - Median Total Compensation: $140,200
    - Median Base Salary: $120,500
    - Industry: Technology

24. Adobe
    - Median Total Compensation: $140,000
    - Median Base Salary: $125,000
    - Industry: Technology

25. Broadcom
    - Median Total Compensation: $140,000
    - Median Base Salary: $130,000
    - Industry: Technology

9.5b The Wage Curve

wage curve

A curve in a scattergram representing the relationship between relative worth of jobs and pay rates

The relationship between the relative worth of jobs and their pay rates can be represented by means of a **wage curve**. This curve may indicate the rates currently paid for jobs within an organization, new rates resulting from job evaluation, or rates for similar jobs currently being paid by other organizations within the labor market. A curve may be constructed graphically by preparing a scattergram consisting of a series of dots that represent the current pay rates. As shown in Figure 9.7, a freehand curve is then drawn through the cluster of dots in such a manner as to leave approximately an equal number of dots above and below the curve. The wage curve can be relatively straight or curved. This curve can then be used to determine the relationship between the value of a job and its pay rate at any given point on the line.

9.5c Pay Grades

pay grades

Groups of jobs within a particular class that are paid the same rate

From an administrative standpoint, it is generally preferable to group jobs into **pay grades** and to pay all jobs within a particular grade the same rate or rate range. When the classification system of job evaluation is used, jobs are grouped into grades as part of the evaluation process. When the point system is used, however, pay grades must be established at selected intervals that represent either the point or the evaluated monetary value of these jobs. The graph in Figure 9.8 illustrates a series of pay grades designated along the horizontal axis at 50-point intervals.

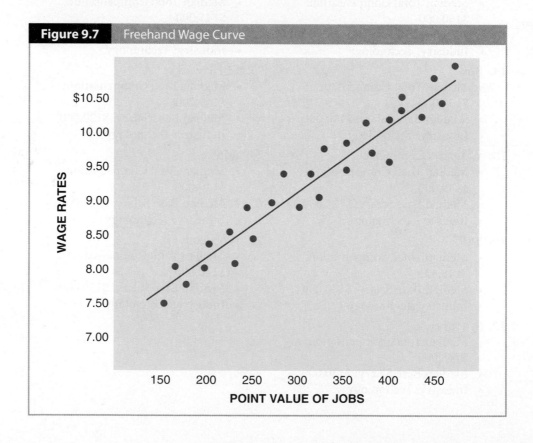

Figure 9.7   Freehand Wage Curve

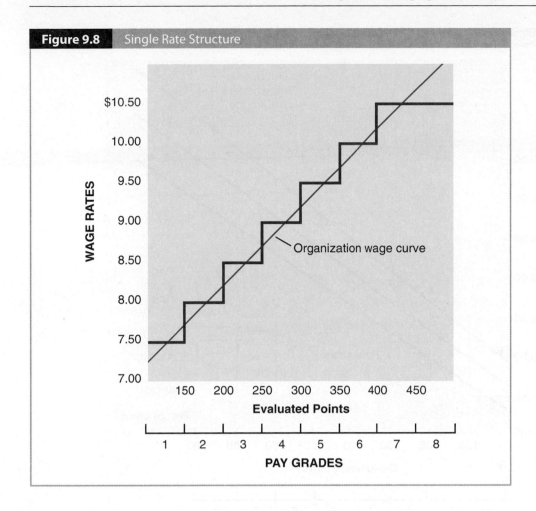

Figure 9.8 Single Rate Structure

Organization wage curve

WAGE RATES

$10.50
10.00
9.50
9.00
8.50
8.00
7.50
7.00

150   200   250   300   350   400   450

Evaluated Points

1   2   3   4   5   6   7   8

PAY GRADES

The grades within a pay structure may vary in number.[33] The number is determined by such factors as the slope of the wage curve, the number and distribution of the jobs within the structure, and the organization's wage administration and promotion policies. The number utilized should be sufficient to permit difficulty levels to be distinguished but not so great as to make the distinction between two adjoining grades insignificant.

9.5d Rate Ranges

Although a single rate may be created for each pay grade, as shown in Figure 9.8, it is more common to provide a range of rates for each pay grade. The rate ranges may be the same for each grade or proportionately greater for each successive grade, as shown in Figure 9.9. Rate ranges constructed on the latter basis provide a greater incentive for employees to accept a promotion to a job in a higher grade.

Rate ranges generally are divided into a series of steps that permit employees to receive increases up to the maximum rate for the range on the basis of merit or seniority or a combination of the two. Most salary structures provide for the ranges of adjoining pay grades to overlap. The purpose of the overlap is to permit an employee with

Figure 9.9	Rate Range Structure

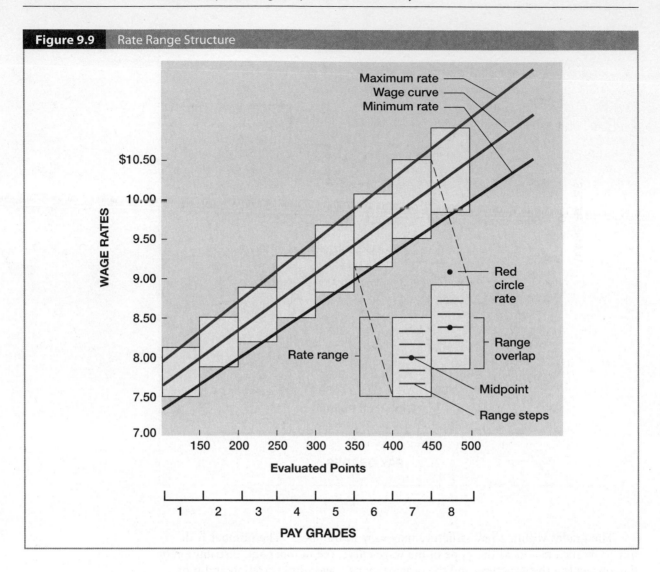

experience to earn as much as or more than a person with less experience in the next higher job classification.

The final step in setting up a wage structure is to determine the appropriate pay grade into which each job should be placed on the basis of its evaluated worth. Traditionally, this worth is determined on the basis of job requirements without regard to the performance of the person in that job. Under this system, the performance of those who exceed the requirements of a job may be acknowledged by merit increases within the grade range or by promotion to a job in the next higher pay grade.[34]

Organizations may pay individuals above the maximum of the pay range when employees have high seniority or promotional opportunities are scarce. Wages paid above the range maximum are called **red circle rates**. Because these rates are exceptions to the pay structure, employers often "freeze" these rates until all ranges are shifted upward through market wage adjustments.

red circle rates
Payment rates above the maximum of the pay range

9.5e Competence-Based Pay

The predominant approach to employee compensation is still the job-based system. Unfortunately, such a system often fails to reward employees for their skills or the knowledge they possess or to encourage them to learn a new job-related skill. Additionally, job-based pay systems may not reinforce an organizational culture stressing employee involvement or provide increased employee flexibility to meet overall production or service requirements. Therefore, organizations such as Frito-Lay, Nortel Networks, Sherwin-Williams, and Honeywell have introduced competence-based pay plans.

Competence-based pay, also referred to as skill-based pay or knowledge-based pay, compensates employees for the different skills or increased knowledge they possess rather than for the job they hold in a designated job category.[35] Regardless of the name, these pay plans encourage employees to earn higher base wages by learning and performing a wider variety of skills (or jobs) or displaying an array of competencies that can be applied to a variety of organizational requirements. For example, in a manufacturing setting, new tasks might include various assembly activities carried out in a particular production system or a variety of maintenance functions. Within service organizations, employees might acquire new knowledge related to advanced computer systems or accounting procedures. Organizations will grant an increase in pay after each skill or knowledge has been mastered and can be demonstrated according to a predetermined standard.

Competence-based pay systems represent a fundamental change in the attitude of management regarding how work should be organized and how employees should be paid for their work efforts. The most frequently cited benefits of competence-based pay include greater productivity, increased employee learning and commitment to work, improved staffing flexibility to meet production or service demands, and reduced effects of absenteeism and turnover, because managers can assign employees where and when needed. Competence-based pay also encourages employees to acquire training when new or updated skills are needed by an organization.

Unfortunately, competence-based plans bring some long-term difficulties. Some plans limit the amount of compensation employees can earn, regardless of the new skills or competencies they acquire. Thus, after achieving the top wage, employees may be reluctant to continue their educational training. Perhaps the greatest challenge in paying individuals for their skills, knowledge, and competencies is developing appropriate measures. It is difficult to write specific knowledge and skill descriptions for jobs that employees perform and then establish accurate measures of acquired skills or knowledge.

competence-based pay
Pay based on an employee's skill level, variety of skills possessed, or increased job knowledge

Broadbanding

Organizations that adopt a competency-based or skill-based pay system frequently use broadbanding to structure their compensation payments to employees. **Broadbanding** simply collapses many traditional salary grades into a few wide salary bands. Broadbands may have midpoints and quartiles, or they may have extremely wide salary ranges or no ranges at all. Banding encourages lateral skill building while addressing the need to pay employees performing multiple jobs with different skill level requirements. Additionally, broadbands help eliminate the obsession with grades and, instead, encourage employees to move to jobs in which they can develop in their careers and add value to the organization. Paying employees through broadbands enables organizations to consider job responsibilities, individual skills and competencies, and career mobility patterns in assigning employees to bands.[36] In all, such pay tools help more effectively implement a compensation strategy.

broadbanding
Collapses many traditional salary grades into a few wide salary bands

9.6 Government Regulation of Compensation

In addition to data from salary surveys and competence-based assessments, compensation implementation is also subject to state and federal regulations. A majority of states have minimum wage laws or wage boards that fix minimum wage rates on an industry-by-industry basis. When an employee is subject to both the state and federal minimum wage laws, the employee is entitled to the higher of the two minimum wages (see Highlights in HRM 3 for state minimum wage laws). Most states also regulate hours of work and overtime payments.

Wage and Hour Provisions

It's important to know the difference and details between minimum wage, overtime, and compensatory time.

Minimum Wage Rate	- The minimum wage prescribed by federal law has been raised many times, from an original figure of $0.25 per hour to $7.25 per hour on July 24, 2009. This is where the minimum wage stands today (see Highlights in HRM 5 for the federal minimum wage poster that employers are required to display). - Assessed every few years and adjusted for cost-of-living factors (e.g., consumer price index). - Applies to actual earning rate BEFORE any added overtime premiums.
Overtime Wage Rate	- 1.5 times the base rate must be paid for all hours worked over 40 during a given week. - Base wage rate must include incentive payments or bonuses received during that period. - Employees paid on piecework basis must receive premium for overtime work.
Compensatory Time (Comp Time)	- When employees are given time off in return for overtime work. - Granted at 1.5 times the number of hours worked as overtime.

*The FLSA does not require severance pay, sick leave, vacation, or holidays.

Under the FLSA, an employer must pay an employee for whatever work the employer "suffers or permits" the employee to perform, even if the work is done away from the workplace and even if it is not specifically expected or requested. This condition could likely occur when employees work away from headquarters and are unsupervised or when they telecommute on a frequent basis.

Minimum Wage and Pay Compression

pay rate compression
Compression of pay between new and experienced employees caused by the higher starting salaries of new employees; also the differential between hourly workers and their managers

Some argue that increases in the minimum wage may lead to pay compression. **Pay rate compression** means that differences between low- and high-paying jobs decrease. It occurs when less experienced, often junior employees, earn as much or more than experienced employees due to high starting salaries for new employees. It also occurs when the minimum wage requirements push up salaries for lower tier salaries but not for higher tier. Both lower- and higher-paid jobs experience pay compression. For example, if starting hourly wages for preschool teachers is $9.00 and preschool teacher aides is $7.25, a minimum wage increase to $9.00 would bring both to essentially the same starting wage (the U.S. median salary for preschool teachers is $12.23, while the bottom 10 percent make $9.00).[37]

The reasons pay compression occurs are usually more market based than government based. For example, the scarcity of qualified applicants in computers, engineering,

Minimum Wage Laws in the States

Note: Where federal and state law have different minimum wage rates, the higher standard applies.

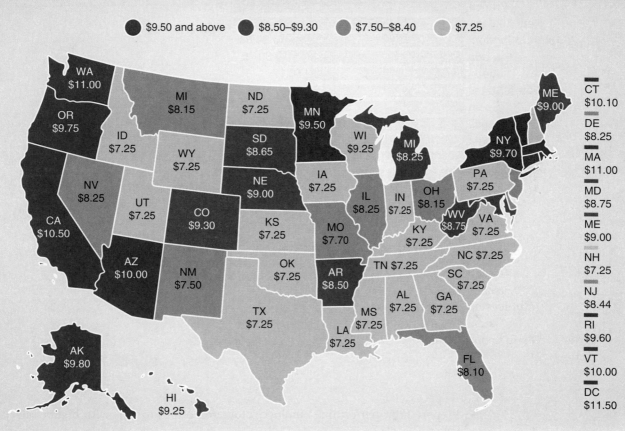

2017 MINIMUM WAGE BY STATE

● $9.50 and above   ● $8.50–$9.30   ● $7.50–$8.40   ○ $7.25

State	Wage
WA	$11.00
OR	$9.75
MI	$8.15
ID	$7.25
ND	$7.25
MN	$9.50
WY	$7.25
SD	$8.65
WI	$9.25
MI	$8.25
ME	$9.00
NV	$8.25
UT	$7.25
NE	$9.00
IA	$7.25
NY	$9.70
PA	$7.25
CA	$10.50
CO	$9.30
KS	$7.25
IL	$8.25
IN	$7.25
OH	$8.15
WV	$8.75
VA	$7.25
AZ	$10.00
NM	$7.50
MO	$7.70
KY	$7.25
NC	$7.25
OK	$7.25
AR	$8.50
TN	$7.25
SC	$7.25
TX	$7.25
MS	$7.25
AL	$7.25
GA	$7.25
LA	$7.25
AK	$9.80
FL	$8.10
HI	$9.25

State	Wage
CT	$10.10
DE	$8.25
MA	$11.00
MD	$8.75
ME	$9.00
NH	$7.25
NJ	$8.44
RI	$9.60
VT	$10.00
DC	$11.50

and other professional and technical fields has forced starting salaries for these occupations to be at or near the salaries paid employees with considerable experience and seniority. Pay compression can also occur when hourly employees, at the top of their pay grades, earn only slightly less than managers at the low end of their pay grades.

Identifying pay rate compression and its causes is far simpler than implementing organizational policies to alleviate its effect. Organizations wishing to minimize the problem may incorporate the following ideas into their pay policies:

- Reward high-performance and merit-worthy employees with large pay increases.
- Design the pay structure to allow a wide spread between hourly and supervisory employees.

Worldwide Minimum Wages

Minimum Wages Around The World

Australia	$16.88
France	$12.09
New Zealand	$11.18
United Kingdom	$9.83
Canada	$9.75
Japan	$8.17
United States	$7.25
Spain	$5.57
Greece	$5.06
South Korea	$4.31
Portugal	$4.19
Hong Kong	$3.87
Argentina	$3.79
Poland	$2.83
Brazil	$1.98
Russia	$0.97
China	$0.80
Mexico	$0.66
Phillipines	$0.61
Afghanistan	$0.57
India	$0.28
Sierra Leone	$0.03

- Prepare high-performing employees for promotions to jobs with higher salary levels.
- Provide equity adjustments for selected employees hardest hit by pay compression.[38]

Since pay rate compression is largely an internal pay equity concern, if not addressed fairly, it can cause low employee morale, leading to issues of reduced employee performance, hard feelings between employees, higher absenteeism and turnover, and even delinquent behavior such as employee theft.

Child Labor Provisions

Another concern with the minimum wage is that the "floor" it imposes makes it more difficult for high school students and young adults to find jobs. Many employers who might otherwise be willing to hire these individuals are unwilling to pay them the same rate as adults because of their lack of experience.

Age 16 is the basic minimum age required for employment. At age 16 youth can be employed for unlimited hours in any occupation that is not declared hazardous by the

The Federal Wage Poster

EMPLOYEE RIGHTS
UNDER THE FAIR LABOR STANDARDS ACT
THE UNITED STATES DEPARTMENT OF LABOR WAGE AND HOUR DIVISION

FEDERAL MINIMUM WAGE

$5.85 PER. HOUR	$6.55 PER HOUR	$7.25 PER HOUR
BEGINNING JULY 24, 2007	BEGINNING JULY 24, 2008	BEGINNING JULY 24, 2009

OVERTIME PAY
At least $1\frac{1}{2}$ times your regular rate of pay for all hours worked over 40 in a workweek.

YOUTH EMPLOYMENT
An employee must be at least **16** years old to work in most non-farm jobs and at least **18** to work in non-farm jobs declared hazardous by the Secretary of Labor.

Youths **14** and **15** years old may work outside school hours in various non-manufacturing, non-mining, non-hazardous jobs under the following conditions:

No more than
- **3** hours on a school day or **18** hours in a school week;
- **8** hours on a non-school day or **40** hours in a non-school week.

Also, work may not begin before **7 a.m.** or end after **7 p.m.**, except from June 1 through Labor Day, when evening hours are extended to **9 p.m.** Different rules apply in agricultural employment. For more information, visit the YouthRules! Web site at **www.youthrules.dol.gov**.

TIP CREDIT
Employers of "tipped employees" must pay a cash wage of at least $2.13 per hour if they claim a tip credit against their minimum wage obligation. If an employee's tips combined with the employer's cash wage of at least $2.13 per hour do not equal the minimum hourly wage, the employer must make up the difference. Certain other conditions must also be met.

ENFORCEMENT
The Department of Labor may recover back wages either administratively or through court action, for the employees that have been underpaid in violation of the law. Violations may result in civil or criminal action.

Civil money penalties of up to $11,000 per violation may be assessed against employers who violate the youth employment provisions of the law and up to $1,100 per violation against employers who willfully or repeatedly violate the minimum wage or overtime pay provisions. This law prohibits discriminating against or discharging workers who file a complaint or participate in any proceedings under the Act.

ADDITIONAL INFORMATION
- Certain occupations and establishments are exempt from the minimum wage and/or overtime pay provisions.
- Special provisions apply to workers in American Samoa and the Commonwealth of the Northern Mariana Islands.
- Some state laws provide greater employee protections; employers must comply with both.
- The law requires employers to display this poster where employees can readily see it.
- Employees under 20 years of age may be paid $4.25 per hour during their first 90 consecutive calendar days of employment with an employer.
- Certain full-time students, student learners, apprentices, and workers with disabilities may be paid less than the minimum wage under special certificates issued by the Department of Labor.

For additional information:

1-866-4-USWAGE
(1-866-487-9243)   TTY: 1-877-889-5627

U.S. Wage and Hour Division

WWW.WAGEHOUR.DOL.GOV

U.S. Department of Labor | Employment Standards Administration | Wage and Hour Division

WHD Publication 1088 (Revised June 2007)

| Figure 9.10 | Race and Gender Pay Inequality | | |

Race and Ethnicity	Male Weekly Income	Female Weekly Income	Women's Earnings as % of Male Earnings
All Races	854	691	81.00%
White Alone, not Hispanic	879	710	81%
Black or African American only	665	599	90%
Asian only	1055	770	73%
Hispanic or Latino (any race)	592	521	88%

Source: Bureau of Labor Statistics, Current Population Survey, "Table 37: Median Weekly Earnings of Full-time Wage and Salary Workers by Selected Characteristics, 2012," Annual Averages (2013). http://www.census.gov/hhes/www/cpstables/032010/perinc/new05_001.htm

U.S. secretary of labor. For example, a 16-year-old could not work as a coal miner, but she could work at the local snow-cone shack. Children ages 14 and 15 can also be hired in specified jobs outside of school hours for limited periods of time each day and each week. Employees under 20 years old can be paid $4.25 per hour during their first 90 calendar days with an employer. Such pay is considered training pay. Finally, employers of "tipped employees" must pay at least $2.13 per hour if they claim a tip credit against their minimum wage obligations. If an employee's tips combined with the employer's pay of at least $2.13 do not equal the minimum hourly wage, the employer must make up the difference.[39]

Pay Equity Provisions

Laws exist to protect employees against pay discrimination. Yet, pay discrimination is still found in many companies today. For example, in 2017 Wells Fargo paid $35.5 million as part of a settlement of a putative class-action lawsuit that alleged discrimination against African American advisors. A group of African American brokers and trainees alleged that they had been excluded from certain business opportunities and higher-up teams because of race. In addition to the monetary settlement, Wells Fargo agreed to set up resources to focus on recruiting more diverse trainees and hire from a more diverse applicant pool, along with other changes to their management training.[40] Figure 9.10 further examines pay inequality based on race and gender.

LO 4

What tools would you use to determine if your company's pay was appropriate for the market?

9.7 Compensation Assessment

Getting your compensation system up and running is not the end of your task as a manager. Once it has been implemented, assessing the effectiveness of your compensation system is vitally important to linking compensation with strategy. With the right measures, you can (1) help the company detect potential compensation problems, (2) make compensation decisions more transparent, and (3) improve the alignment of compensation decisions with organizational objectives. The **compensation scorecard** collects and displays the results for all the measures that a company uses to monitor and compare compensation among internal departments or units. While different companies will use different measures of compensation, the scorecard creates a comparative tool within the organization that can reinforce desired outcomes that are unique to the company's strategy.

Managers in companies without compensation scorecards often struggle to know if the promotions, raises, bonuses, and pay adjustments they make are in line with the rest of the organization and its strategy. A scorecard improves transparency of how people are rewarded and makes managers responsible for how they spend company money. Most compensation scorecards are completed once a year by HR.

For example, Figure 9.11 represents an example of a compensation scorecard. Each functional department in the company reports the average performance rating received by its employees on a scale of 1 (low) to 5 (high). This measure helps to show managers where they are in terms of evaluating their employees. Average merit increases are also gathered. The company had budgeted enough money for a 4 percent increase, on average. If the average merit increase you give your employees is above this 4 percent level, then the additional money needed to compensate employees in your function will need to be drawn from elsewhere in the company. Grade inflation is the growth or decline of the average salary grade distribution. It shows whether or not you vary in pay raises on a year-to-year basis. Compa ratio is a measure of the appropriateness of the salaries given by a function. In essence it is an internal benchmark of salaries. Functions with a compa ratio below 100 percent are considered to be paying their employees below the company norm. Finally, a measure of the percent of annual incentives in relation to organizational targets helps to assess whether a function is meeting its targets and paying its employees in accordance with those objectives.[41]

compensation scorecard

Displays the results for all the measures that a company uses to monitor and compare compensation among internal departments or units

Figure 9.11	Sample Compensation Scorecard				
Function	Average Performance Rating (1–5)	Average Merit Increase (4% Budget)	Grade Inflation	Compa Ratio	Annual Incentive (% of Target)
Marketing	3.4	4.3%	–3%	101%	100%
R&D	3.2	4.4%	0%	98%	102%
Production	4.0	4.2%	12%	96%	105%
Sales	4.1	3.4%	8%	99%	100%
Customer Service	3.6	3.6%	17%	88%	110%

* **Grade inflation** is determined by calculating the percentage change in the number of employees in each grade in comparison to the year before.
** **Compa ratio** is actual salary divided by the midpoint of the salary range. It is a gauge of the appropriateness of the organization's salary ranges.
*** **The direct correlation** between profit growth over a three-year period relative to LTI expense.

Source: Reprinted by permission of The Segal Group, Inc., parent of The Segal Company and its Sibson Consulting Division. © 2011. All rights reserved.

Summary

LO ① Establishing strategic compensation programs requires an assessment of organizational objectives in relation to specific employment goals—employee retention for continued growth, compensation distribution to ensure employees feel treated fairly, communication of compensation methods to increase employee understanding of organizational objectives, and adherence to a budget for cost efficiencies, for instance. Compensation must reward employees for past efforts (pay for performance) while motivating employees' future performances. Internal and external equity of the pay program affects employees' concepts of fairness. Organizations must balance each of these concerns while still remaining competitive. The ability to attract and retain qualified employees while controlling labor costs is a major factor in allowing organizations to remain viable in the domestic or international markets.

LO ② The basis on which compensation payments are determined and the way they are administered can significantly affect employee productivity and the achievement of organizational goals. Internal influences include the employer's compensation policy, worth of the job, performance of the employee, and employer's ability to pay. External factors influencing pay rates include labor market conditions, area pay rates, cost of living, outcomes of collective bargaining, and legal requirements.

LO ③ Wage surveys determine the external equity of jobs. Data obtained from surveys will facilitate establishing the organization's wage policy while ensuring that the employer does not pay more, or less, than needed for jobs in the relevant labor market. The wage structure will be determined based on wage surveys, but will vary based on job function and individual skill differences. Companies use wage curves, pay grades, and rate ranges to group jobs together and to allow for individual employee differences within each type of job. These wage structures will also depend upon the legal requirements around wage.

LO ④ The effectiveness of a compensation system can be assessed by using a compensation scorecard. The scorecard collects and displays where all departments and functions sit in terms of their relative compensation. It increases the transparency of compensation systems, the accountability of managers, and helps companies align their compensation decisions with organizational objectives.

Key Terms

broadbanding

compensation scorecard

competence-based pay

consumer price index (CPI)

escalator clauses

exempt employees

Hay profile method

hourly work

job classification system

job evaluation

job ranking system

nonexempt employees

pay equity

pay grades

pay rate compression

pay-for-performance standard

piecework

point system

real wages

red circle rates

wage and salary survey

wage curve

work valuation

HRM **Experience**

Why This Salary?

A question frequently asked is, "Why is that person paid more than I am when we both perform the same job?" The answer to this question lies in understanding the components of the pay mix as discussed in this chapter. While we may disapprove of the idea that someone is paid more or less than we are for similar work; nevertheless, factors both internal and external to the organization influence the final salary paid to a job or a specific person. Often we have little control over the pay mix factors. However, at other times, we can improve our wage by gaining additional job experience or seniority or by obtaining increases in job knowledge or skills. This project is designed to give you experience in understanding why jobs are paid different salaries.

Assignment

Shown here are the annual median salaries paid in some of the fastest growing occupations in America based on expected growth rates from now until 2024. Study the salaries paid to these workers and then answer the questions that follow as to why the differences in salaries exist. Relate these reasons to the internal and external factors of the pay mix that are discussed in the text.

Occupation	Median Annual Salary
Wind turbine service technician	$51,050
Physical therapist	$84,020
Statistician	$80,110
Ambulance driver	$23,740
Genetic counselors	$72,090
Interpreter and translator	$44,190
Optometrist	$103,900

1. What factors may account for the wide differences among salaries for different occupations?
2. What factors may account for the differences among salaries for the identical occupation in the same organization?
3. What factors may account for the differences among salaries for the identical occupation in different organizations?

You may work individually or in teams to complete this skill-building exercise. The *Occupational Outlook Handbook* published by the U.S. Bureau of Labor Statistics can be found at http://www.bls.gov.

Discussion Questions

LO 1 Tomax Corporation has 400 employees and wishes to develop a compensation policy to correspond to its dynamic business strategy. The company wishes to employ a high-quality workforce capable of responding to a competitive business environment. Suggest different compensation objectives to match Tomax's business goals.

LO 2 Since employees may differ in terms of their job performance, would it not be more feasible to determine the wage rate for each employee on the basis of his or her relative worth to the organization? Explain.

LO 3 Describe the basic steps in conducting a wage and salary survey. What are some factors to consider? One of the objections to granting wage increases on a percentage basis is that the lowest-paid employees, who are having the most trouble making ends meet, get the smallest increase, while the highest-paid employees get the largest increase. Is this objection a valid one? Explain.

LO 4 What is a compensation scorecard and how does it help align a company's strategy with its compensation system?

CASE STUDY Pay Decisions at Performance Sports

Katie Perkins's career objective while attending Rockford State College was to obtain a degree in small business management and to start her own business after graduation. Her ultimate desire was to combine her love of sports and a strong interest in marketing to start a mail-order golf equipment business aimed specifically at beginning golfers.

After extensive development of a strategic business plan and a loan in the amount of $75,000 from the Small Business Administration, Performance Sports was begun. Based on a marketing plan that stressed fast delivery, error-free customer service, and large discount pricing, Performance Sports grew rapidly. At present the company employs 16 people: 8 customer service representatives earning between $11.25 and $13.50 per hour; 4 shipping and receiving associates paid between $8.50 and $9.50 per hour; 2 clerical employees each earning $8.25 per hour; an assistant manager earning $15.25 per hour; and a general manager with a wage of $16.75 per hour. Both the manager and assistant manager are former customer service representatives.

Perkins intends to create a new managerial position, purchasing agent, to handle the complex duties of purchasing golf equipment from the company's numerous equipment manufacturers. Also, the mail-order catalog will be expanded to handle a complete line of tennis equipment. Since the position of purchasing agent is new, Perkins is not sure how much to pay this person. She wants to employ an individual with 5 to 8 years of experience in sports equipment purchasing.

While attending an equipment manufacturers' convention in Las Vegas, Nevada, Perkins learns that a competitor, East Valley Sports, pays its customer service representatives on a pay-for-performance basis. Intrigued by this compensation philosophy, Perkins asks her assistant manager, George Balkin, to research the pros and cons of this payment strategy. This request has become a priority because only last week two customer service representatives expressed dissatisfaction with their hourly wage. Both complained that they felt underpaid relative to the large amount of sales revenue each generates for the company.

Questions

1. What factors should Perkins and Balkin consider when setting the wage for the purchasing agent position? What resources are available for them to consult when establishing this wage?

2. Suggest advantages and disadvantages of a pay-for-performance policy for Performance Sports.

3. Suggest a new payment plan for the customer service representatives.

CASE STUDY An In-N-Out Pay Strategy: Costa Vida's Decision to Boost Pay

For many businesses in today's belt-tightening economy, decisions on pay need to be strategic to ensure that employees are treated fairly and to ensure that businesses can remain viable. This requires knowing what your competitors pay their employees and knowing your own salary budget. But knowing what your competitors are paying can be both valuable and painful.

As a primary stakeholder and former CEO of Costa Vida, a fast-growing chain of fresh Mexican restaurants, Nathan Gardner knew he was competing against some restaurant chains with competitive compensation systems. Costa Vida is a fresh Mexican grill featuring Baja-inspired foods that are made from scratch daily. Following a trip to Cabo San Lucas on the Baja Coast in Mexico, Costa Vida founders JD and Sarah Gardner were inspired with a vision: Bring the freshly made local cuisine with the vibrant lifestyle to the United States. They started their first restaurant in 2001, and after just 13 years, Costa Vida has more than 50 franchises in Arizona, California, Colorado, Florida, Idaho, Illinois, Nevada, New Mexico, Missouri, Oklahoma, Oregon, Texas, Washington, Wyoming, and Utah, and as of 2017, 3 locations in Canada.

One of the main challenges Costa Vida faces is the fierce competition for customers as well as employees. "You'd be surprised how much of a difference having good employees in all areas of the business makes," commented Nathan.

"For the fast-casual food industry," remarked Nathan, "you are dependent upon your people. If you don't treat your people well, they won't treat your customers well. If your customers aren't treated well, you have no business." For months, Nathan agonized over how he could develop a competitive compensation plan that matched the objectives of the organization, but that fell in line with the tight budget of each individually owned franchise unit. He stated, "We, of course, leave the final compensation decision to the franchise owner, but we do all we can to educate and persuade our franchisees to be competitive and fair. In the long run, this is how they can maintain a superior level of customer satisfaction."

Nathan pointed out that a strong benchmark for them has been In-N-Out Burger. In-N-Out started in California and is known for its great compensation package. They start out all their new "associates" (aka employees) at a minimum of $10 an hour. They also offer flexible schedules to accommodate school and other activities, paid vacation, free meals, and a 401k retirement plan. For full-time associates they provide medical, dental, vision, life, and travel insurance coverage. Their reason for paying so high is based on a strategy that lower turnover and more committed workers will lead to better service. "What In-N-Out does for their employees is truly amazing," commented Nathan. "We often see employees moving from one fast-food chain to another, but we rarely see employees coming from In-N-Out."

Nathan had a tough challenge ahead in trying to convince his franchise owners and managers to think more strategically about their pay systems. He needed to help them realize that paying wages and offering other compensation benefits that were better than their competitors may mean lower profit margins up front, but that the returns would be greater in the long run. He also needed to offer evidence to show that this was not just about being fair, but it was about being strategic. The restaurant business is a fast and fierce industry and companies come and go all the time. What was it going to take for Costa Vida to stay for the long haul?

Questions

1. Why is it important for pay to be externally fair?
2. Why is it important for pay to be internally fair?
3. What should Costa Vida's compensation strategy look like? Hint: What are the company objectives and how can employee pay help to achieve those objectives?
4. What should the pay structure look like? What pay mix would you recommend?
5. How should Nathan communicate a new compensation strategy to his franchisee owners and managers?
6. What effect will paying higher wages have on Costa Vida in the short term? What effect will it have in the long term? Explain.

Notes and References

1. S. Morris, S. Alvarez, J. Barney, and J. Molloy, "Firm-Specific Human Capital Investments as a Signal of General Value: Revisiting Assumptions about Human Capital and How it is Managed," *Strategic Management Journal* (press, 2017).
2. Jennifer M. George and Gareth R. Jones, *Understanding Organizational Behavior*, 6th ed. (Boston, MA: Prentice Hall, 2012), Chapter 3; Debra L. Nelson and James Campbell Quick, *Organizational Behavior: Science, the Real World, and You*, 8th ed. (Mason, OH: South-Western, Cengage Learning, 2013), Chapter 16.
3. For a frequently referenced book on strategic compensation planning, see Edward E. Lawler III, *Strategic Pay: Aligning Organizational Strategies and Pay Systems* (San Francisco: Jossey-Bass, 1990). See also Susan E. Jackson and Randall S. Schuler, *Managing Human Resources: Through Strategic Partnerships*, 9th ed. (Mason, OH: South-Western, 2006), Chapter 9.
4. Personal interview with Product Development Manager at Google.
5. Daniel Rothberg,. "With No Bosses, How Do Zappos Employees Get Raises?" *Las Vegas Sun*, (July 15, 2015), https://lasvegassun.com/news/2015/jul/15/no-bosses-how-do-zappos-employees-get-raises/; Zappos, "Why Us? Our Core Values." (March 2017), http://jobs.jobvite.com/zappos/p/why#values.

6. Jonathon Trevor, *Can Pay Be Strategic: A Critical Exploration of Strategic Pay in Practice* (London, England: Palgrave Macmillan, 2011).

7. Hai-Ming Chen and Yi-Hua Hsien, "Key Trends in the Total Reward System of the 21st Century," *Compensation and Benefits Review* 38, no. 6 (November–December 2006): 64.

8. Jay Yarow, "This is the Internal Grading System Google Uses for Its Employees—And You Should Use It Too," *Business Insider* (January 6, 2014).

9. Nick Ushkoff, "Can OKRs Be Tied to Compensation?" *Atiim* (March 27, 2017).

10. Stephen Miller, "Study: Pay for Performance Pays Off," *Society for Human Resource Management* (September 14, 2011), https://www.shrm.org/resourcesandtools/hr-topics/compensation/pages/paysoff.aspx

11. Health Care Incentives Improvement Institute (HCI3), "Pay-for-Performance: Will the Latest Payment Trend Improve?" http://www.hci3.org/thought-leadership/why-incentives-matter/pay-performance.

12. For one of the classic articles on equity theory, see J. Stacey Adams, "Integrity in Social Exchange," in L. Berkowitz (ed.), *Advances in Experimental Social Psychology* (New York: Academic Press, 1965), 276–299.

13. Victor H. Vroom, *Work and Motivation* (San Francisco: Jossey-Bass, 1994). This landmark book, originally published in 1964, integrates the work of hundreds of researchers seeking to explain choice of work, job satisfaction, and job performance.

14. Joseph E. Champoux, *Organizational Behavior: Integrating Individuals, Groups, and Organizations*, 5th ed. (New York: Routledge, 2017), Chapter 8.

15. Ariane Hegewisch, Claudia Williams, and Robert Drago, "Pay Secrecy and Wage Discrimination Fact Sheet," *Institute for Women's Policy Research*, ((January 2014).

16. Julie Cook Ramirez, "The End of Secrecy?" *Human Resource Executive Order* (February 4, 2016). http://www.hreonline.com/HRE/view/story.jhtml?id=534359883.

17. Detailed discussion of exempt and nonexempt rules under the Fair Labor Standards Act can be found at http://www.dol.gov.

18. U.S. Department of Labor, "Exemption for Executive, Administrative, Professional, Computer & Outside Sales Employees Under the Fair Labor Standards Act (FLSA)," https://www.dol.gov/whd/overtime/fs17a_overview.pdf.

19. David Lepak and Scott Snell, "The Human Resource Architecture: Toward a Theory of Human Capital Allocation and Development," *Academy of Management Review* 24, no. 1 (1999): 31–48.

20. Konrad Reiher, "Compensation and Benefits: Job Evaluation," *Handbook of Human Resources Management*, Matthias Zeuch (ed.) (2015): 1–14. See also Robert L. Heneman, Peter V. LeBlanc, and Tim L. Reynolds, "Using Work Valuation to Identify and Protect the Talent Pool," *WorldatWork* 11,

no. 2 (Third Quarter 2002): 31–41; James R. Bowers, "Valuing Work: An Integrated Approach," *WorldatWork* 12, no. 2 (Second Quarter 2003): 28–39.

21. Federal Reserve Bank of New York, "Spring 2014 Small Business Credit Survey" (2014), https://www.newyorkfed.org/smallbusiness/Spring2014/index.html.

22. Tracy Lien, "Snap's IPO Could Make Some Employees Millionaires While Others Are Left Out," *LA Times* (February 28, 2017).

23. Jerry Jasinowski, "Reshoring Means More Jobs," *Huffington Post* (October 25, 2013), http://www.huffingtonpost.com/jerry-jasinowski/reshoring_b_4162947.html. See also Jennifer Goforth Gregory, 8 Customized Benefits to Keep Employees Happy," *American Express Open Forum* (October 22, 2012), https://www.americanexpress.com/us/small-business/openforum/articles/8-customized-benefits-to-keep-employees-happy/.

24. For information on the federal job classification system, go to http//www.opm.gov.

25. Emin Kahya, "Revising the Metal Industry Job Evaluation System for Blue-Collar Jobs," *Compensation and Benefits Review* 38, no. 6 (November–December 2006): 49.

26. "Performing Job Evaluations," *Society for Human Resource Management* (October 27, 2016).

27. Lance A. Berger and Dorothy R. Berger, *The Compensation Handbook: A State-of-the-Art Guide to Compensation Strategy and Design*, 5th ed. (New York: McGraw-Hill, 2015). See also Robert L. Heneman, Peter V. LeBlanc, and Howard Risher, "Work Valuation Addresses Shortcomings of Both Job Evaluation and Market Pricing," *Compensation and Benefits Review* 35, no. 1 (January–February 2003): 7–11.

28. Pawel Fiedor, "Job Evaluation for Knowledge-Based Organizations," *European Conference on Knowledge* (September 2013): 860–867.

29. "The True Value of Salary Surveys," *Human Resource Performance Solutions* (March 2014), http://www.hrperformancesolutions.net/files/hrperf/1033/file/whitepapers/03.2014%20WhitepaperTrueValueofSalarySurveys.pdf.

30. The Bureau of Labor, http://www.bls.gov.

31. Nona Tobin, "Can Technology Ease the Pain of Salary Surveys?" *Public Personnel Management* 31, no. 1 (Spring 2002): 65–76.

32. John H. Davis, *Statistics for Compensation: A Practical Guide to Compensation Analysis* (Hoboken, NJ: Wiley, 2011). See also Curt Finch, "How to Create an Effective Pay Structure," *Employee Benefit Plan Review* 61, no. 10 (April 2007): 26.

33. Organizations may have a compensation program that pays a differential based on geographic location. See Thomas J. Atchison, "Branch Office Salary Structure," *Compensation and Benefits Review* 39, no. 3 (June 2007): 35; James R. Guzak, Barbara Crandall, and Hoda Alavinejad. "Compensation and Culture: A Configurational Fit Between Systems

and Culture Types," *Southwest Academy of Management Proceedings* (2017): 88–97, http://www.swamfbd.org/uploads/SWAM_Proceedings_2017.pdf#page=88.

34. Mirta Diaz-Fernandez, Alvaro Lopez-Cabrales, and Ramon Valle-Cabrera, "What Companies Pay For: The Strategic Role of Employee Competencies," *European Journal of International Management* 3, no. 4 (2009): 439–456.

35. PayScale, "The Advantages of Broadbanding" (April 28, 2011), http://www.payscale.com/compensation-today/2011/04/advantages-of-broadbanding.

36. Payscale.com (April 4, 2017), http://www.payscale.com/research/US/Job=Preschool_Teacher%2C_(but_not_Special_Education)/Hourly_Rate.

37. Stephen Bruce, "The 9 Steps to Solving Pay Compression," *HR Daily Advisor* (January 9, 2012), http://hrdailyadvisor.blr.com/2012/01/09/the-9-steps-to-solving-pay-compression/.

38. "Child Labor Bulletin 101 WH-1330," United States Department of Labor. Wage and Hour Division (WHD) (April 4, 2017).

39. Mason Braswell, "Wells Fargo Advisors to Pay $35.5 Million to Settle Race Discrimination Suit." *Advisor Hub* (January 3, 2017), https://advisorhub.com/wells-fargo-advisors-pay-35-5-million-settle-race-discrimination-suit/.

40. Petr Snapka and Andrea Copikova, "Balanced Scorecard and Compensation," *International Conference on Business and Economics Research* 16 (2011), https://images.template.net/wp-content/uploads/2016/06/30090322/Cost-Based-Performance-Scorecard.pdf.

Fuse/Getty Images

CHAPTER **10**

Pay-for-Performance: Incentive Rewards

Learning Outcomes

After studying this chapter, you should be able to

LO 1 Implement a strategic incentive program.

LO 2 Detect when and what types of individual incentives are appropriate.

LO 3 Differentiate how gains may be shared with employees under different group incentive plans like the Scanlon plan and improshare gainsharing systems.

LO 4 Differentiate between profit sharing plans and explain advantages and disadvantages of these programs as an alternative to individual and group incentive systems.

LO 5 Understand how to apply different incentive systems designed for professionals and executives.

Studies show that pay-for-performance plans can increase job satisfaction, commitment to the company, and trust in management—if handled correctly.[1] The process of (1) choosing the right incentive plans based on organizational objectives, (2) setting up performance measures, and (3) administering those incentive plans may seem a bit daunting—especially since so much can go wrong.

In this chapter, we will discuss incentive plans in terms of the objectives they hope to achieve and the various factors that may affect their success. Because many organizations have implemented broad-based incentive programs to differentiate employees and their performance, for discussion purposes we have grouped incentive plans into three broad categories: individual incentive plans, group incentive plans, and enterprise incentive plans, as shown in Figure 10.1.[2] At the end of the chapter, we also discuss some special incentive plans for professional employees and executives.

10.1 Strategic Reasons for Incentive Plans

A major element of strategic compensation management is the use of incentive plans, also called **variable pay** programs. Variable pay programs consist of bonuses, incentives, or recognition for good work. They allow organizations to reward employees for continued contributions. More than 80 percent of companies globally are offering variable pay programs. In fact, 2017 saw a bump in variable pay as many employers were using it to compensate for low increases in fixed pay.[3] Variable pay is more flexible than fixed pay (salaries, hourly wages), as variable pay is attached to fixed costs that allow flexibility to increase, decrease, or maintain future payments to employees as business conditions warrant.[4] Most HR managers see variable pay as strategic because it allows the organization to align its employees' interests and outcomes with those of the organization.

However, an additional strategic component that HR managers seem to forget is that variable pay can be used to exercise fairness and equity within the organization. As

variable pay
Tying pay to some measure of individual, group, or organizational performance

Figure 10.1	Types of Incentive Plans	
Individual	**Group**	**Enterprise**
Piecework	Team compensation	Profit sharing
Standard hour plan	Scanlon plan	Stock options
Bonuses	Improshare	Employee stock ownership plans (ESOPs)
Merit pay		
Lump sum merit pay		
Incentive awards		
Sales incentives		
Professional employee incentive plans		
Executive incentive plans		

a result, variable pay not only motivates employees to do what the organization wants them to do, it also ensures that employees feel the organization is fair and responsive to their individual contributions.

For example, it has been said that "no good deed goes unpunished." For employees who make valuable contributions, this is sometimes not far from the truth. Professors James Oldroyd and Shad Morris pointed out that those with "high potential" are more likely to get burned out and leave their organization than their more average performing peers. The reason? Feelings of pay inequity. Many high-performing employees feel that because of their high performance they are asked to take on additional work and are bombarded with overwhelming amounts of request for help without additional pay. As a result, challenges meant to be energizing can feel like punishment for success if they are not attached to additional rewards.[5]

One of the difficulties faced by companies during difficult times is that they ask everyone to tighten their belts, yet high performers know their market worth and like to be rewarded for it. Furthermore, even employees who are not high performers work harder (and seem happier) when they work for a company that rewards people who deserve it.[6]

Incentive rewards are based entirely upon a pay-for-performance philosophy (see Chapter 9). Incentive pay plans establish a performance "threshold" (a baseline performance level) that an employee or group of employees must achieve to qualify for incentive payments (see Figure 10.2).

Incentive plans create an operating environment that champions a philosophy of shared commitment through the belief that every individual contributes to organizational performance and success.

10.1a Incentive Plans as Links to Organizational Objectives

Contemporary arguments for incentive plans focus on linking compensation rewards, both individual and group, to organizational goals. Specific company goals or objectives might be to lower labor costs, improve customer satisfaction, expand product markets, or maintain high levels of productivity and quality. By meshing compensation and organizational objectives, managers believe that employees will assume "ownership" of their jobs, thereby improving their effort and overall job performance. Incentive pay is highly valued as a compensation strategy to attract and retain top-performing employees.[7] Figure 10.3 summarizes the major advantages of incentive pay programs as noted by researchers and HR professionals.

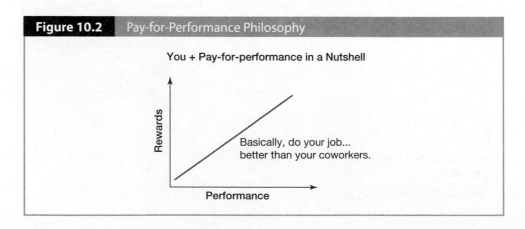

Figure 10.2   Pay-for-Performance Philosophy

Figure 10.3	Advantages of Incentive Pay Programs

- Incentives focus employee efforts on specific performance targets. They provide real motivation that produces important employee and organizational gains.
- Incentive payouts are variable costs linked to the achievement of results. Base salaries are fixed costs largely unrelated to output.
- Incentive compensation is directly related to operating performance. If performance objectives (quantity and/or quality) are met, incentives are paid. If objectives are not achieved, incentives are withheld.
- Incentives foster teamwork and unit cohesiveness when payments to individuals are based on team results.
- Incentives are a way to distribute success among those responsible for producing that success.
- Incentives are a way to increase equity and justice in an organization.
- Incentives are a means to reward or attract top performers when salary budgets are low.

Do incentive plans work? The answer is both yes and no. Various studies, along with reports from individual organizations, show a measurable relationship between incentive plans and improved organizational performance.[8] However, the degree of success obtained depends on several factors including (1) identifying important organizational metrics by which to measure employee performance, and (2) a customized incentive plan which effectively measures employee output and rewards exceptional employee performance.[9] For example, President Trump has supported policies that "financially reward employees who do a good job…" within the government sector. The Department of Defense now requires better linking of performance to rewards such as bonuses and promotions. As a result, the Department of Defense is now more interested in aligning an individual's work quality to organizational objectives.[10]

Unfortunately, studies also show that variable pay plans may not achieve their proposed objectives or lead to organizational improvements. First, incentive plans sometimes fail to satisfy employee expectations for pay gains. Second, management may have failed to give adequate attention to the design and implementation of the plan, leaving employees confused about how incentive payments are calculated. Third, employees may have little ability to affect performance standards. Furthermore, the success of an incentive plan will depend on the environment that exists within an organization. A plan is more likely to work in an organization where morale is high, employees believe they are being treated fairly, and there is harmony between employees and management.[11]

10.1b Requirements for a Successful Incentive Plan

For an incentive plan to succeed, employees must believe in it. Employees must be able to see a clear connection between the incentive payments they receive and their job performance. This connection is more visible if there are objective quality or quantity standards by which they can judge their performance. Management should guard against incentive payments being seen as an *entitlement*. Instead, these payments should be viewed as a reward that must be earned through effort. This perception can be strengthened if the incentive money is distributed to employees in a separate check. Compensation specialist Joanne Sammer notes the following as characteristics of a successful incentive plan[12]:

- Identify important organizational metrics that encourage employee behavior.
- Involve employees. Incentive programs should seem fair to employees.
- Find the right incentive payout. Payout formulas should be simple and understandable.
- Establish a clear link between performance and payout.

10.2 Setting Performance Measures

As we discussed in Chapter 7 on "Appraising and Managing Performance," measuring and differentiating performance among employees is one of the most difficult tasks you will face as a manager. This is especially the case when your assessments are used to distribute rewards.[13] You will need to be able to distinguish between individual contributions and those made by a group. You will need to be able to avoid biases based on who you like and dislike, different personalities, and political agendas. At the group level, you will need to distinguish how much one group contributed over another group, even if the work they do is highly interdependent.[14] In sum, measuring individual, group, and enterprise-level contributions can be extremely complex. Measuring in a way that makes employees feel they are being treated unfairly can lead to serious problems. See Figure 10.4 for details on the do's and don'ts of measuring performance for incentives.

If done correctly, however, measurement can communicate the importance of established organizational goals. For example, if the organization desires to be a

Figure 10.4	Measurement DOs and DON'Ts		
	Individual Pay	**Group Pay**	**Enterprise Pay**
Do	• measure things that are quantitative and simple • measure work that is independent of others' contribution • measure in a way that shows a relationship between work and performance	• measure when work is group interdependent • measure in a way that shows a relationship between work and performance	• measure when work is organizationally interdependent • measure results that employees can control • measure in a way that shows a relationship between work and performance
Don't	• measure based on who you like and dislike • measure based on personalities • measure based on political preferences • measure without considering contributions of peers	• measure without considering contributions of other teams • measure unless there is a mechanism for teams to discipline their "slackers"	• measure unless employees can see how their work actually contributes to the enterprise • measure without considering effects of the environment (e.g., economic downturns)

Setting Performance Measures—The Keys

Establishing meaningful performance measures is one of the important and difficult challenges facing management today. Before managers or supervisors develop and implement organizational measures, they should consider the following guidelines:

- *Performance measures—at all organizational levels—must be consistent with the strategic goals of the organization.* Avoid nonrelevant measures or metrics that are not closely linked to the business or what employees do in their work.

- *Define the intent of performance measures and champion the cause relentlessly.* Demonstrate that performance measures are, in fact, good business management and hold managers and employees accountable for their success.

- *Involve employees.* A critical step in any measurement program is the development of an employee involvement strategy outlining the nature of employee participation, implementation, and ongoing management of the performance management program. Segment the workforce based on the nature of the work and the potential for impact. Consider which metrics require customization. Acceptance of a performance measurement program is heightened when employees "buy into" the process.

- *Consider the organization's culture and workforce demographics when designing performance measures.* For example, organizations with a more traditional hierarchical structure may need more time to introduce performance metrics compared to flatter organizations, which are more fluid and less steeped in control-and-command characteristics.

- *Widely communicate the importance of performance measures.* Performance messages are the principles and guidelines that communicate to employees what the required performance levels are and why the organization needs to achieve those levels of success.

leader in quality, then performance indexes may focus on customer satisfaction, timeliness, or being error free. If being a low-priced producer is the goal, then emphasis should be on cost reduction or increased productivity with lower acceptable levels of quality. While a variety of performance options are available, most focus on quality, cost control, or productivity. Highlights in HRM 1 provides five proven guidelines on how to establish and maintain an effective performance measurement program.

10.3 Administering Incentive Plans

While incentive plans based on productivity can reduce direct labor costs, to achieve their full benefit they must be carefully thought out, implemented, and maintained. A cardinal rule is that thorough planning must be combined with a "proceed with caution" approach. Three of the more important points are:

1. Allowing incentive payments to become pay guarantees defeats the motivational intent of the incentive. Poor performance must go unrewarded.

2. Annual salary budgets must be large enough to reward and reinforce exceptional performance.

3. The overhead costs associated with plan implementation and administration must be determined.

Small Business Application

Administering Incentive Plans for Small Businesses

For small businesses, incentive plans can be both a blessing and a curse. They provide a great way to align the interests of the employees directly with those of the owner, but managing them can also be time consuming and lead to feelings of inequity.

While the potential pitfalls of incentive systems in smalls businesses are great, the potential benefits are worth the risk. The key is to understand these risks and then to manage them. Below are some things small businesses can do to help administer incentive plans:

1. Keep incentive plans simple. The easier it is for employees to know how they can be rewarded, the more likely they will buy into the incentive system.

2. Treat the plan as a work in process. Small business owners need to be open with their employees by communicating that they are trying to reward employees in a fair and equitable manner.

3. Set a minimum requirement around what constitutes average performance. Employees need to know that it is only after the employee exceeds general expectations that the additional rewards begin to kick in.

4. Decide when the rewards will be provided to the employee. The closer you can tie incentives to performance, the more likely you will be able to sustain that behavior.

5. Separate rewards from employees' regular pay. When employees can see that they are actually being given something extra based on their performance, they make a clearer distinction between showing up for work and actually contributing. It is also important to make sure that these bonuses are known by others in the organization, as doing so acts as a reward in and of itself.

6. Refine your measures and make sure employees are happy with them. Communicating with your employees is key to making sure incentive plans do not end up being scrapped the month after they are administered.

LO 2

If Google paid its programmers based on how many programs they wrote per day, what would happen?

straight piecework

An incentive plan under which employees receive a certain rate for each unit produced

differential piece rate

A compensation rate under which employees whose production exceeds the standard amount of output receive a higher rate for all of their work than the rate paid to those who do not exceed the standard amount

10.4 Individual Incentive Plans

One word, *flexibility*, describes the design of individual incentive plans.[15] For example, technology, job tasks and duties, and organizational goals (such as being a low-cost producer) impact the organization's choice of incentive pay programs. Incentive payments may be determined by the number of units produced, achievement of specific performance goals, or productivity improvements in the organization as a whole.

10.4a Piecework

One of the oldest incentive plans is based on piecework. Under **straight piecework**, employees receive a certain rate for each unit produced. Their compensation is determined by the number of units they produce during a pay period. At Steelcase, an office furniture maker, employees can earn more than their base pay, often as much as 35 percent more, through piecework for each slab of metal they cut or chair they upholster. Under a **differential piece rate**, employees whose production exceeds the standard output receive a higher rate for all of their work than the rate paid to those who do not exceed the standard.

The piecework system is more likely to succeed when units of output can be measured readily, the quality of the product is less critical, the job is fairly standardized, and a constant flow of work can be maintained.

Computing the Piece Rate

The incentive rates must be based on hourly wage rates that would otherwise be paid for the type of work being performed. For example, the standard time for producing one unit of work in a job paying $12.75 per hour was set at 12 minutes. The piece rate would be $2.55 per unit, computed as follows:

$$\frac{60 \ (\text{minutes per hour})}{12(\text{standard time per hour})} = 5 \text{ units per hour}$$

$$\frac{\$12.75 (\text{hourly rate})}{5 (\text{units per hour})} = 2.55 \text{ per unit}$$

Piecework: The Drawbacks

Despite their obvious advantages—including their direct tie to a pay-for-performance philosophy—piecework systems have a number of disadvantages that offset their usefulness. One of the most significant weaknesses of piecework, as well as of other incentive plans based on individual effort, is that it may not always be an effective motivator. If employees believe that an increase in their output will provoke disapproval from fellow workers (often referred to as "rate busting"), they may avoid exerting maximum effort because their desire for peer approval outweighs their desire for more money. Also, jobs in which individual contributions are difficult to distinguish or measure or in which the work is mechanized to the point that the employee exercises very little control over output may be unsuited to piecework. Piecework may also be inappropriate in the following situations:

- When quality is more important than quantity.
- When technology changes are frequent.
- When productivity standards on which piecework must be based are difficult to develop.

Importantly, piecework incentive systems can work against an organizational culture promoting workforce cooperation, creativity, or problem-solving because each of these goals can infringe on an employee's time and productivity and, therefore, total pay earned.

10.4b Standard Hour Plan

Another common incentive technique is the **standard hour plan**, which sets incentive rates on the basis of a predetermined "standard time" for completing a job. If employees finish the work in less than the expected time, their pay is still based on the standard time for the job multiplied by their hourly rate. However, while standard hour plans can motivate employees to produce more, employers must ensure that equipment maintenance and product quality do not suffer as employees strive to do their work faster to earn additional income.

standard hour plan
An incentive plan that sets rates based on the completion of a job in a predetermined standard time

10.4c Bonuses

A **bonus** is an incentive payment given to employees beyond their normal base wage. It is frequently given at the end of the year and does not become part of base pay.

bonus
An incentive payment that is supplemental to the base wage

Bonuses can be a powerful tool to increase future performance. For instance, if the link between pay and performance is clearly established, bonuses can be one of the most effective tools to increase future performance. For example, a study on bonuses versus actual pay raises showed that improving one's pay through merit increases by 1 percent would increase future performance by 2 percent. However, if the same money was applied to pay-for-performance bonuses, the employee's performance increases by 15 percent. Indeed, providing a strong pay-for-performance link for bonuses can dramatically improve employee productivity.[16]

A great example of a company that uses bonuses effectively is One Week Bath (https://www.oneweekbath.com/). One Week Bath has a weekly spreadsheet showing the up-to-date profits an employee is making for the company. Employees can see the bonus they have earned so far and view a forecasted profit for the company and personal bonus for the remainder of the year. The bonuses are effective because they're objective, not dependent on some manager's performance assessment. They are also transparent—people know in advance what they will receive and how big it will be.[17]

When some special employee contribution is to be rewarded, a spot bonus is used. A **spot bonus**, as the name implies, is given "on the spot," normally for some employee's effort not directly tied to an established performance standard. Lauren Sejen, compensation expert with Watson Wyatt Worldwide, notes, "I think spot bonuses are one of the most underutilized forms of rewards, given how well employees respond to them. These plans make perfect sense."[18]

spot bonus

An unplanned bonus given for employee's effort unrelated to an established performance measure

10.4d Merit Pay

A merit pay program (merit raise) links an increase in base pay to how successfully an employee performs his or her job. Unlike bonuses, once merit increases are given they become part of base pay, regardless of future performance. Merit raises can serve to motivate if employees perceive the raise to be related to the performance required to earn it.[19] Figure 10.5 shows that as incentive plans become too complex, they can act as a disincentive.

However, research shows that a merit increase in the range of 7 to 9 percent is necessary to serve as a pay motivator.[20] Employees may welcome lower percentage amounts, but low salary increases may not lead to significantly greater effort on the

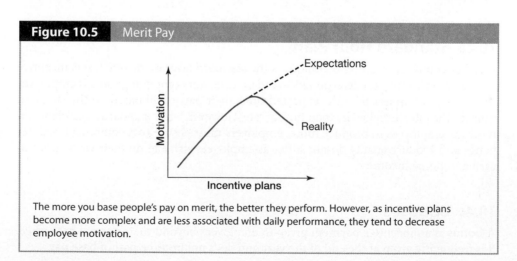

| **Figure 10.5** | Merit Pay |

The more you base people's pay on merit, the better they perform. However, as incentive plans become more complex and are less associated with daily performance, they tend to decrease employee motivation.

part of employees to drive business results. Consequently, with low salary budgets (see Chapter 9), organizations wishing to reward top performers will be required to distribute a large portion of the compensation budget to these individuals.[21] A meaningful merit increase will catch the attention of top performers while sending a signal to poor-performing employees. A strategic compensation policy *must differentiate* between outstanding and good or average performance.

Problems with Merit Raises

Merit raises may not always achieve their intended purpose. As CEO of BetterWorks, Kris Duggan, stated: "It doesn't make sense to only give employees one numeric, formal review. Imagine if your Fitbit gave you your step count at the end of each year. It'd have absolutely no impact on the way you work. Managers should be reviewing employees' work at least quarterly and convening to discuss progress frequently, in some cases weekly or monthly."[22]

Compensation specialists recognize the following problems with merit pay plans:

1. Money available for merit increases may be inadequate to satisfactorily raise all employees' base pay.

2. Managers may have no guidance in how to define and measure performance; there may be vagueness regarding merit award criteria.

3. Employees may not believe that their compensation is tied to effort and performance; they may be unable to differentiate between merit pay and other types of pay increases.

4. Employees and their managers may hold different views of the factors that contribute to job success.

5. Merit pay plans may create feelings of pay inequity.[23]

While there are no easy solutions to these problems, organizations using a true merit pay plan often base the percentage pay raise on **merit guidelines** tied to performance appraisals. For example, a certain pay increase, such as "3 percent," will be tied to a certain performance evaluation, such as "above average." The percentages may change each year, depending on various internal or external concerns such as profit levels or national economic conditions as indicated by changes in the consumer price index. To prevent all employees from being rated outstanding or above average, managers may be required to distribute the performance rating according to some preestablished formula (such as only 10 percent can be rated outstanding). Additionally, when setting merit percentage guidelines, organizations should consider individual performance along with such factors as training, experience, and current earnings.

merit guidelines
Guidelines for awarding merit raises that are tied to performance objectives

10.4e Incentive Awards and Recognition

Incentive awards and employee recognition are an important part of an employer's pay-for-performance compensation strategy. In 2011, a study by the American Psychological Association found that 43 percent of employees feel they receive inadequate nonmonetary awards and recognition for their contributions at work. In fact, almost a third (32 percent) of employees indicated that they intended to seek employment elsewhere within the next year.[24]

For example, if you have worked in a restaurant as a server you will know that a little recognition goes a long way. For example, a popular app used to recognize servers for upselling is called "IncentivizeMe."

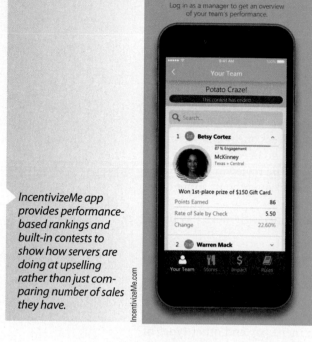

IncentivizeMe app provides performance-based rankings and built-in contests to show how servers are doing at upselling rather than just comparing number of sales they have.

IncentivizeMe gamifies the sometimes daunting task of upselling food. Employees can choose to compete with one another to see who can upsell the most. This app provides performance-based rankings aimed at normalizing sections worked and different shifts, so that employees are judged on their upselling rather than their total sales volume. This app has been especially effective for millennial workers who see fairness in ratings as key to their motivation.[25]

Awards are used to recognize productivity gains, special contributions or achievements, and service to the organization. Popular noncash incentive awards include merchandise, personalized gifts, theater or sports tickets, vacations, dining out, gift certificates or gift cards, and personalized clothing. Employers should take care to tie awards to performance and deliver awards in a timely, sincere, public, and specific way. Most importantly, noncash incentive awards should support business goals and objectives.

A great example of a company good at offering noncash incentives is Atlassian. Atlassian is a software company based in Sydney, Australia. Atlassian focuses on making products for developers and project managers. However, Atlassian does something differently. Every quarter, Atlassian gives its employees 24 hours to innovate however they want. This program is called a ShipIt Day.[26]

Greg Boswell, a strategic business partner and "appreciatologist" at O. C. Tanner, notes, "Employers are now thinking of awards and employee recognition more strategically with programs closely aligned to their business goals"[27] (see Figure 10.6). For example, if quality improvement is a business goal, then recognition needs to be tied to those behaviors that further the achievement of quality. Highlights in HRM 2 provides suggestions for noncash incentive awards based on the generational grouping of employees.

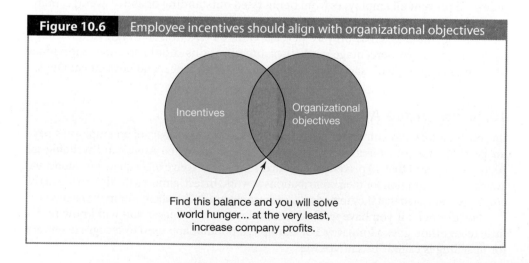

Figure 10.6	Employee incentives should align with organizational objectives

Incentives

Organizational objectives

Find this balance and you will solve world hunger... at the very least, increase company profits.

Lessons Learned: Designing Effective Team Incentives

Will your team incentive program be successful? While there are no exact keys to success, team compensation specialists cite the following as important components of a meaningful team incentive plan.

- Are organizational members—employees and managers—predisposed to a team incentive reward system? Is there a cultural readiness for team compensation? If change is indicated, what information needs to be given to all organizational employees?

- Enlist total employee and managerial support for the incentive effort. While top management support is critical, without the encouragement of employees and middle- and lower-level managers (those directly involved in the program implementation), team incentive programs invariably fail.

- When developing new programs, include representatives from all groups affected by the incentive effort—labor, management, employees. Inclusion, not exclusion, serves to build trust and understanding of the program's intent, and its overall importance to organizational success.

- Establish effective, fair, and precise measurement standards. Selected performance measures should be key indicators of organizational success. Do not attempt to measure everything. Employees should be able to directly influence the performance measures selected. Furthermore, performance measures should be challenging but realistic and obtainable. Standards must encourage increased effort without becoming entitlements.

- Incentive payout formulas must be seen as fair, be easy for employees to calculate, offer payouts on a frequent basis, and be large enough to encourage future employee effort. The goal is to create a pay-for-performance environment. When standards are not met, explain why the reward was not earned.

- Determine how incentive rewards will be distributed. Will team members receive equal dollar awards, or will team members receive differential payments based on such factors as seniority, skill levels, rates of pay, member contributions, and so forth?

- Communicate, communicate, communicate. Constantly champion the benefits of the incentive awards to employees and their contribution to organizational success.

©Caiaimage/Paul Bradbury/Getty Images

Nonmonetary rewards let employees know they are valued, which is why more and more companies are using incentives like these to recognize high performance.

10.4f Sales Incentives

The enthusiasm and drive required in most types of sales work demand that sales employees be highly motivated. Incentive plans must provide a source of motivation that will elicit cooperation and trust.

Unique Needs of Sales Incentive Plans

Incentive systems for salespeople are complicated by the wide differences in the types of sales jobs. These range from department store clerks who ring up customer purchases to industrial salespeople at McGraw-Edison who provide consultation and other highly technical services. Salespeople's performance may be measured by the dollar volume of their sales and by their ability to establish new accounts. Other measures are the ability to promote new products or services and to provide various forms of customer service and assistance that do not produce immediate sales revenues.[28] Performance standards for sales employees are difficult to develop, but if done right can motivate employees to improve performance.

Gamification is one way to provide a fun way to motivate sales teams. Around 50 percent of sales organizations run sales competitions multiple times throughout the year.[29] For example, when companies use games to have employees and teams compete with one another or even teams outside of the office, they tend to see improvements in performance. According to one study, 71 percent of companies who use gamification for their sales associates see anywhere from 11 to 50 percent increases in measured sales performance.[30]

But successful gamification of sales teams is much more than providing simple contests. It consists of doing these six things well:

1. **Reward behaviors immediately.** For example, create an immediate contest between two sales members to see who can make a sale within the next 20 minutes. Immediately provide a $25 Amazon gift card to the person who wins. The idea is to reward behavior immediately after it is performed.

2. **Reward behaviors consistently.** Sales reps are enthusiastic about competitions that align with their goals and that set challenging but realistic benchmarks. Consistency changes gamification from gimmicky, one-off events to a strategic part of team culture.

3. **Reward the correct behaviors.** Sometimes sales contests can reinforce the wrong behaviors, like not helping colleagues with their own sales. Sometimes you can create a contest within a team for highest number of sales assists. For example, John Stockton, former Utah Jazz player, is still remembered for having the highest number of point assists in National Basketball League history.[31]

4. **Use data-driven gamification.** Knowing when employees are most likely to succeed or when lulls may occur in sales can help you strategically start a game or contest between teams when the time is right. Maybe you have a slow hour at 4 p.m. before everyone is ready to go home. Use this time to start a sales competition between teams to boost sales.

5. **Use team games.** When you have one team competing against another team or office it helps drive motivation through camaraderie. Reps work hard not to let their teammates down and feel motivated by a cause greater than themselves.

6. **Use public recognition more often than money.** Sales reps are more motivated by public recognition than they are by prizes and money. As a result, some companies

communicate game outcomes via email and "cc" the boss as well. This may even lead to the boss reaching out to congratulate the employee in a public setting—something that drives employee loyalty.[32]

Types of Sales Incentive Plans

Compensation plans for sales employees may consist of a straight salary plan, a straight commission plan, a combination salary and commission plan, or a sales plus bonus plan.[33] A **straight salary plan** permits salespeople to be paid for performing various duties not reflected immediately in their sales volume. It enables them to devote more time to providing services and building up the goodwill of customers without jeopardizing their income. The principal limitation of the straight salary plan is that it may not motivate salespeople to exert sufficient effort in maximizing their sales volume.

On the other hand, the **straight commission plan**, based on a percentage of sales, provides maximum incentive and is easy to compute and understand. For example, total cash compensation might equal total sales volume times some percentage of total sales, perhaps 2 percent. Straight commission plans encourage aggressive selling, which might be needed in highly competitive industries. Under a straight commission plan, salespeople may be allowed a salary draw. A *draw* is a cash advance that must be paid back as commissions are earned.[34]

However, the straight commission plan is limited by the following disadvantages:

1. Salespeople will stress high-priced products.
2. Customer service after the sale is likely to be neglected.
3. Earnings tend to fluctuate widely between good and poor periods of business, and turnover of trained sales employees tends to increase in poor periods.
4. Salespeople are tempted to grant price concessions.

The **combined salary and commission plan** is the most widely used sales incentive program. For example, the most common pay mix (see "pay mix" in Chapter 9) for salespersons responsible for *new* accounts is 50 percent base pay and 50 percent variable pay. For salespersons servicing *existing* accounts, the pay distribution will lean more toward base pay and less toward commission. The ratio of base salary to commission can be set to fit organizational objectives.

Another type of sales incentive plan is a **salary plus bonus plan**, where the payout can be paid on a monthly, quarterly, or yearly schedule contingent based upon the salesperson achieving targeted sales goals such as number of sales calls made, account servicing, or quality of sales.

10.5 Group Incentive Plans

The emphasis on cost reduction and productivity has led many organizations to implement a variety of group incentive plans. Group plans enable employees to share in the benefits of improved efficiency realized by major organizational units or various individual work teams. These plans encourage a cooperative—rather than individualistic—spirit among all employees and reward them for their total contribution to the organization.

straight salary plan
A compensation plan that permits salespeople to be paid for performing various duties that are not reflected immediately in their sales volume

straight commission plan
A compensation plan based on a percentage of sales

combined salary and commission plan
A compensation plan that includes a straight salary and a commission

salary plus bonus plan
A compensation plan that pays a salary plus a bonus achieved by reaching targeted sales goals

LO **3**
Is there ever a time you would prefer to be paid based on how your team performs versus how you perform?

10.5a Team Compensation

team incentive plan

A compensation plan in which all team members receive an incentive bonus payment when production or service standards are met or exceeded

The **team incentive plan** rewards team members with an incentive when agreed-on performance standards are met or exceeded. Team incentives seek to establish a psychological climate that fosters team member cooperation and a collective desire to fulfill organizational goals and objectives.

One catch with setting team compensation is that not all teams are alike (see Chapter 4). For example, cross-functional teams, self-directed teams, and task-force teams make it impossible to develop one consistent type of team incentive plan. With a variety of teams, managers find it difficult to adopt uniform measurement standards or payout formulas for team pay.[35]

When team compensation is decided upon, organizations typically use the three-step approach to establishing team incentive payments. First, they set performance measures upon which incentive payments are based. Improvements in efficiency, product quality, or reduction in materials or labor costs are common benchmark criteria. For example, if labor costs for a team represent 30 percent of the organization's sales dollars and the organization pays a bonus for labor cost savings, then whenever team labor costs are less than 30 percent of sales dollars, those savings are paid as an incentive bonus to team members. Second, the size of the incentive bonus must be determined. At Thrivent Financial for Lutherans, health insurance underwriters can receive team incentive bonuses of up to 10 percent of base salary. However, the exact level of incentive pay depends on overall team performance and the company's performance over a year. Third, a payout formula is established and fully explained to employees. The team bonus may be distributed to employees equally, in proportion to their base pay or on the basis of their relative contribution to the team.

The following are some noted problems associated with team compensation:

- Individual team members may perceive that "their" efforts contribute little to team success or to the attainment of the incentive reward.

- Team members may be afraid that one individual may make the others look bad, or that one individual may put in less effort than others but share equally in team rewards—the "free-rider" effect.

- Complex payout formulas or insufficient payout rewards.

10.5b Gainsharing Incentive Plans

gainsharing plans

Programs under which both employees and the organization share financial gains according to a predetermined formula that reflects improved productivity and profitability

Gainsharing plans are organizational programs designed to increase productivity or decrease labor costs and share monetary gains with employees. These plans are based on a mathematical formula that compares a baseline of performance with actual productivity during a given period. When productivity exceeds the baseline, an agreed-upon amount of savings is shared with employees. Inherent in gainsharing is the idea that involved employees will improve productivity through more effective use of organizational resources.

There are many variations of gainsharing plans, such as the Scanlon plan and improshare plans. The Scanlon plan emphasizes participative management and encourages cost reductions by sharing with employees any savings resulting from those reductions. Improshare plans are based on the number of finished goods that the employee work teams complete in an established period.

The Scanlon Plan

The **Scanlon plan** is a specific type of gainsharing plan. The philosophy behind the Scanlon plan is that employees should offer ideas and suggestions to improve productivity and, in turn, be rewarded for their constructive efforts. Improvement or gains largely come from "working smarter, not harder." Figure 10.7 illustrates the Scanlon plan suggestion process, including the duties and responsibilities of two important groups—the *shop* and the *screening* committees.

Financial incentives under the Scanlon plan are ordinarily offered to all employees (a significant feature of the plan) on the basis of an established formula. This formula is based on increases in employee productivity as determined by a norm that has been established for labor costs.

Improshare

Improshare—improved productivity through sharing—is another gainsharing program. Individual production bonuses are typically based on how much an employee produces above some standard amount, but improshare bonuses are based on the overall productivity of the *work team*. Improshare output is measured by the number of finished products that a work team produces in a given period. Both production (direct) employees and nonproduction (indirect) employees are included in the determination of the bonus.[36]

scanlon plan

A bonus incentive plan using employee and management committees to gain cost-reduction improvements

improshare

A gainsharing program under which bonuses are based on the overall productivity of the work team

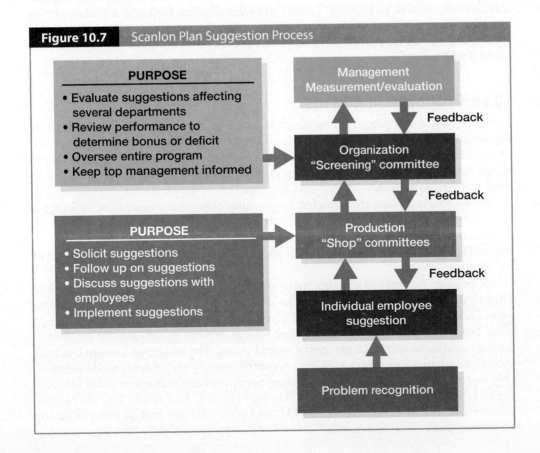

Figure 10.7 Scanlon Plan Suggestion Process

PURPOSE
- Evaluate suggestions affecting several departments
- Review performance to determine bonus or deficit
- Oversee entire program
- Keep top management informed

PURPOSE
- Solicit suggestions
- Follow up on suggestions
- Discuss suggestions with employees
- Implement suggestions

Management Measurement/evaluation

Feedback

Organization "Screening" committee

Feedback

Production "Shop" committees

Feedback

Individual employee suggestion

Problem recognition

The bonus is based on productivity gains that result from reducing the time it takes to produce a finished product. The employees and the company each receive payment for 50 percent of the improvement. Since a cooperative environment benefits all, improshare promotes increased interaction and support between employees and management.

Lessons from the Scanlon Plan and Improshare

Perhaps the most important lesson to be learned from the Scanlon plan and improshare—or any gainsharing program—is that management expecting to gain the cooperation of its employees in improving efficiency must permit them to become involved psychologically as well as financially in the organization. If employees are to contribute maximum effort, they must have a feeling of involvement and identification with their organization, which does not come out of the traditional manager-subordinate relationship.

employee stock ownership plans (ESOPs)

Stock plans in which an organization contributes shares of its stock to an established trust for the purpose of stock purchases by its employees

profit sharing

Profit sharing is any procedure by which an employer pays, or makes available to all regular employees, special current or deferred sums based on the organization's profits

10.6 Enterprise Incentive Plans

Enterprise incentive plans differ from individual and group incentive plans in that all organizational members participate in the plan's compensation payout. Enterprise incentive plans reward employees on the basis of the success of the organization over an extended time period—normally a year, but the period can be longer. Enterprise incentive plans seek to create a "culture of ownership" by fostering a philosophy of cooperation and teamwork among all organizational members. Common enterprise incentive plans include profit sharing, stock options, and **employee stock ownership plans (ESOPs)**.

10.6a Profit Sharing Plans

Profit sharing is any procedure by which an employer pays, or makes available to all regular employees, special current or deferred sums based on the organization's profits. As defined here, profit sharing represents cash payments made to eligible employees at designated time periods, as distinct from profit sharing in the form of contributions to employee pension funds.

Profit sharing plans are intended to give employees the opportunity to increase their earnings by contributing to the growth of their organization's profits. These contributions may be directed toward improving product quality, reducing operating costs, improving work methods, and building goodwill rather than just increasing rates of production.

A popular example of a highly successful profit sharing plan is the one in use at Lincoln Electric. This plan was started in 1934 by J. F. Lincoln, president of the company. Each year the company distributes a large percentage of its profits to employees in accordance with their salary level and merit ratings. It is not uncommon for employees' annual bonuses to exceed 50 percent of annual wages. The success of Lincoln Electric's incentive system depends on a high level of contribution by each employee. Unquestionably there is a high degree of respect among employees and management for Lincoln's organizational goals and for the profit sharing program. As a result, Lincoln Electric has been profitable every year since 1934, and as of 2017 has had 84 years of paying employees profit sharing bonuses.[37]

Variations in Profit Sharing Plans

Profit sharing plans differ in the proportion of profits shared with employees and in the distribution and form of payment. The amount shared with employees may range from 5 to 50 percent of the net profit. In most plans, however, about 20 to 25 percent of the net profit is shared. Profit distributions may be made to all employees on an equal basis, or they may be based on regular salaries or some formula that takes into account seniority and/or merit. The payments may be disbursed in cash, deferred, or made on the basis of combining the two forms of payments.

Weaknesses of Profit Sharing Plans

In spite of their potential advantages, profit sharing plans are also prone to certain weaknesses. The profits shared with employees may be the result of inventory speculation, climatic factors, economic conditions, national emergencies, or other factors over which employees have no control. Conversely, losses may occur during years when employee contributions have been at a maximum. The fact that profit sharing payments are made only once a year or deferred until retirement may reduce their motivational value. If a plan fails to pay off for several years in a row, this can have an adverse effect on productivity and employee morale.

10.6b Stock Options

What do the following companies—Apple, Google, Coca-Cola, Starbucks, Nike, Quaker Oats, and Sara Lee—have in common? The answer: Each of these diverse organizations offers a stock option program to its employees.[38] Stock option plans grant to employees the right to purchase a specific number of shares of the company's stock at a guaranteed price (the option price) during a designated time period.

Organizations that offer stock option programs to employees do so with the belief that there is some incentive value to the systems. By allowing employees to purchase stock, the organization hopes they will increase their productivity, assume a partnership role in the organization, and thus cause the stock price to rise.[39] Highlights in HRM 3 explain how stock option plans work.

Unfortunately, in the wake of various corporate scandals, employee stock option plans have come under attack from stockholder groups, government officials, and the general public. Criticism largely focuses on the extravagance of executive stock option plans and dubious corporate accounting procedures.[40] Nevertheless, despite these faults, stock options continue to be a popular and efficient way to pay for the performance of employees and managers. When stock prices rise, employee stock plans can be financially rewarding to employees.

10.6c Employee Stock Ownership Plans

According to the National Center for Employee Ownership, in 2016 nearly 7,000 organizations have ESOPs for their employees.[41] Columbia Forest Products, Hy-Vee, Publix Super Markets, Herff Jones, The Tribune Co., U.S. Sugar, The Bureau of National Affairs, and Scheels All Sports are organizations with established ESOPs. W. L. Gore and Associates also decided that employee stock ownership was an effective and innovative way to give employees a share of the company's success.

How Stock Option Plans Work

Here is an example of a typical employee stock option plan. An employee is granted the option to purchase 1,000 shares of the company's stock at the current market price of $5 per share (the "grant" price). The employee can exercise the option at $5 per share—typically the exercise price will be equal to the price when the options are granted. Plans allow employees to exercise their options after a certain number of years or when the company's stock reaches a certain price. If the price of the stock increases to $20 per share, for example, the employee may exercise his or her options to buy 1,000 shares at $5 per share and then sell the stock at the current market price of $20 per share.

Companies sometimes revalue the price at which the options can be exercised. This may happen, for example, when a company's stock price has fallen below the original exercise price. Companies revalue the exercise price as a way to retain their employees.

Source: Adapted from "Employee Stock Options Fact Sheet, National Center for Employee Ownership," http://www.nceo.org/.

An ESOP is an employer established trust that qualifies as a tax-exempt employee trust under Section 401(a) of the Internal Revenue Code. Under an ESOP employees do not actually buy shares. Instead, the company contributes its own shares to the plan, contributes cash to buy its own stock (often from an existing owner), or, most commonly, has the plan borrow money to buy stock, with the company repaying the loan. All of these uses have significant tax benefits for the company, the employees, and the sellers. The ESOP holds the stock for employees, and they are routinely informed of the value of their accounts. Stock allocations can be based on employee wages or seniority. When employees leave the organization or retire, they can sell their stock back to the organization, or they can sell it on the open market if it is traded publicly.

Advantages of Employee Stock Ownership Plans

Encouraged by favorable federal income tax provisions, employers use ESOPs to provide retirement benefits for their employees. Favorable tax incentives permit a portion of earnings to be excluded from taxation if that portion is assigned to employees in the form of shares of stock. Employers can therefore provide retirement benefits for their employees at relatively low cost because stock contributions are in effect subsidized by the federal government. ESOPs can also increase employees' pride of ownership in the organization, providing an incentive for them to increase productivity and help the organization prosper and grow.

Problems with Employee Stock Ownership Plans

Generally, ESOPs are more likely to serve their intended purposes in publicly held companies than in privately held ones. A major problem with the privately held company is its potential inability to pay back the stock of employees when they retire. These employees do not have the alternative of disposing of their stock on the open market. Thus, when large organizations suffer financial difficulties and the value of the companies' stocks falls, so does the value of the employees' retirement plan.

Other problems with ESOPs include the following:

- The more retirement income comes from these plans, the more dependent a pensioner becomes on the price of company stock. Future retirees are vulnerable to stock market fluctuations as well as to management mistakes.

- Unlike traditional pension plans, ESOP contributions are not guaranteed by the federally established Pension Benefit Guaranty Corporation (see Chapter 11), a major drawback to employees should their employer face serious financial setbacks or closure.

10.7 Incentives for Professional Employees

LO 5

Do professionals and executives deserve to be incentivized differently than the rest of us?

When it comes to individual, team, and enterprise incentives, professional employees—engineers, scientists, and attorneys, for example—are no different than anyone else. They want to be rewarded for good work. However, where many companies often mess up is by applying the same individual and team-based pay-for-performance principles used in traditional jobs (e.g., manufacturing, clerical). For example, many companies offer cash bonuses to professionals who complete projects on or before deadline dates. They also pay individuals for new patents, publications, or for completing certain tasks within a given time frame. Unfortunately, what often works for employees conducting more specified tasks does not work for employees whose work is ambiguous, complex, and requires creative thought.[42]

It turns out that individual incentives narrow a person's focus. They concentrate the mind. That is why they work in so many circumstances. However, for professional employees, where the task is complex and the solution is not easy to figure out, it is important to motivate employees to be more creative. Pay for performance, unless it is a longer-term incentive, can be problematic in this case. This clip explains why pay for performance can be problematic, if not used wisely: https://www.youtube.com/watch?v=5JB6PZrgZjw

So how should you incentivize your professional workers? Pay is still important, but it should be based more on overall performance over time, and it should not limit them to a set of certain tasks. In other words, make sure your incentives are based around the impact of someone's work and not just that a certain task was completed. Such rewards should provide (1) autonomy to the worker, (2) opportunity to master a skill, and (3) purpose (e.g., helping to build a better organization, curing cancer, alleviating poverty).[43] See Figure 10.8 to understand what areas incentive plans need to cover.

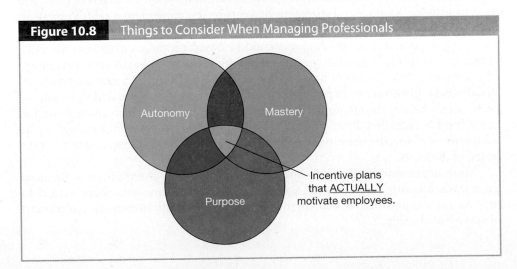

| **Figure 10.8** | Things to Consider When Managing Professionals |

10.8 Incentives for Executives

10.8a The Executive Pay Package

Executive compensation plans consist of five basic components: (1) base salary, (2) short-term incentives or bonuses, (3) long-term incentives or stock plans, (4) benefits, and (5) perks.[44] Each of these elements may receive different emphasis in the executive's compensation package depending on various organizational goals and executive needs.[45]

Executive Base Salaries

Executive base salaries represent between 30 and 40 percent of total annual compensation.[46] An analysis of executive salaries shows that the largest portion of executive pay is received in long-term incentive rewards and bonuses. Regardless, executives of Fortune 500 firms routinely earn an annual base salary in excess of $500,000, with executives in very large corporations earning considerably more. The levels of competitive salaries in the job market exert perhaps the greatest influence on executive base salaries. An organization's compensation committee—normally members of the board of directors—will order a salary survey to find out what executives earn in comparable enterprises.[47] For example, by one estimate, over 90 percent of companies in the Standard & Poor's 500 stock index use a technique called *competitive benchmarking* when setting executive pay or to remain competitive for executive talent.[48] Company boards reason that a CEO who does not earn as much as his or her peers is likely to "take a hike." Comparisons may be based on organization size, sales volume, or industry groupings. Thus, by analyzing the data from published studies, along with self-generated salary surveys, the compensation committee can determine the equity of the compensation package outside the organization.

Executive Short-Term Incentives

Annual bonuses represent the main element of executive short-term incentives.[49] Most organizations pay their short-term incentive bonuses in cash (in the form of a supplemental check), in keeping with their pay-for-performance strategy. By providing a reward soon after the performance and thus linking it to the effort on which it is based, they can use cash bonuses as a significant motivator. Deferred bonuses are used to provide a source of retirement benefits or to supplement a regular pension plan.

Incentive bonuses for executives should be based on the contribution the individual makes to the organization. Incentive bonuses may be based on a percentage of a company's total profits or a percentage of profits in excess of a specific return on stockholders' investments. In other instances, the payments may be tied to an annual profit plan whereby the amount is determined by the extent to which an agreed-upon profit level is exceeded. Payments may also be based on performance ratings or the achievement of specific objectives established with the agreement of executives and the board of directors.

More organizations are tying operational yardsticks to the traditional financial gauges when computing executive pay. Called *balanced scorecards*, these yardsticks may measure things such as customer satisfaction, the ability to innovate, or product or service leadership.[50]

Executive Long-Term Incentives

Stock options are the primary long-term incentive offered to executives.[51] The principal reason driving executive stock ownership is the desire of both the company and outside investors for senior managers to have a significant stake in the success of the business. Figure 10.9 highlights several common forms of long-term incentives.

Short-term incentive bonuses are criticized for causing top executives to focus on quarterly profit goals to the detriment of long-term survival and growth objectives. Important to stockholders are such performance results as growth in earnings per share, return on stockholders' equity, and, ultimately, stock price appreciation. A variety of incentive plans, therefore, have been developed to tie rewards to these performance results, particularly over the long term. Additionally, stock options can serve to retain key executive personnel when exercising the options is linked to a specified vesting period, perhaps two to four years (this type of incentive is called "golden handcuffs").

Executive Benefits

The benefits package offered to executives may parallel one offered to other groups of employees. Various programs for health insurance, life insurance, retirement plans, and vacations are common. However, unlike other employee groups, the benefits offered to executives are likely to be broader in coverage and free of charge. Additionally, executives may be given financial assistance in the form of trusts for estate planning, payment of mortgage interest, and legal help.[52]

Executive Perks

perquisites
Special nonmonetary benefits given to executives; often referred to as *perks*

Perquisites (or perks) are nonmonetary rewards given to executives and are a means of demonstrating the executive's importance to the organization. Some examples of perks may include company plane/car, large insurance policies, financial planning, income

Figure 10.9	Types of Long-Term Incentive Plans
Stock options	Rights granted to executives to purchase shares of their organization's stock at an established price for a fixed period of time. Stock price is usually set at market value at the time the option is granted.
Stock appreciation rights (SARs)	Cash or stock award determined by increase in stock price during any time chosen by the executive in the option period; does not require executive financing.
Stock purchase	Opportunities for executives to purchase shares of their organization's stock valued at full market or a discount price, often with the organization providing financial assistance.
Phantom stock	Grant of units equal in value to the fair market value or book value of a share of stock; on a specified date the executive will be paid the appreciation in the value of the units up to that time.
Restricted stock	Grant of stock or stock units at a reduced price with the condition that the stock not be transferred or sold (by risk of forfeiture) before a specified employment date.
Performance units	Grants analogous to annual bonuses except that the measurement period exceeds one year. The value of the grant can be expressed as a flat dollar amount or converted to a number of "units" of equivalent aggregate value.
Performance shares	Grants of actual stock or phantom stock units. Value is contingent on both predetermined performance objectives over a specified period of time and the stock market.

tax preparation, and chauffeur service along with family perks of children's education, spouse travel, and estate planning. However, the dark side of perks is that they are viewed as wasteful spending and overly lavish. Even so, perks may save executive time or improve executive health.

Highlights in HRM 4 shows the more common perks offered to executives.

10.8b Executive Compensation: Ethics and Accountability

In 2017, the chief executives of American companies got a collective raise of 3.1 percent, which is not much different than the 3.0 percent average salary increases for management and salaried employees.[53] But 3.1 percent of executive pay is much more than that of an average salaried employee.

Almost three in four Americans think CEOs and top-level executives are overpaid. Yet at the same time, most Americans still underestimate how much CEOs make. When asked how much the average CEO is paid in the largest 500 U.S. companies, the median guess was about $1 million per year.[54]

So what is the real answer? The median compensation for CEOs of the biggest 500 U.S. companies is $10.3 million—10 times what most Americans think.[55] Consider the total compensation drawn by the following executives, shown in Figure 10.10.[56]

While the average American may believe executives are overpaid, corporate compensation committees justify big bonuses in the following ways[57]:

1. Large financial incentives are a way to reward superior performance.
2. Business competition is pressure-filled and demanding.
3. Good executive talent is in great demand.
4. Effective executives create shareholder value.

Others justify high compensation as a fact of business life, reflecting market compensation trends.

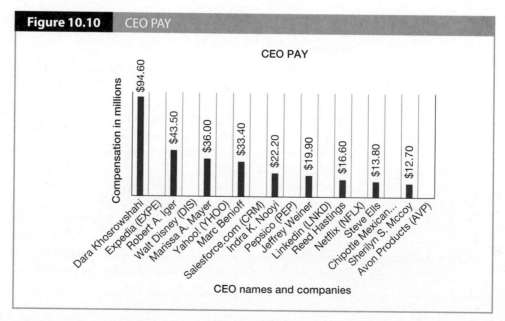

Figure 10.10   CEO PAY

"200 Highest-Paid CEOs 2016," *New York Times,* http://www.equilar.com/reports/38-2-new-york-times-200-highest-paid-ceos-2016.html

Nevertheless, with the large compensation packages awarded to top-level executives, cries for performance accountability and openness abound. Many argue that such exorbitant pay gaps are not only bad for the reputations of firms that pay them, but also that such gaps can create discontent in a general population—threatening the very foundation on which pay for performance was established. Just think of the presidential election won by Donald Trump. Part of his platform was that the pay difference between the average worker and top-level executives was too great.[58] While not all executive pay is exorbitant and not all executive performance is poor, nevertheless angry employees, union groups, government officials, and stockholders argue for change.

10.8c Executive Compensation Reform

Several important changes will impact future executive compensation. First, the Internal Revenue Service (IRS) always looks for tax code violations in connection with hefty executive pay packages. The IRS makes executive pay a part of every corporate audit.[59] Second, the Securities and Exchange Commission has disclosure rules that require companies listed on the New York Stock Exchange and NASDAQ to disclose the true size of their top executive pay packages. Companies must reveal details on accumulated pension benefits, deferred compensation, and perks that exceed more than $10,000 in total value. Also, companies must provide a plain-English table that summarizes executives' various forms of compensation.[60] Third, the Financial Accounting Standards Board (FASB) requires that stock options be recognized as an expense on income statements. Companies and compensation committees must now weigh the benefits provided by stock option programs against the potential charge to earnings.[61] Finally, the Dodd–Frank Wall Street Reform and Consumer Protection Act (Pub. L. 111–203) requires companies to disclose the median total compensation of all its employees in comparison to the total CEO compensation and gives shareholders of a company "say on pay," which means that voting shareholders of a company must ultimately approve of its executive salaries.

Summary

LO 1 The success of an incentive pay plan depends on the organizational climate in which it must operate, employee confidence in it, and its suitability to employee and organizational needs. Importantly, employees must view their incentive pay as being equitable and related to their performance. Performance measures should be quantifiable, be easily understood, and bear a demonstrated relationship to organizational performance.

LO 2 Piecework plans pay employees a given rate for each unit satisfactorily completed. Employers implement these plans when output is easily measured and when the production process is fairly standardized. Bonuses are incentive payments above base wages paid on either an individual or team basis. A bonus is offered to encourage employees to exert greater effort.

Standard hour plans establish a standard time for job completion. An incentive is paid for finishing the job in less than the preestablished time. These plans are popular for jobs with a fixed time for completion.

Paying employees a straight salary allows them to focus on tasks other than sales, such as service and customer goodwill. A straight commission plan causes employees to emphasize sales goals. A combination of salary and commission or bonus provides the advantages of both the straight salary and the straight commission form of payments.

LO 3 The Scanlon and improshare gainsharing plans pay bonuses to employees unrelated to profit levels. Each of these plans encourages employees to maximize their performance and cooperation through suggestions offered to improve organizational performance.

The Scanlon plan pays an employee a bonus based on saved labor cost measured against the organization's sales value of production. The improshare bonus is paid when employees increase production output above a given target level.

LO 4 Profit sharing plans pay employees sums of money based on the organization's profits. Cash payments are made to eligible employees at specified times, normally yearly. The primary purpose of profit sharing is to provide employees with additional income through their participation in organizational achievement. Employee commitment to improved productivity, quality, and customer service will contribute to organizational success and, in turn, to their compensation. Profit sharing plans may not achieve their stated gains when employee performance is unrelated

to organizational success or failure. This may occur because of economic conditions, other competition, or environmental conditions. Profit sharing plans can have a negative effect on employee morale when plans fail to consistently reward employees.

LO 5 Professionals not wanting to move into administrative positions are often offered different tracks where they can continue to increase in their compensation and status without moving into management. This may mean that these professionals have more say in decisions in the company—maybe even more say than their managers. Executives are often offered very elaborate incentives based on how well the company does. Because executives stand to gain more from the decisions they make, they also often stand to lose more.

Key Terms

bonus

combined salary and commission plan

differential piece rate

employee stock ownership plans (ESOPs)

gainsharing plans

improshare

merit guidelines

perquisites

profit sharing

salary plus bonus plan

Scanlon plan

spot bonus

standard hour plan

straight commission plan

straight piecework

straight salary plan

team incentive plan

variable pay

Discussion Questions

LO 1 Working individually or in groups, identify the factors for a successful incentive plan.

LO 2 Contrast the differences between straight piecework, differential piece rate, and standard hour plans. Explain where each plan might best be used.

LO 2 A frequently heard complaint about merit raises is that they do little to increase employee effort. What are the causes of this belief? Suggest ways in which the motivating value of merit raises may be increased.

LO 2 What are the reasons behind the different payment methods for sales employees?

LO 3 What are the reasons for the success of the Scanlon and improshare plans?

LO 4 Because of competitive forces within your industry, you have decided to implement a profit sharing plan for your employees. Discuss the advantages of profit sharing and identify specific characteristics that will ensure success for your plan.

LO 5 Create a list of different types of incentives companies can offer professionals not interested in administrative positions.

HRM **Experience**

Awarding Salary Increases

Because pay for performance is an important factor governing salary increases, managers must be able to defend the compensation recommendations they make for their employees. Merit raises granted under a pay-for-performance policy must be based on objective appraisals if they are to achieve their intended purposes of rewarding outstanding employee performance. As managers know, however, they must deal with other factors that can affect salary recommendations. These may include the opinions of the employee's peers or extenuating circumstances such as illness or family responsibilities. The purpose of this exercise is to provide you with the experience of granting salary increases to employees based on their work performance and other information.

Assignment

Following are the work records of five employees. As their supervisor, you have just completed their annual appraisal reviews, and it is now time to make recommendations for their future salary. Your department budget has $5,780 allocated for salary increases. Distribute the $5,780 among your employees based on the descriptions for each subordinate.

a. Janet Jenkins currently earns $41,000. Her performance appraisal rating was very high. She is respected by her peers and is felt to be an asset to the work group. She is divorced and has three young children to support.

b. Russell Watts earns a salary of $36,000. His annual performance appraisal was average. Several members of the work group have spoken to you about the difficulty involved in Russell's job. They feel that it is a tough and demanding job and that he is doing his best.

c. Jack Perkins earns $31,250. His performance appraisal was below average, and he seems to have difficulty adjusting to his coworkers. Jack has had a difficult time this past year. His wife passed away early in the year, and his father has recently been diagnosed as terminally ill.

d. Rick Jacobson earns $28,000. His performance appraisal was above average. He is respected by his peers and is generally considered to be a "good guy."

e. Paula Merrill earns $28,850. Her performance appraisal was very high. Her peers are upset because they feel that she is working only to provide a second income. Moreover, her peers see her as trying to "show them up."

Share your results with other class members. Be prepared to explain your allocation of money.

CASE STUDY ❶ United States Auto Industry Back on Top ... of CEO Pay

During the financial crisis, many executives' pay was stifled, reduced, or even withheld. Among the hardest hit was the U.S. auto industry. Shareholder groups, union leaders, political officials, and the general public all demanded change in the way auto industry executives were getting rich while their cars were getting poor. For example, Ford made some major cuts for its executives and its employees.

This is why people were shocked to find out that for 2011 the CEO of Ford, Alan Mulally, was to receive $56.5 million in stock awards. Even today, it is one of the richest pay packages ever given to a top executive in the auto industry—and it is even after all the clamor over sky-high executive paychecks. Is it too much?

That depends on who you ask. For most, it seems unreasonable that a boss would make more than 1,000 times the pay of the average worker. However, if you ask Ford workers who have seen Mulally steer Ford back from the edge of bankruptcy, they probably would not complain too much. If you asked Ford's shareholders, it would be hard for them to overlook the fact that Ford shares have gone from $1.56 when Mulally first took over to $14 a share. If you ask Ford dealers, they may be too busy selling one of the strongest lineups of cars around to answer.

Of course, no one really knows if Ford would have been sitting in such a good position regardless of Mulally. On one hand, there are plenty of factors, such as a national economic recovery, that led to Ford's improvements that Mulally clearly could not have had a finger on. On the other hand, there are plenty of companies that would be willing to pay $50 million if they knew their company would rebound as Ford has under Mulally.

Questions

1. Are CEOs and key corporate executives worth the large pay packages they receive? Explain.

2. Do you agree with Peter Drucker that corporate executives should receive compensation packages no larger than a certain percentage of the pay of hourly workers? Explain.

3. Will the Dodd–Frank Wall Street Reform and Consumer Protection Act giving shareholders the right to vote on executive pay influence the size of these packages in the future? Explain.

Source: Adapted from Phil LeBeau, "Mulally and Bill Ford Collect $100 Million Pay Package," *CNBC* (March 8, 2011).

CASE STUDY Team-Based Incentives: Not Your Usual Office

Done-Deal Paper Inc. operates throughout central Pennsylvania with offices in Scranton, Harrisburg, and Altoona. Providing paper and paper needs to most of Central Pennsylvania, Done-Deal is one of the top two competitors in the area.

In January 2018, Conner Carell, office manager of one of the branch offices for Done-Deal, somehow convinced company president and CEO Bailey Zucker that they needed to change the way their sales representatives were incentivized. He argued, "putting our sales reps into teams will not only increase cooperation, but it will increase sales … right now there are too many sales being lost that could have been won through a team effort." Most of the time, sales made to clients required multiple interactions by multiple reps anyway. Bailey agreed with Conner and pointed out that teamwork can also improve morale and synergy. Based on these assessments, Conner organized his 20 sales reps into 4 teams of 5 reps. Sales teams would pool their commissions regardless of who initiated and worked on the sale. After the first year of this team-based incentive program, sales commissions across the four groups varied dramatically. For instance, the highest paid employees in a team made, on average, $50,000 more than the lowest paid team members.

During August 2016, Conner sent to all 20 sales reps a survey requesting feedback on the satisfaction with teams and, specifically, the team-based incentive rewards program. While survey results were generally positive, not everyone was happy in the office. Problems could be grouped into the following categories:

1. Some sales representatives believed that various team members did not "buy into" the team concept and were simply "free riding"—benefiting from the efforts of higher performing reps.

2. There was a general feeling that some teams were assigned difficult regions that prevented them from achieving higher sales.

3. Teams did not always display the motivation and synergy expected, since "bickering" was prevalent between stars and their lesser performing peers. Average performers complained that star reps made them look bad.

4. At least a third of the sales staff felt the incentive rewards program was unfair and asked for a return to individual sales incentives.[62]

Questions

1. Do results from the survey illustrate typical complaints about teams and specifically about team incentive rewards? Explain.

2. If appropriate, what changes would you recommend to improve the incentive reward program? Be specific.

3. Would management have benefited from employee involvement in the initial design and implementation of the program? Explain.

Notes and References

1. Chidiebere Ogbonnaya, Kevin Daniels, and Karina Nielsen, "Research: How Incentive Pay Affects Employee Engagement, Satisfaction, and Trust," *Harvard Business Review* (March 15, 2017).

2. Patricia K. Zingheim and Jay R. Schuster, "Designing Pay and Rewards in Professional Service Companies," *Compensation and Benefits Review* 39, no. 1 (January–February 2007): 55.

3. "WorldatWork 2016–2017 Salary Budget Survey," WoarldatWork.com; Stephen Miller, "Bonus Binge: Variable Pay Outpaces Salary," *Society for Human Resource Management* (August 11, 2016).

4. Kerry Chou, "Hedge Your Bets with Variable Pay," *WorldatWork* (2011), http://www.worldatwork.org/adimComment?id=48615.

5. James Oldroyd and Shad Morris, "Catching Falling Stars: A Human Resource Response to Social Capital's Detrimental Effect of Information Overload on Star Employees," *Academy of Management Review* (July 2012): 396–418.

6. Jean Martin and Conrad Schmidt, "How to Keep Your Top Talent," *Harvard Business Review* (May 2010): 54–61.

7. John A. Menefee and Ryan O. Murphy, "Rewarding and Retaining the Best," *Benefits Quarterly* 20, no. 3 (Third Quarter 2004): 13–21; Anthony Nyberg, "Retaining Your High Performers: Moderators of the Performance-Job Satisfaction-Voluntary Turnover Relationship," *Journal of Applied Psychology* 95, no. 3 (2010): 440–453.

8. Enno Siemsen, Sridhar Balasubramanian, and Aleda V. Roth, "Incentives That Induce Task-Related Effort, Helping, and Knowledge Sharing in Workgroups," *Management Science* 53, no. 10 (October 2007): 1533.

9. Ann Bares, "Incentive Plan Design Begins with Good Questions," *Workforce Management* (October 2008); Fay Hansen, "Control and Customization," *Workforce Management* 86, no. 19 (November 5, 2007): 42, http://www.workforce.com/articles/14112; Luis R. Gomez-Mejia, Pascual Berrone, and Monica Franco-Santos, *Compensation and Organizational Performance: Theory, Research and Practice* (Armonk, NY: M. E. Sharpe Publishing, 2010).

10. Joe Abusamra, "Here Comes Pay for Performance!" *Federal Times* (March 8, 2017).

11. M. Franco-Santos, "Performance Measurement Issues, Incentive Application and Globalization," in L. R. Gomez-Mejia and S. Werner (eds.), *Global Compensation: Foundations and Perspectives* (London: Routledge, 2008), 41–56.

12. Joanne Sammer, "Weighing Pay Incentives," *HR Magazine* 52, no. 6 (June 2007): 64.

13. M. Franco-Santos. "Performance Measurement Issues, Incentive Application and Globalization," in L. R. Gomez-Mejia and S. Werner (eds.), *Global Compensation: Foundations and Perspectives* (London: Routledge, 2008), 41–56.

14. J. M Welbourne and L. R. Gomez-Mejia, "Team-based Incentives," in L. A. Berger and D. R. Berger (eds.), *The Compensation Handbook: A State of the Art Guide to Compensation Strategy and Design* (New York: McGraw-Hill, 2008).

15. George T. Milkovich and Jerry M. Newman, *Compensation*, 10th ed. (Boston: McGraw Hill Irwin, 2010).

16. Michael C. Sturman, "Using Your Pay System to Improve Employees' Performance: How You Pay Makes a Difference," *Cornell Hospitality Report* 6, no. 13 (2006): 4–20.

17. Bill Fotsch and John Case, "How to Build Incentive Plans That Actually Work," *Forbes* (August 24, 2015).

18. Chris Taylor, "On-the-Spot Incentives," *HR Magazine* 49, no. 5 (May 2004): 80–84.

19. Don Hellriegel and John W. Slocum, Jr., *Organizational Behavior*, 12th ed. (Mason, OH: South-Western, 2009), Chapter 6.

20. Employee perceptions of appropriate pay raises likely depend on the employer's ability to pay and the economics of the period. For example, when it is known that an employer's ability to pay is great and the economics of the industry are strong, then employees will expect larger percentage merit raises.

21. Susan J. Wells, "No Results, No Raise," *HR Magazine* 50, no. 5 (May 2005): 76.

22. Dana Wilkie, "Instead of Rating Performance with Numbers, How About Adjectives?" *Society for Human Resource Management* (July 6, 2016).

23. Stephen Miller, "Employers Seek Better Approaches to Pay for Performance," *Society for Human Resource Management* (February 8, 2016); David E. Terpstra and Andre L. Honoree, "Employees Responses to Merit Pay Inequity," *Compensation and Benefits Review* 37, no. 1 (January/February 2005): 51.

24. Donna M. Airoldi, "Two New Studies Show Significant Lack of Workplace Satisfaction and Employee Recognition," *Incentive* (March 9, 2011), http://www.incentivemag.com/News/Industry/Articles/Two-New-Studies-Show-Significant-Lack-of-Workplace-Satisfaction-and-Employee-Recognition/.

25. Ward Olgreen, "Modern-Day Motivation for Restaurant Employees," *IncentiveMag* (March 10, 2017).

26. https://www.atlassian.com/company/shipit (March 21, 2017).

27. Charlotte Garvey, "Meaningful Tokens of Appreciation," *HR Magazine* 49, no. 9 (August 2004): 102.

28. Beitelspacher, L.S., Baker, T.L., Rapp, A. and Grewal, D., 2017. Understanding the long-term implications of retailer returns in business-to-business relationships. *Journal of the Academy of Marketing Science*, pp.1–21.

29. "Sales Performance Optimization Study: 2016 Key Trends Analysis," *CSO Insights*, 2016 Miller Heimen Group, Inc.

30. Bob Marsh, "Gamification and Sales: Is It Working?" Salesforce Blog (March 21, 2017), https://www.salesforce.com/blog/2013/08/gamification-and-sales.html.

31. http://www.espn.com/nba/history/leaders/_/stat/assists (March 21, 2017).

32. Jonathan Lautaha, "7 Sales Gamification Secrets to Drive Productivity," Insidesales.com blog (February 5, 2016).

33. Jim Stockmann, "Change on the Horizon: An Analysis of Sales Compensation Practices," *Workspan* (April 2007): 41.

34. Amy Lyman, "Nordstrom—Great Service for Over 100 Years: Best Company for 25 Years," *2009 Great Place to Work Institute*, www.greatplacetowork-conference.com.

35. George T. Milkovich and Jerry M. Newman, *Compensation*, 10th ed. (Boston: McGraw Hill Irwin, 2010).

36. The standard of improshare's measurement system is the base productivity factor (BPF), which is the ratio of standard direct labor hours produced to total actual hours worked in a base period. The productivity of subsequent periods is then measured by enlarging standard direct labor hours earned by the BPF ratio to establish improshare hours (IH). The IH is then compared with actual hours worked in the same period. If earned hours exceed actual hours, 50 percent of the gain is divided by actual hours worked to establish a bonus percentage for all employees in the plan.

37. https://www.glassdoor.com/Reviews/Lincoln-Electric-Reviews-E3658.htm (March 22, 2017).

38. Jason Kovac, "Stock Options," *Workspan* (August 2006): 23. See also Seymour Burchman and Blair Jones, "The Future of Stock Options: From Starring Role to Ensemble Player," *WorldatWork* 13, no. 1 (First Quarter 2004): 29–38.

39. Mamdough Farid, Vincent Conte, and Harold Lazaus, "Toward a General Model for Executive Compensation," *Journal of Management Development* 30, no. 1 (2011): 61–74; Ira T. Kay and Steve Seelig, "Revising the Use of a Management Stock Purchase Plan to Increase Management Ownership," *Journal of Deferred Compensation* 11, no. 3 (Spring 2006): 24.

40. Chris Matthews and Matthew Heimer, "The 5 Biggest Corporate Scandals of 2016," *Fortune* (December 28, 2016); Raquel Meyer Alexander, Mark Hirchey, and Susan Scholz, "Backdating Employee Stock Options: Tax Implications," *The CPA Journal* 77, no. 10 (October 2007): 24. See also T. Thomas Cottingham III, "The Stock Options Backdating Scandal: Critical First Response," *Risk Management* 54, no. 6 (June 2007): 12.

41. Based on research conducted by The National Center for Employee Ownership (NCEO) in 2016. The NCEO is a private, nonprofit membership and research organization that serves as the leading source of accurate, unbiased information on employee stock ownership plans (ESOPs), broadly granted employee stock options and related programs, and ownership culture. The NCEO can be reached at http://www.nceo.org or by phone at (510) 208–1300.

42. Dan Ariely, Anat Bracha, and Stephan Meier, "Doing Good or Doing Well? Image Motivation and Monetary Incentives in Behaving Prosocially," *American Economic Review* 99, no. 1 (2009): 544–555; Karl Duncker and Lynne Lees, "On Problem Solving," *Psychological Monographs* 58, no. 5 (1945).

43. D. H. Pink, *Drive: The Surprising Truth about What Motivates Us.* (New York: Penguin, 2011).

44. Mark Reilly and Brian Enright, "A New Approach to Executive Compensation," *Workspan* (August 2007): 45.

45. Seymour Burchman and Blair Jones, "Executive Compensation as a Support for Growth Strategy," *WorldatWork* 15, no. 3 (Third Quarter 2006): 39.

46. Total annual compensation is the sum of an executive's annual and long-term compensation. Annual compensation consists of salary, bonus, and other yearly pay. Long-term compensation consists of stock awards, the value of any stock options exercised during the year, and any other long-term compensation (such as payouts from long-term incentive plans, director's fees, and special bonuses).

47. Edward E. Lawler III and David Finegold, "CEO Compensation: What Board Members Think," *WorldatWork* 16, no. 3 (Third Quarter 2007): 38.

48. "2017 Salary Guide," CEO Update, 2017; Mercedes Erickson, "Peer Benchmarking and Trends in Executive Compensation: 2016 Update," *Audit Analytics*, http://www.auditanalytics.com/blog/peer-benchmarking-and-trends-in-executive-compensation-2016-update/.

49. Brandon Cherry, "Executive Bonus Plans: Recent Trends in Equity Compensation," *Workspan* (January 2007): 22.

50. Darrell Rigby and Barbara Bilodeau, "Selecting Management Tools Wisely," *Harvard Business Review* 85, no. 12 (December 2007): 20.

51. Brad Hill and Christine Tande, "What's Next for Executive Incentives Now That Options Are Limited?" *Workspan* (September 2007): 47.

52. Pam Delaney, "Filling the Executive Benefits Gap," *Workspan* (November 2007), 69.

53. *WorldatWork* 2016–2017 Salary Budget Survey (2017).

54. Kara Brandeisky, "Most Americans Can't Guess the Average CEO's Salary. Can You?," *Money* (February 5, 2016).

55. Ibid.

56. "200 Highest-Paid CEOs 2016," *New York Times*, http://www.equilar.com/reports/38-2-new-york-times-200-highest-paid-ceos-2016.html

57. Steven N. Kaplan, "Are CEOs Overpaid?" *WorldatWork* 16, no. 3 (Third Quarter 2007): 22. See also Ira Kay and Steve Van Putten, *Myths and Realities of Executive Pay* (Cambridge, MA: Cambridge University Press, 2007); Jessica Marquez, "5 Questions: in Defense of CEO Pay," *Workforce Management* 86, no. 16 (September 27, 2007): 8.

58. Tim Perry, "Candidate Donald Trump Thought CEO Pay Was Too High. Does the SEC?" CBSNews.com (February 9, 2017).

59. Louis Lavelle, "Everybody Should Be a Little Nervous," *Business Week* (December 22, 2003): 42.

60. Seymour Burchman and Blair Jones, "A New Day for Executive Compensation," *Workspan* (January 2007): 15. See also "Out at Home Depot," *Business Week* (January 15, 2007): 56.

61. Mark Gimein, "The Bottom Line on Options," *Business Week* (April 3, 2006): 32. See also Peter Burrows, "Is Steve's Job Untouchable?" *Business Week* (January 15, 2007): 28.

62. Fictional case adapted from the Network Cable, Inc. case.

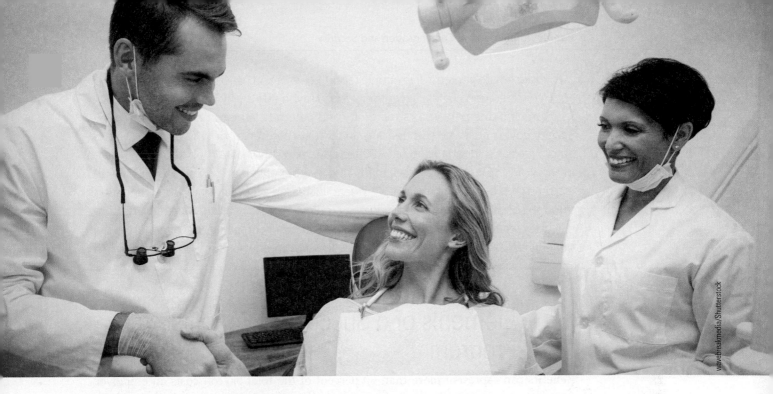

CHAPTER **11**

Employee Benefits

Learning Outcomes

After studying this chapter, you should be able to

LO ❶ Detect cost-effective strategies companies use to develop benefits plans.

LO ❷ Identify and explain the employee benefits required by law.

LO ❸ Describe the types of work-life benefits that employers may provide.

LO ❹ Describe the different types of retirement programs and pension plans and the regulations related to them.

Approximately three in five people report benefits and perks being among their top considerations before accepting a job.[1] Maybe this is why companies like Netflix provide one paid year of maternity and paternity leave to new parents, or why Spotify covers costs for egg freezing and fertility assistance, or why Airbnb gives its employees an annual stipend of $2,000 to travel and stay in an Airbnb listing anywhere in the world.[2] Despite how cool many of these benefits may be, the cost of providing them has been climbing sharply. Due to increased access to employer information through social media and search engines, employees are increasingly aware of the benefits they receive and how they compare to what other companies are offering. Hence, benefits act as a key source of advantage (or disadvantage) for companies.

11.1 Elements of a Successful Benefits Program

Benefits can represent more than 50 percent of the total payroll costs an employer pays, depending upon the types of benefits it offers. Some benefits are legally required, whereas others are voluntarily granted by employers. Figure 11.1 shows the proportion of total pay U.S. organizations, on average, pay to their employees in the form of benefits, and a breakdown of how much goes to each.

Benefits are expensive, which is why companies pay close attention to them. Health care costs, which have been growing at double and triple the rate of inflation, are of particular concern. Managers are also concerned about the affordable health

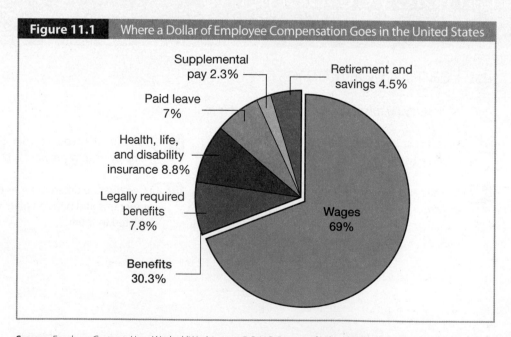

Figure 11.1 Where a Dollar of Employee Compensation Goes in the United States

Supplemental pay 2.3%
Retirement and savings 4.5%
Paid leave 7%
Health, life, and disability insurance 8.8%
Legally required benefits 7.8%
Benefits 30.3%
Wages 69%

Source: *Employer Costs per Hour Worked* (Washington DC: U.S. Bureau of Labor Statistics: 2011), http://www.bls.gov/news.release/ecec.t01.htm.

care laws proposed by Congress in 2017. We will discuss more about health care reform later in the chapter along with health care cost-containment measures firms are implementing.

Many forces must be kept in balance for a benefits program to succeed. For example, a firm's managers must consider how to fund its benefits program and sustain it, as well as the tax consequences related to it. The needs of a company's employees also must be considered because they can differ significantly from firm to firm. If the firm's industry is unionized, this will affect the types of benefits the firm is likely to have to offer. So will the benefits its competitors are offering and the organization's strategic objectives. Microsoft, for example, picks up the full tab for medical care for all of its U.S. employees and their dependents, which is unusual. But Microsoft does so because one of its strategic objectives is to attract the top talent in the country. The benefits plan also needs to be compatible with the organization's strategic compensation plan (see Chapter 9), including its total rewards strategy.[3]

11.1a Selecting Benefits

In designing a benefits program, a firm can purchase detailed compensation data or hire outside firms to help in the designing process. Before a new benefit is introduced, its need should first be determined through consultation with employees. Designing benefits programs with employee participation means employees are more satisfied with the final benefits plan. And employees who are satisfied with their benefits are more likely to be satisfied with their jobs. Opinion surveys are also a common method for obtaining employee input. Many organizations establish committees composed of managers and employees to administer, interpret, and oversee their benefits policies. The Leadership and Learning Center in Salem, Massachusetts, a professional development organization, has decreased turnover from 40 percent in the 1990s to the single digits in recent years. The reason? A benefits committee. Twice a year, employees break into committees to administer benefits survey and revise the benefits plan, giving employees much more responsibility and say in their own benefits packages.[4]

Flexible Benefits

To serve their intended purpose, employee benefits programs must adapt to the changes that are continually occurring within our society. As you have learned, three generations of employees now occupy the workplace, and each places a different priority on their benefits. Consequently, firms have to think about designing a benefits strategy that appeals to each group. For example, Millennial employees are probably less likely to be concerned with having pensions than babyboomers. Likewise, Generation X employees who are raising their families are more likely to want family-friendly benefits and health care for their dependents than babyboomers and Millennial employees. There are also more single-parent families and two-earner couples in the workplace than there have been in the decades past. As you can see, benefits programs need to take into account a highly diversified workforce to attract highly capable employees.

To make it easier to accommodate the individual needs of different employees, a wide range of organizations have begun offering **flexible benefits plans**, also known as **cafeteria plans**. Rather than one-size-fits-all plans, these plans allow individual employees to choose the benefits that are best suited to their particular needs. They also prevent certain benefits from being wasted on employees who have no need for them. Furthermore, companies realize they can get a better return on investment by tailoring

LO 1
What makes benefits so expensive? Would you rather have the additional money being paid for your benefits?

flexible benefits plans (cafeteria plans)
Benefit plans that enable individual employees to choose the benefits that are best suited to their particular needs.

benefits to an employee's stage of life or family status.[5] Compensation specialists often see flexible benefits plans as ideal. Employees select the benefits of greatest value to them, while employers manage benefits costs by limiting the dollars employees have to spend.

Typically, employees are offered a basic or core benefits package of life and health insurance, sick leave, and vacation. Requiring a core set of benefits ensures that employees have a minimum level of coverage to protect against unforeseen financial hardships. Employees are then given a certain amount of funds to purchase whatever other benefits they need through the plan. Other benefit options might include prepaid legal services, financial planning, dental insurance, and long-term care insurance. Some of the less-routine options include elder care, public transportation vouchers, and even pet insurance. These are optional, since not every employee will need or want services such as these, so they are optional.

11.1b Administering Benefits

With the wide variety of benefits offered to employees today, administering an organization's benefits program can be both costly and time-consuming. Even for small employers with 30 to 40 employees, keeping track of each employee's use of a benefit or request for a change of benefits can be cumbersome. Fortunately, online employee benefit systems have become mainstream for both large and small employers. Employees are provided with passwords that allow them to get information about their benefits plans, enroll in their plans of choice, change their coverage, or simply inquire about the status of their various benefit accounts without contacting a HR representative. Online benefits systems are often referred to as *employee self-service (ESS) systems* and can result in significant cost savings in benefits administration, improving accuracy of decisions, decreasing processing time, and greater employee satisfaction.[6] This system is so successful because it gives employees the information and responsibility of personalizing and tracking their own benefits.

As with the benefits themselves, it can be helpful to obtain feedback on different online systems a firm is investigating and adopting by asking employees to "test drive" them. If a system is difficult to navigate, employees will end up calling the human resources department for assistance, defeating the purpose of the system.

11.1c Communicating Employee Benefits

Communicating the costs of benefits is a key part of an effective benefits strategy. One survey from a research and consulting firm found that 4 of 10 U.S. employees lack any knowledge of the costs of their benefits, and of the 60 percent who think they know the cost of their benefits, only 15 percent could provide a reasonable estimate.[7] But even as employees become more aware of the cost of their benefits, many of them still do not realize exactly what employers are paying or why they try to keep benefits costs down.

Communicating employee benefits information improved significantly with the passage of the Employee Retirement Income Security Act (ERISA) in 1974. The act requires that employees be informed about their pension and certain other benefits in a manner calculated to be understood by the average employee. Additionally, employees can sue their employers for misleading them about health and welfare benefits under ERISA.

In one settlement, Providence Health & Services, a nonprofit hospital chain, paid $352 million to settle a proposed class action accusing the organization of using religious affiliation as church exemption to avoid ERISA requirements of minimum funding and failing to protect employees' retirement plans.[8] This and other settlements underscore the importance of communicating benefit information accurately and unambiguously.

When communicating employee benefits, the best advice is to use multiple media techniques. Different employee groups have different ways of learning and distinct preferences for how they receive information. Also, the level of complexity of the benefit information being communicated is likely to determine media selection.[9] Because about a third of IKEA's employees are Millennials, the company was worried if it only mailed out benefit information to these employees, many of them would not bother to open the packages. So in addition to mailing information the company used Twitter to send a weblink to its benefits site and remind employees about the firm's benefit enrollment deadline. "We wanted to talk to our co-workers in a way they are talking," says Beth Gleba, corporate information manager for IKEA, North America.[10]

Samsung is a company using its own technology to build employee engagement to help recruit and retain talent. In 2012, Samsung switched to an online, flexible benefits portal called Highlights, but still struggled to get the staff to take advantage of the choices and flexibility of the benefits plan. So to communicate the benefits package of Highlights, Samsung rebranded the package and its communication strategy. Not only was the Highlights interface easier to access and use, but Samsung passed out gifts to the staff like a piggy bank or a pedometer with the Highlights logo to highlight the new wealth and lifestyle benefits categories. They also used online materials, text messages, and physical posters and infographics to get employees to think more seriously about the benefits offered alongside salary. Samsung, once struggling to engage staff about their benefits, now has reached the stage where 95 percent of its employees have used Highlights.[11]

Some general pointers for designing benefits information regardless of the medium include the following:

- Avoid complex language when describing benefits. Clear, concise, and understandable language is a must.
- Explain the purpose behind a benefit and the value it offers employees. Be upfront about the pros and cons of different benefit plans.
- Use graphics whenever possible to make the information understandable at a glance.
- Provide numerous examples to illustrate how a benefit choice might affect different types of employees, depending upon their personal circumstances.

Even if employees can access their benefits information online, most firms periodically mail out printed benefit statements that detail the status of an employee's benefits. See the Highlights in HRM 1 for an example of how to calculate your total compensation based on salary and benefits. Notice how the employee's total compensation is highlighted so that the full value of the benefits received is easier to see.

Cost Containment Strategies

Many firms have either begun requiring employees to pay part of the cost of their benefits or, if they were already doing so, increasing the amounts they pay in the form of premiums, copays, and deductibles. In addition, it is not uncommon for larger companies to cut the health care plans they once provided their retirees.

Employers must use a variety of techniques to communicate the complexities of benefits programs to their employees.

Source: http://blogs.intel.com/jobs/

Containing Medical Benefits Costs

What is causing the growth in health care costs? The rise has been attributed to many factors. One is the overuse of costly health care services by consumers. This is part of the reason why firms have turned to health savings accounts and **high-deductible health insurance plans (HDHPs)**. In conjunction with HDHPs, employees are provided with a *health care spending account (HSA)* they and their employers can contribute to on a pretax basis. In addition, employees can deduct the amounts they contribute from their earnings when they pay their income taxes. An advantage of HSAs is that the funds remaining in the account at the end of the year belong to the employee, even if he or she leaves the company. Employees often like HDHPs for this reason and because the regular premiums deducted from their paychecks for insurance are generally lower than they are with other types of health care plans such as health maintenance organizations (HMOs) and preferred provider organizations (PPOs).

The downside is that with an HDHP, when employees receive treatment, they have to pay either a percentage of their care or all of it until they meet a high threshold called a deductible. These expenses are generally higher than the copays and deductibles associated with other types of plans. Because of this, employees are more conscious of medical costs. They have an incentive to spend their health care funds wisely and over

high-deductible health insurance plan (HDHP)
A medical insurance plan characterized by high deductibles but lower premiums for workers and a health spending account to which employers contribute funds employees can keep should they leave the organization.

time to increase the value of their health savings accounts. For this reason, HDHPs are sometimes referred to as *consumer-driven plans*.

HDHPs do seem to help control costs. However, because they work differently and require higher out-of-pocket costs for employees, HR managers need to carefully explain how they work and show employees how much long-term savings they can accumulate for their long-term medical care. Also, some studies have shown that employees with HSAs tend to put off preventive care so as to grow their HSAs. This can be a mistake if an employee later develops a serious and costly disease that could have been prevented with early screening and treatment.

Because HMOs and PPOs offer discounted rates, they have become another vehicle for reducing costs. **Health maintenance organizations (HMOs)** are organizations of physicians and other health care professionals that provide a wide range of services to subscribers and their dependents on a prepaid basis. Employees pay a small fixed fee called a copay, often $25 or $30, whenever they get medical treatment. Employers pay a fixed annual fee to the HMO to cover the majority of their employees' medical costs. Because they must provide all covered services for a fixed dollar amount, HMOs generally emphasize preventive care and early intervention. Employees who sign up for the plan must choose a general-practice physician, called a *primary-care physician*, from the HMO's list of doctors. Their primary-care physicians provide them with their basic medical care. However, to see a specialist, employees need a referral from their primary-care physicians. This helps keep costs down as well, because specialists charge fees that are generally higher than those charged by primary-care physicians. The copays employees pay to see specialists are also slightly higher, which gives employees an incentive to see their primary-care physicians first.

A **preferred provider organization (PPO)** is a group of physicians who establish an organization or a network of doctors that guarantee lower costs to the employer through lower service charges or agreed-on utilization controls (such as a reduced number of diagnostic tests per employee). Unlike HMOs, where employees may have limited choices when it comes to the doctors they see, PPOs allow employees to select their doctor of choice from a wider list of physicians (participating doctors). Normally, a number of physicians are available to choose from for different medical needs, and employees do not need a referral to see a specialist. Small copays are a common feature of PPOs as well. Employees also have the option of using a doctor outside of the PPO, but it costs more.

Employers sometimes couple PPOs and HMOS with different types of tax-advantaged accounts employees can use to pay their out-of-pocket health care expenses such as their copays, the cost of prescription drugs, and so forth. A *health reimbursement account (HRA)* allows employees to be reimbursed by their companies for their out-of-pocket expenses. Employees do not have to pay taxes on the amounts they are reimbursed, which is what they would have to do if the reimbursements were made through their paychecks. A *flexible spending account (FSA)* is another type of account employees use to pay for their health-related expenses. Employees fund these accounts by having money deducted from their paychecks. The money deducted is not subject to taxes, so workers have more to spend on their health care than they would without the accounts. Companies can make contributions to FSAs as well. A disadvantage of FSAs is that funds not used by the end of the plan year revert back to one's employer.

In addition, many companies—even Fortune 500 companies—are limiting the plans employees can choose from to all but the least expensive ones and conducting audits to be sure non-eligible dependents of employees are not being covered.

health maintenance organizations (HMOs)
Organizations of physicians and health care professionals that provide a wide range of services to subscribers and dependents on a prepaid basis.

preferred provider organization (PPO)
A network of physicians who establish an organization that guarantees lower health care costs to employers and their employees.

Containing Dental, Optical, and Mental Health Benefits Costs

Dental plans are designed to help pay for dental care costs and to encourage employees to receive regular dental attention. Like medical plans, dental care plans may be operated by insurance companies, dental service corporations, those administering Blue Cross/Blue Shield plans, HMOs, and groups of dental care providers. Typically, the insurance pays a portion of the charges, and the subscriber pays the remainder. Optical benefits work in a similar way. These benefits generally cover or offset the cost of seeing an optometrist once or twice a year as well as the cost of contact lenses and glasses purchased periodically.

Almost all workers with health coverage receive mental health benefits as part of their plans. However, prior to 2009, most plans had limits on inpatient hospital stays and outpatient visits, and the copays were often higher than they were for medical-care copays. The Mental Health Parity and Addiction Equity Act of 2008 changed that. In terms of the costs and access to care, the law requires group health plans to treat mental health benefits the same way they do medical and surgical benefits.[12]

Containing Additional Costs

An aging U.S. population, high obesity rates, and the health problems associated with them are three other reasons cited for rising health care costs. To combat these problems, companies are offering employees lower health care premiums for adopting healthy habits and activities. Wellness programs (discussed shortly) are a part of this effort. Conversely, firms are also penalizing employees for unhealthy habits by charging them higher health care premiums for habits such as smoking.[13] To help cope with the rising costs of drugs, companies are encouraging their employees to use generic drugs and buy 90-day supplies through designated mail-order pharmacies that provide them at a discount.

One of the more dramatic moves companies are making is waiving the deductibles and copays for medical tourism. This means employees can pay less if they are willing to travel abroad for medical procedures where they often cost only a fraction of what they do in the United States.[14] Figure 11.2 shows the countries Americans most utilize for treatment abroad and the approximate cost of procedures as a percentage of U.S. costs.

Many employers offer incentives for employees who take care of their health, such as discounts on health club memberships.

Lucky Business/Shutterstock.com

Value-Based Health Initiatives

A small but growing number of employers are turning to what is being called *value-based health initiatives*. Value-based initiatives focus on more than cost-cutting. Companies pursuing this strategy look at the medical care their employees most use and need—such as treatment for asthma, high blood pressure, or diabetes—and target benefits and health programs toward them. For example, Cerner Corporation, an electronic health record system for health

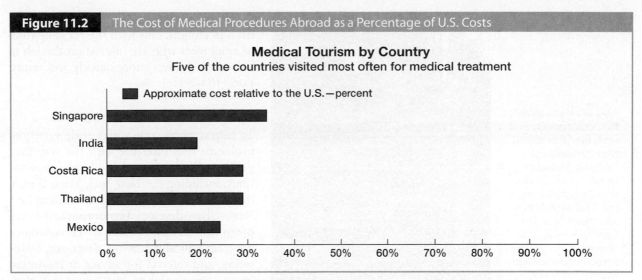

Figure 11.2   The Cost of Medical Procedures Abroad as a Percentage of U.S. Costs

Medical Tourism by Country
Five of the countries visited most often for medical treatment

■ Approximate cost relative to the U.S.—percent

Singapore	
India	
Costa Rica	
Thailand	
Mexico	

0% 10% 20% 30% 40% 50% 60% 70% 80% 90% 100%

Source: Adapted from *Reuters*, Deloitte, and the research findings of Joseph Woodman, the author of *Patients Without Borders*.

care providers like hospitals and clinics, noticed that many of their employees didn't purchase the medicine they needed to handle their anxiety or depression. So they reduced the out-of-pocket costs and waived copayments for prescriptions for antidepressants for employees and their families. Because of this policy change, Cerner Corporation employees were more likely to use or start a new medication for anxiety or depression and reported positive health outcomes.[15]

Wellness Programs

Wellness programs are employer-sponsored programs designed to encourage employees to maintain and improve their health and well-being by getting regular checkups, eating properly, exercising, and managing their stress levels so as to prevent costly and protracted illnesses. The Home Depot has a broad corporate wellness program to prioritize employee health and demonstrates the kinds of strategies other firms can use when formulating their own wellness programs. The Home Depot offers resources like healthy cooking and physical fitness programs with such resources as cookbooks, discounts to health club chains, and chats with coaches to set goals and create a 12-week journey to better health; health challenges every summer for a chance to win cash prizes; smoking cessation programs with free one-on-one coaching and nicotine patches; free onsite flu shots; and wellness recognition programs where employees nominate one employee who sets and achieves their wellness goal for a prized patch to wear on their apron and recognition from The Home Depot.[16]

Disease Management Programs

Via medically trained personnel, **disease management programs** provide patients and their caregivers with information on monitoring and treating medical conditions, while coordinating communication between them, their health care providers, employers, and insurers. Bank One Corporation of Chicago developed such a program when managers noticed high absenteeism among employees with diabetes, asthma, and depression.

wellness programs
Employer-sponsored programs designed to encourage employees to maintain and improve their health and well-being by getting regular checkups, eating properly, exercising, and managing their stress levels so as to prevent costly and protracted illnesses.

disease management programs
Programs that provide patients and their caregivers with information on monitoring and treating medical conditions, while coordinating communication between them, their health care providers, employers, and insurers.

Walk while you work? To combat obesity and other health problems, GlaxoSmithKline, Humana, Mutual of Omaha, and Best Buy have begun utilizing treadmill desks like the one shown here. The treadmills move at a slow speed so employees do not get hot and sweaty and out of breath.

Richard Sennott/Tribune Content Agenc- LLC / Alamy

employee assistance programs (EAPs)

Services provided by employers to help workers cope with a wide variety of problems that interfere with the way they perform their jobs.

Disease management programs can also be used in conjunction with the rehabilitation of employees who are injured on the job to help them recover more quickly and return safely to work.

Employee Assistance Programs

To help workers cope with a wide variety of problems that interfere with the way they perform their jobs, all kinds of organizations, including the New York Mets, USAA, the Los Angeles Police Department, and Levi Strauss, have developed **employee assistance programs (EAPs)**. An employee assistance program typically provides diagnosis, counseling, and referral for advice or treatment when necessary for problems related to alcohol or drug abuse, emotional difficulties, and financial or family difficulties.[17] The main intent is to help employees solve their personal problems or at least to prevent problems from turning into crises that affect their ability to work productively. To handle crises, many EAPs offer 24-hour hotlines employees can call. After Cerner Corporation offered its employees an EAP program, the company's outpatient mental health care costs declined by nearly 41 percent.[18]

Counseling Services

An important part of an EAP is the counseling services it provides to employees. While most organizations expect managers to counsel subordinates, some employees may have problems that require the services of professional counselors. Most organizations refer such individuals to outside counseling services such as family counseling services, marriage counselors, and mental health clinics. Some organizations have a clinical psychologist, counselor, or comparable specialist on staff to who employees may be referred.

LO 2

Does the government require too many or too few benefits for employees?

11.2 Employee Benefits Required by Law

Legally required employee benefits constitute 19 percent of the benefits package that employers provide. These benefits include employer contributions to social security, unemployment insurance, and workers' compensation insurance. We will discuss each of these benefits.

11.2a Social Security Insurance

The Social Security Act was designed to protect workers against the loss of earnings resulting from old age and unemployment. The act was later amended to include disability, or, in the case of dependents, the death of the worker supporting them. Together the programs have become referred to as Old Age, Survivors, and Disability Insurance (OASDI). According to the Social Security Administration, in 2017 over 62 million people received retirement benefits from social security.[19]

A Personalized Statement of Benefits Costs

ABC Corporation

Your Total Compensation Report

Enclosed is a personalized Statement prepared specifically for you. This statement shows the contributions made by your company toward your total compensation package. As you review this statement, you will see that the value of your benefits, added to your annual pay, produce your total compensation. The statement is designed to show how much your service is valued by your company.

Thank you for your service,

Jonathan Bigg, President

Chris Smith
123 Maple Street
Pittsburgh, PA 15212

Department: Marketing

	Base Pay		Other Cash Benefits		Company-Paid Benefits		Total Compensation
	$40,000	+	$1,600	+	$19,579	=	$61,179

Pay		
Base Pay Total	$	**40,000**
Salary	$	40,000
Other Income Total	$	**1,600**
Holiday Bonus	$	200
Annual Bonus	$	500
Performance Bonus	$	900

Total Compensation Package
(Your Base Pay and Company-Paid Benefits)

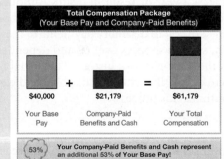

$40,000	+	$21,179	=	$61,179
Your Base Pay		Company-Paid Benefits and Cash		Your Total Compensation

53% Your Company-Paid Benefits and Cash represent an additional 53% of Your Base Pay!

Additional Company Perks
Free Coffee Service
Annual Holiday Gala
Annual Company Picnic

Benefits	Company Contribution			Your Contribution	
Insurance Benefits Total	$	6,917		$	4,703
Health Insurance	$	5,770		$	2,885
Dental Insurance	$	577		$	288
Vision Insurance	$	344		$	--
Short-Term Disability	$	133		$	--
Long-Term Disability	$	93		$	--
Aflac Short-Term Disability	$	--		$	680
Aflac Personal Accident	$	--		$	522
Aflac Cancer	$	--		$	328
Retirement Benefits Total	$	3,425		$	4,175
Social Security	$	2,579		$	2,579
Medicare	$	596		$	596
401K	$	250		$	1,000
Time Off Benefits Total	$	3,320		$	--
PTO	$	3,320		$	--
Mandated Benefits Total	$	1,747		$	--
Federal Unemployment	$	56		$	--
State Unemployment	$	179		$	--
Worker's Compensation	$	1,512		$	--
Special Benefits Total	$	4,170		$	--
Free Parking	$	2,400		$	--
Fun Fridays Food Fests	$	250		$	--
Cell/PC/Technology	$	600		$	--
Education/Training	$	920		$	--
Benefits Total	$	19,579		$	8,878

69% Your Company-Paid Benefits represent 69% of your Total Benefits!

OASDI has become nearly universal for work performed in the United States, covering approximately 96 percent of the American workforce. Workers excluded from coverage include railroad workers and civil service employees covered by their own systems as well as farmers, domestic workers, and the self-employed whose earnings do not meet certain minimum requirements.[20] The Social Security program is supported by means of a tax levied against an employee's earnings that must be matched by the employer in each pay period. In 2017, the tax was 6.2 percent, though the percentage can vary depending on economic conditions.[21] The tax revenues are used to pay three major types of benefits: (1) retirement benefits, (2) disability benefits, and (3) survivors' benefits. Because of the continual changes that result from legislation and administrative rulings, as well as the complexities of making determinations of an individual's rights under social security, we will describe these benefits only in general terms.

Retirement Benefits

To qualify for retirement benefits, a person must have reached retirement age and be fully insured. A *fully insured person* has earned 40 credits—a maximum of 4 credits a year for 10 years, based on annual earnings, a figure adjusted annually. The amount of monthly social security retirement benefits is based on earnings, adjusted for inflation, over the years an individual is covered by social security. Under Social Security guidelines, an individual's *full retirement age* depends on the year of his or her birth. Workers born after 1928 can collect full benefits once they've earned 40 credits, about 10 years of work.[22] Because of longer life expectancies, for those born after that date, the age to collect full benefits has been gradually raised to age 67.

Disability Benefits under Social Security

Social Security pays benefits to people who cannot work because they have a medical condition that is expected to last at least a year or result in death. Although some government programs provide money to people with partial disabilities or short-term disabilities, Social Security does not.[23] In addition to disability payments to the worker, certain members of an employee's family, such as spouses over 62 and dependent children, may qualify for benefits based on the person's work history. The Social Security Administration uses a five-step process to decide if a worker is disabled and eligible to collect benefits. Highlights in HRM 2 outlines this process.

Survivor's Benefits

Survivors' benefits represent a form of life insurance paid to members of a deceased person's family who meet the eligibility requirements.[24] Survivors' benefits can be paid only if the deceased worker had credit for a certain amount of time spent in work covered by social security. The exact amount of work credit needed depends on the worker's age at death. As with other benefits discussed earlier, the *amount* of benefit survivors receive is based on the worker's lifetime earnings doing work covered by social security.

Medicare

The Social Security Administration also administers the Medicare program, which is funded by a separate payroll tax. Retired people age 65 or older are eligible for Medicare, which includes both medical and hospital insurance and prescription drug coverage.[25] The program helps with the cost of health care, but it does not cover all medical expenses or the cost of most long-term care.[26] A portion of the payroll taxes is paid by

Who Is Eligible to Collect Disability Payments under the Social Security Act?

If you experience a disability, the Social Security Administration in conjunction with a state agency will use the following five-step process to determine if you are eligible to collect benefits.

1. **Are you working?** If you are working and your earnings average more than a certain amount each month, you will generally not be considered disabled. The amount changes each year. If you are not working, or your monthly earnings average this amount or less, a state agency will then look at your medical condition.

2. **Is your medical condition "severe"?** For the state agency to decide that you are disabled, your medical condition must significantly limit your ability to do basic work activities—such as walking, sitting, and remembering—for at least one year. If your medical condition is not that severe, the state agency will not consider you disabled. If your condition is that severe, the state agency goes on to step 3.

3. **Is your medical condition on the List of Impairments?** The state agency has a list of impairments that describes medical conditions that are considered so severe that they automatically mean that you are disabled as defined by law. If your condition

(or combination of medical conditions) is not on this list, the state agency looks to see if your condition is as severe as a condition that is on the list. If the severity of your medical condition meets or equals that of a listed impairment, the state agency will decide that you are disabled. If it does not, the state agency goes on to step 4.

4. **Can you do the work you did before?** At this step, the state agency decides if your medical condition prevents you from being able to do the work you did before. If it does not, the state agency will decide that you are not disabled. If it does, the state agency goes on to step 5.

5. **Can you do any other type of work?** If you cannot do the work you did in the past, the state agency looks to see if you would be able to do other work. It evaluates your medical condition, your age, education, past work experience, and any skills you may have that could be used to do other work. If you cannot do other work, the state agency will decide that you are disabled. If you can do other work, the state agency will decide that you are not disabled.

Source: *Disability Benefits*, SSA Publication No. 05-10029 (Washington, DC: U.S. Social Security Administration, 2010), www.ssa.gov/diplan/dqualify5.htm.

workers and matched by their employers. In 2017, workers and their employers each paid 1.45 percent on every dollar of salary or wages paid.[27] Medicare is also financed in part by monthly medical premiums deducted from social security recipient's checks.

One of the concerns employers have about Medicare relates to the eligibility age. As explained, it is currently 65, but legislators are considering increasing the age to 67 as they have done with social security.[28]

11.2b Unemployment Insurance

Unemployment insurance is part of a national program administered by the U.S. Department of Labor under the Social Security Act and coordinated with the states. It protects workers who lose their jobs through no fault of their own. Employers entirely foot the bill for this benefit via a payroll tax, which can vary widely by the state. The rates firms pay also depend upon their layoff records, or what is referred to as their *experience ratings*. Generally speaking, a firm with a record of laying off large numbers of employees will have to pay a higher rate than those that do not. This means that companies most likely to lay people off will have to pay a larger share of unemployment taxes that end up going to their former workers. In addition, these tax rates will vary from one state to the next. As you can see, unemployment taxes are something HR managers must consider when they make decisions about where to locate their operations and hire employees as well as lay them off.

Employees who are laid off are generally eligible for up to 26 weeks of unemployment insurance benefits during their unemployment. During periods of high unemployment, the federal government has sometimes passed legislation extending the amount of weeks employees can collect benefits.

Workers eligible for unemployment benefits must submit an application for unemployment compensation with their state employment agencies, register for available work, and be willing to accept any suitable employment that may be offered to them. However, the term "suitable" gives individuals considerable discretion in accepting or rejecting job offers. The amount of compensation workers are eligible to receive, which also varies by the state, is determined by a worker's previous wage rate and length of employment.

11.2c Workers' Compensation Insurance

workers' compensation insurance
State-mandated insurance provided to workers to defray the loss of income and cost of treatment due to work-related injuries or illness.

Workers' compensation insurance is a system whereby employers purchase private or state-funded insurance to cover employees injured at work. Workers' compensation law is governed by statutes in every state. Therefore, specific laws vary with each jurisdiction. For example, each state has different regulations governing the amount and duration of lost income benefits, including provisions for medical and rehabilitation services and how the state system is administered. Workers' compensation laws also provide death benefits to surviving spouses and dependents.

Workers' compensation insurance covers workers injured on the job, whether injured on the workplace premises, elsewhere, or in an auto accident while on business. It does not matter if the employee was at fault. In addition, workers that collect compensation cannot sue their employers for their injuries unless gross negligence by the employer led to the injury or the employer lacked the level of insurance required by law. Workers' compensation insurance also covers certain work-related illnesses. Before any workers' compensation claim will be allowed, the work-relatedness of the disability must be established. Also, the evaluation of the claimant by a physician trained in occupational medicine is an essential part of the claim process.

While employers in all states pay "workers' comp" insurance, the amount they pay—through payroll taxes—varies. Like with unemployment insurance rates, the rate an employer pays depends upon its experience rating, which is based on various factors including the company's frequency and severity of employee injuries (referred to as the company's experience rating). Not surprisingly, organizations will strive to have good safety records (see Chapter 12 on creating a safe work environment) in order to pay a lower payroll tax rate.

11.2d COBRA Insurance

We first discussed COBRA in Chapter 3. Recall that the Consolidated Omnibus Budget Reconciliation Act mandates that employers make health care coverage—at the same rate the employer would pay—available to employees, their spouses, and their dependents on termination of employment, death, or divorce.[29] The coverage must be offered for 18 to 36 months, depending on qualifying guidelines.

11.2e Benefits Provided by the Patient Protection and Affordable Care Act

In 2010, the Patient Protection and Affordable Care Act (PPACA) became law. This act, along with the Health Care and Education Reconciliation Act of 2010, comprises the health care reform platform that went into effect in 2014.

The key provisions all employers need to consider are the following:

- Firms that employ 50 or more people who work 30 or more hours per week but do not offer them health insurance will have to pay a penalty to the government. Also, firms with 200 full-time employees are required to automatically enroll new full-time employees in their health care plans.
- Employers must offer coverage for their employee's children until they turn 26.
- No copays or deductibles can be charged to employees and their dependents for certain "essential" health care services, which are generally preventive care related.
- Lifetime dollar limits on key health care benefits are not allowed.
- Employees cannot lose their insurance coverage solely because of an honest mistake they or their employers made on their insurance applications.

As of 2017, the Affordable Care Act was being contested by President Trump and the Republican congressional leaders. They insisted that they would retain the crucial part of the law: the promise that people can buy insurance even if they've had illnesses in the past. However, some of the proposed changes included opt-out provisions that would not require insurers to cover a standard, minimum package of benefits to everyone. Insurers would also be able to charge more for people who have prior illness.[30]

11.2f Benefits Provided under the Family and Medical Leave Act

The Family and Medical Leave Act (FMLA) applies to employers having 50 or more employees during 20 or more calendar workweeks in the current or preceding year.[31] A covered employer must grant an eligible employee up to a total of 12 workweeks of unpaid leave in a 12-month period for one or more of the following reasons:

- Birth of and care for a newborn child
- Adoption or foster care placement of a child
- Care for an immediate family member (spouse, child, or parent) with a serious medical condition
- Serious health condition of the employee[32]

Under the FMLA, employees are eligible to take leave if they have worked for their employers for at least 12 months, have at least 1,250 hours of service, and work in organizations that have 50 or more employees within a 75-mile radius. An employer can require that the need for medical leave be supported by a certification issued by a health care provider. Highlights in HRM 3 shows the federally required poster for the FMLA. In studying the poster, note the other important stipulations, such as enforcement and unlawful acts, which are of direct concern to managers.

Parents of newborn children are guaranteed 12 weeks of unpaid leave under the provisions of the Family and Medical Leave Act.

OJO Images Ltd / Alamy

This law affects an organization's benefits program in several of its provisions: It mandates continuation of medical coverage, it prohibits loss of accrued benefits, it provides for restoration of benefits after leave, it permits substitution of paid leave and vacation during leave, it makes communication and notice compulsory, and it prohibits waiver of benefits. On return from FMLA leave, an employee must be restored to his or her original job or to an "equivalent" job. Equivalent jobs are those identical to the original job in terms of pay, benefits, and other employment terms and conditions.

Employers need to check their state employee-leave laws as well. Some states provide rights to employees that are greater than those provided by the FMLA. Wisconsin is an example. Two states—California and New Jersey—require employers to provide paid leave to parents following childbirth or adoption.[33]

In January 2008, Congress passed the National Defense Authorization Act that amended the FMLA to provide eligible employees working for covered employers new leave rights related to military service. Specifically, an eligible employee who is the spouse, son, daughter, parent, or next of kin of a covered service member who is recovering from a serious illness or injury sustained in the line of duty on active duty is entitled to up to 26 weeks of leave in a single 12-month period to care for the service member. Importantly, managers or supervisors with legal or administrative questions regarding the FMLA are advised to seek assistance from HR before proceeding with an employee's FMLA leave request. Also, employers cannot penalize employees for requesting or taking FMLA leave in an employment action including hiring, promotion, transfer, training, disciplinary action, or awards for attendance (not missing work).

Your Rights under the Family and Medical Leave Act

Employers are required to provide employees with this general notice about FMLA, which must be posted at the worksite (or electronically) and published in an employee handbook or given to new employees upon hire.

EMPLOYEE RIGHTS AND RESPONSIBILITIES
UNDER THE FAMILY AND MEDICAL LEAVE ACT

Leave Entitlement

Eligible employees who work for covered employers can take up to 12 weeks of unpaid, job-protected leave in a 12-month period for the following reasons:
- The birth of a child or placement of a child for adoption or foster care
- To bond with a child (leave must be taken within 1 year of the child's birth or placement)
- To care for the employee's spouse, child, or parent, who has a qualifying serious health condition
- For the employee's own qualifying serious health condition that makes the employee unable to perform the employee's job
- For qualifying exigencies related to the foreign deployment of a military member who is the employee's spouse, child, or parent

An eligible employee who is a covered servicemember's spouse, child, parent, or next of kin may also take up to 26 weeks of FMLA leave in a single 12-month period to care for the servicemember with a serious injury or illness.

An employee does not need to use leave in one block. When it is medically necessary or otherwise permitted, employees may take leave intermittently or on a reduced schedule.

Employees may choose, or an employer may require, use of accrued paid leave while taking FMLA leave. If an employee substitutes accrued paid leave for FMLA leave, the employee must comply with the employer's normal paid leave policies.

Benefits and Protections
While employees are on FMLA leave, employers must continue health insurance coverage as if the employees were not on leave.

Upon return from FMLA leave, most employees must be restored to the same job or one nearly identical to it with equivalent pay, benefits, and other employment terms and conditions.

An employer may not interfere with an individual's FMLA rights or retaliate against someone for using or trying to use FMLA leave, opposing any practice made unlawful by the FMLA, or being involved in any proceeding under or related to the FMLA.

Eligibility Requirements
An employee who works for a covered employer must meet three criteria in order to be eligible for FMLA leave. The employee must:
- Have worked for the employer for at least 12 months
- Have at least 1,250 hours of service in the 12 months before taking leave*

- Work at a location where the employer has at least 50 employees within 75 miles of the employee's worksite

*Special "hours of service" requirements apply to airline flight crew employees.

Requesting Leave
Generally, employees must give 30-day advance notice of the need for FMLA leave. If it is not possible to give a 30-day notice, an employee must notify the employer as soon as possible and, generally, follow the employer's usual procedures.

Employees do not have to share a medical diagnosis, but must provide enough information to the employer so it can determine if the leave qualifies for FMLA protection. Sufficient information could include informing an employer that the employee is or will be unable to perform his or her job functions, that a family member cannot perform daily activities, or that hospitalization or continuing medical treatment is necessary. Employees must inform the employer if the need for leave is for a reason for which FMLA leave was previously taken or certified.

Employers can require a certification or periodic recertification supporting the need for leave. If the employer determines that the certification is incomplete, it must provide a written notice indicating what additional information is required.

Employer Responsibilities
Once an employer becomes aware that an employee's need for leave is for a reason that may qualify under the FMLA, the employer must notify the employee if he or she is eligible for FMLA leave and, if eligible, must also provide a notice of right and responsibilities under the FMLA. If the employee is not eligible, the employer must provide a reason for ineligibility.

Employers must notify its employees if leave will be designated as FMLA leave, and if so, how much leave will be designated as FMLA leave.

Enforcement
Employees may file a complaint with the U.S. Department of Labor, Wage and Hour Division, or may bring a private lawsuit against an employer.

The FMLA does not affect any federal or state law prohibiting discrimination or supersede any state or local law or collective bargaining agreement that provides greater family or medical leave rights.

For additional information or to file a complaint:
1-866-4US-WAGE (1-866-487-9243) TTY: 1-877-889-5627
www.dol.gov/whd

U.S. Department of Labor | Wage and Hour Division
WHD Publication 1420 Revised April 2016

U.S. Wage and Hour Division

WHD Publication 1420 Revised January 2009

Note: Other federally required posters are reproduced in Chapters 3, 9, and 12M.

LO 3
What additional types of benefits would be most attractive to you?

11.3 Work-Life Discretionary Benefits

Eddie Bauer, an outdoor clothing and equipment supplier, offers its employees take-out dinners and one paid "balance day" off a year. eBay sets aside spaces at its San Jose, California, campuses as prayer and meditation rooms where employees can "decompress" during the workday. Ben & Jerry's employees have access to a nap room. At Mitre, a nonprofit researcher, employees can take up to a week of paid time off to help with scouting trips or volunteer projects. These organizations, like many others, are seeking to create a work-life organizational climate that allows employees to balance their work with their personal needs. Why? One research report shows that 60 percent of employees prefer to have work-life balance benefits, and that employees are 20 percent more engaged in and satisfied with their job when they've hit the right work-life balance.[34] And work-life balance programs not only retain talent but can be a factor in attracting and recruiting potential employees. And as Millennials trend toward dominating the job market, attracting this demographic means adjusting programs to include the kinds of benefits they want, like 401(k) matching, onsite nutritionists, corporate-wide community events and challenges, the ability to work from home, and opportunities to volunteer or contribute to social causes.[35] To appeal to this broad demographic group and other employees concerned about the environment, some companies have begun offering their employees "green" benefits. Clif Bar & Company gives employees $6,500 toward the purchase of a hybrid car.

11.3a Child and Elder Care

Consider this: Every week, child care providers in the United States look after nearly 11 million children under the age of 5 whose parents are working.[36] This, combined with increased employment of women with dependent children, illustrates the unprecedented demand for child care arrangements. Some employers, such as Fel-Pro, Merck, Syntex, Baptist Hospital of Miami, and Ben & Jerry's, promote onsite or near-site child care centers. Employer-sponsored dependent care spending accounts allow employees to set aside a portion of their pay before taxes to care for a dependent child. If a mom has to travel with a breastfeeding child, Zillow will pay for them to ship their breast milk back home; and Facebook provides $4,000 in "Baby Cash" to employees with a newborn.[37]

Similarly, according to a study of AARP and the National Alliance for Caregiving, today more than 39 million Americans are caring, unpaid, for an elderly parent. The term **elder care**, as used in the context of employment, occurs when an employee provides care to an elderly relative while remaining actively at work. The majority of caregivers are women.[38]

Beyond the loss of organizational productivity and higher employee costs, a growing concern of employers is the negative effects of caregiving on employee health. Not surprisingly, caregivers in the workforce suffer higher levels of physical, emotional, and financial stress since they find it difficult to respond to the demands of balancing work and family.[39] To help employees meet the challenges of caregiving, organizations may offer elder care counseling, educational fairs and seminars, printed resource materials, support groups, and special flexible schedules and leaves of absence.[40] Employers may also band together for better elder care. The Partnership for Elder Care—a consortium of American Express, JPMorganChase, Philip Morris, and other companies—use the resources of the New York City Department of Aging, a public information and aging

elder care

Care provided to an elderly relative by an employee who remains actively at work.

support agency. In addition, an increasing number of employers supply or subsidize temporary care for employees' elders and children when their regular arrangements fall through so these employees can come to work. A benefit such as this is referred to as a **backup care program**. Home Depot, for example, offers a backup care program to its employees. The program provides a discount to employees who need spur-of-the-moment care so they can come to work.

backup care program
A benefit program whereby an employer provides or subsidizes temporary care for its employee's elders or children when their regular arrangements fall through.

11.3b Payment for Time Not Worked

The "payment for time not worked" category of benefits includes paid vacations, bonuses given in lieu of paid vacations, payments for holidays not worked, paid sick leave, military and jury duty, and payments for absence due to a death in the family or other personal reasons. Figure 11.1 showed that these benefits consti-tute another large expenditure—7 percent—of an employer's total payroll costs, on average.[41]

Paid time off is not mandatory in the United States, though. This contrasts sharply with the policies other countries around the world, including Austria, Peru, Spain, the United Arab Emirates, Finland, and Italy, where employees must be given 30 paid days off annually.[42] In fact, until recently China was the only other country that did not offer any paid time off. Now the United States is the only one.[43]

Vacations with Pay

Despite the fact that vacation pay is not required in the United States, most employers generally agree that vacations are essential to the well-being of an employee. Research shows that workers who use their vacation time are more productive and less prone to job-related burnout.[44] Exactly how much paid vacation time firms provide their employ-ees varies by a firm's industry, locale, size, and other factors. Employees in the United States who work for large companies often get 10 paid days of vacation a year. To qualify for longer vacations of 3, 4, or 5 weeks, one may expect to work for 7, 15, and 20 years, respectively.

Most companies require their employees to take their vacation days by the end of the year or forfeit them ("use it or lose it"). An increasing number of employees say they are too busy at work to take all the vacation days they are allotted. According to one survey, Americans hand back more than $21 billion in unused vacation dollars to their employers each year.[45] Some companies, however, let their employees "roll over" at least some of their vacation days to the following year. Of those that do, the average they allow workers to roll over is 20 days, according to a survey by the Society for Human Resources Management.[46]

Paid Holidays

The federal government recognizes 10 legal public holidays, which are shown in Figure 11.3. However, private employers are not required to offer employees these days off or pay employees for them. Many companies do, though. Organizations that have to remain open during holidays (emergency services providers such as hospitals, transpor-tation companies, etc.) often pay employees who work on holidays extra pay for doing so. Many organizations also give workers an additional 2 or 3 days off at their discretion for personal use.

Of course, not all employees celebrate all the holidays their companies recog-nize, particularly Christian holidays. A variety of arrangements can be made for these

---

Figure 11.3   Federally Recognized Holidays in the United States

- New Year's Day, January 1
- Martin Luther King, Jr. Day, the third Monday in January
- President's Day, the third Monday in February
- Memorial Day, the last Monday in May
- Independence Day, July 4
- Labor Day, the first Monday in September
- Columbus Day, the second Monday in October
- Veterans Day, November 11
- Thanksgiving Day, the fourth Thursday in November
- Christmas Day, December 25

---

employees. For example, they might be allowed to work the holidays and then take off other days as a substitute. Or they might be allowed to use personal days, vacation days, or, as a last resort, take the holidays they do not want to work off without pay. Another trend is to give all employees a certain number of paid days they can use as holidays whenever they want.

Sick Leave

There are several ways in which employees may be compensated during periods when they are unable to work because of illness or injury. Most public employees, as well as many in private firms, receive a set number of sick leave days each year to cover such absences. Where permitted, sick leave that employees do not use can be accumulated

Small Business Application

Creative Benefit Strategies Can Help Small Businesses Compete

Although competing with large companies on the basis of benefits might seem impossible, small business owners still have some other "cards" they can play that bigger companies might not offer. For example, if they cannot offer extensive benefits, it is not uncommon for small businesses to offer stock or shares in the company to their employees. Flexible work hours and arrangements are also a low-cost strategic benefit small businesses can offer their employees without first having to cut through a lot of corporate red tape.

Another way small businesses can augment their benefits programs is by partnering with companies that offer discount programs to employers' workers. Price Optical offers a discount program for employers who are not able to provide vision benefits for their employees. Discounts for homeowners, automobile and group life insurance, dental and chiropractic care, health club memberships, and weight-control programs are other benefits small businesses can procure on behalf of their employees as well as tickets to entertainment events and product discounts.

Finally, if a small business wants its employees to have benefits but does not want to either provide or administer them, it can contract with a professional employer organization (PEO). Recall from Chapter 1 that a PEO is typically a larger company that for a fee takes over the management of a smaller company's HR tasks and can provide employees with benefits that small companies cannot afford.

Sources: Gwen Moran, "The Business of Better Benefits," *Entrepreneur* (May 2011), http://www.workforce.com; Vicki Powers, "Green Benefits Helpful in a Down Economy," *Workforce Management* (May 2009), http://www.workforce.com; "Cost Shifting Initiatives," *Broad Reach Benefits* [blog] (February 15, 2011), http://broadreachbenefits.com/blog.

to cover prolonged absences. Accumulated vacation leave may sometimes be used as a source of income when sick leave benefits have been exhausted. Some employers also make group insurance that provides income protection during a long-term disability available. As discussed earlier in the chapter, worker's compensation partially reimburses the income employees lose during absences resulting from job-related injuries.

Sabbaticals

A **sabbatical** is paid (or unpaid) time away from a job for 4 or more weeks that employees take off to renew themselves before returning to work. Historically, sabbaticals have been associated with academia, but in the 1960s, companies, including McDonald's, began to adopt them. *Fortune* magazine has added sabbaticals to their criteria for naming the 100 Best Companies to Work For.[47] For example, Epic Systems Corporation, a Wisconsin-based health care software company, offers employees a paid 4-week sabbatical to pursue their creative talents after 5 years at the company. For small businesses that need to temporarily cut their payroll costs, unpaid sabbaticals can be a short-term alternative to layoffs and a way to reward valuable employees who never previously imagined they would be able to take a significant amount of time off to pursue other activities.

sabbatical
Paid (or unpaid) time away from a job for 4 or more weeks employees take off to renew themselves before returning to work.

Severance Pay

Severance pay is a one-time payment sometimes given to an employee who is being involuntarily terminated. The severance pay may cover only a few days' wages or wages for several months. The pay received usually depends on the employee's years of service. Employers that are downsizing often use severance pay as a means of lessening the negative effects of unexpected termination of employees. Other triggers for severance pay include job elimination, voluntary separation programs, or refusal of a reassignment or relocation. Employees who quit do not ordinarily receive severance pay. An employee who accepts severance pay is generally required to sign a release agreement waiving his or her right to take any kind of legal action against the company. To avoid legal action, companies sometimes offer severance pay to employees fired for cause.

severance pay
A one-time payment sometimes given to an employee who is being involuntarily terminated.

Supplemental Unemployment Benefits

While not required by law, in cyclical industries, unemployment compensation is augmented by **supplemental unemployment benefits (SUBs)** paid for by employers. The mining industry is an example. If the price of a metal being mined falls sharply (which is not an uncommon occurrence), the firms mining the metal often slow down production until the price rises again. SUBs help attract employees to industries such as this. The amount of the benefits is generally determined by an employee's length of service and wage rate.

supplemental unemployment benefit (SUB)
A plan that enables an employee who is laid off to draw weekly benefits from the employer, which draws from a fund created for this purpose, in addition to state unemployment compensation.

11.3c Life Insurance

One of the oldest and most popular employee benefits is group term life insurance, which provides death benefits to beneficiaries and may also provide accidental death and dismemberment benefits. The premium costs are normally paid by the employer, with the face value of the life insurance equal to two times the employee's yearly wages. These programs frequently allow employees to purchase additional amounts of insurance for nominal charges. In addition, many companies allow employees to purchase life insurance for their spouses and dependents via their company plans. This is an attractive benefit because the rates employees pay for the insurance is often lower when purchased through their company plans.

11.3d Long-Term Care Insurance

Long-term care insurance is designed to pay for nursing home and other medical-related costs during old age. Because the workforce is aging and people are living longer, a small but growing number of employers are finding that long-term care insurance can be a strategic benefit to attract and retain employees, particularly workers caring for older parents and relatives. Many of these employees have experienced firsthand the challenges of caring for aging loved ones who were unable to prepare properly for their long-term needs.

11.3e Other Benefits and Services

Credit Unions

Credit unions exist in many organizations to serve the financial needs of employees and attract potential employees. They offer a variety of deposits as well as other banking services and make loans to their members. Although the employer may provide office space and a payroll deduction service, credit unions are operated by the employees under federal and state legislation and supervision. Because credit unions are owned by their members, they often charge lower banking fees and offer loans at lower rates. Generally, credit unions are located near an employer's facility, making it fast and convenient for employees to do their banking there. The service employees receive is also often more personal than the service they would get from bigger banks.

Educational Assistance

Proactive employers view educational assistance programs, also called tuition aid, as a strategic business tool to support talent management and develop leadership.[48] To be eligible for tuition aid, an employee may have to meet a length of service requirement and show that classes taken relate to job performance or organizational career development. Employers may pay full or partial tuition costs plus related expenses such as books and supplies. For example, PwC offers its employees $1,200 per year for student loan debt reimbursement.[49]

Figure 11.4 shows some of the other benefits firms are offering employees that we have not already mentioned in this chapter. In summary, although benefits are expensive, they can be a good way for a company to differentiate itself, strengthen its employer "brand" to attract top talent, and retain that talent. However, both small and large employers need to implement their benefit plans strategically as well as continually monitor their effectiveness and costs.

LO 4

Are companies today offering sufficient retirement benefits?

Retirement Programs

Airline pilots are legally required to retire at age 65. However, for most other professions in the United States there is no law mandating a retirement age. Therefore, whether an employee elects to retire depends on various factors such as personal and financial condition and health, other family obligations, the extent to which he or she receives satisfaction from work, and the ability to meet changing job demands.

Preretirement and Phased Retirement Programs

Although most people eagerly anticipate retirement, many of them find that it requires a major financial lifestyle adjustment. Employers sometimes offer preretirement planning seminars and workshops to help make employees aware of the kinds of adjustments they may need to make when they retire. The topics covered can include pension plans,

Figure 11.4	Other Benefits Organizations Offer Employees

- Business travel insurance
- Time off for children's school activities
- Work-at-home arrangements/telecommuting
- Onsite cafeterias and take-home food
- Onsite laundry, dry cleaning, and hair-dressing services
- Employee referral bonuses
- Donation-gift matching
- Adoption assistance
- Onsite nurses and doctors
- Shuttle services for commuters
- Onsite massage services
- College scholarships

health insurance coverage, Social Security and Medicare, personal financial planning, wellness and lifestyles, and the process of adjusting to being around one's spouse 24/7!

To help older workers get used to the idea of retirement, some organizations experiment with "retirement rehearsal." Polaroid, for example, offers employees an opportunity to try out retirement through an unpaid 3-month leave program and allows its employees to gradually cut their hours before retirement. This kind of program is referred to as **phased retirement**. Formal phased retirement programs are common in other countries but rarer in the United States because employees often need to get their health care coverage through their employers until they turn 65. At this point they can go on Medicare. However, as more babyboomers want to continue to work and employers seek to retain them, the number of phased retirement programs is expected to grow.

phased retirement
A program that allows its employees to gradually cut their hours before retiring.

11.3f Pension Plans

Pensions reward employees for their years of service with a company by providing them with income when they retire. However, like with other discretionary benefits, the decision whether to offer a pension plan is up to the employer.

Types of Pension Plans

There are two major ways to categorize pension plans: (1) according to contributions made by the employer and (2) according to the amount of pension benefits to be paid. In a **contributory plan**, contributions to a pension plan are made jointly by employees and employers. In a **noncontributory plan**, the contributions are made solely by the employer. When pension plans are classified by the amount of pension benefits to be paid, there are two basic types: defined benefit plan and defined contribution plan. Under a **defined benefit plan**,[50] the amount an employee is to receive on retirement is specifically set forth. The amount employees collect is usually based on their years of service, average earnings during a specific period of time, and age at time of retirement. While a variety of formulas exist for determining pension benefits, the one used most often is based on the employee's average earnings (usually over a 3- to 5-year period immediately preceding retirement), multiplied by the number of years of service with the organization. A deduction is then made for each year the retiree is under age 65. For

contributory plan
A pension plan in which contributions are made jointly by employees and employers.

noncontributory plan
A pension plan in which contributions are made solely by the employer.

defined benefit plan
A pension plan in which the amount an employee is to receive on retirement is specifically set forth.

Many baby boomers in the United States are continuing to work long past the traditional retirement age of 65.

racom/Shutterstock.com

example, an employee with a 4-year preretirement annual salary of $55,000 and 30 years of service may receive a yearly retirement payment of $23,000.

A **defined contribution plan** establishes the basis on which an employer will contribute to the pension fund. The contributions may be made through profit sharing, thrift plans, matches of employee contributions, employer-sponsored individual retirement accounts (IRAs), and various other means. The amount of benefits employees receive on retirement is determined by the funds accumulated in their accounts and how well the investments purchased with the funds have grown over time. In other words, the amount employees get is not certain. As a result, these plans pose more financial risk for employees than defined benefit plans do. However, employers have come to prefer them because they do not have to shoulder all of the responsibility of funding them. In 1989, 39 percent of private sector employees were covered by defined benefit pension plans. Today, only 18 percent are.[51] Even Fortune 100 firms are scrapping their defined benefit plans. According to a survey by the HR consulting firm Watson Wyatt, today most Fortune 100 companies now offer their new salaried employees only a defined contribution plan.

401(k) Savings Plans

401(k) plans started to become extremely popular as an employee-savings vehicle beginning in the 1980s. This is a type of defined contribution plan named after section 401(k) of the Internal Revenue Code. The plan allows employees to save through payroll deductions that reduce their taxable income and have their contributions matched by the employer. Usually the employer matches the employee contributions at the rate of 25 to 50 cents for every worker dollar contributed.

401(k) plans have been widely embraced by companies as a replacement for costly defined benefit pension funds. Today, about 60 percent of households nearing retirement

defined contribution plan

A pension plan that establishes the basis on which an employer will contribute to the pension fund.

have 401(k)-type of accounts.[52] However, unlike defined benefit pension plans, which guarantee payments based on years of service, the 401(k) plan guarantees nothing. The return depends entirely on how much money goes into the plan, the rate of return on the investments purchased with the funds contributed, and, with stock-funded plans, the price of the company's stock. Economic downturns and stock market crashes take a heavy toll on 401(k) accounts.

Cash Balance Pension Plans

Along with 401(k) saving plans, a significant development in pension planning has been cash balance saving plans.[53] With cash balance plans, the employer makes a yearly contribution into an employee's retirement savings account.[54] The contributions are based on a percentage of the employee's pay—typically 4 percent. Additionally, the employee's account earns annual interest, often tied to the 30-year Treasury rate. For example, an employee earning $35,000 a year would receive a yearly contribution of $1,400 to his or her account. After a year, the account would receive an interest credit of around 5 percent. Employees can normally roll their account balances into a personal IRA should they change jobs.

Federal Regulation of Pension Plans

Private pension plans are subject to federal regulation, including vesting rules, under ERISA.[55] **Vesting** is a process that guarantees pension-plan participants will receive their pensions when they reach retirement age, regardless of their employment status at that time. In other words, the benefits cannot be revoked, even if the employee no longer works for the company. Vesting prevents companies from laying off employees before they retire so they are unable to collect their pensions. Under ERISA, all pension plans must provide employees with vested rights to their accrued benefits after they meet a certain minimum years of service, say, 5 years. So, for example, an employee leaves the company prior to the minimum years of service, the person would lose any money the firm contributed to his or her pension. However, employers can pay out a departing employee's vested benefits if the present value of the benefit is small.

Vesting

A guarantee of accrued pension benefits to participants at retirement age, regardless of their employment status at that time.

The Employee Retirement Income Security Act also requires minimum funding standards be followed to ensure pension benefits will be available to employees when they retire.[56] Currently the pensions of many older companies are underfunded, however. GM, Chrysler, U.S. Steel, and Delta Air Lines are among them. In addition, many state and local governments are facing billions in pension shortages due to the last recession. Equally worrisome are the number of pension plans in danger of failing altogether.

The Employee Retirement Income Security Act also created the Pension Benefit Guaranty Corporation (PBGC), a federal government agency. The PBGC ensures that if a plan is terminated, guaranteed minimum benefits are paid to participants. When companies go through bankruptcy proceedings, they often try to cancel their pension obligations, leaving employees to rely on the PBGC for retirement income. Unfortunately for retirees, the monthly pension payments from the PBGC are often significantly less than those promised under a company's original retirement plan. Another growing concern is that the PBGC—which has a $34 billion deficit of its own that has been growing annually—will be unable to meet its financial obligations.[57] The PBGC is supported by premiums paid by employers. To improve its funding situation, the agency has asked Congress to allow it to increase the premiums it charges employers.

11.3g Domestic Partner Benefits

More employers are granting benefits to employees who establish *domestic partnerships*, which can consist of both same-sex and unmarried opposite-sex couples. Viacom, Gannett Company (publisher of *USA Today*), Levi Strauss, Silicon Graphics, Warner Bros., and Stanford University are among the many organizations that offer benefits to domestic partners of employees. Most Fortune 500 companies now provide benefits to same-sex partners.

The definition of a domestic partnership varies from company to company. However, Apple Computer's definition, which is as follows, is typical: A domestic partner, the company says, is "a person over age 18 who shares living quarters with another adult in an exclusive, committed relationship in which the partners are responsible for each other's common welfare." Employers that offer domestic partnership coverage typically require employees to sign an "Affidavit of Domestic Partnership" attesting that they meet certain conditions such as the following:

- A minimum age requirement
- A requirement that the couple live together
- A specification of financial interdependence
- A requirement that the relationship be a permanent one
- A requirement that each not be a blood relative[58]

Organizations that offer benefits to domestic partners are simply extending current benefits, normally full medical and dental plans, to all employees.

HR decisions about domestic partnership benefits need to take into account local and state laws and how they are being implemented. For example, several California cities, including Berkeley, Los Angeles, Oakland, and San Francisco, have adopted an ordinance that requires all companies with city contracts to extend domestic partner benefits to their employees who reside in the city or who work on contracts for the city.[59]

Summary

LO 1   The cost of health care programs has become the major concern in the area of employee benefits. Organizations are taking a variety of approaches to contain health care costs. Included among them are the relative preference shown for each benefit by managers and employees, the estimated cost of each benefit and the total amount of money available for the entire benefits package, and how it compares to the competition. Through committees and surveys, a benefits package can be developed to meet employees' needs. Through the use of flexible benefit, or cafeteria plans, employees are able to choose the benefits that are best suited for their individual needs.

LO 2   Nearly a quarter of the benefits package that employers provide is legally required. These benefits include employer contributions to social security, unemployment insurance, workers' compensation insurance, and state disability insurance. Social security taxes collected from employers and employees are used to pay three major types of benefits: (1) retirement benefits, (2) disability benefits, and (3) survivors' benefits. Payroll deductions and taxes are also legally required to fund the government program, Medicare. Medicare provides medical and hospital insurance and prescription drug coverage for people over 65.

LO **3** Included in the category of benefits that involve payments for time not worked are vacations with pay, paid holidays, sick leave, and severance pay. Some companies offer their employees paid sabbaticals. A typical practice in the United States is to give employees 10 days of vacation leave and 10 holidays. In addition to vacation time, most employees, particularly in white-collar jobs, receive a set number of sick leave days. A one-time payment of severance pay may be given to employees who are being terminated. Other types of discretionary benefits that employers typically provide include EAPs, counseling services, educational assistance plans, child care, and elder care.

LO **4** For most professions in the United States, there is no mandatory retirement age. The topics covered can include pension plans, health insurance coverage, Social Security and Medicare, personal financial planning, wellness and lifestyles, and the general process of adjusting to retirement. Whether to offer a pension plan is the employer's prerogative. However, once a plan is established, it is then subject to federal regulation under ERISA to ensure that benefits will be available when an employee retires. Two pension plans are available—defined benefit and defined contribution. With a defined benefit plan, the amount an employee receives on retirement is based on years of service, average earnings, and age at time of retirement. Two of the most significant trends are the growth of 401(k) plans and cash balance pension plans, both of which are defined contribution plans.

Key Terms

backup care program

contributory plan

defined benefit plan

defined contribution plan

disease management programs

elder care

employee assistance programs (EAPs)

flexible benefits plans (cafeteria plans)

health maintenance organizations (HMOs)

high-deductible health insurance plan (HDHP)

noncontributory plan

phased retirement

preferred provider organization (PPO)

sabbatical

severance pay

supplemental unemployment benefit (SUB)

vesting

wellness programs

workers' compensation insurance

Discussion Questions

LO **1** Many organizations are concerned about the rising cost of employee benefits and question their value to the organization and to the employees. In your opinion, what benefits are of greatest value to employees? To the organization? Why?

LO **2** Employers are required by law to provide specific benefits to employees. What laws mandate benefits to employees, and what are the provisions of those laws?

LO **3** Working in teams of 3 or 4, assume your team was hired as a benefits consultant to a small business having 50 to 60 employees. What benefits do you believe this employer should offer, given limited resources? Justify your reasons for offering these benefits.

LO **4** Describe 401(k) pension plans, listing their advantages and disadvantages.

Understanding Employer Benefit Programs

This exercise will help you more fully understand the benefits discussed in this chapter. Additionally, you will explore, in detail, the benefits and services offered by your employer and other employers in your area.

Assignment

Working in teams of four to six individuals, obtain information on the benefits package offered by your employer or other employers in your area. Once the information is gathered, be able to identify (1) each benefit offered, (2) what the benefit provides the employee, (3) employee eligibility (if required), and (4) how the benefit is paid for (employer, employee, or a combination of both). Compare benefit packages. Be prepared to discuss your findings with the class.

CASE STUDY **1** Adobe's Family-Friendly Benefits: An Unexpected Backlash

Adobe Consulting Services (ACS), a provider of HR software application systems, prides itself on the variety of benefits it offers employees. In addition to health care, pension, and vacation benefits, the company also offers an attractive family-friendly benefits package including flexible schedules, child and elder care assistance, counseling services, adoption assistance, and extended parental leave. Unfortunately, sometimes the company's progressive work-life policy experiences a backlash from several employees, as the following case illustrates.

In March 2011, Teresa Wheatly was hired by Adobe as a software accounts manager. With excellent administrative and technical skills, plus 4 years of experience at Adaptable Software, Adobe's main competitor, Teresa became a valued addition to the company's marketing team. As a single mother with two grade-school children, Teresa received permission to take Fridays off. She was also allowed to leave work early or come in late to meet the demands of her children. Teresa is one of 11 software account managers at Adobe.

The problem for Adobe, and particularly for Janis Blancero, director of marketing, began in the fall of 2011. On September 15, Dorothy McShee, citing "personal reasons"—which she refused to discuss—requested a 4-day workweek for which she was willing to take a 20 percent cut in pay. When Dorothy asked for the reduced work schedule, she sarcastically quipped, "I hope I don't have to have kids to get this time off." On October 3, Juan Batista, a world-class marathon runner, requested a flexible work hours arrangement to accommodate his morning and afternoon training schedule. Juan was registered to run the London, England, marathon in May 2013. Just prior to Juan's request, Susan Woolf asked for and was granted an extended maternity leave to begin after the birth of her first child in December.

If these unexpected requests are not enough, Blancero has heard comments from senior account managers about how some employees seem to get "special privileges," while the managers work long hours that often require them to meet around-the-clock customer demands. Janis has adequate reason to believe that there is hidden tension over the company's flexible work hours program. Currently, Adobe has no formal policy on flexible schedules. Furthermore, with the company's growth in business combined with the increasing workload of software account managers and the constant service demands of some customers, Blancero realized that she simply cannot grant all the time-off requests of her employees.

Questions

1. Do managers like Janis Blancero face a more complicated decision when evaluating the personal requests of employees versus evaluating employees' individual work performance? Explain.

2. **a.** Should Adobe establish a policy for granting flexible work schedules? Explain.

   b. If you answered yes, what might that policy contain?

3. If you were Janis Blancero, how would you resolve this dilemma? Explain.

CASE STUDY ❷ Evaluate the Work-Life Climate in Your Company

What is the quality of the work-life environment in your company? The following survey provided by the Work and Family Connection will help provide a "case analysis" of the climate in your organization. Answers to the 20 questions will provide clear insights about your company's position in the work-life area.

Agree or Disagree with the Following Statements

1. My manager or supervisor treats my work-life needs with sensitivity.

2. It is usually easy for me to manage the demands of both work and home life.

3. My career path at this company is limited because of the pressure of home life demands.

4. My job at this company keeps me from maintaining the quality of life I want.

5. My manager or supervisor is supportive when home life issues interfere with work.

6. My manager or supervisor focuses on results, rather than the time I am at my desk.

7. My manager or supervisor has a good understanding of flexible work hour practices.

8. If I requested a flexible work arrangement, my manager or supervisor would support me.

9. My manager or supervisor is often inflexible or insensitive about my personal needs.

10. I believe my manager or supervisor treats me with respect.

11. My manager or supervisor allows me informal flexibility as long as I get the job done.

12. My manager or supervisor tends to treat us like children.

13. My manager or supervisor seldom gives me praise or recognition for the work I do.

14. My manager or supervisor seems to care about me as a person.

15. I would recommend this company to others.

16. The work I do is not all that important to this company's success.

17. If I could find another job with better pay, I would leave this organization.

18. If I could find another job where I would be treated with respect, I would take it.

19. If I could find another job where I could have more flexibility, I would take it.

20. I am totally committed to this company.

For a perfect score, you should answer "Disagree" to questions 3, 4, 9, 12, 13, 16, 17, 18, and 19 and "Agree" to all the rest, 1, 2, 5, 6, 7, 8, 10, 11, 14, 15, and 20.

To score, begin by giving yourself 20 points. Then deduct one point for every "wrong" response from the total score.

If your score is 18 to 20: Congratulations! Your organization is leading the nation in flexibility and supportiveness.

If your score is 14 to 17: Your organization is probably more supportive and flexible than most, but you have room to grow.

If your score is 11 to 13: You could be open to other job offers in the race for talent among employees.

If your score is 10 or less: Your managers will need help to manage the twenty-first-century workforce.

Source: Used with permission of the Work and Family Connection, 5195 Beachside Drive, Minnetonka, Minnesota 55343; 1-800-487-7898, or http://www.workfamily.com.

Notes and References

1. "Glassdoor's 5 Job Trends to Watch in 2016," Glassdoor team (January 12, 2016).

2. "Top 20 Employee Benefits & Perks," Glassdoor Team (February 3, 2016).

3. "Total Rewards" is all of the tools available to an employer that may be used to attract, motivate, and retain employees. Total rewards include everything the employee perceives to be of value resulting from the employment relationship.

4. Mark Harbeke, "5 Workplace Committees to Form and Their Business Benefits," Inc.com (January 5, 2011), http://www.inc.com/guides/2011/01/5-workplace-committees-to-form-and-their-business-benefits.html.

5. Barbara A. W. Eversole, Donald L. Venneberg, and Cindy L. Crowder, "Creating a Flexible Organizational Culture to Attract and Retain Talented Workers Across Generations," *Advances in Developing Human Resources* 14, no. 4 (2012): 607–25.

6. Dianna L. Stone, Diana L. Deadrick, Kimberly M. Lukaszewski, and Richard Johnson, "The influence of technology on the future of human resource management," *Human Resource Management Review* 25, no. 2 (June 2015): 216–31.

7. Stephen Miller, "Employees Value Benefits, Don't Understand Costs," *Society for Human Resource Management* (April 20, 2011).

8. Kat Greene, "Providence Health to Pay $352M To End ERISA Suit," *Law360* (October 24, 2016).

9. JoAnn Davis, "Communication: It Is More Than Distributing Information," *Employee Plan Benefits Review* 62, no. 1 (July 2007): 5.

10. Jeremy Smerd, "Tweeting Benefits in 140 Characters or Less," *Workforce Management* (August 2009), http://www.workforce.com.

11. Robert Crawford, "Samsung Evolves Benefits Strategy," *Employee Benefits* (November 5, 2014), https://www.employeebenefits.co.uk/issues/november-2014/samsung-evolves-benefits-strategy/.

12. Jeffrey A. Buck, "The Looming Expansion And Transformation of Public Substance Abuse Treatment under the Affordable Care Act," *Health Affairs* 30, no. 8 (2011): 1402–10.

13. Bahaudin G. Mujtaba and Frank J. Cavico, "A Review of Employee Health and Wellness Programs in the United States," *Public Policy and Administration Research* 355, no. 4. (2013): 1–16.

14. Corinne Marie Karuppan, "Employer-Based Coverage and Medical Travel Options: Lessons for Healthcare Managers," *Journal of Healthcare Management* 59, no. 3 (May/June 2014): 210–23.

15. Kimberly J. Reid, Kathleen M. Aguilar, Eric Thompson, and Ross M. Miller, "Value-Based Benefit Design to Improve Medication Adherence for Employees with Anxiety or Depression," *American Health & Drugs Benefits* 8, no. 5 (July-August 2015): 263–71.

16. "The Fortune 100 and Their Fitness and Wellness Programs," *Health Fitness Revolution* (August 15, 2015), http://www.healthfitnessrevolution.com/fortune-100-fitness-wellness-programs/.

17. Jodi M. Jacobson and Paul Sacco, "Employee Assistance Program Services for Alcohol and Other Drug Problems: Implications for Increased Identification and Engagement in Treatment," *The American Journal on Addictions*, 21, no. 5 (2012): 468–75.

18. Charlotte Huff, "Employers Collaborate to Customize Health Coverage," *Workforce* (October 18, 2010), http://www.workforce.com/2010/10/18/employers-collaborate-to-customize-health-coverage/.

19. "Social Security Administration Fact Sheet," (April 4, 2017), https://www.ssa.gov/news/press/factsheets/basicfact-alt.pdf.

20. Since the Social Security Act is continually subject to amendment, readers should refer to the literature provided by the nearest Social Security office for the most current details pertaining to the tax rates and benefit provisions of the act.

21. "Contribution and Benefit Base," *Social Security Administration* (March 28, 2017), https://www.ssa.gov/oact/cola/cbb.html.

22. "How You Earn Credits," *Social Security Administration* (2017), https://www.ssa.gov/pubs/EN-05-10072.pdf.

23. As an example, the Social Security Administration manages the Supplemental Security Income (SSI) program, which makes payments to people with low incomes who are age 65 or older or are blind or have disabilities. However, SSI is not paid for by social security taxes but by U.S. Treasury's general funds.

24. "How You Earn Credits," *Social Security Administration* (2017), https://www.ssa.gov/pubs/EN-05-10072.pdf.

25. Ibid.

26. You may think that Medicaid and Medicare are the same. Actually, they are two different programs. Medicaid is a state-run program that provides hospital and medical coverage for people with low income and little or no resources. Each state has its own rules about who is eligible and what is covered under Medicaid. Some people quality for both Medicare and Medicaid. For more information about the Medicaid program, contact your local medical assistance agency, social services, or welfare office.

27. "Tax Topic 751–Social Security and Medicare Withholding Rates," *Internal Revenue Service* (March 28, 2017), https://www.irs.gov/taxtopics/tc751.html.

28. "Raising Medicare Age Could Cost Employers $4.5 Billion," *Workforce Management* (March 2011), http://www.workforce.com.

29. COBRA, P.L. 99–272, 100 Stat. 82 (1986).

30. Margot Sanger-Katz, "Republican Health Proposal Would Undermine Coverage for Pre-Existing Conditions," *The New York Times* (April 4, 2017).

31. FLMA, P.L. 103–3, 107 Stat. 6 (1993).

32. A "serious health condition" means an illness, injury, impairment, or physical or mental condition that involves any period of incapacity or treatment connected with patient care.

33. Janet Walsh, "Americans Value Moms, but Policies Don't," *Huffington Post* (May 5, 2011), http://www.huffingtonpost.com.

34. Natalie Hackbarth, Aaron Brown, and Henry Albrecht, "Workplace Well-Being: Provide Meaningful Benefits to Energize Employee Health, Engagement, and Performance," *Quantum Workplace* (2016), www.limeade.com/content/uploads/2016/12/Workplace-Well-Being_FINAL.pdf.

35. Ibid.

36. "Child Care in America: 2016 State Fact Sheets," *Child Care Aware of America* (2016), www.usa.childcareaware.org/wp-content/uploads/2016/07/2016-Fact-Sheets-Full-Report-02-27-17.pdf.

37. "Top 20 Employee Benefits & Perks," Glassdoor Team (February 3, 2016).

38. "Caregiving in the U.S.: 2015 Report," *AARP and National Alliance for Caregiving* (June 2015), www.aarp.org/content/dam/aarp/ppi/2015/caregiving-in-the-united-states-2015-report-revised.pdf.

39. Ibid.

40. Bill Mulcany, "Why You Should Be Caring for Your Caregivers," *Workspan* (June 2007): 37.

41. Bureau of Labor Statistics. U.S. Department of Labor, *Employer Costs for Employee Compensation* (September 2013).

42. "Mandatory Time Off around the Globe," *Open Forum* (May 2, 2011), http://www.openforum.com.

43. Rebecca Ray, Milla Sanes, and John Schmidt, "*No-Vacation Nation Revisited*," Center for Economic and Policy Research (2013).

44. Oi Ling Siu, Cary L. Cooper, and David R. Phillips, "Intervention Studies on Enhancing Work Well-Being, Reducing Burnout, and Improving Recovery Experiences among Hong Kong Health Care Workers and Teachers," *International Journal of Stress Management* 21, no. 1 (2014).

45. Catherine A. Allen, "Burned Out?" *Life Science Leader* (May 3, 2011), http://www. lifescienceleader.com.

46. "No One in the Private Sector Gets Unlimited Vacation and Sick Leave," *Politifact* (January 28, 2011), http://www.politifact.com.

47. Catherine A. Allen, "Burned Out?" *Life Science Leader* (May 3, 2011), http://www.lifescienceleader.com.

48. Dorothy Martin, "Tuition Assistance Programs as a Strategic Investment: The Importance of Measurement," *Society for Human Resource Management* (September 1, 2016), https://www.shrm.org/hr-today/trends-and-forecasting/special-reports-and-expert-views/pages/dorothy-martin.aspx.

49. "Top 20 Employee Benefits & Perks," Glassdoor Team (February 3, 2016).

50. "Types of Retirement Plans," *United States Department of Labor* (March 28, 2017), https://www.dol.gov/general/topic/retirement/typesofplans.

51. Wiatrowski, William J., "The Last Private Industry Pension Plans: A Visual Essay," Bureau of Labor Statistics. Rep. 2012. Print.

52. E. S. Browning, "Boomers Find 401(k) Plans Fall Short," *Wall Street Journal* (February 19, 2011), Print.

53. Jessica Marquez, "Cash-Balance Plans Make a Comeback," http//www.workforce.com/section/02/feature/25/16/23/index.html.

54. "Cash Balance Pension Plans," U.S. Department of Labor (January 2014),. www.dol.gov/sites/default/files/ebsa/about-ebsa/our-activities/resource-center/faqs/faq_consumer_cashbalanceplans.pdf.

55. ERISA, P.L. 93-406, 88 Stat. 829 (1974).64

56. Carolyn Hirschman, "Overseeing Pension Management," *HR Magazine* 49, no. 7 (July 2004): 66.

57. Michael A. Fletcher, "Pension Benefit Guarantee Corp. Running $34 Billion Deficit," *Washington Post* (November 2012).

58. Pay and Leave Administration, *U.S. Office of Personal Management*, http://www.opm.gov.

59. "Domestic Partner Benefits: Facts and Background," *Employee Benefit Research Institute* (February 2009), www.ebri.org/pdf/publications/facts/0209fact.pdf.

danchooalex/Getty Images

CHAPTER **12**

Promoting Safety and Health

Learning Outcomes

After studying this chapter, you should be able to

LO 1 Summarize the general provisions of the Occupational Safety and Health Act (OSHA).

LO 2 Describe the measures managers and employees can take to create a safe work environment.

LO 3 Identify ways to control and eliminate various on-the-job health hazards.

LO 4 Describe the programs organizations utilize to build better health among their workforces.

Close to 90 percent of all companies in the United States use some form of health and safety program. Safety programs are plans of action to prevent accidents or occupational diseases. Health programs are plans of action to encourage the health and wellness of employees. Health and safety programs ensure that employees stay safe and healthy so they can continue to work. This lowers costs for the company. However, current research shows that health programs not only save the company money through fewer sick days, workers' compensation, disability payments, and replacing employees who are injured or killed, but these programs also increase employee productivity. "When you give people the tools and the opportunity to be physically and mentally healthier, it's not just that they're more likely to be at work," said Lamar Pierce, professor at Washington University. "Those employees are also more likely to be productive."[1]

12.1 Safety and Health: It's the Law

Consider the facts shown in Figure 12.1.

The total impact of worker injury and death is roughly $140 billion per year. See the breakdown of where these costs occur in Figure 12.2.

Providing workers a safe and healthy environment is not just good for business and the right thing to do. It is the law. In 1970 Congress passed the Occupational Safety and Health Act (OSHA).[2] The mission of OSHA is to "assure the safety and health of America's workers by setting and enforcing standards; providing training, outreach, and education; establishing partnerships; and encouraging continual improvements in workplace safety and health" (see Figure 12.3).

Despite the figures in the infographic, the act has been very effective in reducing the number of injuries resulting in lost work time, the incident rate of specific injuries such as back problems, and the number of job-related deaths. Today, most employees report that the safety conditions in their organizations are very good.

LO 1
Why do you think so many safety and health laws have been enacted?

12.1a OSHA's Coverage

OSHA covers all private sector employees and public employees in state and local governments. Self-employed workers are not covered by the law. Federal agencies are required to establish and maintain a safety and health program that is monitored by OSHA.

12.1b OSHA Standards

One of the responsibilities of OSHA is to develop and enforce mandatory job safety and health standards. These standards cover the workplace, machinery and equipment, materials, power sources, processing, protective clothing, first aid, and administrative requirements. To comply with OSHA, employers need to become familiar with those

Figure 12.1	Job Safety Statistics, 2016

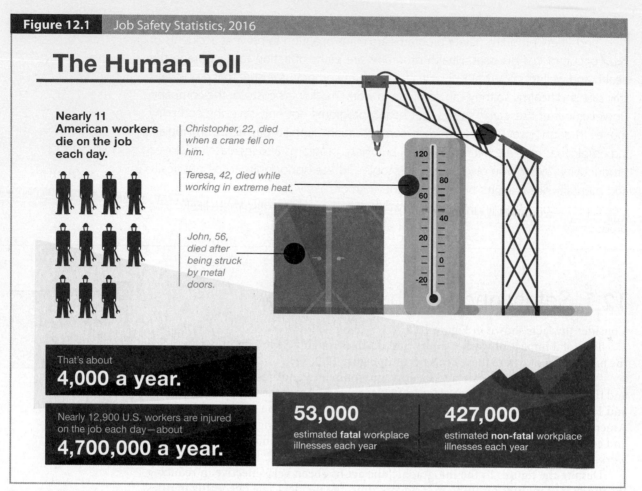

The Human Toll

Nearly 11 American workers die on the job each day.

Christopher, 22, died when a crane fell on him.

Teresa, 42, died while working in extreme heat.

John, 56, died after being struck by metal doors.

That's about
4,000 a year.

Nearly 12,900 U.S. workers are injured on the job each day—about
4,700,000 a year.

53,000
estimated **fatal** workplace illnesses each year

427,000
estimated **non-fatal** workplace illnesses each year

Source: © 2016 National Safety Council. http://www.nsc.org/measure/pages/jse-infographic.aspx.

standards that are applicable to their establishments and to ensure that their employees use personal protective gear and equipment when required for safety. Employers can be cited and fined if they do not comply with OSHA standards.[3]

OSHA can begin standards-setting procedures on its own initiative or on petition from other parties, including the Secretary of Health and Human Services (HHS) and the National Institute for Occupational Safety and Health (NIOSH). Other bodies that may also initiate standards-setting procedures are state and local governments and any nationally recognized standards-producing organization, employer, or labor representative (see Figure 12.4). NIOSH, however, is the major source of standards. As an agency of the Department of Health and Human Services, it is responsible for conducting research on various safety and health problems, including the psychological factors involved.[4]

Figure 12.2 Cost of Worker Injury and Death

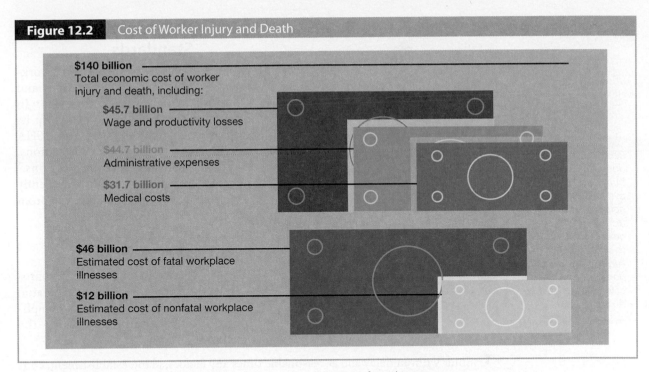

$140 billion
Total economic cost of worker
injury and death, including:

$45.7 billion
Wage and productivity losses

$44.7 billion
Administrative expenses

$31.7 billion
Medical costs

$46 billion
Estimated cost of fatal workplace
illnesses

$12 billion
Estimated cost of nonfatal workplace
illnesses

Source: © 2016 National Safety Council. http://www.nsc.org/measure/pages/jse-infographic.aspx.

Figure 12.3 OSHA Mission

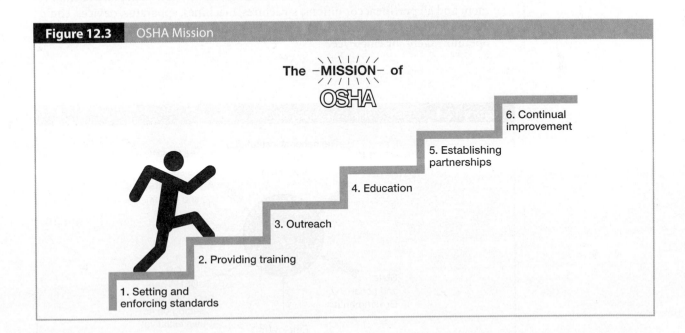

The ‒MISSION‒ of
OSHA

6. Continual
improvement

5. Establishing
partnerships

4. Education

3. Outreach

2. Providing training

1. Setting and
enforcing standards

Because it slowed them down, the workers who built New York's skyline in the early 1900s were actually discouraged from using safety devices such as ropes to prevent falls. Not surprisingly, a disproportionate number of workers fell to their deaths.

SSPL/Getty Images

12.1c Enforcing OSHA Standards

OSHA is authorized to conduct workplace inspections, issue citations, and impose penalties on employers. In recent years OSHA has stepped up its enforcement activities. In 2016, OSHA conducted 31,948 federal inspections, and 43,105 state plan inspections.[5] Figure 12.5 shows the most frequently violated OSHA standards resulting from these federal and state inspections.

Workplace Inspections

Under OSHA, "upon presenting appropriate credentials to the owner, operator, or agent in charge," an OSHA compliance officer is authorized to do the following:

- Enter without delay and at reasonable times any factory, plant, establishment, construction site or other areas, workplace, or environment where work is performed by an employee of an employer; and

- Inspect and investigate during regular working hours, and at other reasonable times, and within reasonable limits and in a reasonable manner, any such place of employment and all pertinent conditions, structures, machines, apparatus, devices, equipment and materials therein, and to question privately any such employer, owner, operator, agent, or employee.[6]

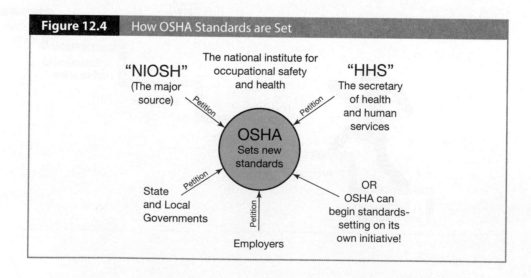

Figure 12.4	How OSHA Standards are Set

"NIOSH"
(The major source)

The national institute for occupational safety and health

"HHS"
The secretary of health and human services

Petition

Petition

OSHA
Sets new standards

State and Local Governments

Petition

Petition

Employers

OR
OSHA can begin standards-setting on its own initiative!

| Figure 12.5 | Most Frequently Violated OSHA Standards |

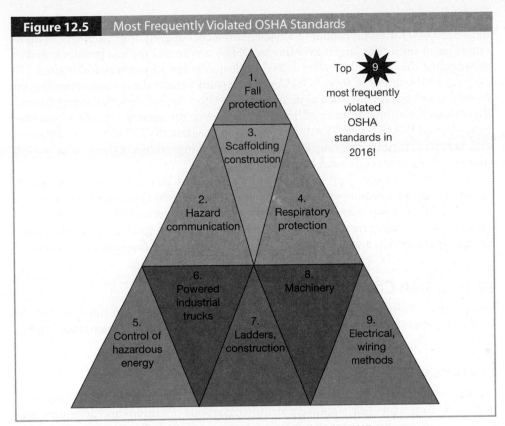

Source: https://www.osha.gov/oshstats/commonstats.html. Accessed April 11, 2017.

Citations and Penalties

OSHA citations may be issued immediately following the inspection or later by mail. Citations tell the employer and employees which regulations and standards are alleged to have been violated and the amount of time allowed for their correction. The employer must post a copy of each citation at or near the place the violation occurred for three days or until the violation is abated, whichever is longer.

Under the act, OSHA may cite the following violations and propose the following penalties:

- Other-Than-Serious: A violation that has a direct relationship to job safety and health but one unlikely to cause death or serious physical harm. Such a penalty could be as low as $100; however, OSHA may propose a penalty of up to $12,675 for each violation depending upon the circumstances.

- Serious: A violation for which there is substantial probability that death or serious physical harm could result *and* the employer knew, or should have known, of the hazard. The average penalty imposed by OSHA for serious violations is now $3,000 to $4,000. The maximum penalty is $12,675 for each violation.

- Willful: A violation that the employer intentionally and knowingly commits or a violation that the employer commits with plain indifference to the law. OSHA may propose penalties of up to $126,749 for each violation.[7]

If a willful violation results in the death of an employee, OSHA can assess penalties up to $250,000 for an individual or $500,000 for a corporation, imprisonment of up to 6 months, or both. The largest ever fine by OSHA was an $82 million penalty levied in 2009 against the oil giant BP after a 2005 explosion killed 15 workers and injured 170 others at a BP refinery in Texas.[8] OSHA can adjust any penalty downward depending on the employer's good faith (such as demonstrating effort to comply with the act), history of previous violations, and size of business.[9] However, the agency can adjust penalties upward, too. OSHA's Severe Violator Enforcement Program (SVEP) identifies employers with repeated, serious citations, and, among other things, subjects them to increased, multi-worksite inspections and higher penalties.

An example of the SVEP in action was when OSHA issued 57 citations for safety violations and $3.4 million in fines to a Japanese-owned auto manufacturing company called Sunfield Incorporated in 2016. The fines were in response to Sunfield's failure to disconnect machinery from a power supply, failure to prevent sudden movement before maintenance/service, and failure to train workers in operating machine presses safely.[10]

12.1d OSHA Consultation Assistance

Besides helping employers identify and correct specific hazards, OSHA can help employers develop and implement effective workplace safety and health programs that emphasize preventing worker injuries and illnesses.

Onsite Consultation

OSHA provides free onsite consultation services. Consultants from the state government or private contractors help employers identify hazardous conditions and determine corrective measures. Employers also may receive training and education services.[11] No citations are issued in connection with a consultation, and the consultant's files cannot be used to trigger an OSHA inspection. Additionally, the consultations may qualify employers for a 1-year exemption from routine OSHA inspections.

Cooperative Programs

Voluntary, cooperative relationships among employers, employees, unions, and OSHA can be a useful alternative to traditional OSHA enforcement procedures. There are four specific cooperative programs—alliances, strategic partnerships, voluntary protection programs, and the Safety and Health Achievement Recognition Program.[12] Figure 12.6 describes the roles of each cooperative program.

12.1e Responsibilities and Rights under OSHA

Both employers and employees have certain responsibilities and rights under OSHA. We will discuss only those that relate directly to the management of human resources.

Employers' Responsibilities and Rights

In addition to providing a hazard-free workplace and complying with the applicable standards, employers must inform all their employees about the safety and health requirements of OSHA. Specific employer responsibilities are listed in OSHA's publication *All about OSHA* and illustrated in Highlights in HRM 1. Employers are also required to keep certain records and to compile and post an annual summary of work-related

Figure 12.6	Cooperative Programs

Cooperative programs:

1. Alliances	2. Strategic partnership programs (SPPs)	3. Voluntary protection programs (VPPs)	4. Safety and health achievement recognition program (SHARP)
Organizations collaborate with OSHA to improve safety health.	Long-term Agreements between Employers and OSHA to improve safety and health.	Try to establish a cooperative relationship between Employers and OSHA (the middle-men) There are 3: 1. Star 2. Merit 3. Demonstration	A certification program that recognizes small employers with exemplary achievements in workplace safety and health.

injuries and illnesses. From these records, organizations can compute their *incidence rate*—the number of injuries and illnesses per 100 full-time employees during a given year. The standard formula for computing the incidence rate is shown by the following equation, in which 200,000 equals the base for 100 full-time workers who work 40 hours a week, 50 weeks a year:

$$\text{Incidence rate} = \frac{\text{Number of injuries and illnesses} \times 200,000}{\text{Total hours worked by all employees during period covered}}$$

It is the employer's responsibility to provide employees with protective equipment when necessary and ensure it is used. Employers must also provide their workers with safety training and be prepared to discipline employees for failing to comply with safety rules. In addition, employers must not discriminate against employees who exercise their rights under the act by filing complaints with OSHA.[13]

Employees' Responsibilities and Rights

Employees are required to comply with all applicable OSHA standards, to report hazardous conditions, and to follow all employer safety and health rules and regulations, including those prescribing the use of protective equipment. Workers have a right to demand safe and healthy conditions on the job without fear of punishment. They also have many rights that pertain to requesting and receiving information about safety and health conditions.[14] For example, most states—and federal law—require that employers provide information to employees about the hazardous chemicals they handle. Commonly known as **right-to-know laws**, these statutes require employers and manufacturers to give employees information about the toxic and hazardous substances they could come into contact with on the job and what the health risks related to those substances are.

right-to-know laws
Laws that require employers to advise employees about the hazardous chemicals they handle.

What Are My Responsibilities under the OSH Act?

If you are an *employer* the OSH Act covers, you must:

- Meet your general duty responsibility to provide a workplace free from recognized hazards that are causing or are likely to cause death or serious physical harm to employees, and comply with standards, rules, and regulations issued under the act.
- Be familiar with mandatory OSHA standards and make copies available to employees for review upon request.
- Inform all employees about OSHA.
- Examine workplace conditions to make sure they conform to applicable standards.
- Minimize or reduce hazards.
- Make sure employees have and use safe tools and equipment (including appropriate personal protective equipment) and that such equipment is properly maintained.
- Use color codes, posters, labels, or signs when needed to warn employees of potential hazards.
- Establish or update operating procedures and communicate them so that employees follow safety and health requirements.
- Provide training required by OSHA standards (hazard communication, lead, etc.).
- Report to the nearest OSHA office within eight hours of any fatal accident or one that results in the hospitalization of three or more employees.
- Keep OSHA-required records of work-related injuries and illnesses, and post a copy of the totals from the last page of OSHA No. 200 during the entire month of February each year. (This applies to employers with 11 or more employees.)
- Post, at a prominent location within the workplace, the OSHA poster (OSHA 2203) informing employees of their rights and responsibilities. (In states operating OSHA-approved job safety and health programs, the state's equivalent poster and/or OSHA 2203 may be required.)

- Provide employees, former employees, and their representatives access to the Log and Summary of Occupational Injuries and Illnesses (OSHA 200) at a reasonable time and in a reasonable manner.
- Provide access to employee medical records and exposure records to employees or their authorized representatives.
- Cooperate with the OSHA compliance officer by furnishing names of authorized employee representatives who may be asked to accompany the compliance officer during an inspection. (If none, the compliance officer will consult with a reasonable number of employees concerning safety and health in the workplace.)
- Not discriminate against employees who properly exercise their rights under the act.
- Post OSHA citations at or near the worksite involved. Each citation, or copy thereof, must remain posted until the violation has been abated, or for three working days, whichever is longer.
- Abate cited violations within the prescribed period.

If you are an *employee* the OSH Act covers, you should:

- Read the OSHA poster at the job site.
- Comply with all applicable OSHA standards.
- Follow all employer safety and health rules and regulations, and wear or use prescribed protective equipment while engaged in work.
- Report hazardous conditions to the supervisor.
- Cooperate with the OSHA compliance officer conducting an inspection if he or she inquires about safety and health conditions in your workplace.
- Exercise your rights under the act in a responsible manner.

Source: *OSH Act, OSHA Standards, Inspections, Citations and Penalties* (Washington, DC: Occupational Safety and Health Administration, May 20, 2011), http://www.osha.gov.

12.2 Promoting a Safe Work Environment

LO 2
What are some of the safety programs at your college?

Typically, a firm's HR department or the industrial relations department is responsible for its safety program. The HR department typically coordinates the safety communication and training programs, maintains safety records required by OSHA, and works closely with managers and supervisors in a cooperative effort to make the program a success.

12.2a Creating a Culture of Safety

Lower-level operational managers and supervisors have traditionally been the bedrock for encouraging health and safety in their organizations.[15] Indeed, one study by the American Institute of Plant Engineers showed that there was a direct correlation between an increase in the commitment to safety by managers and a decrease in accidents (see Figure 12.7).

However, firms today try to create a "culture" of safety within their organizations that goes beyond managing operational processes and reducing accidents.[16] A culture of safety exists when everyone within an organization consciously works to improve its safety and health conditions. HR managers play a key role in this effort. "HR executives should be the point persons on creating and making sure that a corporate safety culture exists," Carolyn Merritt, the late chairperson of the U.S. Chemical Safety Board (CSB) once noted. "These are the people who have their fingers on the culture pulses of the organization."[17] The Highlights in HRM 2 will help you assess your knowledge and awareness of safety and health issues.

Some companies periodically conduct **fitness-for-duty evaluations** on their current employees. Fitness-for-duty evaluations are similar to prehire physical exams but can be done any time during employment. They determine an employee's physical, mental, and emotional fitness and are most often used for safety or security-sensitive positions. For example, federal rules require nuclear-plant workers to undergo random fitness-for-duty evaluations on the job to determine if they have been using alcohol or drugs.

fitness-for-duty evaluations
Evaluations randomly conducted to determine an employee's physical, mental, and emotional fitness for a job.

The Key Role of the Supervisor

Like HR managers, supervisors play a key role in their employer's safety programs. One of a supervisor's major responsibilities is to communicate to an employee the need to work safely.[18] Proper work procedures, the use of protective clothing and devices, and potential hazards should be explained thoroughly.[19] Moreover, supervisors must continually observe employees at work, reinforce safe practices, and immediately correct behaviors that are unsafe.[20]

Proactive Safety Training Programs

In certain occupational areas, safety and health training is legally required. For example, employers regulated by a federal agency called the Pipeline and Hazardous Materials Safety Administration

Marcel Thomas/Getty Images

OSHA regulations mandate the use of protective equipment in recognized hazardous conditions.

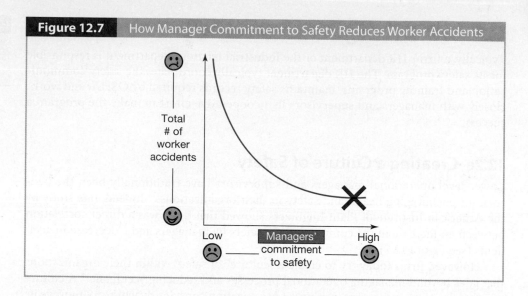

Figure 12.7   How Manager Commitment to Safety Reduces Worker Accidents

are legally required to provide their employees with environmental-safety protection training. When training is mandated, employers must keep accurate records of all employee education. Violations can incur criminal penalties.

Most organizations have a safety awareness program that entails the use of several different media. Safety lectures and courses and printed and audiovisual material are common.[21] The use of games has also become an interactive way to provide employees with safety training. Costco and Amazon.com, for example, have successfully used a product called *Safety Bingo* to motivate employees on a daily basis to create a safety-conscious atmosphere and remind them of their safety goals.[22]

HR professionals and safety directors in particular advocate employee involvement when designing and implementing safety programs.[23] Employees can offer valuable ideas regarding specific safety and health topics to cover, instructional methods, and proper teaching techniques. Furthermore, employees are more likely to embrace safety training when they feel a sense of ownership in the instructional program.[24]

12.2b Enforcing Safety Rules

Firms communicate specific safety rules and regulations in a variety of ways, including through supervisors, bulletin board notices, employee handbooks, and signs attached to equipment. In additional to safety labels and signs, many companies prominently display in their workplaces the number of consecutive days they have operated without an injury. The idea is to motivate employees to keep the injury-free "streak" going and possibly set new records for injury-free performance.

12.2c Investigating and Recording Accidents

The supervisor and a member of the safety committee should investigate every accident, even those considered minor. Such an investigation may determine the factors contributing to the accident and reveal what corrections are needed to prevent it from happening again.

Test Your Safety Smarts

Take the following quiz to evaluate your knowledge and awareness of safety and health issues. The answers are found at the end of this chapter.

1. True or False? Employers have the right to be told by an Occupational Safety and Health Administration (OSHA) compliance officer the reason why it is undergoing a workplace inspection by the government agency.

2. True or False? Employers have the legal right to have a company representative accompany OSHA compliance officers on inspections.

3. True or False? OSHA requires employers to give its inspectors access to employees when inspecting medical and safety records of their firms.

4. True or False? In order to correct potential health and safety problems, employers have the right to know the name of an employee who files a complaint with OSHA.

5. Which causes more accidents: unsafe acts or unsafe conditions?

6. True or False? Employers are required to provide employee training on OSHA standards.

7. True or False? Employers are required to allow OSHA inspectors on premises for unannounced inspections.

8. True or False? Employers have 24 hours to report to OSHA accidents that result in a fatality.

OSHA requirements mandate that employers with 11 or more employees maintain records of work-related occupational injuries and illnesses.[25] As stated in an earlier section, OSHA also requires a Log of Work-Related Injuries and Illnesses (OSHA Form 300) to be maintained by the organization. All recordable cases are to be entered in the log. A **recordable case** is any injury or illness that results in any of the following: death, days away from work, restricted work or transfer to another job, or medical treatment beyond first aid. Other problems employers must record as work-related include loss of consciousness or diagnosis of a significant injury or illness by a health care professional.[26] Figure 12.8 illustrates OSHA's diagram for classifying accidents under the law. For every recordable case written in the log, an Injury and Illness Incident Report (OSHA Form 301) is to be completed. OSHA Form 301 requires answers to questions about the case. Each year OSHA Form 300A, Summary of Work-Related Injuries and Illnesses, must be completed and posted in a conspicuous place or places where notices to employees are customarily posted. Remember, when completing all OSHA forms, employers must not list the name of an injured or ill employee if the case has "privacy concerns," such as those involving sexual assault, HIV infection, and mental illness.[27]

We conclude our discussion of OSHA by showing the OSHA poster that employers are required to display at the workplace (see Highlights in HRM 4 later in the chapter).

> **recordable case**
> Any occupational death, illness, or injury to be recorded in the log (OSHA Form 300).

12.2d Safety Hazards and Issues

Workers face many different safety hazards on the job, which differ depending upon their occupations. It is impossible to discuss all of them in this chapter. However, we will discuss a number of hazards that have been getting a great deal of attention from HR managers and firms lately.

Figure 12.8 Guide to Recording Cases under the Occupational Safety and Health Act

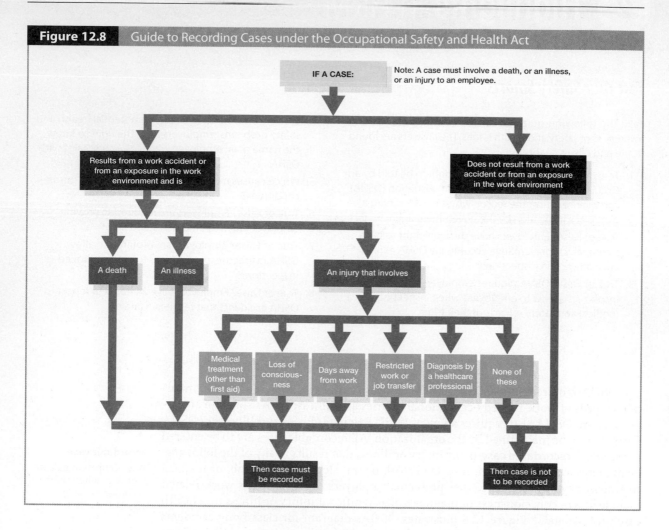

Fatigue

Few safety issues have been in the news more lately than employee fatigue. You have probably heard about air traffic controllers who have fallen asleep on the job and could not be awakened by pilots trying to contact them. Fatigue is more of a problem in organizations that operate around the clock or have night shifts. Studies show that 30 to 50 percent of night-shift workers report falling asleep at least once a week while on the job, according to Dr. Charles Czeisler, chief of sleep medicine at Brigham and Women's Hospital in Boston.[28]

Fatigue may not result in life-or-death consequences for most jobs. Nonetheless managers, employees, and the public are concerned about how it affects workplace safety and performance. The regulations in certain industries limit the number of hours employees can work per shift. The airline industry is one such industry. However, even with the limits, workers are finding themselves fatigued. Some experts say downsizing may be a factor as fewer workers are being asked to cover more shifts. Recently the U.S. government vowed it would give air traffic controllers an extra hour off between shifts to combat fatigue. Continental has given its pilots permission to call in and report if they're too fatigued to fly.

Although OSHA currently has no fatigue standard, it is seeking to establish one, and unions are increasingly negotiating fatigue contracts. Employees at Dow Chemical's

Freeport, Texas, facility have negotiated a fatigue standard in their new labor contract. Under the new agreement, employees who work three consecutive 16-hour days must receive a 24-hour break. Employees on regular shifts must get a 48-hour break if they work 21 days in a row.[29]

Distracted Driving

Do you know what the leading cause of worker fatalities each year is? Motor vehicle crashes come in first. Moreover, according to a National Highway Traffic Safety Administration study, people who send text messages while driving are 23 times more likely to crash than other drivers, and distracted driving accounts for 80 percent of all accidents. When it comes to mass transit, the consequences of distracted driving can be catastrophic.

To help prevent distracted driving accidents, a growing number of employers are adopting mandatory cell-phone policies for their employees. A survey of more than 2,000 employers conducted by the National Safety Council found that 58 percent had some type of cell-phone usage policy in place, and roughly one-quarter of those surveyed prohibit both handheld and hands-free devices while driving for some or all employees.[30] Other companies are doing more than establishing policies. OSHA does not have specific regulations on distracted driving.

Workplace Violence

The NIOSH defines workplace violence as "any physical assault, threatening behavior, or verbal abuse occurring in the work setting. It includes, but is not limited to, beatings, stabbings, suicides, shootings, rapes, near suicides, psychological traumas such as threats, obscene phone calls, an intimidating presence, and harassment of any nature such as being followed, sworn at, or shouted at."

Approximately 27 percent of American adults have past or current experience with bullying in the workplace. Bullying is a form of violence; it is the repeated, health-harming mistreatment of one or more persons by one or more other people. It can consist of verbal abuse or offensive behaviors that are threatening, humiliating, intimidating, or interfere with someone's ability to work. For example, bullying can be found when one employee withholds information or resources from another employee, treats the victim in a disrespectful way, interferes with work activities, or prevents someone from expressing themselves. Due to lack of legislation, workplace bullying is currently pursued under Title VII antidiscrimination laws.[31]

In a Zogby poll, 35 percent of American adults said they had been bullied at work. Not only does bullying lead to lower morale, it can result in deadly suicides, violence, and homicides in the workplace.[32] A number of countries around the world, including France and Sweden, have enacted laws against bullying. Today, all U.S. states have an antibullying law.[33]

Reducing Workplace Violence. In addition to protecting workers at high risk of on-the-job assaults, OSHA recommends firms analyze their workplaces to uncover areas of potential violence and develop violence prevention programs and training for their employees. To begin, background checks on job applicants should be conducted to ensure they don't have histories showing a propensity toward aggression or violence.[34] Remember, employers can be sued for negligent hiring if they do not take this step and workplace injury occurs as a result. Managers, supervisors, and employees should also be trained to recognize violence indicators such as those listed in Figure 12.9.

Last, but certainly not least, a firm's HR department must effectively communicate to a firm's employees that it has zero tolerance for violence.[35] Organizations such

Figure 12.9	Violence Indicators: Know the Warning Signs

The following behaviors should be taken seriously when assessing situations of potential violence:

- Direct or veiled threatening statements
- Recent performance declines, including concentration problems and excessive excuses
- Insubordination and severe reactions to criticism
- Prominent mood or behavior changes; despondence
- Preoccupation with guns, knives, or other weapons
- Deliberate destruction of workplace equipment; sabotage
- Fascination with stories of violence or war
- Reckless or antisocial behavior; evidence of prior assaultive behavior
- Aggressive behavior or intimidating statements; yelling or using profanity
- Written messages of violent intent; exaggerated perceptions of injustice
- Serious stress, legal, or financial problems in one's personal life
- Intruding on other people's privacy by pestering, spying on, or stalking them
- Obsessive desire to harm a specific group or person
- Violence against a family member
- Substance abuse

Sources: Adapted from Violence in the Workplace: Risk Factors and Prevention Strategies, NIOSH Bulletin #59; David D. Van Fleet and Ella W. Van Fleet, "Preventing Workplace Violence: The Violence Volcano Metaphor," *Journal of Applied Management and Entrepreneurship* 12, no. 3 (July 2007): 17; Bella L. Galperin and Joanne D. Leck, "Understanding the Violent Offender in the Workplace," *Journal of American Academy of Business* 10, no. 2 (March 2007): 114.

as Garden Fresh, a restaurant chain, Enterprise Rent-a-Car, JetBlue Airways, and Ritz Carlton have formalized workplace violence prevention policies informing employees that aggressive employee behavior will not be tolerated. Employees should encourage employees to report any possible or observed incidents to their firm's HR departments. Some firms have set up hotlines for employees to report incidents without having to fear repercussions for "getting involved."

Workplace Emergencies

According to OSHA, a workplace emergency is an unforeseen situation that threatens employees, customers, or the public; disrupts or shuts down operations; or causes physical or environmental damage. Emergencies can be natural or manmade. In addition to workplace violence, they can include the following:

- Floods
- Hurricanes
- Tornadoes
- Fires
- Toxic gas releases
- Chemical spills
- Radiological accidents
- Explosions
- Civil disturbances and terrorism.

emergency action plans
A plan an organization develops that contains step-by-step procedures for dealing with various emergency situations.

OSHA requires companies to have **emergency action plans** to deal with incidents such as these. An emergency action plan must include, among other things, procedures for reporting a fire or other emergency, evacuating a facility, and accounting for employees after an evacuation. The plan must also include procedures for employees who must remain in facilities to ensure critical plant operations continue, as well as procedures for workers performing rescue and medical duties. A copy of the emergency action plan should either be provided to employees or kept in a convenient location where employees can access it. Organizations with 10 or fewer employees are allowed to communicate their emergency plans orally to employees.

Highlights in HRM 3 shows a readiness-assessment checklist that organizations can complete to determine how prepared they are for an emergency. OSHA Publication 3088, *How to Plan for Workplace Emergencies and Evacuations*, is also a helpful guideline for employers.

Crisis Management Teams

Organizations such as Motorola and Circle K Corporation have implemented formal crisis management teams. These teams, composed of hourly and managerial employees, work in conjunction with HR to conduct initial risk assessment surveys, develop emergency action plans, test them, and perform crisis intervention during emergency events. For example, a crisis management team would investigate a threat reported by an employee. The team's mandate would be to gather facts about the threat, decide whether the organization should intervene, and, if so, determine the most appropriate method of doing so. Figure 12.10 shows what a crisis management team or other manager could do to calm an angry employee, for example.

Crisis management teams and HR managers play a key role when it comes to getting employees back to work and paid on time following an emergency. Crisis management teams are also responsible for disseminating public information and addressing the press.

Figure 12.10	Calming an Angry Employee

If you try to defuse a tense situation, remember that anger frequently results from a person's feeling of being wronged, misunderstood, or unheard. Keep the following tips in mind to guide you.

- Strive to save the employee's dignity during an angry confrontation. Do not attack a person's rash statements or continue a muddled line of thinking.
- Hold all conversations in private. Do not allow the employee to create an embarrassing public situation for himself or herself, yourself, or other employees.
- Always remain calm. Anger or aggressiveness on your part will trigger a similar response in the employee.
- Listen to the employee with an open mind and nonjudgmental behavior. Give the employee the benefit of hearing him or her out.
- Recognize the employee's legitimate concerns or feelings. Agree that the employee has a valid point and that you will work to correct the problem.
- If the employee is very emotional or if the engagement seems out of control, schedule a delayed meeting so people can calm down.
- Keep the discussion as objective as possible. Focus on the problem at hand, not the personalities of individuals. A cornerstone of conflict resolution is to attack the problem, not the personality.
- If the employee appears overly aggressive, withdraw immediately and seek professional help before any further discussion with the employee.
- If your efforts fail to calm the employee, report the incident to your manager, security, or human resource personnel.

Source: Adapted from professional literature on crisis management and seminars attended by the authors.

Emergency Readiness Checklist

Readiness Assessment

How Prepared Is Your Business for an Emergency?	Yes	No	Unsure
1. Does your business know what kinds of emergencies might affect it – both internally and externally?	❏	❏	❏
2. Does your business have a written, comprehensive emergency plan in place to help ensure your safety and take care of employees until help can arrive?	❏	❏	❏
3. Has your business created and practiced procedures to quickly evacuate and find shelter in case of an emergency?	❏	❏	❏
4. Has your business created a communication plan to communicate with employees in an emergency? (Examples include set up a telephone call tree, password-protected page on the company Web site, e-mail alert or call-in voice recording, and a contact list that includes employee emergency contact information.)	❏	❏	❏
5. Has your business talked with utility service providers about potential alternatives and identified back-up options?	❏	❏	❏
6. Has your business determined operations that need to be up and running first after an emergency and how to resume key operations?	❏	❏	❏
7. Has your business created a list of inventory and equipment, including computer hardware, software, and peripherals (such as backed up/protected records and critical data) for business continuity and insurance purposes?	❏	❏	❏
8. Has your business met with your insurance provider to review current coverage in case of an emergency?	❏	❏	❏
9. Does your business promote family and individual preparedness among co-workers (such as emergency preparedness information during staff meetings, newsletters, company intranet, periodic employee e-mails, and via other internal communication tools)?	❏	❏	❏
10. Have emergency shutdown procedures been developed for equipment such as boilers, automatic feeds or other operations that cannot simply be left running in an emergency evacuation?	❏	❏	❏
11. Has your business worked with your community on emergency planning efforts and helped to plan for community recovery?	❏	❏	❏

Readiness Results

Count your number of "Yes" responses to calculate a score. Your score is a *general reflection* of how much you know about emergency planning efforts at your business and/or how prepared your business may be for an emergency.

❏ If you have 8-11 "Yes" responses, you are well on your way to having a comprehensive and effective plan in place.

❏ If you have 4-7 "Yes" responses, while some aspects of your plan may be in place, you have some work to do to fill gaps.

❏ If you have 1-3 "Yes" responses, get started immediately on developing an emergency plan for your business. This training program is a great first step!

Planning for Emergencies
© 2007 National Safety Council

Source: National Safety Council.

12.3 Creating a Healthy Work Environment

LO 3

How are health and safety related? If your workplace is safe, does that mean it is also healthy? Why or why not?

Because of the dramatic impact workplace accidents have, managers and employees sometimes pay more attention to them than health hazards. Accidents happen quickly. The effect of health hazards show up only over time. When they do show up, though, they adversely affect workers, their families, and their companies.

12.3a Ergonomics

One way to help eliminate health hazards in the workplace is via ergonomics. Recall that we discussed ergonomics in Chapter 4 when we looked at job design. Ergonomics focuses on ensuring that jobs are designed for safe and efficient work while improving the safety, comfort, and performance of users. Ergonomics also considers the requirements of a diverse workforce, accommodating, for example, women who may lack the strength to operate equipment requiring intense physical force or Asian Americans who may lack the stature to reach equipment controls.

Ergonomics has proven cost effective at organizations such as Compaq Computer, 3M, Pratt and Whitney, and the U.S. Postal Service and has eliminated, or at least reduced, many repetitive motion injuries, particularly those related to the back and wrist. The key elements of successful ergonomic programs are shown in Figure 12.11.[36]

12.3b Health Hazards and Issues

At one time health hazards were associated primarily with jobs found in manufacturing operations. In recent years, however, hazards in jobs outside of plants, such as in offices, health care facilities, and airports, have been recognized, and methods to lessen these hazards have been adopted.

Figure 12.11   Key Elements for a Successful Ergonomics Program

Companies with award-winning ergonomics programs list the following as common elements of success:

- *Provide notice and training for employees.* Implement a well-publicized ergonomics policy or present ergonomic information in safety policies or training programs. Train employees, supervisors, and managers in basic workplace ergonomics.
- *Conduct preinjury hazard assessment.* Survey the workplace and work processes for potential hazards and adopt measures to lessen the exposure to ergonomic risk factors. Answer the question: "Are certain work areas more prone to ergonomic hazards than others?"
- *Involve employees.* Include employees in risk assessment, recognition of MSD symptoms, design of work-specific equipment or tools, and the setting of work performance rules and guidelines.
- *Plan and execute.* Integrate ergonomic responsibilities into the performance plans for all personnel. Demand accountability for program success.
- *File injury reports.* Encourage early reporting of MSD symptoms or injuries. Refer employees to the company's medical facilities or to the employee's personal physician for treatment.
- *Evaluate and assess the ergonomics program.* Periodically review the effectiveness of the ergonomics program. If the program appears to be ineffective, determine the underlying causes for failure and propose corrective changes.

Job Safety and Health Protection Poster

An ergonomically designed computer workstation like this will reduce the strain on the worker's eyes, neck and shoulders, wrists, and back.

Cumulative Trauma Disorders

Meat cutters, cooks, dental hygienists, textile workers, violinists, flight attendants, office workers at computer terminals, and others whose jobs require repetitive motion of the fingers, hands, or arms are reporting injuries in growing percentages.[37] Known as **cumulative trauma disorders** or repetitive motion injuries, these musculoskeletal disorders are injuries of the muscles, nerves, tendons, ligaments, joints, and spinal discs caused by repeated stresses and strains. One of the more common conditions is *carpal tunnel syndrome*, which is characterized by tingling or numbness in the fingers occurring when a tunnel of bones and ligaments in the wrist narrows and pinches nerves that reach the fingers and the base of the thumb. Without proper treatment, employees with carpal tunnel syndrome can lose complete feeling in their hands.

Ergonomics techniques are also successfully used to improve or correct workplace conditions that cause or aggravate cumulative trauma disorders.[38] Continuous developments in office furniture, video display terminals, tool design, computer keyboards, and adjustable workstations are all attempts to make the work setting more comfortable—and, hopefully, more productive—but also to lessen musculoskeletal disorders. Minibreaks involving exercise and the changing of work positions have been found helpful.

cumulative trauma disorders

Injuries involving tendons of the fingers, hands, and arms that become inflamed from repeated stresses and strains.

Computer Workstation Issues

Figure 12.12 provides a checklist of potential repetitive motion problem areas for employees using computers. Video and computer screens are a particular concern. The problems that managers have to confront in this area fall into three major groups:

1. *Visual difficulties.* Screen operators frequently complain of blurred vision, sore eyes, burning and itching eyes, and glare.[39]
2. *Muscular aches and pains.* Pains in the back, neck, and shoulders are common complaints of screen operators.
3. *Job stress.* Eyestrain, postural problems, insufficient training, excessive workloads, and monotonous work are complaints reported by three-quarters of screen users.

Figure 12.12	Computer Workstation Ergonomics Checklist

Use the following list to identify potential problem areas that should receive further investigation. Any "no" response may point to a problem.

1. Does the workstation ensure proper worker posture, such as
   - Thighs in the horizontal position?
   - Lower legs in the vertical position?
   - Feet flat on the floor or on a footrest?
   - Wrists straight and relaxed?
2. Does the chair
   - Adjust easily?
   - Have a padded seat with a rounded front?
   - Have an adjustable backrest?
   - Provide lumbar support?
   - Have casters?
3. Are the height and tilt of the work surface on which the keyboard is located adjustable?
4. Is the keyboard detachable?
5. Do keying actions require minimal force?
6. Is there an adjustable document holder?
7. Are armrests provided where needed?
8. Are glare and reflections minimized?
9. Does the monitor have brightness and contrast controls?
10. Is there sufficient space for knees and feet?
11. Can the workstation be used for either right- or left-handed activity?

Source: The National Institute for Occupational Safety and Health (NIOSH), *Elements of Ergonomics Programs: A Primer Based on Workplace Evaluations of Musculoskeletal Disorders* (Washington, DC: U.S. Government Printing Office, March 1997).

To capitalize on the benefits of computer screens while safeguarding employee health, Dr. James Sheedy, a screen and vision expert, offers these tips on how to minimize the negative effects of computer use on the eyes and body:

- Place the computer screen 4 to 9 inches below eye level.
- Keep the monitor directly in front of you.
- Sit in an adjustable-height chair with lower back support and with feet flat on the floor.
- Use shades or blinds to reduce the computer screen glare created by window lighting.
- Keep elbows close to body and supported.
- Place wrist and hands in line with forearms.

Chemical Hazards

The OSHA Hazard Communication Standard is the most frequently cited OSHA standard for general industry as well as for the construction industry. The purpose of the law is to ensure the testing and evaluation of chemicals by producers and the distribution of the chemical hazard information to users of the chemical.

All hazardous chemical containers must be labeled with the identity of the contents and must state any appropriate hazard warnings. OSHA-published hazardous chemical regulations known as the Hazard Communication Standard (HCS) prescribe a system for communicating these warnings. It includes a format for **Material Safety Data Sheets (MSDSs)**. MSDSs must include the chemical name of a hazardous substance; all of the risks involved in using it, including any potential health risks; safe handling practices; personal protective equipment needed; first aid in the event of an accident; and information identifying the manufacturer. OSHA-required chemical training includes informing employees of the methods used to detect the presence or release of hazardous chemicals, the physical and health problems posed by hazardous chemicals, and the ways in which employees can protect themselves from chemical dangers.

> **Material Safety Data Sheets (MSDSs)**
> Documents that contain vital information about hazardous substances.

Chemical hazards can affect the reproductive health of either women or men. In an important case concerning women, the U.S. Supreme Court ruled in *International Union v. Johnson Controls* (1991) that employers may not bar women of childbearing age from certain jobs because of potential risk to their fetuses.[40] The Court said that such policies are a form of sex bias that is prohibited by federal civil rights law. The decision has made it important for employers to inform and warn female workers about fetal health risks on the job.

Smoking and Tobacco Smoke

Virtually all large organizations and even smaller ones have initiated smoking policies specifying when and where smoking will be allowed in their organizations, if at all. In developing smoking policies, it is advisable to have the involvement of both smokers and nonsmokers.

Bloodborne Pathogens

You have probably noticed that when technicians clean your teeth or draw your blood, they wear rubber gloves, eye protection, masks, and other protective devices. Exposures to blood and other body fluids occur across a wide variety of occupations and can result

Small Business Application

OSHA Resources for Small Businesses

Meeting all of OSHA's requirements can seem like a daunting task for small businesses, especially ones just setting up shop. Fortunately, for business owners and entrepreneurs, OSHA has a wealth of resources and programs designed to help small businesses. The agency estimates that for every dollar a small business invests in safety in health measures, it can reap as much as $4 to $5 in savings in terms of these costs.

Michael Foods, Inc., an Elizabeth, New Jersey, food company, scheduled an onsite consultation after receiving a letter from OSHA notifying the company that it was a likely candidate for inspection due to its workplace injury and illness rates. "When you want to know if your company is doing all the right things as it relates to health and safety, who better than OSHA to tell you," says Damir Tutundzic, the company's safety manager. Michael Foods went further than just getting a consultation. It followed OSHA's recommendations and now has the SHARP designation. Productivity is up, and at one point the distribution center had worked over 1,500 days without any lost time incidents and over 700 days without a reportable accident. "All of these efforts led to a reduction in workers' compensation costs of nearly $250,000 and 100 percent employee engagement," says Tutundzic.

Source: *Small Business Success Stories* (Washington, DC: Occupational Safety and Health Administration, May 25, 2011), http://www.osha.gov.

in employees contracting diseases. The pathogens of primary concern are the human immunodeficiency virus (HIV), hepatitis B virus (HBV), and hepatitis C virus (HCV). Workers can be exposed to blood through needlestick and other sharp-object injuries, mucous membranes, and skin exposures.

12.3c Building Better Physical and Emotional Health among Employees

LO **4**

How would you describe the physical and emotional health of the people you work with or have worked with in the past? What role do employers play when it comes to the emotional health of their workers?

Along with improving working conditions that are hazardous to employee health, employers today are cognizant of the physical and emotional health of their employees and thus provide them with programs to maintain and improve both.

Recall that we discussed EAPs in Chapter 11. As we have indicated, EAPs can help employees with a range of problems. EAPs can also help workers with relationship, marital, and family problems; anger, depression, anxiety, and stress; and elder care demands. Workplace issues, addiction, and self-improvement are other areas in which EAPs provide workers with help.

Wellness and Weight Issues

In Chapter 11 we mentioned wellness programs. Discovery Communication in Silver Spring, Maryland, provides a wellness center. The company employs a medical assistant, nurse practitioner, and physician who offer health services, including stress management, consultation and techniques, fitness programs, and podiatry care.[41] Google encourages employee wellness through their "small changes" program in which Google headquarters encourages employees to ride scooters to meetings, eat healthier food at their cafeteria with portion sizes in check, be active and playful with their in-office slide and Ping-Pong tables, and take advantage of their onsite physical therapist and chiropractor.[42]

We also mentioned weight-related problems and obesity in Chapter 11. As you know, excess weight can affect the health of a worker and his or her productivity. A study by Duke University researchers, who examined the records of nearly 12,000 university employees, found that obese employees experienced medical costs that were more than five times higher than those of nonobese workers. They also missed eight times the number of workdays, which by some estimates costs companies an estimated $5.5 billion a year in lost productivity.[43] Not surprisingly, employers are launching or improving programs specifically designed to help employees maintain or lose weight by exercising and eating properly.[44] For example, a nutritional component is part of the wellness program of JWT, a New York advertising firm. Nutritional programs address two lifestyle changes: (1) increasing a person's physical exercise (via walking, jogging, bicycling, etc.); and (2) adopting nutritional dietary programs that emphasize eating lots of fruits and vegetables, fish, and low-fat dairy products.[45] Stephanie Pronk, the chief health officer at RedBrick Health, a Minneapolis health technology and services company, notes that employers today are trying to create a "culture of wellness" that makes thinking about maintaining a healthy weight second nature to employees.[46]

stress
Any adjustive demand caused by physical, mental, or emotional factors that requires coping behavior.

Job Stress and Burnout

It is no secret that employees today are more stressed out than they have been in years past. A Gallup poll recently found that 66 percent of employees were dissatisfied with the amount of stress they experience in the workplace.[47] **Stress** is any demand on the individual that requires coping behavior. Stress comes from two basic sources: physical activity and mental or emotional activity. The physical reaction of the body to both types of stress is the same. Psychologists use two separate terms to distinguish between positive and negative forms of stress, even though reactions to the two forms are the same, biochemically. **Eustress** is positive stress that accompanies achievement and exhilaration.[48] This type of stress is regarded as a beneficial force that helps us to forge ahead against obstacles. What is harmful is **distress**. Stress becomes distress when we begin to sense a loss of our feelings of security and adequacy. Helplessness, desperation, and disappointment turn stress into distress.

Burnout is a severe stage of distress. Career burnout generally occurs when a person begins questioning his or her own personal values. Quite simply, the person no longer feels that what he or she is doing is important. Depression, frustration, and a loss of productivity are all symptoms of burnout. Burnout is primarily due to a lack of personal fulfillment in the job or a lack of positive feedback about one's performance.[49] To decrease the chance of burnout, managers should provide role clarity, opportunities to develop, and conduct feedback and goal development sessions with employees on a regular basis.[50]

The causes of workplace stress are many. However, according to a study by Luminari, a national health care company, four factors have a major influence on employee stress (see Figure 12.13):

- **High demand:** having too much to do in too short a time
- **High effort:** having to expend too much mental or physical energy over too long a period
- **Low control:** having too little influence over the way a job is done on a day-to-day basis
- **Low reward:** receiving inadequate feedback on performance and no recognition for a job well done.

Other job stressors include layoffs and organizational restructuring; disagreements with managers or fellow employees; prejudice because of age, gender, race, or religion; inability to voice complaints; and poor working conditions. Even minor irritations such as lack of privacy, unappealing music, and other conditions can be distressful to one person or another.

eustress
Positive stress that accompanies achievement and exhilaration.

distress
Harmful stress characterized by a loss of feelings of security and adequacy.

burnout
A severe stage of distress, manifesting itself in depression, frustration, and loss of productivity.

Figure 12.13	Different Factors that Create Stress for Employees

Job stress places both women and men at risk for fatigue, high blood pressure, cardiovascular problems, depression, and obesity and increases employee susceptibility to infectious diseases. Studies have shown that work-related stress contributes to injuries and illnesses. All of these contribute to higher health care costs and can lower productivity, job satisfaction, and retention.[51] Stress is also the most frequently cited reason employees give for why they would leave a company.[52]

HR professionals are well aware of the negative effects of workplace stress on employees' health and job performance.[53] In one study, the top three sources of stress employers think negatively affect the workplace are lack of work-life balance, inadequate staffing, and technologies that expand availability during nonworking hours.[54] Armed with this awareness, many employers have developed stress management programs to teach employees how to minimize the negative effects of job-related stress.[55] A typical program might include instruction in relaxation techniques, coping skills, listening skills, methods of dealing with difficult people, time management, and assertiveness.

All of these techniques are designed to break the pattern of tension that accompanies stressful situations and to help participants achieve greater control of their lives. Organizational techniques, such as clarifying the employee's work role, redesigning and enriching jobs, correcting physical factors in the environment, and effectively handling interpersonal factors should not be overlooked in the process of teaching employees how to handle stress. Stress management counselors recommend several ways to resolve job-related stress as described in Figure 12.14.

Depression

Emotional problems and personal crises become organizational problems when they affect people's behavior at work and interfere with their job performance.[56] The most prevalent problems among employees are personal crises involving marital, family, financial, or legal matters.[57] Most personal crises are resolved in a reasonable period of time. Unfortunately, when a personal crisis lingers, it can lead to depression. **Depression** is a decrease in functional activity accompanied by persistent symptoms of low spirits, gloominess, and sadness. The National Institute of Mental Health estimates that nearly 7 percent of the adult population experience depression each year.[58]

Fortunately, with available treatment, 80 percent of depressed individuals will significantly improve, usually within a matter of weeks. Managers are in a good position to identify the signs of depression on the job.[59] They include decreased energy on the part of an employee, concentration and memory problems, guilt feelings, irritability,

depression
A negative emotional state marked by feelings of low spirits, gloominess, sadness, and loss of pleasure in ordinary activities.

Figure 12.14	Tips for Reducing Job-Related Stress

- Build rewarding relationships with your coworkers.
- Talk openly with managers or employees about your job or personal concerns.
- Prepare for the future by keeping abreast of likely changes in your job's demands.
- Do not greatly exceed your skills and abilities.
- Set realistic deadlines; negotiate reasonable deadlines with managers.
- Act now on problems or concerns of importance.
- Designate dedicated work periods during which time interruptions are avoided.
- When feeling stressed, find time for detachment or relaxation.
- Do not let trivial items take on importance; handle them quickly or assign them to others.
- Take short breaks from your work area as a change of pace.

and chronic aches and pains that do not respond to treatment. Managers and supervisors who suspect an employee is depressed are encouraged to express their concerns to the person, actively listen to him or her, and—should the depression persist—suggest professional help.[60] Under no circumstances should managers attempt to play amateur psychologist and try to diagnose an employee's condition.[61] Mood disorders such as depression are complex in nature and do not lend themselves to quick diagnoses. Furthermore, in reviewing such cases, the organization should pay particular attention to workplace safety factors because there is general agreement that emotional disturbances are primary or secondary factors in a large portion of industrial accidents and incidents of violence.

Alcoholism

Nearly 6 million working Americans bring their alcohol problems to the workplace.[62] It has been estimated that business and industry lose more than $20 billion each year because of alcoholism. It is a disease that affects both the young and old, is prevalent across the sexes, and affects workers in every occupational category—blue collar and white collar.[63]

The first step in helping the alcoholic is to awaken the person to the reality of his or her situation. A supervisor should carefully document evidence of the person's declining performance on the job and then confront the employee with unequivocal proof to that effect. The employee should be assured that help will be made available without penalty. Because the evaluations are made solely in terms of poor on-the-job performance, a supervisor can avoid any mention of alcoholism and allow such employees to seek aid as they would for any other problem.

Employers must remember that alcoholism is classified as a disability under the Americans with Disabilities Act (ADA—see Chapter 3). Alcoholism is regarded as a disease, similar to a mental impairment. Therefore, a person disabled by alcoholism is entitled to the same protection from job discrimination as any other person with a disability. However, under the ADA, employers can discipline or discharge employees when job performance is so badly affected by alcohol usage that the employee is unable to perform the job.[64]

Drug Abuse

Like alcohol abuse, the abuse of illegal drugs by employees costs businesses billions annually in terms of safety risks, theft, reduced productivity, absenteeism, and accidents. A wide range of employers, including federal contractors and private and public transportation firms, are subject to regulations aimed at eliminating the use of illegal drugs on the job. The federal antidrug initiatives include the following:

1. The Drug-Free Workplace Act of 1988, which requires federal contractors and recipients of federal grants to take specific steps to ensure a drug-free work environment. One of the main provisions of the act is the preparation and distribution of an antidrug policy statement.

2. Department of Defense (DOD) contract rules, which specify that employers entering into contracts with the DOD must agree to a clause certifying their intention to maintain a drug-free workplace.

3. Department of Transportation (DOT) regulations, which require that employees whose jobs include safety- or security-related duties be tested for illegal drug use under DOT rules.

To help employers benefit from being drug-free and to further its mission to help companies maintain safe, healthy, and productive workplaces, the U.S. Department of Labor created the Working Partners for an Alcohol and Drug-Free Workplace. This goal of the agency is to raise awareness about the impact of substance abuse in the workplace and provide employers with substance abuse prevention information. Additionally, the Department's Drug-Free Workplace Advisor provides information to employers about how to establish and maintain an alcohol- and drug-free environment.[65]

The ADA considers an individual with a serious, life-affecting drug problem to be disabled, provided the person is enrolled in a drug treatment program and not currently using drugs. The person's employer therefore must make reasonable accommodations for his or her disability. Reasonable accommodations might include time off from work or a modified work schedule to obtain treatment. As we noted earlier, federal regulations require employers to test their workers for drug use under certain specified conditions.[66]

The abuse of legal drugs can also pose a problem for employees.[67] In fact, unlike marijuana, cocaine, and other illegal drugs, according to Quest Diagnostics, a blood-testing company, both employees' prescribed use and misuse of opiates such as hydrocodone and oxycodone have been rising sharply. Employees who abuse legal drugs—those prescribed by physicians—often do not realize they have become addicted or how their behavior has changed as a result of their addiction. Also, managers should be aware that some employees may be taking legal sedatives or stimulants as part of their medical treatment and that their behavior at work may be affected by their use of these drugs.

Summary

LO 1 The Occupational Safety and Health Act was designed to assure, so far as possible, safe and healthful working conditions for every working person. In general, the act extends to all employers and employees. The Occupational Safety and Health Administration (OSHA) sets health and safety standards, ensures employers and employees comply with them, and provides safety and health consultation and training where needed. Both employers and employees have certain responsibilities and rights under OSHA. Employers not only are required to provide a hazard-free work environment but also must keep employees informed about OSHA requirements and provide them with protective equipment when necessary and ensure they wear it. Under the "right to know" regulations, employers are required to keep employees informed of hazardous substances and instruct them in avoiding the dangers presented. Employees, in turn, are required to comply with OSHA standards, to report hazardous conditions, and to follow all employer safety and health regulations.

LO 2 To provide safe working conditions for their employees, employers typically establish a formal safety program in liaison with their HR departments. The program may have many facets, including providing safety knowledge and motivating employees to use it, making employees aware of the need for safety, and rewarding them for safe behavior. Incentives such as praise, public recognition, and awards are used to involve employees in the safety program. Employers also engage their workers by asking them to join safety committees, help develop safety procedures, observe the safety practices of their coworkers, and investigate any accidents. The maintenance of required records from accident investigations provides a basis for information that can be used to create a safer work environment.

LO **3** Job conditions that are dangerous to the health of employees are now receiving much greater attention than in the past. There is special concern for toxic chemicals that proliferate at a rapid rate and may lurk in the body for years without outward symptoms. Health hazards other than those found in manufacturing operations—such as video display terminals and cumulative trauma disorders—present special problems many firms are addressing with ergonomic solutions. Secondhand smoke and bloodborne pathogens are two other health hazards that have received greater attention in recent years.

LO **4** Along with providing safer and healthier work environments, many employers establish programs that encourage employees to improve their health habits. Wellness programs that emphasize exercise, nutrition, weight control, and avoidance of harmful substances serve employees at all organizational levels. Alternative medicine approaches such as relaxation techniques and hypnosis, chiropractic care, acupuncture, homeopathy, herbal therapy, special diets, massage, and so forth are also used to help employees with a variety of health problems.

Key Terms

burnout

cumulative trauma disorders

depression

distress

emergency action plan

eustress

fitness-for-duty evaluation

Material Safety Data Sheets (MSDSs)

recordable case

right-to-know laws

stress

Discussion Questions

LO **1** When OSHA was enacted in 1970, it was heralded as the most important new source of protection for the U.S. worker in the second half of the twentieth century. From the information in this chapter, what is your opinion about the effectiveness or the ineffectiveness of the act? Should it be expanded, or should businesses have more freedom to determine safety standards for their workers?

LO **2** What steps should management take to increase the motivation of their employees to operate safely?

LO **3** An unhealthy work environment can lower productivity, contribute to low morale, and increase medical and workers' compensation costs. Consider ways to improve the work environment.

LO **4** To live a healthier life, medical professionals say we need to identify those things we currently do that either impair or contribute to our health. Discuss with others a way to develop a lifetime program for a healthy lifestyle.

CASE STUDY Rambo Goes Violent

The facts of the case are straightforward. A shop floor dispute at an automobile parts manufacturing plant in Hamilton, Iowa, ended with one worker killing another. At about 2:00 p.m., police responded to a report of a fight that erupted between two employees. When members of the Hamilton Police Department's Violent Crime Unit arrived, they found Mark Lomas seriously injured. Lomas, 30, died 3 hours later at Good Samaritan Memorial Hospital. The other employee, Thomas Waycross, was charged with second-degree murder.

During the investigation of the incident, employees noted that Lomas and Waycross often "bickered" when working together. One employee remarked that Waycross liked to "act tough." Another employee claimed that Waycross had a "Rambo-type" personality. It was widely known that management had told both employees to "learn to get along" or quit.

When asked about the incident, police spokesperson Kathy Calder remarked, "Employers must be vigilant when monitoring for signs of potential workplace violence." Nancy Lomas, Mark's wife, has filed a negligence lawsuit against the company.

Questions

1. What are some violence indicators an employee might display?

2. What are some actions management can take to help prevent workplace violence?

3. How can employees protect themselves against workplace violence?

Source: Adapted from a case known to one of the authors. All names are fictitious.

CASE STUDY Too Much Fatigue and Stress? You Decide

Job fatigue and stress are significant problems faced by employees and their managers. Unfortunately, when a case of depression arises as a result, trying to resolve the problem may be difficult—sometimes leading to conflict—as this case illustrates.

Donald Knolls was an air traffic control supervisor for International Gateway Airport (IGA), an airport serving a major metropolitan area. Donald began to experience depression-related problems largely due to severe stress and fatigue on the job. A few months later, he requested and was granted a disability leave for treatment of his illness. After 8 months, his personal physician, an expert in depression treatment and a licensed consulting psychologist, agreed that he was sufficiently improved to return to his former position.

IGA then sent Donald to the physician it had used when Donald first requested his disability leave. After an extensive evaluation, the doctor concluded that while Donald had made considerable strides in overcoming his depression, he should not be immediately returned to his former supervisory

position because the conditions of the job had not changed and he was apt to find the stress too great. Instead, he recommended that Donald be returned to a nonsupervisory position on a 6-month trial basis, with the case to be reviewed at the end of that time. IGA followed the advice of its doctor and did not return Donald to a supervisory position. Donald, angered by management's decision, filed a grievance through IGA's alternative dispute resolution procedure, a procedure that could end in binding arbitration.

During several meetings between Donald and management, the employer maintained that it had the right to rely on the medical opinion of "a fair and impartial" doctor who had determined that Donald should not be returned to the position that was the cause of his original stress-related emotional problems. Additionally, management pointed out to Donald that IGA's disability leave provision states that it "may require appropriate medical documentation if it believes an employee is not fit to return to his or her former position."

Donald responded, through an attorney he hired to represent his position, that the disability leave provisions were clear but, nevertheless, biased against an employee because they completely disregarded the opinion of his physician and psychologist. According to Donald, "Why bother to get expert medical opinions if they are dismissed?" He further noted, "I have never felt better. I'm really ready to get back to my job." Finally, Donald's lawyer contended that Donald was the victim of discrimination based on his former state of depression: "What happened to Donald would not have happened if his illness had been a more conventional physical injury."

ANSWERS TO HIGHLIGHTS IN HRM 2

1. True
2. True
3. True
4. False

Questions

1. When conflicting medical opinions are presented, should the advice of a medical expert count more heavily than the opinion of a general physician? Explain your answer.

2. Is the charge of discrimination presented by Donald's lawyer relevant to this case? Explain your answer.

3. If you were presented with this case, what decision would you reach? Explain.

Source: *Small Business Success Stories* (Washington, DC: Occupational Safety and Health Administration, May 25, 2011), http://www .osha.gov.

5. Unsafe acts (85 percent of all accidents)
6. True
7. False
8. False (8 hours)

Notes and References

1. Erika Ebsworth-Goold, "Working Well by Being Well: The Bottom Line Benefits of Corporate Wellness Programs," *The Source* (St. Louis: Washington University, August 24, 2016).
2. P.L. 91-596, 91st Congress, S. 2193, December 29, 1970.
3. OSHA publishes many pamphlets pertaining to various aspects of the act, such as employee workplace rights and voluntary compliance programs. All OSHA publications can be downloaded at no cost from the agency website at http:// www.osha.gov; you may also call (800) 321-OSHA or fax a request to (202) 693–2498.
4. *All about OSHA*, 14.
5. https://www.osha.gov/oshstats/commonstats.html (April 11, 2017).
6. *All about OSHA*, 21.
7. https://www.osha.gov/penalties/ (April 11, 2017).
8. https://www.osha.gov/dep/enforcement/top_cases.html (April 11, 2017).
9. *All about OSHA*, 21.
10. Kent Mallett, "OSHA Fines Sunfield $3.4 Million for Safety Violations," *USA Today* (July 1, 2016).
11. For a comprehensive list of compliance requirements of OSHA standards or regulations, refer to Title 29 of the Code of Federal Regulations at www.osha.gov or call (800) 321-OSHA.
12. *All about OSHA*, 31.
13. *All about OSHA*, 13.
14. Ibid., 5.
15. Roy Maurer, "Making Safety Committees Work," *Society for Human Resource Management* (August 8, 2013): 1.
16. Ibid., 2.
17. Jessica Marquez, "Creating a Culture of Safety," *Workforce Management* 86, no. 8 (April 23, 2007): 1.
18. Robert Pater, "Next Level Safety Cultures," *Occupational Health and Safety* (May 2008).
19. Oregon OSHA, "Supervisor Responsibilities," *Health and Safety Resource Magazine* 21 (December 2011): 7.
20. Carol Leaman, "The Future of Safety Training," *Occupational Health and Safety* (September 2013).
21. Ismael E. Garza, "Increasing Safety Awareness in the Workplace: Measuring the Emotional, Cognitive and Rhetorical Effectiveness of Informational Illustrations Used in Safety Documents," *University of Houston-Downtown* (December 2009): 80.
22. "How to Make Safety Training Fun," *Workplace Safety Experts* (June 2011).
23. Aruna Vayuvegula, "Learning Activities for Making Safety Training Fun," *CommLab India* (January 2012).

24. E. Kevin Kelloway and Cary L. Cooper, *Occupational Health and Safety for Small and Medium Sized Enterprises*, (Edward Elgar Publishing, 2011), 45.

25. OSHA considers an injury or illness to be work-related if an event or exposure in the work environment either caused or contributed to the resulting condition or significantly aggravated a preexisting injury or illness. Work-relatedness is presumed for injuries and illnesses resulting from events or exposure occurring in the work environment. OSHA defines the work environment as "the establishment and other locations where one or more employees are working or are present as a condition of their employment. The work environment includes not only physical locations, but also the equipment or materials used by the employee during the course of his or her work."

26. For complete information on the recording and reporting of illnesses and injuries, see OSHA Publication 3169, *Recordkeeping*, particularly Sections 1904.5 (determination of work-relatedness) and 1904.7 (general recording criteria). See also the OSHA website at http://www.osha.gov.

27. If employers have a "privacy concern case," they may not enter the employee's name on the OSHA 300 log. Instead, they should enter "privacy case" in the space normally used for the employee's name. This will protect the privacy of the injured or ill employee when another employee, a former employee, or an authorized employee representative is provided access to the OSHA 300 log. Privacy cases must be recorded on a separate confidential list. Employers must consider the following injuries or illnesses privacy concern cases: (i) an injury or illness to an intimate body part of the reproductive system; (ii) an injury or illness resulting from a sexual assault; (iii) mental illnesses; (iv) HIV infection, hepatitis, or tuberculosis; (v) needlestick injuries and cuts from sharp objects that are contaminated with another person's blood or other potentially infectious material; and (vi) other illnesses, if the employee independently and voluntarily requests that his or her name not be entered on the log.

28. Randolph P. Schmid, "Odd Work Schedules Pose Health Risk," *ABC News* (April 16, 2011), http://abcnews.go.com.

29. L.M. Sixel, "Working: Beyond Exhausted, but Still on the Job," *Houston Chronicle* (May 5, 2011), http://www.chron.com; https://www.osha.gov/OshDoc/data_Hurricane_Facts/faq_longhours.html (April 11, 2017).

30. Julie Ferguson, "Distracted Driving and Employer's Policies," *HR Web Café* (November 1, 2009), http://www.hrwebcafe.com.

31. Alev Dudek, "Workplace Bullying, A Form of Violence Pursued Under Title VII," *The Huffington Post* (February 3, 2017).

32. Roy Maurer, "Workplace-Bullying Laws on the Horizon?" *Society for Human Resource Management* (July 2013): 3.

33. Deborah Temkin, "All 50 States Now Have a Bullying Law. Now What?" *Huffington Post* (April 27, 2015).

34. W. Barry Nixom and Kim Kerr, Background Screening and Investigation: Managing Hiring Risk from the HR and Securities Perspectives, (Elsevier, August 2011), 28.

35. Marcia K. Korow, "How Reflective Is Our Policy?" *Nursing Management* 39, no. 1 (January 2008): 37; see also Scott R. Gane, "Avoiding Violent Outcomes," *Security Management* 51, no. 6 (June 2007): 140.

36. John P. Baeseman and Douglas Newhand, "The Ergonomically Correct Workplace," *Document Processing Technology* 15, no. 7 (December 2007): 20.

37. Emil Jacob, "The Future of Computer Ergonomics," *Occupational Health and Safety* (September 2011); see also Joshua S. Berger and Roy Garvin, "Microcentrifuge Tube Ergonomics and the Required Force of Opening," *Occupational Health and Safety* (July 2010).

38. Michael S. Zedalis and Keitha Kessler, "Frequently Asked Questions: Ergonomics and Hand Protection," *Occupational Health and Safety* 76, no. 4 (April 2007): 64.

39. Reid Goldsborough, "Keeping Your Eyes Healthy in Front of a Computer Screen," *TECH Directions* 66, no. 10 (May 2007): 12.

40. The Supreme Court decision in *International Union v. Johnson Controls* may be found in 59 U.S. Law Week 4029.

41. Judy Ashley, "Building a Culture of Wellness the Discovery Way," *Workspan* (July 2007): 43.

42. The Greatest Team, "The 46 Healthiest Companies to Work for in America," *Greatest* (October 2013); see also Joshua Love, "Five Reasons Corporate Wellness Is More Important Than Ever," *Forbes* (September 2013); see also Mary Lorenze, "7 Habits of Highly Successful Corporate Wellness Programs," *CareerBuilder* (July 2010).

43. Dale Kaplan and Park Dietz, "Use Employee Assistance to Manage Risk," *Occupational Health and Safety* 76, no. 7 (July 2007): 82.

44. Josh Cable, "Shedding Pounds Good for Bottom Line," *Occupational Hazards* 69, no. 10 (October 2007): 18.

45. Jeremy Smerd, "Young and Unhealthy: Urgent Care Required," *Workforce Management* 86, no. 15 (September 10, 2007): 36.

46. "Obesity Programs Are Latest Wellness Focus," *HR Focus* 84, no. 7 (July 2007): 12.

47. "U.S. Workers' Satisfaction with Job Dimensions Increases," *Gallup* (August 29, 2016), http://www.gallup.com/poll/195143/workers-satisfied-job-dimensions.aspx.

48. Kerry Sulkowicz, "Stressed for Success," *Business Week* (May 21, 2007): 18.

49. Gary M. Stern, "Employee Burnout: Around the Corner? Already Here?" *Fortune, CNN Money* (May 2012).

50. "U.S. Workers' Satisfaction with Job Dimensions Increases."

51. http://www.watsonsyatt.com/research/reports.asp.

52. Jenna Goudreau, Gail Edmondson, and Michelle Conlin, "Dispatches from the War on Stress: Business Begins to Reckon with the Enormous Costs of Workplace Angst," *Business Week*

(August 6, 2007): 74; see also Michael R. Frone, "Are Work Stressors Related to Employee Substance Use? The Importance of Temporal Context Assessments of Alcohol and Illicit Drug Use," *Journal of Applied Psychology* 93, no. 1 (January 2008): 199.

53. "Will Stress Be Your Next Wellness Target?" *HR Focus* 85, no. 1 (January 2008): 12.

54. Tower Watson, "2013/2014 Staying@Work Report: U.S. Executive Summary," *National Business Group on Health*, No. 29407 (2013): 6.

55. Ashley Weinberg, Cary L. Cooper, and Dr. Valerie J Sutherland, *Organizational Stress Management: A Strategic Approach* (Palgrave Macmillan, September 2010), 234.

56. Dale Kaplan and Park Dietz, "Use Employee Assistance to Manage Risk," *Occupational Health and Safety* 76, no. 7 (July 2007): 82.

57. Gary M. Stem, "Not Tonight, Dear," *The Conference Room Review* 44, no. 2 (March/April 2007): 38.

58. James Hunter, "Research on Depression," *National Institute of Mental Health and PsychCentral* (October 2013), https://www.nimh.nih.gov/health/statistics/prevalence/any-anxiety-disorder-among-adults.shtml.

59. "Treating Depression Improves Productivity," *Industrial Engineer* 40, no. 1 (January 2008): 11.

60. "Depression Outreach Can Boost Productivity," *HR Focus* 84, no. 12 (December 2007): 12.

61. The HR Specialist, "ADA Warning for Bosses: You're not Qualified to Diagnose Employees' Mental Illness," *Discrimination and Harassment in Human Resources, Business Management Daily* (November 2012).

62. Pearl Jacobs and Linda Scaain, "Alcohol Abuse in the Workplace: Developing a Workable Plan of Action," *Research in Business & Economics Journal* (March 2010): 1.

63. Mindy Chapman, "Drugs and Alcohol Workplace Trends," *Occupational Health and Safety* 76, no. 8 (August 2007): 32.

64. *The Employer's Legal Handbook*, see section on preventing discrimination.

65. Information regarding the U.S. Department of Labor's efforts to create a drug-free workplace can be found at http://www.dol.gov.

66. Kathy Gurchiek, "Employer Testing Credited for Lower Drug-Use Rates," *HR Magazine* 52, no. 6 (June 2007): 36.

67. Andrew Powell, "Prescription for a Hazardous Workplace," *Occupational Health and Safety* (September 2013).

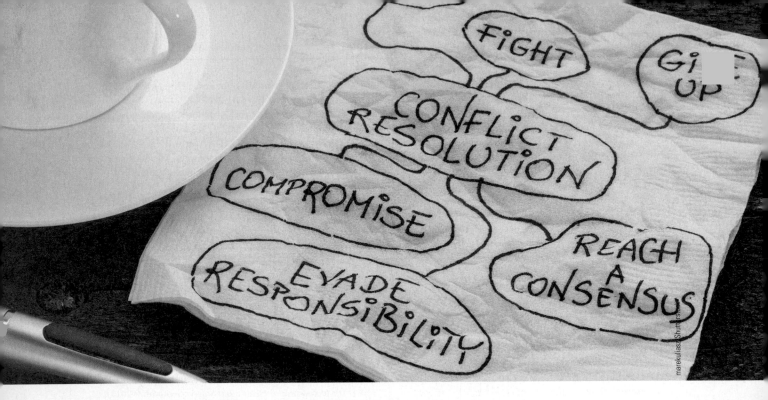

marekulias/Shutterstock

CHAPTER **13**

Employees Rights and Discipline

Learning Outcomes

After studying this chapter, you should be able to

LO ① Explain the concepts of employee rights and employer responsibilities.

LO ② Identify and explain what the privacy rights of employees are.

LO ③ Establish disciplinary policies and differentiate between the two approaches to disciplinary action.

LO ④ Identify the different types of alternative dispute resolution methods.

n this chapter, we discuss the rights of employees, the privacy they can expect in the workplace, and employee discipline. Companies without clear policies and procedures for dealing with employee rights and discipline can end up losing lots of money and, worst of all, ruining their reputation.

This is where HR managers play a crucial role. To be effective they must stay abreast of current laws, agency regulations, and court rulings, establish written employment policies based on this information, and educate the staff members in their organizations about them.

13.1 Employee Rights and Privacy

Employee rights can be defined as the guarantees of fair treatment that workers expect in return for their services to an employer. These expectations become rights when they are granted to employees by the courts, legislatures, or employers. Included among those rights are the rights of employees to protest unfair disciplinary actions, to question genetic testing, to have access to their personal files, to challenge employer searches and monitoring, and to be largely free from employer discipline for off-duty conduct.[1]

The evolution of employee rights is a natural result of the evolution of societal, business, and employee interests.[2] However, legal scholars recognize that the protection of employee privacy rights extends only so far; federal and state courts generally view the privacy rights of employees as minimal. As attorney Benjamin J. Cook notes, "When employers clearly state that there is no expectation of privacy, it's hard to argue that a reasonable person could have such an expectation."

For example, consider the issue of camera surveillance. Generally, it is legal to install cameras in the workplace (except for installations in bathrooms and locker rooms), as long as employees are informed about them. However, after pornography was discovered on one of its computers, a California children's home for abused children installed hidden surveillance cameras in an office shared by two employees. The person who had accessed the pornography was never caught. However, the two employees who shared the office later discovered the camera and were upset they were being monitored. They claimed their privacy rights had been violated, but the Supreme Court of California ruled against them, saying that their employer had a legitimate business reason for conducting the surveillance.[3]

employee rights
Guarantees of fair treatment that become rights when they are granted to employees by the courts, legislatures, or employers.

13.1a Employee Rights versus Employer Responsibilities

Balanced against employee rights is the employer's responsibility to provide a safe workplace for employees while guaranteeing safe, quality goods and services to consumers.[4] An employee who uses drugs may exercise his or her privacy right and refuse to submit to a drug test. But should that employee produce a faulty product as a result of drug impairment, the employer can be held liable for any harm caused by that product. Employers must therefore exercise *reasonable care* in the hiring, training, and assignment of employees to jobs.[5]

It is here that employee rights and employer responsibilities often come into conflict (see Figure 13.1).

LO 1
Are the rights you have as a citizen of the United States the same as the rights you have as an employee?

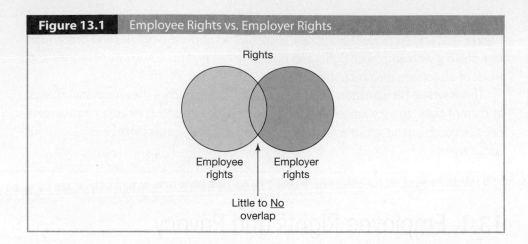

Figure 13.1   Employee Rights vs. Employer Rights

Rights

Employee rights

Employer rights

Little to <u>No</u> overlap

When employers fail to honor the rights of employees, it can result in costly lawsuits, damage the organization's reputation, and hurt employee morale. But the failure to protect the safety and welfare of employees or consumer interests can invite litigation from both groups.

13.1b Negligent Hiring

negligence
The failure to provide reasonable care when such failure results in injury to consumers or other employees.

In Chapter 6, we discussed negligent hiring. In law, **negligence** is the failure to use a reasonable amount of care when such failure results in injury to another person. A general responsibility exists for employers to exercise *reasonable care* in preventing employees from intentionally harming other employees during the course of their work.[6]

Unfortunately, when one employee commits a violent act against another employee or an employee willfully defames another employee through email messages communicated at work, the employer may face a negligent-hiring lawsuit claiming that the employer should have used more reasonable care in the hiring of its employees.[7] A negligent-hiring lawsuit can seem like a "Catch-22" for an employer. In the remainder of this section, we will discuss various rights employees have come to expect from their employers.

13.1c Job Protection Rights

It is not surprising that employees should regard their jobs as a right that should not be taken away without "just cause" (a good reason) for doing so. However, although employees might believe they have a right to their jobs, there are no laws in the United States guaranteeing them as much, as you will see shortly.

psychological contract
Expectations of a fair exchange of employment obligations between an employee and employer.

Nonetheless, workers have certain expectations about the employment relationships they have with their employers.[8] This expectation is referred to as the **psychological contract**. It consists of an employer and an employee's beliefs about the mutual obligations they have toward one another.[9] For example, in exchange for their talents, energies, and technical skills, workers expect employers to provide fair compensation, steady work, job training, and promotions.

Employment-at-Will

The employment relationship has traditionally followed the common-law doctrine of employment-at-will. An **employment-at-will relationship** is created when an employee agrees to work for an employer for an unspecified period of time. Because the duration of the employment is indefinite, it can, in general, be terminated at the whim of either party.[10]

Does the employment-at-will doctrine give managers and supervisors the unrestricted right of termination? No.[11] First, as we have emphasized throughout this text, federal and state laws, court decisions, and administrative rulings restrict termination decisions. For example, as you learned in Chapter 3, people cannot be fired because of certain characteristics such as their race, gender, and so forth. Second, in unionized organizations, union collective bargaining agreements limit automatic discharges. These agreements specify the kinds of infractions that can lead to termination.

Not all employers operate on the at-will principle, however. Some have written policies that require good cause to terminate an employee. In any case, despite the at-will doctrine, in today's litigious environment, most employers are very cautious about terminating employees. Barry Roseman, employment attorney, notes, "Employers increasingly need to operate under the premise that they have to 'prove' that an employee's conduct or action warrants termination, if they hope to prevail in court."

Wrongful Discharge

Approximately 2 million workers are discharged each year.[12] A substantial number of these employees sue their former employers for **wrongful discharge**. A wrongful discharge is one that is illegal. Wrongful discharge suits challenge an employer's right under the employment-at-will concept to unilaterally terminate employees.[13] Various state courts now recognize the following three important exceptions to the employment-at-will doctrine:

1. *Violation of public policy.* This exception occurs when an employee is terminated for refusing to commit a crime; for reporting criminal activity to government authorities; for disclosing illegal, unethical, or unsafe practices of the employer; or for exercising employment rights. See Figure 13.2 for examples of public policy violations.

2. *Implied contract.* This exception occurs when employees are discharged despite the employer's promise (expressed or implied) of job security or contrary to established termination procedures. An employer's oral or written statements may constitute a contractual obligation if they are communicated to employees and employees rely on them as *conditions of employment.*[14]

3. *Implied covenant.* This exception occurs when an employer has acted with a lack of good faith and fair dealing. For example, an employer would be doing so if it were to terminate a salesperson simply to avoid having to pay him or her a commission. By inflicting harm without justification, the employer violated the implied covenant between the two parties.

The confusion and conflict between the traditional rights of employers to terminate at will and the rights of employees to be protected from unjust discharge are far from resolved. HR specialists recommend firms follow the suggestions given in Figure 13.3.[15] Next, let's look at some situations that can result in wrongful discharge suits.

employment-at-will relationship
The right of an employer to fire an employee without giving a reason and the right of an employee to quit when he or she chooses.

wrongful discharge
A discharge, or termination, of an employee that is illegal.

Figure 13.2	Discharges That Violate Public Policy

An employer may not terminate an employee for:
- Refusing to commit perjury in court on the employer's behalf
- Cooperating with a government agency in the investigation of a charge or giving testimony
- Refusing to violate a professional code of conduct
- Reporting Occupational Safety and Health Administration (OSHA) infractions
- Refusing to support a law or a political candidate favored by the employer
- Whistle-blowing, or reporting illegal conduct by the employer
- Informing a customer that the employer has stolen property from the customer
- Complying with summons to jury duty

Figure 13.3	Tips to Avoid Wrongful Employment Termination Lawsuits

- *Terminate an employee only if there is an articulated reason.* An employer should have clearly articulated, easily understandable reasons for discharging an employee. The reasons should be stated as objectively as possible and should reflect company rules, policies, and practices.
- *Set and follow termination rules and schedules.* Make sure every termination follows a documented set of procedures. Procedures can be from an employee handbook, a supervisory manual, or even an intraoffice memorandum. Before terminating, give employees notices of unsatisfactory performance and improvement opportunities through a system of warnings and suspensions.
- *Document all performance problems.* A lack of documented problems in an employee's personnel record may be used as circumstantial evidence of pretextual discharge if the employee is "suddenly" discharged.
- *Be consistent with employees in similar situations.* Document reasons given for all disciplinary actions, even if they do not lead to termination. Terminated employees may claim that exception-to-the-rule cases are discriminatory. Detailed documentation will help employers explain why these "exceptions" did not warrant termination.

Whistle-Blowing

whistle-blowing

Complaints to governmental agencies by employees about their employers' illegal or immoral acts or practices.

Employees engage in **whistle-blowing** when they report an employer's illegal actions, immoral conduct, or illegal practices to governmental agencies charged with upholding the law. A number of federal and state laws protect whistle-blowers from retaliation from their employers.[16]

The Sarbanes–Oxley (SOX) Act protects whistle-blowers employed in publicly traded companies.[17] The law encourages whistle-blowing by motivating publicly held companies to promote a more open culture that is sympathetic to employees who have a "reasonable belief" that a law has been violated. Federal employees are covered by the federal Whistleblower Protection Act (WPA).[18] The Notification and Federal Employee Antidiscrimination and Retaliation Act (No FEAR Act) requires federal agencies to be more accountable for violations of antidiscrimination and whistle-blower protection laws. The False Claims Act (FCA) and Dodd–Frank Wall Street Reform and Consumer Protection Act protect and financially reward whistle-blowers who expose

Christian Science Monitor/Getty Images

Google, owner of Nest, set up an internal website for employees to report whistleblowers. After paying $200 million in fines due to one whistle-blower at Nest, the company now encourages employees to air their frustrations by talking to management before talking to the press.

fraud related to governmental programs and wrongdoing related to consumer financial products or services, respectively. OSHA administers the whistle-blowing provisions in 15 federal statutes protecting whistle-blowers in such industries as airline, nuclear power, and public transportation.

Not only is whistle-blowing a protected right of employees, but also these cases result in embarrassment for employers, harassment for employees, and large fines for employers that are found guilty.[19] For example, in 2016 news broke that Barney Jones, former employee of the smart-home company Nest, exposed the company to the U.K. government for not paying appropriate taxes. Nest, which happens to be owned by Google, ended up paying nearly $200 million in fines and fees.[20]

To prevent cases such as these, HR professionals recommend companies implement a whistle-blowing policy that encourages employees to report illegal or immoral conduct internally rather than externally. The policy should provide for the safeguard of employee rights, a complete and unbiased investigation of the incident, a speedy report of findings, and an appeals procedure for employees who are dissatisfied with company findings. You can rest assured that Nest now has a website for employees to blow the whistle internally before they have to go outside the company to find justice. The website also encourages employees to stop friends from leaking important information. You could say it promotes whistle-blowing on whistle-blowers.[21]

Implied Contract

Because a majority of Americans work without an employment contract, under certain conditions these employees may be granted contractual employment rights. This can occur when an implied promise by the employer suggests some form of job security to the employee. Once these explicit or implicit promises of job security have been made, courts have generally prohibited the employer from terminating the employee without first exhausting the conditions of the contract. The following are some examples of how an implied contract may become binding:

- Telling employees their jobs are secure as long as they perform satisfactorily and are loyal to the organization.
- Stating in the employee handbook that employees will not be terminated without the right of defense or access to an appeal procedure.
- Urging an employee to leave another organization by promising higher wages and benefits, then reneging on those promises after the person has been hired.

Employers can lessen their vulnerability to implied contract lawsuits by prudent managerial practices, training, and HR policies. HR experts recommend the following approaches:

1. Training supervisors and managers not to imply contract benefits in conversations with new or present employees.

2. Including in employment offers a statement that an employee may voluntarily terminate his or her employment with proper notice and may be dismissed by the employer at any time and for a justified reason.

3. Including employment-at-will statements in all employment documents—for example, employee handbooks, employment applications, and letters of employment[22] (see Highlights in HRM 1).

4. Having written proof that employees have read and understood the employment-at-will disclaimers provided to them.

Explicit Contracts

Explicit employment contracts are formal written (signed) agreements that grant to employees and employers agreed-upon employment benefits and privileges. The contracts normally state the period of employment, terms and conditions of employment (e.g., salary and benefits), and severance provisions. Explicit contracts are popular with executives, senior managers, and people with highly technical or professional skills and abilities. When an employee has an explicit contract, he or she cannot be dismissed at will.

In today's highly competitive environment, before hiring employees, employers sometimes impose certain restrictions, or provisions, in explicit contracts. The most widely used restrictions are:

- *Nondisclosure of information agreement.* This provision forbids employees from revealing proprietary information outside the company, either during or following their employment. Courts widely enforce these agreements.
- *Intellectual property agreement.* This provision grants to an employer the ownership of an idea, invention or process, or work of authorship developed by the employee during the time of employment. Such an agreement expressly states that the employer retains all rights, titles, and interests in ideas that are subject to patent laws and developed during the employee's period of hire.
- *Noncompete agreement.* This provision prevents ex-employees from either becoming a competitor or working for a competitor for a designated period of time, for example, 1 or 2 years.[23] Noncompete agreements are designed to protect confidential information, customer relations, and other valuable assets.[24]

- *Nonpiracy agreements*. These agreements prohibit ex-employees from soliciting clients or customers of former employers for a specific period of time *and* from disclosing or making use of confidential employer information.

Explicit contracts are enforceable in court when either the employee or employer violates any provisions of the agreement.

Constructive Discharge

It is increasingly common for employees to quit or resign from their jobs because the intolerable acts of their employers left them no choice. This situation is referred to as a **constructive discharge**. That is, the employees were "forced" to resign because of intolerable working conditions purposefully placed upon them by the employer.[25] In a leading constructive discharge case, *Young v. Southwestern Savings and Loan Association*, the court noted:

> The general rule is that if the employer deliberately makes an employee's working conditions so intolerable that the employee is forced into involuntary resignation, then the employer has encompassed a constructive discharge and is as liable for any illegal conduct involved therein as if he had formally discharged the aggrieved employee.

The courts, by formulating the constructive discharge doctrine, attempt to prevent employers from accomplishing covertly what they are prohibited by law from achieving overtly.[26]

constructive discharge
An employee's voluntary termination of his or her employment because of harsh, unreasonable employment conditions placed on the individual by the employer.

Discharge as a Result of Retaliation

Title VII of the Civil Rights Act, the Age Discrimination in Employment Act, the Americans with Disabilities Act, and other employment laws prohibit employers from retaliating against employees when they exercise their rights under these statutes

The Bratz-versus-Barbie doll war isn't child's play. What's the fight about? Mattel says the toy's inventor, Carter Bryant, designed the doll when he was working for Mattel, so it should be a Mattel product. Bryant says he invented the toy on his own time, and when Mattel showed no interest in the product, he sold the idea to rival toymaker MGA.

AP Images/PRNews-Foto/MGA Entertainment

Examples of Employment-at-Will Statements

Employment handbooks frequently include an opening statement that employees are employed at will; that is, there are no duration guarantees. They also typically state that no supervisors or managers, except specified individuals (i.e., the HR director or company president), have the authority to promise any employment benefit—including salaries, job positions, and the like. All handbooks should include a disclaimer that expressly provides that all employment policies and benefits contained in the handbook are subject to change or removal at the sole and exclusive discretion of the employer.

Two examples of at-will statements are as follows:

I acknowledge that if hired, I will be an at-will employee. I will be subject to dismissal or discipline without notice or cause, at the discretion of the employer. I understand that no representative of the company, other than the president, has authority to change the terms of an at-will employment and that any such change can occur only in a written employment contract.

I understand that my employment is not governed by any written or oral contract and is considered an at-will arrangement. This means that I am free, as is the company, to terminate the employment relationship at any time for any reason, so long as there is no violation of applicable federal or state law. In the event of employment, I understand that my employment is not for any definite period or succession of periods and is considered an at-will arrangement. That means I am free to terminate my employment at any time for any reason, as is the company, so long as there is no violation of applicable federal or state law.

Note of Caution: Because at-will employment is governed by state laws, in order for an employer to preserve its at-will status, it must follow the regulations of its jurisdiction. This includes the writing of employment-at-will statements.

(see Chapter 3). Employees may believe retaliation occurs when managers transfer them to lower-rated jobs, deny them salary increases or promotions, impose on them unrealistic job assignments, or become belligerent or uncommunicative with them after they file discrimination complaints or receive a favorable settlement.[27]

To prevent retaliation charges, employers should implement a separate anti-retaliation policy and train managers and supervisors in acceptable and unacceptable methods to resolve employee complaints.[28] A key component to any anti-retaliation policy is to treat employees with dignity and respect. Other suggestions to reduce retaliation discharges include the following:

- Take no adverse employment action against employees when they file complaints. Let them know you take their complaints seriously and are looking into them.

- Keep complaints confidential.

- Be consistent and objective in your treatment of employees. Evaluate employees on how well they perform, not on their personalities.

- Harbor no animosity toward employees when they file discrimination lawsuits. Treat every employee the way you would want to be treated—fairly.

Discharges and the WARN Act

In 1989, Congress passed the Worker Adjustment and Retraining Notification (WARN) Act, which requires organizations with more than 100 employees to give employees and their communities 60 days' notice of any closure or layoff affecting 50 or more full-time employees.[29] Notice must be given to collective bargaining representatives, unrepresented employees, the appropriate state dislocated worker agency, and the highest elected local official. Terminated employees must be notified individually in writing. The act allows for several exemptions, including "unforeseeable circumstances" and "faltering businesses."

13.1d Privacy Rights

The right of privacy is the freedom from unwarranted government or business intrusion into one's personal affairs. It involves the individual's right to be given personal autonomy and to be left alone.[30] Not surprisingly, employees strongly defend their right to workplace privacy. Meanwhile, employers defend their right to monitor employees' activities when they directly affect a business, its productivity, workplace safety, and/or morale.[31] So who is right? Employers or employees? (See Figure 13.4.)

In this section, we will discuss some of the most pressing privacy issues being debated by employees and employers today and how they are being resolved.

Substance Abuse and Drug Testing

As you learned, in the United States companies can legally test workers for drugs. But can they do so under any and all circumstances? The answer is no. Certain restrictions apply. In the private sector, drug testing is largely regulated by individual states. Pro-drug testing states generally permit testing, provided that strict testing procedures are followed.[32] By contrast, states with restrictive drug-testing laws generally prohibit testing for drugs except in very specific circumstances and for drugs listed in state regulations.[33]

Federal regulations and laws restrict drug testing as well. Recall from Chapter 3 that the Equal Employment Opportunity Commission does not allow job applicants to be tested before they are extended offers. The Americans with Disabilities Act protects employees who have been addicted to drugs and are recovering from them. And some drugs that would otherwise be illegal, such as opiates and medical marijuana, are legitimately prescribed for certain conditions.[34]

Safety Sensitive Positions. Drug testing is most prevalent among employees in sensitive positions within the public sector, in organizations doing business with the federal government, and in public and private transportation companies. Since the passage of the Drug-Free Workplace Act of 1988, applicants and employees of federal contractors have become subject to testing for illegal drug use. Barring state and federal laws that restrict or prohibit drug testing, however, private employers generally have a right to

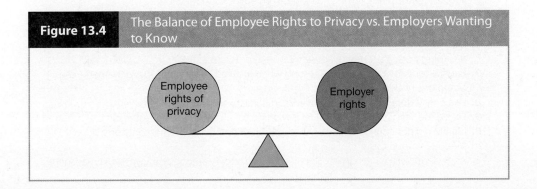

| Figure 13.4 | The Balance of Employee Rights to Privacy vs. Employers Wanting to Know |

LO **2**

What are the privacy settings on your Facebook page? Do you think your employer, or prospective employer, should be allowed to look at it?

require employees to submit to the tests. The exception is unionized workforces. Drug-testing programs for these employees must be negotiated by their unions.

Criticisms of Drug Testing.   In Chapter 6, we explained that studies have failed to show that drug testing makes the workplace safer and that alcohol appears to create more problems than drugs.[35] Another criticism of drug tests, including urinalysis and hair tests, is that they do not reveal if a person is currently under the influence of a drug. Illegal substances remain in urine for various periods of time: cocaine for approximately 72 hours, marijuana for 3 weeks or longer.[36] Therefore, an employee can test positive for a drug days or weeks after using it but not be impaired on the job. Alcohol will not show up in a urinalysis or hair test. For that, a breathalyzer, blood, or saliva test must be used. The question becomes, Which test should an employer use?

Organizations also have to ensure that any samples taken from employees are properly handled and that accredited labs are used to test them. The results of the tests must be kept confidential and provided only to those who need to know—for example, supervisors or HR staff members—and not to other coworkers or disinterested managers.

For reasons such as these, companies have become less aggressive about drug testing than they were in decades past when the tests first found their way into the workplace. Today, most companies only test when reasonable suspicion or probable cause exists. Figure 13.5 shows an example of a drug-free workplace policy.

Impairment Testing

impairment testing
Also called fitness-for-duty or performance-based testing, it measures whether an employee is alert enough to work.

An alternative to drug testing is to evaluate an employee's suitability for work through **impairment testing**. Also called fitness-for-duty or performance-based testing, impairment testing measures whether an employee is alert enough to work. One impairment test requires an employee to keep a cursor on track during a video game-like simulation. Test results, when compared against baseline data gathered earlier on the employee, mimic those of a sobriety test. One advantage of impairment testing is that it focuses on

Figure 13.5	Recommendations for a Drug-Free Workplace Policy

1. Adopt a written zero tolerance drug-free workplace policy and provide a copy to all employees. A signed copy should be placed in the employee's personnel file.
2. Post "We Are a Drug-Free Workplace" signs where employees will widely observe them.
3. Provide employees with substance abuse prevention educational materials. Arrange substance abuse awareness training for employees and managers.
4. Consider performing preemployment drug testing on all new hires.
5. Advise employees that they are subject to drug testing when "reasonable suspicion" exists.
6. Provide for follow-up testing to ensure that an employee remains drug-free after returning from a substance abuse treatment program.
7. Provide for post-accident drug testing when justified by property loss or damage, serious injury, or death.
8. Use only federally or state-approved/certified labs for analysis.
9. Utilize the services of a medical review officer for all positive drug test results.
10. Maintain strict confidentiality of all test results. Provide information only on a "need-to-know" basis.
11. Apply terms of a written policy strictly, fairly, and equally among employees and managers.

workplace conduct rather than off-duty behavior. Furthermore, it identifies employees who are impaired because of problems that a drug test cannot spot: fatigue, stress, and alcohol use.

13.1e Digital Surveillance

Why do companies use surveillance and other technology to watch what their employees do? One reason is employee theft, such as the stealing of merchandise, supplies, or equipment, the selling of information such as customer lists and trade secrets, embezzlement, and so on.[37] Monitoring quality control, ensuring the safety of employees, and eliminating the amount of time they spend surfing the Web and doing personal business on company time are other reasons.[38] Next, let us look at some of the most common methods of surveillance, and the employer–employee rights associated with them.

Camera Surveillance

DuPont uses long-distance cameras to watch employees on its loading docks. The Cheesecake Factory, a restaurant chain, uses video surveillance of kitchens, dining rooms, and hostess stations to monitor how workers treat customers and each other. Most high-end hotels have cameras in their facilities to protect both workers and guests. Employers also install cameras in their parking lots and remote workplace areas to help improve safety. Few federal laws protect workers from being watched. In general, employers can train video cameras on their employees without significant legal concerns as long as they have a legitimate business reason for doing so and inform employees they are doing as much. States, however, set their own regulations.

Employers are not the only ones with cameras, though. You might be surprised to know that employees' cameras have become a new issue firms are dealing with. In just a few seconds, a coworker with a camera phone can take offensive pictures of his or her coworkers in private or embarrassing situations and disseminate them around the world via the Web.[39] In 2017, a McDonalds employee was fired for posting a video showing rats running around inside the fast-food chain. The video led to health inspectors closing down the restaurant and the employee losing her job.[40] Small cameras and camera phones can also be used to quickly and efficiently conduct industrial espionage and steal a company's patents and trade secrets. As a result, some employers ban the use of these devices in the workplace unless employees are given special permission to use them. Workers in Apple's testing

NO CAMERA NO TRIPOD NO FLASH

NO SELFIE STICKS NO RECORDING TURN OFF MOBILE

NO DRONE CAMERA NO ACTION CAMERA NO CAMCORDER

sahua d/Shutterstock

Many companies ban the use of personal recording devices to prevent the leak of confidential information to the outside world.

rooms are required to cover up devices with black cloaks when they are working on them so the company can be assured no "rogue" cameras are being used to take pictures of the products.[41]

Phone Conversations and Text Communications

In general, employers have the right to monitor calls, text and direct messages sent from their telecommunications devices, provided they do so for compelling business reasons and employees have been informed that their communications will be monitored. However, a federal law, the Electronic Communications Privacy Act (ECPA), places some limitations on that right.[42] The ECPA restricts employers from intercepting wire, oral, or electronic communications. For example, under the law, if an employee receives a personal call, the employer must hang up as soon as he or she realizes the call is personal. However, if employees are told *not* to make personal calls or send text messages from their business phones, the ECPA no longer applies, and their communications may be monitored.

Email, Internet, and Computer Use

Many employees are unaware that their employers can monitor what they do online and fire or discipline them based on that information.[43] According to a recent report by the American Management Association, more than a quarter of employers have fired workers for misusing email, and about a third have fired workers for misusing the Internet.[44] Until recently, employers were allowed to monitor any and all email communications their employees sent from work computers. However, court rulings have limited employer's rights somewhat. For example, some courts have ruled that employers can monitor incoming and outgoing data on their *own* email systems but not email sent via outside email systems such as Yahoo, Google, and AOL systems. One firm discovered this the hard way after monitoring an employee who was planning to go to work for a competitor. She believed her emails sent on her employer's computer, but via a nonwork email system, were private. A New Jersey court agreed with her.[45]

Other privacy issues relate to Internet sites employees are allowed to access. More and more companies are banning social media at work. They see the negative effects it has on productivity and even on their own reputation. For example, when a photo of a Taco Bell employee licking taco shells was posted on social media, the fast-food giant naturally took a lot of heat.

As the use of Instagram, SnapChat, and other social media platforms continues to grow, their abuse in the workplace continues to grow as well. According to one study, more than 70 percent of businesses have had to take disciplinary action against employees for misusing social media.[46] (See Figure 13.6 for reasons employees use social media.)

Companies can legally create electronic communication policies that limit employees' Internet use. Blocking employees from accessing sites such as Facebook, eBay, gambling, and pornographic websites has also become a common tactic for firms.

The measures employees need to take to protect their laptops and what to do if they are stolen should also be part of an electronic policy.[47] If they go missing, a mountain of valuable corporate data can fall into the wrong hands. Likewise, policies surrounding electronic storage devices such as USB drives are also being adopted by organizations. Studies have shown that people own a lot of USB drives and often don't keep good track of them and what they contain. USB drives can also infect a company's computers and servers with viruses.

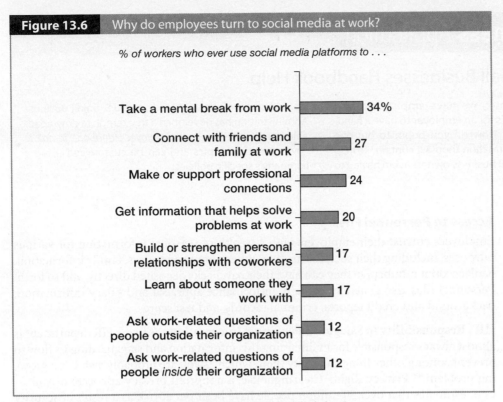

Figure 13.6   Why do employees turn to social media at work?

% of workers who ever use social media platforms to . . .

- Take a mental break from work — **34%**
- Connect with friends and family at work — **27**
- Make or support professional connections — **24**
- Get information that helps solve problems at work — **20**
- Build or strengthen personal relationships with coworkers — **17**
- Learn about someone they work with — **17**
- Ask work-related questions of people outside their organization — **12**
- Ask work-related questions of people *inside* their organization — **12**

Source: "Survey conducted Sept. 11–21, 2014. "Social Media and the Workplace."

Searches

Can employers search employees' work lockers, desks, suitcases, toolboxes, and general work areas without their knowledge? Generally speaking, yes. However, random searches of employees' personal belongings without probable cause should be avoided. Even if a firm has probable cause, legal experts advise that a company should first look at the information it has from available sources such as security cameras, timecards, and so forth to see whether the search is truly warranted. Body searches should be done only under emergency situations. If conducted, the searches should be made by a security officer and a person of the same sex.

A firm that reserves the right to search employees under warranted circumstances should have a written plan as to the privacy employees can expect.

1. The search policy should be clearly outlined in a firm's employee handbook. The handbook should explain that searches will not be conducted without a compelling reason.

2. When possible, searches should be conducted in private.

3. The employer should attempt to obtain the employee's consent prior to the search.

4. The search should be conducted in a humane and discreet manner to avoid infliction of emotional distress.

5. The penalty for refusing to consent to a search should be specified.

Small Business Application

SBA Offers Small Businesses Handbook Help

Throughout this chapter, we have emphasized how extremely important it is for an employer to have a handbook. The question is, How do you begin to put one together, and what information should it contain? To help entrepreneurs and small business owners avoid having to create handbooks from scratch, the U.S. Small Business Administration has developed a free template downloadable from its site. The basic *Employee Handbook Template* covers multiple topics and can be customized using a company's specific policies.

Access to Personnel Files

Employees entrust their employers with a wealth of personal information for various purposes, including their social security numbers, home addresses, family information, bank account numbers so they can have their paychecks deposited directly, and so forth. Personnel files also generally contain performance appraisal and salary information, background and credit reports, criminal records, and test scores.

HR's Responsibility to Safeguard Personnel Information. A firm's HR department is almost always responsible for maintaining this information and safeguarding its flow to prevent, among other things, identity theft, which as you are probably aware is a growing problem.[48] Privacy Rights Clearinghouse, a nonprofit privacy advocate organization, estimates that over 50 million people have been put at risk as a result of security breaches. For example, Adobe suffered a data breach during which hackers stole 38 million users' credit card records and login information.[49] Moreover, in 2017 Amalgamated Sugar Company, out of Boise, Idaho, suffered a breach when personal information of 2,858 employees was lost to cyberattackers.[50]

HR managers need to take the lead when it comes to safeguarding employee information. Under the Privacy Act of 1974, federal agencies must safeguard the personal information of their employees. Figure 13.7 shows the steps employers can take to safeguard employees' personal information. Also, as you learned in Chapter 3, employees' medical and genetic information must be kept confidential in a separate file from any employee's other personnel information.

Employee Access to Personnel Files. Legislation at the federal level and various states laws permit employees to inspect their own personnel files. How much access is allowed varies from state to state.[51] The states that grant employees the privilege to see their personnel files generally provide:

- The right to know of the existence of one's personnel file
- The right to inspect one's own personnel file
- The right to correct inaccurate data in the file

Typically, if a state law allows employees to examine their files, employers can insist that someone from HR, or a supervisor, be present to ensure that nothing is taken, added, or changed. Even in the absence of specific legislation, most employers give their employees access to their personnel files. Employment professionals recommend that organizations develop a policy on employee files that includes, as a minimum, the points noted in Figure 13.7.

Figure 13.7	Guidelines for Safeguarding Personnel Files

- Define exactly what information is to be kept in employee files. Do not collect information from employees or applicants you do not need or use. Do not collect information that could be viewed as discriminatory or could form the basis for an invasion-of-privacy suit.
- Identify the individuals allowed to view personnel files and when and why they should be allowed to do so. Keep employee records in a locked and secured area that only qualified personnel can access on a need-to-know basis. Maintain a log that shows who accessed what records and when.
- Specify where, when, how, and under what circumstances employees may review or copy their files.
- Do not use social security numbers as employee identifiers. Rather, use random identifiers and keep the social security numbers as narrowly distributed as possible. Do not print social security numbers on people's paychecks or send documents to employees via mail or e-mail that contain their social security numbers. The exception are IRS documents mailed at year end for tax purposes.
- Use encryption software that translates personnel data into a code that can only be accessed using a key or password.
- Do not give out information about employees over the phone. The person might claim they are a prospective employer or banker looking to help process a loan for an employee but in reality could be a debt collector, stalker, or person engaging in identity theft. Instead tell the person to send you a written authorization form signed by the employee that allows you to disclose the information. When you receive the form, verify it with the employee.
- Audit employment records on a regular basis to remove irrelevant, outdated, or inaccurate information.
- Use up-to-date digital and/or hardware-based methods, thoroughly wipe all data from the hard drive and removable magnetic media of any obsolete computers discarded or sold by the company, and physically destroy any data CDs or DVDs containing company and employee information.
- Shred and securely dispose of any paper records containing sensitive company and employee information.

Source: Adapted from "Employee Rights and Identity Theft," *Texas Workforce Commission*, accessed June 2, 2011, http://www.twc.state.tx.us.

Off-Duty Employee Conduct

Consider the following case. On Monday morning, the owner of ABC Corporation reads in the newspaper that a company employee has been charged with robbery and assault on a local convenience store owner. The employee has been released pending trial. A phone call to the employee's supervisor reveals that the employee has reported to work. What should the owner do?

A number of states have passed laws that prohibit employers from disciplining or firing employees for activities they pursue offsite on their own time as long as they are legal.[52] However, even when the activities are illegal, court rulings have suggested that the conduct may not, in some circumstances, be a lawful justification for employee discipline. Organizations that want to discipline employees for off-duty misconduct must establish a clear relationship between the misconduct and its negative effect on other employees or the organization.[53] This might be established, for example, in cases in which off-duty criminal misconduct (such as child molestation) creates a disruptive impact on the workplace. Another example might be when the public nature of the employee's job (such as police or fire department personnel) creates an image problem for the organization. However, before banning specific off-duty behavioral conduct, employers are advised to obtain legal advice.

Off-Duty Employee Speech

Some organizations have social networking and blogging policies that restrict employees from making disparaging remarks about their firms or its supervisors, or otherwise casting their organizations in a bad light. The First Amendment prohibits the government—not private employers—from telling us what we can and cannot say.

However, like off-duty conduct, state laws and courts have tried to balance the rights of employees with those of their employers in this regard.[54] The National Labor Relations Act, which allows workers to form unions, protects the rights of employees to talk to one another about their working conditions.

Meanwhile, employees need to realize that what they say online can put their employers in an awkward situation to which they are going to feel compelled to respond. Moreover, online posts that are racist, sexist, demean or harass one's coworkers, and reveal confidential company information are not likely to be legally protected. They can also be career enders for employees.

Workplace Romances

Workplace romances create a dilemma for organizations. Acceptable behavior in a consensual relationship between employees can become harassing behavior if one party to the relationship no longer welcomes the conduct, and it may result in violence should a scorned lover seek violent revenge at the work site. Of particular concern is an employer's liability if a coworker, supervisor–subordinate, or other power-differentiated romance goes sour and leads to charges of sexual harassment.[55] Furthermore, workplace romances can lead to employee charges of favoritism against a coworker involved in a supervisor–subordinate romance. These "reverse harassment" claims are based on preferential treatment given an employee engaged in a romantic affair. Workplace romances can also create morale problems when other employees feel unfairly treated; such situations can lead to jealousy, resentment, and hard feelings[56] (see Figure 13.8).

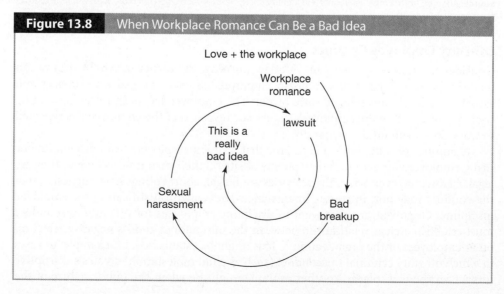

Figure 13.8	When Workplace Romance Can Be a Bad Idea

Love + the workplace

Workplace romance

lawsuit

This is a really bad idea

Sexual harassment

Bad breakup

As we mentioned in Chapter 3, although some companies have strict anti-fraternization policies, such a policy can lead to lawsuits. However, recall that the rights of companies to control the legal, off-duty conduct of their employees are limited. Sexual harassment policies have become the preferred way to deal with the issue. Some employers have dating parties sign *consensual relationship agreements* stating that they will not let their relationship affect the work environment or sue their employer should the relationship go sour.[57]

Body Art, Grooming, and Attire

Tattoos and body piercings are increasingly popular. Nearly half of Millennials (47 percent) and over a third of Generation Xers (36 percent) have one or more tattoos. This stands in stark contrast to only 13 percent of babyboomers having a tattoo.[58]

A relationship with a fellow astronaut fizzled, and Nowak was later arrested for attempting to kidnap her former lover's new girlfriend. The girlfriend was able to escape unharmed from Nowak, who was later discovered and arrested. NASA didn't institute a nonfraternization policy following the incident, but it did beef up its screening policies to help screen out candidates with psychological issues.

Matt Stroshane/Getty Images

However, employers have the right to establish reasonable standards for grooming, attire, tattoos, and facial piercings and to require employees to abide by those standards.[59] An at-will employee who does not do so can be let go. However, policies on appearance should reflect the nature of the organization and its industry, the types of safety concerns it faces, and not impinge on an employee's religious rights.[60]

Dean Drobot/Shutterstock

According to some, tattoos help Millennials declare their identity with conviction.

discipline

A tool, used to correct and mold the practices of employees to help them perform better so they conform to acceptable standards.

13.2 Disciplinary Policies and Procedures

When managers are asked to define the word *discipline*, their most frequent response is that discipline means punishment (see Figure 13.9).

However, in the context of management, **discipline** does not mean punishment. Rather, discipline is a tool used to correct the practices of employees to help them perform better so they conform to acceptable standards. Many organizations, such as Bank of America and Adobe, define *discipline* in their policy manuals as training that "corrects, molds, or perfects knowledge, attitudes, behavior, or conduct." Figure 13.10 lists the more common disciplinary problems identified by managers.

It goes without saying that disciplinary actions should be taken only for justifiable reasons and that employees should be treated fairly and consistently. Good guidelines will help a firm not only avoid lawsuits but also prevent creating a poisonous atmosphere at work that can lead to low morale among employees and high turnover.

13.2a The Result of Inaction

Even when it's justified, managers don't generally enjoy disciplining their employees. However, failing to do so generally aggravates a problem that eventually must be resolved.

Figure 13.11 presents a disciplinary model that illustrates the areas where provisions should be established. The model also shows the logical sequence in which disciplinary steps must be carried out to ensure enforceable decisions. Should discipline become

Figure 13.9	The True Definition of Discipline

Discipline ≠ Punishment
⤷ = Constructive Training

Figure 13.10	Common Disciplinary Problems

ATTENDANCE PROBLEMS
- Unexcused absence
- Chronic absenteeism
- Unexcused or excessive tardiness
- Leaving without permission

DISHONESTY AND RELATED PROBLEMS
- Theft
- Falsifying employment application
- Willfully damaging organizational property
- Punching another employee's time card
- Falsifying work records

WORK PERFORMANCE PROBLEMS
- Failing to complete work assignments
- Producing substandard products or services
- Failing to meet established production requirements

ON-THE-JOB BEHAVIOR PROBLEMS
- Bullying
- Intoxication at work
- Insubordination
- Horseplay
- Smoking in unauthorized places
- Fighting
- Gambling
- Failing to use safety devices
- Failing to report injuries
- Carelessness
- Sleeping on the job
- Using abusive or threatening language with supervisors
- Possessing illegal narcotics or alcohol
- Possessing of firearms or other weapons
- Sexual harassment

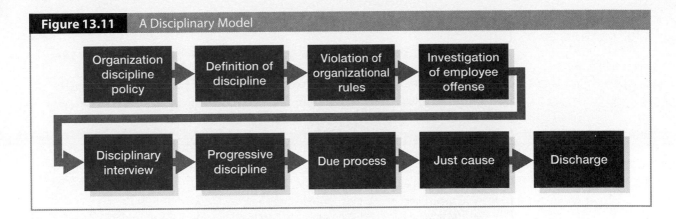

Figure 13.11 A Disciplinary Model

Organization discipline policy → Definition of discipline → Violation of organizational rules → Investigation of employee offense →

Disciplinary interview → Progressive discipline → Due process → Just cause → Discharge

necessary, the employee's immediate supervisor is the logical person to apply the company's disciplinary procedures and monitor the employee's improvement, although the HR departments should develop and ensure disciplinary policy and action conform to current laws.

13.2b Setting Organizational Rules

Setting an organization's rules is the foundation for an effective disciplinary system. These rules govern the type of behavior expected of employees. The following suggestions can help HR managers and their firms when they are considering the rules the organization should adopt and how they should be implemented:

1. The rules must be reasonable and relate to the safe and efficient operation of the organization.

2. The rules as well as the consequences for breaking them should be written down and widely disseminated to all employees. Neglecting to communicate the rules is a major reason disciplinary actions taken against employees are reversed.[61]

3. The rules should be clearly explained. Employees are more likely to accept a rule if they understand the reason behind it.

4. Employees should sign a document stating that they have read and understood the organizational rules.

5. The rules should be reviewed periodically—perhaps annually—especially those rules critical to work success.

13.2c Investigating a Disciplinary Problem

Figure 13.12 lists seven questions to consider when investigating an employee offense. Attending to each question will help ensure a full and fair investigation while providing reliable information free from personal prejudice.

Documenting Misconduct

When a manager fails to record the misconduct of employees, it can undermine a firm's efforts to deal with the behavior. A manager's records of employee misconduct are considered business documents, and as such they are admissible evidence in arbitration hearings, administrative proceedings, and courts of law.

Figure 13.12	Questions to Consider during Disciplinary Investigations

1. In very specific terms, what is the offense charged?
   - Is management sure it fully understands the charge against the employee?
   - Was the employee really terminated for insubordination, or did the employee merely refuse a request by management?
2. Did the employee know he or she was doing something wrong?
   - What rule or provision was violated?
   - How would the employee know of the existence of the rule?
   - Was the employee warned of the consequence?
3. Is the employee guilty?
   - What are the sources of facts?
   - Is there direct or only indirect evidence of guilt?
   - Has anyone talked to the employee to hear his or her side of the situation?
4. Are there extenuating circumstances?
   - Were conflicting orders given by different supervisors?
   - Does anybody have reason to want to "get" this employee?
   - Was the employee provoked by a manager or another employee?
5. Has the rule been uniformly enforced?
   - Have all managers applied this rule consistently?
   - What punishment have previous offenders received?
   - Were any other employees involved in this offense?
6. Is the offense related to the workplace?
   - Is there evidence that the offense hurt the organization?
   - Is management making a moral judgment or a business judgment?
7. What is the employee's past work record?
   - How many years of service has the employee given the organization?
   - How many years or months has the employee held the present job?
   - What is the employee's personnel record as a whole, especially his or her disciplinary record?

The most significant cause of inadequate documentation, however, is that managers often do not know what constitutes good documentation. The documentation need not be lengthy, but to be complete it should include the following eight items:

1. The date, time, and location of the incident(s)
2. The behavior exhibited by the employee (the problem)
3. The consequences of that action or behavior on the employee's overall work performance and/or the operation of the employee's work unit
4. Prior discussion(s) with the employee about the problem
5. The disciplinary action to be taken and the improvements expected should be documented
6. The consequences of failing to make the improvements by a certain follow-up date
7. The employee's reaction to the supervisor's attempt to change his or her behavior
8. The names of witnesses to the incident (if applicable)

To ensure that the documentation is as accurate as possible, a manager should record the previous eight items immediately after an incident takes place while it is still fresh in his or her mind.

The Investigative Interview

Before any disciplinary action is initiated, an investigative interview should be conducted to make sure the employee is fully aware of the organization's rules and that he or she has not followed them.[62] The interview should concentrate on how the offense violated the performance and behavior standards expected. Most important, the employee must be given a full opportunity to explain his or her side of the issue.[63]

Employees do not have the right to have an attorney present during an investigative interview. However, in *NLRB v. Weingarten, Inc.*, the Supreme Court upheld a National Labor Relations Board ruling in favor of a unionized employee's right to have a union representative with him or her during an investigative interview—if the employee reasonably believes that discipline could result from the interview.[64] Currently, nonunion employees do not have the right to have a coworker present in an investigatory interview that may lead to disciplinary action.

13.2d Approaches to Disciplinary Action

Assuming a thorough investigation shows that an employee has violated a rule, a firm can take one of two approaches to disciplinary action: progressive discipline and positive discipline.

Progressive Discipline

Progressive discipline is the application of corrective measures by increasing degrees. Progressive discipline is designed to motivate an employee to correct his or her misconduct voluntarily. A number of factors must be considered in determining how severe a disciplinary action should be. Some of the factors to consider are listed in Figure 13.12.

progressive discipline
The application of corrective measures by increasing degrees.

The typical progressive discipline procedure includes four steps. From an oral warning (or counseling), the action may progress to a written warning, to a suspension without pay, and ultimately to discharge only as a last resort. When progressive discipline is applied properly:

1. Employees always know where they stand regarding offenses.
2. Employees know what improvement is expected of them.
3. Employees understand what will happen next if improvement is not made.

Positive Discipline

Some HR professionals believe that the intimidating and adversarial nature of progressive discipline keeps it from achieving the intended purpose. For these reasons, organizations such as Saint Alphonsus Regional Medical Center, Ocean Spray, Banner Health, Pennzoil, and Bay Area Rapid Transit have instead used an approach called **positive, or nonpunitive discipline**. Positive discipline is based on the concept that employees must assume responsibility for their personal conduct, job performance, and careers.[65]

positive, or nonpunitive discipline
A system of discipline that focuses on early correction of employee misconduct, with the employee taking total responsibility for correcting the problem.

Positive discipline requires a cooperative environment in which the employee and the supervisor engage in a joint discussion to agree on a way to resolve the performance issue. The employee then bears the sole responsibility of implementing the solution. Rather than reprimands, the supervisor provides the employee with reminders to improve his or her performance.

Positive discipline is implemented in three steps. The first is the conference between the employee and the supervisor to find a solution to the problem. If improvement does not occur after the first step, the supervisor holds a second conference with the employee to determine why the solution agreed to in the first conference did not work. At this stage, however, a written reminder is given to the employee. This document states the new or repeated solution to the problem, with an affirmation that the improvement is the responsibility of the employee and a condition of his or her continued employment.

When both conferences fail to produce the desired results, the third step is to give the employee a one-day *decision-making leave* (a paid leave). The purpose of this paid leave is for the employee to decide whether he or she wishes to continue working for the organization. Employees given a decision-making leave are instructed to return the following day with a decision either to make a total commitment to improve their performance or to quit the organization. If a commitment is not made, the employee is dismissed with the assumption that he or she lacked responsibility toward the organization.

13.2e Discharging Employees

Because discharging a worker poses serious consequences for the employee—and possibly for the organization—it should be undertaken only after a deliberate and thoughtful review of the situation.[66] If an employee is fired, he or she may file a wrongful discharge suit claiming the termination was "without just or sufficient cause," implying a lack of fair treatment by management.

How does an employer know if it has just cause to terminate an employee? This question is not easily answered, but standards governing discharges do exist in the form of rules developed in the field of labor arbitration.[67] These rules consist of a set of guidelines that are applied by arbitrators to determine if a firm had just cause for a termination. These guidelines are normally set forth in the form of questions, provided in Figure 13.13. For example, before discharging an employee, did the manager forewarn the person of possible disciplinary action? A no answer to any of the seven questions in the figure generally means that just cause was not established and that the decision to terminate was arbitrary, capricious, or discriminatory. The significance of these guidelines is that they are being applied not only by arbitrators, but also by judges in wrongful discharge suits. It is critical that managers at all levels understand the just cause guidelines, including their proper application.

Figure 13.13	"Just Cause" Discharge Guidelines

1. Did the organization forewarn the employee of the possible disciplinary consequences of his or her action?
2. Were management's requirements of the employee reasonable in relation to the orderly, efficient, and safe operation of the organization's business?
3. Did management, before discharging the employee, make a reasonable effort to establish that the employee's performance was unsatisfactory?
4. Was the organization's investigation conducted in a fair and objective manner?
5. Did the investigation produce sufficient evidence of proof of guilt as charged?
6. Has management treated this employee under its rules, orders, and penalties as it has other employees in similar circumstances?
7. Did the discharge fit the misconduct, considering the seriousness of the proven offense, the employee's service record, and any mitigating circumstances?

Informing the Employee

Regardless of the reasons for a discharge, it should be done with personal consideration for the employee affected. Every effort should be made to ease the trauma a discharge creates.[68] The employee must be informed honestly, yet tactfully, of the exact reasons for the action. Doing so can help the employee face the problem and adjust to the termination in a constructive way.

To gain confidence, a supervisor might want to discuss, and even rehearse, with his or her peers and an HR manager the upcoming termination meeting to ensure that all important points are covered and presented in the best way possible. Although managers agree that there is no single right way to conduct the discharge meeting, the following guidelines will help make the discussion more effective:

1. Come to the point within the first 2 or 3 minutes, and list in a logical order all reasons for the termination.[69]

2. Be straightforward and firm, yet tactful, and remain resolute in your decision.

3. Make the discussion private, businesslike, and fairly brief.

4. Do not mix the good with the bad. Trying to sugarcoat the problem sends a mixed message to the employee.

5. Avoid making accusations against the employee and injecting your personal feelings into the discussion.

6. Avoid bringing up any personality differences between you and the employee.

7. Provide the employee with any severance pay information, and let the person know about the status of his or her benefits and coverage.

8. Explain how you will handle employment inquiries from future employers looking to hire the person.[70]

Termination meetings should be held in a neutral location, such as a conference room, to prevent the employee from feeling unfairly treated. The manager should never provoke the employee. Should the employee become belligerent, agitated, or show signs of hostility, the meeting should be stopped immediately and the firm's HR department and security notified.

It is common for managers or security officers to accompany employees back to their work areas to collect their belongings and then escort them off the premises. However, this should be done as discreetly as possible to lessen any embarrassment the employee may experience.

A manager who terminates an employee should keep the details of the termination private and not disparage the person when talking to other people, including other managers, customers, and the person's former coworkers. It gives the terminated employee grounds to sue the manager and firm for defamation.

Due Process

Despite the at-will employment doctrine, most people believe that employees should not be disciplined without the protection of due process. HR managers normally define **due process** as the employee's right to be heard—the right of the employee to tell his or her side of the story regarding the alleged infraction of organizational rules. Employers risk having their terminations overturned—even when they are justified—when employees are denied due process.

due process
Procedures that constitute fair treatment, such as allowing an employee to tell his or her story about an alleged infraction and defend against it.

LO 4

What pros and cons do you think employees who agree to settle their grievances via alternative dispute resolution methods face?

13.2f Alternative Dispute Resolution Procedures

In unionized workplaces, grievance procedures are stated in virtually all labor agreements. In nonunion organizations, however, **alternative dispute resolution (ADR)** methods are often used.[71] ADR methods address employee discharges and complaints outside of court, which is generally faster and cheaper for both parties. Employers often ask workers to sign ADR agreements when they receive their offer letters or sign their employee handbooks.

Although the right to require employees to sign ADR agreements is supported by court decisions, to be enforceable—they must be fair and equitable to both employees and employers.[72] Employers can't "stack the deck" against employees by imposing rules on employees that clearly favor the employer. As one legal expert has noted, "As much as possible, the agreement should provide employees with the same rights and remedies that they would have enjoyed had their day in court been available to them."[73] Next we will look at some of the different types of alternative dispute resolution methods organizations use.

alternative dispute resolution (ADR)

A term applied to different employee complaint or dispute resolution methods that do not involve going to court.

Step-Review Systems

A **step-review system** is based on a preestablished set of steps—normally four—for the review of an employee's complaint by successively higher levels of management. These procedures are patterned after the union grievance systems we will discuss in Chapter 14. For example, they normally require that the employee's complaint be formalized as a written statement. Managers at each step are required to provide a full response to the complaint within a specified time period, perhaps 3 to 5 working days.

An employee is sometimes allowed to bypass meeting with his or her immediate supervisor if the employee fears reprisal from this person. Unlike appeal systems in unionized organizations, however, nonunion appeal procedures ordinarily do not provide for a neutral third party—such as an arbitrator—to serve as the judge of last resort. In most step-review systems, the president, chief executive officer, vice president, or HR director acts as the final authority, and this person's decision is not appealable. Some organizations give employees assistance in preparing their complaint cases. For example, an employee who desires it may be able to get advice and counsel from a designated person in the HR department before discussing the issue with management.

step-review system

A system for reviewing employee complaints and disputes by successively higher levels of management.

Peer-Review Systems

A **peer-review system**, also called a complaint committee, is composed of equal numbers of employee and management representatives. The employees on the committee are normally elected by secret ballot by their coworkers for a rotating term, whereas the managers are assigned, also on a rotating basis. A peer-review system functions as a jury because its members weigh evidence, consider arguments, and, after deliberation, vote independently to render a final decision.

The peer-review system can be used as the sole method for resolving employee complaints, or it can be used in conjunction with a step-review system. For example, if an employee is not satisfied with management's action at step 1 or 2 in the step-review system, the employee can submit the complaint to the peer-review committee for final resolution. A benefit of the peer-review system is the sense of justice that it creates among employees.

peer-review system

A system for reviewing employee complaints that utilizes a group composed of equal numbers of employee representatives and management appointees. The group weighs evidence, considers arguments, and, after deliberation, votes to render a final decision.

Open-Door Policy

The idea behind an **open-door policy** is that to facilitate communication and the free exchange of ideas, every manager's office door should be open to every employee. The policy is also an old standby method for settling employee complaints. In an organization that has such a policy, an employee is allowed to contact various managers above his or her immediate supervisor for various reasons, including grievances; the levels may extend as high as a vice president, president, or chief executive officer. The person who acts as "the court of last resort" is the HR director or a senior staff official.

There are some problems associated with open-door policies, however. One is that some managers do not like to listen honestly to employee complaints. As an employee once told the authors of this text, "My manager has an open-door policy, but the door is only open one inch." Because of this, employees are often reluctant to approach managers with their problems. One way to make an open-door policy work better is to ensure employees with grievances first try to work out their problems with their immediate supervisors before contacting higher-up managers. This way, the chain of command isn't violated, and the supervisor of the employee who aired the grievance does not feel as if he or she was not given a chance to resolve the issue.

open-door policy
A policy of settling grievances that identifies various levels of management above the immediate supervisor for employee contact.

Ombudsman System

An **ombudsman** is a designated individual from whom employees may seek counsel for the resolution of their complaints. The ombudsman listens to an employee's complaint and attempts to resolve it by seeking an equitable solution between the employee and the supervisor. Because the ombudsman has no authority to finalize a solution to the problem, compromises are highly possible, and all parties concerned tend to feel satisfied with the outcome.

To function successfully, ombudsmen must be able to operate in an atmosphere of confidentiality that does not threaten the security of the managers or subordinates who are involved in a complaint. It is recommended that they have access to high levels of management to ensure that employee complaints receive fair treatment.

ombudsman
A designated individual from whom employees may seek counsel for resolution of their complaints.

Mediation

Along with arbitration, mediation is fast becoming a popular way to resolve employee complaints. During **mediation**, which is also discussed in Chapter 14 in conjunction with labor agreements, a neutral person (mediator) helps employees and managers negotiate and reach a voluntary agreement acceptable to both parties. The essence of mediation is compromise. The **mediator** holds a meeting with the employee and management, listens to the position of each side, gathers facts, and then through discussion, suggestions, and persuasion obtains an agreement that satisfies the needs and requirements of both sides.

A mediator serves primarily as a fact finder and as an open channel of communication between the parties. Unlike arbitrators, mediators have no power or authority to force either side toward an agreement. They must use their communication skills and the power of persuasion to help the parties resolve their differences (see Figure 13.14). A cornerstone of mediation is that the parties maintain control over the settlement outcome.[74]

Mediation is a flexible process that can be shaped to meet the demands of the parties. Settlements fashioned through mediation are generally readily acceptable by the parties, thus promoting a favorable working relationship.

mediation
The use of an impartial neutral to reach a compromise decision in employment disputes.

mediator
A third party in an employment dispute who meets with one party and then the other to suggest compromise solutions or to recommend concessions from each side that will lead to an agreement.

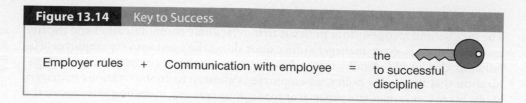

Figure 13.14   Key to Success

Employer rules   +   Communication with employee   =   the [key] to successful discipline

Arbitration

Private employers may require that employees settle their disputes through arbitration.[75] Arbitration, which is fully explained in Chapter 14, works like this: The employee and employer present their cases, or arguments, to an arbiter, who is typically a retired judge. He or she then makes a decision that the parties have agreed to be bound by. Arbitration is used primarily to resolve discrimination suits related to age, gender, sexual harassment, and race.[76] Other workplace issues such as promotions, compensation, discipline, and application of company policies can be arbitrated if an employer's arbitration program allows it.

While arbitration agreements normally mandate that employees arbitrate their discrimination claims and may prevent workers from suing their employers in court, they cannot prohibit employees from filing discrimination charges with the EEOC and other government agencies in an effort to pursue their statutory rights. In *EEOC v. Waffle House Inc.*,[77] the U.S. Supreme Court ruled that even when an employee has signed a mandatory arbitration agreement, if it chooses to, the EEOC can file a suit in its own name and recover monetary damages for the individual. Writing for the Court, Justice John Paul Stevens noted, "The EEOC has the authority to pursue victim-specific relief regardless of the forum that the employer and the employee have chosen to resolve their dispute."[78]

Discussion and compromise are cornerstones of employment mediation, which is a highly effective method of resolving disputes.

Noel Hendrickson/Blend Images/Alamy

13.3 Managerial Ethics in Employee Relations

Beyond what is required by the law is the question of organizational ethics and the ethical—or unethical—behavior engaged in by managers. **Ethics** can be defined as a set of standards of acceptable conduct and moral judgment. Ethics provides cultural guidelines—organizational or societal—that help us decide between proper or improper conduct.[79] How a firm treats its employees largely distinguishes an ethical organization from an unethical one. In an ethical organization, managers are honest in their dealings with employees, and each group has mutual respect for the other.[80]

As you learned earlier in the book, many organizations have their own codes of ethics that govern how they deal with their employees and the public. These written codes focus attention on an organization's ethical values and provide a basis for its managers to evaluate their plans and actions. HR departments have been given a greater role in communicating an organization's values and standards, monitoring compliance with its code of ethics, and enforcing the standards throughout the organization. Organizations now have ethics committees and ethics ombudsmen to provide training in ethics to employees. The ultimate goal of ethics training is to avoid unethical behavior and adverse publicity; to gain a strategic advantage; and most of all, to treat employees in a fair and equitable manner, recognizing them as productive members of the organization.

ethics
A set of standards of conduct and moral judgments that help to determine right and wrong behavior.

Summary

LO 1 Workers have certain expectations about the employment relationship they have with their employers, including the mutual obligations they have to one another. Included among those expectations are a certain degree of privacy and fair and equitable treatment while on the job. Employers, however, have the responsibility to monitor the activities of their workers to provide a safe and secure workplace free from harmful employee acts. When the perceived rights of employees differ from the reasonable responsibilities of management, conflict can result.

LO 2 Once employed, employees expect certain privacy rights, such as the freedom from unwarranted intrusion into their personal affairs. Laws and court cases related to workplace privacy generally attempt to balance employees' legitimate expectation of privacy against the need of employers to supervise and control the efficient operations of the organizations. Testing for substance abuse and searching and monitoring employees while on the job and off are among the many privacy-rights issues employers and their workers face.

LO 3 A firm's HR professionals, in combination with other managers, should establish disciplinary policies, or rules, that relate to the safe and efficient operation of the organization. The rules should be written down, explained, widely communicated within the organization, and consistently applied. They should also be revised regularly as laws, regulations, and court rulings change. An investigation of an infraction begins with properly documenting the infraction. To determine the severity of the disciplinary measure, managers need to know whether the employee knew of the rule that was violated, any extenuating circumstances that might justify the employee's conduct, the employee's past work record, and various other factors.

LO 4 Alternative dispute resolution procedures are ways to resolve disputes out of court while ensuring employees receive fair treatment. The most common forms of ADRs are step-review systems, peer-review systems, the open-door system, the ombudsman system, mediation, and arbitration.

Key Terms

alternative dispute resolution (ADR)

constructive discharge

discipline

due process

employee rights

employment-at-will relationship

ethics

impairment testing

mediation

mediator

negligence

ombudsman

open-door policy

peer-review system

positive, or nonpunitive discipline

progressive discipline

psychological contract

step-review system

whistle-blowing

wrongful discharge

Discussion Questions

LO 1 Explain three areas in which employee rights and employer responsibilities could result in conflict. How might this conflict arise?

LO 2 What are the legislative and court restrictions on employer drug testing in both the private and the public sectors?

LO 3 Discuss why documentation is so important to the disciplinary process. What constitutes correct documentation?

LO 4 What do you think would constitute an effective alternative dispute resolution system? What benefits would you expect from such a system? If you were asked to rule on a discharge case, what facts would you analyze in deciding whether to uphold or reverse the employer's action?

CASE STUDY 1 Discharged for Off-Duty Behavior

In 2015, Chad Shanks, the official social media manager for the Houston Rockets, tweeted at the end of a game with the Dallas Mavericks the following:

Source: Twitter

After sending out the tweet, he got 7,600 retweets and 5,000 favorites. The Dallas Mavericks, whose mascot is a horse, responded by tweeting, "Not very classy, but we still wish you guys the best of luck in the next round."

Though responses were quite positive from Rockets fans, the Rockets decided to fire Chad for the tweet. The Rockets also apologized for the tweet, saying it was in "very poor taste & not indicative of the respect we have for the @dallasmavs & their fans." After he was fired, Chad followed up with a tweet from his personal account:

Source: Twitter

In an interview later, Chad commented that "leading up to our series with Dallas, there were some harsh quotes about our team from Mark Cuban and former Rocket Chandler Parsons was returning after saying some negative things about the city, so the rivalry between the two organizations was at an all-time high." He figured this was his chance to take a jab at the Mavs. He meant it to be just a play on taking an old horse out to pasture that would get Rockets fans even more pumped up. He said he was quite confused that people would equate pretend violence on an emoji horse with actual violence on a real horse.

Chad's job was to stir up interest from fans and have fun with social media. His boss told him on numerous accounts that his job was to "take the [twitter] account to subversive places" and do everything he could to give the fans engaging content. Up until this point, Chad was considered one of the best social media experts out there and he had always pulled through for the Rockets. It just didn't seem fair to be fired over this one incident.

Questions

1. Given the facts of this case, should Chad have been discharged? Why or why not?

2. Should the social media manager of a company be held to a higher standard of personal conduct than others in the company? Explain.

3. Should management have considered Chad's past work record before deciding on discharge? Explain.

Sources: Adi Joseph, "Exclusive Q&A: Rockets' fired social media manager explains ill-fated tweet," *SportingNews* (April 29, 2015); Calvin Watkins, "Rockets fire social media manager after tweet directed at Mavericks," *ESPN* (April 30, 2015); Mike Foss, "The Houston Rockets fire man behind that creepy tweet to the Dallas Mavericks," *USA Today* (April 30, 2015).

CASE STUDY 2   You Can't Fire Me! Check Your Policy

Supervisors report that discharging an employee is one of the toughest tasks they perform as managers. Furthermore, termination for absenteeism can be particularly difficult due to the causes of absenteeism and, in some cases, the past work record of the employee. This case illustrates a typical absentee problem faced by management.

Hattie Mae was employed by Beach Electrical Systems for 9 years. For the first 6 years of her employment, she was considered a model employee. Hattie's annual performance reviews were always above average or exceptional, and she was described by her managers as a loyal and dedicated employee. However, things changed rapidly in 2010 when Hattie became, as her current manager stated, "an absentee problem."

According to HR department records, in 2014 and 2015 Hattie was absent 12 percent and 19 percent of the time, respectively. Her worst year was 2016, when she was absent 27.2 percent of the time. However, unlike other absent employees, Hattie was always absent because of genuine and verifiable illnesses or work-related accidents. Hattie's supervisor had talked to her periodically about her attendance problem, but she was never given an official warning notice—oral or written—that she would be fired if her attendance record did not improve.

The incident that caused her termination occurred on Thursday, May 20, 2017. On that day her manager notified all department employees (eight in total) that they would need to work overtime on Saturday, May 22, 2017, to complete a critical order for a highly valued and important customer. All employees agreed to work on Saturday, except Hattie, who cited "personal reasons," which she refused to disclose, for her refusal to work.

On Monday, May 24, 2017, her supervisor, with concurrence from the department manager, terminated her employment for "unsatisfactory attendance." Hattie did not dispute the attendance record; however, she filed a grievance through the company's alternative dispute resolution procedure alleging that management did not discharge her according to the organization's published disciplinary policy. She pointed to the section in the policy manual that states, "Employees will be warned for absenteeism before they are terminated." Hattie maintained that she was never officially warned as required. Management replied that Hattie was well aware of her absentee problem but that warning her would have served no purpose since she was unable to prevent her continued illnesses from occurring. Additionally, her refusal to work overtime on Saturday was a further indication of her lack of concern for her job or the welfare of the company.

Questions

1. What role, if any, should Hattie's past work record play in this case? Explain your answer.

2. Does management have a right to know why employees refuse to work overtime? Why or why not?

3. Evaluate the arguments of Hattie Mae and management in this case.

4. If you were a member of the company's peer-review complaint committee, how would you vote in this case? What facts would cause you to vote this way?

Source: Based on an arbitration case heard by George W. Bohlander. Names have been changed.

Notes and References

1. "Off-Duty Conduct Privacy," United Employees Law Group (March 6, 2017); "How to Get More Control Over 'Virtual' Workplace Devices," *HR Focus* 84, no. 6 (June 2007): 9. See also John D. Canoni, "Location Awareness Technology and Employee Privacy Rights," *Employee Relations Law Journal* 30, no. 1 (Summer 2004): 26.

2. Michael Orey, "Fear of Firing," *Business Week* (April 23, 2007): 52.

3. David J. Walsh, *Employment Law for Human Resource Practice* (Mason, OH: South-Western, 2007), Chapter 17.

4. Jeffery A. Mello, "Introduction: The Evolving Nature of the Employment Relationship: Reconsidering Employee Responsibilities and Rights," *Employee Responsibility and Rights Journal* 15, no. 3 (September 2003): 99.

5. Mike McKee, "California Supreme Court Narrows Workplace Privacy," *Law.com* (August 5, 2009), http://www.law.com.

6. "Background Checks Are on the Rise," *HR Focus* 84, no. 7 (July 2007): 51.

7. Maria Greco Danahar, "Retailer Sued over Clerk's Conduct," *HR Magazine* 52, no. 6 (June 2007): 141.

8. Donna Scimia, "A Common Sense Approach to Reducing Liability in Today's Workplace," *Employee Relations Law Journal* 33, no. 2 (Autumn 2007): 23.

9. Rita Zeidner, "How Deep Can You Probe?" *HR Magazine* 52, no. 10 (October 2007): 57. See also Jena McGregor, "Background Checks That Never End," *Business Week* (March 20, 2006): 40.

10. Robert Del Campo, "Psychological Contract Violation: An Individual Difference Perspective," *International Journal of Management* 24, no. 1 (March 2007): 43.

11. Ellen Dannin, "Why At-Will Employment Is Bad for Employers and Just Cause Is Good for Them," *Labor Law Journal* 58, no. 1 (Spring 2007): 5.

12. "Job Openings and Labor Turnover Summary," Bureau of Labor Statistics (March 16, 2017), https://www.bls.gov/news.release/jolts.nr0.htm.

13. *Adair v. United States*, 2078 U.S. 161 (1908).

14. "How At-Will Employment Is Changing," *HR Focus* 84, no. 10 (October 2007): 1.

15. Patric J. Cihon and James Ottavio Castagnera, *Employment and Labor Law*, 6th ed. (Mason, OH: South-Western, 2008), 3–4.

16. Lawrence Peikes, "Employer Pays for Reneging on a Promise," *HR Magazine* 49, no. 3 (March 2004): 109.

17. Quiang Lin and Brian H. Kleiner, "New Developments Concerning Termination in Violation of Public Policy," *Management Research Review Feature Edition*, no. 4 (2010): 111; Susan H. Roos, "Fired Fendi Manager Bags over $1 Million," *HR Magazine* 52, no. 6 (June 2007): 141.

18. David C. Lindsay and Sabrina Rockoff, "State Regulations Update: Beyond Sarbanes-Oxley: State Law Protection in the Era of the Whistleblower," *Employment Relations Today* 34, no. 1 (Spring 2007): 69. See also Paul D. Scott, "Whistleblowers Wanted," *Journal of Accountancy* 203, no. 5 (May 2007): 86.

19. U.S.C.S. § 1514A (a) (2002). See D. Bruce Shine, "Pity the Sox Whistleblower: Pity the Sox Lawyer Whistleblower!" *Labor Law Journal* 58, no. 4 (Winter 2007): 228.

20. David Connett, "Barney Jones: Meet the Whistleblower Who Helped Expose Google's Tax Avoidance," *Independent* (January 29, 2016).

21. Eugine Kim, "Google Reportedly Has an Internal Site for Employees to Report Whistle-Blowers," *Business Insider* (June 2, 2016).

22. Benisa Berry, "Organizational Culture: A Framework and Strategies for Facilitating Employee Whistleblowing," *Employee Responsibilities and Rights Journal* 16, no. 1 (March 2004): 1.

23. "*Toussaint v. Blue Cross and Blue Shield of Michigan*: Employee Rights and Wrongful Discharge, 408 Mich. 579, 292 N.W.2d 880 (1980)," *Michigan Bar Journal* (March 2009): 15.

24. "Employee Handbooks: Have You Updated Yours Lately?" *HR Focus* 83, no. 7 (July 2006): 5.

25. Howard J. Rubin and Gregg A. Gilman, "Will Garden Leaves Blossom in the States," *Employee Relations Law Journal* 33, no. 2 (Autumn 2007): 3. See also Brian L. Lemer and Jeffrey K. Geldens, "Ensuring Fair Play: Using Common Law to Protect against Unfair Competition from Former Employees," *Employee Relations Law Journal* 32, no. 3 (Winter 2006): 41.

26. Steven M. Gutierrez, Joseph D. Neguse, and Steven Collis, "The Human Limits of Human Capital: An Overview of Non-compete Agreements and Best Practices for Protecting Trade Secrets from Unlawful Misappropriation," *Employee Relations Law Journal* (Summer 2010): 64.

27. Jonathan A. Segal, "I Quit! Now Pay Me," *HR Magazine* 49, no. 10 (October 2004): 129.

28. Martha Crumpacker, "The U.S. Supreme Court Clarifies Constructive Discharge under Title VII: Responsibilities and Opportunities for Human Resources Practitioners," *Public Personnel Management* 36, no. 1 (Spring 2007): 1.

29. Rebecca M. Archer and Stephen T. Lanctot, "Are Your Hands Tied? A Practical Look at Employee Claims for Retaliation," *Employee Relations Law Journal* 33, no. 1 (Summer 2007): 53.

30. 29 U.S.C.A. §§ 2101–2109 (2001).

31. Janis Procter-Murphy, employment attorney, interview by author, December 9, 2007.

32. "Balancing HR Systems with Employee Privacy," *HR Focus* 83, no. 11 (November 2006): 11.

33. Diana Cadrain, "Are Your Employee Drug Tests Accurate?" *HR Magazine* 48, no. 1 (January 2003): 41. Diana Cadrain, "Are Your Employee Drug Tests Accurate?" *HR Magazine* 48, no. 1 (January 2003): 41.

34. "If You're Asked to Take a Drug Test," *Nolo*, accessed June 1, 2011, http://www.nolo.com.

35. "New Year, New Scams, New Risks—What to Watch for Now," *Security Director's Report* 11, no. 2 (February 2011): 1.

36. "If You're Asked to Take a Drug Test," *Nolo*, accessed June 1, 2011, http://www.nolo.com.

37. "Constitution Limits Pre-employment Drug Testing by Public Employers," *Venulex Legal Summaries* (2008 Q1): 1; "Drug Testing Is Common and Codified at Many Workplaces," *HR Focus* 83, no. 6 (June 2006): 9; "New Developments Question the Use of Drug Tests in the Workplace," *Safety Director's Report* 4, no. 9 (September 2004): 3–6; "Fired for Blogging," accessed June 3, 2011, http://www.nolo.com; Sandy Smith, "What Every Employer Should Know about Drug Testing in the Workplace," *Occupational Hazards* 66, no. 8 (August 2004): 45–48.

38. T. L. Stanly, "Workplace Drug Testing and the Growing Problem of Methampheta-mines," *Supervision* 68, no. 8 (August 2007): 3.

39. William I. Sauser Jr., "Employee Theft: Who, How, Why, and What Can Be Done," *S.A.M. Advanced Management Journal* 72, no. 3 (Summer 2007): 13.

40. Andrea Marvin, "Video Shows Rats Running Around McDonald's," *ABCNews* (February 10, 2017).

41. Adrienne Fox, "Caught in the Web," *HR Magazine* 52, no. 12 (December 2007): 35.

42. "Employee Rights and Identity Theft," *Texas Workforce Commission*, accessed June 2, 2011, http://www.twc.state.tx.us.

43. Brad Stone and Ashlee Vance, "Apple's Obsession with Secrecy Grows," *New York Times* (June 22, 2009), http://www.nytimes.com.

44. Electronic Communications Privacy Act, 18 U.S.C. § 2510–2720.

45. Rita Zeidner, "Keeping E-mail in Check," *HR Magazine* 52, no. 6 (June 2007): 70.

46. "Top Ten Reasons Companies Block Social Media at Work," *Work Place Answers* (March 29, 2016).

47. Mark Szakonyi, "Big Brother at Work," *Portfolio* (February 8, 2010), http://www.portfolio.com.

48. Paul E. Paray, "N.J. Supreme Court Sides with Employee on Email Privacy Case," Digital Risk Strategies [blog] (April 5, 2010), http://blog.digitalriskstrategies.com.

49. "Why It's Time to Update Your Privacy Policies," *HR Focus* 84, no. 4 (April 2007): 3.

50. Steve Bertel, "Amalgamated Sugar Suffers Cyber Security Breach; 2,858 Workers' Personal Info Stolen," *ABCNews* (February 24, 2017).

51. Dan Caterinicchia, "Safeguarding HR Information," *HR Magazine* 50, no. 11 (November 1, 2005): 55–59.

52. Diane Cadrain, "Setting the Records Straight," *HR Magazine* 52, no. 6 (June 2007): 82.

53. "Fired for Blogging," accessed June 3, 2011, http://www.nolo.com.

54. Cynthia F. Cohen and Murray E. Cohen, "On-Duty and Off-Duty: Employee Rights to Privacy and Employers Right to Control in the Private Sector," *Employee Responsibilities and Rights Journal* 19, no. 4 (December 2007): 235.

55. Julianne Pepitone, "Facebook Firing Settled out of Court," *CNNMoney* (February 8, 2011), http://money.cnn.com.

56. Charles A. Pierce, Brandee J. Broberg, Jamie R. McClure, and Herman Aquinis, "Responding to Sexual Harassment Complaints: Effects of a Dissolved Workplace Romance on Decision Making Standards," *Organizational Behavior and Human Decision Processes* 95, no. 1 (September 2004): 83.

57. Judy Greenwald, "Employers Are the Losers in the Dating Game," *Workforce Management*, http://www.workforce.com/section/09/feature/24/93/98/index.html.

58. "Tattoo Takeover: Three in Ten Americans Have Tattoos, and Most Don't Stop at Just One," *The Harris Poll* (February 10, 2016).

59. Kathryn Tyler, "Sign in the Name of Love," *HR Magazine* 53, no. 2 (February 2008): 41.

60. "How Companies Are Dealing with Workplace Body Art Issues," *HR Focus* 81, no. 4 (April 2004).

61. George W. Bohlander and Donna Blancero, "A Study of Reversal Determinants in Discipline and Discharge Arbitration Awards: The Impact of Just Cause Standards," *Labor Studies Journal* 21, no. 3 (Fall 1996): 3–18.

62. Jathan W. Janove, "Private Eye 101," *HR Magazine* 49, no. 7 (July 2004): 127.

63. Mollica Kelly, "Perceptions of Fairness," *HR Magazine* 49, no. 6 (June 2004): 169.

64. *NLRB v. Weingarten Inc.*, 95 S.Ct. 959 (1975), 402 U.S. 251, 43 L.Ed.2d. 171.

65. Readers interested in the pioneering work on positive discipline should see James R. Redeker, "Discipline, Part 1:

Progressive Systems Work Only by Accident," *Personnel* 62, no. 10 (October 1985): 8–12; James R. Redeker, "Discipline, Part 2: The Nonpunitive Approach Works by Design," *Personnel* 62, no. 11 (November 1985): 7–14.

66. Stephen P. Postalakis, "Avoiding a Sticky Situation: A Guide to Firing an Employee," *Catalyst 2002* (March/April 2007): 22.

67. For an excellent explanation of just cause discharge guidelines, see Frank Elkouri and Edna Asper Elkouri, *How Arbitration Works*, 5th ed. (Washington, DC: Bureau of National Affairs, 1997).

68. Jack and Suzy Welch, "The Right Way to Say Goodbye," *Business Week* (March 25, 2007): 144.

69. Elizabeth Agnvall, "Case Closed. Now What?" *HR Magazine* 53, no. 2 (February 2008): 69.

70. Nancy Hatch Woodward, "Smoother Separations," *HR Magazine* 52, no. 6 (June 2007): 94.

71. Michael Orey, "The Vanishing Trial: As Court Battles Become More Rare, Some Experts Fear the Effects on the Law," *Business Week* (April 30, 2007): 38.

72. Louise Lamothe, "Avoiding Potholes in Mandatory Arbitration: A Look at Recent California Decisions," *Dispute Resolution Journal* 58, no. 2 (May–June 2003): 18. See also D. Diane Hatch, James T. Hall, Mark T. Kobata, and Marty Denis, "Law

Firm's Arbitration Procedures Rules Unfair," *Workforce Management* 86, no. 13 (July 23, 2007): 10.

73. Walsh, *Employment Law for Human Resource Practice*, 19.

74. Ruth D. Raisfeld, "How Mediation Works: A Guide to Effective Use of ADR," *Employee Relations Law Journal* 33, no. 2 (Autumn 2007): 30.

75. Jennifer J. Froehlich, "The New Company Unions: Mandatory Individual Employment Arbitration Agreements and Section 8 (a) (2) of the National Labor Relations Act," *Labor Law Journal* 58, no. 3 (Fall 2007): 195.

76. Elizabeth F. R. Gingerich, "Enforcing Arbitration Agreements in Discrimination Claims: Judicial Reconsideration," *Employee Relations Law Journal* 33, no. 4 (Spring 2008): 61.

77. *EEOC v. Waffle House Inc.*, 534 U.S. 279 (2002).

78. "EEOC May Sue Even If Arbitration Agreement Exists," *HR Focus* 79, no. 3 (March 2002): 2.

79. Betsy Stevens, "Corporate Ethical Codes: Effective Instruments for Influencing Behavior," *Journal of Business Ethics* 78, no. 4 (April 2008): 601.

80. Jennifer Schramm, "Perception on Ethics," *HR Magazine* 49, no. 11 (November 2004): 176.

CHAPTER **14**

The Dynamics of Labor Relations

Learning Outcomes

After studying this chapter, you should be able to

LO 1 Reflect upon reasons that employees join unions.

LO 2 Describe the process by which unions organize employees and gain recognition as their bargaining agent.

LO 3 Outline the challenges faced by HR managers when union representation is voted into a company.

LO 4 Discuss the bargaining process and the bargaining goals and strategies of a union and an employer.

LO 5 Describe a typical union grievance procedure and explain the basis for arbitration awards.

Monkey Business Images/Shutterstock

Mention Labor Day and most people think of the start of the football season, shopping Labor Day sales, mourning the unofficial end of summer, or complaining about that one time they needed to renew their driver's license and the DMV closed early. Labor Day, without all of its modern trappings, is a federal holiday honoring the American labor movement and its contributions to worker health, safety, well-being, and productivity.

Mention labor movements and trade unions, and most people will have a more polarized opinion, whether considering the adversarial relationship between employees and higher-ups and strikes, or industrial democracy, fairness, opportunity, and equal representation.[1] And some may wonder if unions are still relevant today, in an era with worker safety laws and globalization.

Unions are still at large, influencing policies and helping workers in a range of different ways. Union-trained military veterans are helping to rebuild New York's World Trade Center complex. Union letter carriers save lives by alerting officials if an elderly person hasn't been collecting his or her mail. Even the TV shows you watch are the product of one of America's most unionized industries.[2]

14.1 The Labor Relations Process

National Labor Relations Board (NLRB)
The agency responsible for administering and enforcing the Wagner Act. It serves the public interest by reducing interruptions in production or service caused by labor—management strife.

labor relations process
A logical sequence of five events: (1) workers desire collective representation, (2) the union begins its organizing campaign, (3) the NLRB representation process begins, (4) collective negotiations lead to a contract, and (5) the contract is administered.

Individually, employees may be able to exercise relatively little power in their relationship with employers. If individual employees believe they are not being treated fairly, then they may organize into unions and bargain with the employer collectively. **Unions** represent an organized association of workers formed to further the interests of the individuals working for an employer. The ability of workers to form a union and collectively bargain with an employer is a legal right granted by the **National Labor Relations Board (NLRB)**.

When workers decide to unionize, the labor relations process begins. As Figure 14.1 illustrates, the **labor relations process** consists of a logical sequence of five events: (1) workers desire collective representation, (2) the union begins its organizing campaign, (3) the NLRB representation procedure begins, (4) collective negotiations lead to a contract, and (5) the contract is administered. Laws and administrative rulings influence each of the separate events by granting special privileges to or imposing defined constraints on workers, managers, and union officials.[3]

For example, when Gawker Media workers became tired of the instability of their employment environment, they decided to start an organizing campaign. The campaign was spearheaded by Hamilton Nolan, one of Gawker's senior writers. Even though Gawker is a digital media outlet populated by 20- and 30-something college grads who start with a decent salary of $40,000 to $50,000 a year and great benefits, employees felt

Figure 14.1 The Labor Relations Process

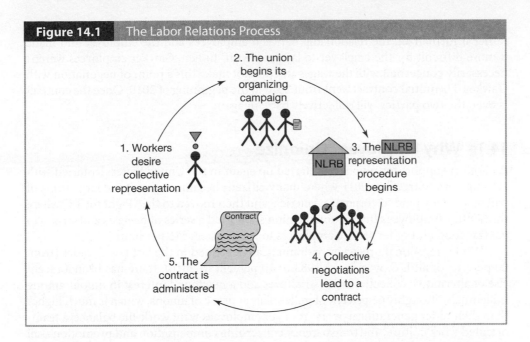

that a union could provide a safety net during uncertain times. Once they decided they wanted collective representation, employees had to choose a union to help with the organizing campaign. They chose to work with the Writers Guild of America East to help with the campaign. When the union was finally recognized and formalized through the NLRB representation process, Gawker employees collectively bargained and came up with a contract between the union and the employer.

Daryl L/Shutterstock

Occupy Wall Street represented a labor movement against economic inequality worldwide.

The new contract didn't necessarily impose many new demands on the employer, rather it formalized the relationship between employees and the employer and made it more difficult for the employer to lay people off. In fact, Gawker employees weren't necessarily concerned with the wages and did not make this a point of negotiation with Gawker. The initial contract went from 2016 to the beginning of 2019. Once the contract is over, the two parties will collectively bargain again.

14.1a Why Employees Unionize

A surge of support for unions has started up again in the United States. It started with "Occupy Wall Street" in 2011 where many citizens became angry at the large sums of bail out money paid to corporate America, and then moved to the "Fight for 15" where the Service Employees International Union supported a series of protests and strikes to get fast-food and other service employers to pay workers $15 per hour.[4]

While traditional unions have dramatically declined in the last few decades (from 20 percent of all U.S. workers in 1983 to 10 percent in 2016), there has been a recent rise of alternative collective labor structures and a newfound interest in unions among millennials.[5] Roughly 66 percent of millennials approve of unions, which is much higher than their older generational peers. Younger employees want work-life balance, a team-oriented work culture, and transparency concerning compensation and promotion—all values similar to those espoused by unions.[6]

Just because millennials share similar values as unions, however, doesn't mean they will easily join them. Like many corporations, unions are predisposed to nontransparent beauracracies that play political games to negotiate higher wages for workers. However, millennials aren't as interested in having more pay. Rather, they are more interested in equality and transparency. Young people tend to see the value of tackling problems from a collective level, rather than just as individuals. In this regard, employees see unions as a way to achieve results they cannot achieve acting individually.

LO 1

While unionization in the private sector is declining, certain industries, such as the hospitality industry, are gaining ground in unionization. If you were a service worker in a hotel, what factors would make you want to join a union? (See Figure 14.2 for some hints.)

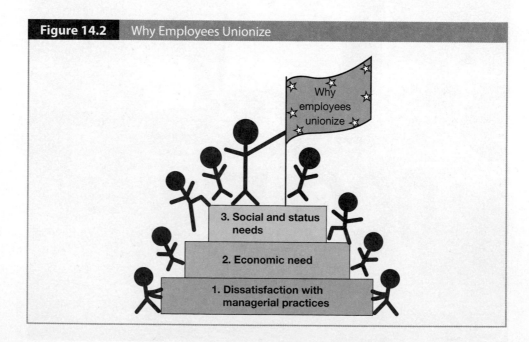

Figure 14.2   Why Employees Unionize

Why employees unionize

3. Social and status needs

2. Economic need

1. Dissatisfaction with managerial practices

Millennial protestors tackle problems as a collective which lends way to employees using unions to achieve results that are otherwise unattainable as individuals.

FernandoPodolski/Getty Images

- **Dissatisfaction with management.** Employees may seek unionization when they perceive that managerial practices regarding promotion, transfer, shift assignment, or other job-related policies are administered in an unfair or biased manner. Employees cite favoritism shown by managers as a major reason for joining unions. Furthermore, the failure of employers to give employees an opportunity to participate in decisions affecting their welfare may encourage union membership.

- **Economic needs.** Dissatisfaction with wages, benefits, and working conditions appears to provide the strongest reason to join a union. According to Union Plus, a nonprofit for union members, benefits of union membership include: union employees make an average of 30 percent more than nonunion workers; 92 percent of union workers have job-related health coverage versus 68 percent of nonunion workers; and union workers are more likely to have guaranteed pensions than nonunion employees.

- **Social and Status Needs.** Employees whose needs for recognition and social affiliation are being frustrated may join unions as a means of satisfying these needs. Through their union, they have an opportunity to fraternize with other employees who have similar desires, interests, problems, and gripes. Such concerns often revolve around job insecurity, broken promises, lack of autonomy, double standards, hopelessness, humiliation, and lack of recognition. Employees (especially Millennials) may join unions to benefit in the equality and teamwork that organization membership may provide. Additionally, the union enables them to put leadership talents to use as officers of the union and representatives of fellow employees. One study found that employees became **union stewards** so that they could be seen as "a fellow your buddies look to" and as a person who "stands up to the boss."

Of the factors mentioned, organizing campaigns based on social concerns (e.g., justice, equality, and teamwork) are more successful than campaigns based on dissatisfaction with management or even economic issues.[7] In other words, employees today are more interested in being treated fairly and working collectively.

union steward

An employee who as a nonpaid union official represents the interests of members in their relations with management.

14.1b Challenges of Unions to Management

Though unions provide many potential benefits for employees, this tends not to be the case for the employer. In fact, most employers would prefer to not have to deal with unions. While employers have been known to exploit workers, unions have also been known to exploit employers. For example, one union organizer named Steve told us that as a machine operator for a small assembly plant he brought in the union to help organize the workers. The union ended up putting so much pressure on the company that the company had to shut down because it could not compete with other nonunion shops.[8]

Unions typically attempt to achieve greater participation in management decisions that affect their members. Specifically, these decisions may involve such issues as the subcontracting of work, productivity standards, and job content. Employers quite naturally seek to claim many of these decisions as their exclusive *management prerogatives—* decisions over which management claims exclusive rights.

For example, these terms can determine what corrective action is to be taken in directing and in disciplining employees. When disciplining employees, supervisors must be certain they can demonstrate *just cause* (see Chapter 13) for their actions. Additionally, specific contract language can also reduce the supervisor's ability to manage in such areas as scheduling, training, transfers, performance evaluation, and promotions. Under provisions of the labor agreement, supervisors may have to promote employees by seniority rather than by individual merit.

Finally, unions can create divisions between management and workers, making it difficult to foster a team spirit within the organization where everyone is working for a common organizational cause. To avoid these constraints, many organizations try to ensure the work environment is a place where people are well compensated, management is supportive and collaborative with workers, and all people are treated equally.[9]

14.1c Union Avoidance Practices

There are things companies can do from an HRM perspective to decrease the chances that their employees will want to form a union in the first place, thus avoiding the union organizing campaign altogether. Specifically, there are six practices or principles companies can adopt to decrease the chances of employees wanting to unionize (Figure 14.3).[10]

The first practice has to do with *pay*. As discussed in Chapter 9, not only do above-market wages and benefits potentially increase performance and decrease turnover, they also decrease the likelihood that employees will want to unionize. For example, very few companies that have above-market wage and benefits policies have unions.

The second practice is to *promote more employees from within* and to do it often. People like to feel that they are progressing and that there is a chance for growth and advancement. Opportunities for career advancement help to bolster hope and a sense of equity in work environments where employees who do a good job are recognized and given chances to better their positions in the organization.

Third, *conduct cultural audits*. As discussed in Chapter 2, cultural audits provide managers with a picture of what the company needs. It tells management how employees feel about what is going on in the organization and the quality of the working environment. Organizations can then take this information and facilitate developmental programs for employees, focus more on employee needs, and correct problems before

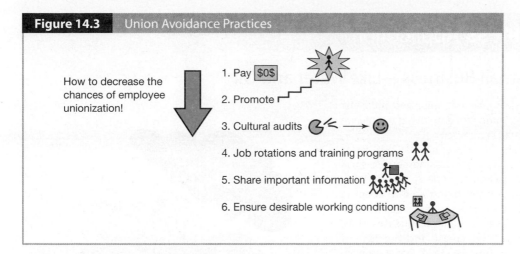

Figure 14.3 Union Avoidance Practices

How to decrease the chances of employee unionization!

1. Pay 0
2. Promote
3. Cultural audits
4. Job rotations and training programs
5. Share important information
6. Ensure desirable working conditions

they become too large. Attitude surveys also provide a way for employees to feel they are being listened to. Management must take care with these surveys, however. Organizations that do not respond to or act upon this valuable feedback risk developing even more discontent in their workforce, as employees feel that their suggestions are not valued.

The fourth practice is to *offer job rotations and training programs.* In Chapter 7 we talk about effective ways to manage training programs and job rotation assignments. Specifically, job rotations help reduce burnout, which can lead to people either leaving their jobs or feeling trapped and hopeless. Job rotations also lead to increased employee satisfaction. If variety is the spice of life, then job rotation is the spice of work. This leads to increased commitment to the organization.

Fifth, *share information with employees about the state of the organization.* Companies that practice open book management are more likely to earn the trust and commitment of their employees to avoid push back from unions and consumers at financial troubles.[11] For example, in 2011 Delta Airlines brought back call center jobs to the United States from Jamaica. CEO Richard Anderson said that "one of the ways to mitigate the impact of the recession is to insource work." In 2009, Delta also closed a call center in India, sparking a trend among airlines and U.S. companies in general to bring back jobs.[12] But open management helps ensure employees understand the management decisions and are less likely to turn to a union when they aren't receiving enough transparency.

Finally, organizations should *make sure they have desirable working conditions.* While it is not feasible to make the working environment pleasant in all industries, an organization should make sure its work environment for its employees is equally desirable as other firms in the same industry. This means having appropriate and sufficient lighting, ergonomic workspaces, and a nonhostile environment. It is important to recognize that these strategies react to the conditions cited at the beginning of the chapter as the main reasons why workers unionize. Because these conditions are under the direct control of management, they can be changed to help discourage or prevent unionization.

LO 2

What steps should employees take to unionize? What steps can employers take in trying to stop the union from organizing? See Highlights in HRM to test your labor relations know-how.

14.1d Organizing Campaigns

Once employees desire to unionize, a formal organizing campaign may be started either by a union organizer or by employees acting on their own behalf.[14] Contrary to popular belief, most organizing campaigns are begun by employees rather than by

Small Business Application

Unions and Small Business—Like Water and Oil

While most small businesses are not unionized and prefer it that way, it is not uncommon for employees to unionize even when they are small in number.

So why, then, might employees of small businesses want to unionize? Usually when businesses are small they are much less formal and more personal. This informality presents advantages in being able to adapt to the environment and devote needed resources to building the business. However, as small businesses grow, the benefits of informality decrease and the costs of having informal relationships increase. Some employees may begin to feel singled out—or worse yet, left out. Such situations sow seeds of discontent. To reduce the threat of unionization among small businesses, employers must consider when to hire an HR specialist to help manage the people and work culture more effectively.

A firm with only a few employees cannot afford a full-time HR specialist to deal with work culture issues. Illustrated here are a few conditions to help you understand when to appoint a specialist to deal with these issues.[13]

However, if these practices don't work and your employees still decide they want to pursue organizing a union, there are things management can do to stop the union from organizing.

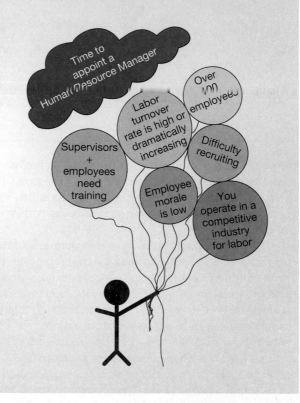

union organizers. Large national unions such as the United Auto Workers, the United Brotherhood of Carpenters, the United Steelworkers, and the Teamsters, however, have formal organizing departments whose purpose is to identify organizing opportunities and launch organizing campaigns.

Organizing Steps

Terry Moser, former president of Teamster Local 104, once told the authors that the typical organizing campaign follows a series of progressive steps that can lead to employee representation. The organizing process as described by Moser normally includes five steps (Figure 14.4).

Step 1 The first step begins when employees and union officials meet up to explore the possibility of unionization. During these discussions, employees investigate the advantages of labor representation, and union officials begin to gather information on employee needs, problems, and grievances. Labor organizers also seek specific information about the employer's financial health, supervisory styles, and organizational policies and practices. To win employee support, labor organizers must build a case *against* the employer and *for* the union. (See Highlights in HRM 2 to see how unions have evolved over the years.)

Figure 14.4 The five steps to organizing a union

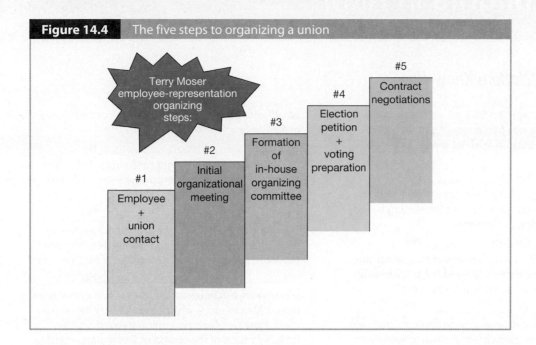

Step 2 As an organizing campaign gathers momentum, the organizer schedules an initial union meeting to attract more supporters. The organizer uses the information gathered in step 1 to address employee needs and explain how the union can secure these goals. Two additional purposes of organizational meetings are (1) to identify employees who can help the organizer direct the campaign and (2) to establish communication chains that reach all employees.

Step 3 The third important step in the organizing drive is to form an in-house organizing committee composed of employees willing to provide leadership to the campaign. The committee's role is to interest other employees in joining the union and in supporting its campaign. An important task of the committee is to have employees sign an **authorization card** indicating their willingness to be represented by a labor union in collective bargaining with their employer. At least 30 percent of the employees must sign authorization cards before the NLRB will hold a representation election.[16]

authorization card
A statement signed by an employee authorizing a union to act as a representative of the employee for purposes of collective bargaining.

Step 4 If a sufficient number of employees support the union drive, the organizer seeks a government-sponsored election. A representation petition is filed with the NLRB, asking that a secret ballot election be held to determine whether employees actually desire unionization. Before the election, a large publicity campaign is directed toward employees, seeking their support and election votes. This is a period of intense emotions for the employees, the labor organization, and the employer.

Step 5 Union organizing is concluded when the union wins the election. The NLRB "certifies" the union as the legal bargaining representative of the employees. Contract negotiations now begin; these negotiations represent another struggle between the union and employer. During negotiations, each side seeks employment conditions favorable to its position. Members of the in-plant organizing committee and the union organizer attempt to negotiate the employees' first contract. In about one out of four

Test Your Labor Relations Know-How

1. An auto mechanic applied for a job with an automotive dealership. He was denied employment because of his union membership. Was the employer's action lawful?

   _____Yes _____No

2. During a labor organizing drive, supervisors questioned individual employees about their union beliefs. Was this questioning permissible?

   _____Yes _____No

3. When members of a union began wearing union buttons at work, management ordered the buttons to be removed. Was management within its rights?

   _____ Yes _____ No

4. While an organizing drive was under way, an employer agreed—as a social gesture—to furnish refreshments at a holiday party. Was the employer acting within the law?

   _____ Yes _____ No

5. A company distributed to other antiunion employers in the area a list of job applicants known to be union supporters. Was the distribution unlawful?

   _____ Yes _____ No

6. During a union organizing drive, the owner of Servo Pipe promised her employees a wage increase if they would vote against the union. Can the owner legally make this promise to her employees?

   _____ Yes _____ No

7. Do employees have the right to file unfair labor practice charges against their employer even when the organization is nonunion?

   _____ Yes _____ No

8. The union wishes to arbitrate a member's grievance, which management has demonstrated is completely groundless. Must management arbitrate the grievance?

   _____ Yes _____ No

9. John Green, a maintenance engineer, has a poor work record. Management wishes to terminate his employment. However, Green is a union steward, and he is highly critical of the company. Can management legally discharge this employee?

   _____ Yes _____ No

10. During an organizing drive, an office manager expressed strong antiunion beliefs and called union officials "racketeers," "big stinkers," and a "bunch of radicals." He told employees who joined the union that they "ought to have their heads examined." Were the manager's comments legal?

    _____ Yes _____ No

Answers are found at the end of this chapter.

---

union campaigns, unions are unable to secure a first contract after winning a representation election.[17] Should the union fail to obtain an agreement within 1 year from winning the election, the Taft-Hartley Act allows the employees to vote the union out through a NLRB "decertification" election.

Aggressive Organizing Tactics

Without question, a strategic objective of the labor movement is to become more aggressive and creative in its organizing tactics. Unions have been shocked into developing these "revolutionary" organizing strategies to compensate for a decline in membership and to counteract employer antiunion campaigns. (Both topics will be discussed later in the chapter.) To accomplish their agenda of "vitalizing" the labor movement, unions employ the following organizing weapons—in varying degrees—to achieve their goals:

1. *Political involvement.* Unions have become more selective in their support of public officials, giving union funds to candidates who specifically pledge

What Happened to the American Labor Union?

Review this video in MindTap to learn more about the time period from the first government-mediated settlement in 1838 when President Van Buren facilitated the negotiation of a strike by shipyard workers, to the creation of the Federal Mediation and Conciliation Service (FMCS) in 1947, to the Occupational and Health Safety Act, to the Fight for $15 today.[15]

support for prolabor legislation. During the 2016 U.S. presidential election, Donald Trump won the support of many union members who typically vote Democrat. Exit polls revealed that 43 percent of union households voted for Mr. Trump. For big labor, this was a harsh reminder that the political preferences of its members are not as set in stone as the union's leadership, which backed Hillary Clinton. Large unions in the United States are now reconsidering their political affiliations as a result of the actions President Trump has taken to try to bring jobs back to America.[18]

2. *Neutrality agreements.* Neutrality agreements secure a binding commitment from the employer to remain neutral during the organizing drive. The employer agrees that managers will not campaign against or disparage the union and will only provide facts about the union when questioned by employees. Furthermore, the employer agrees to accept a card check to recognize the union if the union produces sufficient employee-signed authorization cards.[19]

Trump wins 2016 presidential election with help of many unions workers.

Aaron P. Bernstein/Getty Images

3. *Organizer training.* Traditionally, organizing has been a part-time work. Today, the AFL-CIO's Organizing Institute is actively training a new generation of professional, highly skilled, full-time organizers. Organizers who successfully complete the training program are usually hired by local and national unions. They work to assist workers to gain representation. They do this by educating workers about their rights, identify and develop leadership skills, and run campaigns for union recognition.

4. *Corporate campaigns.* Unions may enlist political or community groups to boycott the product(s) of a targeted company. Other tactics include writing newspaper editorials chastising specific company decisions; filing charges with administrative agencies such as OSHA, the Department of Labor, and the NLRB; and pressuring an organization's financial institution to withhold loans or demand payments.

5. *Information technology.* Social media is fast becoming an effective union organizing tool. Websites exist that link employees to union literature, union membership applications, and individual union web pages. "Cyberunions" seek to apply computer technology to all aspects of organizing activity.[20] For example, some union organizing efforts have used hashtags to bring attention to their campaigns. The #fightfor15 and #ourwalmart are two examples of effective efforts to bring people together for protests and rallies. Coworker.org also created a platform to gather petitions from low-wage workers who otherwise lack the ability to collectively organize because they are scattered across multiple locations. Finally, another effort unions can use is the Worker's Lab. Launched in 2015, the Worker's Lab is like a venture capital fund for worker organizing movements. The funds are used to support innovative alt-labor movements that will lead to more innovative organized labor unions.[21]

14.1e Employer Tactics Opposing Unionization

Employers use a two-pronged campaign to fight unionization. First, when possible, employers stress the favorable employer–employee relationship they have experienced in the past without a union. Employers may emphasize any advantages in wages, benefits, or working conditions the employees may enjoy in comparison with those provided by organizations that are already unionized. "While you have a right to join a union," the employers may remind their employees, "you also have a right not to join one and to deal directly with the organization free from outside interference."

Second, employers emphasize any unfavorable aspects of unionism including strikes, the payment of union dues and special assessments, and published abuses of members' legal rights, along with any false promises made by the union in the course of its campaign. Union rules on member conduct, such as being fined for crossing a picket line, are emphasized to employees. Employers may also use government statistics to show that unions commit large numbers of unfair labor practices. Employers may initiate legal action should union members and/or their leaders engage in any **unfair labor practices (ULPs)** during the organizing effort.

Within the limits permitted by the Taft-Hartley Act, employers can express their views about the disadvantages of being represented by a union. However, when counteracting a union campaign, managers must not threaten employees with loss of jobs or loss or reduction of other employment benefits if they vote to unionize. Nor may

unfair labor practices (ULPs)

Specific employer and union illegal practices that deny employees their rights and benefits under federal labor law.

United Food and Commercial Workers International Union Authorization Card

United Food & Commercial Workers International Union

Affiliated with AFL-CIO-CLC

AUTHORIZATION FOR REPRESENTATION

I hereby authorize the United Food & Commercial Workers International Union, AFL-CIO-CLC, or its chartered Local Union(s) to represent me for the purpose of collective bargaining.

_____ (Print Name)   _____ (Date)

_____ (Signature)   _____ (Home Phone)

_____ (Home Address)   _____ (City)   _____ (State)   _____ (Zip)

_____ (Employer's Name)   _____ (Address)

_____ (Hire Date)   _____ (Type Work Performed)   _____ (Department)

Day Shift _____   Night Shift _____   Full Time _____   Part-Time _____

_____ (Hourly Rate)   _____ (Day Off)

Would you participate in an organizing committee?   Yes _____   No _____

---

employers offer new or improved employee benefits or higher wages as a means of getting employees to vote "no union." Highlights in HRM 4 lists some of the activities in which managers or supervisors should not engage.[22]

14.1f How Employees Become Unionized

The employees to be organized constitute the bargaining unit to be covered by the labor agreement. The NLRB defines a **bargaining unit** as a group of two or more employees who have common employment interests and conditions and may reasonably be grouped together for purposes of collective bargaining. If an employer and a union cannot agree on who should be in the bargaining unit, an appropriate bargaining unit will be determined by the NLRB on the basis of a similarity of interests (such as wages, job duties, or training) among employees within the unit. For example, in hospitals, the NLRB has designated separate units for nurses, technicians, doctors, maintenance employees, office clerical personnel, all other nonprofessionals, and guards.

bargaining unit
A group of two or more employees who share common employment interests and conditions and may reasonably be grouped together for purposes of collective bargaining.

14.1g NLRB Representation Election

If it succeeds in signing up 30 percent of employees within the bargaining unit, the union petitions for a NLRB-conducted election. The petition to hold representation elections usually is initiated by the union, although employers, under certain circumstances, have the right to petition for one (see Highlights in HRM 5). Prior to the election, the NLRB holds a *pre-election hearing* with the employer and union, or unions, seeking

LO 3

If the union wins the vote, what does this mean for the HR manager?

Employer "Don'ts" during Union Organizing Campaigns

Union organizing drives are emotionally charged events. Furthermore, labor law, NLRB rulings, and court decisions greatly affect the behavior and actions of management and union representatives. During the drive, managers and supervisors should avoid the following:

- Attending union meetings, spying on employee-union gatherings, or questioning employees about the content of union meetings
- Questioning present or current employees about their union sentiments, particularly about how they might vote in a union election
- Threatening or terminating employees for their union support or beliefs

- Changing the working conditions of employees because they actively work for the union or simply support its ideals
- Supplying the names, addresses, and phone numbers of employees to union representatives or other employees sympathetic to the union
- Promising employees improvements in working conditions (wage increases, benefit improvements, and so on) if they vote against the union
- Accepting or reviewing union authorization cards or prounion petitions because employees' names are listed on these documents

---

to represent the employees. At this meeting several important issues are determined, including verification of the authorization cards, the NLRB's jurisdiction to hold the election, determination of the bargaining unit (if contested by the parties), the date of the election, and the voting choice(s) to appear on the ballot. The ballot lists the names of the unions that are seeking recognition and also provides a choice of "no union." See Highlights in HRM 3 for an example of a union authorization card.

After the election is held, the winning party is determined on the basis of the number of actual votes, not on the number of members of the bargaining unit. For example, suppose the bargaining unit at XYZ Corporation has 100 employees, but only 27 employees voted in the election. A union receiving 14 yes votes among the 27 voting (a majority) would be declared the winner, and the union would bargain for all 100 employees. By law the union would be granted **exclusive representation** over all bargaining unit employees.[23] The union is *certified* by the NLRB as the bargaining agent for at least a year or for the duration of the labor agreement. Once the union is certified, the employer is obligated to begin negotiations leading toward a labor agreement. An important statistic in labor relations is the win/loss record of unions in certification elections. In 1950, the union win rate in elections held by the NLRB was 74.5 percent. This percentage dropped dramatically to 60.2 percent in 1965 and to 48.2 percent in 1995. In 2016, the NLRB held 1,496 conclusive representation elections, of which 68 percent resulted in union wins.[24]

Some of the different types of unions include craft unions, industrial unions, and employee associations. **Craft unions** include the International Association of Machinists, United Brotherhood of Carpenters, and United Association of Plumbers and Pipefitters. Unions that represent unskilled and semiskilled workers employed along industry lines are known as **industrial unions** (Figure 14.5). The American Union of Postal Workers is an industrial union, as are the United Auto Workers; United Steelworkers; American Federation of State, County, and Municipal Employees; and Office and Professional Employees International Union. While this distinction still exists, technological changes, union mergers, and competition among unions for members have helped

exclusive representation
The legal right and responsibility of the union to represent all bargaining unit members equally, regardless of whether employees join the union or not.

craft unions
Unions that represent skilled craft workers.

industrial unions
Unions that represent all workers—skilled, semiskilled, unskilled—employed along industry lines.

Figure 14.5	Different Types of Unions

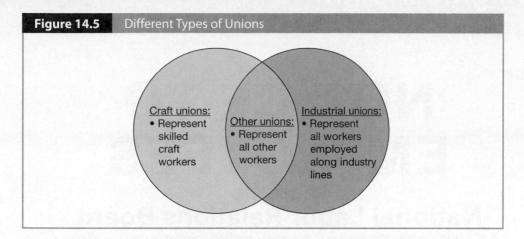

Craft unions:
• Represent skilled craft workers

Other unions:
• Represent all other workers

Industrial unions:
• Represent all workers employed along industry lines

reduce it. Today skilled and unskilled workers, white-collar and blue-collar workers, and professional groups are being represented by both types of union. For example, the UAW represents workers in diverse industries from auto manufacturing to agriculture, health care to higher education.[25]

While technically not a union, **employee associations** represent various groups of professional and white-collar employees. Examples of employee associations include the National Education Association, Michigan State Employees Association, American Nurses' Association, and Air Line Pilots Association. In competing with unions, these associations, for all purposes, may function as unions and become just as aggressive as unions in representing members.

employee associations
Labor organizations that represent various groups of professional and white-collar employees in labor–management relations.

Public Unions

Involvement of unions for federal, state, and local government employees has been an area of important activity since the early 1960s. Today unions represent more than 34.4 percent of all government workers in the United States (compared with just 11 percent in 1960).[26]

Imagesource/Photo Library

One of the functions of a union steward is to discuss issues with management as they arise. Here, a steward is discussing a safety issue with the site manager.

NLRB Election Poster

NOTICE TO EMPLOYEES

FROM THE
National Labor Relations Board

A PETITION has been filed with this Federal agency seeking an election to determine whether certain employees want to be represented by a union.

The case is being investigated and NO DETERMINATION HAS BEEN MADE AT THIS TIME by the National Labor Relations Board. IF an election is held Notices of Election will be posted giving complete details for voting.

It was suggested that your employer post this notice so the National Labor Relations Board could inform you of your basic rights under the National Labor Relations Act.

YOU HAVE THE RIGHT under Federal Law

- To self-organization
- To form, join, or assist labor organizations
- To bargain collectively through representatives of your own choosing
- To act together for the purposes of collective bargaining or other mutual aid or protection
- To refuse to do any or all of these things unless the union and employer, in a state where such agreements are permitted, enter into a lawful union-security agreement requiring employees to pay periodic dues and initiation fees. Nonmembers who inform the union that they object to the use of their payments for nonrepresentational purposes may be required to pay only their share of the union's costs of representational activities *(such as collective bargaining, contract administration, and grievance adjustments)*.

It is possible that some of you will be voting in an employee representation election as a result of the request for an election having been filed. While NO DETERMINATION HAS BEEN MADE AT THIS TIME, in the event an election is held, the NATIONAL LABOR RELATIONS BOARD wants all eligible voters to be familiar with their rights under the law IF it holds an election.

The Board applies rules that are intended to keep its elections fair and honest and that result in a free choice. If agents of either unions or employers act in such a way as to interfere with your right to a free election, the election can be set aside by the Board. Where appropriate the Board provides other remedies, such as reinstatement for employees fired for exercising their rights, including backpay from the party responsible for their discharge.

NOTE:

The following are examples of conduct that interfere with the rights of employees and may result in the setting aside of the election.

- Threatening loss of jobs or benefits by an employer or a union
- Promising or granting promotions, pay raises, or other benefits to influence an employee's vote by a party capable of carrying out such promises
- An employer firing employees to discourage or encourage union activity or a union causing them to be fired to encourage union activity
- Making campaign speeches to assembled groups of employees on company time within the 24-hour period before the election
- Incitement by either an employer or a union of racial or religious prejudice by inflammatory appeals
- Threatening physical force or violence to employees by a union or an employer to influence their votes

Please be assured that IF AN ELECTION IS HELD every effort will be made to protect your right to a free choice under the law. Improper conduct will not be permitted. All parties are expected to cooperate fully with this Agency in maintaining basic principles of a fair election as required by law. The National Labor Relations Board, as an agency of the United States Government, does not endorse any choice in the election.

NATIONAL LABOR RELATIONS BOARD
an agency of the
UNITED STATES GOVERNMENT

THIS IS AN OFFICIAL GOVERNMENT NOTICE AND MUST NOT BE DEFACED BY ANYONE

FORM NLRB-666 (5-90)

✦ U.S. Government Printing Office: 1990-270-693/10127

As unions and employee associations of teachers, police, firefighters, and state employees have grown in size and political power, they have demanded the same rights to bargain and strike that private-sector employees have.

While public sector and private sector collective bargaining have many features in common, a number of factors differentiate the two sectors. For example, there are no national boards, like the NLRB in the private sector, that govern public sector labor relations. Public sector collective bargaining falls within the separate jurisdiction of each state, and great diversity exists among the various state laws.

14.2 The Bargaining Process

Those unfamiliar with contract negotiations often view the process as an emotional conflict between labor and management, complete with marathon sessions, fist pounding, and smoke-filled rooms. In reality, negotiating a labor agreement entails long hours of extensive preparation combined with diplomatic maneuvering and the development of bargaining strategies. Furthermore, negotiation is only one part of the **collective bargaining process.** (See Figure 14.7 later in the chapter.) Collective bargaining also may include the use of economic pressures in the form of strikes and boycotts by a union. Lockouts, plant closures, and the replacement of strikers are similar pressures used by an employer. In addition, either or both parties may seek support from the general public or from the courts as a means of pressuring the opposing side.

collective bargaining process
The process of negotiating a labor agreement, including the use of economic pressures by both parties.

14.2a Preparing for Negotiations

Preparing for negotiations includes assembling data to support bargaining proposals and forming the bargaining team. This permits collective bargaining to be conducted on an orderly, factual, and positive basis with a greater likelihood of achieving desired goals. Assuming that the labor agreement is not the first to be negotiated by the parties, preparation for negotiations ideally start soon after the current agreement has been signed. This practice allows negotiators to review and diagnose weaknesses and mistakes made during the previous negotiations while the experience is still current in their minds.

Normally, each side has four to six representatives at the negotiating table. The chief negotiator for management is the vice president or manager for labor relations; the chief negotiator for the union is the local union president or national union representative. Others making up management's team may include representatives from accounting or finance, operations, employment, legal, or training. The local union president is likely to be supported by the chief steward, various local union vice presidents, and a representative from the national union. Importantly, it is widely accepted that the conduct of the negotiators strongly influences individual bargaining sessions and the outcomes reached. According to one experienced negotiator, "The conduct of negotiations largely depends on the relationship and attitude of negotiators toward one another. If you want conflict in your bargaining sessions, just start off attacking the other side."

 LO 4

How do you ensure that the bargaining process does not become highly adversarial?

14.2b Gathering Bargaining Data

Employers gather economic data primarily in the areas of wages and benefits. However, internal data relating to grievances, disciplinary actions, transfers, promotions, overtime, and former arbitration awards are useful in formulating and supporting the employer's bargaining position. The supervisors and managers, who must live with and administer the labor agreement, can be very important sources of ideas and suggestions concerning changes that are needed in the *next* agreement.

When negotiating contracts, union bargainers talk about "taking wages out of competition." This term refers to having similar contract provisions—particularly concerning wages and benefits—between different companies in order to prevent one employer from having a favorable labor cost advantage over another. For example, the United Auto Workers representing workers at both General Motors and Ford will seek similar contract provisions. Furthermore, this allows unions to show their members that they are receiving wages and benefits comparable to those of other employees doing like work. Other negotiated labor agreements, particularly at the local and regional levels, play a significant part in settling the terms of the labor agreement.

14.2c Developing Bargaining Strategies and Tactics

Both management and union negotiators approach bargaining with a defined strategy. In tough economic periods, the employer's strategy might be cost containment or specific reductions in wages or benefits such as health care or pension costs. Conversely, in times of economic growth—when a union strike would harm sales—the employer will be more willing to meet union demands. The employer's strategy should also consider proposals the union is likely to submit, goals the union is striving to achieve, and the extent to which it may be willing to make concessions or to resort to strike action in order to achieve these goals.

At a minimum, the employer's bargaining strategy must address these points:

- Likely union proposals and management responses to them
- A listing of management demands, limits of concessions, and anticipated union responses
- Development of a database to support management bargaining proposals and to counteract union demands
- A contingency operating plan should employees strike

Certain elements of strategy are common to both the employer and the union. Generally, the initial demands presented by each side are greater than those it actually may hope to achieve.[27] This is done to provide room for concessions. Moreover, each party usually avoids giving up the maximum it is capable of conceding to allow for further concessions that may be needed to break a bargaining deadlock.

The negotiation of a labor agreement can have some of the characteristics of a poker game, with each side attempting to determine its opponent's position while not revealing its own.[28] Each party normally tries to avoid disclosing the relative importance that it attaches to a proposal so that it will not be forced to pay a higher price than is necessary to have the proposal accepted. As in buying a new car, the buyer and seller employ a lot of strategy to obtain the best outcome possible.

14.2d Negotiating the Labor Agreement

While there is no "exact" way to negotiate a labor agreement, typically each side focuses on one issue or several related issues until agreement is reached.[29] For each bargaining issue to be resolved satisfactorily, the point at which agreement is reached must be within limits that the union and the employer are willing to accept. In a frequently cited bargaining model, Ross Stagner and Hjalmar Rosen call the area within these two limits the **bargaining zone**. In some bargaining situations, such as the one illustrated in Figure 14.6, the solution desired by one party may exceed the limits of the other party. Thus that solution is outside the bargaining zone. If that party refuses to modify its demands sufficiently to bring them within the bargaining zone or if the opposing party refuses to extend its limit to accommodate the demands of the other party, a bargaining deadlock results.[30] For example, when bargaining a wage increase for employees, if the union's lowest limit is a 4 percent increase and management's top limit is 6 percent, an acceptable range—the bargaining zone—is available to both parties. If management's top limit is only 3 percent, however, a bargaining zone is not available to either side, and a deadlock is likely to occur. Figure 14.6 shows that as bargaining takes place, several important variables influence the negotiators and their ability to reach agreement within the bargaining zone.

bargaining zone
An area in which the union and the employer are willing to concede when bargaining.

14.2e Good-Faith Bargaining

The Taft-Hartley Act requires an employer to negotiate in good faith with the union's representatives over conditions of employment (the same obligation applies to the union representatives).[31] Good faith requires meetings to be held at reasonable times and places to discuss employment conditions. It requires also that the proposals submitted by each party be realistic. In discussing the other party's proposals, each side must offer reasonable counterproposals for those it is unwilling to accept. Finally, both parties must sign the written document containing the agreement reached through negotiations.

14.2f Interest-Based Bargaining

U.S. labor–management negotiations are characterized as adversarial. With adversarial bargaining, negotiators start with defined positions, and through deferral, persuasion, trade, or power, the parties work toward the resolution of individual bargaining demands. Unfortunately, as noted by one labor negotiator, "adversarial bargaining does little to establish a long-term positive relationship based on open communications and trust. By its nature, it leads to suspicion and compromise."[32] To overcome these negative feelings, labor and management practitioners may use a nonadversarial approach to negotiating.

Interest-based bargaining is based on the identification and resolution of mutual interests rather than the resolve of specific bargaining demands.[33] Interest-based bargaining is "a problem-solving process conducted in a principled way that creates

interest-based bargaining
Problem-solving bargaining based on a win-win philosophy and the development of a positive long-term relationship.

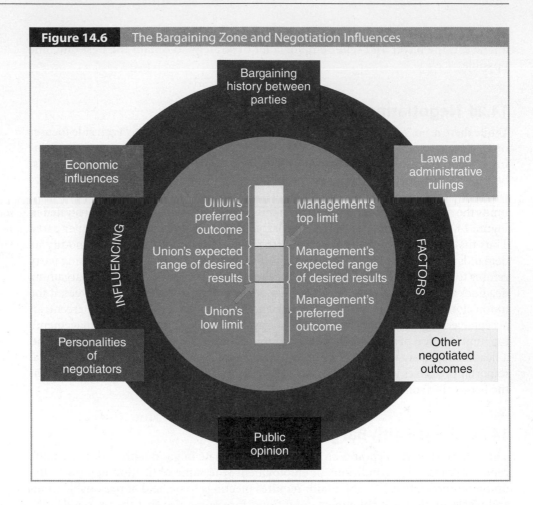

Figure 14.6   The Bargaining Zone and Negotiation Influences

effective solutions while improving the bargaining relationship." The focus of bargaining strategy is to discover mutual bargaining interests with the intent of formulating options and solutions for mutual gain.[34] Rather than using proposals and counterproposals as a means of reaching agreement (as with adversarial negotiations), participants use brainstorming, consensus decision-making, active listening, process checking, and matrix building to facilitate the settlement of issues. An underlying goal of interest-based bargaining is to create a relationship for the future based on trust, understanding, and mutual respect.

14.2g Management and Union Power in Collective Bargaining

bargaining power

The power of labor and management to achieve their goals through economic, social, or political influence.

Fortunately, the great majority of labor–management negotiations are settled peacefully. However, should negotiations become deadlocked, bargaining can become highly adversarial as each side will now employ its bargaining power to achieve its desired ends. The party's **bargaining power** consists of its economic, political, and social influence to achieve its demands at the expense of the other side.

Union Bargaining Power

The bargaining power of the union may be exercised by striking, picketing, or boycotting the employer's products or services. A strike is the refusal of a group of employees to perform their jobs. Unions usually seek strike authorization from their members to use as a bargaining ploy to gain concessions that will make a strike unnecessary. A strike vote by the members does not mean they actually want or expect to go out on strike. Rather, it is intended as a vote of confidence to strengthen the position of their leaders at the bargaining table.

When a union goes on strike, it pickets the employer by placing people at business entrances to advertise the dispute and to discourage others from entering the premises. Because unions often refuse to cross another union's picket line, the pickets may serve to prevent the delivery and pickup of goods or performance of other services. For example, a Teamster truck driver may refuse to deliver produce to a food store whose employees are out on strike with the United Food and Commercial Workers Union.

Another economic weapon of the union is the *boycott*, which is a refusal to patronize the employer. For example, production employees on strike against a hand tool manufacturer might picket a retail store that sells the tools made by the struck employer. Unions will also use handbills, radio announcements, email campaigns, and newspaper ads to discourage the purchase of the employer's product or service.

Management Bargaining Power

When negotiations become deadlocked, the employer's bargaining power largely rests on being able to continue operations in the face of a strike *or* to shut down operations entirely.

A strike is one way union members can exercise their bargaining power.

Ethan Miller/Getty Images

Should employees strike the organization (referred to as an economic strike), employers have the legal right to hire replacement workers. With this right, employers acquire a bargaining weapon equal in force to the union's right to strike. As one observer noted, "The availability of a worker replacement strategy improves management's ability to battle a union head-on in the way that unions have battled employers for decades."

In extreme situations, the employer may elect to lock out its employees. The lockout is a bargaining strategy by which the employer denies employees the opportunity to work by closing its operations. Besides being used in bargaining impasses, lockouts may be used by employers to combat union slowdowns, damage to their property, or violence within the organization that may occur in connection with a labor dispute. Employers may still be reluctant to resort to a lockout, however, because of their concern that denying work to regular employees might hurt the organization's image.

14.2h Resolving Bargaining Deadlocks

Unions and employers in all types of industries—sports, transportation, entertainment, manufacturing, communication, and health care—have used mediation and arbitration to help resolve their bargaining deadlocks.[35] As discussed in Chapter 13, mediation is a voluntary process that relies on the communication and persuasive skills of a mediator to help the parties resolve their differences. The federal government is likely to become involved in labor disputes through the services of the FMCS.

arbitrator
A third-party neutral who resolves a labor dispute by issuing a final decision in the disagreement.

Unlike a mediator, an **arbitrator** assumes the role of a decision maker and determines what the settlement between the two parties should be. In other words, arbitrators write a final contract that the parties *must* accept. Compared with mediation, arbitration is not often used to settle private sector bargaining disputes. In the public sector, where strikes are largely prohibited, the use of *interest arbitration* is a common method to resolve bargaining deadlocks. Generally, one or both parties are reluctant to give a third party the power to make the settlement for them. Consequently, a mediator typically is used to break a deadlock and assist the parties in reaching an agreement. An arbitrator generally is called on to resolve disputes arising in connection with the administration of the agreement, called *rights arbitration* or *grievance arbitration*, which will be discussed shortly.

14.3 The Labor Agreement

When negotiations are concluded, the labor agreement becomes a formal *binding* document listing the terms, conditions, and rules under which employees and managers agree to operate. Highlights in HRM 6 shows some of the major articles in a labor agreement and also provides examples of some new and progressive contract clauses. Two important items in any labor agreement pertain to the issue of management rights and the forms of security afforded to the union.

14.3a The Issue of Management Rights

Management rights have to do with the conditions of employment over which management is able to exercise exclusive control. Almost without exception, the labor agreement contains a *management rights* clause. This clause states that "management's authority is

Items in a Labor Agreement

Typical clauses will cover:

- Wages
- Vacations
- Holidays
- Work schedules
- Management rights
- Union security
- Transfers
- Discipline
- Training
- Grievance procedures
- No strike/no lockout clause
- Overtime
- Safety procedures
- Severance pay
- Seniority

- Pensions and benefits
- Outsourcing
- Work rules

Progressive clauses will cover:

- Employee access to records
- Limitations on use of performance evaluation
- Elder care leave
- Flexible medical spending accounts
- Protection against hazards of technology equipment (VDTs)
- Limitations against electronic monitoring
- Procedures governing drug testing
- Bilingual stipends
- Domestic partnership benefits
- Employee involvement programs

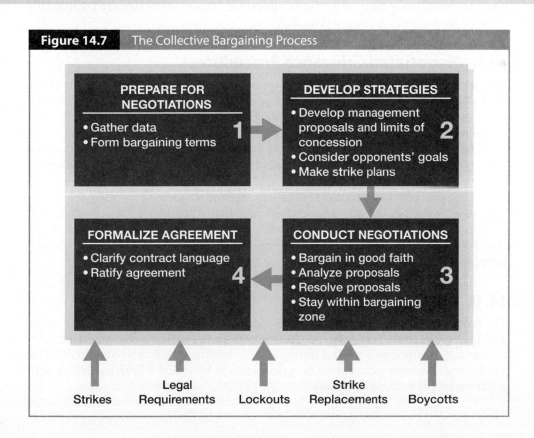

Figure 14.7 | The Collective Bargaining Process

PREPARE FOR NEGOTIATIONS
- Gather data
- Form bargaining terms

1

DEVELOP STRATEGIES
- Develop management proposals and limits of concession
- Consider opponents' goals
- Make strike plans

2

FORMALIZE AGREEMENT
- Clarify contract language
- Ratify agreement

4

CONDUCT NEGOTIATIONS
- Bargain in good faith
- Analyze proposals
- Resolve proposals
- Stay within bargaining zone

3

Strikes Legal Requirements Lockouts Strike Replacements Boycotts

supreme in all matters except those it has expressly conceded in the collective agreement, or in those areas where its authority is restricted by law." Management rights might include the right of management to determine the products to produce, to determine the location of production or service facilities, or to select production equipment and procedures.

14.3b Union Security Agreements

union security agreement
Where an employer and the union agree on the extent to which the union may compel employees to join the union and how the dues will be collected.

As we noted at the beginning of this chapter, unions must represent all bargaining unit members equally regardless of whether employees join the union or not. In exchange for this obligation, union officials will seek to negotiate some form of compulsory membership as a condition of employment. This form of agreement where an employer and the union agree on the extent to which the union may compel employees to join the union and how the dues will be collected is known as the **union security agreement**.

LO 5
How would you resolve a complaint about your boss making you do work that is not in your contract?

14.4 Administration of the Labor Agreement

Negotiation of the labor agreement, as mentioned earlier, is usually the most publicized and critical aspect of labor relations. Nevertheless, as managers in unionized organizations know, the bulk of labor relations activity comes from the day-to-day administration of the agreement because no agreement could possibly anticipate all the forms that disputes may take. In addition, once the agreement is signed, each side will naturally interpret ambiguous clauses to its own advantage. These differences are traditionally resolved through the grievance procedure.

14.4a Negotiated Grievance Procedures

grievance procedure
A formal procedure that provides for the union to represent members and nonmembers in processing a grievance.

The **grievance procedure** typically provides for the union to represent the interests of its members (and nonmembers as well) in processing a grievance. It is considered by some authorities to be the heart of the bargaining agreement, or the safety valve that gives flexibility to the whole system of collective bargaining.[36]

The grievance procedure is normally initiated by the union—or an individual employee—when it feels management has violated some article of the labor agreement. In one case, the union filed a grievance against a supervisor when it believed the supervisor promoted an employee out of seniority order—called a bypass grievance. A significant benefit of the grievance procedure is that it provides a formal and orderly procedure for the union to challenge the actions of management without resort to force. One authority has noted, "The grievance procedure fosters cooperation, not conflict, between the employer and the union."[37]

14.4b Grievance Arbitration

rights arbitration
Arbitration over interpretation of the meaning of contract terms or employee work grievances.

The function of **rights arbitration** is to provide the solution to a grievance that a union and an employer have been unable to resolve by themselves. As mentioned earlier, arbitration is performed by a neutral third party (an arbitrator or impartial umpire). This third party's decision dictates how the grievance is to be settled.[38] Both parties are obligated to comply with the decision.

Under the **fair representation doctrine**, unions have a legal obligation to provide assistance to members who are pursuing grievances. Because members can bring suit against their unions for failing to process their grievances adequately, many union officers are reluctant to refuse taking even weak grievances to arbitration.

Arbitration Hearing

In our experience, employees unfamiliar with arbitration find the process confusing and often stressful. This is true for employees in the nonunion, as well as the union, setting. Arbitration hearings have the appearance of a court hearing but without many of the formalities of a court proceeding. The process begins with the swearing-in of witnesses and the introduction of the *submission agreement*. The submission agreement is a statement of the problem to be resolved. Such a statement might read: "Was the three-day suspension of Alex Hayden for just cause? If not, what is the appropriate remedy?" The parties will then make opening statements, followed by the presentation of facts and evidence, and the oral presentation of witnesses. The hearing will conclude with each side making summary statements that are arguments in support of its position.

In arbitrating a dispute, it is the responsibility of the arbitrator to ensure that each side receives a fair hearing during which it may present all of the facts it considers pertinent to the case. The primary purpose of the hearing is to assist the arbitrator in obtaining the facts necessary to resolve a human relations problem rather than a legal one. The arbitrator, therefore, has a right to question witnesses or to request additional facts from either party. After conducting the hearing and receiving post-hearing briefs (should the parties choose to submit them), the arbitrator customarily has 30 days in which to consider the evidence and render an award. In most labor contracts, the costs of arbitration are shared equally by the parties.

Arbitration Award

The arbitration award is a formal written document given to both sides. As in grievance procedures, there is no specific format to an arbitration award, but typically the award contains five parts: (1) submission agreement, (2) facts of the case, (3) positions of the parties, (4) opinion of the arbitrator, and (5) decision rendered. As might be expected, the decision of the arbitrator is of major importance to the parties. However, the reasoning behind the decision—the opinion—is equally important since it can provide guidance concerning the interpretation of the labor agreement and the resolution of future disputes arising from its administration. In pointing out the merits of each party's position, the reasoning that underlies the award can help lessen the disappointment and protect the self-esteem of those representing the unsuccessful party. The opinion will also evaluate the evidence presented by each side in support of its position and, in discipline cases, whether management had just cause for the action taken against an employee. (See Chapter 13 for a discussion of just cause in arbitration.)

Because of the importance and magnitude of arbitration in both the union and nonunion setting, the process by which arbitrators make decisions and the factors that influence those decisions are of continuing interest to managers. Typically, arbitrators use four factors when deciding cases:

1. The wording of the labor agreement (or employment policy in nonunion organizations)
2. The submission agreement as presented to the arbitrator

fair representation doctrine
A doctrine under which unions have a legal obligation to assist both members and nonmembers in labor relations matters.

3. Testimony and evidence offered during the hearing
4. Arbitration criteria or standards (similar to standards of common law) against which cases are judged

In practice, arbitration decision-making is not an exact science. In fact, the decisions of arbitrators can be rather subjective. Arbitrators can, and do, interpret contract language differently (e.g., what "just cause discharge" actually means), they assign varying degrees of importance to testimony and evidence, they judge the truthfulness of witnesses differently, and they give arbitration standards greater or lesser weight as they apply to facts of the case. Each of these influences introduces subjectivity into the decision-making process.[39]

14.5 Contemporary Challenges to Labor Organizations

We conclude our discussion of labor relations by highlighting two important issues facing unions today: decrease of union membership and foreign competition and technological advances.

14.5a Decrease in Union Membership

A major challenge confronting organized labor is to halt the decline in union membership. The magnitude of the problem is illustrated by statistics that show how union membership has declined in total numbers and as a percentage of the total civilian labor force. Representing only 10 percent of American workers, the loss of union jobs reflects, in part, the decline in U.S. manufacturing jobs, coupled with the failure of unions to draw membership from among the white-collar and service ranks, where the labor force is growing more rapidly.[40] Other reasons for the decline in union membership include the following:

- A shift from traditional unionized industries (manufacturing, mining) to high-technology industries (information technology, health care)[41]
- Growth in the employment of part-time and temporary workers
- Growth in small businesses, in which unionization is more costly and difficult to perform
- Globalization of the workforce particularly among low-wage employers[42]

What are labor organizations doing to stem the decline in union membership? The answer, according to one union official, is "energized organizing." First, unions are targeting workers they have long ignored: low-wage service workers on the bottom tier of the U.S. economy—for example, janitors, maids, and service workers; food service employees; and retail clerks. Furthermore, unions see recent immigrants, the fastest-growing segment of working people, as a potent prospect for union growth.[43]

Richard Trumpka takes on both political parties to question the way politicians have failed to address the inability of the future generation to earn as much money as their parents.

Chip Somodevilla/Getty Images

Second, the AFL-CIO has embraced an aggressive unionization strategy. Richard Trumka, president of the AFL-CIO, argued that "Republicans, and too many democrats, have rigged our economy to enrich the select few... There is a Wall Street wing that seeks to undermine Donald Trump's promises to workers." Trumka pointed out the efforts that unions are taking to organize white-collar workers such as graduate students and technology professionals, as well as hotel and fast-food workers.[44]

14.5b Globalization and Technological Change

The importation of steel, consumer electronics, automobiles, clothing, textiles, and shoes from foreign countries creates a loss of jobs in the United States for workers who produce these products. Furthermore, foreign subsidiaries of American corporations such as Carrier, Westinghouse, and Xwerox have been accused by labor unions of exporting the jobs of U.S. workers. As a result, unions are demanding more government protection against imports, seeking to protect U.S. jobs from low-cost overseas producers. To add to that, in recent years, the service sector of the U.S. economy has witnessed the outsourcing of white-collar jobs to foreign employers in locations such as India and Indonesia.

More and more Americans are worried about their jobs being filled by people in other countries. **Offshoring**, defined as work that was previously carried out in one country to another, has been examined with great fear and trepidation in the last 20 years. The United States is now at a critical crossroads in how we deal with offshoring of American jobs. There is no question that most of the recent growth in U.S. companies comes from outside of the country. Companies argue that to remain competitive

offshoring
Work that was previously carried out in one country is moved to another country.

against foreign companies they must take advantage of lower cost labor in countries like India and China—perpetuating the continual loss of union jobs in the United States. Statistics show that between 2001 and 2013, the United States lost 3.2 million jobs to China alone.[45]

To bring back jobs, President Trump started renegotiating the North Atlantic Trade Agreement to ensure fewer jobs were going to Mexico and staying in the United States. But using trade barriers and punishing American companies for sending jobs outside the United States has major implications for the competitiveness of American companies, and employees as well. Such pressures could cause companies to send their headquarters to other countries.

Moreover, most of the job loss that occurs in the United States is a result of technology advances rather than globalization.[46]

Improvements in computer technology and highly automated operating systems have lowered the demand for certain types of employees. Decline in membership in the auto, steel, rubber, and transportation unions illustrates this fact. As previously discussed, technological advances have also diminished the effectiveness of strikes because highly automated organizations are capable of maintaining satisfactory levels of operation with minimum staffing levels during work stoppages. So, what does this all mean for unions and employers?

Summary

LO 1 Studies show that workers unionize for different economic, psychological, and social reasons. While some employees may join unions because they are required to do so, most belong to unions because they are convinced that unions help them improve their wages, benefits, and most importantly, equality. Employee unionization is largely caused by dissatisfaction with managerial practices and procedures.

LO 2 A formal union organizing campaign is used to solicit employee support for the union. Once employees demonstrate their desire to unionize through signing authorization cards, the union petitions the NLRB for a secret ballot election. If 51 percent of those voting in the election vote for the union, the NLRB certifies the union as the bargaining representative for all employees in the bargaining unit.

LO 3 Once a group of employees gets 30 percent of their peers within the bargaining unit to sign a petition, then the NLRB steps in and monitors an election to see if the employees can unionize. If the employees choose to unionize, then a particular union that has agreed to collectively represent the employees in negotiations will try to come to an agreement with the company on certain changes.

LO 4 Negotiating a labor agreement is a detailed process. Each side prepares a list of proposals it wishes to achieve while additionally trying to anticipate proposals desired by the other side. Bargaining teams must be selected, and all proposals must be analyzed to determine their impact on and cost to the organization. Both employer and union negotiators are sensitive to current bargaining patterns within the industry, general cost-of-living trends, and geographical wage differentials. Managers establish goals that seek to retain control over operations and to minimize costs. Union negotiators focus their demands around improved wages, hours, and working conditions. An agreement is reached when both sides compromise their original positions and final terms fall within the limits of the parties' bargaining zone.

Traditionally, collective bargaining between labor and management has been adversarial. Presently, there is an increased interest in nonadversarial negotiations—negotiations based on mutual gains and a heightened respect between the parties. What the FMCS calls interest-based bargaining is one form of nonadversarial negotiations.

LO 5 When differences arise between labor and management, they are normally resolved through the grievance procedure. Grievance procedures are negotiated and thus reflect the needs and desires of the parties. The typical grievance procedure consists of three, four, or five steps—each step having specific filing and reply times. Higher-level managers and union officials become involved in disputes at the higher steps of the grievance procedure. The final step of the grievance procedure may be arbitration. Arbitrators render a final decision to problems not resolved at lower grievance steps.

The submission agreement is a statement of the issue to be solved through arbitration. It is simply the problem the parties wish to have settled. The arbitrator must answer the issue by basing the arbitration award on four factors: contents of the labor agreement (or employment policy), submission agreement as written, testimony and evidence obtained at the hearing, and various arbitration standards developed over time to assist in the resolution of different types of labor–management disputes. Arbitration is not an exact science because arbitrators give varying degrees of importance to the evidence and criteria by which disputes are resolved.

Key Terms

arbitrator	exclusive representation	offshoring
authorization card	fair representation doctrine	rights arbitration
bargaining power	grievance procedure	unfair labor practices (ULPs)
bargaining unit	industrial unions	union
bargaining zone	interest-based bargaining	union steward
collective bargaining process	labor relations process	union security agreement
craft unions	National Labor Relations Board	
employee associations	(NLRB)	

Discussion Questions

LO 1 Contrast the arguments concerning union membership that are likely to be presented by a union with those likely to be presented by an employer.

LO 2 Describe the steps in the traditional organizing drive.

LO 3 Describe what it means for HR managers when employees win an election to unionize. What can HR do at this point to make sure the employees' and company's interests align?

LO 4 Of what significance is the bargaining zone in the conduct of negotiations? What are some influences affecting negotiated outcomes? The

negotiations between data services international and its union have become deadlocked. What form of bargaining power does each side possess to enforce its bargaining demands? What are the advantages and disadvantages of each form of bargaining power for both the employer and union?

LO 5 a. What are some of the actions being taken by unions to cope with the contemporary challenges they face?

b. How can companies respond to the labor changes that result from increased technology and globalization?

HRM **Experience**

Learn about Unions

Unions, like businesses, are dynamic and varied. Some unions are very large, such as the United Auto Workers (UAW) and the American Federation of State, County and Municipal Employees (AFSCME), and represent workers nationally or even internationally. Others are smaller in size—for example, the Writers Guild of America East (WGAE) or the Air Traffic Controllers Association (ATCA)—and represent only specific groups of employees or organize only in a designated geographic area. This exercise will help you learn more about unions.

Assignment

Working individually or in teams, select four or five different unions or employee associations and report on the following. Vary your selections (large/small, public/private, and so on) to widen your understanding of labor organizations.

- History of the union
- Membership size and type of employees represented
- Mission of the union
- Structure of the union, including its major departments
- National officers
- Names of employers with whom they have an agreement
- Special benefits they offer members
- Other interesting or pertinent information

The AFL-CIO website (http://www.afl-cio.org) provides a list of all unions—and their websites—affiliated with the federation. National unions and their locals along with library research can also provide information. Be prepared to present your findings during a class discussion.

CASE STUDY The New Union Battles: Public Unions vs. Rich World Governments

While private sector unions may be rapidly declining in the United States, public sector unions are still strong … or at least were. In 2011, public sector unions representing teachers, prison guards, police officers, railworkers, and civil servants were dealt a blow by their employers—the government. At the forefront of the battle was the issue of collective bargaining. And it began in Wisconsin.

But this is not the first time Wisconsin has been at the forefront of collective bargaining. The Wagner Act of 1934 did not grant public employees the right to collective bargaining. In the 1950s and 1960s public sector employees pushed for collective bargaining rights. Finally, in 1959 Wisconsin became the first state to grant this right to public employees. In a dramatic turn of events, Wisconsin is now the first to repeal collective bargaining rights for its public sector employees.

After a standoff with state Democrats and prounion demonstrators, Wisconsin governor Scott Walker and the state legislature decided that public employees did not have the right to collective bargaining. This set off a chain reaction in other states. For example, in 2017 lawmakers in Iowa proposed a bill to prohibit collective bargaining for state employees. This crackdown on collective bargaining could now act as a model for President Trump to overhaul the federal workforce. Scott Walker said that he spoke with Vice President Mike Pence about "how they may take bits and pieces of what we did" with the union law and "apply it at the national level." However, these are only the words of Walker; President Trump hasn't said anything about it yet. Either way, public sector employees are concerned about their future.

President Trump and Wisconsin Governor Walker during a campaign rally in 2016.

Chip Somodevilla/Getty Images

Questions

1. Why are politicians so interested in trying to repeal collective bargaining rights for public sector employees?

2. What risks does losing their collective bargaining rights hold for public employees?

3. As an elected politician charged with major cuts in your state budget, how would you negotiate with the public sector unions? As a public sector union leader, how would you negotiate with the state legislature?

Sources: Thomas Kochan, "Protective Bargaining: How to Prevent the Labor Wars," *Boston Review* (March 23, 2011), http://www .bostonreview.net/BR36.2/thomas_kochan_wisconsin_labor_ wars .php; "The Battle Ahead: The Struggle with Public-Sector Unions Should Be about Productivity and Parity, not Just Spending Cuts," *The Economist* (January 6, 2011), http://www.econo-mist.com /node/17851305; David Morris, "When Unions Are Strong, Americans Enjoy the Fruits of Their Labor," *Huffington Post* (April 8, 2011), http://www.huffingtonpost.com/david-morris/ when-unions-are-strong-am _b_846802.html; Clay Masters, "Iowa Moves to Restrict Collective Bargaining for Public Sector Workers," *NPR* (February 14, 2017); Associated Press, "Scott Walker's Wisconsin Could Be a Model for Trump on Unions," *The Denver Post* (February 6, 2017).

CASE STUDY ❷ The Arbitration Case of Jesse Stansky

At the arbitration hearing, both parties were adamant in their positions. Nancy Huang, HR manager of Phoenix Semiconductor, argued that the grievant, Jesse Stansky, was justly terminated for arguing and hitting a coworker—a direct violation of company policy and the employee handbook. Stansky argued that he had been a good employee during his 10 years of employment.

The submission agreement governing the case read, "It is the employer's position that just cause existed for the discharge of Mr. Jesse Stansky and the penalty was appropriate for the offense committed." Additionally, the employer introduced into evidence the labor agreement, which defined just cause termination as follows:

Just cause shall serve as the basis for disciplinary action and includes, but is not limited to: dishonesty, inefficiency, unprofessional conduct, failure to report absences, falsification of records, violation of company policy, destruction of property, or possession or being under the influence of alcohol or narcotics.

Stansky was hired as a systems technician on November 20, 2003, a position he held until his termination on October 25, 2017. According to the testimony of Huang, Phoenix Semiconductor strived to maintain a positive and cordial work environment among its employees. Fighting on the job was strictly prohibited. Stansky's performance evaluation showed him to be an average employee, although he had received several disciplinary warnings for poor attendance and one 3-day suspension for a "systems control error." Stansky was generally liked by his coworkers, and several testified on his behalf at the arbitration hearing.

The termination of Stansky concerned an altercation between himself and Gary Lindekin, another systems technician. According to witnesses to the incident, both Stansky and Lindekin became visibly upset over the correct way to calibrate a sensitive piece of production equipment. The argument—one witness called it no more than a heated disagreement—lasted approximately 3 minutes and concluded when Stansky was seen forcefully placing his hand on Lindekin's shoulder. Lindekin took extreme exception

to Stansky's behavior and immediately reported the incident to management. After interviews with both Stansky and Lindekin and those who observed the incident, Huang, Samantha Lowry, the employee's immediate supervisor, and Grant Ginn, department manager, decided that Stansky should be terminated for unprofessional conduct and violation of company policy.

Questions

1. Which arguments should be given more weight: those based on company policy, the employee handbook, and the labor agreement or mitigating factors given by the grievant and his witnesses? Explain.

2. How might unprofessional conduct be defined? Explain.

3. If you were the arbitrator, how would you rule in this case? Explain fully the reasons for your decision.

Source: Adapted from an arbitration heard by George W. Bohlander. All names are fictitious.

Answers to Highlights in HRM 1

1. No. Applicants are considered as employees and, as such, are protected under the law.

2. No. Individual questioning of employees about their union membership or activities is unlawful.

3. No. Except in specific situations (e.g., to promote safety), employees have the right to wear union insignia.

4. Yes.

5. Yes. Blacklisting of job applicants or employees is against labor law.

6. No. During an organizing drive, an employer cannot promise improvements in wages or benefits as a means of defeating the union.

7. Yes. Both nonunion and union employers are subject to unfair labor practice charges.

8. Yes. When a grievance arbitration clause exists in a labor agreement, management must arbitrate cases that seem baseless.

9. Yes. Employees can be disciplined or discharged for work-related misconduct but not solely because of their union affiliations or union sentiments.

10. Yes. Antiunion remarks are not unlawful, provided they are not coercive.

Notes and References

1. Pandej Chintrakam, "Labor Unions and Income Inequality: Evidence from US States," *Journal of Applied Sciences* 11, no. 20 (2011): 3530–3533.

2. Donna Brazile, "What Have Unions Done for Us?" *CNN* (September 4, 2012), http://www.cnn.com/2012/09/04/opinion/brazile-unions/.

3. For an expanded model of the labor relations process, see John Dunlop, *Industrial Relations Systems* (New York: Henry Holt, 1958), Chapter 1. This book is a classic in the labor relations field. Also, those interested in labor relations may wish to explore in greater detail the historical developments of the U.S. labor movement. Much can be learned about the current operations of labor organizations and the philosophies of labor officials from labor's historical context. A brief but comprehensive history of labor unions can be found in undergraduate labor management textbooks such as those listed among these references.

4. Kavi Guppta, "Will Labor Unions Survive in the Era of Automation?" *Forbes* (October 12, 2016); Nina Foo, "Millennials Are the Key to Saving Unions," *Organizer* (February 8, 2017); Lydia Saad, "Americans' Support for Labor Unions Continues to Recover," *Gallup* (August 17, 2015).

5. Sara Horowitz, "Will Gawker Employees' Decision to Organize Make Unions Cool Again?" *Fast Company* (April 24, 2015).

6. Foo, "Millennials Are the Key to Saving Unions"; Saad, "Americans' Support for Labor Unions Continues to Recover."

7. Foo, "Millennials Are the Key to Saving Unions"; Saad, "Americans' Support for Labor Unions Continues to Recover"; Kate Bronfenbrenner, "The Role of Union Strategies in NLRB Certification Elections," *Industrial and Labor Relations Review* 50, no. 2 (1997): 195–212.

8. Personal conversation (May 1, 2017).

9. "Challenges Continue for Organized Labor in 2017," *Law 360* (March 15, 2017); Selena Maranjian, "Unions: Good or Bad?" *The Motley Fool* (November 22, 2014).

10. Barbara L. Rau, "The Diffusion of HR Practices in Unions," *Human Resources Management Review* 22, no. 1 (2012): 27–42.

11. Shad S. Morris, "Book Review of Offshoring of American Jobs," *Human Resource Management* 50, no. 2 (2011): 303–306.

12. Tracey E. Schelmetic, "Delta to Shut Down Contact Center in Jamaica; Bring Jobs to U.S.," *TMCnet* (January 14, 2011).

13. Forbes Human Resources Council, "5 Reasons Your Small Business Needs a Human Resources Professional," *Forbes* (November 3, 2016), https://www.forbes.com/sites/forbeshumanresourcescouncil/2016/11/03/5-reasons-your-small-business-needs-a-human-resources-professional/#2163c28385f2.

14. William H. Holley, Kenneth M. Jennings, and Roger S. Wolters, *The Labor Relations Process* (New York: Cengage Learning, 2011).

15. While most employers will readily negotiate with the union once it is certified as the bargaining representative of employees, other employers will continue to vigorously oppose unionization. This may be accomplished by taking a very aggressive bargaining posture against union demands. NLRB statistics show that unions file a large number of unfair labor practice charges [8(a)(5) violations] when they believe employers illegally hinder the bargaining process.

16. "Union Organizing: Authorization Cards: What Steps Should an Employer Take When Presented with Union Authorization Cards?" *Society for Human Resources Management* (June 1, 2012), https://www.shrm.org/resourcesandtools/tools-and-samples/hr-qa/pages/authorizationcardpresentation.aspx.

17. Neil King Jr., Thomas M. Burton, and Kris Maher, "Political Fight over Unions Escalate," *Wall Street Journal* (February 22, 2011), http://online.wsj.com/news/articles/SB10001424052748703800204576158851079665840.

18. Richard Berman, "Union Support for Donald Trump Gives Big Labor Chance to Catch Up," *The Washington Times* (February 6, 2017).

19. "Organizing Institute: Three-Day Training," *AFL-CIO*, http://www.aflcio.org/Get-Involved/Become-a-UnionOrganizer/Organizing-Institute/Three-Day-Training

20. Arthur B. Shostak, *The Cyberunion Handbook: Transforming Labor Through Computer Technology* (New York: Routledge, 2015).

21. Kati Sipp, "The Internet vs. The Labor Movement: Why Unions Are Latecomers to Digital Organizing," *New Labor Forum* (April 23, 2016).

22. Neil Bucklew, Christopher N. Ellison, and Jeffrey D. Houghton, "Shared Governance and Academic Collective Bargaining in American Higher Education: A Potential Model for US Participation in the Global Experience of Works Councils and Codetermination," *Journal of Collective Bargaining in the Academy* 4, no. 1 (2013): 1–13.

23. "Election Report for Cases Closed," *FY 2016* (May 1, 2017): 1.

24. See UAW website at www.uaw.org.

25. "Union Members Summary," *Bureau of Labor Statistics* (May 1, 2017).

26. Leigh Thompson, *The Mind and Heart of the Negotiator*, 3rd ed. (Upper Saddle River, NJ: Prentice Hall, 2004).

27. John Valery White, "How to Play Your Hand: Lessons for Negotiators from Poker," *UNLV Gaming Law Journal* 2, no. 2 (2011).

28. Joel Cutcher-Gershenfeld, Thomas Kochan, John-Paul Ferguson, and Betty Barrett, "Collective Bargaining in the Twenty-First Century: A Negotiations Institution at Risk," *Negotiation Journal* 23, no. 3 (July 2007): 249.

29. Ross Stagner and Hjalmar Rosen, *Psychology of Union-Management Relations* (Belmont, CA: Wadsworth, 1965), 95–97. This is another classic in the field of labor–management relations.

30. The National Labor Relations Board offers an excellent book on the National Labor Relations Act. This book discusses good-faith bargaining as well as other important legal issues—for example, employers covered by the law, unfair labor practices, and election procedures. See *Basic Guide to the National Labor Relations Act* (Washington, DC: U.S. Government Printing Office, 1997).

31. Joe Stanley, interview by author, January 5, 2008, Phoenix, AZ.

32. The FMCS has a complete and comprehensive program to train labor and management negotiators in the art and techniques of interest-based bargaining (IBB). Information on the IBB program can be obtained from the FMCS national headquarters at 2100 K Street, N.W., Washington, DC 20427 or from FMCS district offices.

33. Leonard J. Marcus, Barry C. Dorn, and Eric J. McNulty, "The Walk in the Woods: A Step-by-Step Method for Facilitating Interest-Based Negotiation and Conflict Resolution," *Negotiation Journal* 28, no. 3 (2012): 337–349.

34. Roger J. Peters and Deborah Bavarnick Mastin, "To Mediate or Not to Mediate: That Is the Question," *Dispute Resolution Journal* 62, no. 2 (May—July 2007): 14.

35. *Grievance Guide*, 12th ed. (Washington, DC: BNA Books, 2007); Paul J. Gollan and David Lewin, "Employee Representation in Non-Union Firms: An Overview," *Industrial Relations: A Journal of Economy and Society*, 52, no. s1 (2013): 173–193.

36. Vera Riggs, Labor-Management Relations Conference, August 11, 2007, Phoenix, AZ.

37. Arbitration awards are not final in all cases. Arbitration awards may be overturned through the judicial process if it can be shown that the arbitrator was prejudiced or failed to render an award based on the essence of the agreement.

38. Lawrence Mishel, "Unions, Inequality, and Faltering Middle-Class Wages," *Issue Brief*, 342 (2012).

39. Lydia Dishman, "These Are the Jobs with the Most Potential in 2017," *Fast Company* (January 6, 2017); David Welch, "Twilight of the UAW," *Business Week* (April 10, 2006): 62.

40. Matthew J. Slaughter, "Globalization and Declining Unionization in the United States," *Industrial Relations* 46, no. 2 (April 2007): 329; "Why Trade Unions Are Declining," *The Economist* (September 29, 2015), www.economist.com/blogs/economist-explains/2015/09/economist-explains-19.

41. Lance Compa, "Labor at a Crossroads: How Unions Can Thrive in the 21st Century," *The American Prospect* (January 27, 2015), http://prospect.org/article/labor-crossroads-how-unions-can-thrive-21st-century.

42. Yuki Noguchi, "AFL-CIO's Trumka Says Both Parties Have Lost Focus on U.S. Workers," *NPR* (April 4, 2017).

43. Will Kimball and Robert E. Scott, "China Trade, Outsourcing and Jobs," *Economic Policy Institute* (December 11, 2014), http://www.epi.org/publication/china-trade-outsourcing-and-jobs/.

44. Kimberly Amadeo, "How Outsourcing Jobs Affects the U.S. Economy," *The Balance* (March 30, 2017).

CHAPTER **15**

International Human Resources Management

Learning Outcome

After studying this chapter, you should be able to

LO 1 Explain the political, economic, sociocultural, and technological factors in different countries that HR managers need to consider.

LO 2 Identify the types of organizational forms used for competing internationally.

LO 3 Explain how domestic and international HRM differ. Discuss the recruitment, selection, training, compensation, and performance appraisal needs for different types of employees working across borders.

LO 4 Explain how labor relations differ around the world.

515

Have you ever noticed that much of what you buy is not made in the United States? The shirt you are wearing right now was probably made in Bangladesh, Vietnam, Indonesia, or China. The brand, of course, may be American (e.g., Abercrombie & Fitch, Hollister, American Eagle), but that just means that the company is headquartered here. In fact, despite antiglobalization sentiments, most companies today are involved in international business in one way or another.

Managing human resources across these international settings may help to leverage specialized skills, provide cheaper labor, or even bring new ideas into the company. However, managing human resources internationally makes everything all the more complicated.[1] Such complications arise as each country possesses unique political policies, economic situations, social and cultural norms, and technological capacities. The first part of this chapter describes some of the environmental factors that affect the work of managers in a global setting. We show how a political, economic, sociocultural, technological (PEST) analysis can help you to more effectively assess the threats and opportunities presented to HRM in a global setting. Just as with domestic operations, the dimensions of the environment form a context in which HRM decisions in foreign countries are made. Next, we show how companies respond to these environmental complications. We examine the different forms companies will take to help them compete in a global environment—international, multidomestic, global, and transnational. In many respects, these organizational forms influence the kinds of managerial and human resource issues a company faces. A major portion of this chapter deals with the various HR activities involved in the recruitment, selection, development, and compensation of employees working abroad. However, as we explain later in this chapter, workers stationed all over the United States are increasingly finding themselves working virtually with people from other cultures who speak different languages. This creates challenges not only for them but also for firms' HR managers.

<table>
<tr><td>LO ❶

What is the first thing you think about when you read the word "PEST"?</td></tr>
</table>

15.1 Analyzing Your International Environment

In Chapter 1, we highlighted some of the global trends affecting human resource management. Because political, economic, social, and technological conditions are constantly shifting across the world, how people are managed in those changing environments will shift as well. To systematically help companies manage in the global environment, political, economic, sociocultural, and technological (PEST) analysis acts as an audit of a company's environmental influences to help it determine its strategy and HR response.

Conducting a PEST analysis entails scanning different contextual environments to understand the long-term trends and how they might impact a company.[2] As an HR manager, PEST analysis can help you to (1) spot business or personnel opportunities, and it gives you advanced warning of threats, (2) spot trends in the business environment so you can proactively adapt to these changes, (3) avoid implementing

HR practices in a particular country where they may fail, and (4) break free of old habits and assumptions about how people should be managed to help bring about innovative ideas for the entire company.

We begin by showing you how to perform a PEST analysis (Figure 15.1)—something completely different from an analysis of issues you may be facing with household insects and rodents.

15.1a Political Factors

First, **political factors** are assessed by examining a country's labor laws, property rights, and patents. For example, when the Ohio-based welding company Lincoln Electric started operations in Brazil, they were not able to offer their yearly bonus program based on performance because any bonuses paid for two consecutive years become a legal entitlement.[3]

In many countries, particularly those in Africa, property rights are poorly protected by governments. Whoever has the political power or authority can seize others' property with few or no repercussions. Civil unrest can also lead to the poor enforcement of property rights. Companies have less incentive to locate factories or invest in countries experiencing strife. Another issue relates to intellectual property rights—rights related to patents, trademarks, and so forth.

15.1b Economic Factors

Economic factors consist of trends around market and trade cycles, specific industry changes, customer preferences, and country economic growth forecasts. For example, in 1995, the World Trade Organization (WTO) was formalized as a cooperative forum for country leaders to come together and increase free trade across the world. As of 2017, the WTO member countries represent over 164 member nations and cover 97 percent of all international trade.[4] In addition, countries are continually negotiating free trade agreements with each other in hopes of increasing their economic activity and power.

Since China joined the WTO in 2001, its economy has grown dramatically, drastically altering its political and trading relationships with many nations. In a strange twist of fate, Xi Jinping, the leader of the communist world and China's president, has taken to defending free trade and globalization, whereas Donald Trump, leader of the free world and America's president, has taken to attacking them.[5]

political factors
external factors including labor laws, property rights, and patent processes.

economic factors
external factors including the strength or weakness of markets, stability of trade cycles, specific industry conditions, customer preferences, and government's economic policies.

In 2016 South Africa's parliament approved a bill allowing the government to take land from individual and corporate owners if it is in the public interest. "South Africa Approves Land Expropriation Bill," BBC News, May 26, 2016.

Figure 15.1   PEST Analysis

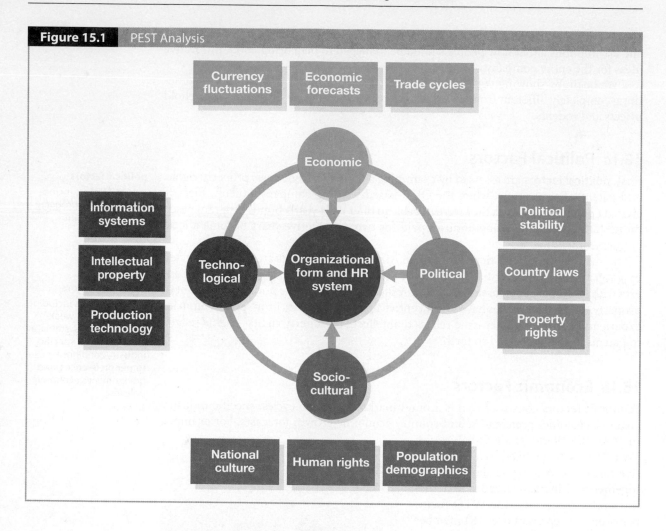

15.1c Sociocultural Factors

sociocultural factors
external factors including method and style of communications, religions, values and ideologies, education standards, and social structure

Beyond the economic issues just mentioned, a country's **sociocultural factors** (communications, religion, values and ideologies, education, and social structure) also have important implications when it comes to a company's decision about when and how to do business there. Because of low labor costs and language similarities, many U.S. companies have found India an attractive place to locate their facilities, particularly call centers. Moreover, the U.S. military's long-term stay in Panama developed a bilingual workforce that already understands the U.S. work culture. Now that the Panama Canal has been expanded to accommodate new, larger freight ships, the United States is looking to take advantage of these close ties and cultural similarities in the workforce there.[6]

By recognizing and accommodating different ideologies, religious beliefs, communication styles, education systems, and social structures, managers stand a better chance of understanding the culture of a **host country**—a country in which an international business operates. Even in countries that have close language or cultural links, HR practices can be dramatically different. For example, night shifts may be taboo. Employers might be expected to provide employees with meals while at work and transportation

host country
A country in which an international corporation operates.

In some countries, like Malaysia, corporate leaders fashion "personnel sharia", which represent human resource rules to ensure that employees exhibit ethical and moral values in their conduct at work. (source: Sloane-White, P. 2011. Working in the Islamic Economy: Sharia-ization and the Malaysian workplace. Sojourn: Journal of Social Issues in Southeast Asia, 26(2), 304-334.)

between home and work. In most of the Islamic Middle East, it is completely acceptable to ask coworkers very personal questions about their children, especially their sons, but never about their wives.[7]

In another example, Netflix has had challenges in expanding internationally. In 2015, Netflix had about 30 employees who were initially uncomfortable with Netflix's culture of bluntness, so at odds with their home culture of communicating in subtler ways. Netflix is currently working to reconcile company and national culture, both with different communication preferences.[8]

15.1d Technological Factors

Related to a country's sociocultural norms, where it stands technologically also influences the threats and opportunities that foreign companies face. **Technological factors** refer to the maturity of manufacturing equipment, information systems, technology platforms, research funding, and consumer access to technology. Even in less-developed countries where manufacturing is typically stronger due to low cost of labor and high cost of capital-intensive equipment, labor-saving technology is becoming more affordable and accessible. Take, for instance, a textile factory in Vietnam. It is more cost effective for the factory to purchase high-tech threading equipment to spin the cotton into thread than to hire hundreds of people to thread the cotton by hand, even when the average wage for such employees is less than $100 a month.

While advances in technology have pushed for more service-based jobs, information systems and technology platforms have also increased the rate at which these services can be traded across countries. Along with the creation of the WTO, 1995 also signifies the beginning of the Internet era. America Online (AOL) went public in 1995 to mark the beginning of Integrated technology platforms that could be shared instantaneously across the world. *Integrated technology platforms* represent common operating

technological factors
external factors pertaining to the technological infrastructure and investments, information systems, manufacturing equipment, and consumer access to technology

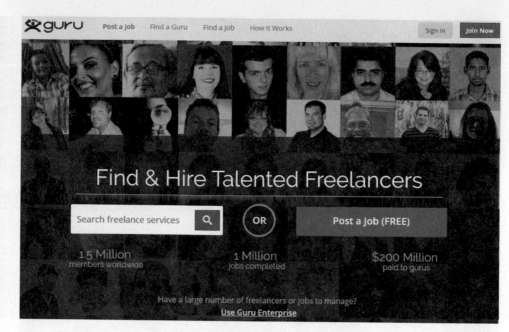

Guru.com helps you connect to talent from all over the world.

systems such as Microsoft Windows 10 that can be used across multiple computers connected through the Internet. Through these common platforms, work becomes less specific to particular companies and countries.

In this era, employees become empowered to compete without the need of a large company. For example, many websites such as guru.com have developed an online marketplace where individuals can offer various services and compete for business throughout the world. Imagine you are interested in developing a new website for your company. By going to the Internet you can select various individuals offering these specific services. They may be from Manila, Mumbai, Manhattan, or Munich. In sum, these PEST factors shift the way companies are formed and how they manage their human resources.

15.1e Analyzing Your International Operations

LO 2

How might a PEST analysis decide how you run your business in a foreign location?

International business operations can take several different forms. A large percentage carry on their international business with only limited facilities in foreign countries. Others, particularly Fortune 500 corporations, have extensive facilities and personnel in various countries of the world. Dell, for example, actually employs more people outside the United States than within it. Managing these resources effectively and integrating their activities to achieve global advantage is a challenge to the leadership of these companies.

Figure 15.2 shows four basic types of organizations and how they differ in the degree to which international activities are separated to respond to the local regions and integrated to achieve global efficiencies. The **international corporation** is essentially a domestic firm that builds on its existing capabilities to penetrate overseas markets. Companies such as Honda, General Electric, and Procter & Gamble used this approach to gain access to Europe—they essentially adapted existing products for overseas markets without changing much else about their normal operations.

international corporation

A domestic firm that uses its existing capabilities to move into overseas markets.

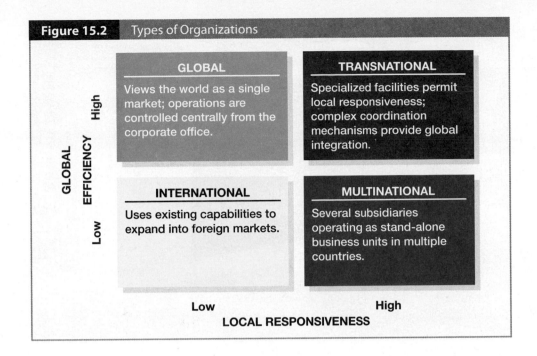

Figure 15.2   Types of Organizations

GLOBAL EFFICIENCY (vertical axis: Low to High)
LOCAL RESPONSIVENESS (horizontal axis: Low to High)

GLOBAL
Views the world as a single market; operations are controlled centrally from the corporate office.

TRANSNATIONAL
Specialized facilities permit local responsiveness; complex coordination mechanisms provide global integration.

INTERNATIONAL
Uses existing capabilities to expand into foreign markets.

MULTINATIONAL
Several subsidiaries operating as stand-alone business units in multiple countries.

A **multidomestic corporation (MDC)** is a more complex form that usually has fully autonomous units operating in multiple countries. Shell, Philips, and ITT are three typical MDCs. These companies have traditionally given their foreign subsidiaries a great deal of latitude to address local issues such as consumer preferences, political pressures, and economic trends in different regions of the world. Frequently these subsidiaries are run as independent companies without much integration. The **global corporation**, on the other hand, can be viewed as a multinational firm that maintains control of its operations worldwide from the country in which it is headquartered. Japanese companies, such as Matsushita and NEC, tend to treat the world market as a unified whole and try to combine their activities in each country to maximize their efficiencies on a global scale. These companies operate much like a domestic firm, except that they view the whole world as their marketplace.

Finally, a **transnational corporation** attempts to achieve the local responsiveness of an MDC while also achieving the efficiencies of a global firm. To balance this global/local dilemma, a transnational corporation uses a network structure that coordinates specialized facilities positioned around the world. By using this flexible structure, a transnational corporation provides autonomy to its operations in foreign countries but brings these separate activities together into an integrated whole. For most companies, the transnational form represents an ideal rather than a reality. McDonald's is an example of a transnational corporation, especially with culture-specific food items, like India's vegetarian McAloo Tikki, the McKebab in Israel, or a Hawaiian Deluxe Breakfast complete with spam, rice, eggs, and hashbrowns. With 31,000 restaurants across 119 countries serving 58 million people each day, it makes sense that McDonald's overseas revenue makes up nearly 65 percent of their total revenue, and that they cater McDonalds' core burger-fries-and-shakes menu to local tastes.[9]

multidomestic corporation (MDC)
A firm with independent business units operating in multiple countries.

global corporation
A firm that has integrated worldwide operations through a centralized home office.

transnational corporation
A firm that attempts to balance local responsiveness and global scale via a network of specialized operating units.

McDonald's McAloo Tikki can only be found in India.

Although various forms of organization exist, in this chapter we will generally refer to any company that conducts business outside its home country as an international business. With the global environment being filled by companies originating from different countries and operating in multiple cultures, increased pressure is being placed on the HRM function. International HRM is being seen more and more as a key source of competitive advantage for international businesses. HR units can no longer operate as separate groups attached only by a common brand and finances. HR managers must more effectively manage and move people across country borders. In the next section of this chapter we examine the different HR practices used to manage in these complex circumstances.

LO **3**

Do you think it would be difficult to work as an expatriate?

expatriates, or home-country nationals

Employees from the home country who are on international assignment.

host-country nationals

Employees who are natives of the host country.

third-country nationals

Employees who are natives of a country other than the home country or the host country.

15.2 Managing Your International Operations

When a company expands globally, HR managers are generally responsible for ensuring that operations are staffed with the right people. There are three main ways a company can staff an international operation. First, the company can send people from its home country. These employees are often referred to as **expatriates, or home-country nationals**. Second, it can hire **host-country nationals**, natives of the host country, to do the managing. Third, it can hire **third-country nationals**, natives of a country other than the home country or the host country. Most corporations use all three for staffing their multinational operations.[10] It is important to note, however, that host countries sometimes restrict their choices by passing laws and regulations designed to employ host-country individuals. Tax incentives, tariffs, and quotas are frequently implemented by the host country to encourage local hiring.

As shown in Figure 15.3, at early stages of international expansion, organizations often send home-country nationals to establish activities (particularly in less-developed countries) and to work with local governments. This is generally very costly.

Figure 15.3	Changes in International Staffing over Time

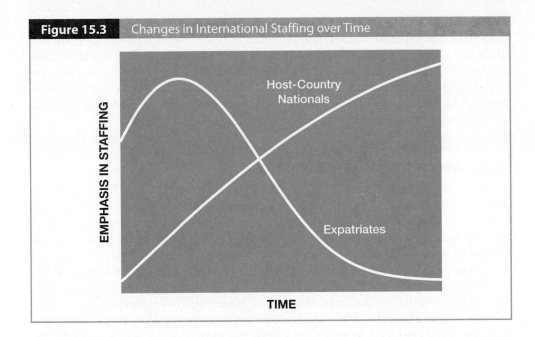

Traditionally, expatriates have received generous salaries, automobiles, full relocation services, private schooling for their children, trips home, and other perks. These services frequently end up costing more than $300,000 yearly, on average, making the cost of a typical 3-year expatriate assignment more than $1 million.

In recent years, there has also been a trend to send expatriates on shorter, project-based assignments (1 to 6 months versus 1 to 3 years) and to shift more quickly toward hiring host-country nationals. This has three main advantages:

1. Hiring local citizens is generally less costly than relocating expatriates. Local citizens also know the cultural and political landscape of the country and are often more likely to be able to gain the support of local staff members.

2. Since local governments usually want good jobs for their citizens, foreign employers may be required to hire locally.

3. Most customers want to do business with companies (and people) they perceive to be local versus foreign.

Because U.S. companies want to be viewed as true international citizens, there has also been a trend away from hiring expatriates to head up operations in foreign countries, especially European countries. ABB, Eli Lilly, and PepsiCo, which have strong regional organizations, have tended to replace their U.S. expatriate managers with local managers as quickly as possible. In addition to hiring local managers to head their foreign divisions and plants, more companies are using third-country nationals. Third-country nationals are often multilingual and already acclimated to the host country's culture—perhaps because they live in a nearby region. Thus, they are also less costly to relocate and sometimes better able to cope culturally with foreign environments.

Companies tend to continue to use expatriates only when a specific set of skills is needed or when individuals in the host country require development. Typically, expatriate assignments fail when the expatriate is selected because of his or her technical skills alone, rather than the ability to adapt to the host country. For example, U.S. managers value their time as a commodity, and therefore are more focused on productivity and efficiency. However, this kind of manager may be frustrated by—and even frustrating to—host-country nationals in countries like China, where *quanxi*, or connections, are more important than money.[11] To help their expatriates adapt in Asia and elsewhere, firms are finding it helpful to pair them with local "buddies," or host-country mentors, or even complete cultural training before departing.

15.2a Recruiting Internationally

Improved telecommunications and travel have made it easier to match up employers and employees of all kinds worldwide. For example, in 2017 we worked with Microsoft to help them improve the recruiting and connectedness of their employees located all over the world. The majority of their current and potential employees are located outside the United States. This is the case for most large corporations.

HR departments must be particularly responsive to the cultural, political, and legal environments both domestically and abroad when recruiting internationally. Companies such as Starbucks, Lockheed Martin, and Honeywell have made a special effort to create codes of conduct for employees throughout the world to ensure that standards of ethical and legal behavior are known and understood. Lockheed Martin has a strong international ethics program to ensure all decisions throughout the company are made with integrity. For example, their vision statement stresses the following factors: (a) doing what is right, (b) respecting others, and (c) performing with excellence. All employees are required to undergo business conduct and compliance training. This training helps employees deal with difficult issues related to export control, insider trading, international business practices, kickbacks and gratuities, and the Truth in Negotiations Act. The programs are offered in over 21 languages.[12]

The regulatory environment outside the United States often differs substantially. The regulations range from those that cover procedures for recruiting and screening to their working conditions, pay and incentives, and retirement provisions. In Japan, for example, criminal background checks on candidates are not allowed. In France, employees can only work 35 hours per week until overtime and rest days start to be required.[13] Virtually all countries have work permit or visa restrictions that apply to foreigners.

work permit or visa

A government document granting a foreign individual the right to seek employment.

A **work permit or visa** is a document issued by a government granting authority to a foreign individual to seek employment in that government's country. Since 9/11, getting skilled foreign workers into the United States has been difficult for companies. However, since 2017 the U.S. government has made it even more difficult for workers to get a work permit or H1B Visa. H1B Visas were created to import specialized technological and scientific talent that we don't have sufficiently available in the United States. This is particularly difficult news for companies like Google, Apple, LinkedIn, and SnapChat, who already have a difficult time finding qualified tech workers. According to one study, the United States has a shortage of about 110,000 computer science jobs annually.[14] Yet, students who come from foreign countries to attend school in the United States are finding it more difficult to get jobs with U.S. companies.

As a result, many Indian and Chinese living in the United States are being heavily recruited by companies and governments to work back in their home countries. For example, one former Microsoft employee was denied an H1B Visa and went home to India and started his own company. It's now valued at over $7 billion. That's a lot of lost tax revenue and jobs for the United States. Making matters worse, other countries have

A visa is issued to foreign individuals granting them the right to work in that country.

become less restrictive than the United States in terms of granting foreign residents citizenship and work permits. The United Kingdom, for example, gives graduates of the world's top 50 business schools an automatic right to work in the United Kingdom for a year. In addition, the European Union is contemplating introducing a "blue card" system designed to expedite the EU citizenship of talented employees.[15] Whatever the employee's destination, HR managers need to ensure that work permits and visas are applied for early in the relocation process.

In terms of recruiting at the executive level, companies use executive recruiting firms such as Heidrick & Struggles in the United States or Spencer Stuart in the United Kingdom. At lower levels, as Chapter 7 explained, companies recruiting abroad often need to advertise their firms and employment "brand" to recruits who are not familiar with it. In countries such as India and China, an employer's reputation is extremely important to candidates' families—sometimes more important than pay.

Many employers have learned that the best way to find workers in these less well-developed countries is through referrals and radio announcements because many people lack sufficient reading or writing skills. Other firms use international recruiting firms to find skilled labor abroad. As we have explained, some countries, in fact, require the employment of locals if adequate numbers of skilled people are available. Specific exceptions are sometimes granted (officially or unofficially) for contrary cases, as for Mexican farm workers in the United States and for Italian, Spanish, Greek, and Turkish workers in Germany and the Benelux countries (Belgium, the Netherlands, and Luxembourg). Foreign workers invited to perform needed labor are usually referred to as **guest workers**. Foreign workers with H2B Visas can come to the United States for a maximum of 9 months to perform temporary, nonagricultural seasonal work that is one-time only. These types of visas are often used in conjunction with recruiting workers for entry-level positions in hotels and restaurants during peak travel seasons.

guest workers
Foreign workers invited to perform needed labor.

Although hiring nonnationals can result in lower direct labor costs for a company, the indirect costs—those related to housing, language training, health services, recruitment, transportation, and so on—can be substantial. Some companies competing in industries with acute talent shortages are nonetheless finding the expenditures worthwhile. Nursing is one such industry. (See the Case Study at the end of the chapter.)[16]

Apprenticeships

A major source of trained labor in European nations is apprenticeship training programs (described in Chapter 7.) In Europe, a dual-track system of education directs a large number of youths into vocational training. The German system of apprenticeship training, one of the best in Europe, provides training for office and shop jobs under a three-way responsibility contract between the apprentice, his or her parents, and the organization. At the conclusion of their training, apprentices can work for any employer but generally receive seniority credit with the training firm if they remain in it. France has been able to draw on its "Grandes Écoles" for centuries. Created during the Renaissance to fulfill a need that universities were not meeting at the time, the Grandes Écoles educate prospective engineers up to the equivalent level of master of engineering.

Staffing Transnational Teams

transnational teams
Teams composed of members of multiple nationalities working on projects that span multiple countries.

In addition to focusing on individuals, it is also important to note that companies are increasingly using transnational teams to conduct international business. **Transnational teams** are composed of members of multiple nationalities working virtually on projects that span multiple countries. Aware that many products developed in developed economies will have a limited market in developing economies, companies such as P&G, GE, and Tata Motors have turned to transnational teams to help develop low-cost but high-quality products for the poor. For example, Tata Motors developed the Tata Nano, a car for nearly $2,000. As the cheapest car in the world, the Tata Nano was developed by a large transnational team, with suppliers in different countries designing specific parts to meet a price-sensitive threshold.[17]

Teams such as these are especially useful for performing tasks that the firm as a whole is not yet structured to accomplish. For example, they may be used to transcend the existing organizational structure to customize a strategy for different geographic regions, transfer technology from one part of the world to another, and communicate between headquarters and subsidiaries in different countries. Sometimes companies send employees on temporary assignments abroad as part of transnational teams lasting perhaps a few months. This might be done to break down cultural barriers between international divisions or disseminate new ideas and technologies to other regions. In other instances, employees are transferred for extended periods of time. Years ago, Fuji sent 15 of its most experienced engineers from Tokyo to a Xerox facility in Webster, New York. Over a 5-year period, the engineers worked with a team of U.S. engineers to develop the "world" copier. The effort led to a joint venture that has lasted for decades. Fuji-Xerox now employs approximately 10,000 people globally at 13 companies around the world.[18]

The fundamental task in forming a transnational team is assembling the right group of people who can work together effectively to accomplish the goals of the team. Many companies try to build variety into their teams in order to maximize responsiveness to the special needs of different countries. Cross-cultural training can benefit transnational teams by helping them overcome language and cultural barriers they face.

15.2b Selecting Employees Internationally

Selecting employees in a foreign country environment can be difficult. When embarking on hiring employees in a new country, a firm's international HR managers should get to know the local market and customs in hiring. This will help the firm understand what to look for in an employee. When GE first entered India, it did not realize that much of the effective hiring was done through family ties and friendship networks. Not wanting to appear biased, GE at first did not allow such practices. However, after struggling to select good recruits, GE finally incorporated peer and family referral systems into their selection practices. This led to selection of employees who stayed within the organization much longer.

To better understand the local market, there are a few things firms can do. First, international HR managers should get to know the universities, technical schools, and primary schools in the area. More than ensuring qualifications, schools provide extensive networks to future employees and provide insight on the type of hires managers would want to select. This means taking time to understand how the local schools operate. In many developing countries, higher education systems are underdeveloped and either do not provide enough future employees or employees with suitable skills. For example, Rolls-Royce and Intel have both become involved in the development of school curriculum for both managerial and engineering skill development. By partnering with local universities, Rolls-Royce and Intel offer funding and curriculum design to better prepare students for the work environment. At their own expense, these companies see such costs as investments in future employees as well as a chance to shape the skills they need to run their companies in those countries.

Second, international HR managers should develop networks in the business and government communities. Because many companies' reputations may not precede them, they must use personal networks to develop trust in the company. An international HR manager's job will not be just to select the right people that come to the office but to go out and select the right people within the community. For instance, when Unilever, a large British–Dutch consumer products company, opens up operations in a foreign environment it often becomes heavily involved in the local community by conducting community feedback meetings, local education programs, and environmental studies. The company's heavy involvement in the local environment helps to rapidly build its local reputation, which increases its knowledge of potential new hires.[19]

Finally, to effectively select employees in a local environment, international HR managers must understand the employees of the firm's competitors. As they map out and get to know key employees in competing organizations, they develop a better understanding of what to look for in other employees while building up a new pool of applicants to recruit in the future. For example, companies such as Exxon and Marriott, as well as smaller companies, will turn to employees of competing companies because they already know that these employees have the necessary skills and abilities to survive in their company. This is especially important to note, as more and more domestic companies are hiring away foreign international firms' employees, with the lure of patriotism and staying power of a local company.

Selecting Global Managers

What if an organization cannot find the appropriate talent in the local country? What if a firm is opening up operations in a foreign country but needs managers who know the ins and outs of the company or who have company specific expertise? In this case,

global manager
A manager equipped to run an international business.

organizations need to select managers from one country and move them to another. Levi Strauss has identified the following six skill categories for the **global manager**, or manager equipped to run an international business:

- The ability to seize strategic opportunities
- The ability to manage highly decentralized organizations
- An awareness of global issues
- Sensitivity to diversity issues
- Competence in interpersonal relations
- Community-building skills[20]

If a candidate for expatriation is willing to live and work in a foreign environment, an indication of his or her tolerance of cultural differences should be obtained. On the other hand, if local nationals have the technical competence to carry out the job successfully, they should be carefully considered for the job before the firm hires a domestic candidate and sends the person abroad. As we explained, most corporations realize the advantages to be gained by staffing international operations with host-country nationals wherever possible.

Selecting home-country and third-country nationals requires that more factors be considered than in selecting host-country nationals. While the latter must of course possess managerial abilities and the necessary technical skills, they have the advantage of familiarity with the physical and **cultural environment** and the language of the host country. We can break the advantages and disadvantages of hiring global managers from these three different groups.

cultural environment
The communications, religion, values and ideologies, education, and social structure of a country.

Colgate-Palmolive, Whirlpool, and Dow Chemical have further identified a set of **core skills** that they view as critical for success abroad and a set of **augmented skills** that help facilitate the efforts of expatriate managers. These two types of skills are shown in Highlights in HRM 1. Many of these skills are not significantly different from the skills managers need to succeed domestically. Although in years past the average U.S. expatriate manager was an American-born Caucasian, more companies today are seeing the advantages of assigning expatriates depending on their ethnicity. But such a decision needs to be considered carefully. For example, an Indian candidate applying for a position in India may never have actually visited the country or may not relate well to the culture. Ultimately, the candidate best qualified for the job should be sent. In the past, women were overlooked for global managerial positions—perhaps because companies believed they would fare poorly in foreign, male-dominated societies or because they believed women have less desire to go abroad. Today women comprise around 25 percent of expatriates.[21] Moreover, multiple studies show that women expatriates perform just as well as men.[22]

core skills
Skills considered critical to an employee's success abroad.

augmented skills
Skills helpful in facilitating the efforts of expatriate managers.

Several steps are involved in selecting individuals for an international assignment, and the sequencing of these activities can make a big difference:

Step 1: Begin with self-selection. Employees should begin the process years in advance by thinking about their career goals and how interested they are in working abroad. Companies such as EDS and Deloitte give their employees self-selection instruments to help them consider the pros and cons of international assignments. Performance Program Inc.'s Overseas Assignment Inventory and the International Mobility Assessment test, developed by Tucker International, are two such tests.

Step 2: Create a candidate pool. After employees have self-selected, organizations can build a database of candidates for international assignments. Information in the database might include availability, languages, country preferences, and skills.

Skills of Expatriate Managers

Core Skills

- Experience
- Decision making
- Resourcefulness
- Adaptability
- Cultural sensitivity
- Team building
- Maturity

Augmented Skills

- Technical skills
- Negotiation skills
- Strategic thinking
- Delegation skills
- Change management

Step 3: Assess candidates' core skills. From the short list of potential candidates, managers can assess each candidate in terms of their technical and managerial readiness relative to the needs of the assignment.

Step 4: Assess candidates' augmented skills and attributes. As Figure 15.4 shows, expatriate selection decisions are typically made based upon the technical competence of candidates as well as their professional and international experience. In addition, organizations are beginning to pay more attention to an individual's ability to adapt to different environments. How well a person adjusts depends on his or her flexibility, emotional maturity and stability, empathy for the culture, language and communication skills, resourcefulness and initiative, prior international experience, exposure to different cultures, and diplomatic skills. If these skills are lacking, no amount of technical competency is likely to result in a successful assignment.[23]

Figure 15.4	Expatriate Selection Criteria

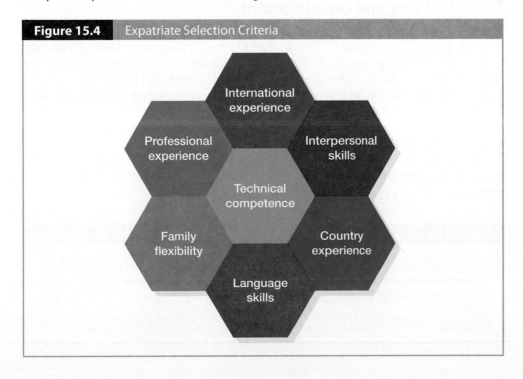

failure rates
The percentage of expatriates who do not perform satisfactorily.

Even companies that believe they have selected the best candidates frequently experience high expatriate **failure rates**. Figure 15.5 shows the major causes of assignment failure. Poor cultural fit is a major reason why assignments fail. For example, although China is among the easiest countries to which to attract Western expatriates, it is also one of the hardest places for them to succeed because the country's culture is so different.

A lack of expatriate support from headquarters is another major cause. Expatriates often describe themselves as "out of sight and out of mind." This highlights the importance of headquarters maintaining close contact with them to see how they are faring.

Yet another big factor is a spouse's inability to adjust to his or her new surroundings. Today, more companies are preparing families by offering them cultural and language training. ARAMCO, a Saudi Arabian corporation, has such a program. The program includes practical information such as how to deal with Saudi Arabia's transportation systems, where to shop, day-to-day finances, and an explanation of the differences between the beliefs and customs of Saudis and people from other cultures.[24]

There are number of ways to improve the success of expatriate assignments. Ultimately the expatriate must find a way to adjust to the demands of their company, the country environment, and their family needs. Employees who share a common vision with the company are willing to undergo difficulties for the organization. Employees who take time to understand the culture and market in which they are operating will be better able to cope with unexpected changes and demands. Finally, employees who have family members that are supportive and interested in an overseas assignment are much more successful in their international assignments. As a result, expatriates stand a greater chance of being able to successfully adjust to their international positions. See Figure 15.6 to examine how these three factors must be aligned to ensure expatriate adjustment. In addition, training and development for both expatriates and their spouses can have a big impact.

15.2c Training and Development

Although companies try to recruit and select the very best people to send abroad, once they are selected, it is critical to their success to provide them with training. Not only is this type of training important for expatriate managers, it is also important for the foreign employees they will ultimately supervise. For example, to know and understand how the Japanese or Chinese negotiate contracts or how business people from Latin America view the enforcement of meeting times can help expatriate managers and their employees deal with each other more successfully. The biggest mistake managers can make is to assume that people are the same everywhere.

Apart from developing talent for overseas assignments, most companies have found that good training programs also help them attract the employees they need from host countries.

Figure 15.5   Causes of Expatriate Assignment Failure

- Family adjustment
- Lifestyle issues
- Work adjustment
- Bad selection
- Poor performance
- Other opportunities arise
- Business reasons
- Repatriation issues

Figure 15.6	Expatriate Adjustment Factors

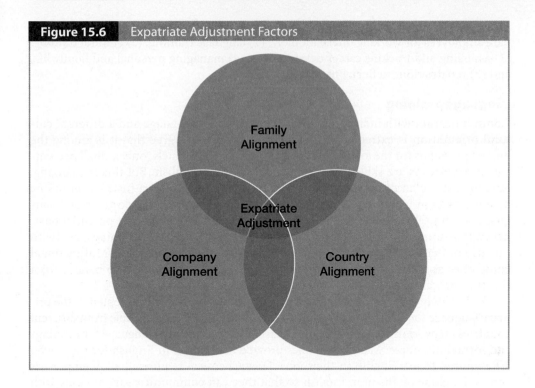

15.2d Content of Training Programs

Lack of training is one of the principal causes of failure among employees working internationally. Those working internationally need to know as much as possible about (1) the country where they are going, (2) that country's culture, and (3) the history, values, and dynamics of their own organizations. Figure 15.7 gives an overview of what one needs to study for an international assignment. In many cases, the employee and his or her family can obtain a great deal of general information about the host country, including its culture, geography, social and political history, climate, food, and so on, via the Internet, books, and podcasts.

Figure 15.7	Preparing for an International Assignment

To prepare for an international assignment, one should become acquainted with the following aspects of the host country:

1. Social and business etiquette
2. History and folklore
3. Current affairs, including relations between the host country and the United States
4. Cultural values and priorities
5. Geography, especially its major cities
6. Sources of pride and great achievements of the culture
7. Religion and the role of religion in daily life
8. Political structure and current players
9. Practical matters such as currency, transportation, time zones, and hours of business
10. The language

However, at least five essential elements of training and development programs prepare employees for working internationally: (1) language training, (2) cultural training, (3) assessing and tracking career development, (4) managing personal and family life, and (5) repatriation—a final, but critical, step.[25]

Language Training

Communication with individuals who have a different language and a different cultural orientation is extremely difficult. Most executives agree that it is among the biggest problems for the foreign business traveler. Unfortunately, only a small percentage of Americans are skilled in a language other than English. But this is changing. Students who plan careers in international business should start instruction in one or more foreign languages as early as possible. Some companies do their own language training. When ARCO Products, a U.S. firm, began exploring potential business opportunities in China, its HR department set up a language training class (with the help of Berlitz International) in conversational Mandarin Chinese. Multinational companies as well as businesses that outsource work abroad stand to benefit from this type of training.

Fortunately for most Americans, English is almost universally accepted as the primary language for international business. Particularly when many people from different countries are working together, English is usually the designated language for meetings and formal discourse. Many companies provide instruction in English for those who are required to use English in their jobs. Dow Chemical requires that all employees across the globe be fluent in English so that they can communicate more easily with one another. Even with an interpreter, much is missed. The following list illustrates the complexities of the communication process in international business.

1. In England, to "table" a subject means to put it on the table for present discussion. In the United States, it means to postpone discussion of a subject, perhaps indefinitely.

2. In the United States, information flows to a manager. In cultures in which authority is centralized (such as Europe and South America), the manager must take the initiative to seek out the information.

3. Getting straight to the point is uniquely American. Many Europeans, Arabs, Asians, and others resent the directness of American-style communication.

4. In Japan, there are 16 ways to avoid saying "no."

5. When something is "inconvenient" to the Chinese, it is most likely downright impossible.

6. In most foreign countries, expressions of anger are unacceptable; in some places, public display of anger is taboo.

7. The typical American must learn to treat silences as "communication spaces" and not interrupt them.

8. In general, Americans must learn to avoid gesturing with the hand. A couple of cases in point: When former President Richard Nixon traveled to Brazil in the 1950s, he waved and gave the "A-OK" sign to the country's citizens. But in Brazil, the gesture is considered obscene and insulting. Nonverbal communication training can help businesspeople avoid some of these communication pitfalls. Highlights in HRM 2 illustrates that some of our everyday gestures have very different meanings in other cultures.[26]

Nonverbal Communications in Different Cultures

Calling a Waiter

In the United States, a common way to call a waiter is to point upward with the forefinger. In Asia, a raised forefinger is used to call a dog or other animal. To get the attention of a Japanese waiter, extend the arm upward, palm down, and flutter the fingers. In Africa, knock on the table. In the Middle East, clap your hands.

Insults

In Arab countries, showing the soles of your shoes is an insult. Also, an Arab may insult a person by holding a hand in front of the person's face.

A-Okay Gesture

In the United States, using the index finger and the thumb to form an "o" while extending the rest of the fingers is a gesture meaning okay or fine. In Japan, however, the same gesture means money. Nodding your head in agreement if a Japanese uses this sign during your discussion could mean you are expected to give him some cash. In Brazil the same gesture is considered a seductive sign to a woman and an insult to a man.

Eye Contact

In Western and Arab cultures, prolonged eye contact with a person is acceptable. In Japan, on the other hand, holding the gaze of another is considered rude. The Japanese generally focus on a person's neck or tie knot.

Handshake and Touching

In most countries, the handshake is an acceptable form of greeting. In the Middle East and other Islamic countries, however, the left hand is considered the toilet hand and is thought to be unclean. Only the right hand should be used for touching.

Scratching the Head

In most Western countries, scratching the head is interpreted as lack of understanding or confusion. To the Japanese, it indicates anger.

Indicating "No"

In most parts of the world, shaking the head left and right is the most common way to say no. But among the Arabs, in parts of Greece, Yugoslavia, Bulgaria, and Turkey, a person says no by tossing the head up, sometimes clicking the tongue at the same time. In Japan, no can also be said by moving the right hand back and forth.

Agreement

In addition to saying yes, Africans will hold an open palm perpendicular to the ground and pound it with the other fist to emphasize "agreed." Arabs will clasp their hands together, forefingers pointed outward, to indicate agreement.

Source: S. Hawkins, *International Management* 38, no. 9 (September 1983): 49. Copyright 1983 by Reed Business Information Ltd. Reprinted with permission.

Cultural Training

Cross-cultural differences represent one of the most elusive aspects of international business, but successfully done, it tends to improve the satisfaction and success of expatriates and their employers.[27] Brazilians tend to perceive Americans as always in a hurry, serious, reserved, and methodical, whereas the Japanese view Americans as relaxed, friendly, and impulsive. Why do these different perceptions exist, and how do they affect the way we do business across borders? People's attitudes and behaviors are influenced, in large part, by the culture and society in which they have been educated and trained. Each culture has its expectations for the roles of managers and employees. An American manager in Asia once complained that meetings held in his foreign place of employment accomplished nothing. He was used to arriving at a final decision during meetings. But to his Asian coworkers, meetings were solely a place in which to share ideas. Decisions were to be made before or after the meeting. Being successful abroad depends on a person's ability to understand the way things are normally done and to recognize that changes cannot be made abruptly without considerable resistance, and possibly antagonism, on the part of local nationals.

A wealth of data from cross-cultural studies reveals that nations tend to cluster along certain cultural dimensions such as their work goals, values, needs, and attitudes toward work. Using data from eight comprehensive studies of cultural differences, Simcha Ronen and Oded Shenkar have grouped countries into the clusters shown in Figure 15.8. Ronen and Shenkar point out that while evidence for the grouping of countries into Anglo, Germanic, Nordic, Latin European, and Latin American clusters appears to be quite strong, clusters encompassing the Far Eastern and Arab countries are ill-defined and require further research, as do clusters of countries classified as independent. Many areas, such as Africa, have not been studied much at all. It should also

Figure 15.8 A Synthesis of Country Clusters

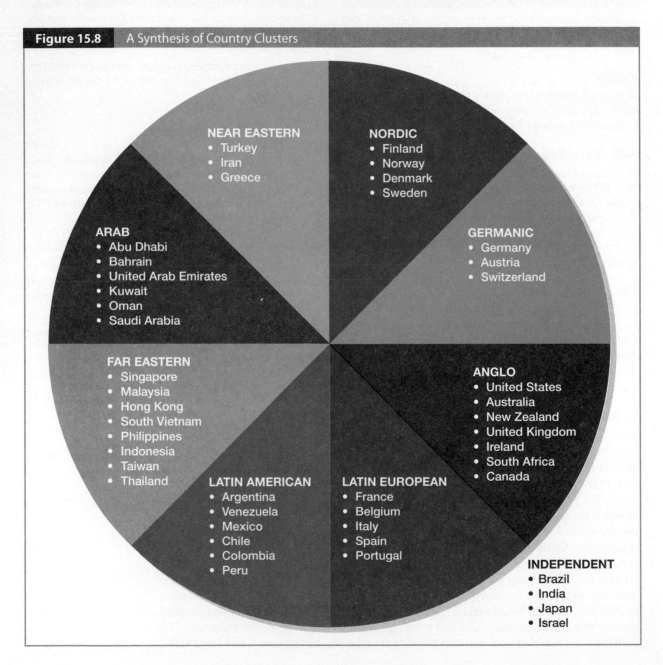

be noted that the clusters presented in Figure 15.8 do not include Russia and the former satellites of the Soviet Union. Those countries, if added to the figure, would likely fall between the Near Eastern and Nordic categories.

Studying cultural differences can help managers identify and understand work attitudes and motivation in other cultures. When compared with the Japanese, for example, Americans may feel little loyalty to their organizations. In Japan, employees are more likely to feel a strong loyalty to their company, although this has been changing. Japanese companies no longer universally guarantee an employee a job for life, and layoff decisions are increasingly being made based on merit, not seniority—a practice unthinkable in the country in the past. Latin Americans tend to view themselves as working not only for a particular company, but also for an individual manager. Thus managers in Latin American countries can encourage performance only by using personal influence and working through individual members of a group. In the United States, competition has been the name of the game; in Japan, Taiwan, and other Asian countries, cooperation is more the underlying philosophy.[28]

One of the important dimensions of leadership, whether in international or domestic situations, is the degree to which managers invite employee participation in decision making. While it is difficult to find hard data on employee participation across different countries, careful observers report that American managers are about in the middle on a continuum of autocratic to democratic decision-making styles. Scandinavian and Australian managers also appear to be in the middle. South American and European managers, especially those from France, Germany, and Italy, are toward the autocratic end of the continuum. Japanese managers are at the most participatory end. Because Far Eastern cultures and religions tend to emphasize harmony, group decision-making predominates there.[29]

Assessing and Tracking Career Development

International assignments provide some definite developmental and career advantages. For example, working abroad tends to increase a person's responsibilities and influence within the corporation. In addition, it provides a person with a set of experiences that are uniquely beneficial to both the individual and the firm. In this way, international assignments enhance a person's understanding of the global marketplace and offer the opportunity to work on a project important to the organization.[30] Furthermore, research shows that international assignments increase a person's creative problem-solving skills and receptivity to new ideas.[31]

In recent years, U.S. companies have become a melting pot of CEOs. Increasingly, foreign-born CEOs are making up the Fortune 500 top slots. Executive recruiters say corporate boards are asking for leaders with experience outside of the United States. Foreign-born expatriates tend to be greater risk takers and harder workers. They are people who have left their home countries and communities to set off on their own.[32]

To maximize the career benefits of a managerial assignment, a candidate should ask two key questions before accepting a foreign post.

1. Do the organization's senior executives view the firm's international business as a critical part of their operation?
2. Within top management, how many executives have a foreign-service assignment in their background, and do they feel it important for one to have overseas experience?

Managing Personal and Family Life

culture shock

Perpetual stress experienced by people who settle overseas.

As noted previously, one of the most frequent causes of an employee's failure to complete an international assignment is personal and family stress. **Culture shock**—a disorientation that causes perpetual stress—is experienced by people who settle overseas for extended periods. The stress is caused by hundreds of jarring and disorienting incidents such as being unable to communicate, having trouble getting the telephone to work, being unable to read the street signs, and a myriad of other everyday matters that are no problem at home. Soon minor frustrations become catastrophic events, and one feels helpless and drained, emotionally and physically.

In Chapter 5, we explained that more and more employers are assisting two-career couples in terms of finding suitable employment in the same location. To accommodate dual-career partnerships, some employers offer spouses career and life planning counseling, continuing education, intercompany networks to identify job openings in other companies, job-hunting or fact-finding trips, and help securing work permits abroad.

Repatriation

repatriation

The process of transition for an employee home from an international assignment.

An increasing number of companies such as Monsanto, 3M, EDS, and Verizon are developing programs specifically designed to facilitate **repatriation**—that is, helping employees make the transition back home. Repatriation programs are designed to prepare employees for adjusting to life at home (which at times can be more difficult than adjusting to a foreign assignment).

Unfortunately, not all companies have career development programs designed for repatriating employees or do not do an effective job of it. Employees often lament that their organizations are vague about repatriation, their new roles within the company, and their career progression. In many cases, employees abroad have learned how to run an entire international operation—or at least significant parts of it. When they return home however, their responsibilities are often significantly diminished. Some surveys have found that up to 60 percent of expatriates believed their careers had not advanced

A foreign assignment can be an excellent step in a person's career. But to be successful, expatriates often need extensive training on their host countries' languages, cultural differences, business practices, and other related issues.

View Stock/Alamy

Repatriation Checklist

Before they go:

- Make sure there is a clear need for the international assignment. Develop a clear set of objectives and expectations and time frames in which they should be met.
- Make sure that your selection procedures are valid. Select the employee and also look at and involve the employee's family.
- Provide (or fund) language and cultural training for the employee and the employee's family.
- Offer counseling and career assistance for the spouse.
- Establish career planning systems that reward international assignments and lead to promotion and knowledge sharing.
- Jointly establish a developmental plan that focuses on the goal to be achieved.
- Tie performance objectives to the achievement of the goal.
- Identify mentors who can be a liaison and support person from home.
- Keep communications open so that the expatriate is aware of job openings and opportunities.

- Arrange for frequent visits back home (for the employee and the family). Make certain they do not lose touch with friends and relatives.

When they come back home:

- Throw a "welcome home" party and arrange for a meeting with other former expatriates.
- Offer counseling to ease the transition.
- Arrange conferences and presentations to make certain that knowledge and skills acquired away from home are identified and disseminated.
- Set up an expatriate database to help other employees who go abroad later.
- Get feedback from the employee and the family about how well the organization handled the repatriation process.

Sources: Adapted from Bennet & Associates, Price Waterhouse, and Charlene Marmer Solomon, "Repatriation Planning Checklist," *Personnel Journal* 14, no. 1 (January 1995): 32; Yamasaki, Yukiko. "Why Do Some Employees Readjust to Their Home Organizations Better Than Others? Job Demands-Resources Model of Repatriation Adjustment" (2016); Charlene Marmer Solomon, "Global HR: Repatriation Planning," *Workforce* (2001), special supplement: 22–23.

after returning home.[33] It is also not at all uncommon for employees to return home after a few years to find that there is *no* position for them in the firm and that they no longer know anyone who can help them—their longtime colleagues have moved to different departments or even different companies. This frequently leaves the repatriated employee feeling alienated. Wondering about their future also creates stress for them and their families while they are abroad.

Even when employees are successfully repatriated, their companies often do not fully utilize the knowledge, understanding, and skills developed on their assignments. This hurts the employee, of course, but it also hurts the firm's chances of utilizing the employee's expertise to gain a competitive advantage. Not surprisingly, expatriates frequently leave their companies within a year or two of coming home. Monsanto's repatriation program is designed not only to smooth the employee's return to the home organization but to ensure that the expatriate's knowledge and experience are fully used. To do so, returning expatriates get the chance to showcase their new knowledge in debriefing sessions. Some companies also create databases of expatriates to help other employees who go abroad later.[34] Of course, if a firm is able to retain its current repatriates, it will have better success recruiting future expatriates. A repatriation checklist is shown in Highlights in HRM 3.

15.3 Compensation

One of the most complex areas of international HRM is compensation. Different countries have different norms for employee compensation. For Americans, while nonfinancial incentives such as prestige, independence, and influence may be motivators, money is likely to be the driving force. Other cultures are more likely to emphasize respect, family, job security, a satisfying personal life, social acceptance, advancement, or power. Since there are many alternatives to money, the rule is to match the reward with the values of the culture. In individualistic cultures, such as the United States, pay plans often focus on individual performance and achievement. However, in collectively oriented cultures such as Japan and Taiwan, pay plans focus more on internal equity and personal needs.[35]

In general, a guiding philosophy for designing pay systems might be "think globally and act locally." That is, executives should normally try to create a pay plan that supports the overall strategic intent of the organization but provides enough flexibility to customize particular policies and programs to meet the needs of employees in specific locations. After a brief discussion of compensation practices for host-country employees and managers, we will focus on the problems of compensating expatriates.

15.3a Compensation of Host-Country Employees

As shown in Figure 15.9, minimum wages vary dramatically from country to country. Minimum wage workers in manufacturing positions in Luxembourg make over $22,000 per year. By contrast, in Mexico, minimum wage workers earn less than $2,000 per year, on average. Host-country employees are generally paid on the basis of productivity, time spent on the job, or a combination of these factors. In industrialized countries, pay is generally by the hour; in developing countries, pay is generally by the day. The piece-rate method is quite common. In some countries, including Japan, seniority is an important element in determining employees' pay rates. In Italy, Japan, and some other countries, it is customary to add semiannual or annual lump sum payments equal to 1 or 2 months' pay. These payments are not considered profit sharing but an integral part of the basic pay package. Profit sharing is legally required for certain industry categories in Mexico, Peru, Pakistan, India, and Egypt among the developing countries and in France among the industrialized countries.

Employee benefits can range dramatically from country to country as well. In France, for example, benefits comprise a much higher proportion of people's pay than they do in the United States. In contrast to 10 vacation days in the United States, workers in the United Kingdom, France, and the Netherlands receive about 25 days of paid vacation. Workers in Sweden and Austria receive 30 days. Whereas in the United States most benefits are awarded to employees by employers, in other industrialized countries most of them are legislated or ordered by governments.[36]

Because the largest cost for most companies is labor, it plays a prime role in international HR decision making. However, some people believe that companies are overcapitalizing on worldwide compensation differences. Many firms have generated bad press for charging hundreds of dollars for their individual products while the people who make them earned only a few cents on the dollar. This has led to international political protests, as was mentioned in Chapter 1, and pressure on firms to exercise greater global social responsibility.

Figure 15.9	Hourly Wages in Different Countries

Dataset: Real minimum wages

	Pay period	Annual
	Unit	Dollar
	Time	2016
Country		
Luxembourg		22,836.1
Netherlands		22,209.8
Australia		21,967.2
Belgium		21,170.2
Germany		20,847.4
France		20,413.6
New Zealand		19,346.4
Ireland		18,942.8
United Kingdom		17,568.3
Canada		16,792.4
Japan		15,292.1
United States		14,892.1
Slovenia		14,520.8
Korea		14,440.9
Israel		13,059.7
Spain		12,317.4
Turkey		12,074.8
Poland		11,977.5
Greece		11,492.1
Portugal		10,941.1
Costa Rica		10,859.7
Hungary		9,155.1
Slovak Republic		8,980.0
Estonia		8,595.0
Czech Republic		8,399.1
Lithuania		8,319.6
Latvia		7,829.6
Chile		6,998.3
Colombia		6,950.2
Brazil		4,753.6
Russian Federation		3,199.2
Mexico		1,895.7

Data extracted on 03 May 2017 00:00 UTC (GMT)
Source: OECD.stat (Data are calculated in terms of purchasing power parity [PPP].)

Student protesters put pressure on University of Southern California to stop using sweatshop labor in the manufacturing of USC school apparel.

AP Images/Lee Jin-man

Nike is just one example of a company that has experienced the pressure from protesting groups first hand. They soon realized they couldn't afford to ignore the problem any longer. The bad press finally took a toll on Nike's bottom line. As a result, Nike now monitors all its partner factories to ensure that workers are not underage, that pay is competitive, and that working conditions are compliant with international standards. Over 100 full-time staff are dedicated to monitoring these partner factories. While this costs Nike around $11 million per year, they have unexpectedly realized additional cost savings as their monitoring staff are also able to help the factories with streamlining the work processes, training managers, and decreasing corrupt practices by the factories.[37]

15.3b Compensation of Host-Country Managers

In the past, the compensation of host-country managers has been based on local salary levels. Today, however, more companies are offering their host-country employees a full range of training programs, benefits, and pay comparable with their domestic employees back in the country of origin but adjusted for local differences. These programs are known as **global compensation system**.

global compensation system

A centralized pay system whereby host-country employees are offered a full range of training programs, benefits, and pay comparable with a firm's domestic employees but adjusted for local differences.

According to a survey by the HR consulting firm Watson Wyatt, companies are split evenly as to whether they have central (global) compensation systems or decentralized (local) systems. Companies with centralized systems report having higher effectiveness and satisfaction levels with their compensation systems, and more companies are saying they are moving toward centralized systems. Unilever, for example, used to leave the compensation arrangements largely to the boss of a region or a big country. Now brand managers in different countries increasingly compare notes so they see potential discrepancies based on market differences and expatriate assignments. So, the company moved from a narrow grading structure to five global work levels.[38]

15.3c Compensation of Expatriate Managers

If the assignment is going to be successful, the expatriate's compensation plan must be competitive, cost-effective, motivating, fair, easy to understand, consistent with international financial management, relatively easy to administer, and simple to communicate. To be effective, an international compensation program must:

1. Provide an incentive to leave the United States
2. Allow for maintaining an American standard of living
3. Provide for security in countries that are politically unstable or present personal dangers
4. Include provisions for good health care
5. Reimburse the foreign taxes the employee is likely to have to pay (in addition to having to pay domestic taxes) and help him or her with tax forms and filing
6. Provide for the education of the employee's children abroad, if necessary
7. Allow for maintaining relationships with family, friends, and business associates via trips home and other communication technologies
8. Facilitate the expatriate's reentry back home when the assignment is finished.
9. Be in writing[39]

For short-term assignments, usually those that are project based, expatriates are frequently given per diem (per day) compensation. These managers might reside in hotels and service apartments instead of leasing houses. They are also less likely to bring their family members with them. The assignment becomes more like a commuting assignment in which the expatriate spends the week in the host country and returns home on the weekend.

For longer-term assignments, there are two basic types of compensation systems. The first is **home-based pay**, based on the **balance sheet approach**, a system designed to equalize the purchasing power of employees at comparable positions living overseas and in the home country and to provide incentives to offset qualitative differences between assignment locations.[40] The balance sheet approach generally comprises the following steps:

Step 1: Calculate base pay. Begin with the home-based gross income, including bonuses. Deduct taxes, Social Security, and pension contributions.

Step 2: Figure cost-of-living adjustment (COLA). Add a cost-of-living adjustment to the base pay. Typically, companies do not subtract when the international assignment has a lower cost of living. Instead, they allow the expatriate to benefit from the negative differential. Often a housing allowance is added in here as well.

Step 3: Add incentive premiums. General mobility premiums and hardship premiums compensate expatriates for separation from family, friends, and domestic support systems; usually 15 percent of base salary, although in recent years, some companies have reduced this amount. Oftentimes incentive premiums are paid for hazardous duty or harsh conditions the expatriate might experience while abroad. Expatriates who locate to war zones, for example, can sometimes earn three times their base salary.

Step 4: Add assistance programs. These additions are often used to cover added costs such as moving and storage, automobile, and education expenses.

home-based pay
Pay based on an expatriate's home country's compensation practices.

balance sheet approach
A compensation system designed to match the purchasing power in a person's home country.

The differentials element is intended to correct for the higher costs of overseas goods and services so that in relation to their domestic peers expatriates neither gain purchasing power nor lose it. It involves a myriad of calculations to arrive at a total differential figure, but in general, as we have said, the cost typically runs between three and five times the home-country salary. Fortunately, employers do not have to do extensive research to find comparative data. They typically rely on data published quarterly by the U.S. State Department for use in establishing allowances to compensate U.S. civilian employees for costs and hardships related to assignments abroad.

Recently, **split pay** plans have become popular among companies. Under a split pay system, expatriates are given a portion of their pay in the local currency to cover their day-to-day expenses. The rest of their pay is distributed in their home currency to safeguard their earnings should changes in foreign exchange rates or inflation adversely affect their pay.

Another type of compensation system is **host-based pay**. Companies are under pressure to move expatriates to host-based pay because it is generally less costly. Host-based pay is compensation that is equivalent to that earned by employees in the country where the expatriate is assigned. This process is called **localization**. When an employee is localized, his or her compensation is set on par with local standards and practices. Incentive premiums are generally phased out, and the employee pays only local taxes and falls under the social benefit programs established by the government of the host country.

Usually the decision to localize an employee depends on whether he or she will ultimately remain abroad or return home. In many companies, the decision depends on whether the employee or the employer is the driving force behind the localization. An expatriate employee with a strong desire to remain in the host country beyond the planned length of assignment (perhaps because he or she married a local or has simply fallen in love with the country) is likely to be more amenable to localization.

split pay
A system whereby expatriates are given a portion of their pay in the local currency to cover their day-to-day expenses and a portion of their pay in their home currency to safeguard their earnings from changes in inflation or foreign exchange rates.

host-based pay
Expatriate pay comparable to that earned by employees in a host country.

localization
Adapting pay and other compensation benefits to match that of a particular country.

15.3d Performance Appraisal

As we noted earlier, individuals frequently accept international assignments because they know that they can acquire skills and experiences that will make them more valuable to their companies. Frequently, however, it can be difficult for the home office to evaluate the performance of employees working abroad. Even the notion of performance evaluation is indicative of a U.S. management style that focuses on the individual, which can cause problems in Asian countries such as China, Japan, and Korea and Eastern European countries such as Hungary and the Czech Republic. Performance appraisal problems can contribute to failure rates among expatriates and actually derail an individual's career rather than enhance it.[41]

Who Should Appraise Performance?

In many cases, an individual working internationally has at least two allegiances: one to his or her home country (the office that made the assignment) and the other to the host country in which the employee is currently working. Superiors in each location frequently have different information about the employee's performance and may also have very different expectations about what constitutes good performance. For these reasons, the multirater (360-degree) appraisal discussed in Chapter 8 is popular among global firms. There are exceptions, however. For example, Thai workers do not see it as their business to evaluate their bosses, and Thai managers do not think subordinates are in any way qualified to assess them. Before implementing a different appraisal process, HR managers need to understand how the process is likely to be received in the host country.[42]

The notion of individual performance evaluation reflects a U.S. management style divergent from the norms of Eastern European and Asian countries.

©Rob Marmion/Shutterstock.com

Home versus Host-Country Evaluations

Domestic managers who have not worked abroad are frequently unable to understand an expatriate's or host-country manager's experiences, value these employees, or accurately measure their contribution to the organization. Geographical distances create communication problems for expatriates and home-country managers, although e-mail, instant messaging, and other HR information systems technologies have begun to close the gap.[43] Still, local managers with daily contact with the person are more likely to have an accurate picture of his or her performance. Host-country evaluations can sometimes be problematic.

Even if the formal appraisal is conducted in the home office and promotion, and pay and other administrative decisions are made there, most HR experts agree that performance evaluations should try to balance the two sources of appraisal information. If there is much concern about cultural bias, it may be possible to have people of the same nationality as the expatriate conduct the appraisal.

Performance Criteria

Because expatriate assignments are so costly, many HR managers are increasingly under pressure to calculate the return on investment of these assignments. What did the firm get for the million dollars it spent to send an expatriate abroad? Has the expatriate achieved the goals set forth in the assignment in the appropriate time frame? Obviously, the goals and responsibilities inherent in the job assignment are among the most important criteria used to evaluate an individual's performance, and different goals necessitate measuring different criteria. The criteria are tied to the various reasons employees were sent abroad in the first place—whether it was part of a goal to transfer technical skills or best practices, as a result of a merger or new division, to improve a division's financial performance, or to develop managerial talent.

There are five steps related to calculating the ROI of an assignment:

1. Defining the assignment's objectives
2. Agreeing on the quantifiable measurements for the assignment
3. Developing an equation that converts qualitative behavior into quantifiable measurements
4. Evaluating the expatriate's performance against these measurements
5. Calculating the ROI (This can be a complex cost accounting or a simple calculation to see if the expatriate covered the cost of keeping them on assignment.)

Companies also look at how well the total cost of the assignment was managed, taking into account any tax efficiencies and whether the right mix of expatriates, third-country nationals, and locals were used to minimize the assignment's costs.[44] The danger with ROI calculations, however, is that there is a temptation to resort to using "easy" criteria such as productivity, profits, and market share to measure an expatriate's performance. These criteria may be valid, but they are still deficient if they do not capture the full range of an expatriate's responsibility. Other, more subtle factors should be considered as well. Leadership development, for example, involves a much longer-term value proposition. In many cases, an expatriate is an ambassador for the company, and a significant part of the job is cultivating relationships with citizens of the host country.

Providing Feedback

Performance feedback in an international setting is clearly a two-way street. Although the home-country and host-country superiors may tell an expatriate how well he or she is doing, it is also important for expatriates to provide feedback regarding the support they are receiving, the obstacles they face, and the suggestions they have about the assignment. More than in almost any other job situation, expatriates are in the very best position to evaluate their own performance.

In addition to ongoing feedback, an expatriate should have a debriefing interview immediately on returning home from an international assignment. These repatriation interviews serve several purposes.

1. They help expatriates reestablish old ties with the home organization and may prove to be important for setting new career paths.
2. The interview can address technical issues related to the job assignment itself.
3. The interview can address general issues regarding the company's overseas commitments, such as how relationships between the home and host countries should be handled.
4. The interview can be very useful for documenting insights an individual has about the region. These insights can then be incorporated into training programs for future expatriates. However, if the learning is not shared, then each new expatriate to a region may have to go through the same cycle of adjustment.[45]

See Figure 15.10 to understand the pros and cons of using expatriates, host-county nationals, or third-country nationals to manage your overseas operations.

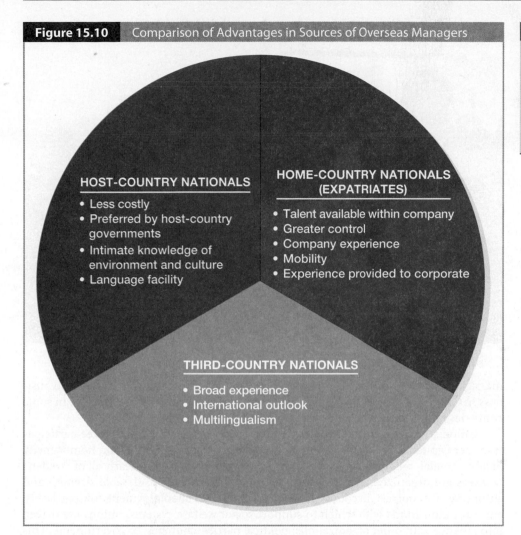

Figure 15.10 Comparison of Advantages in Sources of Overseas Managers

HOST-COUNTRY NATIONALS
- Less costly
- Preferred by host-country governments
- Intimate knowledge of environment and culture
- Language facility

HOME-COUNTRY NATIONALS (EXPATRIATES)
- Talent available within company
- Greater control
- Company experience
- Mobility
- Experience provided to corporate

THIRD-COUNTRY NATIONALS
- Broad experience
- International outlook
- Multilingualism

LO 4

Do you think there should be some international standard for labor rights? If so, what should that standard be and how should it be enforced?

15.4 Analyzing the International Labor Environment

A country's labor environment plays a large role in international business and HR decisions. As we have said, wages and benefits vary dramatically across the world as do safety, child, and other legal regulations. In many countries, the regulation of labor contracts is profound and extensive. Labor unions around the world differ significantly as well. Differences exist not only in the collective bargaining process, but also in the political-legal conditions.

For example, the EU prohibits discrimination against workers in unions, but in many other countries, including countries in Central America and Asia, labor unions are illegal. China has only one union, the All-China Federation of Trade Unions (ACFTU), a Communist Party institution that for decades has aligned itself more closely with

While employees at Walmart and Sam's Club in China have little bargaining power, being part of the ACFTU gives them a collective sense of identity.

management than workers. As Walmart discovered, Western firms that want to do business in China have to reach collective bargaining agreements with the ACFTU. In some countries, only workers at larger firms are allowed to organize.[46]

Union strength depends on many factors, such as the level of employee participation, per capita labor income, mobility between management and labor, homogeneity of labor (racial, religious, social class), and unemployment levels. Nearly all of Sweden's workers are organized, giving the unions in this country considerable strength and autonomy. By contrast, in countries with relatively high unemployment, low pay levels, and no union funds with which to support social welfare systems, unions are driven into alliance with other organizations: political parties, churches, or governments. This is in marked contrast to the United States, where the union selected by the majority of employees bargains only with the employer, not with other institutions. By contrast, the unions in many European countries (such as Sweden) have a great deal of political power and are often allied with a particular political party. When employers in these countries deal with unions, they are, in effect, dealing indirectly with governments.

In a number of countries, however, including Japan, Germany, New Zealand, and the United Kingdom, unions have been losing some of their power. Ironically, the power of the unions to gain high wages and enforce rigid labor rules has been blamed for hurting competitiveness, particularly in European countries. Laws make it difficult to fire European employees, so workers are hired only sparingly. Unemployment benefits are very generous, so people tend to remain unemployed for longer rather than seek work.

15.4a Collective Bargaining in Other Countries

We saw in Chapter 14 how the collective bargaining process is typically carried out in companies operating in the United States. When we look at other countries, we find that the process can vary widely, especially with regard to the role of government.

Collective bargaining can take place at the firm, local, or national levels. In Australia and New Zealand for most of the twentieth century, labor courts had the authority to impose wages and other employment conditions on a broad range of firms (many of which were not even privy to the suits brought before the courts). In the United Kingdom and France, the government intervenes in all aspects of collective bargaining. Government involvement is only natural where parts of industry are nationalized.

In developing countries, the governments commonly have representatives present during bargaining sessions to ensure that unions with relatively uneducated leaders are not disadvantaged in bargaining with skilled management representatives. Still, in these countries a union may do little more than attempt to increase wages and leave the rest of the employment contract unchanged. In more-developed countries, goals related to other aspects of the employment relationship, such as workweek lengths, safety requirements, and grievance procedures, are more likely to be pursued.

15.4b International Labor Organizations

The most active of the international union organizations has been the International Trade Union Confederation (ITUC), which has its headquarters in Brussels. The ITUC is a confederation of 311 national trade union centers, representing 176 million trade union members in 162 countries and territories. The ITUC's mission is to promote worker rights and interests through international cooperation between trade unions, campaigning, and advocacy with governments and global institutions.[47]

Another active and influential organization is the International Labour Organization (ILO), a specialized agency of the United Nations created in 1919. The ILO perhaps has had the greatest impact on the rights of workers throughout the world. It promotes the rights of workers to organize, the eradication of forced and child labor, and the elimination of discrimination. The organization has been effective because it involves nation-states as well as workers and their employers. Agenda 2030 for Sustainable Development places decent work for all at the heart of the ILO's current initiative.[48]

Around the world, collective bargaining processes vary widely. The ILO and other international labor organizations promote the rights of workers to organize.

AP Images/Lee Jin-man

15.4c Labor Participation in Management

In many European countries, provisions for employee representation are established by law. An employer may be legally required to provide for employee representation on safety and hygiene committees, worker councils, or even boards of directors. While their responsibilities vary from country to country, worker councils basically provide a communication channel between employers and workers. The legal codes that set forth the functions of worker councils in France are very detailed. Councils are generally concerned with grievances, problems of individual employees, internal regulations, and matters affecting employee welfare.

codetermination

Representation of labor on the board of directors of a company.

A higher form of worker participation in management is found in Germany, where representation of labor on the board of directors of a company is required by law. This arrangement is known as **codetermination** and often referred to by its German word, *Mitbestimmung*. While sometimes puzzling to outsiders, the system is fairly simple. Company shareholders and employees are required to be represented in equal numbers on the supervisory boards of large corporations. Power is generally left with the shareholders, and shareholders are generally assured the chairmanship. Other European countries and Japan either have or are considering minority board participation.[49]

Each of these differences makes managing human resources in an international context more challenging. But the crux of the issue in designing HR systems is not choosing one approach that will meet all the demands of international business. Instead, organizations facing global competition must balance multiple approaches and make their policies flexible enough to accommodate differences across national borders. Throughout this book we have noted that different situations call for different approaches to managing people, and nowhere is this point more clearly evident than in international HRM.

Summary

LO 1 Analyzing the political, economic, socio-cultural, and technological factors affecting your company can help to (1) spot business or personnel opportunities, (2) spot trends in the business environment (3) avoid inappropriate HR practices, and (4) break free of old habits.

LO 2 There are four basic ways to organize for global competition: (1) the international corporation is essentially a domestic firm that has leveraged its existing capabilities to penetrate overseas markets; (2) the multidomestic corporation has fully autonomous units operating in multiple countries in order to address local issues; (3) the global corporation has a worldview but controls all international operations from its home office; and (4) the transnational corporation uses a network structure to balance global and local concerns.

LO 3 International HRM consists of managing three different types of employees—home-country nationals (expatriates), host-country nationals, and third-country nationals. Managing each set of employees requires different approaches to recruitment, selection, training, and compensation.

LO 4 In many European countries—Germany, for one—employee representation is established by law. Organizations typically negotiate the agreement with the union at a national level, frequently with government intervention. In other countries, union activity is prohibited or limited to only large companies. European unions have much more political power than many other unions around the world, although their power has declined somewhat due to globalization forces. The International Confederation of Free Trade Unions (ICFTU) and International Labour Organization (ILO) are among the major worldwide organizations endeavoring to improve the conditions of workers.

Key Terms

augmented skills

balance sheet approach

codetermination

core skills

cultural environment

culture shock

economic factors

expatriates, or home-country
  nationals

failure rates

global compensation system

global corporation

global manager

guest workers

home-based pay

host country

host-based pay

host-country nationals

international corporation

localization

multidomestic corporation (MDC)

political factors

repatriation

sociocultural factors

split pay

technological factors

third-country nationals

transnational corporation

transnational teams

work permit or visa

Discussion Questions

LO ① In recent years, we have observed an increase in foreign production throughout the world. What PEST factors would you consider to be most relevant to H&M's HR managers when trying to figure out if they should open up a plant in Vietnam to make clothes?

LO ② What major HR issues must be addressed as an organization moves from an international form to a multinational, global, and transnational form?

LO ③ a. Starbucks is opening new stores abroad every day, it seems. If you were in charge, would you use expatriate managers or host-country nationals to staff the new facilities? Explain your thinking.

b. This chapter places considerable emphasis on the role spouses play in terms of the success of an overseas manager. What other steps should companies take to increase the likelihood of a successful experience for all parties involved?

c. Talk with a foreign student on your campus; ask about his or her experience with culture shock on first arriving in the United States. What did you learn from your discussion? If the cost of living is lower in a foreign country than in the United States, should expatriates be paid less than they would be at home? Explain your position. Who should ultimately decide whether an employee should be localized or not? If grooming a talented individual for a leadership role is an important outcome of a foreign assignment, how can this be worked into a performance appraisal system? How would a manager assess leadership accomplishments?

LO ④ a. What are the major differences between labor–management relations in Europe and those in the United States?

b. Do you believe that codetermination will ever become popular in the United States? Explain your position.

An American (Expatriate) in Paris

There is often a great deal of work involved in setting up expatriate assignments. The administrative requirements can be far ranging and extend beyond the employee to also include family issues. Suppose you were faced with the following scenario. What would be the most pressing considerations that you would need to address?

The Scenario

You are the head of HR for Sarip International, a consulting firm specializing in hotel and restaurant management. Your firm is opening an office in Paris, France, and Jim Verioti, director of sales and marketing, has been asked to assume responsibilities for the expansion. Jim understands that the expatriate assignment will last 2 to 3 years, and although he has traveled to Europe for work on several occasions, this is his first long-term assignment overseas. He has a lot of questions about what he can expect and also some personal constraints.

Jim and his wife Betty have just moved into their new home (their mortgage is around $1,750 per month). In addition, Betty is an elementary school teacher and doesn't really know how the move will affect her job security. Their three children, Veronica (14), Reggie (12), and Archie (10), are of an age at which school considerations are very important. A friend told them about the American School in Paris, and this is a consideration. None of the Veriotis speak French.

Assignment

Working in teams of four to six individuals, put together the package that would allow Jim to move his family to Paris while still maintaining his present lifestyle (his current annual salary is $160,000 plus incentives). Address at least the following issues:

1. Visas and permits
2. Relocation allowance and housing
3. Language and culture training
4. Spousal employment concerns
5. Health/medical/insurance issues
6. Compensation and incentives
7. Education for the children

The following websites may be helpful to you, but other resources may prove valuable as well:

- U.S. embassy in Paris (https://fr.usembassy.gov/)
- French consulates in the United States (https://france.visahq.com/)
- Expatica.com (http://www.expatica.com/fr/main.html)
- Americans in Paris (http://www.americansinfrance.net)
- Easy Expat (http://www.easyexpat.com/paris_en.htm)
- Centers for Disease Control and Prevention (http://wwwn.cdc.gov/travel/default.aspx)
- American School in Paris (http://www.asparis.org/about)
- Medibroker (insurance) (http://www.medibroker.com)
- Travlang (currency calculator) (http://www.travlang.com/money/)

CASE STUDY ➊ How about a 900 Percent Raise?

Registered nurse Carmen Lopez wants a raise—so she's leaving Mexico and moving to California to take a job at Desert Valley Medical, a hospital near Los Angeles, where her income will increase tenfold. "I was making US$500 a month in Mexico, and in the U.S. I will be making between $25 and $28 an hour," Lopez says. Lopez, upon finishing her U.S. nursing exam, will be joining nine other Mexican nurses at Desert Valley Medical.

As U.S. baby boomers age, the number of registered nurses in the United States is not keeping up. The U.S. government forecasts that 1.2 million nursing vacancies will emerge by 2022. Lopez and her colleagues were recruited by MDS Global Medical Staffing in Los Angeles. Roger Viera, cofounder of MDS Global Staffing, says he and his business partner have invested $1 million, and the Mexican government added another $1 million, to open a nurse residency program in Mexico that trains and certifies nurses to work in the United States. "We only recruit qualified nurses. They must have a four-year bachelor of science degree and four years of work experience," Viera says. MDS expects to recruit from Mexico's 12 nursing schools and from Costa Rica in the near future.

MDS has also recruited Maria de la Cruz Gonzalez, who says she's excited about this opportunity to emigrate with her husband and work as a nurse in the United States. "The hospitals offer us a two-year contract where our nuclear family can come along to live with us in the U.S.," she says. MDS gives the nurses 3 months of paid rent and transportation, provides placement with client hospitals, and provides training in technology and language. They will be able to work in U.S. hospitals for 2 years under a North American Free Trade Agreement visa.

Donna Smith, chief nursing officer at Desert Valley Medical, says she is happy to have the Mexican nurses join her staff and believes that they are as qualified as U.S. nurses. But, she says, they will need more technical experience before they can go to work, since technology is different in the hospitals of Mexico. "We will provide them with extra training once they get here," she says.

Questions

1. Is recruiting nurses abroad a good idea for U.S. hospitals facing worker shortages?

2. Can you think of any cultural problems U.S. hospitals might encounter as a result?

3. What long-term recruiting measures should U.S. hospitals strive for?

Sources: Condensed from Aisha Belone, "How About a 900 Percent Raise? Mexican Nurses Head North to Cure the Ballooning U.S. Health Care Labor Shortage," *Latin Trade* 12 no. 7 (July 2004): 30; Rebecca Grant, "The U.S. Is Running Out of Nurses," *The Atlantic* (February 3, 2016).

CASE STUDY ❷   A "Turnaround" Repatriate Plan: U.S. Company Moves Indian Workers Back Home

In an unusual move, a seriously ailing Dallas software company, i2 Technologies, resettled 209 Indian engineers, programmers, and managers in their South Asian homeland on a voluntary basis to help stem losses as it laid off thousands of other employees. A series of corporate crises led to the mass repatriation back to India.

Many returnees had worked in Texas, Massachusetts, and California for 5 to 7 years on H1B Visas designed for temporary, highly skilled workers, although about 10 percent had acquired permanent residency green cards or U.S. citizenship. They found the company's Move to India Program too good to turn down—even if it meant a pay cut of 50 percent or more. None was pressured by management to return, said Gunaranjan "Guna" Pemmaraju, a 30-year-old engineer, who returned home. The returnees, many graduates of India's top technical universities, were confident of finding other U.S. jobs if i2 laid them off and were prepared to "change industries if need be," he asserted.

"When I left America, I actually kissed the ground," Pemmaraju said. "It helped me grow as an individual, and it enriched my thought process." Significantly, though, Pemmaraju says the quality of life in his middle-class Bangalore neighborhood is comparable—with a few minor downsides that he and his wife are willing to accept. Although their pay shrank in dollar terms, the repatriates are relatively better off in India.

"If we were in the top 25 percent in the United States, we're in the top 5 percent here," said one repatriate.

"We may not have 54-inch TV sets, but we have more of a sense of community and belonging here," another added.

Pemmaraju relies on DSL Internet access, fields morning calls from Dallas colleagues on a cell phone, and watches satellite TV while pedaling his new exercise bike. Instead of a Honda Accord, he drives a much smaller Suzuki Zen sedan.

For i2, the wage and benefit savings are helping it edge toward profitability. The company says the savings have been substantial. At its peak, i2 employed 6,349 people, with about 800 in India. It has since scaled down to 2,500 workers, 1,100 of whom are based in Bangalore.

Pemmaraju's family expresses no regrets about returning, yet they retain fond memories of the United

States, a country of "milk and honey"—not to mention seven-layer Taco Bell burritos and Krispy Kreme doughnuts. Pemmaraju was tickled by a recent call to a fast-food restaurant in Bangalore. "A guy answered the phone saying, 'Thank you for calling Pizza Hut. Would that be for delivery or carry out?' he said. It's just what they said in Arlington [Texas]!"

Questions

1. Does repatriation represent a good financial strategy for firms with international employees?

2. Besides cost savings, does i2 have anything to gain by repatriating its Indian employees?

3. What type of repatriation preparation training do you think i2's repatriates should receive before going home?

Source: Condensed from Barry Shlachter, "Software Firm Resettles Indian Workers in Turnaround Plan," *Fort Worth* (Texas) *Star-Telegram* (via Knight-Ridder/Tribune Business News), June 24, 2004.

Notes and References

1. Shad S. Morris, Daniel Chng, Jian Han, Bi-Juan Zhong, and Oded Shenkar, "Leveraging Local Talent for Global Learning in Multinational Enterprises' Foreign Subsidiaries," Working Paper (2017).

2. PESTLE analysis factsheet, Chartered Institute of Personnel and Development (CIPD) (October 15, 2015), https://www.cipd.co.uk/knowledge/strategy/organisational-development/pestle-analysis-factsheet.

3. Jordan Siegel and Barbara Zepp Larson, "Labor Market Institutions and Global Strategic Adaptation: Evidence from Lincoln Electric," *Management Science* 55, no. 9 (2009): 1527–1546.

4. See www.wto.org for more information on the World Trade Organization.

5. Larry Elliott and Graeme Wearden, "Xi Jinping Signals China Will Champion Free Trade if Trump Builds Barriers," *Guardian* (January 17, 2017).

6. "The Panama Canal Expansion: Changes Beyond the Waterway," Knowledge@Wharton (June 3, 2016), http://knowledge.wharton.upenn.edu/article/panama-canal-expansion-changes-beyond-waterway/; Steven Mufson, "An Expanded Panama Canal Opens for Giant Ships," *Washington Post* (June 26, 2016).

7. S. Vollmer, "How to Mind Your Manners in the Middle East: CPAs Who Do Business in the Region Need to Know the Cultural Rules," *Journal of Accountancy* 219, no. 1 (2015): 42; Ruchika Tulshyan, "Quirkiest Cultural Practices from Around the World," *Forbes* (March 18, 2010).

8. Caroline Fairchild, "Netflix Redefined American Company Culture. Will It Do the Same Abroad?" *CNBC* (June 20, 2016), www.cnbc.com/2016/06/20/netflix-redefined-american-company-culture-will-it-do-the-same-abroad.html.

9. Robert Johnson, "17 Awesome McDonald's Dishes You Can't Buy in America," *Business Insider* (June 16, 2011), http://www.businessinsider.com/mcdonalds-meals-around-the-world-2011-6?op=1/#donalds-hawaiian-deluxe-breakfast-12.

10. Carla Joinson, "No Returns," *HRMagazine* 47, no. 11 (November 2002): 70–77; Frank Jossi, "Successful Handoff," *HRMagazine* 47, no. 10 (October 2002): 48–52; Steve Bates, "Study Discovers Patterns in Global Executive Mobility," *HRMagazine* 47, no 10 (October 2002): 14; Morgan McCall and George Hollenbeck, "Global Fatalities: When International Executives Derail," *Ivey Business Journal* 66, no. 5 (May/June 2002): 74–78; Leslie Gross Klass, "Fed Up with High Costs, Companies Thin the Ranks of Career Expats," *Workforce Management* 83, no. 10 (October 1, 2004): 84.

11. Valerie Berset-Price, "Training: The Solution to the Expat Challenge," *Training Magazine* (May 4, 2012), https://trainingmag.com/content/training-solution-expat-challenge.

12. Readers interested in codes of conduct and other ethical issues pertaining to international business might read Nadar Asgary and Mark Mitschow, "Toward a Model for International Business Ethics," *Journal of Business Ethics* 36, no. 3 (March 2002): 238–246; Diana Winstanley and Jean Woodall, "The Adolescence of Ethics in Human Resource Management," *Human Resource Management Journal* 10, no. 4 (2000): 45; J. Brooke Hamilton and Stephen Knouse, "Multinational Enterprise Decision Principles for Dealing with Cross-Cultural Ethical Conflicts," *Journal of Business Ethics* 31, no.1 (May 2001): 77–94; Michael Maynard, "Policing Transnational Commerce: Global Awareness in the Margins of Morality," *Journal of Business Ethics* 30, no. 1 (March 2001): 17–27.

13. Adam Chandler, "Au Revoir to France's 35-Hour Workweek?" *The Atlantic* (March 10, 2016).

14. Michael Solomon, "H1B Visas: Why They're Broken and What We Can Do," *Huffington Post* (March 20, 2017).

15. Ben Wildavsky, "Reverse Brain Drain: How Much Should the U.S. Worry?" *The Chronicle of Higher Education* (March 28, 2011); "Keeping Out the Wrong People: Tightened Visa Rules Are Slowing the Vital Flow of Professionals into the U.S.," *Business Week* no. 3902 (October 4, 2004): 90; "Security Delays Hurt U.S. Business," *Legal Times* (August 23, 2004);

"Skilled Workers Leave in Reverse Brain Drain," *Fort Worth Star Telegram* (August 25, 2007): 9A.

16. "Society: Affirmative Action? Oui! At Long Last, France Takes a Page from America in Order to Manage Diversity—and Bring Minorities into Elite Schools," *Newsweek International* (April 12, 2004): 30; Leo D'Angelo Fisher, "The Hunt for a New Work Order," *BRW* 30, no. 9 (May 15, 2008): 46–52.

17. Martin Aschmoneit and Dijana Janevska, "Closing the Gap between Frugal and Reverse Innovation: Lessons Learned from the Case of the Tata Nano," Linköping University Department of Management and Engineering (2013).

18. https://www.linkedin.com/company-beta/163911/ (May 2, 2017); see Fuji Xerox website for detailed information about the company, http://www.fujixerox.com/eng/; Andrea Poe, "Selection Savvy," *HRMagazine* 47, no. 4 (April 2002): 77–83; "Exploiting Opportunity: Executives Trade Stories on Challenges of Doing Business in Global Economy," *Business Mexico* 15, no. 2 (February 2005): 54–58.

19. https://www.unilever.com/careers/ (May 2, 2017).

20. Sheree R. Curry, "Offshoring Swells Ranks of 'Returnees' Working Back in Their Native Countries," *Workforce Management* 84, no. 2 (February 1, 2005): 59; Yochanan Altman and Susan Shortland, "Women and International Assignments: Taking Stock—a 25-Year Review," *Human Resource Management* 47, no. 2 (Summer 2008): 199–216; Handan Kepir Sinangil and Deniz S. Ones, "Gender Differences in Expatriate Job Performance," *Applied Psychology: An International Review* 52, no. 3 (July 2003): 461–475; "More Women Sent on International Assignment," *Compensation & Benefits* 39, no. 2 (March–April 2007): 14–15.

21. *BGRS* Global Mobility Trends Report (2016), http://globalmobilitytrends.bgrs.com/#/data-highlights.

22. Nina Cole and Yvonne McNulty, "Why Do Female Expatriates 'Fit-in' Better Than Males?" *Cross Cultural Management*, 18, no. 2 (2011); Robert O'Connor, "Plug the Expat Knowledge Drain," *HRMagazine* 47, no. 10 (October 2002): 101–107; Andrea Graf and Lynn K. Harland, "Expatriate Selection: Evaluating the Discriminant, Convergent, and Predictive Validity of Five Measures of Interpersonal and Intercultural Competence," *Journal of Leadership & Organizational Studies* 11, no. 2 (Winter 2005): 46–63.

23. Paula Caligiuri, *Cultural Agility: Building a Pipeline of Successful Global Professionals* (New York: John Wiley & Sons, 2013); Paula Caligiuri, Ibraiz Tarique, and Rick Jacobs, "Selection for International Assignments," *Human Resource Management Review* 19, no. 3 (2009): 251–262; Riki Takeuchi, "A Critical Review of Expatriate Adjustment Research through a Multiple Stakeholder View: Progress, Emerging Trends, and Prospects," *Journal of Management* 36, no. 4 (2010): 1040–1064; Riki Takeuchi, Seokhwa Yun, and Paul Tesluk, "An Examination of Crossover and Spillover Effects of Spousal and Expatriate Cross-Cultural Adjustment on Expatriate Outcomes," *Journal of Applied Psychology* 87, no. 4 (August 2002): 655–666; Andrea Poe, Iris I. Varner, and Teresa M. Palmer, "Role of Cultural Self-Knowledge in Successful Expatriation," *Singapore Management Review* 27, no. 1 (January–June 2005): 1–25; Semere Haile, Marcus D. Jones, and Tsegai Emmanuel, "Challenges Facing Expatriate Performance Abroad," *International Journal of Business Research* 7, no. 5 (2007): 100–105; Margery Weinsten, "China a Double-Edged Sword for Ex-Pats," *Training* 43, no. 11 (November 2006): 12.

24. "Motorola to Increase Operations in China," *The New York Times* (November 8, 2001), C4; Peter J. Buckley, Jeremy Clegg, and Hui Tan, "Knowledge Transfer to China: Policy Lessons from Foreign Affiliates," *Transnational Corporations* 13, no. 1 (April 2004): 31–73; Neeraj Kataria and Shweta Sethi, "Making Successful Expatriates in Multinational Corporations," *Asian Journal of Business and Economics* 3, no. 3.4 (2013): 1–12.

25. Managers who are interested in setting up a language training program or who wish to evaluate commercially available language training programs should consult the "Standard Guide for Use-Oriented Foreign Language Instruction." The seven-page guide is put out by the American Society for Testing and Materials (ASTM), (610) 832-9585, http://www.astm.org. See also "Why Top Executives Are Participating in CEIBS and IESE's Joint Global Management Programme," *PR Newswire* (July 19, 2004); John Okpara and Jean Kabongo, "Cross-Cultural Training and Expatriate Adjustment: A Study of Western Expatriates in Nigeria," *Journal of World Business* 46, no. 1 (2011): 22–30.

26. Jared Wade, "The Pitfalls of Cross-Cultural Business," *Risk Management* 51, no. 3 (March 2004): 38–43; Semere Haile, Marcus D. Jones, and Tsegai Emmanuel, "Challenges Facing Expatriate Performance Abroad," *International Journal of Business Research* 7, no. 5 (2007): 100–105.

27. Vipin Gupta, Paul Hanges, and Peter Dorman, "Cultural Clusters: Methodology and Findings," *Journal of World Business* 37, no. 1 (Spring 2002): 11–15; Jane Terpstra-Yong and David Ralston, "Moving Toward a Global Understanding of Upward Influence Strategies: An Asian Perspective with Directions for Cross-Cultural Research," *Asia Pacific Journal of Management* 19, no. 2 (August 2002): 373–404; Hsiu-Ching Ko and Mu-Li Yang, "The Effects of Cross-Cultural Training on Expatriate Assignments," *Intercultural Communication Studies* 1 (2011): 158–174.

28. David C. Thomas and Mark F. Peterson, *Cross-Cultural Management: Essential Concepts* (Thousand Oaks, CA: Sage Publications, 2014); Ping Ping Fu et al., "The Impact of Societal Cultural Values and Individual Social Beliefs on the Perceived Effectiveness of Managerial Influence Strategies: A Meso Approach," *Journal of International Business Studies* 35, no. 4 (July 2004): 33; Geert Hofstede, *Culture's Consequences: Comparing Values, Behaviors, Institutions, and Organizations across Nations* (Thousand Oaks, CA: Sage, 2001).

29. Justin Martin, "The Global CEO: Overseas Experience Is Becoming a Must on Top Executives' Resumes, According to This Year's Route to the Top," *Chief Executive* 195 (January–February 2004): 24–31; Alizee B. Avril and Vincent P. Magnini, "A Holistic Approach to Expatriate Success," *International Journal of Contemporary Hospitality Management* 19, no. 1 (2007): 53–64; David C. Thomas and Mark F. Peterson, "The Manager as Decision Maker: Cross-Cultural Dimensions of Decision-Making," in *Cross-Cultural Management: Essential Concepts* (Thousand Oaks, CA: Sage Publications, 2014).

30. David Lipschultz, "Bosses from Abroad," *Chief Executive* 174 (January 2002): 18–21; Denis Lyons and Spencer Stuart, "International CEOs on the Rise," *Chief Executive* 152 (February 2000): 51–53; "U.S. Companies with Foreign-Born Executives," *Workforce Management* 83, no. 7 (July 1, 2004): 23;

31. Leung and C. Chiu, "Multicultural Experience, Idea Receptiveness, and Creativity," *Journal of Cross-Cultural Psychology* 41, no. 5–6 (2010): 723–741; W. Maddux and A. Galinsky, "Cultural Borders and Mental Barriers: The Relationship Between Living Abroad and Creativity," *Journal of Personality and Social Psychology* 96, no. 5 (2009): 1047–1061

32. Sharon Gillenwater, "Immigrant CEOs: What Global Citizens Bring to American Business," *Boardroom Insiders* (March 23, 2016).

33. Charles M. Vance, Yvonne McNulty, Yongsun Paik, and Jason D'Mello, "The Expat-preneur: Conceptualizing a Growing International Career Phenomenon," *Journal of Global Mobility* 4, no. 2 (2016): 202–224; Daomi Lin, Jiangyong Lu, Xiaohui Liu, and Xiru Zhang, "International Knowledge Brokerage and Returnees' Entrepreneurial Decisions," *Journal of International Business Studies* 47, no. 3 (2016): 295–318; Phyllis Tharenou and Natasha Caulfield, "Will I Stay or Will I Go? Explaining Repatriation by Self-Initiated Expatriates," *Academy of Management Journal* 53, no. 5 (2010): 1009–1028. Mark C. Bolino, "Expatriate Assignments and Intra-Organizational Career Success: Implications for Individuals and Organizations," *Journal of International Business Studies* 38, no. 5 (September 2007): 819–835.

34. M. Kraimer, M. Bolino, and B. Mead, Themes in Expatriate and Repatriate Research over Four Decades: What Do We Know and What Do We Still Need to Learn? *Annual Review of Organizational Psychology and Organizational Behavior* 3 (2016); 83–109; Lynette Clemetson, "Special Report on Globalization: The Globe Trotters," *Workforce Management* (December 2010); Calvin Reynolds, *Guide to Global Compensation and Benefits* (New York: Harcourt, 2001); Gary Parker, "Establishing Remuneration Practices across Culturally Diverse Environments," *Compensation & Benefits Management* 17, no. 2 (Spring 2001): 23–27; Timothy Dwyer, "Localization's Hidden Costs," *HRMagazine* 49, no. 6 (June 2004): 135–141.

35. Caroline Fisher, "Reward Strategy Linked to Financial Success: Europe," *Benefits & Compensation International* 32, no. 2 (September 2002): 34–35; "Comparative Analysis of Remuneration: Europe," *Benefits & Compensation International* 31, no. 10 (June 2002): 27–28; Fay Hansen, "Currents in Compensation and Benefits: International Trends," *Compensation and Benefits Review* 34, no. 2 (March–April 2002): 20–21.

36. Donald C. Dowling Jr., "Avoid These Global Compensation and Global Benefits Plan Obstacles," *Society for Human Resource Management* (April 22, 2014), https://www.shrm.org/resourcesandtools/hr-topics/global-hr/pages/global-compensation-benefits-plans.aspx; Chao Chen, Jaepil Choi, and Shu-Cheng Chi, "Making Justice Sense of Local-Expatriate Compensation Disparity: Mitigation by Local Referents, Ideological Explanations, and Interpersonal Sensitivity in China-Foreign Joint Ventures," *Academy of Management Journal* 45, no. 4 (August 2002): 807–817.

37. Richard Locke, "Does Monitoring Improve Labor Standards? Lessons from Nike," *Industrial and Labor Relations Review* 61, no. 1 (2007): 3–31; Greg Distelhorst, Jens Hainmueller, and Richard M. Locke, "Does Lean Improve Labor Standards? Management and Social Performance in the Nike Supply Chain," *Management Science* (2016); Ashley Lutz, "How Nike Shed Its Sweatshop Image to Dominate the Shoe Industry," *Business Insider* (June 6, 2015), http://www.businessinsider.com/how-nike-fixed-its-sweatshop-image-2015-6.

38. Patricia Zingheim and Jay Schuster, "How You Pay Is What You Get," *Across the Board* 38, no. 5 (September–October 2001): 41–44; "Benefits for Expatriate Employees: International," *Benefits & Compensation International* 31, no. 10 (June 2002): 26–27; Steven P. Nurney, "The Long and Short of It: When Transitioning from a Short-Term to a Long-Term Expatriate Assignment, Consider the Financial Implications," *HRMagazine* 50, no. 3 (March 2005): 91–95.

39. "Designing Global Compensation Systems," *Society for Human Resource Management* (April 3, 2017), https://www.shrm.org/resourcesandtools/tools-and-samples/toolkits/pages/designingglobalcompensation.aspx; Stephan Kolbe, "Putting Together an Expat Package: As More and More Companies Adopt an International Outlook, They Are Increasingly Sending Staff on Overseas Assignments—Usually Involving a Complex Relocation Package," *International Money Marketing* (September 2004): 33.

40. Nick Royle, "Three Expatriate Compensation Approaches," *The Global Talent Mobility Company* (May 5, 2011), http://msigbs.com/blog/global-compensation-payroll-administration/three-expatriate-compensation-approaches/; the U.S. State Department Index of Living Costs Abroad can be found on the Web at http://www.state.gov/travel.

41. "International Assignment: Performance Management: How Can a Company Manage an Expatriate Employee's Performance?" *Society for Human Resource Management* (November 30, 2012), https://www.shrm.org/resourcesandtools/tools-and-samples/hr-qa/pages/expatriateperformance.aspx.

42. Paula Caligiuri, "The Big Five Personality Characteristics as Predictors of Expatriate's Desire to Terminate the Assignment and Supervisor-Rated Performance," *Personnel Psychology* 53, no. 1 (Spring 2000): 67–88; Calvin Reynolds, "Global Compensation and Benefits in Transition," *Compensation and Benefits Review* 32, no. 1 (January–February 2000): 28–38; Charlene Marmer Solomon, "The World Stops Shrinking," *Workforce* 79, no. 1 (January 2000): 48–51; Stephenie Overman, "Mentors without Borders: Global Mentors Can Give Employees a Different Perspective on Business Matters," *HRMagazine* 49, no. 3 (March 2004): 83–87; Agneš Slavic, Nemanja Berber, and Bojan Lekovic, "Performance Management in International Human Resource Management: Evidence from the Cee Region," *Serbian Journal of Management* 9, no. 1 (2014): 45–58.

43. Frank Jossi, "Successful Handoff," *HRMagazine* 47, no. 10 (October 2002): 48–52; Paula Caligiuri, David Day, and Shirley Puccino, "Worldwide Practices and Trends in Expatriate Compensation and Benefits," *Benefits & Compensation Digest* 44, no. 1 (January 2007): 34–38; Eric Krell, "Evaluating Returns on Expatriates," *HRMagazine* 50, no. 3 (March 2005): 60–65.

44. B. Sebastian Reiche, Günter K. Stahl, Mark E. Mendenhall, and Gary R. Oddou, *Reading and Cases in International Human Resources Management*, 6th ed. (New York: Routledge, 2016).

45. Bernhard Ebbinghaus and Jelle Visser, *The Societies of Europe: Trade Unions in Western Europe since 1945* (London, England: Palgrave Macmillan, 2000); John Pencavel, "Unionism Viewed Internationally," *Journal of Labor Research* 26, no. 1 (Winter 2005): 65–98; "Membership Required," *Economist* 87, no. 8591 (August 2, 2008): 66; Jeremy Smerd, "Unions Reverse Decline," *Workforce Management* 87, no. 2 (February 4, 2008): 1–3.

46. Randall S. Schuler, Susan E. Jackson, and Ibraiz Tarique, "Global Talent Management and Global Talent Challenges: Strategic Opportunities for IHRM," *Journal of World Business* 46 (2011): 506–516; Christopher Rhoads, "Germany Faces Storm over Tech Staffing—Labor Groups Are Enraged by Proposal to Import Badly Needed Workers," *The Wall Street Journal* (March 7, 2000): A23; "European Workplaces Tighten Policies as Countries Struggle to Compete Worldwide," *Pittsburgh (Pennsylvania) Post-Gazette* (via Knight-Ridder/Tribune Business News) (November 28, 2004).

47. http://www.ituc-csi.org/ (May 2, 2017).

48. http://www.ilo.org/wcmsp5/groups/public/---dgreports/---dcomm/documents/publication/wcms_374809.pdf (May 2, 2017).

49. Herbert Spiro, "Co-Determination in Germany," *The American Political Science Review* 48, no. 4 (December 1954): 1114–1127; Yuko Nishimura, "Reconstructing Minority Identities in 21st Century Japan," *Global Ethnographic Journal for Ethnographic Research* (January 23, 2012), http://oicd.net/ge/index.php/reconstructing-minority-identities_yukonishimura/.

CHAPTER **16**

Implementing HR Strategy: High-Performance Work Systems

Learning Outcomes

After studying this chapter, you should be able to

LO 1 Discuss how a firm's strategy can be achieved with a high-performance work system and what its fundamental principles are.

LO 2 Describe how a high-performance work system is designed, and explain how its components must align horizontally and vertically to support one another and a firm's strategy.

LO 3 Recommend processes for implementing and evaluating a high-performance work system.

LO 4 Discuss a high-performance work system's potential outcomes for both employees and the organization.

So you have finished reading 15 chapters on HRM. Congratulations—textbooks do not always make for the most gripping reading. But before you close this book, think about the following question: What is more difficult—designing effective HR practices or implementing them as one system?

Most HR textbooks simply end after each individual aspect of HRM is introduced and explained. But in today's competitive environment, many organizations are discovering that it is how the pieces are *combined* together and put into practice that makes all the difference. After all, managers typically do not focus on staffing, training, and compensation practices in isolation from one another. These HR practices are implemented into an overall system to enhance employee involvement and performance. So now that we have talked about the individual pieces, let's talk about how they fit together into a *high-performance work system*. Understand that this is not a piece of software. Rather, a **high-performance work system (HPWS)** is the combination of HR practices, work structures, and processes specific to a firm that maximizes the knowledge, skills, commitment, flexibility, and resilience of employees, which in turn enhances a firm's competitiveness.

An HPWS can take an organization from being good to great. Consider the Dallas Cowboys. The Cowboys have recruited top talent and paid them top dollar. The owner of the Cowboys, Jerry Jones, has also replaced the Cowboys' coaches multiple times. Although the team has won its division a number of times in recent years, it hasn't (at least at the time of this writing), won a Super Bowl since 1996. Even making the playoffs has been a rare occurrence for the Cowboys. As one HR professional and writer puts it: "Talent might be the fuel of a business's performance, but it's the organization that makes it over the finish line first that really counts."[1] Put another way, it's not enough for organizations to improve just their various HR practices—employee recruitment, rewards, and retention, and so forth. They have to improve their "people processes" as an entire system aligned with their strategies. If some of the "pieces of the puzzle" don't fit, the firm is bound to lose the game.

high-performance work system (HPWS)

A specific combination of HR practices, work structures, and processes that maximizes knowledge, skill, commitment, flexibility, and resilience of a firm's employees.

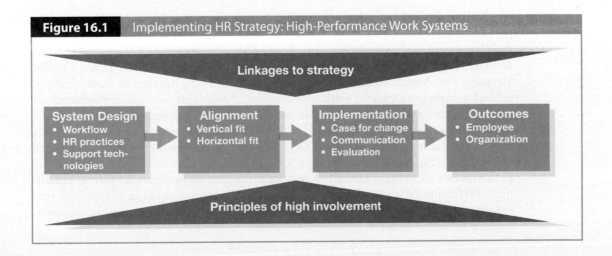

| **Figure 16.1** | Implementing HR Strategy: High-Performance Work Systems |

Linkages to strategy

System Design
- Workflow
- HR practices
- Support technologies

Alignment
- Vertical fit
- Horizontal fit

Implementation
- Case for change
- Communication
- Evaluation

Outcomes
- Employee
- Organization

Principles of high involvement

In this chapter, we will look at how the various pieces of the HR puzzle fit together to implement a firm's strategy. We will start by discussing the fundamental principles that guide the development of high-performance work systems and the potential benefits that can occur as a result. Then we will outline the various components of the system, the work-flow design, HR practices, management processes, and supporting technologies. (See Figure 16.1.) We will also describe the ways in which an organization tries to tie together, or align, all the pieces of the system and link them with its strategy. We end the chapter with a discussion of the processes organizations use to implement high-performance work systems as well as the outcomes that benefit both employees and the organization as a whole.

LO ①

As an employee, how do you think a high-performance work system might benefit you personally? What drawbacks might you experience because of such a system?

16.1 Fundamental Principles

In Chapter 1, we noted that organizations face a number of important strategic and competitive challenges such as adapting to global competition, harnessing technology, improving productivity, and containing costs. We also noted some very important employee concerns that must be addressed, such as managing a diverse workforce with different educational skills, recognizing employee rights, and adjusting to the new work attitudes of employees and their desire for work-life balance. We now know that the best organizations go beyond simply balancing these sometimes competing demands; they create work environments that blend these concerns to simultaneously get the most from their employees and meet their needs while reaching the short-term and long-term goals of the organization.

The four simple but fundamental principles that underlie a high-performance work system are as follows and illustrated in Figure 16.2:

- Egalitarianism and engagement
- Shared information and trust
- Knowledge development
- Performance-reward linkage[2]

These principles are the building blocks for managers who want to create high-performance work systems. We will use the principles as a framework for the rest of the chapter. In addition, it should be noted that in a review and statistical analysis of 92 studies involving more than 19,000 organizations, researchers James Combs, Yongmei Liu, Angela Hall, and David Ketchen identified a number of major findings related to high-performance work systems. First, the systems have a larger influence on the performance of organizations than other highly visible governance practices, such as the independence of a firm's board of directors. Second, because of their synergistic effects, the elements of the systems have a larger impact when they are implemented as a bundle. Third, the systems have a significant effect regardless of whether the performance of firms is measured in operational terms or financial terms. Finally, high-performance work systems can be successfully implemented in all types of organizations, including both manufacturing and service organizations, and in organizations of different sizes.

| Figure 16.2 | Underlying Principles of High-Performance Work Systems |

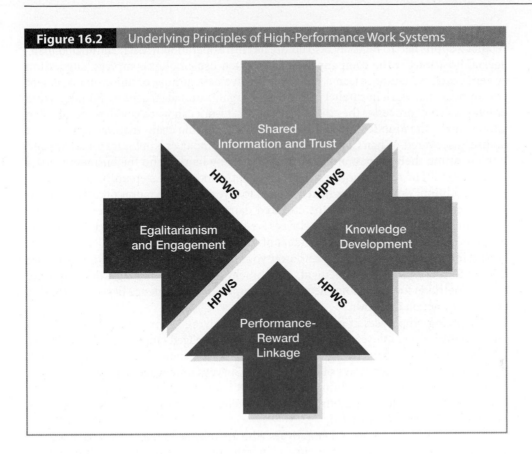

16.1a Egalitarianism and Engagement

People want a sense that they are members, not just workers, in an organization. Status and power differences tend to separate people and magnify whatever disparities exist between them. The "us versus them" battles that have traditionally raged between managers, employees, and labor unions are increasingly being replaced by more cooperative approaches to managing work. More egalitarian work environments lessen status and power differences and, in the process, increase collaboration and teamwork. When this happens, productivity can improve if people who once worked in isolation from (or in opposition to) one another begin to work together.

Nucor Steel has an egalitarian work environment and remarkable loyalty and productivity of its employees, each of whom is listed alphabetically on the company's annual report. Upper-level managers at Nucor do not enjoy better insurance programs, vacation schedules, holidays, or have corporate cars, jets, executive dining rooms, or designated parking places. In fact, benefits such as Nucor's profit sharing plan, scholarship program, employee stock purchase plan, bonus plan, and service awards program are not available to Nucor's officers at all. At the Swedish-based company IKEA, hierarchical differences aren't prominent, in part because egalitarianism is a Swedish value. Employees are on a first-name basis and sit side-by-side at IKEA desks in an open-floor arrangement with their managers. Few managers even have business cards.[3]

Moving power downward in organizations—that is, empowering employees—frequently requires structural changes that involve more than rearranging the furniture and getting rid of executive parking spaces. Recall from Chapter 2 how the online shoe retailer Zappos had to radically restructure its entire operation when it eliminated managerial positions at the company. Managers often use employee surveys, suggestion systems, quality assurance teams, employee involvement groups, or union-management committees that work in parallel with existing organizational structures. Simply asking employees what processes they think work or don't work can work wonders. That's what Chip Conley, the founder Joie de Vivre Hotels, a California chain that was teetering on failure, discovered. When Conley began asking the company's employees for advice and implementing their suggestions, they began working harder, and the business made a turnaround. "The more you give people a voice, the more they step up," Conley says.[4]

In addition, workflows can be redesigned to give employees more control and influence over decision making. At the cultured dairy product manufacturer Old Home Foods in St. Paul, Minnesota, all employees are involved in the decision-making process of the business. Says one of the founders of the company, Peter Arthur: "To be a successful independent, you need to empower your employees and let them know they are critical to success."[5] Job enlargement, enrichment, and self-managing work teams are typical methods for increasing the power of employees to influence decisions, suggest changes, or act on their own.

Involving employees in decision making and giving them the power to act also tends to increase employee engagement. Recall that engaged employees are employees who consistently perform at high levels, are enthusiastic about what they do, and look for better, more efficient ways of doing things. Surveys on engagement statistics vary. Recently in a large survey conducted by the HR consulting firm Aon Hewitt, only 24 percent of U.S. employees said they were highly engaged on the job; worse yet, 63 percent said they were not engaged.

Disengaged employees and employees who are only semiengaged can cost a company dearly. The French bank Société Générale found this out when a junior-level trader lost billions of the bank's money making illicit trades. Some experts believe that a number of Société Générale employees were perhaps aware that there was a problem but did not report it, possibly because of poor employee engagement. "There's plenty of evidence that suggests that strategic human resources management and high-performance work systems are foundational in driving employee engagement," says Ellie Maggio, the managing director of Emend Management Consultants in Toronto, Canada. "If an organization is strategic about human resources, they're going to have higher engagement."[6]

16.1b Shared Information and Trust

The principle of shared information is critical to the success of employee empowerment and involvement initiatives in organizations. In the past, employees were hired to do narrowly defined jobs and not given a great deal of information about their firms. One of the underlying ideas of high-performance work systems is that workers are intimately acquainted with the nature of their own work and are therefore in the best position to recognize problems and devise solutions to them. Only individuals and teams can transform an organization. Organizations, cultures, and processes cannot; they can only support or stifle the efforts of individuals and teams that do.[7] However, without timely and accurate information about the business, employees can do little more than simply carry out orders rather than understand the overall direction of the business or contribute fully to its success.

When employees are given timely information about business performance, plans, and strategies, they are more likely to make good suggestions for improving the business and to cooperate in major organizational changes. They are also likely to feel more committed to new courses of action if they take part in the decision making, and happier, which seems to be at least one key to high-performance work systems, research shows.[8] They will "know more, do more, and contribute more."[9]

Shared information shifts organizations away from command and control toward employee commitment. It also shifts the relationship between employers and employees—from one that is merely transactional to one that is more relational. A study of Chinese hospitals found that HPWSs don't work as well when employees and employers view their relationship as merely an exchange of labor for money (transactional). Employees just end up exhausted by the extra demands put on them.

By contrast, when employees and employers have a more relational view—they see that the firm's commitment to its employees and vice versa as long term—an HPWS is more likely to succeed.[10] Sharing key information with employees indicates you trust them and that your commitment to them is long term. So does having a certain amount of job security, which in turn gives employees confidence to experiment with new ideas and products without having to worry about getting fired if they fail. Thus, trust can make the difference between firms like Apple that are able to innovate and adapt to change versus firms that are merely able to improve their productivity, quality, or cost savings.[11]

16.1c Knowledge Development

Knowledge development is the twin sister of information sharing. As a former CEO of Harley-Davidson, noted, "The only thing you get when you empower dummies is bad decisions faster." High-performance work systems depend on the shift from touch labor to knowledge work. Employees today need a broad range of technical, problem-solving, and interpersonal skills to work either individually or in teams on cutting-edge projects. Because of the speed of change, knowledge and skill requirements must also change rapidly. In today's work environment, employees must learn continuously. Stopgap training programs may not be enough. Companies have found that employees in high-performance work systems need to learn in "real time," on the job, using innovative new approaches to solve novel problems. At Ocean Spray's Henderson, Nevada, plant, making employees aware of the plant's progress has been a major focus. A real-time scoreboard on the Henderson plant floor provides workers with streaming updates of the plant's vital stats, including average cost per case, case volumes filled, filling speeds, and injuries to date. When people are better informed, they do better work. "We operate in real time, and we need real-time information to be able to know what we have achieved and what we are working towards," says an Ocean Spray manager.

16.1d Performance-Reward Linkage

It is not uncommon for employees to intentionally or unintentionally pursue outcomes that are beneficial to them but not necessarily to the organization as a whole. A corollary of this idea, however, is that things tend to go more smoothly when there is some way to align the interests of an organization and its employees. When companies reward their employees based on their performance, workers naturally pursue outcomes that are mutually beneficial to themselves and the organization. When this happens, some amazing things can result. For example, supervisors do not have to constantly watch to make sure that employees do the right thing. Instead, employees are more likely to go out of their way—above and beyond the call of duty—to make certain that their coworkers are getting the help they need, systems and processes are functioning efficiently, and the firms' customers are happy.

As Case Study 2 at the end of the chapter explains, every 4 weeks, the natural foods grocer Whole Foods calculates the profit per labor hour for every team in every store. Teams that exceed a certain threshold get a bonus in their next paycheck. Performance-based rewards such as these ensure that employees share in the gains that result from any performance improvement. This also ensures fairness and tends to focus employees on the organization.

LO **2**

Have you ever moved a piece of furniture in your house or dorm room and noticed that once you did, everything else needed to be moved, too? How do you think this same principle might work when it comes to high-performance work systems?

16.2 Designing High-Performance Work Systems

No two firms, even those that compete against one another, are exactly the same. Consequently, their best practices have to be different as well. However, some clear trends in work design, HR practices, leadership roles, and information technologies tell us what high-performance work systems look like.[12] Some of these are summarized in Figure 16.3.

16.2a Work-Flow Design and Teamwork

High-performance work systems frequently begin with the way work is designed. Total quality management (TQM), reengineering, Six Sigma, and the like have driven many organizations to redesign their work flows. Firms are focusing on the key business processes that drive customer value—and then create teams responsible for those processes. Recall that this is the idea behind self-directed work teams. Federal Express redesigned its delivery process to give truck drivers responsibility for scheduling their own routes and for making necessary changes quickly. FedEx drivers work together as a team to identify bottlenecks and solve problems that slow delivery. To facilitate this, advanced communications equipment was installed in the delivery trucks to help teams of drivers balance routes among those with larger or lighter loads.[13] By redesigning the work flow around key business processes, companies such as Federal Express have been able to establish a work environment that facilitates teamwork, takes advantage of its employees' skills and knowledge, empowers employees to make decisions, and provides them with more meaningful work.[14]

In most cases, a "homegrown" process and procedures developed by a firm's managers and employees work better than one adopted from elsewhere. Each organization has unique circumstances, and parties are more likely to commit to procedures they create and own. Homegrown processes can also give a firm a competitive advantage because they are harder for competitors to imitate.

A common mistake organizations often make is focusing on either top-down changes driven by executives or bottom-up changes cultivated by the employees. Firms such as Champion International, now a part of International Paper, and ASDA, a low-cost British retailer, are among the many companies that have found that the best results occur when managers and employees work together.[15] At MTS, a telecommunications company based in the Canadian province of Manitoba, unions and company managers design, select, and implement new procedures together.

Figure 16.3   Design Aspects of High-Performance Work Systems

	Egalitarianism	Shared Information	Knowledge Development	Performance-Reward Linkage
Work flow				
• Self-managed teams	■	■	□	□
• Empowerment	■	■	■	□
Staffing				
• Selective recruiting	□	□	■	□
• Team decision making	■	■	□	□
Training				
• Broad skills	□	□	■	□
• Cross-training	■	■	■	□
• Problem solving	■	■	■	□
• Team training	□	■	■	□
Compensation				
• Incentives	■	□	□	■
• Gainsharing	■	■	■	■
• Profit sharing	■	■	■	■
• Skill-based pay	■	□	■	■
Leadership				
• Few layers	■	■	■	□
• Coaches/facilitators	■	■	■	□
Technologies				
• HRIS	□	■	□	□
• Communications	■	■	■	□

HR personnel need to be intimately involved with the development of new procedures too. Most HR managers have a good idea of what works in a particular firm and what does not. Thus, the recruiting, evaluation, and reward systems devised by a firm's HR department can have a huge impact on how well high-performance work systems are implemented.

16.2b Complementary Human Resources Policies and Practices

Work redesign, in and of itself, does not result in a high-performance work system. Neither does total quality management or reengineering. Other supporting elements of HRM are needed. For example, several studies suggest that both the performance of employees and their satisfaction are much higher when organizations combine their changes in work-flow design with HR practices that encourage skill development and employee involvement.[16] Next, let's look at some of these key HR practices.

Staffing Practices

Many high-performance work systems begin with highly directive recruitment and selection practices. The recruitment tends to be both broad and intensive in order to get the best pool of candidates from which to choose. Human resources information systems have made it easier for firms to compile an inventory of their talent and search for employees with the specific skills they need. Talented employees "come up to speed" more quickly and take less time to develop. At Whole Foods Market, Zappos, and W.L. Gore, team members select their teammates. This practice gives employees more control over decisions about who their coworkers will be and forges relationships more quickly than if new members were simply assigned to a team.[17]

Too often, however, organizations try to save money by doing a superficial job of hiring. As a consequence, they run the risk of hiring the wrong people and spending more on training them or on outplacement and severance programs if they are let go or quit, followed by additional recruiting costs to hire their replacements. Other hiring pitfalls include simply looking for skills and experience in candidates and not looking for cues to see if they are truly engaged employees capable of contributing adequately to a high-performance work system. Says Jennifer Anderson, the VP of recruiting for the bank Capital One: "We seek candidates with an entrepreneurial mindset who have the courage to challenge the status quo."[18]

How can you tell if candidates have the "right stuff"? Kris Dunn, an HR executive and writer, suggests asking candidates behavioral questions such as the following: "Tell me about a time in a past job that you got really excited about something you were working on. Now tell me about a situation at work in which you got bored." If a candidate struggles to come up with relevant examples, there is no reason to think the person will be a fully engaged employee in your company.[19]

Training and Development

Like recruitment and selection, training focuses on ensuring employees have the skills they need to assume greater responsibility in a high-performance work environment. At the grocery chain Publix, managers are responsible for developing succession plans for employees to help them reach their full potential. Employees submit information about Publix jobs they are interested in. They then log onto computers in the breakroom

High-performance work systems have helped many auto manufacturers improve production and quality.

Fabrizio Costantini/Getty Images

and elsewhere to take training courses related to them and are matched with job openings as they occur. Virtually all of Publix's managers began their careers as entry-level employees with the company. Todd Jones, the company's CEO, started his career with the company as a bagger.[20]

Schindler Elevator, the world's second-largest manufacturer of elevators, provides a 60-hour prehire training program of instruction and testing in such subjects as orientation/company history, safety, plant policies and procedures, just-in-time (JIT) techniques, and basic shop math. The company also has an apprenticeship program. Schindler's emphasis on teamwork, engagement, and continuous improvement requires employees to develop a broader understanding of work processes performed by others around them rather than rely on just knowing their own jobs.

Recall that cross-training involves training employees in jobs in areas closely related to their own. Cross-training is very important for a HPWS. Nurses in the perinatal unit of Cincinnati-based TriHealth implemented cross-training to facilitate teamwork and cooperation across units; the training also helps nurses identify trouble spots that can occur in several of the jobs and allows them to suggest areas for improvement.

Compensation and Benefits

Another important piece of a high-performance work system is the compensation package. Because high-performance work systems ask many different things from employees, it is difficult to isolate one single approach to pay that works for everyone. As a consequence, many companies are experimenting with alternative compensation plans. In order to link pay and performance, high-performance work systems often include some type of employee incentives. Pushing decision making down to front-line roles usually requires higher compensation for two reasons: Leaders often need to pay more to attract highly skilled people, and the higher pay can be used to reward high performance, says Alec Levenson, senior research scientist at the Center for Effective Organizations at the University of Southern California in Los Angeles.[21] At Henry Ford Health System, a Detroit-area hospital network, employees' monetary performance incentives are tied to the system's strategic plan. If the system exceeds its financial targets, and if a business unit also achieves its targets and budget, then employees are awarded commensurately.[22] In 2010, Hilcorp Energy, a Houston firm, awarded every employee either a new car or $50,000 for meeting a 5-year challenge for doubling the firm's value, production rate, and oil and gas reserves. When employees doubled Hilcorp's numbers again in 2015, each one of them received $100,000.[23]

Other organizational incentives such as gain sharing, profit sharing, and employee stock ownership plans focus employee efforts on outcomes that benefit both themselves and the organization as a whole. The Scanlon Plan, Rucker Plan, and Improshare, three systems discussed in Chapter 10, have been used by companies to elicit employee suggestions and reward them for contributions to productivity.

High-performance work systems can also incorporate skill-based pay plans. By paying employees based on the number of different job skills they have, organizations such as Shell Canada and Honeywell have created both a broader skill base among employees and a more flexible pool of people to rotate among interrelated jobs. Both of these qualities are beneficial in a high-performance work environment and may justify the extra compensation. Honeywell has even experimented with what it calls "intracapital"—a pool of money employees can spend on capital improvements if the company meets its profitability goals.[24] Lastly, more companies are connecting their firm's corporate responsibility goals with their compensation systems. Whole Foods, the retailer Marks & Spencer, and Tesco, a global grocer and merchandiser, are among the companies that incorporate sustainability targets into their performance goals. Whole Foods and Tesco's goals include community-involvement initiatives as well.[25]

Recall that in addition to linking pay and performance, high-performance work systems are also based on the principle of egalitarianism. This encourages employees to be more involved and committed.[26] At Henry Ford Health System each staff member within a business unit—including physicians—gets the same incentive reward if the unit's goals are met, which in a recent year averaged about $800.[27] At Tesco, the bonuses staff members and executives receive are tied to meeting the company's corporate social responsibility goals as is the pay for the firm's board of directors.[28] Open pay plans that allow employees to know what everyone else makes is a compensation system used to create a more egalitarian environment.

Of course, not every company can afford to offer its employees incentive pay or profit sharing, let alone a car or a $100,000. As we have explained, every company has to develop its own practices. To better match their HR practices with their workforces and retain hourly and lower wage workers in high-turnover industries, some firms utilize programs that motivate employees by offering them more flexibility and other work-life benefits. Kaiser Permanente and Marriott have implemented a range of practices, such as giving employees flexible start and end times to their work shifts and the ability to take paid time off for a few hours to take care of their personal business rather than having to take an entire day off if they don't need it.[29] Lyft and other companies are utilizing ATM-like systems that allow workers to cash out their pay as soon as they earn it, rather than waiting for a paycheck.[30]

Management Processes and Leadership

Organizations such as Motorola, Doubletree Hotels, American Express, and Reebok International found that the success of any high-performance work system depends on first changing the roles of managers and team leaders. With fewer layers of management and a focus on team-based organization, the role of managers and supervisors is substantially different in an environment of high-performance work systems. Managers and supervisors are seen more as coaches, facilitators, and integrators of team efforts.[31] Rather than autocratically imposing their demands on employees and closely monitoring workers, managers share responsibility for decision making with employees, help them become better decision makers, and troubleshoot and innovate on their own. Typically, the term *manager* is replaced by the term *team leader*. In a growing number of cases, leadership is shared among team members. It's not uncommon to rotate team leaders at various stages in team development. That way, different individuals can assume functional leadership roles when their particular expertise is needed most.

16.2c Supportive Information Technologies

Communication and information technologies are yet one more piece that has to be added to the framework of high-performance work systems. Technologies of various kinds create an infrastructure vital for communicating and sharing information. Sally Corporation is a Florida-based company that makes robotic human and animal creatures for movies and theme parks. The firm uses information technology to assign employees to various project teams and to budget and track their time spent on them. GE is attempting to use machine learning, HR data, and LinkedIn information to correlate the career paths of successful executives and candidates who might one day take their places to sustain the company's performance.

But information technologies need not be high tech. The richest communication occurs face to face. The important point is that high-performance work systems cannot succeed without timely and accurate communications. (Recall the principle of shared information.) Typically the information needs to be about business plans and goals, unit and corporate operating results, incipient problems and opportunities, and competitive threats.[32]

16.3 Strategic Alignment

Each of these practices we have discussed highlights the individual pieces of a high-performance work system. As we discussed in Chapter 2, careful planning helps ensure that the pieces fit together and are linked with the overall strategic goals of the organization. Figure 16.4 summarizes the internal and external linkages needed to fit high-performance work systems together.

16.3a Ensuring Horizontal Fit

Chapter 2 noted that **horizontal fit**, or alignment, occurs when all *internal* elements of a work system—HR practices, work designs, management processes, and technologies—reinforce one another. The synergy achieved through overlapping work and HR practices is at the heart of what makes a high-performance system effective.

horizontal fit
The situation in which all the internal elements of the work system reinforce one another.

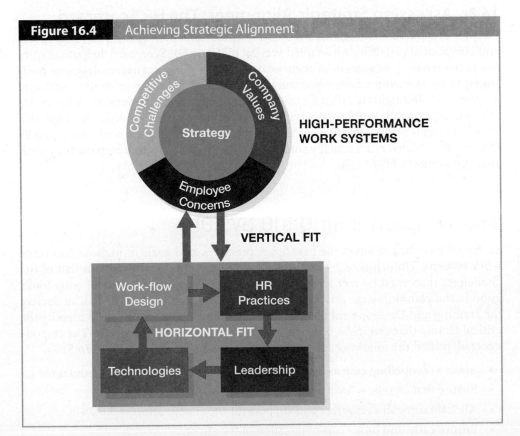

| **Figure 16.4** | Achieving Strategic Alignment |

For example, an improved selection system may be of no use if it is not working in conjunction with a firm's training and development activities. The two components would be working at cross purposes. Moreover, changes in one component will affect all of the other components because the pieces are interdependent.

16.3b Establishing Vertical Fit

To achieve **vertical fit**, or vertical alignment, high-performance work systems must support the organization's strategies given its external competitive challenges, organizational values, and the concerns of employees.[33]

Xerox uses a planning process known as "Managing for Results," which begins with a statement of corporate values and priorities and establishes clear goals for the organization. Each business unit establishes annual objectives based on these goals, and the process cascades down through every level of management. Ultimately, each employee within Xerox has a clear "line of sight" to the values and goals of the organization, so he or she can see how individual effort makes a difference.[34]

Efforts such as these help focus the design of high-performance work systems on a firm's strategic priorities. Objectives such as innovation, faster speed to market, cost containment, quality enhancement, and better customer service directly influence what is expected of employees and the skills they need to be successful. High-performance work systems are designed to link employee initiatives to those strategies.

16.3c Assessing Strategic Alignment: The HR Scorecard

Chapter 2 introduced the balanced scorecard, which helps managers link strategic goals and operational activities. An adapted version of it, the HR Scorecard, helps managers assess the strategic alignment of their work systems.[35] First, managers diagnose horizontal fit by assessing whether particular HR practices reinforce or conflict with one another (see Highlights in HRM 1A). Second, managers assess the extent to which their HR practices result in employment stability and teamwork (see Highlights in HRM 1B). Third, the degree of vertical fit is evaluated by assessing the degree to which the results the workforce delivers are actually connected with the elements that help the firm excel (see Highlights in HRM 1C).

16.4 Implementing the System

So far we have talked about the principles, practices, and goals of high-performance work systems. Unfortunately, these design issues pose probably less than half of the challenges that must be met to ensure an HPWS is successful. Much of what looks good in the planning stage gets messy during implementation. The American Society for Training and Development (ASTD) asked managers and consultants to identify the critical factors that can make or break a high-performance work system. The respondents identified the following actions as necessary for success (see Figure 16.5):

- Make a compelling case for change linked to the company's business strategy.
- Ensure that change is "owned" by senior and line managers.
- Allocate sufficient resources and support for the change effort.
- Ensure early and broad communication of the effort.

Diagnosing Horizontal Fit

This chart estimates the degree to which the various HR management subsystems work together. Think of the degree of fit and internal consistency as a continuum from −100 to +100, and assign a value in that range to each relationship. Examples of the extremes and midpoints on that continuum are as follows:

−100: The two subsystems work at cross purposes.
0: The two subsystems have little or no effect on one another.
+100: Each subsystem is mutually reinforcing and internally consistent.
DNK: Don't know or have no opinion.

	HR Plan-ning	Recruit-ing and Selection	Training and Devel-opment	Performance Management and Appraisal	Compensa-tion and Benefits	Work Organi-zation (e.g., Teams)	Commu-nication Systems	HR Performance Measurement	
								Cost	Value Creation
HR planning	—	−30	0	−20	0	0	0	0	0
Recruiting and selection		—	0	−10	−20	−30	0	30	−40
Training and development			—	0	0	0	0	30	−10
Performance management and appraisal				—	0	−30	20	0	−20
Compensation and benefits					—	−50	0	40	0
Work organiza-tion (e.g., teams)						—	0	0	0
Communication systems							—	0	0
HR performance measurement									

Source: Brian Becker, Mark Huselid, and Dave Ulrich, *The HR Scorecard* (Cambridge, MA: Harvard University Press, 2001).

- Ensure that teams are implemented in a systemic way.
- Establish methods for measuring the results of the change.
- Ensure continuity of leadership and appoint "champions" of the initiative.[36]

16.4a Building a Business Case for Change and Engaging Stakeholders

Change can be threatening because it asks people to abandon the old ways of doing things and accept new approaches that, to them at least, are untested. Figure 16.6 shows how to "build a bridge" with the firm's stakeholders such as its employees, the unions it

1B Highlights in HRM

Testing the Alignment of the HR System with HR Deliverables

Indicate on a scale of −100 to +100 the degree to which the following HR system elements facilitate the HR deliverables shown. Examples of the extremes and midpoints on that continuum are as follows:

−100: This dimension is counterproductive for enabling this deliverable.

0: This dimension has little or no effect on this deliverable.

+100: This dimension significantly enables this deliverable.

DNK: Don't now or have no opinion.

	HR Planning	Recruiting and Selection	Training and Development	Management and Appraisal	Compensation and Benefits	Work Organiza-tion (e.g., Teams)	Communication Systems
Employment stability	0	0	0	0	−50	−20	0
Team-based behaviors	0	0	−30	−20	−40	0	0
Strategy-focused behaviors	0	0	0	0	40	0	0
High-talent staffing level	0	−50	0	−50	0	0	0

1C Highlights in HRM

Testing the Alignment of HR Deliverables

Indicate on a scale of −100 to +100 the degree to which each HR deliverable in the following chart enables each strategic driver. Empty cells indicate this is not a key deliverable for a particular driver. Examples of the extremes and midpoints on that continuum are as follows:

−100: This deliverable is counterproductive for enabling this driver.

0: This deliverable has little or no effect on this driver.

+100: This deliverable significantly enables this driver.

DNK: Don't know or have no opinion.

Strategic Performance Drivers	HR Deliverable			
	Employment Stability among Senior R&D Staff	Team-Based Behaviors	Strategy-Focused Performance	High-Talent Staffing Level
1. Shorten product development times	−80	−30	30	
2. Enhance customer focus and responsiveness	−20		−20	
3. Enhance productivity		−10	−50	−40
4. Develop and successfully manage joint ventures	−10	−50		

570

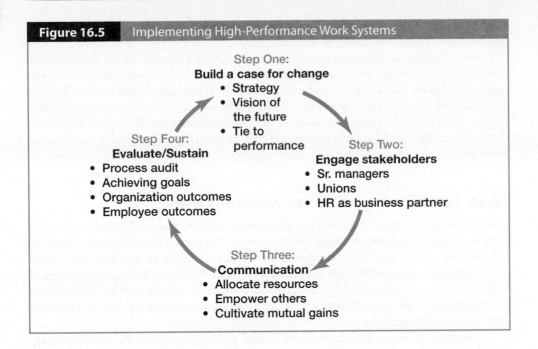

Figure 16.5 Implementing High-Performance Work Systems

Step One:
Build a case for change
- Strategy
- Vision of the future
- Tie to performance

Step Two:
Engage stakeholders
- Sr. managers
- Unions
- HR as business partner

Step Three:
Communication
- Allocate resources
- Empower others
- Cultivate mutual gains

Step Four:
Evaluate/Sustain
- Process audit
- Achieving goals
- Organization outcomes
- Employee outcomes

works with, and other groups when implementing a high-performance work systems.[37] One way is to show the groups where the business is today—its current performance and capabilities. Then show them where the organization needs to be in the future. The gap between today and the future represents a starting point for discussion. When executives at TRW wanted to make a case for change to high-performance work systems, they used employee attitude surveys and data on turnover costs. The data provided enough

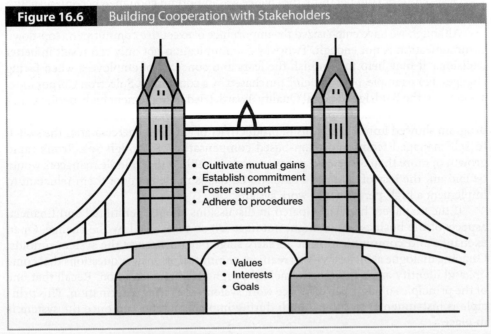

Figure 16.6 Building Cooperation with Stakeholders

- Cultivate mutual gains
- Establish commitment
- Foster support
- Adhere to procedures

- Values
- Interests
- Goals

Source: Adapted from the Conference Board of Canada.

ammunition to get a conversation going about needed changes and sparked some suggestions about how they could be implemented.

Some research studies have found that unions can be a barrier to high-performance work systems, perhaps because unions are concerned that the efficiencies achieved might be so great that workers can be eliminated.[38] To help get unions on board, managers should try to create "win-win" situations in which all stakeholders, including unions, gain from the implementation of high-performance work systems. Organizations such as Shell and Novartis have found that "interest-based" (win-win) approaches work best.

16.4b Establishing a Communications Plan

Building support for an HPWS and implementing it will be more readily accomplished if a top manager champions or promotes the system. The person should spend a substantial amount of time communicating with employees about the change and the reasons for it, and then, along with other top managers, work closely with middle managers to make it happen. Because middle managers operate in the trenches of an organization amid both its people and processes, they can have a big impact on a firm's performance and how fast changes take place.[39]

Nonetheless, major transformations should not be shouldered by middle managers. It needs to be clear to employees that the CEO and senior managers are intimately involved with and committed to the change. When Harley-Davidson tried to institute employee involvement groups without first demonstrating their own personal commitment to the program, employees were apathetic about it. They concluded that the changes were just "another program" put in place by HR. Similarly, the CEO of a business consulting company was adamant that his vice presidents understand a new initiative and give a short speech about it at an introductory session. On the day of the program's launch, however, the CEO himself did not show up. The message to the vice presidents was clear. The CEO did not think the change was important enough to become an active participant. Not surprisingly, the change was never implemented.[40]

Although we have emphasized the importance of executive commitment, top-down communication is not enough. Two-way communication not only can result in better decisions, it may help to diminish the fears and concerns of employees when facing changes. For example, prior to being purchased by a competitor, Solectron Corporation, a winner of the Baldrige National Quality Award, tried to implement high-performance work systems to capitalize on the knowledge and experience of its employees. A pilot program showed immediate gains in productivity of almost 20 percent after the switch to self-managed teams and team-based compensation. Although Solectron's rapid growth of more than 50 percent per year made it unlikely that middle managers would be laid off, the loss of control to empowered teams made many of them reluctant to implement a high-performance work system.

If the managers had participated in discussions about operational and financial aspects of the business, they might not have felt so threatened by the change. Open exchange and communication at an early stage pay off later as the system unfolds. Ongoing dialogue at all levels helps reaffirm commitment, answer questions that come up, and identify areas for improvement throughout implementation. Recall that one of the principles of high-performance work systems is sharing information. This principle is instrumental to success both during implementation and once the system is in place.

Navigating the Transition to High-Performance Work Systems

Different organizations implement high-performance work systems in different ways. In start-up firms, managers have the advantage of being able to put everything in place at once. However, when organizations have to be retrofitted, the process can be a bit more cumbersome. For example, when Honeywell switched to a high-performance work system in one of its plants, employees attended training programs and participated in the redesign of their jobs while the plant was shut down and being reequipped with new technology. When the new plant was reopened, self-managing teams were put in place, and a new pay system was implemented for the high-performance workforce.[41]

Not every organization has the luxury of suspending operations while changes are put in place. For example, in already existing organizations, the pieces of the system often have to be changed incrementally rather than as a total program. Establishing an implementation plan that provides a timetable for redesigning the work flow and training employees can keep the effort from bogging down.

Adhering to New Procedures

Following the new procedures required to implement an HPWS is often the hardest part of the job. As one HR executive puts it, "Procedure is the 'rug' on which alliances [a firm's stakeholders] stand. Pull it out by making a unilateral management determination or otherwise changing the rules of the game, and the initiative will falter. Procedure keeps the parties focused."[42]

HR managers are in a good position to help employees in transition handle what they are going through in terms of changes. When the old ways of doing things are abandoned, many experienced employees begin to feel like beginners again on the job. This can be stressful and sometimes polarizes employees. To cope, many people, including managers, are likely to revert to older routines. Ford and Texas Instruments created special units to facilitate their transitions to high-performance work systems. The consumer-goods maker Unilever created a team of senior line and HR managers to help prevent relapses.[43]

16.4c Evaluating and Sustaining the Success of the System

Once high-performance work systems are in place, they need to be monitored and evaluated over time. First, there should be a **process audit** to determine whether the system has been implemented as it was designed and whether the principles of high-performance work systems are being reinforced. Employee-related questions such as the following might be included in the audit:

process audit
Determining whether the high-performance work system has been implemented as designed.

- Are employees actually working together, or is the term "team" just a label?
- Are employees getting the information they need to make empowered decisions, and are they engaged?
- Are training programs helping employees develop the knowledge and skills they need?
- Are employees being rewarded for good performance and useful suggestions?
- Are employees treated fairly so that power differences are minimal?
- Are quality-of-life goals being achieved for employees?

To determine whether the HPWS is succeeding, managers should look at metrics such as the following:

- Are the behaviors the organization desires being exhibited on the job?

- Are quality, productivity, flexibility, and customer service objectives being met?
- Is the organization more competitive than in the past?

Implementing an HPWS is one thing. Sustaining it is another. As with any change activity, there will be missteps during the system's implementation for any number of reasons. Xerox Corporation found that when it implemented teams without also changing its compensation system to support teamwork, it got caught in a bad transition. The teams actually performed worse than employees working alone. In other words, building and fostering high-performance work systems can't be a piecemeal approach.

Because the work teams in an HPWS are performing at their peak, burnout can be a problem. If there aren't enough staff members to manage the volume of work, stress is almost guaranteed. Employee poaching by competitors can occur, too. Motorola's Indian division strategically recruited its employees and put together a high-performance work system, only to have them hired away by a competitor. Consequently, Motorola had to look for new ways to motivate and retain the division's workforce.

Small Business Application

Are Your Employees Engaged, or Do You Need an HPWS?

Companies with disengaged workforces suffer from problems that do not seem to get better, including excessive employee turnover, lower productivity, and profits. When employees are engaged, however, the results can be much different. One Gallup study reported that firms with top engagement scores had 18 percent higher productivity and 16 percent higher profitability. Another study found that engaged employees outperform other employees and are far less likely to leave their organizations. In a small business, engagement can have an even bigger impact because the margin for error when it comes to success or failure is so thin.

As a small-business owner, how do you know if your employees are engaged or not? One way would be to survey them. Gallup has come up with a 12-question survey designed to gauge employee engagement that includes:

- Do you have the materials and equipment you need to do your work right?
- At work, do you have the opportunity to do what you do best every day?
- In the last seven days, have you received recognition or praise for doing good work?
- Does your supervisor, or someone at work, seem to care about you as a person?
- Is there someone at work who encourages your development?
- At work, do your opinions seem to count?

Business author Barb Taylor Krantz has another idea about how to measure engagement: Just talk to your employees. A CEO of a large company can't talk to all of the firm's employees, but a small-business person can. What motivates them to achieve, which aspects of their jobs are most satisfying, and how they can contribute more in those areas? What challenging goals can they set for their own development? If your employees can't answer these questions, chances are good they are not engaged.

So how can you increase the engagement of employees other than by asking them to work harder than they already are? Simply looking for a quick fix to engagement won't work, says HR blogger Gautam Ghosh. "For world-class companies like Southwest Airlines, employee engagement is a way of life that's taken them years to build into their cultures. It's not a strategy or program to them. It's just part of their corporate DNA."

Instead you may have to look at your firm's culture, rethink how you operate, and implement the concepts in this chapter. Two other good publications that can help a small business implement an HPWS are *The HR Scorecard: Linking People, Strategy, and Performance* and *The Power of Full Engagement: Managing Energy, Not Time, Is the Key to High Performance and Personal Renewal*.

Sources: Duckjung Shin and Alison M. Konrad, "Causality between High-Performance Work Systems and Organizational Performance," *Journal of Management* 43, no. 4 (April 2017): 973; Barb Krantz Taylor, "Are Employees Going Above and Beyond?" *The Bailey Group* (July 10, 2009), http://www.thebaileygroup.com; "The Backlash against Employee Engagement," RiseSmart (April 2, 2010), http://www.risesmart.com.

Finally, high-performance work systems should be periodically reevaluated in terms of new organizational priorities and initiatives. Because a high-performance work system is built to deliver value to customers and thereby increase a firm's strength, as their needs change, so too should the system. When change occurs, it should be guided by a clear understanding of the business needs and exhibit a close alignment with strategy.

16.5 Outcomes of High-Performance Work Systems

LO **4**

Is having a high-performance work system enough to give a firm a competitive advantage?

Organizations achieve a wide variety of outcomes from high-performance work systems and effective HR management. We have categorized these outcomes in terms of either *employee concerns* such as quality-of-work-life issues and job security or *competitive challenges* such as the firm's performance, productivity, and profitability. Throughout the text, we have emphasized that the best organizations find ways to achieve a balance between these two sets of outcomes and pursue activities that improve both.

16.5a Employee Outcomes and Quality of Work Life

Properly implemented, managed, and monitored, high-performance work systems offer employees many potential benefits. Because the systems emphasize learning, people can take more risks, generate new ideas, and make mistakes, which in turn can actually lead to new products, services, and markets. As Richard Carlton, a former executive of 3M, put it, "You can't stumble if you're not in motion."[44] Because employees are more informed and have more latitude to decide how to achieve their goals, they are likely to feel they have a bigger role to play and that their opinions and expertise are valued more. As a result, they are more likely to be satisfied on the job and find their career-growth needs are being met. In addition, workers are likely to have more job security because their skills are higher and their potential to contribute to the organization is greater. This makes them more marketable to other organizations.

Conversely, when employees are underutilized, the performance of an organization suffers, and employees develop poor work attitudes and habits. Some years ago, the British Land Rover Company, a manufacturer of four-wheel-drive vehicles, found itself saddled with a notorious reputation for poor quality and productivity. Then it underwent a fundamental transformation. The company instituted extensive training (including giving every employee a personal training fund to be used on any subject), implemented more team-based production methods, reduced the number of separate job classifications, developed more cooperative relations with organized labor, and began a total quality program. As a result of these changes, productivity, quality, and the company's sales soared. However, despite massive evidence documenting the effectiveness of the new system, BMW, which later bought the company, began to dictate changes after taking over Land Rover—changes that ultimately undid its transformation.[45]

16.5b Organizational Outcomes and Competitive Advantage

Several organizational outcomes can also result from using high-performance work systems. These outcomes include greater innovation for a firm, greater flexibility, higher productivity, lower costs, better responsiveness to customers, and higher revenues and profits.

For example, a study of 962 firms in multiple industries showed that high-performance work systems resulted in an annual increase in profits of more than $3,800 per employee. Another study of 62 automobile plants showed that those implementing high-performance work systems had 47 percent better quality and 43 percent better productivity.[46]

However, although benchmarks such as these are indicative of success, they may not be enough to sustain an organization's competitive advantage. Recall that in Chapter 2 we said that organizations can create a sustainable competitive advantage through people if they focus on four criteria. The same criteria hold for high-performance work systems:

- *Valuable:* High-performance work systems increase value by establishing ways to increase innovation and efficiency, decrease costs, improve processes, and provide something unique to customers.

- *Rare:* High-performance work systems help organizations develop and harness skills, knowledge, and abilities that are not equally available to all organizations.

- *Difficult to imitate:* High-performance work systems are designed around team processes and capabilities that cannot be transported, duplicated, or copied by rival firms.

- *Organized:* High-performance work systems combine the talents of employees and rapidly deploy them in new assignments with maximum flexibility.[47]

These criteria clearly show how high-performance work systems, in particular, and human resources management, in general, are instrumental in achieving competitive advantage through people.

However, for all their potential, implementing high-performance work systems is not an easy task. The systems are complex and require close partnering among all of a firm's stakeholders. Ironically, this very complexity can lead to a competitive advantage. The ability to integrate business and employee concerns is indeed rare, and doing it in a way that adds value to customers is especially noteworthy. Organizations such as Google and Southwest Airlines have been able to do it, and as a result they enjoy a competitive advantage.

Land Rover vehicles were notoriously known for their poor quality until a company-wide transformation resulted in better quality and productivity.

Daniel Jones/Alamy

Summary

LO 1 High-performance work systems are specific combinations of HR practices, work structures, and processes that maximize the knowledge, skills, commitment, and flexibility of employees. The systems are based on the principles of shared information and trust, knowledge development, performance-reward linkages, and egalitarianism and employee engagement.

LO 2 High-performance work systems are composed of several interrelated components. Team members are carefully selected and undergo extensive training, including cross training, and often share leadership duties. Integrated information technology systems can help ensure that employees have the information they need to make timely and productive decisions. To align the interests of employees with those of the organization, the reward systems associated with high-performance work systems are performance-based and often include group and organizational incentive pay and sometimes skill-based pay. When all the pieces of the system support and complement one another, high-performance work systems achieve horizontal fit. When the system is aligned with the competitive priorities of the organization as a whole, it achieves vertical fit as well.

LO 3 Implementing high-performance work systems within existing organizations often has to be done in stages. The implementation is much more likely to go smoothly if a business case is first made for the HPWS and fully communicated to employees. Gaining the support of the firm's various stakeholders is essential. A company's HR department can be an invaluable partner when it comes to implementing an HPWS. HR personnel can also help establish a transition structure to shepherd the implementation through its various stages and reassure employees they will be successful working in the new system. Once the system is in place, it should be evaluated in terms of its processes, outcomes, sustainability, and ongoing fit with strategic objectives of the organization.

LO 4 When implemented effectively, high-performance work systems benefit both employees and their organizations and can provide a company with a sustainable competitive advantage.

Key Terms

high-performance work system (HPWS)

horizontal fit

process audit

vertical fit

Discussion Questions

LO 1 Do you think the fundamental principles of getting employees highly involved with their work provides an adequate context for designing high-performance work systems? What other concerns or guidelines for developing high-performance work systems would you suggest?

LO 2 Although achieving both horizontal and vertical fit are important for high-performance work systems, which do you consider more critical and why?

LO 3 This chapter emphasizes the processes required to implement a high-performance work system. What are the most critical steps to successfully implementing one?

LO 4 Do high-performance work systems always result in a win-win situation for employers and their employees? Why or why not?

Assessing the Strategic Fit of High-Performance Work Systems

High-performance work systems are potentially power-ful tools. However, ensuring all HR practices support one another and the principles of an HPWS is not always easy. Some HR practices might support the HPWS while others work against it. It takes only one misaligned practice to crash the whole system. Recall that the HPWS principles include the following:

- Egalitarianism and engagement
- Shared information and trust
- Knowledge development
- Performance-reward linkage

Assignment

The following figure lists the main HR practices used at Egan Clothiers, Ltd. Working in teams of four to six, assess the extent to which you believe each HR practice supports (or works against) each of the HPWS principles.

1. For each cell in the matrix, insert a number indicat-ing the extent to which you believe the HR practice

supports the principle or is counterproductive. The scale runs from –5 (strongly counterproductive) to 5 (very supportive). Zero indicates neither support nor detriment.

2. When you are done filling in each cell, add the num-bers across each row to determine how supportive each HR practice is of all of the principles. Which HR practice is the most supportive? Which HR practice is the least supportive?

3. Add each column to see how the overall set of HR practices supports each principle. Which principle is most strongly supported? Which principle is the big-gest concern?

4. Add the rows and/or columns to see how well the HPWS is supported overall. What changes would you recommend to improve the system?

Note: This figure corresponds to the integrative case on Egan Clothiers, Ltd., in the back of the text. The exercise can be used in conjunction with the case, or you may simply refer to the case as background reading.

EGAN CLOTHIERS, LTD.

HPWS PRINCIPLES

HR PRACTICES		Egalitarianism	Shared Information	Knowledge Development	Performance-Reward Linkage	
STRUCTURE	• Cross-functional team					Row 1
	• Department rotation					Row 2
STAFFING	• Select for experience					
	• Promote from within					
TRAINING	• Retail selling skills					
	• Customer service					
REWARDS	• Results appraisal					
	• Forced distribution					
	• Individual incentives					
TECHNOLOGY	• HR information system					
	• Post performance					
		Column 1	Column 2	Column 3	Column 4	**TOTAL**

SCORING KEY

5 = strongly supports the principle
0 = neutral
–5 = strongly counterproductive

CASE STUDY ① How Implementing an HPWS Fortified the Snack-Food Maker Snyder's-Lance

When Greg Flickinger became the director of manufacturing for the snack-food maker Snyder's-Lance's Charlotte, North Carolina, facility, he was determined to build from scratch the kind of high-performance workforce he led when he worked for a competing firm. Many organizations take piecemeal approaches to improving their firms. But Flickinger knew that one-off plans for improvement would not result in sustained improvements for the plant—especially given the fact that nearly 1,000 employees worked at the Charlotte site producing more than 500 types of products. What the Charlotte plant needed was an all-encompassing high-performance work system.

The first step in developing the HPWS was to create a vision for it that could be defined succinctly and communicated easily to all staff members. Ultimately the vision was defined as follows: "To nurture a transition from a traditional work system to an employee-centric high-performance work system (HPWS) with a cultural foundation rooted in total employee involvement and focused on continuous improvement."

The details inherent in the vision then shaped the foundation of a formal but very simple and direct mission: "Take care of your people and deliver your numbers." This statement was front and center in every meeting, every communication, and every initiative that was undertaken. It provided the rallying cry and aligned everyone across the site with a concept that was easily translated into something real that people could get their minds around, says Flickinger.

To implement the HPWS, the company completely restructured the way the plant was led. The hierarchical structure of supervisors, department managers, and superintendents were eliminated. Team leaders, line leaders, and technical support leaders were put in place instead. The line leadership concept was the most critical role in the development of the plant's culture of accountability. A line leader was assigned to each line and was responsible for all of its output—from raw materials and ingredients in the door through to the finished product out the door. In essence, each line leader owned the success of all aspects of his or her line 24 hours a day. This created a single point of accountability. The technical support leaders became the support group for line leaders by providing them expertise in areas such as reliability engineering, system engineering, line changeovers, and sanitation.

Another milestone in the development of the HPWS was cross-training everyone, including salaried employees. Employees had one month to learn all the jobs and determine who would work what job. They had to learn to work together as a team in a very different way than they had ever worked before. This gave everyone on the line an opportunity to walk in the shoes of everyone else and take another step forward toward building trust and respect among salaried and hourly employees.

After the HPWS was completely implemented, the Charlotte plant experienced financial results no one thought possible:

- A 40 percent reduction in waste
- A 41 percent reduction in accidents
- A 52 percent reduction in consumer complaints

These metrics signaled that the HPWS had been effective. Moreover, the improvements were sustained in following years. What made these gains even more significant was that the performance improvements were made with negligible capital investment. The results were driven through a focus on people and processes.

Implementing an HPWS isn't an easy process, though, says Flickinger. Sustained results do not come overnight. Above all, empowering an organization at the individual level doesn't mean that a firm's managers can walk away from their guidance, prioritization, and, above all, support roles, he says. "As a leader, you have to make sure the effort touches every employee individually and in a real way. Make the tough decisions to ensure you are taking care of your people, and remember, above all else, sustained success begins and ends with them."

Questions

1. Identify how Synder's-Lance engages its employees.

2. Why might it be more effective to implement an entire new system like an HPWS rather than make incremental changes at a production facility like the one in Charlotte? Couldn't the large-scale changes create chaos in a plant its size?

Sources: Adapted from Greg Flickinger, "How Snyder's-Lance Transformed Its Plant into a High Performance Work System," *Food Processing* (2011): http://www.foodprocessing.com.

CASE STUDY 2   Whole Foods Market Faces Whole New Challenge

In this chapter we talked about how hierarchical, command-and-control types of organizational structures are giving way to high-performing work systems— systems characterized by egalitarianism, knowledge and information sharing, employee empowerment, and reward and performance linkages. Such a system has pretty well summed up Whole Foods Market, the world's leading natural and organic foods grocer. Whole Foods started out in 1980 with one small store in Austin, Texas. Today it employs nearly 19,000 employees in more than 450 stores in North America and the United Kingdom.

The company's HR practices have been a big part of its success. Whole Food isn't "run" by executives and store managers but by in-store teams. Each team is responsible for one area of the store, such as baked goods, meat, poultry, and so forth, and is empowered to make product, pricing, and staffing decisions. This high degree of decentralization allows the stores to better tailor their offerings and services to meet the needs of the communities, which helps them be more competitive.

The decentralized approach begins with hiring. The company found that centralized, online recruiting left local stores awash with resumes but not much knowledge about applicants. Applicants can still submit resumes online, but now each store has its own human resources department that aids in hiring and recruiting and in-store kiosks where applicants can apply.

Many interviews at Whole Foods Market are conducted by teams of employees. Once an applicant is hired, he or she is assigned to one of the store's teams for a trial period, after which the team members vote to determine if the person deserves a full-time spot on the team. The same process is used at the corporate level for employees who want to join the firm's marketing, human resources, finance, and IT departments.

The voting is crucial in part because it affects workers' paychecks. The teams are treated as separate profit centers and rewarded with monthly bonuses if their labor costs are under budget. Consequently, nobody wants to vote in a slacker. Not surprisingly, the company does not do a lot of monitoring of its employees. They do it themselves. "We don't have lots of rules handed down from headquarters in Austin,"

John Mackey, the founder of the company and CEO, has said. "Peer pressure enlists loyalty in ways that bureaucracy doesn't."

Speaking of bureaucracy, in many companies CEOs earn literally hundreds of times what the average worker does. Not at Whole Foods. Mackey's salary and those of other executives are capped at 19 times the average annual salary of a full time employee. Employees also vote on company-wide initiatives, and full-timers get 100 percent of their health care costs paid for.

Nearly 8 out of 10 employees say that the training Whole Foods offers helps them advance professionally. Employees are encouraged to pursue continuing education through the company's online training portal or certifications such as the American Cheese Society Certified Cheese Professional exam, green recycling classes, cooking seminars, and work-related field trips. Invariably, Whole Foods lands on Fortune's 100 Best Companies to Work For list each year. "I love working at Whole Foods, and I hope to grow with this company for years and years to come," says one of its employees. "This company empowers me and makes me feel valued and valuable."

The current challenge for Whole Foods is sustaining that environment—and the firm's success. Recently the company has been facing greater competition from lower-priced grocers like Trader Joe's and regional grocers that sell organic food, and the company's earnings and stock value have fallen. Whole Foods has responded by lowering its prices, creating a customer loyalty program, and rolling out a chain of smaller, lower priced stores called 365 to attract younger and less-affluent consumers. The company has also laid off workers, reduced the number of full-time employees, and lowered some wages. (Whole Foods' labor costs are reportedly equal to about 20 percent of its sales—twice the industry standard.)

However, some industry analysts think the changes aren't enough and that Whole Foods has been too slow to reposition itself in the marketplace. "What's happened in the natural food sector is that the world has changed very fast around it," says Joe Dobrow, a health food writer and book author. "Now there isn't very much that is unique to Whole Foods anymore."

In 2017 a hedge fund purchased about 8 percent of the Whole Foods stock and began pressuring the company to operate more like big-box grocers such as Costco and Walmart to boost its revenues and share price. The changes would likely include offering fewer product choices to customers, implementing a central distribution system, and centralized operations—or even selling the company outright to make as much money as possible for investors. Later in the year, Amazon.com bought Whole Foods Market for $13.7 billion.

Questions

1. Why don't all companies treat their employees like Whole Foods does? Are there downsides of doing so?

2. Do you think Whole Foods will have to change its HR practices to better compete? Are the practices no longer vertically or horizontally aligned with the firm's strategy? Or does the firm's strategy need to change?

Sources: Alexandra Stevenson, "Whole Foods Pressured by Activist Investor Jana Partners," *New York Times* (April 10, 2017); Tom Philpott "Employees Are Bitter as Whole Foods Chops Jobs and Wages," *Mother Jones* (October 3, 2015), http://www.motherjones.com; "Celebrating Great Workplace Cultures," *Great Place to Work Institute* (2013), http://www.greatplacetowork.com; "Whole Foods Market Named to 2013 'World's Most Ethical Companies' List," *MarketWatch* (March 6, 2013), http://www.marketwatch.com; Gary Hael and Bill Breen, "Creating a Community of Purpose: Management Innovation in Action," Harvard Business School Press, 2007; "Whole Foods Market's Unique Work Culture and Practices," ICMR (2006), http://www.icmrindia.org; Frank Roche, "HR Lessons from Whole Foods," KnowHR, http://www.knowhr.com.

Notes and References

1. Diane Landsman, "Talent Management at the Best Workplaces," *Talent Management* (April 4, 2007), http://talentmgt.com.

2. Rebecca R. Kehoe and Patrick M. Wright, "The Impact of High-Performance Human Resource Practices on Employees' Attitudes and Behaviors," *Journal of Management* 39, no. 2 (2013): 366–391; D. A. Nadler and M. S. Gerstein, "Designing High-Performance Work Systems: Organizing People, Work, Technology, and Information," *Organizational Architecture* (San Francisco: Jossey-Bass, 1992), 195–208; E. Lawler III, Susan Albers Mohrman, and Gerald E. Ledford, *Creating High Performance Organizations: Practices and Results of Employee Involvement and Total Quality Management in Fortune 1000 Companies* (San Francisco: Jossey-Bass, 1995); Edward Lawler III, Susan Albers Mohrman, and George Benson, *Organizing for High Performance: Employee Involvement, TQM, Reengineering, and Knowledge Management in the Fortune 1000*: The CEO Report (San Francisco: Jossey-Bass, 2001). See also David Nadler, Michael Tushman, and Mark Nadler, *Competing by Design: The Power of Organizational Architecture* (New York: Oxford University Press, 1997); Jody Gitell Hoffer, "Relationships and Resilience," *Journal of Applied Behavioral Science* 44, no. 1 (March 2008): 25–47.

3. Beth Kowitt, "At Ikea, No Ranks, No Rancor," *Fortune* (March 15, 2016): 202.

4. Verne Harnish, "Five Ways to Keep Employees Excited," *Fortune* (December 3, 2012), 40.

5. Tae-Youn Park and Jason D. Shaw, "Turnover Rates and Organizational Performance: A Meta-Analysis" (2013): 268; J. B. Arthur, "Effects of Human Resource Systems on Manufacturing Performance and Turnover," *Academy of Management Journal* 37 (1994): 670–687; M. Huselid, "The Impact

of Human Resource Management Practices on Turnover, Productivity, and Corporate Financial Performance," *Academy of Management Journal* 38 (1995): 635–672; Mark A. Youndt, Scott A. Snell, James W. Dean, Jr., and David P. Lepak, "Human Resource Management, Manufacturing Strategy, and Firm Performance," *Academy of Management Journal* 39, no. 4 (August 1996): 836–866; John F. Tomer, "Understanding High-Performance Work Systems: The Joint Contribution of Economics and Human Resource Management," *The Journal of Socio-Economics* 30, no. 1 (January 2001): 63; Kris Dunn, "Rules of Engagement," Workforce Management Online (July 2008).

6. Arnold B. Bakker, Evangelia Demerouti, and Ana Isabel Sanz-Vergel, "Burnout and Work Engagement: The JD–R Approach," *Annual Review Organizational Psychology, Organ. Behavior* 1, no. 1 (2014): 389–411; Rasha Mourtada, "Bosses Fan the Flames of Burnout," *Globe and Mail* (June 8, 2011), http://www.theglobeandmail.com.

7. "Developing and Sustaining High-Performance Work Teams," *SHRM* (July 23, 2017), https://www.shrm.org.

8. Linda Anderson, "A Little Something for the Weekend," *Financial Times* (June 3, 2011), http://www.ft.com.

9. Carlton P. McNamara, "Making Human Capital Productive," *Business and Economic Review* 46, no. 1 (October–December 1999): 10–13; Meagan Stovel and Nick Bontis, "Voluntary Turnover: Knowledge Management—Friend or Foe?" *Journal of Intellectual Capital* 3, no. 3 (2002): 303–322.

10. M. Zhang, C. Zhu, P. Dowling, and T Bartram, "Exploring the Effects of High-Performance Work Systems (HPWS) on the Work-Related Well-Being of Chinese Hospital Employees," *International Journal of Human Resource Management* 24, no. 16 (December 2013): 3196–3212.

11. Hui Zhang and Lanyun Wang, "The Description and Evaluation on the Modern Mechanism of High-Performance Work Systems," *Modern Management* 3, no. 5 (October 2013): 135–140.

12. Steven D. Silver, "Designing Technology for Managing the Information Exchange of Decision Making Teams," *Decision Support Systems* 61 (2014): 136–146; Martin Eppler and Oliver Sukowski, "Managing Team Knowledge: Core Processes, Tools and Enabling Factors," *European Management Journal* 18, no. 3 (June 2000): 334–341; Andrea Foote, "One in a Million: Ocean Spray Henderson Has Parlayed Hard Work and Dedication into a Remarkable Operations Milestone," *BeverageWorld* 122, no. 8 (August 15, 2003): 22–29; Rick Frattali, "The Company That Teaches Together Performs Together," T+D 61, no. 7 (July 2007), http://www.astd.org.

13. Sheng Wang, Raymond A. Noe, and Zhong-Ming Wang, "Motivating Knowledge Sharing in Knowledge Management Systems: A Quasi–Field Experiment," *Journal of Management* 40, no. 4 (2014): 978–1009; Jeffrey Kling, "High Performance Work Systems and Firm Performance," *Monthly Labor Review* (May 1995): 29–36; Chad Kaydo, "Top of the Charts: FedEx," *Sales and Marketing Management* 150, no. 7 (July 1998): 46, 48; Michael Trachtman, "Roving Internet Appliances," *Web Techniques* 6, no. 10 (October 2001): 55–57; Richard Shulman, "Just Say the Word," *Supermarket Business* 56, no. 6 (June 15, 2001): 19–20; "Customer Service Excellence: Continuously Delighting Your Customers," *PR Newswire* (February 24, 2005), http://www.prnewswire.com

14. Mark Chen, "Applying the High-Performance Work Teams to EPC," *AACE International Transactions* (2002): PM61-PM67; Valerie Sessa, "Supporting Work Team Effectiveness: Best Management Practices for Fostering High Performance," *Personnel Psychology* 53, no. 2 (Summer 2000): 457–460.

15. Amina Malik, Laxmikant Manroop, and Pankaj C. Patel, "An Empirical Examination of the Relationship between HPWS and Firm Performance," *Academy of Management Proceedings* 2016, no. 1 (2016); Martha Gephart and Mark Van Buren, "Power of High Performance Work Systems," Training & Development 50, no. 10 (October 1996): 21–36; Michael Beer, "How to Develop an Organization Capable of Sustained High Performance: Embrace the Drive for Results-Capability Development Paradox," *Organizational Dynamics* 29, no. 4 (Spring 2001): 233–247.

16. Karina Van De Voorde and Susanne Beijer, "The Role of Employee HR Attributions in the Relationship between High-Performance Work Systems and Employee Outcomes," *Human Resource Management Journal* 25 no. 1 (2015): 62–78; Lawler, Mohrman, and Ledford, *Creating High Performance Organizations*; Eileen Appelbaum, Thomas Bailey, Peter Berg, and Narne Kalleberg, *Manufacturing Advantage: Why High-Performance Work Systems Pay Off* (Ithaca, NY: Cornell University Press, 2000); Gil Preuss and Brenda Lautsch, "The Effect of Formal versus Informal Job Security on Employee Involvement Programs," *Relations Industrielles* 57, no. 3 (Summer 2002): 517–539; Wendy S. Becker, "*Manufacturing Advantage: Why High-Performance Work Systems Pay Off*," Personnel Psychology 56, no. 2 (Summer 2003): 549–553.

17. Liang-Chih Huang et al., "High Performance Work Systems, Employee Well-being, and Job Involvement: An Empirical Study," *Personnel Review* 45, no. 2 (2016): 296–314; Laurie J. Bassi and Mark E. Van Buren, "Sustaining High Performance in Bad Times," *Training & Development* 51, no. 6 (June 1997): 32–42; Michael J. Stevens and Michael A. Campion, "Staffing Work Teams: Development and Validation of a Selection Test for Teamwork Settings," *Journal of Management* 25, no. 2 (1999): 207–228.

18. Christopher Tkaczyk, "Tips from Recruiters at the 100 Best Companies," *Fortune* (March 15, 2016): 90.

19. Carolee Coleter, "To Build a Productive Team, Interview Effectively," *Natural Foods Merchandiser* 25, no. 12 (December 2004): 27; Kris Dunn, "Rules of Engagement," *Workforce Management Online* (July 2008).

20. Christopher Tkaczyk, "My Five Days of 'Bleeding Green,'" *Fortune* (March 15, 2016), http://www.fortune.com.

21. Alec Levenson, "The Value of High Performance Work Design," *Talent Economy* (November 7, 2017), http://www.talenteconomy.io.

22. Douglas McCarthy, Kimberly Mueller, and Jennifer Wrenn, "Henry Ford Health System: A Framework for System Integration, Coordination, Collaboration, and Innovation," *Commonwealth Fund* (August 2009), http://www.common-wealthfund.org.

23. Chris Matthews, "This Company Gave Every One of Its Employees a $100K Christmas Bonus," *Fortune* (December 11, 2015), http://fortune.com; Erica Frey, "Hilcorp Energy," *Fortune* (August 12, 2013), 14.

24. Rosemary Batt and Lisa Moynihan, "The Viability of Alternative Call Centre Production Models," *Human Resource Management Journal* 12, no. 4 (2002): 14. For more information on the potential application of "intracapital," see Gifford Pinchot, "Free Intraprise," *Executive Excellence* 18, no. 1 (January 2001): 10; Frank Giancola, "Skill-Based Pay—Issues for Consideration," *Benefits & Compensation Digest* 44, no. 5 (May 2007): 1–15.

25. Rod Newing, "Targets Are Linked to Pay by Early Adopters," *Financial Times* (June 7, 2011), http://www.ft.com.

26. David Paper, James Rodger, and Parag Pendharker, "A BPR Case Study at Honeywell," *Business Process Management Journal* 7, no. 2 (2001): 85–93. See also Robert McNabb and Keith Whitfield, "Job Evaluation and High Performance Work Practices: Compatible or Conflictual?" *Journal of Management Studies* 38, no. 2 (March 2001): 293–312; Leslie A. Weatherly, "Performance Management: Getting It Right from the Start," *HRMagazine* 49, no. 3 (March 2004): S1–S11.

27. Douglas McCarthy, Kimberly Mueller, and Jennifer Wrenn, "Henry Ford Health System: A Framework for System Integration, Coordination, Collaboration, and Innovation," *Commonwealth Fund* (August 2009), http://www.common-wealthfund.org.

28. Rod Newing, "Targets Are Linked to Pay by Early Adopters," *Financial Times* (June 7, 2011), http://www.ft.com.

29. Rachel Emma Silverman, "For Hourly Jobs, White-Collar Perks," *Wall Street Journal* (October 8, 2011), B8.

30. Stacy Cowley, "New Payday Options for Making Ends Meet," *New York Times* (July 4, 2016), https://www.nytimes.com.

31. Warren Bennis, "The Future Has No Shelf Life," *Executive Excellence* 17, no. 8 (August 2000): 5–6; Peggy Holman, "Culture Change," *Executive Excellence* 17, no. 7 (July 2000): 16; Clinton Longenecker, "Building High Performance Management Teams," *Industrial Management* 43, no. 6 (November–December 2001): 21–26; Wendy S. Becker, "Manufacturing Advantage: Why High-Performance Work Systems Pay Off," *Personnel Psychology* 56, no. 2 (Summer 2003): 549; Srivastava Pallavi and Jyotsna Bhatnagar, "Turnaround at Motorola India—Mobile Devices Business through the HR Lever," *The Journal for Decision Makers* 33, no. 1 (January–March 2008): 119–129.

32. W. Randy Evans and Walter D. Davis, "High-Performance Work Systems as an Initiator of Employee Proactivity and Flexible Work Processes," *Organization Management Journal* 12, no. 2 (2015): 64–74; Keith Newton, "The High Performance Workplace: HR-Based Management Innovations in Canada," *International Journal of Technology Management* 16, no. 1–3 (1998): 177–192; Georg Von Krogh, Kazuo Ichijo, and Ikujiro Nonaka, *Enabling Knowledge Creation: How to Unlock the Mystery of Tacit Knowledge and Release the Power of Innovation* (New York: Oxford University Press, 2000); Lawler, Mohrman, and Benson, *Organizing for High Performance.*

33. Patrick M. Wright and Scott A. Snell, "Toward a Unifying Framework for Exploring Fit and Flexibility in Strategic Human Resource Management," *Academy of Management Review* 23, no. 4 (October 1998): 756–772; Clair Brown and Michael Reich, "Micro-Macro Linkages in High-Performance Employment Systems," *Organization Studies* 18, no. 5 (1997): 765–781; S. A. Snell, M. Shadur, and P. M. Wright, "Human Resources Strategy: The Era of Our Ways," in M. A. Hitt, R. E. Freeman, and J. S. Harrison (eds.), *Handbook of Strategic Management* (London: Blackwell, 2002), 627–649.

34. Björn Michaelis, Joachim D. Wagner, and Lars Schweizer, "Knowledge as a Key in the Relationship between High-Performance Work Systems and Workforce Productivity," *Journal of Business Research* 69, no. 5 (2015): 1035–1044; Van Buren and Werner, "High Performance Work Systems," 15–23; Gilbert Probst, Steffen Raub, and Kai Romhardt, *Managing Knowledge—Building Blocks for Success* (New York: Wiley, 2000). For a similar example of horizontal fit within European firms, see Sue Hutchinson, John Purcell, and Nick Kinnie, "Evolving High Commitment Management and the Experience of the RAC Call Center," *Human Resource Management Journal* 10, no. 1 (2000): 63–78.

35. Brian Becker, Mark Huselid, and Dave Ulrich, *The HR Scorecard: Linking People, Strategy, and Performance* (Cambridge, MA: Harvard Business School Press, 2001).

36. Jongwook Pak and Seongsu Kim, "Team Manager's Implementation, High Performance Work Systems Intensity, and Performance: A Multilevel Investigation," *Journal of Management* (2016): 0149206316646829; Arup Varma, Richard W. Beatty, Craig Eric Schneier, and David O. Ulrich, "High Performance Work Systems: Exciting Discovery or Passing Fad?" Human Resource Planning 22, no. 1 (1999): 26–37; Martha Gephart and Mark Van Buren, "Power of High Performance Work Systems," *Training & Development* 50, no. 10 (October 1996): 21–36; Foote, "One in a Million: Ocean Spray Henderson," 22–29.

37. Takao Katom, Hideaki Miyajima, and Hideo Owan, *Does Employee Stock Ownership Work?* Research Institute of Economy, Trade and Industry (RIETI; 2016); Louise Clarke and Larry Haiven, "Workplace Change and Continuous Bargaining," *Relations Industrielles* 54, no. 1 (Winter 1999): 168–191; Ruth Wright, "Forging Sustainable Alliances in a New Economy," *Canadian Business Review* (Summer 1995): 20–24; Sukanya Sengupta, "The Impact of Employee-Share-Ownership Schemes on Performance in Unionised and Non-Unionised Workplaces," *Industrial Relations Journal* 39, no. 3 (May 2008): 170–190.

38. Akhtar Mahmood, Muhammad Kashif Khurshid, and Usman Ali, "The Impact of High Performance Work System on Employees Attitude: The Mediating Role of Human Resource Flexibility," *Journal of Contemporary Management Sciences* 2, no. 1 (2017): 83–124; Wenchuan Liu, James P. Guthrie, Patrick C. Flood, and Sarah Maccurtain, "Unions and the Adoption of High Performance Work Systems: Does Employment Security Play a Role?" *Industrial & Labor Relations Review* 63, no. 1 (October 2009): 109.

39. Ethan R. Mollick, "People and Process, Suits and Innovators: The Role of Individuals in Firm Performance," *Social Science Research Network* (June 27, 2010), http://papers.ssrn.com.

40. Karina Van De Voorde and Susanne Beijer, "The Role of Employee HR Attributions in the Relationship between High-Performance Work Systems and Employee Outcomes," *Human Resource Management Journal* 25, no. 1 (2015): 62–78; Varma, Beatty, Schneier, and Ulrich, "High Performance Work Systems," 26–37; Gephart and Van Buren, "Power of High Performance Work Systems"; "Making Change Work—for Real," *HRFocus* 80, no. 1 (January 2003): S1.

41. Judith A. Neal, Cheryl L. Tromley, Ernie Lopez, and Jeanne Russell. "From Incremental Change to Retrofit," *The Academy of Management Executive* 9, no. 1 (February 1995): 42–54.

42. Wright, "Forging Sustainable Alliances," 20–24; Hannele Rubin, "How CEOs Get Results," *Chief Executive* (February 2001): 8.

43. Randa A. Wilbur, "Making Changes the Right Way," *Workforce* (March 1999): S12–S13; Gephart and Van Buren, "Power of High Performance Work Systems"; Irena St. John-Brooks, "CEOs See HR as Helping to Lead Organizational Efforts: USA," *Benefits & Compensation International* 32, no. 1 (July/August 2002): 73–74; "Human Resources Role Transformed

at Deutsche Bank," *Human Resource Management International Digest* 10, no. 5 (2002): 12–14; Michael Svoboda and Silke Schroder, "Transforming Human Resources in the New Economy: Developing the Next Generation of Global HR Managers at Deutsche Bank AG," *Human Resource Management* 40, no. 3 (Fall 2001): 261–273; "HR Advice: Manage Transition—Not Just Change," *HR Briefing* (November 15, 2002): 1–2; "HR Must Seize Major Role over Change Management," *Personnel Today* (May 20, 2003): 8.

44. Liang-Chih Huang et al., "High Performance Work Systems, Employee Well-Being, and Job Involvement: An Empirical Study," *Personnel Review* 45, no. 2 (2016): 296–314; "How to Take the 'Non' out of Your Non-Performers," *Human Resource Department Management Report* (February 2005): 1–5; Paul Lukas and Maggie Overfelt, "3M, a Mining Company Built on a Mistake, Stuck It Out until a Young Man Came Along with Ideas about How to Tape Those Blunders Together as Innovations—Leading to Decades of Growth," *Fortune* (April 1, 2003), http://money.cnn.com/smallbusiness.

45. Jeffrey Pfeffer, "When It Comes to 'Best Practices'—Why Do Smart Organizations Occasionally Do Dumb Things?" reprinted from *Organizational Dynamics*, Summer 1996 with permission from Elsevier; Cordelia Brabbs, "Rover's White Knight," *Marketing* (May 18, 2000): 28; Georg Auer, "Burela to Instill Quality Culture at Land Rover," *Automotive News* 75, no. 5902 (November 6, 2000): 32x–32z; Ronald W. Pant, "Land Rover History Lesson," *Truck Trend* 8, no. 3 (May–June 2005): 12; Bradford Wernle, "Solihull Must Do 'a Halewood' to Survive; Jaguar Plant Is the Example Land Rover Factory Must Follow," *Automotive News Europe* 9, no. 19 (September 20, 2004): 39.

46. P. Kumar, AMUDHA, "High Performance Work Systems and Organizational Success," *Journal of Human Resource* 2, no. 6 (2011): 1–11; Martha A. Gephart and Mark E. Van Buren, "The Power of High Performance Work Systems," *Training & Development* 50, no. 10 (October 1996): 21–36.

47. John Purcell, "Best Practice and Best Fit: Chimera or Cul-de-Sac?" *Human Resource Management Journal* 9, no. 3 (1999): 26–41; Snell, Shadur, and Wright, "Human Resources Strategy: The Era of Our Ways," 627–649; Patrick M. Wright, Benjamin Dunford, and Scott A. Snell, "Human Resources and the Resource-Based View of the Firm," *Journal of Management* 27, no. 6 (2001): 701–721.

CASE 1

Microsoft's MACH Program Designed to Help Millennial Grads Make a Difference—Fast

Like many companies, Microsoft has been faced with the challenge of finding ways to accelerate the careers of new hires. The tech firm's executives found that its fast-track program was not especially helpful when it came to onboarding millennial employees. As Leigh Cresswell, a millennial education business manager for Microsoft, put it, too often millennials aren't given challenging work when they are first hired, which can be frustrating for them and lead to turnover. That is what happened to Cresswell at her previous employer, a multinational maker of office equipment. Their onboarding program was "just training; they didn't understand what we wanted, which was to have an impact and a voice straight away."

Microsoft did not want to make the same mistake. To deal with this issue, attract top graduates, and begin utilizing their skills quickly, the company launched the "Microsoft Academy for College Hires," or MACH for short. The 2-year program is designed to provide top new university graduates hired into the company's Evangelism, Finance, IT, Marketing, Operations, and Sales and Services organizations with onboarding courses, hands-on training, coaching, and networking opportunities. The main objective of MACH [https://careers.microsoft.com/students/mach] is not only to onboard new graduates so they can start adding value to their teams quickly, but also to more fully orient them to efficiently navigate the corporate culture and politics. MACH pushes new hires to make a more valuable contribution earlier in their career. So it's not just an onboarding program about helping people understand how they can fit into the Microsoft culture. Rather, it's about orienting people within Microsoft to drive innovation and change early in their career.

Thousands of individuals have gone through MACH since its inception. One of them, Francesco Esposito, noted that because new grads have small or nonexistent professional networks and are typically entering a large corporation for the first time, they can have a hard time launching their careers. Graduates of the MACH noted that the program not only helped them network with senior employees, but also connect with other Microsoft employees around the world. MACH has expanded to include participants in 70 countries who attend global and regional conferences with each other. This has given participants a worldwide group of peers who can provide them with support as they transition from school to the working environment. The global aspect also had the added benefit of exposing them to vastly different opportunities and parts of the company.

According to Maryann Baumgarten, who managed the development of the curriculum for the MACH program, Microsoft learned that the program needs to follow several key steps to have maximum impact. In the first year, MACH students focus on moving from the academic world to Microsoft's corporate environment. "It's a critical first step in employee retention as we help them to understand our culture, strategy, and customers," Baumgarten explains. In the second year, the participants go through career coaching and peer reviews to help them determine which career paths in the company will best suit their needs. Once a path is determined, they can choose mentors whom they can job shadow to learn more about the job's duties and responsibilities.

To facilitate the job-shadowing process, senior employees fill out an online form to make themselves available for the MACH program, but they can opt out as needed for specific time periods. The form identifies the mentor's top three skill sets, languages, and geographical location. This makes it easier for a junior employee to find a suitable match. The form also allows junior employees to search for available mentors and request career-shadowing time. To help senior employees become good mentors who can help develop and retain young workers, Microsoft offers them classes on generational milestones and characteristics as well as scenario training.

Since its start, the MACH program seems to be speeding up the contributions of millennials and improving their job satisfaction at Microsoft. "We believe that betting on young talent means bringing in new ideas to continue empowering people and organizations around the world, a key aspect in an industry that does not respect tradition, only innovation," said Elizabeth Arredon, a university recruiter for Microsoft. Joseph Ibarra, a MACH grad, is also a supporter of the program. "I've seen alumni at the MACH events, people who have accelerated quickly throughout the company and won some of Microsoft's most prestigious awards. It's really inspirational to see people come to the company and have a huge influence. It shows it can be done, even at a company with so many people."

Questions

1. How does orientation differ from onboarding?

2. Why do you think Microsoft implemented the MACH program? Can you see any drawbacks of doing so?

3. How might the program improve Microsoft's employer brand and help it attract talent?

Sources: Elliot Bullman, "Microsoft Seeks Mexican Millennials to Change the World," *The Yucatan Times* (January 22, 2017), http://www.theyucatantimes.com/2017/01/microsoft-seeks-mexican-millennials-to-change-the-world/; Microsoft Careers. https://careers.microsoft.com/students/mach (Accessed May 18, 2017); Andrew Weiss, "What Microsoft Wants Its New Grads to Know," *IT World* (July 2, 2012), http:www.itworld.com; Jennifer J. Salopek, "Onboarding Program Indoctrinates New Workers at MACH Speed," *Workforce Management* (June 2011), http://www.workforce.com; Randy Woods, "Grooming New Hires with Microsoft's MACH Program," *NWjobs* (March 13, 2010), http://blog.nwjobs.com; "Case Study: A Customized Office and SharePoint Solution for Microsoft's Internal Career Shadowing Program," 3sharp.com (July 7, 2011), http://www.3sharp.com.

Trains and Training at BNSF Railway

By its nature, the railroad industry can be a dangerous one in which to work. Consequently, railway workers must be equipped with the knowledge, tools, focus, and skills to work safely. At BNSF Railway, safety is of the upmost importance. As new hires come on board, BNSF provides training through multiple methods, including on-the-job training in the field with input from experienced employee mentors and safety assistants or safety coordinators. Formal training is provided for many positions at the company's Technical Training Center (TTC) in Overland Park, Kansas, as well as in the field.

Newly hired conductors at BNSF, for example, have an interim period before they are officially hired. Candidates must successfully respond to a panel interview. During the interview, BNSF's interviewers communicate the challenges of working for a railroad along with BNSF's safety vision. Candidates also must pass safety and rules exams, and complete either a 13- or 15-week intensive training program (depending on the location), which includes classroom and on-the-job training. The program culminates in a final exam which, when passed, qualifies students as conductors.

United Transportation Union (UTU) training coordinators help with the first week of training and pair students with experienced conductors who mentor students during the on-the-job training segment. Once the new hires are paired, the experienced conductors play a significant role in conductor training, teaching 9 to 10 weeks of the 13- to 15-week program. "I particularly focus on deadly decisions—and consequences of at-risk behaviors," says one of the UTU's training coordinators.

To further integrate a new conductor, a division's UTU training coordinators provide enhanced safety training specific to the conductor's location. This includes an overview of the local terrain and environmental extremes that a potential employee is likely to encounter. In Montana, for example, trainers help employees understand the challenges of operating through the mountains and in winter conditions.

Of course, the training at BNSF isn't just for new hires. For those on a managerial track, the company offers mentoring, safety leadership training, and an annual company-wide initiative called "People Leader Training." It is designed to develop the leadership capabilities of employees via a competitive railroad simulation and a 12-week online program that utilizes case studies, social learning, and gamification principles. BNSF also cross-trains its Transportation trainers. They become qualified to train locomotive engineers and conductors, as well as provide training on simulators and rules and remote train-control. This effectively increases BNSF's training capacity while also expanding individual trainers' areas of specialty.

Questions

1. What methods does BNSF use as part of its comprehensive training system for new hires? How do the methods differ for employees on a managerial track?

2. Explain the company's team approach to training. How does cross-training the company's trainers benefit BNSF?

3. What is the purpose of explaining during interviews BNSF's safety practices and on-the-job working challenges?

Sources: Excerpted/adapted from "Trainers Carry Forward BNSF's Safety Vision to New Hires," *Railway* (Spring 2011): 16–17; "Additional 2016 Best Award Winners," *Association for Training and Development* (October 5, 2016), https://www.td.org.

Job Analysis and Hiring Decisions at Ovania Chemical Company

Background

Ovania Chemical Corporation is a specialty chemicals producer of polyethylene terephthalate (PET) thermoplastic resins primarily used to make containers for soft drinks and bottled water, as well as packaging for food and pharmaceutical products. Although it's smaller than other chemical producers that produce globally, Ovania has competed successfully in the specialty chemical business. Its main plant is located in Steubenville, Ohio, which is positioned along the Ohio River midway between Pittsburgh, Pennsylvania, and Wheeling, West Virginia. Over the years, advances in technology have altered the nature of chemical production, and like other firms in the industry, Ovania Chemical is constantly taking steps to stay abreast of them. Not surprisingly, these technological changes have been accompanied by redesign in employee jobs. In fact, over the last 3 years, there have been drastic changes in both the number and the kinds of jobs being performed by employees. The latest change at the Steubenville plant involves the job transformation of the system analyzer position.

The System Analyzer

Because chemical production involves highly integrated process technologies, someone is needed who can monitor all of the individual components simultaneously. The system analyzer is primarily responsible for this monitoring function. It is one of the most prestigious nonmanagerial jobs in the entire plant, and its importance is likely to grow.

Formerly, the position was classified as that of a semiskilled maintenance technician, but as the plant has become more automated, the requirements for the system analyzer job have become much more extensive. Knowledge of pneumatics, hydraulics, information technology, programming, scheduling, and electrical wiring are all increasingly critical aspects of this job.

The three men who currently hold the position admit that they will be incapable of performing adequately in the future. It is estimated that within 2 years, the tasks, duties, and responsibilities of the system analyzer will have changed by more than 70 percent. For these reasons, the decision was made to recruit and select three new people for the rapidly transforming position.

Job Analysis and New Position Analysis

Forming a selection committee were Ovania's Steubenville plant manager, Ravi Sarabe; the HR manager, Emily Claire; and two senior engineers, Dave Packley and Mary Young. With the help of two consultants, they first conducted a job analysis for the new position of system analyzer. Although they had to make some predictions about what the nature of the job would be in the future, they collectively felt they had created an accurate depiction of the requirements for someone who would occupy the position. Figure 3.1 shows a list of the major performance dimensions of the job and a subsample of specific tasks characteristic of each dimension.

From this list of tasks, the selection committee then delineated a set of 12 KSAOs required for anyone in the system analyzer position (as shown in Figure 3.2). The numbers beside each ability indicate the tasks (see Figure 3.1) to which it is related. The abilities marked with an asterisk (*) were considered by the committee to be "critical." Any applicant not scoring well on each of the critical dimensions would be considered unqualified for the job.

Anticipated Selection Process

The committee hoped to find the best available talent for the job and therefore wanted to recruit externally for it. However, Ovania's top managers were

Figure 3.1	Performance Dimensions (Duties and Tasks)

Maintaining Spares and Supplies

1. Anticipates future need for parts and supplies and orders them.

2. Stocks parts and supplies in an orderly fashion.

3. Maintains and calibrates test equipment.

Troubleshooting

4. Applies calibration standards to verify operation by subjecting the system to known standards.

5. Decides whether the problem is in the sensor, in the processor, in the process stream, and/or in the sample system.

6. Uses troubleshooting guides in system manuals to determine the problem area.

7. Uses test equipment to diagnose the problem.

8. Makes a general visual inspection of the analyzer system as a first troubleshooting step.

9. Replaces components such as printed circuit boards and sensors to see if the problem can be alleviated.

Handling Revisions and New Installations

10. Makes minor piping changes such as size, routing, and additional filers.

11. Makes minor electrical changes such as installing switches and wires and making terminal changes.

12. Uses common pipefitting tools.

13. Uses common electrical tools.

14. Reads installation drawings.

Record-Keeping

15. Maintains system files showing historical record of work on each system.

16. Maintains loop files that show the application of the system.

17. Updates piping and instrument drawings if any changes are made.

18. Maintains Environmental Protection Agency records and logbooks.

19. Disassembles analyzers to perform repairs onsite or back in the shop.

20. Replaces damaged parts such as filters, electronic components, light source, lenses, sensors, and values.

21. Uses diagnostic equipment such as oscilloscopes, ohmmeters, and decade boxes.

22. Tests and calibrates repaired equipment to ensure that it works properly.

23. Reads and follows written procedures from manuals.

Routine Maintenance

24. Observes indicators on systems to ensure that there is proper operation.

25. Adds reagents to systems.

26. Decides whether the lab results or the system is correct regarding results (i.e., resolves discrepancies between lab and analyzer results).

27. Performs calibrations.

Figure 3.2	Abilities and Tasks

Numbers represent tasks cited in Figure 3.1. Asterisks indicate abilities considered critical by the committee.

Skills	Task Numbers
*Finger dexterity	3, 4, 7, 9, 10, 11, 12, 13, 19, 20, 21, 22, 25, 27
*Mechanical comprehension	3, 5, 6, 8, 9, 10, 12, 13, 7, 14, 19, 20, 22, 23, 24, 27, 11, 17
*Numerical ability	11, 3, 4, 24, 10, 21, 12, 13, 14, 27
*Spatial ability	2, 4, 5, 9, 10, 11, 14, 19, 20
*Visual pursuit	3, 4, 5, 6, 7, 8, 9, 10, 11, 14, 16, 17, 19, 20, 21, 22, 27
*Detection	2, 3, 5, 6, 8, 9, 10, 14, 19, 20, 23, 7
Oral comprehension	1, 2, 5, 6, 26, 7, 8, 9, 19, 21, 25
Written comprehension	1, 15, 16, 17, 18
Deductive reasoning	1, 5, 3, 6, 7, 8, 9, 10, 11, 19, 21, 20, 22, 2, 26, 27
Inductive reasoning	1, 3, 5, 6, 7, 8, 9, 10, 11, 19, 21, 20, 22, 2, 26, 27
Reading comprehension	3, 6, 14, 7, 22, 23, 21, 9, 27
Reading scales and tables	3, 4, 7, 8, 9, 21, 23, 24, 27, 2, 6, 14

also deeply committed to promoting from within. Ultimately the committee decided to recruit both internally and externally for the new position. The committee also decided to encourage the firm's current system analyzers to reapply for the job.

Because there was a 2-year lead time before the newly transformed position would be put in place, the committee was very careful not to include in the selection battery any skills or knowledge that could reasonably be trained for within that 2-year period. Only aptitude or ability factors were incorporated into the selection process rather than achievement tests.

The three present system analyzers were white males. However, since Ovania Chemical had a rather unenviable history of employment discrimination charges, the decision was made to have applicants undergo a battery of tests but not look at their previous experience. The committee believed this would encourage minorities and women to apply for the new position regardless of their prior experience in the field.

However, there was some concern about prejudice if a woman or minority member were to get the job. Several employees at the company said they wondered if a woman would be willing to get into the treatment tanks to check gauge readings. All of these factors, taken together, made for a very sensitive selection process. Ovania's managers, however, were dedicated to making the procedures and decisions fair and objective.

Fifty-six employees applied for the new position of system analyzer. Twenty-one were female; fifteen were African American. Only two of the three current system analyzers reapplied for the new position. The company decided that an overall total score of 800 on the 12 tests would be the cutoff score in order for an applicant to be seriously considered for the system analyzer position. This criterion resulted in the primary pool of 20 candidates shown in Figure 3.3. It should be noted that although each of the aptitude tests has been published, standardized (100 points possible for each test), and validated for other jobs, the same is not true of the system analyzer job because it's a new position. Therefore, whether the tests are predictive depends upon content validity judgments made by the managers of the company. The final cutoff scores and methods for combining the multiple predictors are problematic for the selection committee as well.

Figure 3.3	Primary Pool of Candidates

Name	Race	Sex	External/ Internal	Finger Dexterity	Mechanical Comprehension	Numerical Ability	Spatial Ability	Visual Pursuit	Detection	Oral Comprehension	Written Comprehension	Deductive Reasoning	Inductive Reasoning	Reading Comprehension	Reading Scales and Tables	=	
Baldwin, T.	W	M	I	83	76	78	76	69	71	90	70	74	72	88	92	=	941
Bittner, D.	W	M	E	92	62	88	89	96	85	90	94	93	89	97	87	=	1062
Bohlander, G.	W	M	E	67	78	74	70	76	62	80	69	71	76	78	82	=	883
Buffett, J.	B	M	E	87	97	89	61	94	93	75	90	85	96	85	80	=	1032
Denny, A.	B	F	I	92	88	72	72	78	79	69	76	81	83	81	78	=	949
Egan, M.	W	F	E	93	80	76	98	76	88	93	92	93	78	81	92	=	884
Granger, D.	W	F	I	82	82	79	75	77	73	72	80	81	77	70	80	=	856
Haney, H.	W	M	E	82	76	76	71	69	80	62	76	75	74	78	67	=	810
Kight, G.	W	F	E	65	75	72	67	80	74	62	47	66	67	60	80	=	815
Kovach, S.	W	M	E	82	87	85	85	83	88	81	80	80	83	84	80	=	998
Laukitis, T.	B	F	E	87	97	63	89	93	90	91	85	86	96	88	89	=	1054
Lesko, B.J.	B	F	I	83	84	89	91	80	82	86	88	85	84	90	89	=	1031
Rom, D.	B	M	I	80	60	67	66	67	62	74	80	67	72	75	66	=	835
Sara, E.	W	F	I	89	91	77	93	90	91	88	78	98	80	80	76	=	1021
Sauder, C.	W	F	E	76	72	78	81	80	72	73	77	75	79	82	82	=	927
Sherman, A.	W	F	I	91	82	78	93	92	94	89	77	95	77	81	92	=	1041
Snell, J.	W	M	E	80	85	84	81	81	80	89	88	84	86	81	82	=	1001
Timothy, S.	W	F	E	82	78	76	71	69	80	62	76	76	70	71	67	=	878
Whitney, J.	W	M	I	67	71	70	76	76	62	81	69	71	76	78	82	=	815
Wright, P.	W	M	I	80	60	57	56	57	62	74	80	69	72	75	65	=	887

Questions

1. How would you go about conducting a job analysis for a job that does not yet exist?

2. What reasons did the selection committee have for selecting only those factors that could not be acquired in a 2-year training program?

3. Should the concern for women getting down into the dirty treatment tanks have been a selection issue?

4. Would the test battery and selection procedure decided on be defensible in court?

Ill-Fated Love at Centrex Electronics

Juanita Hernandez-Canton never imagined she would lose her job at Centrex Electronics Corporation (CEC). Unfortunately, after 6 years of employment, the last 2 as a senior product engineer in CEC's military/space division in Atlanta, Hernandez-Canton made a mistake: she fell in love.

CEC is highly regarded as a quality employer in the electronics industry. It is a multinational corporation with engineering services and production facilities in Spain, Canada, Hong Kong, Mexico, and Germany. With more than 12,000 employees in the United States, the firm has been named as one of the country's top 100 organizations to work for by several studies. The firm is known as a top-paying corporation with proactive employee relations policies.

Kathryn Garner, the vice president of human resources for CEC, is credited with establishing many positive employee rights policies, including those covering electronic communications, drug testing, search and surveillance, access to employee records, same-sex partner benefits, and off-duty conduct. The corporation allows employees to marry except in cases where one employee is in a direct reporting relationship with the other.

Hernandez-Canton joined Centrex Electronics shortly after graduating from Georgia State University in 2012. At that time she was married to Tom Canton, her college sweetheart. In 2015, Canton died suddenly. As a single parent, his widow then became dependent upon her job for the majority of her family's support.

Hernandez-Canton enjoyed rapid promotions through various engineering positions. She also had been awarded the firm's Engineering Distinction Award for her research and development work in metallography. But in January 2017, a week after receiving a significant raise, she was called into the firm's human resources department. The question from the military/space division manager was clear and direct:

"Are you dating Mike Domzalski?" Domzalski was a former CEC senior engineer who in 2015 had gone to work for International Technologies, a direct competitor of CEC. There was no denying the romance. The two had dated while Domzalski was with CEC, and he still remained friends with other Centrex Electronics Engineers. It was widely known among Hernandez-Canton's friends that she was "extremely fond" of Domzalski.

Now, chastised for her involvement, Hernandez-Canton was ordered to forget about Domzalski or be demoted. After the meeting she told a friend, "I was so socialized in CEC culture and so devoted to my job that I thought seriously about breaking up with Mike." As she later testified in court, however, she never got the chance because she was dismissed the day after the meeting with her manager.

At the root of Hernandez-Canton's dismissal was a corporate policy regarding the leakage of confidential product information. The policy seeks to avoid situations where an employee of CEC might be compromised into providing sensitive or confidential information to an employee of a competing organization. Hernandez-Canton's work in research and development made her subject to the following CEC policy:

> Employees performing jobs where they have access to sensitive or confidential information which could benefit competitors are prohibited from being married to or from having a romantic relationship with individuals employed by competing organizations.

Since Domzalski's work at International Technologies was similar to Hernandez-Canton's at CEC, the corporation felt their "romantic relationship" made her discharge appropriate. Feeling aggrieved, Hernandez-Canton engaged the services of an attorney specializing in employee rights claims. In preparing her wrongful discharge suit, the attorney told her that given the nature of her case, he believed she could win the lawsuit. Furthermore, while gathering background information for the trial, the attorney discovered something that her former division manager did not know. Shortly before her discharge, the chairman of CEC had declared that "CEC employees are responsible for their own off-the-job behavior. We are concerned with an employee's off-the-job conduct only when it reduces the employee's ability to perform normal job assignments."

A jury trial in state court upheld the wrongful discharge suit and awarded Hernandez-Canton $425,000 in back pay and punitive damages. Like other trials, however, this one took its toll on the parties involved. "I couldn't function for 4 or 5 months after the trial, I was so emotionally upset and drained," Hernandez-Canton said. She is now employed as an engineer for

a medical-device maker; she and Domzalski are no longer dating. "It was a bad experience all around," she says. "There was a real sense of belonging and a feeling of personal job worth at CEC. If I had my way, I'd take my old job back today."

Questions

1. What exceptions to the employment-at-will doctrine would the attorney have used to file the lawsuit?

2. Comment on the confidential information policy adopted by Centrex Electronics. Do you agree with the way it is used? Explain.

3. Is dating a "romantic relationship"? Explain.

Source: This case is adapted from an actual situation known to the authors. All names are fictitious.

Pepper Construction Group: Change in Safety Leads to Decline in Injuries and Illnesses

Dave Pepper, the third-generation owner of Pepper Construction, met with his insurance group to review the group's annual summary of safety performance. To his surprise, Pepper Construction's experience modification rate (EMR) placed them in the bottom third of the group. The EMR compares the frequency and severity of workers' compensation claims between companies of similar size operating in the same type of business and reflects the degree to which a particular company's experience is better or worse than the industry as a whole. At the time, Pepper Construction Group's EMR was 0.71, nearly 30 percent better than the national average for general contractors, but two-thirds of the insurance group members were even better. Safety performance was good, but not good enough.

The Solution

Pepper Construction had begun to develop a long-range strategic planning initiative. The initial goals set by the company's leaders were related to business growth—profit, efficiency, information technology, and production—but not one mentioned safety. Pepper reminded his team members that the company's most valuable asset has always been its people, and he encouraged them to shift their focus. It was as if a light went on within his management group. They fully embraced the commitment to safety and saw that it would protect the company's greatest asset—their people. The strategic plan shifted, and safety became the first priority. Their initial goals remained, but safety was now the foundation on which profit, growth, and productivity would be built.

Senior management, along with a newly formed safety committee, developed the following TEAM safety mission statement to communicate the company's commitment to an accident free workplace:

- Training for all employees.
- Empowerment where everyone has the authority to say "no" to unsafe conditions.
- Action—the commitment to taking the steps necessary to protect employees and continuously strive to improve the safety program.
- Motivation—making sure the safety of the company's people is the top priority, above all else.

The challenge was to communicate the safety mission through the entire company, from the hourly craftsmen through the executive level. Previous annual safety seminars included every craftsman in the company, often more than 600 people in the same lecture hall listening to lectures and generic training topics. To emphasize their commitment to safety, Pepper and Ken Egidi, the president of Pepper Construction Company, held much smaller meetings limited to no more than 40 people. They took the time to shake every employee's hand and made it very clear that everyone had the right, and responsibility, to work safely.

Pepper and his team worked hard to ensure all employees knew the company was serious about safety. They put in place additional resources to support this goal. For example, the company hired a new corporate safety director, increased training opportunities, and formed trades safety committees.

Pepper Construction now offers safety training in Spanish, including an OSHA-developed training program that consists of a 10-hour course and first-aid training. The company also provides comprehensive safety orientations on every job site. In addition, the company provides safety seminars for the trades.

These seminars include up to 4 hours of training specific to the skills needed by the craftspeople, such as powered lift training, fall protection, and emergency response. Almost 90 percent of the company's current craftspeople have completed OSHA's 30-hour construction safety course.

Pepper Construction has also worked through OSHA's cooperative programs to improve its safety performance. The company is a gold level participant in OSHA Region V's Strategic Partnership with the Builders Association. The goals of this strategic partnership include reducing injuries, illnesses, and fatalities in construction by addressing key industry hazards, promoting recognition for construction safety excellence, and sharing best practices. Gold level participants must meet a number of requirements, including the implementation of a comprehensive safety and health management program and maintaining an injury/illness rate at least 10 percent lower than the Bureau of Labor Statistics (BLS) rate for their industries.

Pepper Construction is also a participant in the OSHA Challenge Program, a three-stage process to implement an effective system to prevent fatalities, injuries, and illnesses. An electronic tool that breaks down the actions, documentation, and results desired is provided by OSHA to participating companies as well. Pepper Construction is also applying for recognition under OSHA's Voluntary Protection Programs (see Chapter 12).

The Impact

Since the strategic planning initiative and subsequent restructuring of the safety and health program, Pepper Construction Company has seen a dramatic decrease in OSHA-recordable injury and illness rates. The firm is now well below the national average incidence rate in the construction industry.

When asked about the return on investment, Pepper has said the biggest benefit he has seen is the improved company culture: "Our workers are looking after each other, watching out for hazards and eliminating them—and really caring for their fellow employees." Pepper's improved safety culture has also spread to its subcontractors. When Pepper Construction bids out jobs, it reviews each subcontractor's safety and health records. All subcontractors are prequalified, and no bids are awarded to subcontractors that do not meet the company's safety performance standards.

As a result of Pepper Construction's increased scrutiny of its subcontractors' safety records, it has removed contractors from its list of prequalified contractors because of poor safety performance. For example, several years ago an iron worker was observed standing on the rail of an aerial lift without proper fall protection. Because the steel erecting company officials did not consider this a serious safety problem, they were removed from the job site and did not work on another Pepper Construction site for 4 years. After this contractor initiated an intensive safety management program, their performance improved; they are currently applying for reinstatement to Pepper Construction's prequalified contractors list.

Questions

1. How does the Pepper Construction's "TEAM" mission help keep the company on track toward better safety?

2. Why should Pepper Construction be concerned about the safety of its subcontractors?

Source: Paul Flentge, "Change in Safety Culture at Pepper Construction Group Leads to Dramatic Decline in Injuries and Illnesses," *Success Stories and Case Studies* (Washington, D.C.: Occupational Safety and Health Administration), (July 2010), http://www.osha.gov/.

Realigning HR Practices at Egan's Clothiers

At the end of fiscal year 2017, revenues at Egan's Clothiers, Inc. had increased 12 percent over 2016 and had increased at a compounded rate of 14 percent over the past 5 years. That is the good news. The bad news is that costs have risen at an even more rapid rate, thereby shrinking the company's gross margins. As a consequence, Egan's profitability (measured as return on sales and return on net assets) has actually fallen by 6 percent over the past 3 years.

The drop in profitability at Egan's is particularly worrisome. In fact, according to Egan's chief financial officer, Richard Coyle, if something is not done immediately to control material and labor costs, as well as administrative expenses, the company may need to restructure its operations. In the short run, Coyle, company president Karen Egan, and vice president of HR Pam McCaskey have put an indefinite freeze on all hiring. They are also contemplating laying off nearly one-quarter of Egan's sales staff and are weighing the benefits of cutting back on HR-related expenses such as training. Compared to others in the industry, the firm's labor costs are very high.

Company Background

Gene Egan and Pat Pollock opened their first store in Baldwin, New York, in 1958. The company grew rapidly and now operates a chain of 34 medium-sized stores located throughout Connecticut, New York, Pennsylvania, and New Jersey. Since the beginning, Egan's customers have been primarily middle-class and upper middle-class families purchasing sportswear, dresswear, and fashion accessories. The company has established a longstanding tradition of quality and customer service. In addition to its 34 stores, the company also maintains 2 distribution centers and its administrative offices

in Stamford, Connecticut. The total employment currently stands at approximately 2,400 people: 15 executives, 40 staff specialists, 40 store managers, 215 sales managers, 250 administrative personnel, 1,600 salespeople, and 240 distribution workers. Except for the employees at the distribution centers, the company is not presently unionized. However, it is no secret that Egan's management has been trying very hard recently to keep current labor organizing activities to a minimum, viewing it as a threat to the company's success.

Egan's HR department has been called upon to conduct a program audit of various personnel practices utilized at Egan's. The purpose of this audit is to assess the impact of Egan's HR policies and practices on employee outcomes (e.g., performance, employee satisfaction, absenteeism, and turnover). The objective of the audit is to identify specific problem areas where policy adjustments may be necessary. The final report to the executive staff will include the HR department's evaluation of any current problems and the changes it recommends.

Human Resources Management History

Over the past 5 years, Egan's has made several changes in order to implement the best HR practices possible. Partially, this has been to circumvent unionization efforts, but primarily it is indicative of Egan's longstanding belief that success in retailing depends on the competencies and efforts of its employees.

The commitment to HR is demonstrated by the fact that in 2017 the company spent $1.3 million on a new human resources information system (HRIS). Also, Egan's has maintained an ongoing training program for the past 5 years to help sales-people improve their retail selling skills (RSS) and customer service. The annual cost of this program has been roughly $750,000.

To ensure its employees provide customers with top-notch service, the company's selection standards are substantially higher than its competitors. Whereas other retail companies typically hire inexperienced high school students, Egan's generally requires some retailing or sales experience before considering an applicant for employment. Although this policy increases Egan's overall labor costs, managers are confident that the added expense is well justified over the long run. However, recently even the strongest proponents of HR have been wondering if it might be a good idea to cut back on training, given the company's current financial picture.

By far the most problematic and volatile HR issues at Egan's have revolved around promotions and salary increases. Because the company promotes from within and distributes raises on a company-wide basis, comparisons generally have to be made across employees in different jobs and departments. To help prevent subjectivity and bias when making these decisions, Egan's links these rewards to objective measures of performance. Specifically, rather than utilizing subjective managerial evaluations of employee performance, ongoing sales results are maintained for each employee through the HRIS. On the basis of this information, each department manager assigns each employee one of five categories:

Superior—top 10 percent

Very good—next 20 percent

Good—middle 40 percent

Fair—lower 20 percent

Poor—lowest 10 percent

Administrative decisions are then made across departments utilizing these standardized distributions. To provide constant feedback to each employee about his or her relative performance, data are updated and posted daily. Eagan's managers believe the feedback motivates employees. There are also no surprises when the time comes for semiannual performance appraisal interviews. Since the changes have been made in the performance appraisal system, there has not been one formal complaint by employees about

salary or promotion decisions. However, the company's sales managers have mentioned occasionally that they do not feel as comfortable now that they are required to assign employees to the "fair" and "poor" categories.

HR Outcomes

Despite the concerted efforts of Egan's management to create a first-rate system of human resources management, there are several troubling issues facing the company. The HR practices are not having their desired effects. For example, there have been recent complaints that employees have not been as patient or courteous with customers as they should be. This was best summarized by Paul Kelly, a store manager in White Plains, New York, who noted, "My people are beating up the clientele in order to make a sale—the very opposite of what the RSS program trains them to do." This lapse in customer service is frustrating to management since the RSS training has proven effective in the past. Additionally, there seems to be a great deal of competition within departments that is hurting a team effort. Although intergroup rivalries between departments have always been viewed as normal and healthy, the lack of intragroup cohesiveness is seen as a problem. The company is also facing greater competition from retailers that sell clothing strictly online and can keep their prices lower because they don't have to maintain brick-and-mortar stores.

Additionally, Egan's has been plagued with increases in lost and damaged merchandise. Management attributes this to the fact that storage rooms are disorganized. This is in sharp contrast to the selling floors, which have remained fairly well ordered and uncluttered. Nevertheless, inventory costs have been increasing at an alarming rate.

Everyone notices that something is wrong. But the behavior patterns are perplexing. Absenteeism has decreased by 23 percent, but employee turnover has actually increased from 13 percent to over 29 percent, thereby increasing labor costs overall. Unfortunately, many of those who left the company (43 percent) were rated as very good to superior employees.

As executives in the company look at these trends, they are understandably concerned. The success of the company and its reputation for quality and service depend on solid investments in HR to ensure the best possible workforce. However, the expenses are eroding the company's profits, and worse, it now looks like these investments are not paying off.

Questions

1. What overall changes could you recommend to the executive team at Egan's about its HR practices?

2. What are the pros and cons of Egan's performance appraisal system? Do you think it identifies the best employees? Do you think it helps develop employees to perform the best they can?

3. Can increased sales be linked directly and/or indirectly to the appraisal system? How about some of the other performance effects? How would you change the system?

4. How do you account for the fact that absenteeism has decreased at Egan's while turnover has increased?

A Performance Appraisal Snafu

Research has shown that the performance appraisal process, particularly the interaction between employees and managers, is a key determinant affecting employee motivation and productivity. Understandably, managers can view the appraisal of employee performance as a "Catch-22": The slightest mistake can cause employee resentment, as this case illustrates.

Marcus Singh, a naturalized U.S. citizen from India, is a research economist in the Office of Research and Evaluation in the city of Newport, Oregon. He is 40 years old and has worked for the city of Newport for the past 10 years. During that time, Singh has been perceived by his supervisors as an above-average performer. However, due to the small size of the department and the close working relationship between employees and management, a formal evaluation of employees was considered unnecessary. Instead, feedback and coaching were used. About 10 months ago, Singh was transferred from the department's industrial development unit to the newly formed Office of Research and Evaluation. Other employees were also transferred as part of an overall reorganization.

Victoria Popelmill, the department's director, issued a directive to all unit heads to formally evaluate the performance of their subordinates. Attached to her memorandum was a copy of a new performance appraisal form to be used in conducting the evaluations. Garth Fryer, the head of the Office of Research and Evaluation, decided to allow his subordinates some input in the appraisal process. (In addition to Garth Fryer, the Office of Research and Evaluation comprised Marcus Singh, five other research economists—Jason Taft, Susan Mussman, Richard Gels, Marsha Fetzer, and Juan Ortiz—and one administrative assistant, Connie Millar.) Fryer told each of the researchers to complete both a self-appraisal and a peer appraisal. After reviewing these appraisals, Fryer completed the final and official appraisal of each researcher. Before sending the forms to Popelmill's office, Fryer met with each researcher individually to review and explain his ratings. Each researcher signed the appraisal and indicated agreement with the ratings.

About a week after submitting the appraisals to the director, Fryer received a memorandum from Popelmill stating that his evaluations were unacceptable. Fryer was not the only unit head to receive this memorandum; in fact, they all received the same note. On examination of the completed appraisal forms from the various departments, the director had noticed that not one employee was appraised in either the "fair" or "satisfactory" category. In fact, most employees were rated as "outstanding" in every category. Popelmill felt that the unit heads were too lenient and asked them to redo the evaluations in a more objective and critical manner. Furthermore, because the department's compensation budget for salary increases was largely based on a distribution of employee ratings, evaluating all employees as outstanding would result in raises that exceeded the city's budget limits.

Garth Fryer explained the director's request to his subordinates and asked them to redo their appraisals with the idea of being more objective this time. However, the new appraisals were not much different from the first ones. Believing he had no choice in the matter, Fryer unilaterally formulated his own ratings and discussed them with each employee.

Marcus Singh was not pleased when he found out that his supervisor had rated him one level lower on each category (compare Figure 7.1 and Figure 7.2). Although he signed the second appraisal form, he indicated on the form that he did not agree with the evaluation. Jason Taft, another researcher in the Office of Research and Evaluation, continued to receive all "outstanding" ratings on his second evaluation.

Like Singh, Taft has a master's degree in economics, but he has been working for the city of Newport for less than 2 years and is only 24 years old. Taft had

Figure 7.1	Employee Appraisal Form

Employee Name: <u>Marcus Singh</u>   Date: <u>October 4, 2017</u>
Job Title: <u>Economist/Researcher</u>
Please indicate your evaluation of the employee in each category by placing a check mark (✓) in the appropriate block.

	Outstanding	Good	Satisfactory	Fair	Unsatisfactory
KNOWLEDGE OF JOB Assess overall knowledge of duties and responsibilities of current job.	☑	☐	☐	☐	☐
QUANTITY OF WORK Assess the volume of work under normal conditions.	☐	☑	☐	☐	☐
QUALITY OF WORK Assess the neatness, accuracy, and effectiveness of work.	☐	☑	☐	☐	☐
COOPERATION Assess ability and willingness to work with peers, superiors, and subordinates.	☐	☑	☐	☐	☐
INITIATIVE Assess willingness to seek greater responsibilities and knowledge. Self-starting.	☐	☑	☐	☐	☐
ATTENDANCE Assess reliability with respect to attendance habits.	☑	☐	☐	☐	☐
ATTITUDE Assess disposition and level of enthusiasm. Desire to excel.	☑	☐	☐	☐	☐
JUDGMENT Assess ability to make logical decisions.	☐	☑	☐	☐	☐

Comments on ratings: <u>Valuable employee!</u> _____

Supervisor's signature: *Garth Fryer*
Department: <u>Office of Research and Evaluation</u>   Date: <u>October 4, 2017</u>
Employee's signature: *Marcus Singh*
Does the employee agree with this evaluation? ___X___ Yes _____ No

also worked closely with Garth Fryer before being transferred to his new assignment 10 months ago. Recently, the mayor of the city had received a letter from the regional director of a major government agency praising Jason Taft's and Garth Fryer's outstanding research. Marcus Singh's working relationship with Garth Fryer and Jason Taft and with others in the department has been good. On some occasions, though, he has found himself in awkward disagreements with his coworkers in certain areas.

After Singh and Taft had signed the appraisals, Garth Fryer forwarded them to Popelmill's office, where they were eventually added to the employees' permanent files. When pay raises were awarded

Figure 7.2	Employee Appraisal Form

Employee Name: <u>Marcus Singh</u>   Date: <u>October 18, 2017</u>

Job Title: <u>Economist/Researcher</u>

Please indicate your evaluation of the employee in each category by placing a check mark (✓) in the appropriate block.

	Outstanding	Good	Satisfactory	Fair	Unsatisfactory
KNOWLEDGE OF JOB Assess overall knowledge of duties and responsibilities of current job.	☐	☑	☐	☐	☐
QUANTITY OF WORK Assess the volume of work under normal conditions.	☐	☐	☑	☐	☐
QUALITY OF WORK Assess the neatness, accuracy, and effectiveness of work.	☐	☐	☑	☐	☐
COOPERATION Assess ability and willingness to work with peers, superiors, and subordinates.	☐	☐	☑	☐	☐
INITIATIVE Assess willingness to seek greater responsibilities and knowledge. Self-starting.	☐	☐	☑	☐	☐
ATTENDANCE Assess reliability with respect to attendance habits.	☐	☑	☐	☐	☐
ATTITUDE Assess disposition and level of enthusiasm. Desire to excel.	☐	☑	☐	☐	☐
JUDGMENT Assess ability to make logical decisions.	☐	☐	☑	☐	☐

Comments on ratings: <u>Marcus needs to increase the quantity of his work to receive higher ratings. Also, he should take a greater initiative in his job.</u>

Supervisor's signature: *Garth Fryer*

Department: Office of Research and Evaluation   Date: <u>October 18, 2017</u>

Employee's signature: *Marcus Singh*

Does the employee agree with this evaluation? _____ Yes__ X __ No

in the department 3 weeks later, Marcus Singh did not receive a merit raise. He was told that it was due to his less-than-outstanding appraisal. He did, however, receive the general increase of $2,500 given to all employees regardless of their performance appraisals. This increase matched the increase in inflation for the Newport, Oregon, area.

Singh has refused to speak one word to Garth Fryer since they discussed the appraisal, communicating only through Connie Millar or in writing. Singh has lost all motivation and complains bitterly to his colleagues about his unfair ratings. While he reports to work at 8 A.M. sharp and does not leave until 5 P.M. each day, he has been observed to spend a lot of time on Facebook and surfing the Internet while at work.

Questions

1. What do you see as the problems in this case? Explain.

2. Could these problems have been avoided? How?

3. Comment on the advantages and disadvantages of using peer evaluations in the appraisal process.

4. What can be done to resolve the problem with Marcus Singh?

Source: This case was adapted from a case prepared by James G. Pesek and Joseph P. Gronenwald of Clarion University in Pennsylvania.

The Last Straw for Aero Engine

The meeting lasted only 10 minutes, since all those present quickly agreed that Tom Kinder should be fired. According to management, Kinder had caused the company numerous problems over the last 18 months, and the incident on Saturday was "the straw that broke the camel's back." Plant managers believed they had rid themselves of a poor employee, one the company had offered many opportunities for improvement. It seemed like an airtight case, one the union could not win if taken to arbitration.

Tom Kinder had worked for the Aero Engine Company for 14 years prior to being terminated. He was initially employed as an engine mechanic servicing heavy-duty diesel engines. For his first 9 years with Aero Engine, he was considered a model employee by his supervisors and plant management. Kinder was also well liked by his fellow employees. His performance appraisals were always marked "exceptional," and his personnel folder contained many commendation letters from customers and supervisors alike. Supervisor Chen Lee described Kinder as "devoted to his job of building and repairing engines." Through company-sponsored training classes and courses taken at a local trade school, Kinder had acquired the knowledge and experience to build and repair specialty engines used in arctic oil exploration.

The Aero Engine Company, with headquarters in the Midwest, was engaged primarily in the production and maintenance of specialty engines used in drilling, heavy manufacturing, and diesel transportation. The company had experienced very rapid growth in sales volume, number of products produced, and the size of its workforce since 2015. (At the time of Kinder's termination, the company employed about 1,700 employees.) Aero Engine avoided hiring new personnel and then laying them off when they were no longer needed. Company policy stated that layoffs were to be avoided except in extreme circumstances. When heavy workloads arose, the natural solution to the problem was to schedule large amounts of overtime and to hire temporary employees through one of the local temporary help services.

Kinder's work problems had begun approximately 5 years prior to his discharge when he went through a very emotional and difficult divorce. He was a devoted family man, and the divorce was a shock to his values and his way of life. The loss of custody of his children was particularly devastating to his mental well-being. He became sullen, withdrawn, and argumentative with his supervisors. Several of his close friends said they thought he was depressed. Aero Engine has a comprehensive employee assistance program (EAP) for employees experiencing personal and family problems. Kinder's supervisor, Gordon Thompson, had recommended the services of the EAP to him, but it was unknown if he had used counseling since the EAP program is voluntary and confidential. Management professes that it took a very proactive and humanistic approach toward Kinder, an employee the company valued and respected. However, regardless of the company's concern for Kinder, his work performance had become problematic.

An absenteeism problem developed and continued until his discharge. Over the 18 months prior to this termination, Tom was absent 27 complete days and 9 partial days and was tardy 19 times. Twelve months before termination, he had been given a written warning that his attendance must improve or he would face further disciplinary action, including possible discharge. Unfortunately, his attendance did not improve; however, he received no further disciplinary action until his discharge on Monday, June 9, 2016.

Management had experienced problems other than absenteeism with Kinder. The quantity and quality of his work had decreased to only an acceptable level of performance. His supervisor had discussed this with him on two occasions, but no disciplinary action was ever instituted. Furthermore, during heavy production periods Kinder would either refuse to work overtime assignments or, once assigned, would often fail to report for work. It was an incident that occurred during a Saturday overtime shift that caused his discharge.

On Saturday, June 7, Kinder was assigned to a high-priority project that required him to build a specialty engine for a large and loyal customer. The big new engine was needed to replace a smaller engine that had exploded on an Alaskan drilling rig. The engine was being built in a newly constructed plant building located one-half mile from the company's main production facilities. At approximately 9:15 A.M. that Saturday, Gordon Thompson had walked over to the new building to check on the progress of the engine. As Thompson passed by a window, he noticed Kinder sitting at a desk with his feet up, reading a magazine. The supervisor decided to observe him from outside the building. After about 25 minutes, Kinder had not moved, and Thompson returned to the plant to report the incident to Glenn Navarro, the plant production manager. Neither the supervisor nor the production manager confronted Kinder about the incident.

At 8:15 the next Monday morning, supervisor Thompson and production manager Navarro met with the director of human resources to review Kinder's total work performance. After this short meeting, all those present decided he should be fired. His discharge notice read, "Terminated for poor work performance, excessive absenteeism, and loafing." At 10:15 that morning Kinder was called into Navarro's office and discharged. Navarro then handed him his final paycheck, which included 8 hours of work for Monday.

Questions

1. Comment on the handling of this case by the supervisor, production manager, and director of human resources.

2. How much concern should organizations show employees before taking disciplinary action for personal family problems? Explain.

3. To what extent were consistent discipline and due process applied prior to the discharge?

4. If Kinder's discharge went to arbitration, how would you decide the case? Why? What arguments would labor and management present to support their respective positions?

Source: This case is based on an actual arbitration. All names are fictitious.

Employee Selection and Training at Meadowbrook Golf and Golf Ventures West

Meadowbrook Golf, headquartered in Championsgate, Florida, is a leader in golf course management, maintenance, and supplies in the United States. Today the organization is composed of four companies that meet the demands of the market: Meadowbrook Golf provides the management, International Golf Maintenance provides the maintenance, and Golf Ventures East and West are the golf supply arms of the business.

Ron Jackson is the CEO of Meadowbrook. The turf business is a highly specialized, tight-knit industry. The company's strong reputation was built on its expertise in providing superior products and services to golf courses and municipalities. Jackson knew the only way he could take the company to the next level was to not only find the right people with the specific experience they needed but to find a way to keep them happy and motivated so they would stay.

Jackson learned about a behavioral assessment tool called Predictive Index, produced by the Wellesley, Massachusetts—based management consulting company PI Worldwide, and brought it into Meadowbrook as a way to help the managers understand what motivated their employees to come to work every day. Meadowbrook also realized that their top performers possessed very similar behavioral characteristics. Using this information, Meadowbrook was able to incorporate this information into its hiring process.

Golf Ventures West (GVW), the supply division of Meadowbrook in the western United States, offers equipment that ranges from a string trimmer to a $70,000 rotary motor, along with fertilizer, seed, and specialty products. Mike Eastwood, the president of GVW, had the best talent in the industry, long-time clients, and very low turnover. While it all seemed idealistic, Eastwood had a problem. He needed his team to sell more. The challenge was how to identify what they needed in sales training to help them grow their sales.

When sharing his concerns with Jackson, Eastwood learned that the publishers of the Predictive Index also offered a selling training tool that identified the strengths of salespeople and areas for their development as well as offered customer-focused sales (CFS) training. To explore the tool further, he and his senior management team took the assessment themselves. The results accurately identified Eastwood's selling style. His general managers, most with over 30 years in the industry, scored in the mid to high range.

Next, Eastwood gave his sales team members the assessment. However, their overall scores were in the mid-to-low range. Eastwood quickly realized that despite the talent of his sales team, 80 percent of them did not know how to sell. The results of the assessment showed most of them were not asking enough investigative questions when speaking with their clients. This was a huge breakthrough. Eastwood's team members then took the CFS workshop to learn how to think like customers do and investigate and uncover their needs.

The results? "My most senior and successful salesperson followed the CFS process and closed a $40,000 deal with a customer that had only purchased from our competitor for the last 10 years," says Eastwood. In another instance, Eastwood had a salesperson who was underperforming but knew he had the potential to be successful. This salesperson went through the sales training and was moved to a new territory. "In 4 months he has sold more in his new territory than he had in a year in his original territory," says Eastwood. Apparently, the training is paying off. Even though golf courses, in general, have been struggling in recent years, Golf Ventures West has expanded its operations to a number of new locations across the country.

Questions

1. Why did Eastwood and his general managers take PI's competency assessment prior to administering it to the company's other salespeople?

2. How did the assessment help uncover the skills gap handicapping Golf Ventures West's salespeople?

3. What does the case indicate about the training "readiness" of the company's salespeople?

Source: Adapted from "Hire Smart, Develop Selling Skills and Manage for Individual and Team Success" *PI Worldwide*, http://www.piworldwide.com.

CASE 10

Newell's Decision to Downsize: An Ethical Dilemma

A particular issue in business ethics is: "What exactly does the term *ethics* mean?" Various writers have described ethics as rules that govern behavior, desired societal values such as respect for justice, or accepted principles of right or wrong. One author noted, "While laws concern what we must do, ethics concerns what we should do."[1]

In the practice of HR, managers and supervisors are continually faced with ethical dilemmas regarding the fair and equitable treatment of employees. Ethical choices abound in areas such as recruitment and selection, employee privacy, whistle-blowing, sexual harassment, and diversity or affirmative action. An important ethical dilemma faced by managers today is the fair and correct way to downsize organizations. The decisions involved in downsizing a workforce are complex and, as one manager stated, "gut-wrenching."

The Need to Downsize

Newell Corporation is a medium-sized manufacturer of navigational systems for commuter and larger airplanes. The company operates two plants—one in Atlanta, Georgia, and the other in Norwood, California. In 2016, the Norwood plant employed 273 employees, most of them engaged in the manufacture and technical support of company products.

Newell is regarded as an excellent place to work by its employees and within the surrounding communities. Employee morale and loyalty have always been high, and job satisfaction studies conducted by the company consistently rate the organization as a fair and equitable place to work. The company's HR policies can be described as proactive and progressive. With its positive reputation, Newell has been able to select new employees from a large pool of job applicants.

One cornerstone of HR policy has been to use the principle of seniority when training, assigning, transferring, and promoting employees. Additionally, with Newell's emphasis on employee retention, employees have experienced and come to expect long and steady employment. Prior to 2014, Newell has never downsized its workforce. Employment growth at the Norwood facility had been moderate and steady.

The racial composition of the company has been predominately Caucasian, for two reasons. First, the racial composition of the company's local labor market has historically been Caucasian. Second, the skill levels needed for the company's technical jobs have come primarily from a trained Caucasian labor force. A review of the company's federally required EEO-1 report showed that Newell had few employees in each of the minority categories listed. This is true for both hourly and managerial positions. However, since then, the demographic characteristics of the local labor market have changed dramatically to include more Hispanics, African Americans, and Asian Americans.

In 2010, Newell experienced a large increase in the demand for its products. To meet customer orders, the Norwood plant hired 27 new manufacturing assemblers and 14 new technical support technicians. With the increased diversity of the external labor force, plus the desire to increase the minority composition of its internal workforce, 34 of the 41 new hires were minorities. It is noteworthy that Newell welcomed the opportunity to rapidly increase the diversity of its workforce for both business and ethical reasons. The following is an excerpt from Newell's statement of vision and values published in July 2015:

> Newell Corporation believes that a work environment that reflects a diverse workforce, values diversity, and honors the worth of its employees benefits the company, its customers, and its employees. Employment decisions will be

1. Terry Halbert and Elaine Ingulli, *Law and Ethics in the Business Environment*, 7th ed. (Mason, OH: Cengage Learning, 2011).

made on these principles while also considering the efficient and effective operation of the organization.

Because many of the minority employees needed to be trained to do the company's manufacturing and technical jobs, the firm spent approximately $1.7 million on entry-level skills training. The integration of minorities into the Norwood facility was seamless and without racial tension.

In 2015, sales for Newell's products once again followed historical patterns. Unfortunately, sales then unexpectedly took a sharp downturn: a 12 percent decline in 2016 and a 23 percent decline in 2017. The causes for the decline in sales were attributed to two new low-wage foreign competitors that had entered the market, a decline in the market demand for the products made by Newell and its competitors, and higher-than-average production costs due to Newell's older, less efficient manufacturing equipment. Future demand for company products was projected to be moderate for 2018, 2019, and 2020.

In February 2017, Tom Malcom, Norwood's director of HR; Steven L. Davis, corporate vice president for manufacturing; and Mary Umali, Norwood's plant manager, decided to downsize the workforce at the Norwood facility. Specifically, they decided to lay off 37 manufacturing employees and 11 technical support personnel. The difficult question faced by senior management was how to lay off employees in a manner that would be fair and equitable to individuals and legally defensible while maintaining the integrity of Newell's HR policies and the productivity of the Norwood plant.

Questions

1. What is the ethical dilemma faced by management in this case? Explain.

2. What specific problems might Newell face in its downsizing decision?

3. What options might Newell employ in its downsizing decision? Explain.

4. How would you downsize the Norwood facility? Explain.

Source: This case was adapted from an actual case known to the authors. All names are fictitious.

CASE 11 — Someone Has to Go: A Tough Layoff Decision

Located in the Los Angeles area, Aero Performance, with 27 employees, is a sales and maintenance company that provides equipment upgrades and general aircraft maintenance to regional airlines, corporate aircraft, and small international carriers. When Aero Performance was created 2 years ago, the company faced little competition, and the robust airline market seemed to present unlimited potential for growth. Unfortunately, industry economics coupled with cost-cutting measures by airlines and new competition from similar airline service companies meant that Aero's business performance was stabilized, and the company experienced losses in certain specialized areas. Airline companies as well as the owners of corporate jets delayed the purchase and installation of Aero's advanced electronic equipment.

Mike Martinez, manager of the technology upgrade unit, faces a tough decision. With a significant downturn in his unit's work, he must lay off one employee. The decision is made particularly difficult because all employees of the unit are qualified employees with average or better work records. Additionally, each employee has a unique personal background directly affecting his or her work life. A summary of the background and work record of each of the four employees follows.

Gary Meadors is married and has two children in high school. He lives modestly in order to send his kids to college. His wife works evenings at a convenience store to assist with family expenses. Meadors has worked 9 years with Aero Performance, 6 years in airline maintenance, and 3 years in the technology upgrade unit. He has learned airline technology largely through technical articles, trade journals, and on-the-job experience. His performance evaluations are average, and he is considered a consistent and reliable employee. His attendance and company loyalty are exceptional.

Brenda Baldwin is the only woman in the technology upgrade unit. She is a single mother with a child in elementary school. Brenda has 3 years of service with Aero Performance, all in Martinez's unit. She joined the company after obtaining an airline technology degree from a well-respected 4-year university. Brenda continues to take evening classes in her field and seems to have, according to Martinez, "the most potential for growth in the company." However, her performance has slipped the past year, and she has been counseled for an attendance problem. She has felt somewhat resented as a female in a traditionally male-dominated industry.

Udit Chopra is a dedicated employee. In fact, everyone says he is "married to his job." He will work long hours to complete technical installations and is regarded as a perfectionist. Udit has a college degree in marketing but has found his home in airline technology. He possesses an excellent ability to persuade Aero Performance customers to upgrade their technology systems. Udit drives a new BMW and is believed to come from a wealthy family.

Craig Cottrell joined Aero Performance 3 years ago, having been hired away from a competitor. He has a total of 12 years of experience in the airline service industry. Craig has a complete understanding of airline technology. Cottrell's work performance the first 2 years with Aero Performance was barely average; however, his work record the past year was evaluated as very high. Currently, he is the top performer in the unit. There has been work friction between him, Baldwin, and Chopra over the selection and installation of cockpit instruments.

	Seniority (Years)	Salary	Performance			
			2014	2015	2016	2017
Gary Meadors	9	$74,250	Avg	Good	Avg	Avg
Brenda Baldwin	3	$81,190		High	Good	Avg
Udit Chopra	5	$78,500	Avg	Good	Good	Good
Craig Cottrell	3	$75,960		Avg	Avg	High

Mike Martinez must make his decision by this Friday. Aero Performance will grant the laid-off employee a severance package to assist in transition to other employment. Martinez is committed to aiding his employee in finding another job in the airline service industry.

Questions

1. What criteria should be used to determine potential layoff candidates? What emphasis, if any, should be given to non-job-related factors such as personal problems or a spouse's need to work? Explain your answer.

2. What should be included in a severance package for laid-off employees? How long should the severance package last?

3. Are there any potential legal implications in Martinez's decision?

4. How would you handle the termination interview?

A

360-degree evaluation A performance evaluation done by different people who interact with the employee, generally on forms compiled into a single document for use in the evaluation meeting conducted by the employee's manager.

Acceptance rate The percentage of applicants who accept a firm's jobs after being offered them.

Adventure-based learning The use of adventures, such as games, trust activities, and problem-solving initiatives, for the personal and social development of participants.

Adverse impact A concept that refers to the rejection of a significantly higher percentage of a protected class for employment, placement, or promotion when compared with the successful, nonprotected class.

Affirmative action A policy that goes beyond equal employment opportunity by requiring organizations to comply with the law and correct any past discriminatory practices by increasing the numbers of minorities and women in specific positions.

Agility A firm's ability make quick changes to gain a competitive advantage.

Alternative dispute resolution (ADR) A term applied to different employee complaint or dispute resolution methods that do not involve going to court.

Applicant tracking system (ATS) A system recruiters use to post job openings, screen résumés and uploaded profiles, contact via email potential candidates for interviews, and track the time, costs, and other metrics related to hiring people.

Apprenticeship training A system of training in which a worker entering the skilled trades is given thorough instruction and experience, both on and off the job, in the practical and theoretical aspects of the work.

Arbitrator A third-party neutral who resolves a labor dispute by issuing a final decision in the disagreement.

Assessment center test A process by which managerial candidates are evaluated at an assessment center as they participate in a series of situations that resemble what they might need to handle on the job.

Augmented skills Skills helpful in facilitating the efforts of expatriate managers.

Authorization card A statement signed by an employee authorizing a union to act as a representative of the employee for purposes of collective bargaining.

B

Backup care program A benefit program whereby an employer provides or subsidizes temporary care for its employee's elders or children when their regular arrangements fall through.

Balance sheet approach A compensation system designed to match the purchasing power in a person's home country.

Balanced scorecard (BSC) A measurement framework that helps managers translate strategic goals into operational **objectiv**es.

Bargaining power The power of labor and management to achieve their goals through economic, social, or political influence.

Bargaining unit A group of two or more employees who share common employment interests and conditions and may reasonably be grouped together for purposes of collective bargaining.

Bargaining zone An area in which the union and the employer are willing to concede when bargaining.

Behavior modeling A learning approach in which work behaviors are modeled, or demonstrated, and trainees are asked to mimic them.

Behavior modification A technique that operates on the principle that behavior that is rewarded, or positively reinforced, will be exhibited more frequently in the future, whereas behavior that is penalized or unrewarded will decrease in frequency.

Behavior observation scale (BOS) A behavioral approach to performance rating that measures the frequency of observed behavior.

Behavioral description interview (BDI) An interview in which an applicant is asked questions about what he or she actually did in a given situation.

Behaviorally anchored rating scale (BARS) A behavioral approach to performance rating that consists of a series of vertical scales, one for each important dimension of job performance.

Benchmarking The process of looking at your practices and performance in a given area and then comparing them with those of other companies.

Blended learning The use of both in-person classroom learning and online learning.

Bona fide occupational qualification (BFOQ) A suitable defense against a discrimination charge only when age, religion, sex, or national origin is an actual qualification for performing the job.

Bonus An incentive payment that is supplemental to the base wage.

Branding A company's efforts to help existing and prospective workers understand why it is a desirable place to work.

Broadbanding Collapses many traditional salary grades into a few wide salary bands.

Burnout A severe stage of distress, manifesting itself in depression, frustration, and loss of productivity.

Business environment Factors in the external environment that a firm cannot directly control but that can affect its strategy and performance.

Business necessity A work-related practice that is necessary to the safe and efficient operation of an organization.

C

Calibration A process whereby managers meet to discuss the performance of individual employees to ensure their employee reviews are in line with one another.

Career paths Lines of advancement in an occupational field within an organization.

Career plateau A situation in which for either organizational or personal reasons the probability of moving up the career ladder is low.

Charge form A discrimination complaint filed with the EEOC by employees or job applicants.

Chief diversity officer (CDO) A top executive responsible for implementing a firm's diversity efforts.

Chief ethics officers A high-ranking manager directly responsible for fostering the ethical climate within the firm.

Chief learning officers A high-ranking executive responsible for fostering employee learning and development within the firm.

Codetermination Representation of labor on the board of directors of a company.

Collective bargaining process The process of negotiating a labor agreement, including the use of economic pressures by both parties.

Combined salary and commission plan A compensation plan that includes a straight salary and a commission.

Compensation scorecard Displays the results for all the measures that a company uses to monitor and compare compensation among internal departments or units.

Compensatory model A selection decision model in which a high score in one area can make up for a low score in another area.

Competence-based pay Pay based on an employee's skill level, variety of skills possessed, or increased job knowledge.

Competency assessment An analysis of the sets of skills and knowledge needed for decision-oriented and knowledge-intensive jobs.

Competitive environment Consists of a firm's specific industry, including the industry's customers, rival firms, new entrants, substitutes, and suppliers.

Computer-administered (automated) interview Interviews in which the questions are administered to applicants via computers. The interviews can be conducted at a firm's facilities, using kiosks, online, or via phone.

Concurrent validity The extent to which the test scores of current employees correlate with their job performance.

Construct validity The extent to which a selection tool measures a theoretical construct or trait.

Constructive discharge An employee's voluntary termination of his or her employment because of harsh, unreasonable employment conditions placed on the individual by the employer.

Consumer price index (CPI) A measure of the average change in prices over time in a fixed "market basket" of goods and services.

Content validity The extent to which a selection instrument, such as a test, adequately samples the knowledge and skills needed to do a particular job.

Contrast error A performance rating error in which an employee's review is biased either upward or downward because of comparison with another employee just previously evaluated.

Contributory plan A pension plan in which contributions are made jointly by employees and employers.

Cooperative training A training program that combines practical on-the-job experience with formal educational classes.

Core capabilities Integrated knowledge sets within an organization that distinguish it from its competitors and deliver value to customers.

Core skills Skills considered critical to an employee's success abroad.

Core values The strong and enduring beliefs and principles that guide a firm's decisions and are the foundation of its corporate culture.

Corporate social responsibility The responsibility of the firm to act in the best interests of the people and communities affected by its activities.

Craft unions Unions that represent skilled craft workers.

Criterion-related validity The extent to which a selection tool predicts, or significantly correlates with, important work behaviors.

Critical incident method A job analysis method used to identify both desirable and undesirable behaviors that resulted in either a very good outcome or a very bad outcome on the job.

Cross-training The process of training employees to do multiple jobs within an organization.

Cross-validation Verifying the results obtained from a validation study by administering a test or test battery to a different sample (drawn from the same population).

Cultural audits Audits of the culture and quality of work life in an organization.

Cultural environment The communications, religion, values and ideologies, education, and social structure of a country.

Culture shock Perpetual stress experienced by people who settle overseas.

Cumulative trauma disorders Injuries involving tendons of the fingers, hands, and arms that become inflamed from repeated stresses and strains.

Customer evaluation A performance evaluation that includes evaluations from both a firm's external and internal customers.

D

Defined benefit plan A pension plan in which the amount an employee is to receive on retirement is specifically set forth.

Defined contribution plan A pension plan that establishes the basis on which an employer will contribute to the pension fund.

Dejobbing Refers to a process of structuring organizations not around jobs but around projects that are constantly changing.

Demotion A downward transfer that moves an individual into a lower-level job that can provide developmental opportunities.

Depression A negative emotional state marked by feelings of low spirits, gloominess, sadness, and loss of pleasure in ordinary activities.

Differential piece rate A compensation rate under which employees whose production exceeds the standard amount of output receive a higher rate for all of their work than the rate paid to those who do not exceed the standard amount.

Disabled individual Any person who (1) has a physical or mental impairment that substantially limits one or more of the person's major life activities, (2) has a record of such impairment, or (3) is regarded as having such an impairment.

Discipline A tool, used to correct and mold the practices of employees to help them perform better so they conform to acceptable standards.

Disease management programs Programs that provide patients and their caregivers with information on monitoring and treating medical conditions, while coordinating communication between them, their health care providers, employers, and insurers.

Disparate treatment A situation in which protected class members receive unequal treatment or are evaluated by different standards.

Distress Harmful stress characterized by a loss of feelings of security and adequacy.

Downsizing The planned elimination of jobs.

Due process Procedures that constitute fair treatment, such as allowing an employee to tell his or her story about an alleged infraction and defend against it.

E

E-learning Learning that takes place via electronic media.

Economic factors external factors including the strength or weakness of markets, stability of trade cycles, specific industry conditions, customer preferences, and government's economic policies.

Elder care Care provided to an elderly relative by an employee who remains actively at work.

Emergency action plans A plan an organization develops that contains step-by-step procedures for dealing with various emergency situations.

Employee assistance programs (EAPs) Services provided by employers to help workers cope with a wide variety of problems that interfere with the way they perform their jobs.

Employee associations Labor organizations that represent various groups of professional and white-collar employees in labor–management relations.

Employee empowerment Giving employees the power to initiate change, thereby encouraging them to take charge of what they do.

Employee engagement A situation in which workers are enthusiastic and immersed in their work to the degree that it improves the performance of their companies.

Employee leasing The process of dismissing employees who are then hired by a leasing company (which handles all HR-related activities) and contracting with that company to lease back the employees.

Employee profiles A profile of a worker developed by studying an organization's top performers to recruit similar types of people.

Employee rights Guarantees of fair treatment that become rights when they are granted to employees by the courts, legislatures, or employers.

Employee stock ownership plans (ESOPs) Stock plans in which an organization contributes shares of its stock to an established trust for the purpose of stock purchases by its employees.

Employee team A group of employees working together toward a common purpose, in which members have complementary skills, members' work is mutually dependent, and the group has discretion over tasks performed.

Employment-at-will relationship The right of an employer to fire an employee without giving a reason and the right of an employee to quit when he or she chooses.

Entrepreneur One who starts, organizes, manages, and assumes responsibility for a business or other enterprise.

Environmental scanning Systematic monitoring of the major external forces influencing the organization.

Equal employment opportunity (EEO) The treatment of individuals in all aspects of employment—hiring, promotion, training, etc.—in a fair and nonbiased manner.

Equal Employment Opportunity Commission (EEOC) The EEOC's work consists of formulating EEO policy and approving all litigation involved in maintaining equal employment opportunity. The EEOC's guidelines are not federal law but administrative rules and regulations published in the *Federal Register*.

Ergonomics The process of studying and designing easy-to-use equipment and systems so the physical well-being of employees isn't compromised and work gets done more efficiently.

Error of central tendency A performance rating error in which all employees are rated about average.

Escalator clauses Clauses in labor agreements that provide for quarterly cost-of-living adjustments in wages, basing the adjustments on changes in the consumer price index.

Essay method A trait approach to performance rating that requires the rater to write a statement describing an employee's behavior.

Ethics A set of standards of conduct and moral judgments that help to determine right and wrong behavior.

Eustress Positive stress that accompanies achievement and exhilaration.

Exclusive representation The legal right and responsibility of the union to represent all bargaining unit members equally, regardless of whether employees join the union or not.

Exempt employees Employees not covered by the overtime provisions of the Fair Labor Standards Act.

Expatriates, or home-country nationals Employees from the home country who are on international assignment.

Experiential learning The process of learning by "doing," reflecting on it, critically analyzing it, and applying it in new situations or settings.

F

Failure rates The percentage of expatriates who do not perform satisfactorily.

Fair employment practices (FEPs) State and local laws governing equal employment opportunity that are often more comprehensive than federal laws and apply to small-business employers.

Fair representation doctrine A doctrine under which unions have a legal obligation to assist both members and nonmembers in labor relations matters.

Fitness-for-duty evaluations Evaluations randomly conducted to determine an employee's physical, mental, and emotional fitness for a job.

Flexible benefits plans (cafeteria plans) Benefit plans that enable individual employees to choose the benefits that are best suited to their particular needs.

Flextime Flexible working hours that give employees the option of choosing daily starting and quitting times, provided that they work a set number of hours per day or week.

Forced distribution A performance ranking system whereby raters are required to place a certain percentage of employees into various performance categories.

Forced-choice method A trait approach to performance rating that requires the rater to choose from statements designed to distinguish between successful and unsuccessful performance.

Four-fifths rule A rule of thumb followed by the EEOC in determining adverse impact for use in enforcement proceedings.

Functional job analysis (FJA) A job analysis approach that utilizes an inventory of the various types of work activities that can constitute any job.

Furloughing A situation in which an organization asks or requires employees to take time off for either no pay or reduced pay.

G

Gainsharing plans Programs under which both employees and the organization share financial gains according to a predetermined formula that reflects improved productivity and profitability.

Global compensation system A centralized pay system whereby host-country employees are offered a full range of training programs, benefits, and pay comparable with a firm's domestic employees but adjusted for local differences.

Global corporation A firm that has integrated worldwide operations through a centralized home office.

Global manager A manager equipped to run an international business.

Graphic rating scale method A trait approach to performance rating whereby each employee is rated according to a scale of characteristics.

Grievance procedure A formal procedure that provides for the union to represent members and nonmembers in processing a grievance.

Guest workers Foreign workers invited to perform needed labor.

H

Hay profile method A job evaluation technique using three factors—knowledge, mental activity, and accountability—to evaluate executive and managerial positions.

Health maintenance organizations (HMOs) Organizations of physicians and health care professionals that provide a wide range of services to subscribers and dependents on a prepaid basis.

High-deductible health insurance plan (HDHP) A medical insurance plan characterized by high deductibles but lower premiums for workers and a health spending account to which employers contribute funds employees can keep should they leave the organization.

High-performance work system (HPWS) A specific combination of HR practices, work structures, and processes that maximizes knowledge, skill, commitment, flexibility, and resilience of a firm's employees.

Home-based pay Pay based on an expatriate's home country's compensation practices.

Homeshoring The practice of outsourcing work to domestic workers who work out of their homes.

Horizontal fit A situation in which all the internal elements of the work system reinforce one another.

Host country A country in which an international corporation operates.

Host-country nationals Employees who are natives of the host country.

Host-based pay Expatriate pay comparable to that earned by employees in a host country.

Hourly work Work paid on an hourly basis.

Human capital The knowledge, skills, and capabilities of individuals that have economic value to an organization.

Human capital readiness The process of evaluating the availability of critical talent in a company and comparing it to the firm's supply.

Human resources information system (HRIS) A computerized system that provides current and accurate HR-related data for the purposes of control and decision-making.

Human resources management (HRM) The process of managing human talent to achieve an organization's objectives.

Human resources planning (HRP) The process of anticipating and providing for the movement of people into, within, and out of an organization.

I

Impairment testing Also called fitness-for-duty or performance-based testing, it measures whether an employee is alert enough to work.

Improshare A gainsharing program under which bonuses are based on the overall productivity of the work team.

Independent contractors Workers who are self-employed and do project work on a contract basis for different organizations.

Industrial engineering A field of study concerned with analyzing work methods and establishing time standards.

Industrial unions Unions that represent all workers—skilled, semiskilled, unskilled—employed along industry lines.

Informational interview A conversation you have with someone in a career you are interested in to gather information about it.

Instructional objectives The desired outcomes of a training program.

Interest-based bargaining Problem-solving bargaining based on a win–win philosophy and the development of a positive long-term relationship.

Internal labor markets Labor markets in which workers are hired into entry-level jobs and higher-level jobs are filled from within.

International corporation A domestic firm that uses its existing capabilities to move into overseas markets.

J

Job An activity people do for which they get paid, particularly as part of the trade or occupation they occupy.

Job analysis The process of obtaining information about a job by determining its duties, tasks, or activities.

Job characteristics model A job design theory that purports that three psychological states (experiencing meaningfulness of the work performed, responsibility for work outcomes, and knowing the results of the work performed) result in a jobholder's improved work performance, internal motivation, and lower absenteeism and turnover.

Job classification system A system of job evaluation in which jobs are classified and grouped according to a series of predetermined wage grades.

Job crafting A naturally occurring phenomenon whereby employees mold their tasks to fit their individual strengths, passions, and motives better.

Job description A statement of the tasks, duties, and responsibilities of a job to be performed.

Job design An outgrowth of job analysis that improves jobs through technological and human considerations in order to enhance organization efficiency and employee job satisfaction.

Job enlargement The process of adding a greater variety of tasks to a job.

Job enrichment Enhancing a job by adding more meaningful tasks and duties to make the work more rewarding or satisfying.

Job evaluation A systematic process of determining the relative worth of jobs to establish which jobs should be paid more than others within an organization.

Job progressions The hierarchy of jobs a new employee might experience, ranging from a starting job to jobs that successively require more knowledge and/or skill.

Job ranking system The simplest and oldest system of job evaluation by which jobs are arrayed on the basis of their relative worth.

Job rotation The process whereby employees rotate in and out of different jobs.

Job shadowing The process of observing someone in his or her work environment to see if the job is of interest to you.

Job sharing An arrangement whereby two part-time employees do a job normally held by one full-time employee.

Job specifications A statement of the specific knowledge, skills, and abilities of a person who is to perform a job needs.

Just-in-time training Electronic training delivered to trainees when and where they need it to do their jobs.

K

Knowledge workers Workers whose responsibilities extend beyond the physical execution of work to include planning, decision-making, and problem-solving.

L

Labor relations process A logical sequence of five events: (1) workers desire collective representation, (2) the union begins its organizing campaign, (3) the NLRB representation process begins, (4) collective negotiations lead to a contract, and (5) the contract is administered.

Learning management system (LMS) Online system that provides a variety of assessment, communication, teaching, and learning opportunities.

Leniency or strictness error A performance rating error in which the appraiser tends to give employees either unusually high or unusually low ratings.

Line managers Non-HR managers who are responsible for overseeing the work of other employees.

Localization Adapting pay and other compensation benefits to match that of a particular country.

M

Management by objectives (MBO) A philosophy of management that rates the performance of employees based on their achievement of goals set mutually by them and their managers.

Management forecasts The opinions (judgments) of supervisors, department managers, experts, or others knowledgeable about the organization's future employment needs.

Manager and/or supervisor evaluation A performance evaluation done by an employee's manager and often reviewed by a manager one level higher.

Markov analysis A method for tracking the pattern of employee movements through various jobs in a firm.

Material Safety Data Sheets (MSDSs) Documents that contain vital information about hazardous substances.

Mediation The use of an impartial neutral to reach a compromise decision in employment disputes.

Mediator A third party in an employment dispute who meets with one party and then the other to suggest compromise solutions or to recommend concessions from each side that will lead to an agreement.

Mentors Individuals who coach, advise, and encourage employees of a lesser rank.

Merit guidelines Guidelines for awarding merit raises that are tied to performance objectives.

Microlearning Training sessions that take place in a very short timeframe, usually 5 minutes or less.

Mission The basic purpose of the organization as well as its scope of operations.

Mixed-standard scale method A trait approach to performance rating similar to other scale methods but based on a comparison with (better than, equal to, or worse than) a standard.

Mobile recruiting The process of recruiting candidates via their mobile devices.

Multidomestic corporation (MDC) A firm with independent business units operating in multiple countries.

Multiple cutoff model A selection decision model that requires an applicant to achieve some minimum level of proficiency on all selection dimensions.

Multiple hurdle model A selection decision model in which only the applicants with the highest scores at an initial test stage go on to subsequent stages.

N

National Labor Relations Board (NLRB) The agency responsible for administering and enforcing the Wagner Act. It serves the public interest by reducing interruptions in production or service caused by labor—management strife.

Nearshoring Occurs when a firm relocates jobs abroad to nations closer to its domestic market.

Negligence The failure to provide reasonable care when such failure results in injury to consumers or other employees.

Negligent hiring The failure of an organization to discover, via due diligence, that an employee it hired had the propensity to do harm to others.

Nepotism A preference for hiring the relatives of current employees.

Nine-box grid A comparative diagram that includes appraisal and assessment data to allow managers to easily see an employee's actual and potential performance.

Noncontributory plan A pension plan in which contributions are made solely by the employer.

Nondirective interview An interview in which the applicant is allowed the maximum amount of freedom in determining the course of the discussion, while the interviewer carefully refrains from influencing the applicant's remarks.

Nonexempt employees Employees covered by the overtime provisions of the Fair Labor Standards Act.

O

Offshoring The business practice of sending jobs to other countries; work that was previously carried out in one country is moved to another country.

Ombudsman A designated individual from whom employees may seek counsel for resolution of their complaints.

Onboarding The process of systematically socializing new employees to help them get "on board" with an organization.

On-the-job training (OJT) A method by which employees are given hands-on experience with instructions from their supervisor or other trainer.

Open-door policy A policy of settling grievances that identifies various levels of management above the immediate supervisor for employee contact.

Organization analysis An examination of an organization's environment, goals, strategies, performance, and resources so as to determine what training it should do.

Organizational culture The shared values, beliefs, and assumptions people in an organization have.

Orientation The formal process of familiarizing new employees with the organization, their jobs, and their work units.

Outplacement services Services provided by organizations to help terminated employees find a new job.

Outsourcing Contracting outside the organization to have work done that formerly was done by internal employees.

P

Panel interview An interview in which a board of interviewers questions and observes a single candidate.

Passive jobseekers People who are not looking for jobs but could be persuaded to take new ones given the right opportunity.

Pay equity An employee's perception that compensation received is equal to the value of the work performed.

Pay grades Groups of jobs within a particular class that are paid the same rate.

Pay rate compression Compression of pay between new and experienced employees caused by the higher starting salaries of new employees; also the differential between hourly workers and their managers.

Pay-for-performance standard A standard by which managers tie compensation to employee effort and performance.

Peer evaluation A performance evaluation done by one's fellow employees, generally on forms compiled into a single profile for use in the evaluation meeting conducted by the employee's manager.

Peer-review system A system for reviewing employee complaints that utilizes a group composed of equal numbers of employee representatives and management appointees. The group weighs evidence, considers arguments, and, after deliberation, votes to render a final decision.

Performance management The process of creating a work environment in which people can perform to the best of their abilities.

Performance reviews A process in which a manager evaluates an employee's performance relative to the requirements of his or her job and uses the information to show the person where improvements can be made and how.

Perquisites Special nonmonetary benefits given to executives; often referred to as *perks*.

Person analysis The process of determining the specific individuals who need training in an organization.

Phased retirement A program that allows its employees to gradually cut their hours before retiring.

Piecework Work paid according to the number of units produced.

Point system A quantitative job evaluation procedure that determines the relative value of a job by the total points assigned to it.

Political factors To come

Position analysis questionnaire (PAQ) A questionnaire that identifies approximately 300 different tasks to determine the degree to which each is involved in doing a job.

Positive, or nonpunitive discipline A system of discipline that focuses on early correction of employee misconduct, with the employee taking total responsibility for correcting the problem.

Predictive validity The extent to which candidates' test scores match criterion data obtained from them after they have been hired and on the job for a period of time.

Preemployment test An objective and standardized test used to gauge a person's knowledge, skills, abilities, and other characteristics (KSAOs) relative to other individuals.

Preferred provider organization (PPO) A network of physicians who establish an organization that guarantees lower health care costs to employers and their employees.

Process audit Determining whether a high-performance work system has been implemented as designed.

Profit sharing Any procedure by which an employer pays, or makes available to all regular employees, special current or deferred sums based on the organization's profits.

Progressive discipline The application of corrective measures by increasing degrees.

Promotion A change of assignment to a job at a higher level in the organization.

Protected classes Individuals of a minority race, women, older people, and those with disabilities who are covered by federal laws on equal employment opportunity.

Psychological contract Expectations of a fair exchange of employment obligations between an employee and employer.

Q

Quality of fill A metric designed to measure how well new hires that fill positions are performing on the job.

R

Real wages Wage increases larger than rises in the consumer price index, that is, the real earning power of wages.

Realistic job preview (RJP) Informing applicants about all aspects of the job, including both its desirable and undesirable facets.

Reasonable accommodation An attempt by employers to adjust, without undue hardship, the working conditions or schedules of employees with disabilities or religious preferences.

Recency error A performance rating error in which the evaluation is based largely on the employee's most recent behavior rather than on behavior throughout the evaluation period.

Recordable case Any occupational death, illness, or injury to be recorded in the log (OSHA Form 300).

Recruiting process outsourcing (RPO) The practice of outsourcing an organization's recruiting function to an outside firm.

Red circle rates Payment rates above the maximum of the pay range.

Reliability The degree to which an interview, test, or other selection procedures result in consistent information about a candidate.

Repatriation The process of transition for an employee home from an international assignment.

Replacement charts Listings of current jobholders and people who are potential replacements if an opening occurs.

Re-recruiting The process of keeping track of and maintaining relationships with former employees to see if they would be willing to return to the firm.

Reverse discrimination The act of giving preference to members of protected classes to the extent that unprotected individuals believe they are suffering discrimination.

Reverse mentoring A program whereby younger employees are called on to mentor older employees and executives about social media trends, new technology, and marketplace trends.

Rights arbitration Arbitration over interpretation of the meaning of contract terms or employee work grievances.

Right-to-know laws Laws that require employers to advise employees about the hazardous chemicals they handle.

S

Sabbatical An extended period of time in which an employee leaves an organization to pursue other activities and later returns to his or her job.

Salary plus bonus plan A compensation plan that pays a salary plus a bonus achieved by reaching targeted sales goals.

Scanlon plan A bonus incentive plan using employee and management committees to gain cost-reduction improvements.

Selection The process of choosing individuals who are qualified to fill existing or projected job openings.

Selection ratio The number of applicants compared with the number of people to be hired.

Self-evaluation A performance evaluation done by the employee being evaluated, generally on an evaluation form completed by the employee prior to the evaluation meeting.

Sequential interview A format in which a candidate is interviewed by multiple people, one right after another.

Severance pay A one-time payment sometimes given to an employee who is being involuntarily terminated.

Sexual harassment Unwelcome advances, requests for sexual favors, and other verbal or physical conduct of a sexual nature in the working environment.

Similar-to-me error A performance rating error in which an appraiser inflates the review of an employee because of a mutual personal connection.

Situational interview An interview in which an applicant is given a hypothetical incident and asked how he or she would respond to it.

Skill inventories Files of personnel education, experience, interests, skills, and so on that allow managers to quickly match job openings with employee backgrounds.

SMART goals Goals that are specific, measurable, achievable, realistic, and time-based.

Sociocultural factors external factors including method and style of communications, religions, values and ideologies, education standards, and social structure.

Split pay A system whereby expatriates are given a portion of their pay in the local currency to cover their day-to-day expenses and a portion of their pay in their home currency to safeguard their earnings from changes in inflation or foreign exchange rates.

Spot bonus An unplanned bonus given for employee's effort unrelated to an established performance measure.

Spot rewards Programs that award employees on the spot when they do something particularly well during training or on the job.

Staffing table A table that shows a firm's jobs, along with the numbers of employees currently occupying those jobs and future (monthly or yearly) employment requirements.

Stakeholders Key people and groups that have an interest in a firm's activities and that can either affect them or be affected by them.

Standard hour plan An incentive plan that sets rates based on the completion of a job in a predetermined standard time.

Step-review system A system for reviewing employee complaints and disputes by successively higher levels of management.

Straight commission plan A compensation plan based on a percentage of sales.

Straight piecework An incentive plan under which employees receive a certain rate for each unit produced.

Straight salary plan A compensation plan that permits salespeople to be paid for performing various duties that are not reflected immediately in their sales volume.

Strategic human resources management The pattern of human resources deployments and activities that enable an organization to achieve its strategic goals.

Strategic planning Procedures for making decisions about the organization's long-term goals and strategies.

Strategic vision A statement about where the company is going and what it can become in the future.

Stress Any adjustive demand caused by physical, mental, or emotional factors that requires coping behavior.

Structured interview An interview in which a set of standardized questions having an established set of answers is used.

Subordinate evaluation A performance evaluation of a superior by an employee, which is often used for developmental rather than for administrative purposes.

Succession planning The process of identifying, developing, and tracking key individuals for executive positions.

Supplemental unemployment benefit (SUB) A plan that enables an employee who is laid off to draw weekly benefits from the employer, which draws from a fund created for this purpose, in addition to state unemployment compensation.

Sustainability Doing business in a way that does as little harm to the environment and depletes as few natural resources as possible.

SWOT analysis A comparison of one's strengths, weaknesses, opportunities, and threats for strategy formulation purposes.

T

Talent reviews strategic meetings to determine if a company has the human resources it needs to compete in the future.

Task analysis The process of determining a training program's content by studying the tasks and duties a job involves.

Task inventory analysis An organization-specific list of tasks and their descriptions used as a basis to identify components of jobs.

Team evaluation A performance evaluation that recognizes team accomplishments rather than individual performance.

Team incentive plan A compensation plan in which all team members receive an incentive bonus payment when production or service standards are met or exceeded.

Technological factors External factors pertaining to the technological infrastructure and investments, information systems, manufacturing equipment, and consumer access to technology.

Telecommuting The use of personal computers, networks, and other communications technology to do work in the home that is traditionally done in the workplace.

Third-country nationals Employees who are natives of a country other than the home country or the host country.

Time-to-fill Metrics that refer to the number of days from when a job opening is approved to the date a person accepts the job and begins it.

Transfer of training The effective application of principles learned to what is required on the job.

Transfer The placement of an employee in another job for which the duties, responsibilities, status, and pay and benefits are approximately equal to those of the previous job the person held.

Transnational corporation A firm that attempts to balance local responsiveness and global scale via a network of specialized operating units.

Transnational teams Teams composed of members of multiple nationalities working on projects that span multiple countries.

Trend analysis A quantitative approach to forecasting labor demand based on a factor such as sales.

U

Unfair labor practices (ULPs) Specific employer and union illegal practices that deny employees their rights and benefits under federal labor law.

Uniform Guidelines on Employee Selection Procedures A procedural document published in the Federal Register to help employers comply with federal regulations against discriminatory actions.

Union security agreement Where an employer and the union agree on the extent to which the union may compel employees to join the union and how the dues will be collected.

Union steward An employee who as a nonpaid union official represents the interests of members in their relations with management.

V

Validity The degree to which a test or selection procedure actually measures or predicts a person's ability to do a job.

Value creation What a firm adds to a product or service by virtue of making it; the amount of benefits provided by the product or service once the costs of making it are subtracted.

Variable pay Tying pay to some measure of individual, group, or organizational performance.

Vertical fit The situation in which the work system supports the organization's goals and strategies.

Vesting A guarantee of accrued pension benefits to participants at retirement age, regardless of their employment status at that time.

Video interviews Interviews conducted via videoconferencing or over the Web.

Video résumés Short video clips that highlight applicants' qualifications beyond what they can communicate on their résumés.

Virtual job fair Job fairs conducted online.

Virtual teams Teams that utilize telecommunications technology to link team members who are geographically dispersed—often worldwide across cultures and across time zones.

W

Wage and salary survey A survey of the wages paid to employees of other employers in the surveying organization's relevant labor market.

Wage curve A curve in a scattergram representing the relationship between the relative worth of jobs and pay rates.

Wellness programs Employer-sponsored programs designed to encourage employees to maintain and improve their health and well-being by getting regular checkups, eating properly, exercising, and managing their stress levels so as to prevent costly and protracted illnesses.

Whistle-blowing Complaints to governmental agencies by employees about their employers' illegal or immoral acts or practices.

Work permit or visa A government document granting a foreign individual the right to seek employment.

Work valuation A job evaluation system that seeks to measure a job's worth through its value to the organization.

Workers' compensation insurance State-mandated insurance provided to workers to defray the loss of income and cost of treatment due to work-related injuries or illness.

Workforce (HR) analytics The process of gathering and analyzing data to improve a firm's human resources management.

Workforce utilization analysis A process of classifying protected-class members by number and by the type of jobs they hold within the organization.

Wrongful discharge A discharge, or termination, of an employee that is illegal.

Y

Yield ratio The percentage of applicants from a particular source that make it to the next stage in the selection process.

Name Index

Organization Index